Anne Griffith

The Ideology
American Political and
System Myth

H. Mark Roelofs
NEW YORK UNIVERSITY

Gerald L. Houseman
INDIANA UNIVERSITY, FORT WAYNE

The American

IDEOLOGY AND

Political System

MYTH

Macmillan Publishing Co., Inc.
NEW YORK

Collier Macmillan Publishers
LONDON

Copyright © 1983, Macmillan Publishing Co., Inc.

Printed in the United States of America

Macmillan Publishing Co., Inc.
866 Third Avenue, New York, New York 10022

Collier Macmillan Canada, Inc.

Library of Congress Cataloging in Publication Data

Roelofs, H. Mark.
  The American political system.

  Includes bibliographies and index.
  1. United States—Politics and government.
I. Houseman, Gerald L. II. Title.
JK274.R745 1983   320.973   82-9895
ISBN 0-02-402720-0   AACR2

Printing: 1 2 3 4 5 6 7 8   Year: 3 4 5 6 7 8 9 0

ISBN 0-02-402720-0

PREFACE

This is a critical, analytical text on American government.

We believe that it is highly readable, current, and informative. We also believe that its coverage is comprehensive. All the basics are here and embedded in a sufficiency of relevant detail. Throughout the book we have tried to keep a balance between our explication and illustrative materials. In this connection, the boxed material placed throughout all the chapters is especially important, as is the glossary at the book's end.

The strength of the book lies in its analytical power. Many things can be said about American government, most of them true and most of them also contradictory. The subject can easily become not just confusing but paradoxical beyond apparent possibility of explanation. Is the presidency strong or weak? Do political parties matter? What does Congress do, really? It can even be debated whether the American republic is a democracy at all, assuming "democracy" can be defined.

The theme of this book is that these and other paradoxes like them can be explained if each is stated unflinchingly and then made to submit to the distinction between what we call "myth" and what we call "ideology." But there is a second requirement. The distinction between myth and ideology must itself be treated rigorously and rooted in fundamental conceptions about politics and power. When this is done, these terms can be defined by reference to the functions they perform in the political system: myth is the set of ideas, values, and practices by which power in the system is created and legitimated; ideology is the set of ideas, values, and practices by which power is organized and exercised on a day-to-day basis.

Once the myth-ideology distinction has been established, we believe a whole range of paradoxes in American government will yield to explanation. America is indeed a democracy, but ambiguously. In legitimizing myth, it is a Social Democracy, dedicated to egalitarian propositions and founded on the principle of sovereignty of the people. In practical ideology, it is a Liberal Democracy with a powerful elitist bias. The presidency is both strong and weak—strong in myth, weak in ideology. Parties are vital to the American political system—in myth. In ideology they hardly exist. In myth, Congress is the supreme law-making body of the land but of distinctly less significance than the presidency. In ideology, Congress is the political system's primary mechanism for harmonizing the diverse claims of the competing interests; as such, it plays a central and indispensable role in American politics.

There is one matter we do not address. The tone of the book is skeptical about the political system's ability to do anything more than survive indefinitely. Yet at no point do we take up the question of what should be done about it. Some readers may find our reluctance here surprising, if not coy, but we have two reasons for it.

This is a book about what American government is. It is not a book about what American government might be, much less what it ought to be. We simply are not in the business of making recommendations about principles, policies, or persons. As we said at the outset, this is a critical, analytical text.

In the second place, it is our belief that the responsibility for confronting the challenge of what to do about the deficiencies of American government lies with our students, young, bright, and committed. Our hope is that we may help them meet that challenge by providing them with a critical, analytical account of what they are up against. As we say in the book's epilogue, our conclusions can be their beginning.

Acknowledgments

We are grateful to our reviewers: John Champlin of The Ohio State University, Janet Clark of the University of Wyoming, Kathy Ferguson of Siena College, Lawrence Mead of New York University, and Victor Wallis of Indiana University–Purdue University at Indianapolis. They gave unstintingly of their time and intelligence and saved us from many errors while providing constructive suggestions. We are especially grateful to the people at Macmillan, especially John Travis and Gene Panhorst, to Clark Baxter, former senior editor at Macmillan, and to Edward Cone. We also want to acknowledge the help given by four faculty members at Indiana University at Fort Wayne: Donna Bialik, Frank Codispodi, John Modic, and Shmuel Wahli. A special contribution was made by Murray Gibas. Marcie Irey typed a great deal of the manuscript. Finally, we thank each other for enormous hard work, patience, and forgiveness. The good work that appears in this book is of course claimed for ourselves individually, and the faults and excesses we assign, without hesitation, to the other.

H. MARK ROELOFS
GERALD L. HOUSEMAN

THE AMERICAN POLITICAL SYSTEM

MYTH

The People

States

Constitution

C P1 → P ← P2 Cts

Citizens

1. Sovereignty of the People
2. Confederalism
3. Separation of Powers
4. Responsible Two—
   Party Government

POWER

Gettysburg Address

Social Democracy "Equality"

Myth

Legitimization

Governance

Ideology

Declaration of Independence

Liberal Democracy "Freedom"

Protestant | Bourgeois

Individualism

IDEOLOGY

Constitution

Cts.

States

Fed Gov S P R

Rich "Poor"

(The Rest)

1. Constitutionalism
2. Federalism
3. Mixed Government (Ck + Bl)
4. Representative Government
   (Elite Pluralism)

A composite schematic diagram of the American political system. The center of the diagram represents power as American individualism's essential understanding of politics. The right and left halves of the diagram represent the progressive development of the power concept's mythic and ideological components. The left half shows myth's development from the Gettysburg Address's egalitarianism through Social Democracy's understanding of America as a united historic community equipped with the institutions listed in the diagram's lower left-hand corner. The right half of the diagram shows ideology's development from the Declaration of Independence's libertarianism through Liberal Democracy's understanding of America as a framework of law equipped with the institutions listed in the diagram's lower right-hand corner.

CONTENTS

Introduction 1

PRINCIPLES 9

1 The Paradoxes of American Politics 11

Diversity and Consensus in America 14
   A Nation of Individuals and Groups 14
   Diversity, But a Surprising Unity 15
   Importance of Religion 17
   Importance of the Business Ethic 19
American Political Individualism 21
   The Individualist Philosophy 21
   The Roots of Individualism: Hobbes and Locke 21
Schizophrenic Politics 28
   Edwards and Franklin: Separate Paths 29
   Implications 31

2 Power in America 34

Politics and Power 37
   Establishing Power 38
   Legitimation and Governance 39
Myth and Ideology 42
   Legitimacy, A Requisite for Power 45
   National and Political Culture 46
   Myth and Ideology 48

Myth in America   **51**
  Myth and Patriotism   51
  Myth and the Gettysburg Address   54
  Our Primary Myth: A Single People   56
Ideology in America   **57**
  The Dialogues and Practice of Governance   57
  The Founders' View of Government and Society   58
  Minority Rights to be Protected: Calhoun   59
  Ideologically, A System of Elite Rule   60
  In Myth, a System of Popular Democracy   63

3 The Partitioning of Authority: Federalism and the Separation of Powers 67

Federalism: A General Description   **70**
  Purpose and Arrangements for Dividing Power   70
  Operating the System   73
  The Mythic Interpretation of Federalism   77
  The Ideological Interpretation of Federalism   78
Separation of Powers: A General Description   **82**
  The Parliamentary System: A Contrast   84
  American Government: Not "Responsible"   85
  Separation of Powers and Checks and Balances   86
The "Pure" Theory of Separation of Powers   **87**
The Theory of Mixed Government   **89**
  Bicameralism   89
  Mixed Government Theory and Devotion to Law   91
  Presidential Veto   92
  Elitism and the "Democratic Element"   92
A "Bifocal" Vision of American Government   **94**

4 The Processes of the American Political System 96

Political Actors and the Political Process   **97**
  Political Actors: A Classification   97
  Stages of the Political Process   98
The "Normal" Stage—Liberal Democracy   **101**
  The Baronial Elite   102
  Corruption   104

Public Policy and the "Public Interest" 105
Calhounian "Incrementalism" 107

The "Stress" Stage—Social Democracy   **110**
The Rise of Discontent 110
The Social Democratic Vision 111
Elections and Social Democracy: Relegitimation 113

The "Crisis" Stage   **117**
The Civil War, Slavery, and the Pattern of Crisis 117
The Aftermath of Crisis 119

CONSTITUTIONAL STRUCTURES 123

5 The Courts   125

The Judicial System   **128**
The English Legacy 128
Civil and Criminal Law 129
An Independent Judiciary 130

The Organization of Justice   **139**
Judicial Selection 139
Federal Appeals and District Court
  Appointments 141
Powers and Jurisdiction of the Judicial Branch 143

The Special Functions and Purposes of the Supreme   **144**
Court
Ideology, Myth, and the Supreme Court 144
Judicial Review 146
Federal Supremacy and the Commerce Clause 149
Limitations on the Court's Power 150
The Ideological Limitation 154

6 The Congress   160

Congress in Myth and Ideology   **162**
Congress as a Legislature   **164**
The Constitutional Mandate 164
The Legislative Process in Myth 169
Party Organization in Congress 171
The President and Congress 173
The Courts and Congress 174

Representative Government   **174**

The Position and Privileges of Congress
  Members 174

Re-election: The First Priority 179

The Committee System and the Seniority
  System 181

Customs, Folkways, and Reciprocity 182

"Representative" Congress 186

The Investigatory Power and the Oversight
  Function 186

The Legislative Process in Ideology 190

How a Bill Becomes a Law 192

Lobbyists 196

7 The Presidency   **201**

The Presidency: Tradition and Constitutional Position   **204**

Institutionalization of the Presidency 206

A Presidential Perspective 213

The Mythic Role of the Presidency   **215**

Presidential Personalities and Styles 215

The Symbols of the Presidency 217

The Budget Process 221

The Presidency and Foreign Policy 227

The President's Ideological Role   **228**

Budget-Making 229

Foreign Policy 231

Philosophical Limitations 234

The Assassination Threat   **236**

8 State and Local Government   **239**

State and Local Government in the Constitutional System   **240**

Ideology, Myth, and State and Local
  Government 242

Intergovernmental Relations 242

The Structure of State Governments   **245**

Popular Control of Government 246

The Governor 246

The Legislature 248

Legislative Reapportionment 255

The Structure of Local Governments   **257**
City Governments 257
Counties 258
Special Districts 259
Regional Government 260
Financing State and Local Governments   **260**
The Cost of State and Local Governments 260
Types of State and Local Taxes 261
Inequities: The Case of School Financing 261
Federal Grants-in-Aid 263
Revenue Sharing 263
State and Local Government in Social Democratic   **264**
Myth
Citizenship Participation Amid Fragmented
   Government and Fragmented Hopes 264
Social Democratic Myth and the Spirit of Reform 266
Effects of Reform 267
State and Local Government in Liberal Democratic   **271**
Ideology
The Problem of "Representative" Government 272
Social Program Inadequacy 275

THE ADMINISTRATIVE STATE   279

9 The Bureaucracy   281

Bureaucratic Organization   **284**
The Size and Shape of the Federal Government 284
Cabinet Departments 287
Independent Agencies 288
Independent Regulatory Commissions 289
Government Corporations and Coordinating
   Agencies 293
Making and Administering Laws and Regulations 294
Rational Professionalism and Organizational Behavior   **296**
The Rational-Professional Mind 297
Conventional Norms, Terms, and Roles 299
Bureaucratic Practices 302
Reorganizing the Bureaucracy 307
Reform of Bureaucratic Budgeting 310
Freedom of Information Act 314

10 Foreign Policy and National Security   316

Imperial Crusades   319
Myth and Ideology in Foreign and Defense
  Policy 319
Historical Roots of Our Foreign Policy 320
The Foreign Policy Establishment   325
The Constitutional Mandate: President and
  Congress 326
The NSC, NSA, and the CIA 327
The State Department 330
The Defense Department 333
AID and ICA 338
Policy Coordination 339
The Military-Industrial Complex   341

11 Economic Management   348

Models of Economic Management   351
Adam Smith and Free Enterprise 351
Socialism 352
The Mixed Economy: A Response to the Demands of   354
  Ideology
The Eighteenth Century 354
The Nineteenth Century 354
The Great Depression 356
Economic Management Since World War II 358
Supply-Side Economics 360
The Mixed Economy: The Reaction of Myth   361
The Tools of Economic Management   365
Fiscal Policy 365
Monetary Policy 368
Wage-Price Guidelines and Jawboning 373
Wage and Price Controls 375
Conclusion   375

12 The Welfare State   377

Contributory Welfare Programs: The Social Security   381
  System
Solving the Funding Dilemma 382

Social Security Financing: Not Based on Ability to
    Pay 382
Noncontributory Programs   **385**
    The Reagan Cuts 388
Does the Welfare System Work?   **390**
Social Needs and the Purposes of the Welfare State   **392**
    The Invisible Poor 393
    Dependence and Insecurity 393
    Regulation of the Poor 394
Reforming the Welfare System   **396**
The Clouded Future of the Welfare State   **398**

IV

THE PEOPLE 403

13 Mass Myths   **405**

Components of the Social Democratic Myth   **406**
Socialization   **408**
    The Family 409
    Peer Groups 411
    Schools 411
    Mass Media 413
    Cultural Rituals 420
Varieties of Unbelief   **420**
    The Apathetic 422
    The Cynical 422
    The Alienated 423
    The Anomic 423
Public Opinion   **424**
    Measuring Public Opinion: The Polls 425
    Evaluating Polls 427
    Distorting the Political Process 429
    Public Opinion and Public Policy 429
    Other Objective Indicators of Political Attitudes 429

**14 Political Participation, Parties,
and Elections**   **431**

Civic Participation   **434**
    A Profile of Political Participants 434

Organizing the People 435
Organizing Groups 438
Political Parties   **442**
The Mythic Role of Political Parties 442
The Ideological Role of Parties 447
Elections   **455**
The Electoral College 455
Primary Elections 461
Campaigns 462
The Meaning of Elections   **465**

15 Civil Liberties   472

The Bill of Rights   **477**
The First Amendment: Freedom of Speech, Freedom
   of Religion, and Separation of Church and State 477
The Second Amendment and Gun Control 480
The Third Amendment: Quartering Troops Banned 480
Amendments Four, Five, Six, Seven, and Eight: "Due
   Process" 480
The Ninth and Tenth Amendments 483
Threats to the Bill of Rights Freedoms   **483**
The First Amendment Freedoms: Interpretations and   **484**
   Analyses
Free Speech 484
The "Clear and Present Danger" Test 486
Public Safety and "Fighting Words" 488
Obscenity and Censorship 489
Libel and Defamation 490
Free Exercise of Religion 491
The Separation Clause 492
Freedom of Assembly and Freedom of
   Association 494
Equal Protection of the Laws   **495**
The Due Process and Equal Protection Requirements
   of the Fourteenth Amendment 495
Equality and Equal Protection 496
Equal Protection and the Supreme Court 497
Affirmative Action and Equal Employment
   Opportunity 498
Is the Fourteenth Amendment Adequate? 499
Privacy   **503**
Privacy of the Home and the Person 503

Griswold v. Connecticut: Finding the Right of Privacy
in the Constitution 504
The Criminal Law Definition of Privacy 505

16 Corporate America   509

The Modern Business Corporation   509
Roots and History of the Corporation in America   515
Corporate Governance and Perquisites   517
Socialization of the Public by Corporations   520
Political Activities of Corporations   525
Public Policy and Corporate Ideology   530
Taxation and Subsidies 531
Antitrust Policy 534
Policies of Social Responsibility 539
Corporate Ideology in the International Arena   540
The Multinational Corporation 540
Multinational Policies and Activities 542
The Corporate State   543
The Crisis of Reindustrialization 543

Conclusion: The Approaching Crisis   547

Glossary   551

Appendix I: The Declaration of Independence   561

Appendix II: The Constitution of the United States   565

Index   585

Introduction

American politics is paradoxical. We say one thing and do another. Endlessly, we shield our political acts in the rhetoric of noble aspirations. Why does our political life so often appear to be quite different from what it really is?

Our chief executives call with the greatest urgency for broad programs to deal with fiscal crises, urban decay, unemployment, nuclear waste, racial antagonisms, and crime in the streets. Yet years go by with little coherent or constructive action taken to solve these problems. Our legislatures generate welfare programs to aid the poor, but poverty continues to spread on a scale that, in a rich and humane nation, is as scandalous as it is barbaric. The courts insist on protection of the rights of every citizen, including those who admit their criminality, but police brutality is common, justice is delayed and uneven, and conditions in our prisons are regularly described as deplorable.

In our wars, national leaders proclaim dedication to the highest ideals of humanitarianism. But here the paradoxes apply in even more gruesome detail, for the conduct of those wars has been marked by individual incidents and even officially sanctioned policies of unbridled ferocity and brutality. It is not only the Vietnamese who testify to this: our history shows that this barbarity has been meted out to Japanese civilians, Philippine insurgents, American Indians, and the victims of our own Civil War.

Probably the most widely felt paradox in the American political system is that whereas it is in every appearance a true democracy, in practice it falls short of that ideal many times and in serious ways. National slogans about the "sovereignty of the people," patriotic songs about this "sweet land of liberty," monuments to fallen heroes such as Abraham Lincoln, and, above all, the unceasing rhetoric of our politicians during their extended and expensive election campaigns all seek to persuade us that our government is truly of, by, and for the people. Yet we know that major segments of the populace, for no reason other than race, religion, sex, economic condition, lack of education, or some combination of these, have often been systematically excluded from the processes of government. And this is still true, despite a hundred years or more of presidential proclamations, constitutional amendments, statutes, court decisions, and administrators' programs to the contrary.

It is also significant that millions of Americans, the polls tell us, feel "left out" of the system. Over the years, they have come to suspect that our fabled "democracy" is something of a façade, and that the "real" decisions affecting their lives are largely made by self-appointed and self-perpetuating elite groups occupying seats of power mostly hidden from public view and influence. The malaise can be measured in many ways: by the worries expressed about the future of the country in many opinion polls, by the kinds of broad concerns lacking articulated solutions that are displayed for us in the media, and by the decline in voting in presidential elections that has persisted as a steady pattern since 1960—the longest period of voting decline in American history.[1]

This book seeks to confront the paradoxes of the American political system. There is no pretense that the strains and tensions, the ambiguities and deceptions that we see in the American world of politics are just so many occasional accidents, individual mistakes, or pardonable errors. The paradoxes of American politics are real. They are deeply rooted, ongoing characteristics of the system as much as its principal and formal parts are. It is an undeniable fact that the American people are basically of a democratic spirit and wish to see their government faithfully embody that spirit. It is also true that the government which rules them can be undemocratic in many important ways. Perhaps more surprising to those who have learned the highly "patriotic" versions of our history, it can be shown that this government was designed from its very beginning to be "undemocratic."

The central device by which this book confronts facts of this order is the distinction between myth and ideology. This distinction is applied right across the American political system, both to its basic components and to the system itself. All of the major institutions and processes of American government are described and analyzed in detail in the pages to come; but because the myth-ideology distinction is the basic analytic device of the book, and because its twin terms are employed in special ways, a brief and general explanation of these is necessary at the outset.

"Myth" is our national hope. It is what we are taught to believe about ourselves and our government by slogan, song, and saga, but also by folk wisdom, school texts and teachers, and the customs and values implicit in a host of citizenship activities. The most important of these

---

[1] *Statistical Abstract of the United States 1977*, p. 508, quoted in Howard L. Reiter, "Why Is Turnout Down?" *Public Opinion Quarterly*, 43: 297 (Fall 1979).

activities, incidentally, is voting in national, state, and local elections. Myth is our identity as a political people, our traditional, national self-understanding. It is how we picture ourselves and how we wish to be seen in the world. Saying that myth is essentially our national "self-appearance," however, does not downplay its importance. In politics even more than in other spheres of life, appearances are of enormous importance. By appearing at least to ourselves to be a certain kind of people with a particular history, dedicated to a given set of ideals, we become identifiable in a selected and fixed way to ourselves and to others as a nation among nations. It is myth that spells out the meaning of our symbols—the flag, the statues of heroes like Washington and Jefferson, the national anthem, the eagle clutching the olive branch on one side and the weapons of war on the other. It is myth that over the years has given our political institutions the appearance of democracy and dictated that we citizens should vote unfailingly in all elections, cheering the victors in the name of national unity, while consoling the defeated to try again another day.

By believing myth, by believing our government to be in conscientious service to certain ideals, and by accepting it for what it *appears* to be in myth, we prepare ourselves to obey its laws and to support it with our loyalty, our taxes, and, if need be, our lives. We are prepared, in the words of President John F. Kennedy, to suffer any cost, bear any burden, and ask not what our government can do for us, but what we can do for our government.

In short, myth identifies, defines, legitimizes. Myth is that whole body of national lore, symbol, and periodic bouts of activity by which we know and reveal ourselves to be Americans—free, kind, democratic, and proud.

"Ideology" is a much more routine sort of phenomenon. It is the "how to" of politics. Ideology comprises the practical institutions, understandings, assumptions, and values by which authority and authority relationships are established, operated, and maintained. These authority relationships are about who is to do what, how, why, and to whom. Ideology defines roles and institutional relationships in the political system so that men and women in public life can perform the day-to-day tasks of government. Ideology is concerned with persuasion, influence, brokerage, job-seeking, power, and coercion. It is carried out by law and conventional practice and it is the basis of the operative understanding between the casts of characters who make up the world of American politics—judges, bureaucrats, politicians, (whether office-holders or office-seekers), and government workers of every sort.

In a word, ideology is governance.

The terms "myth" and "ideology" are given more extensive explanation in later sections of this book; but it is already possible at this point to set out the overarching theme of the book. The theme is that in America, for a variety of reasons, our national legitimizing myth and our ideology of governance are at odds. We are not, in ideological practice, what we aim to be in mythic aspiration. We are therefore, in a permanent and fundamental sense, false to ourselves. Continually over the decades of our history, we have strained mightily against ourselves. It is in this clash between myth and ideology that the final source of both the dynamic and the paradox of American politics is found.

The reader should note that the terms "myth" and "ideology" are given special meanings in this book that are related to, but do not exactly correspond to, ordinary usage. Ordinary usage might suggest that we distinguish between "myth" and "reality," or, abandoning these terms altogether, that we talk about the difference between "theory" and "practice." But these ordinary usages raise difficulties of their own. First, what is called "myth" in this book is as substantially and functionally *real* as any other part of the political system. Americans over the years really have come to identify themselves in certain ways with freedom, equality, democracy, and other values. Second, the notion that one can logically distinguish between "theory" and "practice" in any serious discussion is not defensible. Is there a "theory" and a "practice" of gravity? The authors grant that defining terms is a slippery business but hope that once they have made clear the meanings they are giving these terms, and also the relevance of these meanings to the problems that must be analyzed, their definitions will be allowed to stand.

The development of this myth-ideology theme through the various chapters involves description and analysis of every major feature of the American political system, from basic principles to particular problems, from legal structures to political processes, from interest group demands to policy implementation and evaluation, from national institutions to state and local government. We hope that the mass of useful information we provide will enable the reader to understand how our political system functions. Knowing information, however, is never enough by itself. Information must be placed in a useful and understandable context so that facts, processes, institutions, opinions, attitudes, behavior, and yes, ideology and myth, can be combined into meaningful relationships. That is why this book has a theme and why this theme is squarely stated at the beginning. By understanding the theme, the reader can be prepared for the wealth of information to come.

The obvious point should be made that information about American government and politics is not available to students in this book alone; while working through the text, readers are urged to study with special care the daily press, weekly newsmagazines, and other current sources as well as the bibliography at the end of each chapter. As a result we hope that the reader will not only know the facts of American politics and government but will also be able to understand and explain them.

The format of the book is closely tied to the theme of the clash in American politics between myth and ideology. The reader should first look ahead and survey the book as a whole to see how the theme makes its way through the topics of the various chapters.

Part 1 is composed of four chapters that lay out the basic myth-ideology dichotomies of the American political system: (1) the rocklike base of the system rooted in an individualism divided against itself; (2) the expression of this divided individualism in the nation's legitimizing myth on the one hand and its ideological patterns of governance on the other; (3) the application of these, in turn, to the system's two fundamental constitutional principles—federalism and the separation of powers—with the consequent ambiguous formulation of each principle; and (4) the product of this whole structure of ambiguity in conflicting visions of the nation's democratic life—the Social Democratic vision of its mythic aspirations and the Liberal Democratic vision of its ideological governance. The fourth chapter of Part 1 is probably the most important chapter in the book. For it is in the conflict between the Social Democracy of America's legitimizing hopes and the Liberal Democracy of its ideological practice, and in the periodic crises arising from the inevitable confrontations between them, that the full scale of the paradox in the American political system can be most comprehensively seen.

In Part 2, the myth-ideology perspective is used to analyze the major units of the American political system—the courts, Congress, the presidency, and state and local government. There will be some surprises here. Myth is a convincing mask. Judging by appearances, most of us believe we know in a general way what these major units of government do. Under the focus of myth-ideology analysis, however, we will find that whereas our courts are in some measure concerned with dispensing justice, their more substantive function is to preserve the legal limitations, just or unjust, within which public and private life goes on in this country. Analysis will further show that Congress, though it is to all mythic appearances a law-making body for all the people and organizes itself dutifully as such, is in ideological practice far more involved in representing special interests and harmonizing as best it can the diversity of claims upon it by a wide array of corporate and other private elites and their bureaucratic allies. Then there is the presidency, a grand and supremely powerful office—in myth. In ideological practice, its possibilities are sharply circumscribed except for its virtually unlimited capacity to regenerate the myth of its own greatness. Finally, we look at state and local government, fabled in tale and textbook as the grassroots of our national democracy. In ideological practice, they reproduce in an extraordinarily literal way the elitist patterns of the national government, especially as exemplified in Congress.

The four chapters of Part 3 examine the administrative state, also viewed in the myth-ideology perspective. The bureaucracy in Washington and in offices across the country is sometimes referred to as the government's "fourth branch." Certainly in number of personnel it is far and away the biggest part of the government and the one that impinges most directly and most frequently on the lives of ordinary citizens. The general significance of its work is matched only by its diversity and extent—economic management, providing essential services, administering the welfare state, running cultural and research programs, protecting our civil liberties, and carrying out military and foreign policy. Nevertheless, the performance of this vast mechanism poses fundamental problems both for our daily lives and for analysis. Bureaucracy by nature is supposed to be a service. Although it may appear to be mostly concerned with serving itself, in principle bureaucracy works for others under the leadership of Congress, the presidency, the judiciary, and other centers of public life. But in the American political system, this leadership is as fragmented and ambivalent as the system itself. In consequence, the bureaucracy, though it is summoned by the system's mythic side to confront pervasive problems with comprehensive programs formulated in the spirit of humanitarianism and the public interest, finds itself splintered, harassed, and frustrated by the ideological forces in the political system that controls it. There is a glacial inevitability in the bureaucracy's slide toward performance marked by confusion, inefficiency, self-serving, and pettiness.

The final section of the book, Part 4, deals with "politics"—the major processes by which citizens and groups of all kinds seek access to, influence upon, and control over governmental personnel, decisions, and programs. The most obvious subjects here are political parties and the elections in which, in myth, parties are historically supposed to be the primary agents. Analysis demonstrates, however, that American political parties seldom perform any of the functions assigned to them in myth and that in ideological practice they barely exist. Elections are primarily of expressive, that is, of emotional significance and serve mostly as rites of regime legitimation. At the practical level, interests that are financially and organizationally powerful enough largely bypass parties and elections and act directly upon the governmental apparatus, issue by issue, through lobbying and other forms of interest group activity. Meanwhile, the rest of the citizenry is systematically socialized, through direct instruction in the schools as well as by other means, into occasionally active but mostly passive acceptance of the dominant myths of the system. The most important of these myths is that the ordinary citizen, through the ballot, has a significant influence on public policymaking and elected officials, who are viewed as "responsible" for all that the government does.

The conclusion of the book directly challenges the reader. Overall, it must be admitted, the book's tone has been clearly skeptical, but it has also been rigorously analytical. It has stated its broad theme, assembled facts around it, analyzed the meanings and relationships of these facts, and pointed to conclusions. But it has made no recommendations. It does not make any now. The American political system *on its own terms* works reasonably well. This is an inescapable conclusion wrought by virtually every fact and strand of analysis presented in the course of this book.

A growing number of alert and concerned citizens will not rest easily with such a conclusion. What is to be done? This is the difficult, profound, and urgent question we face. The answer to it lies with the reader, who must work it out independently. There may be some small comfort in knowing that thinking about what is to be done is necessarily the first step. In the meantime, we must face the facts without flinching, realizing that in both myth and ideology they go to the roots of the system.

PRINCIPLES I

In this part we examine the fundamental principles of the American political system. There are four chapters, each dealing with a separate principle or set of principles.

The first chapter examines the political system's fundamental value, individualism. But the chapter shows that this individualism is divided against itself into Protestant and Bourgeois halves that war against each other.

Chapter 2 shows how this divided individualism is incorporated into the political system's fundamental organizing concept, power. The Protestant side of our individualism produces myths that legitimize power; the Bourgeois side of it produces the ideology in terms of which power is exercised.

Chapter 3 details how this two-sided understanding of power is applied to the political system's major institutional principles, federalism and separation of powers. Both these principles are shown to experience double interpretations, so that federalism means one thing in myth, another in ideology, and separation of powers equally means one thing in myth and something else in ideology.

Chapter 4 gathers all these points and shows how in aggregate they form within the political system two conflicting visions of democracy—the Social Democracy of our great, legitimating political myths and the Liberal Democracy of the ideology of our day-to-day practice of government.

The central theme of these four chapters is that the conflicts in American democracy, the internal tensions that fill it with paradox, are rooted in the system's most fundamental political values and worked out in its most fundamental organizing and institutional principles and processes.

The Paradoxes of American Politics

1

The political career of Richard Milhous Nixon, thirty-seventh president of the United States, was paradoxical. In its final phases, Nixon was elected to the presidency in 1968 by the narrowest of margins but was re-elected four years later by one of the most impressive landslides ever recorded. Then because of the Watergate scandal, less than two years later, he became the first president forced to resign from office.

While many believed he had disgraced the office of president and humiliated the country in the eyes of the world, Nixon was never formally charged with any crime. President Ford gave him a blanket pardon to forestall any charges from being brought, and he has since lived out his life in what any ordinary person would regard as sumptuous if rather lonely luxury with a variety of government benefits such as a large pension and full Secret Service protection.

Many other paradoxes can be found in Nixon's career, some ironic, some bitter indeed. But there is a more profound paradox lying behind his career, the paradox of the Nixon personality. Throughout his political life he tried hard to be "correct" in dress, speech, and action. Methodically and without humor, he ceaselessly aimed to do "the right thing." Yet his public life was blotched almost from the beginning with repeated instances of gross insensitivity, bad judgment, and dubious morality. As his last public crisis drew to a close, many people concluded that Nixon was an evil man, an aberrant figure in American politics. They believed that his career was an unfortunate accident that the constitutional system, with some difficulty, was able in the end to expel. They concluded that the Watergate crisis revealed the strengths and the genius of the American political system. The system somehow manages to be self-correcting. But with the advantage of several years' hindsight, it does not look quite that way.

Before his last crisis of exposure and resignation, Nixon seemed in many respects a quite ordinary American politician to some observers.

The columnist and widely read author Garry Wills, for one, thought that Nixon looked almost typically American, the epitome of the painfully ordinary. In 1969, four years before Nixon's resignation, Wills published *Nixon Agonistes,* a book with the subtitle "The Crisis of the Self-Made Man." It was based on materials and interviews Wills had been collecting for many years and, of course, Wills had no benefit of foreknowledge of the scandals and disgrace that were soon to be exposed. But Wills's book remains among the best biographies of Nixon. The preface opens with these words:

> This book grew out of a series of reportorial assignments that led me to watch the American people make Richard Nixon President, then led me to reflect upon this man elected, these people electing him, the relation of country to President as he took up and wielded powers they had granted him. To say the two deserve each other will, I suppose, be taken as an insult (to one or the other), though I mean the remark in several ways, some complimentary (to both). What is best and weakest in America . . . [is reciprocated in the] strength and deficiencies [of] Richard Nixon.[1]

What Wills found ordinary in Nixon, what made him think Nixon was both a reflection and a projection of essential features of the American political character, was the thought he set out in his book's subtitle, "The Crisis of the Self-Made Man." The same thought is in the second word of the book's title, "Agonistes." The word comes from a Greek root meaning "contest" and is the source of such modern words as "agony" and "agonizing." In the seventeenth century, the English poet John Milton had written a drama about Samson, the blinded giant of the Old Testament, and had called it *Samson Agonistes.* Wills, borrowing from

---

[1] Garry Wills, *Nixon Agonistes: The Crisis of the Self-Made Man* (New York: New American Library, 1969), p. ix.

**BOX 1–1
President Richard
M. Nixon on the
People**

The average American is just like the child in the family. You give him some responsibility and he is going to amount to something. He is going to do something. If, on the other hand, you make him completely dependent and pamper him and cater to him too much, you make him soft, spoiled and eventually a weak individual.

—Quoted in the introduction to *People vs. Government: The Responsiveness of American Institutions,* Leroy N. Rieselbach, ed. (Bloomington: Indiana University Press, 1975).

WE HOLD THESE TRUTHS TO BE SELF-EVIDENT: THAT ALL MEN ARE CREATED EQUAL, THAT THEY ARE ENDOWED BY THEIR CREATOR WITH CERTAIN INALIENABLE RIGHTS, AMONG THESE ARE LIFE, LIBERTY AND THE PURSUIT OF HAPPINESS, THAT TO SECURE THESE RIGHTS GOVERNMENTS ARE INSTITUTED AMONG MEN. WE... SOLEMNLY PUBLISH AND DECLARE, THAT THESE COLONIES ARE AND OF RIGHT OUGHT TO BE FREE AND INDEPENDENT STATES···AND FOR THE SUPPORT OF THIS DECLARATION, WITH A FIRM RELIANCE ON THE PROTECTION OF DIVINE PROVIDENCE, WE MUTUALLY PLEDGE OUR LIVES, OUR FORTUNES AND OUR SACRED HONOUR.

Words of the Declaration of Independence adorn the walls of the Jefferson Memorial in Washington, D.C.

its title for his own, also put this line from Milton's poem at the front of his book on Nixon:

O lastly over-strong against thy self!

This line is a nearly perfect rendering of the central difficulty of the American political character. President Nixon's paradoxical personality, over-strong against himself so that he was his own worst enemy, is nothing more than an extreme expression of it. The division of the American political character against itself is the most enduring and fundamental feature of the American political system, the rock upon which all else is built. Its major elements may be summarized as follows:

1. Politically, as well as economically, religiously, ethnically, and racially, the American people seem to be a marvelous diversity;
2. In fact, politically as well as in other ways, the American people are contained within an extraordinarily narrow and uniform consensus about the whys and hows of politics, the basic tenet of which is a powerful individualism; but . . .
3. This individualism is deeply divided against itself and pulls all those who are committed to it in powerfully contradictory, even self-destructive ways.

This chapter takes up each of these three points, always with the thought that there may be more than a little of Nixon's paradoxical personality in each of us.

Diversity and Consensus in America

A Nation of Individuals and Groups   America is a nation of individuals and, to all appearances, we are a very diverse lot. Some of our diversities are of the sort all nations have, but we seem to make more of them. All nations have divisions between their young and old but, more than elsewhere, the young in America often

**BOX 1–2
Tom Wicker on the People**

New York Times columnist Tom Wicker is typical of many commentators who describe the American people in frustrated and bitter terms. Reviewing the movie *Nashville*, Wicker says that it depicts the "vulgarity, greed, deceit, cruelty, barely contained hysteria, and the frantic lack of root and grace into which American life has been driven by its own heedless vitality . . . the writhings of a culture that does not even know it is choking on exhaust fumes . . . a culture desperately clinging to the idea of value while vulgarizing almost every particular value . . . the American mobility culture, with its autos, obsolete and crunchable the day they're sold, its fastfood parlors, plastic motel rooms, take-out orders, transient sex and junk music."
—Quoted in *Society* 13-93 (January-February 1976).

Question: Compared to ten years ago, do you think blacks in America are a lot better off, a little better off, about the same, a little worse off, or a lot worse off?

Responses of Blacks		Responses of Whites
18%	A lot better off	52%
42	A little better off	39
29	About the same	10
9	A little worse off	2
8	A lot worse off	2

—Survey by NBC/Associated Press, May 28–30, 1980; reported in *Public Opinion* 4:32 (April/May 1981).

appear to have left the old far behind and the two groups seem to hold radically different perspectives on life goals, personal morality, leisure-time activities, respect for authority, and other far-reaching issues. Almost all countries have regional differences, but in America, North and South fought a Civil War of dreadful proportions that is still remembered for great battles nobly lost and even more noble causes still not won. Certainly all nations have social and economic class differences, but ours are more extreme than most of us care to admit. The top 5 percent of American families in terms of income increased their share of the national wealth from 14.4 percent to 15.7 percent between 1972 and 1980, while the lowest 20 percent saw its share decline from 5.5 percent to 5.2 percent. Any number of other studies and indices confirms that since 1972 the gap between rich and poor incomes has been steadily increasing.[2] We have a predominant and affluent middle class but our wealthy citizens are very rich indeed, and the extremity of the conditions of our desperately poor is difficult to match in most Western, industrialized nations.

**Diversity, But a
Surprising Unity**

The real flavor of American diversity is captured only in what our school texts tell us about: that in this land of every climate and geography dwell sizable populations of all races, ethnic types, cultural backgrounds, and religions. In one nation we find large numbers of people who represent every hue of black, yellow, red and white skin. Most nations of the world have secured significant representation on these shores.

[2] U.S. Bureau of the Census, *Population Reports*, and Peter Henle, "Exploring the Distribution of Earned Income," *Monthly Labor Review*, 95: 16–27 (December 1972).

America's religions are symbolic of this diversity. We are said to be a nation of churches and temples, not just Protestant, Catholic and Jewish but every gradation of these. There are more than two hundred fifty recognized, established religions in the United States, but a further fact deepens this diversity. The differences between our nation's groups, denominations, and ethnic and racial affiliations are serious enough to break out fairly often into open antagonisms, and this has been going on at least since the burning of a Catholic monastery in the Massachusetts Bay Colony. Our Civil War has not been repeated and certainly America as a whole throughout its history has had a more or less peaceful time of it compared with the recurring bloodbaths of Ireland, Lebanon, and the Balkans. Nevertheless we still experience serious problems of group, racial, ethnic, and religious tension.

All these observations add up to a serious question about what holds

A great variety of religious and ethnic groups have migrated to America since its beginning, and this process still goes on.

ELLIS ISLAND

The island nearest you was the gateway through which some 12 million persons entered the United States between 1892 and 1954. In 1907 alone more than one million people from many nations landed there. The towered building was the Immigrant Station where all newcomers reported.

Ellis Island was made part of Statue of Liberty National Monument by Presidential Proclamation in May 1965. It is being developed as an immigration memorial.

us together as one nation. On the face of it, it is more than a little surprising that the Civil War happened only once and that, despite the outbreak from time to time of race riots, violent strikes, and the like, the nation has held together in one piece as well as it has.

One reason for this surprising degree of unity is the political system. The authors of the Constitution recognized that America was a land of diversities and they designed our institutions with this thought foremost in their minds. To this end they gave the constitutional system two overriding characteristics. Structurally the system looks loose and fragmented to the point of being disjointed. In operation its flexibility allows for the representation of a range of extraordinarily diverse interests, each of which receives some measure of attention to its special claims. Viewed from another perspective, the political system is an overarching and remarkably durable structure of law that "cages" all of us in one way or another within its confines. Our federal Constitution and the political system it has spawned give us more unity than perhaps we have a reasonable right to expect. No wonder we customarily revere the Constitution, keeping it sealed at the National Archives Building in Washington in a bronze and glass case filled with helium.

There is, all the same, an even more important factor holding us together than the forms of our political institutions. Behind the appearance of great diversity in race, ethnicity, economic class, social affiliations, and religious convictions is an extraordinary measure of allegiance across America to fundamental values and propositions about how and why life should be lived, by whom it should be lived, and what we may reasonably expect from our economic, social and political systems. America has been to an uncommon degree forged into a nation of acutely shared values about what it means to have a nice home, drive a fine car, be a success, worship God, radiate beauty, be open and friendly, get ahead, and expect certain entitlements (see Box 1–4). This sharing of values helps to brace and support our political institutions.

Importance of Religion

This point is well-illustrated by looking again at our religious life. The profusion of our various affiliations is deceptive. It appears we can all believe as we please, however diverse our outlooks; but a common thread outweighs and supplants all these differences. By providing a religion for virtually every taste, the American religious community puts a heavy imperative on each of us to attend some house of worship. Everyone is expected to be religious in one way or another.

As more than one perceptive observer has noticed, the religions of America, at the deeper levels, have much in common.[3] The striking dif-

[3] Will Herberg, *Protestant, Catholic, Jew: An Essay in American Religious Sociology* (Garden City: Doubleday, 1956); H. Richard Niebuhr, *The Social Sources of Denominationalism* (New York: World, 1971).

BOX 1–4
Economic, Social,
and Political Rights
to Which
Americans Believe
They Are Entitled

Asked whether they believed they were morally or legally entitled to a list of certain benefits and rights as citizens, a sample of respondents answered affirmatively in the following percentages to various items:

Prevention of serious crimes in the cities	94%
Effective teaching of reading and writing in school	94
Products certified as safe and not hazardous to health	90
Honest and reliable reporting in the news media	90
Adequate public transportation	90
Adequate housing within each person's means	89
Steadily improving standard of living	88
Legal protection against unauthorized use of confidential personal information	88
Adequate retirement income adjusted for inflation	87
A guaranteed job for all those willing and able to work	85
Being able to buy as much gas as one wants	75
Use of professional services, such as lawyers in public clinics	71
Television programming uncluttered by commercials	63
Graduate or professional schooling free to all qualified	59
Free doctor and hospital care for everyone	55
Free dental care for everyone	53
Four-day workweek, gradually realized	52
Right to use drugs for pleasure	15

—Opinion Research Corporation; published in *Public Opinion* 4:16 (April/May 1981).

ferences in ritual, recited creeds, modes of discipline, and organization occasionally cause sharp disputes. Beneath these cultic differences at the level of operative personal religiosity, however, American Catholics, Jews, Protestants, and other groups share a common and distinctively American emphasis on personalized religion expressed through a need for commitment based on feeling and experience more than intellectual assent or studious reflection. This emphasis is widely distributed throughout various American religious organizations and groups, and its history is one of a steady, pervasive development. To note its effects, one should look past church or synagogue buildings with their characteristic architectural differences to the parking lots where the comings and goings are of a common pattern. Listen to the content of the youth programs and discover how alike in emphasis and concern they are; notice how similar are the manners and speech modes of the priests, rabbis, pastors, and ministers, for all their differences in dress and religious background. This causes us to think that the way of life of virtually all Americans, including many of the religiously indifferent, has a spirit closely related to the personalistic emphases of Evangelical Protestantism. This kind of religiosity places a premium upon individual problems, convictions, and conscience, upon "What *I* think and feel" rather than "This is what my religion says or dictates." In this generalized light, all Americans are strongly affected by this Protestant individualism.

The same conformist pressures to toe the line of a hidden ethical imperative can be seen in another significant area of American life, the business arena. The private enterprise system encourages all to work avidly at their chosen occupation to make a living or, perchance, get rich, sometimes very rich. The result is a vast display of diversity in every field of endeavor. It is true that much of what we call modern capitalism is monopolistic or oligopolistic capitalism in which competition is more shibboleth than fact. Nevertheless, individuals pursue their personal goals and careers, often with remarkable independence and mobility. And there are still some enclaves of venture capitalism and individual entrepreneurship. In business life in America the pursuit of personal profit, whether it be a salary, stock options, or margins of profit, is still the name of the game.

**Importance of the
Business Ethic**

Which is exactly the point. Despite the great diversity of activities undertaken in the American business world, we all are trying to make a living, and more if possible, for ourselves. The point is sometimes put in pejorative terms: everyone is caught up in the rat race. However it may be expressed or described, we can simply note that in American business the pursuit of material reward is the primary motive, and success or failure in this pursuit is the measure of importance (see Box 1–5). Once again, conformity and consensus on essentials lie just behind an outward spectacle of diversity.

The central value affirmed in American business life, moreover, turns out to be the identical central value hidden in American religious life. Whether in faith or in works, Americans are expected to be individualists, and quite radically so. With this kind of agreement in religion and business, we can anticipate that it will show up again in politics.

**BOX 1–5
The American
Dream**

HOUSTON, June 17—One day in 1978, Jeff Carter's accountant called. "You made it," he said.

At the age of 26, Mr. Carter had become a millionaire—four years ahead of the schedule he had set for himself, and just 12 years after he vowed, as an eighth grader in Odessa, Tex., wearing other families' hand-me-downs, that he would never be poor again.

Mr. Carter told the story as he surveyed the Houston skyline from his new office here, where the blondish, athlete-trim young entrepreneur—still more than six months shy of age 30—operates a budding, 17-company mini-empire, founded on oil and real estate, with assets estimated at between $100 million and $200 million, that is said to have made him a millionaire several times over. . . .

But, according to Mr. Carter's plans, all the above is merely prologue.

He'd once been a tennis pro for two years, but saw a limited future. He'd studied as an architect, but that meant working for other people. He read up on the storied names of American wealth, Rockefeller and Hunt and Getty and Mellon, and concluded that if they had what it took, so did he. And he decided to do what they had done.

"My goal," he said in the soft west Texas accent in which he still calls people "sir," was and is to put together "a combination of what I felt were their best assets." The objective now, Mr. Carter said, is nothing less than for him and his three brothers to become "one of the wealthiest families in the world," and one of the greatest. . . .

He works 18-hour days, travels to New York and Geneva in search of investors and money, drives a Mercedes 450, plays tennis when he can, has given up drinking, lunches on Perrier water and salad, dresses in three-piece suits and is getting a divorce from his wife, who, he said, did not like his constant commitment to work and would not move to Houston. . . .

—William K. Stevens, *New York Times*, June 18, 1981.

American Political Individualism

Individualism shows up in American politics in the same deceptive way it does in religion and business. In American political life, there is a constant appearance of almost chaotic diversity, with all kinds of political actors saying and doing every sort of thing with a minimum of coordination and unity. Our two major political parties, the Democrats and the Republicans, are supposed to bring some kind of order to all this confusing variety, but both of these parties are loose coalitions harboring various shades of political diversity. Though to some journalists and political scientists the two parties seem to be narrowing their appeal—the usual landmarks cited are the Goldwater convention of 1964 for the Republicans and the McGovern nomination in 1972 for the Democrats—the fact remains that both parties are still coalitions in organizational and philosophical terms. The GOP includes a "pragmatic" wing and an ultraconservative wing, and it is often alleged that President Ronald Reagan is too closely associated with the latter. The Democrats are represented in Congress by Ron Dellums of California, who is not afraid to embrace some Marxist tenets, and Larry McDonald of Georgia, who is a member of the far Right John Birch Society. Undisciplined variety seems to be what American politics is all about.

But once again, all this variety stems from a stern conformity to an underlying, rigorously supported orthodoxy called individualism. The Founding Fathers recognized this principle as primary and built a restraining "cage" of law around it. We must now discern what this principle means and how it has been affected by our traditions and laws. Individualism, after all, is not just a principle that concerns us as individuals. It is a philosophy about society and government, about how these are to be organized and operated to give primary recognition and status to the individual.

Individualism as a social and governmental philosophy originated in its modern form in seventeenth-century England. Its patron saint is usually said to be John Locke, and it was Locke that Thomas Jefferson, for one, believed he was most directly quoting when he wrote the Declaration of Independence. But it was the philosopher Thomas Hobbes who, some decades before Locke, most fully and originally spelled out modern individualism and its essential tenets. These may be listed as follows:

1. Each individual is a complete unit. Hobbes said the individual is an *ens completum*, a "complete thing," meaning that however each man and woman might depend on others for meeting physical wants, they

**BOX 1–6
The Strong Pull of
Individualism and
Assimilation Works
Against Diversity
and Promotes
Middle-Class Values**

George Foreman, the former world heavyweight champion: "I don't know the fancy words. . . . But I know if you're black, you have to work harder, hope harder, and not let the Man put you off. . . . we're going to make it. But like I can only depend on my fists and my strength, we've got to depend on what we do for ourselves."

—Louis Harris, *The Anguish of Change.* (New York: Norton, 1973), p. 247.

Many of [the] values [of the Mexican-American subculture] . . . are diametrically opposed to the value orientation of the middle class world. . . . For example, in the Mexican-American subculture emphasis is placed on the primary responsibility to family and on maintenance of family ties, on concentrating on the immediate present and consequently leaving events of the future in the hands of God. In the greater society, however, emphasis is placed on the individual and on minimal family ties so as to facilitate both physical (geographic) and social mobility; on achievement of material wealth and related status and privilege. . . .

—Salvador Ramirez, "Employment Problems of Mexican-American Youth," in *Mexican-Americans in the United States*, ed. by John H. Burma (Cambridge: Schenkman, 1970), p. 185.

[In the suburban Jewish home] interest in the Jewish tradition has withered, ceremonies are not adhered to, the basic skills of prayer have been lost; . . . Hebrew is unknown. . . . There is [an abundance of] science, atomic facts, sex and . . . American ways and values. . . .

—L. H. Grunebaum, quoted in Irving Howe, *World of Our Fathers* (New York: Simon and Schuster, 1977), p. 617.

Father Andrew Greeley relates a story . . . on the Irish about an academic colleague of his who for years tried unsuccessfully to get federal money for an 'Irish studies' program. Finally, the academic went to Washington to confront the bureaucrat in the Office of Education who had been turning down his requests. The . . . perplexed scholar asked outright, "Why don't you fund an Irish studies program?" Replied the

BOX 1–6
The Strong Pull of
Individualism and
Assimilation Works
Against Diversity
and Promotes
Middle-Class Values
(Continued)

bureaucrat, "Because the Irish don't count." In one very limited sense, the Washington official was right. Of all the ethnic
groups, the Irish are the most assimilated. Entire generations
of Irish rejected their ethnic past . . . to become "good Americans," and they succeeded.

—Mark R. Levy and Michael S. Kramer, *The Ethnic Factor* (New York: Simon
and Schuster, 1972), p. 139.

are each identifiable selves knowing their own needs and defining
their own ways and means for themselves.

2. The natural relationship between human beings is one of competition for scarce resources. Always active and seeking after material
goods, human beings must be curbed or they will tend toward a condition of "war of all against all."

3. The necessary restraint on our naturally unrestrained desires can be
supplied only by the creation of an absolute sovereign. By the terror
of his ways, he will hold us all in awe and keep the peace. Hobbes
believed that each of us has enough cool reason to see the need for
such a sovereign if only to protect our individual private interests,
and therefore by reasoning (and, incidentally, by reading Hobbes's
Leviathan) we can be persuaded to obey the sovereign and restrain
our excessive impulses within the limits of his law.

These three principles—the "atomistic" individual, the natural condition of war, and the peace-keeping and containing sovereign—may
appear, especially to Americans who feel the truth of these, to be uncomplicated. Nevertheless certain misunderstandings must be avoided.

First, Hobbes is not saying that people are naturally bad or even
"selfish." He is not passing any judgments at all. He thinks he is just
stating the facts on which any well-conceived political enterprise must
be based. People are just as they are; self-centeredness is their natural
state.

Second, Hobbes does not approve of war. He himself was notably
pacific in his personal demeanor. In his old age he recalled his birth in
1588, the year of the Spanish Armada's approach on England, and remarked that in that year his mother had brought forth twins, "myself
and fear." Hobbes's greatest fear was of war and violent death. His
greatest wish was for people to live in security and comfort, free from
war and violence, and able to enjoy the "delectations" of life.

And third, Hobbes's saying that the sovereign must be "absolute"
does not mean that he favors totalitarianism. Logically the sovereign
does not have to be a person at all; the sovereign can simply be the law,

which we should never take into our own hands. Hobbes's sovereign has very limited functions. He is to keep the peace, no more. That is all that calling him "absolute" means. There should not be, in the settlement of any dispute, any appeal beyond the sovereign. If there is, it can only lead to anarchy.

Hobbes and Locke wrote in an England that, although then torn by internal strife, was an ancient land with well-developed standards of civility and public trust. Hobbes and Locke wrote in a most unconscious way as spokesmen for the rising middle class that was bent on bringing to England the bounty of emerging industrialization and capitalism. Their writings assumed this, and their immediate audience assumed far more than they wrote. But England is not America, and when the works of Hobbes and Locke were read far across the Atlantic, there was no saving grace of a well-developed and supportive social context. In provincial eighteenth-century America, the bones of society were bare. Hobbes and Locke were taken literally by American readers. English social individualism became a brute individualism in America that, quite often throughout our history, has legitimized a dog-eat-dog view of politics and society.

One of the most immediate results of the literal reading of Hobbes and Locke is the famous second paragraph of the Declaration of Independence. To this day Americans suppose these few words constitute a

The Declaration of Independence is celebrated in the Tournament of Roses Parade in Pasadena, California.

complete and sufficient political philosophy. They certainly do state a radical individualism, as this rendering with a side commentary shows:

We hold these truths to be self-evident . . .
a statement designed to preclude all argument or debate

that all men . . .
what about women? Indians? black slaves? criminals? children? indentured servants? the very poor, the aged, the sick?

are created equal . . .
so that, as the race of life gets under way, some may become very unequal, but the rest should not complain about it

that they are endowed by their Creator . . .
directly and individually by an otherworldly power and not by society or its agents who are thereby denied the basis for any higher legitimacy

with certain inalienable rights . . .
no obligations? no responsibilities?

that among these are Life, Liberty, and the pursuit of Happiness . . . That to secure these rights, Governments are instituted among Men . . . deriving their just powers from the consent of the governed . . .
Whose happiness? Mine? Yours? The public's?
Having no other function than just to protect rights? How? Each person separately or working as a group? And when? Just once at the beginning, or each day anew?

The Declaration of Independence is rhetoric. It is not surprising that philosophically it raises as many questions as it answers. But there can be no question of its central thrust: each of us is described by its imperatives as persons who are to pursue our own happiness, and we look to our government to give each of us security in that pursuit. It is equally clear from the Declaration that not much else matters.

From the Declaration of Independence through a host of other public statements and documents, it is clear that American citizens and their chosen leaders have disallowed any claim of government powers beyond those specifically consented to; this is also the sense obtained from a reading of the Constitution's Preamble:

We the People of the United States in Order to form a more perfect Union, establish Justice, insure domestic Tranquility, provide for the common defence, promote the general Welfare, and secure the Blessings of Liberty to ourselves and our Posterity, do ordain and establish this Constitution for the United States of America.

*Adoption of the
Declaration of
Independence in
Philadelphia, 1776.*

This same narrow concern with individual pursuits and the protection of them is embedded in another of our founding documents, the Bill of Rights, which is the first ten amendments to the Constitution. Unlike the Declaration of Independence, the Bill of Rights is a legal document with the force of law. It has been the subject of great controversies and interpretations in the courts (see Chapters 5 and 15). It is generally agreed that its central concern, like that of the Declaration, has been to secure usable freedoms for individuals and their interests. All ten of the amendments to the Constitution are concerned with the rights of citizens in their relationship to government; it is quite proper to think of these as rights *against* the government. Originally this meant the federal government in Washington, D.C., but because of the Fourteenth Amendment, added after the Civil War, and the court interpretations of this amendment, the Bill of Rights restrictions have been extended, case by case, to state and local governments as well.

From these foundations, America has become not only an unusually individualistic society but also an extraordinarily legalistic one. The connection is more than accidental. If individuals and their property are to be protected, and if this is the central and all-consuming focus of the political system and its basic documents, then it should be expected that an elaborate legal structure must be established to fulfill these

BOX 1–7
An Individualist
Manifesto: Henry
David Thoreau's
"Civil
Disobedience"
(1848)

I heartily accept the motto, "That government is best which governs least, and I should like to see it acted up to more rapidly and systematically. Carried out, it finally amounts to this, which I also believe—"That government is best which governs not at all;" and when men are prepared for it, that will be the kind of government which they will have. Government is at best but an expedient; but most governments are usually, and all governments are sometimes, inexpedient. The objections which have been brought against a standing army, and they are many and weighty, and deserve to prevail, may also at last be brought against a standing government. The government itself, which is only the mode which the people have chosen to execute their will, is equally liable to be abused and perverted before the people can act through it. Witness the present Mexican War, the work of comparatively a few individuals using the standing government as their tool; for, in the outset, the people would not have consented to this measure. . . .

As for adopting the ways which the State has provided for remedying the evil (of slavery), I know not of such ways. They take too much time, and a man's life will be gone. I have other affairs to attend to. . . . A man has not everything to do, but something; and because he cannot do *everything*, it is not necessary that he should do *something* wrong. It is not my business to be petitioning the Governor or the Legislature any more than it is theirs to petition me. . . . But in this case the State has provided no way; its very Constitution is the evil. This may seem to be harsh and stubborn and unconciliatory; but it is to treat with kindness and consideration the only spirit that can appreciate or deserve it. . . .

—Reprinted in *American Political Thought*, ed. by Kenneth M. Dolbeare (Monterey, Calif.: Duxbury Press, 1981), pp. 231–245.

needs. America has more lawyers per capita than any other country, and it has laws and regulations of every kind to restrain individuals and to protect them from each other and their government. The definition and application of these laws and regulations in daily practice has been the source of endless complexities.

In the actual case-by-case course of events, the Supreme Court and other branches of government have tried to wend their way through these complexities. The issues at stake are vital questions in a free society that go to the heart of our democratic traditions. What is most obvious is that through all this controversy, all sides have sought to preserve the core value—our national individualism. The Bill of Rights, together with a host of laws, documents, and proclamations, have shored up the dignity and safety of the individual's life, limb, and property. The First Amendment, the basis of our human rights from which all of the other freedoms flow, has protected with considerable success the ultimate right—the right of conscience, the right to think and believe, to choose, and to speak for oneself—to be, in short, an individual person.

Schizophrenic Politics

Now we must pull together the foregoing facts and arguments and face the root of our problem. Americans are radical individualists and are allowed in our political system great freedom to practice their individualism. But what, in all this freedom, are they individually expected to do? Again, we return to the Nixonlike Agonistes who strives over-strong against himself. American individualists, in massive contradiction, are pulled in opposite directions by their political traditions, producing a split, or schizophrenic, politics.

American individualism is the central tenet of a larger, broader political tradition called Liberalism. It began with Hobbes and continued not only through Locke, but also Adam Smith and John Stuart Mill in England and, in America, to James Madison, John C. Calhoun, Ralph Waldo Emerson, Henry David Thoreau, and many others (see Box 1–7). It is in this larger context, the broad stream of Liberalism, where American individualism can be seen as a self-dividing entity.

Liberalism has two strands—one religious, the other economic. Both are passionately individualistic. The religious strand is essentially Protestant, whereas the economic strand is essentially middle class, or Bourgeois. The Protestant religious strand pulls the individual primarily through appeals to faith, love, and hope. The Bourgeois strand appeals to the individual through personal interest, profit, and material rewards. Liberalism's Protestant strand has given us not only its churches by the thousands but also its traditions of community fellowship, civic idealism, and social conscience. Liberalism's Bourgeois strand has given America not only its massive economic organizations and accomplishments, but also its hard-headed practicality, its insistence upon political realism, and its willingness to negotiate and compromise.[4]

[4] See, for example, John Kenneth Galbraith, *The New Industrial State* (Boston: Houghton Mifflin, 1967); Richard Hofstadter, *The American Political Tradition and the Men Who Made It* (New York: Knopf, 1948).

Because Liberalism in America developed in isolation from its European origins, its internal divisions have been sharply exaggerated. American Liberals have tended to assert their own versions of the truth without fear of rebuttal or amendment. On the other hand, they have sensed this split within themselves between their Protestant and Bourgeois sides so that on many occasions they have turned upon themselves. In a long succession stretching from the Order of Cincinnatus, the Know-Nothings, the Ku Klux Klan, and campaigns against Communists in government, the American people have demonstrated their recurrent fear of enemies "boring from within."[5] In America, however, there has never been much on which such supposed enemies and their hidden conspiracies might feed. Americans turn upon themselves and find fault with their own behavior, often to the point of wild exaggeration.

The most extreme early example of the strains between the two strands of American Liberalism is the contrast between New England divine Jonathan Edwards and his near contemporary, Benjamin Franklin. Edwards is not widely known today, but when his congregation forced him out of his pastorate in Northampton, Massachusetts, it created one of the great scandals of the eighteenth century. A man of towering intel-

**Edwards and Franklin:
Separate Paths**

[5] Gustavus Myers, *History of Bigotry in the United States* (New York: Capricorn, 1960).

Benjamin Franklin.

lect, he was also a powerful preacher, as his most famous sermon, "Sinners in the Hands of an Angry God," shows. What he most stood for was the notion that conversion, the essential step toward salvation, arises from a wholly personal awareness of sin followed by a consciousness of God's light—a wholly and profoundly private religious experience by the individual of God's presence in oneself.

This was a radical kind of Protestant spiritual individualism. It was exactly matched on the Bourgeois side by Franklin's pragmatic individualism as preached in *Poor Richard's Almanac*, the *Autobiography*, and other writings. Franklin's talents bent toward the natural and applied sciences, and he enjoyed the pleasures of this life and their material rewards in modest measure. He insisted that these were available only on the basis of individual effort and ought not to be otherwise. Franklin's famous saying, "Time is money," should be understood as something more profound than a handy and prudent ethical admonition. In its philosophical dimensions, it means that the measure of our life is the money that passes each day through our hands. It would be hard to imagine a more complete contrast to Edwards's preachment that the pivotal experience in a person's life is the realization of God's immediate grace.

The point is that both Franklin and Edwards were preaching a radical individualism, but they were preaching in opposite directions. Ed-

BOX 1–8
An Overzealous Legalism Can Thwart Our Purposes: A Comment on the "Cage" of American Law

Our constant preoccupation with the constitutionality of legislation rather than with its wisdom tends to preoccupation of the American mind with a false value. The tendency of focusing attention on constitutionality is to make constitutionality synonymous with wisdom, to regard a law as all right if it is constitutional. Such an attitude is a great enemy of liberalism. Particularly in legislation affecting freedom of thought and freedom of speech much which should offend a free-spirited society is constitutional. Reliance for the most precious interests of civilization, therefore, must be found outside of their vindication in courts of law. Only a persistent positive translation of the faith of a free society into the convictions and habits and actions of a community is the ultimate reliance against unabated temptations to fetter the human spirit.

—Supreme Court Justice Felix Frankfurter, dissenting in *West Virginia Board of Education* v. *Barnette* (1943).

wards summoned humankind to God's love, Franklin to personal material aggrandizement. What Edwards condemned as sin, Franklin called
success; what Edwards saw as spiritual achievement, Franklin called
pathetic mystification.

The contrast between Edwards and Franklin is important because it
became the central conflict in the American political mind. The centuries since these men lived have deeply implanted this conflict upon our
consciousness. It has created in our social selves a perpetual restless-
ness that, based on our sense of personal responsibility for all that we
are and do, has caused us to look with ambivalence on every side of our
social and political endeavors. We constantly pursue individual
achievement and personal gain but anxiously doubt what all of it
means. Is achievement found in beating someone to the top, or in loving
them more? Is success measured in power and money, or devotion and
service? These questions plague us when we view the work, and sometimes the corruption, of our public officials. These important questions
were etched, for example, in the lives of nineteenth-century philanthro-
pists like Andrew Carnegie, Andrew Mellon, and John D. Rockefeller—
all of whom amassed enormous fortunes by hard work and, often
enough, dubious means, but contributed spectacularly huge sums to the
nation's cultural and social betterment in a generosity born of guilt.

The political implications of this dualism in the American spirit are **Implications**
striking. We will see it carved in the structures of each of the major
institutions of our political system and in the flow of their processes.
Each of them will be found to display a schizophrenic quality. The
courts, the Congress, the presidency, the systems of state and local government are each invested with an almost religious-type aura of aspiration toward perfection. This reflects in each the idea of testing and constantly retesting whether government of, by, and for the people can long
endure. At the same time each of these major parts of the system performs much more mundanely behind its noble aspirations. Our com-
monplace language signals the shift in emphasis. We say, "Well, ideals
are fine, but in the end you've got to be practical," or "That's all right in
theory, but in practice things don't work quite that way." There are
even books on American politics with titles like "The Theory and Practice of American Government," as if "theory" and "practice" are bound
to be different.

This is the fundamental paradox of the American political system. In
a profound sense, the system gives every appearance and promise of
being a Social Democracy pursuing broad goals of community solidarity, justice, and equality. But to call this our "theory"—when we believe it so strongly and act it out in a host of different ways—is both
unfair and seriously misleading. It is equally true, however, that behind
its sincere appearance and constant promise, the system operates by

paying attention to very different ideas. Success is to the strong and well connected; government is cliquish and elitist. The system is representative but mostly heeds the clashing and persuasive claims of vested interests. At this level, the theory and the practice are united in service to the notion that government is an arena in which the questions are answered as to who gets what, how, and why, and at whose expense.

How can this be? How can a contradiction so sharp continue to persist? How does it work itself out in detail? What language can be used to describe it?

Much of the rest of the book is devoted to answering these questions and demonstrating how the contradictions manage to persist. For example, American presidents by the logic of their office have been compelled to strive to be two things at once. Whether they planned or understood it, they have been pushed into being tribunes of all the people on the one hand, leading them in righteous crusades for human betterment. Simultaneously, they have been compelled to be calculating politicians working for their own advantage by assiduously favoring some groups over others.

In making this kind of assertion, one point must not be lost. This analysis charges no one with hypocrisy, certainly not of a personal, deliberate sort. The political system, not individuals, splits American political life into its discordant halves—its spiritual-like aspirations and its all too pragmatic operations. And each of these halves is real. Both are important and functional parts of the system. America's political aspirations and ideals are sincerely held and fit into fixed patterns over the years, just as do the operative aspects of our political system.

FOR FURTHER READING

BEARD, CHARLES A. *An Economic Interpretation of the Constitution of the United States*. New York: Free Press, 1965. Unique landmark study that indicates the Founders were looking after their own interests.

BECKER, CARL. *The Declaration of Independence*. New York: Vintage, 1942. Classic study of this important document.

DOLBEARE, KENNETH M. ed. *American Political Thought*. Monterey, Calif.: Duxbury, 1981. Collection of readings that acquaints students with some of the major trends in American political thought.

EDELMAN, MURRAY. *The Symbolic Uses of Politics*. Urbana, Ill.: University of Illinois Press, 1964. Demonstrates the importance of symbolism in political words, acts, and deeds.

GALBRAITH, JOHN KENNETH. *The New Industrial State*. Boston: Houghton Mifflin, 1967. Demonstrates the importance of bureaucracy in all American institutions, an importance the author believes surpasses such considerations as profit.

HARRIS, LOUIS. *The Anguish of Change*. New York: Norton, 1973. Traces the development of American public opinion over a recent thirteen-year period.

HARTZ, LOUIS. *The Liberal Tradition in America*. New York: Harcourt Brace Jovanovich, 1955. Often regarded as the conventional wisdom on its subject.

HOFSTADTER, RICHARD. *The American Political Tradition and the Men Who Made It.*
New York: Knopf, 1948. Landmark treatise on the thought of America's leaders from the Founders to Franklin D. Roosevelt.

KRISTOL, IRVING. *On the Democratic Idea in America.* New York: Harper and Row,
1972. A conservative view that eschews democracy, holding that it lacks virtue.

LANE, ROBERT E. *Political Ideology: Why the American Common Man Believes
What He Does.* New York: Free Press, 1962. Considered an important breakthrough in the study of patterns of political socialization of Americans.

LIPSET, SEYMOUR M. *Political Man: The Social Bases of Politics.* Garden City:
Doubleday, 1959. An eminent sociologist links the social base of America to
political attitudes.

MARCUSE, HERBERT. *One-Dimensional Man.* Boston: Beacon Press, 1964. A telling
critique of the political assumptions of American society.

MYERS, GUSTAVUS. *History of Bigotry in the United States.* New York: Capricorn,
1960. The story of our darker side, frighteningly documented.

ROELOFS, H. MARK. *Ideology and Myth in American Politics: A Critique of a National Political Mind.* Boston: Little, Brown, 1976. The work that serves as the
basis of the theme of this text.

2 Power in America

In the shadow of a great factory, the workers march. They carry big sticks. The hired toughs, working for the company, await them. Then all hell breaks loose. The company toughs find that they are surrounded by two groups of workers. The workers use their sticks; the company men fall. A bomb goes off, and a truck, engulfed in flames, rolls into the company's gate. The gate gives way, and the wrought-iron sign above it, "Consolidated Trucking," falls to the ground, symbolizing the end of repression. The workers, after years of injustice, can organize their union.

This evocative scene from the movie *Fist* is fascinating because it graphically presents a transfer of power. Many other films—*All the King's Men* is a good example—depend on the idea of political power to pique and engross our interest. Power is one of the great motives of politics, although it is not the only one. Understanding the nature of power is basic to understanding the American political system.

America's divided, ambivalent individualism is the foundation of its political system. The division within this individualism runs like a geological fault throughout our political system, from the highest national offices to the most obscure local offices. How can this be? The immediate answer is that America's schizophrenic individualism fits into a fundamental division in the nature of political power. It is from this complementarity between the divided nature of power and the fundamental divisions in our individualism that all else in the American political system stems.

Political power is not force. It is a responsive relationship in which one person gets another to do what the first tells the other to do—because for one reason or another they have agreed that power may be exerted by the one over the other. Power has two sides. The primary side involves the consent to have power exerted. The secondary side is the actual exercise of that power. The division in American individualism fits into this basic division of the two sides of power.

In America, the exercise of power is largely carried out in terms of Bourgeois individualism, our practical proclivity for the pursuit of self-interest. On the other hand, we are largely persuaded to grant power to the leaders of the political system by their appeals to our Protestant individualism, to our needs to love one another, and to work for social justice in the interest of the common welfare.

**BOX 2–1
On Power, Politics,
and Society**

I put for a general inclination of all mankind, a perpetual and restless desire of power after power, that ceaseth only in death.
—Thomas Hobbes, *Leviathan*, Chapter 11.

Covenants, without the sword, are but words, and of no strength to secure a man at all. The bonds of words are too weak to bridle men's ambition, avarice, anger, and other passions, without the fear of some coercive power.
—Thomas Hobbes, *Leviathan*, Chapter 17.

Political power comes out of the barrel of a gun.
—Attributed to Mao Tse-tung.

Power, in whatever hands, is rarely guilty of too strict limitations on itself.
—Edmund Burke, "A Letter to the Sherriffs of Bristol," in *Edmund Burke: on Government, Politics and Society*, ed. by B. W. Hill (New York: International Publications Service, 1975), p. 189.

Let us not be in the same cry as the power-seekers. . . . We should keep together aloof from power politics and its contagion. . . . Today, politics has become corrupt. Anybody who goes into it is contaminated. Let us keep out of it altogether. Our influence will grow thereby. The greater our inner purity, the greater shall be our hold on the people, without any effort on our part.
—Mohandas Gandhi, to the members of the Hindustani Talimi Sangh, 1947. Quoted by Raghavan N. Iyer, *The Moral and Political Thought of Mahatma Gandhi* (New York: Oxford University Press, 1973), p. 53.

. . . it is well to seem merciful, fruitful, humane, sincere, religious, and also to be so; but you must have the mind so disposed that when it is needful to be otherwise you may be able to change to the opposite qualities.
—Niccolo Machiavelli, *The Prince Including the Discourses*, trans. Luigi Ricci (New York: Modern Library, 1950), p. 27.

The earth has never yet seen a truly great and virtuous nation, for woman has never yet stood the equal with men.
—Elizabeth Cady Stanton, letter, *Proceedings of the Woman's Rights Convention*, Worcester, Mass., October 23 and 24, 1850 (published 1851).

**BOX 2–1
On Power, Politics,
and Society
(Continued)**

Formal government makes but a small part of civilized life; and when even the best that human wisdom can devise is established, it is a thing more in name and idea than in fact.

—Thomas Paine, "The Rights of Man," in *Thomas Paine: Representative Selections*, ed. by Harry H. Clark rev. ed. (New York: Hill and Wang, 1961)

This has been the situation since the beginning of our republic. The Founding Fathers were leaders of profoundly Bourgeois inclination. Their religious bent was relatively weak and noncommittal. The constitutional system they devised for the governance of America and for the exercise of power reflected this balance in favor of Bourgeois considerations, the practical side of life. But even in the preamble to their document they had to appeal, in seeking support for their work, to broad concerns for social justice. In later decades the appeal for legitimation of the Constitution became a full-throated call to the Protestant conscience. The contrast between the contents of the Constitution and what was appealed to in support of it became more and more pronounced over the years, and then hardened into tradition. This looks well ahead of the present argument, however. What we must do now is appreciate the nature of power and see how the division of American individualism has been able to fit into it.

Politics and Power

Power is the distinguishing feature of politics. Whenever people are demanding power, getting it, or using it, or, on the other hand, giving it, responding to it, or trying to resist it, we can be sure that we would immediately recognize the situation as political.

Power, all the same, is not the essence of politics. The essence of politics is the complex process of talk, argument, and agreement that people go through to create power and then use it. Power as exercised by one group of human beings over another is not the source of politics. It is the consequence of politics.

Power is certainly what politics seems to be about—who has it, for what reason, and over whom. But power is not violence, nor is it necessarily the threat of violence, however much we may tend to associate these concepts. Imagine a father putting his young son to bed. If the child resists so that all the father can do is pick him up and carry him screaming and kicking to bed, we would say that the father had for that time lost control (that is, power) over his son and had to substitute force for power. If the child had quietly done what he was requested to do, however, never mind if with a sour face, then the father's power would be obvious. But never forget that the father's power depends on the acknowledgment of it by the son. Once again, the essence of politics is not power but agreement. Agreement creates power.

Establishing Power

How and why does the agreement to create power come about?

Taking this question step by step, let us begin with the simplest possible definition of power: Power is the ability of a superior to get an inferior to do what he or she would not do otherwise. Figure 2–1 illustrates this definition. Most of us carry this picture in our heads when we think of power in the simplest terms. The picture raises questions. Why does *B* give in to *A*'s commands?

One answer that immediately suggests itself is that *B* is afraid of *A* for some reason. Perhaps *B* is terrified that *A* may use force and cause him or her harm if the commands are not quickly obeyed. This might be the case if *A* was a robber threatening *B* with a gun or a knife. This certainly would be enough to persuade most people to do what they are told. If, however, the situation stops short of the open threat of violence, *A*, by one argument or another, must persuade the *B*s who he or she would order around to give in voluntarily. Only then can *A* have power.

There are many means by which people can be persuaded to do as they are told beyond being threatened with violence. They can be tricked into submission, just as robbers can bluff with a toy gun. Those who would hold power can promise people the things they really want, such as personal rewards, security from attacks by others, leadership in organizing and managing community projects, and a commitment to their personal and general welfare. Would-be leaders also tend to argue that they ought to be obeyed, that they possess a moral authority to command because, for example, they represent the lawful offices of the established government. What all this amounts to is that for power to be obtained it must have been granted, after some kind of persuasion, by those over whom it is to be exercised.

Figure 2–2 incorporates this idea in our original power diagram. As this diagram shows, the persuasive process by which the granting of power is requested and made precedes its exercise. The technical name for this process is "legitimation." It is the process by which governors gain the recognition and the right—that is, the political power—to govern. Often the dialogue through which it takes place is complex, ex-

Figure 2–1. Power—a simple definition.

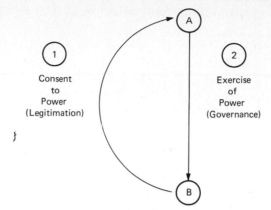

Figure 2–2.
The dialogue of power.

tended, and ongoing. Sometimes it is virtually instantaneous. A policeman calls upon us to halt. In a glance, we notice that he is armed and wearing the uniform of the law, so we stop dead in our tracks.

Our analysis shows that the exercise of power—what we can call the process of "governance"—is distinct from the legitimation process. But it is related to that process and is conditioned by it. Logically, it would seem that the exercise of power must be limited by the terms that granted it. Yet as we shall see, in practical effect the legitimation process can take place in one dialogue and the governance process can be in a quite different one. How different these are in America—and with what consequences—is the substance of this book.

So far our analysis has shown that all government is by consent. The interesting questions have to do with how consent is gained, in what form, and to what extent. Before we can analyze questions of this order, we must note one more preliminary matter. It has been mentioned that in power situations the governors and the governed must be in dialogue. Both sides of the power relationship, the governing side and the legitimation side, are grounded in talk. The whole meaning of power, in the end, is that we do as we are *told*, rather than being compelled by force.

What we should now notice is that we cannot do as we are told or undertake any dialogue with those who would command us unless we understand the language in which we are being addressed. This is a precondition for those who wish to command us and for those of us who wish to legitimate their commands. Before governors and governed can begin their dialogue, they must share a field of meanings in which they speak the same language and understand a whole range of ideas and relationships which either side may bring to bear on their situation. In diagram form, this is shown by Figure 2–3 on page 41.

Legitimation and Governance

The pluralist description of the division of political power in America is associated with mainstream political science and with welfare-state liberalism. In the pluralist view, the political system is made up of groups that make competing claims on the resources of the system. This is true whether we are looking at the national political system, as in David Truman's *Governmental Process,* or at a local system, as in Robert A. Dahl's classic study of decision making in New Haven, *Who Governs?* Government institutions and the other elements of the political system produce *consensus* out of these competing claims. There is always some dissatisfaction, of course, with the political system, but the system is not capable of achieving a perfect equilibrium among all competing groups and claims.

This is recognized by all the competing groups. They adhere to the "rules of the game," and to a marked degree, they show a willingness to abide by the rules and by the decisions and settlements made within the political system. The politics that produces consensus produces, almost by its very nature, a rough sort of justice for the greater part of the claims made by the various interests. If this were not so, too many people would be dissatisfied, there would be no more consensus, and the system would eventually fail to function.

A major root assumption of pluralism is that the system—made up of society and its political institutions—is neutral. The system is not "stacked" against anyone, although it is recognized that there are varying degrees of access to, and success in, the political system. Consensus is often attained by "splitting the difference" in various disputes and in the arena of competing claims so that everyone eventually gets something (though not necessarily at the same time). The neutrality of the system assures that most decisions will be settled well away from the extreme positions of the competing groups.

The power of competing interests and the power of these interests *relative* to one another achieves a certain kind of brokerage. Ideals or values or moral suasion enter into this power equation, as well as such forces as public opinion, the media, past deferral of certain demands, and the economic climate.

**BOX 2–2
The Division of
Political Power in
America: The
Pluralist Thesis
(Continued)**

Another assumption underlying the pluralist thesis and its concept of consensus is that our system is inherently productive, that it gets the best out of everyone, and that it constantly increases the general wealth. The system is seen to a great degree as an admirable mechanism in which there is an ever increasing potential for individual fulfillment. This generates the conclusion, fundamental to the consensus politics of pluralism, that *all* groups have a greater interest in the basic operation of the system and in its well-being *more than* they have an interest in promoting their own particular claims.

Antipluralists question the neutrality of the system, believe that pluralists tend to overstate the equality of competing claims and groups, and assert that the sort of justice meted out to some groups—the poor and minorities, for example—is rough indeed. Pluralism presently appears to be in a state of decline, though we cannot be sure why. Perhaps pluralists have placed too much faith in rationality and have been too optimistic about the results that can be expected from the political system.

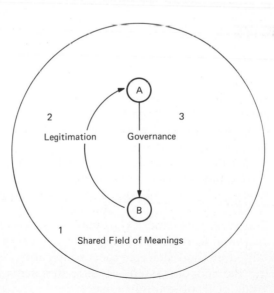

Figure 2–3.
The politics of power.

If we compress this whole discussion into formal definitions, it can be seen that

politics is the process of dialogue by which, in a shared field of meanings, power is created and exercised;

power is the ability of a recognized (legitimated) superior to control (govern), within a shared field of meanings, the behavior of a willing (consenting) inferior.

These are simple definitions. When they are applied to actual features of modern governments such as the American political system, the rudimentary elements that these definitions stress almost disappear from view under layer after layer of practical detail. But these rudimentary elements remain all the same; in fact, they are fundamentally controlling.

It is especially important to stress this fact in the study of American government. Most discussions of American government and politics focus almost exclusively upon how the nation is governed. They say very little about the legitimation process. They neglect to point out that much of the work of the government's various departments is concerned with legitimation as much as or more than it is with governance. Even more serious is the failure to consider carefully the discrepancies and strains between what is said in American politics on its legitimation and governance sides. In these discrepancies between the promises and aspirations of legitimation and the actual capacities for political performance are found both the vital dynamic and the paralyzing immobilism of American government.

Myth and Ideology

Now we must confront more directly the problem of how, within a shared field of meanings, the dialogue of power can produce discrepancies and strains between the talk of legitimation and the talk of governance. The first step is to show how each of these kinds of talk can be embedded in our national culture and can take on lives of their own quite independent of each other.

When a sergeant marches his men out to a parade ground, all concerned have in their minds a set of expectations about the kinds of commands the sergeant might give. The sergeant can command "present arms," "eyes right," or "about face"; but there is a range of commands that sergeants cannot reasonably be expected to give, such as ordering everyone to remove his left shoe. The sergeant and his men seem contained by their shared expectations about each other. If anyone, including the sergeant, steps outside this sense of mutual containment, all kinds of trouble might ensue.

As a more subtle example, imagine an established church group or social club of long standing. In any such community some individuals stand out. Maybe they have been members for many years; maybe they have held a succession of administrative posts; perhaps they have given generously to the group's treasury or have a record of helping to develop and advocate successful policies; or perhaps they are generally liked because of their friendly and always sympathetic manner. One thing seems certain: such people, whether they are men or women and quite apart from their holding any particular office, are influential. Within the group they have powers to sway the views and actions of others. How and why does this kind of influence accumulate, and how far can it extend? Again, this can be explained in the language of expectations. It can be assumed that everyone wants the group to endure and succeed; but this is rarely easy. Decisions, sometimes hard ones, must be taken, cooperation has to be forthcoming and developed, money has to be

The power elite explanation of the American political system asserts that the system is "stacked" against the poor, certain minorities, and those without political or economic resources. An unelected elite, representing only themselves and a relatively small part of the population, is permanently in power and, through a system of shared values and various cues (but not by conspiracy), makes all the important decisions in the political system. This is true whether we are looking at the national political system, as in C. Wright Mills' *The Power Elite*, or at a local system, as in Floyd Hunter's *Community Power Structure*.

In Mills's work, the American elite is described as the top leadership in the political, corporate, and military structures of the country. Mills gave us the term "military-industrial complex." President Dwight Eisenhower gave Mills's work some credence when he alluded to the dangers of this complex in his 1960 Farewell Speech.

This integrated national elite works within a honeycombed environment of financial, family, and school ties. The members of the elite are educated in private schools and for the most part Ivy League universities. They often move between two or even three of the spheres of the political-military-industrial complex, and in doing this they have effectively blurred the line between "private" and "public." Government carries out corporate policies, for example, and corporations act in governmental roles, shifting resources, costs, benefits, and people around to suit their own interests.

This view of the system asserts that there is little movement into or out of elite circles. Nonmembers of the power elite are permitted to join this select circle, however, under rather stringent conditions.

The elitist argument is not a simplistic assertion that the wealthy rule America. It seeks to tell how America is ruled and to what ends. It defines the elite as having an interest in a permanent and large defense establishment, for example, and it quite pessimistically asserts that the system is not really open to any significant change in policies or outlook.

This pessimism contrasts with the advocacy of social and political change often made by those who adhere to the power elite thesis. This has a logic, however, because elite theorists almost invariably claim that the American political system is

BOX 2–3
The Division of
Political Power in
America: The
Power Elite Thesis
(Continued)

repressive and undemocratic in character. They reject plural-ist notions of political balance, competition of claims, and accommodation. In addition, elite theorists draw upon a long tradition in sociology of studies of power elite political and social configurations in various communities across the land. And they draw upon a tradition of suspicions of the American body politic that a centralized elite makes most, or all, of the important political decisions.

Elite theorists are generally blamed for their strident at-tacks upon the system, for their failure to understand the "rules of the American political game," and for their lack of specific evidence that such an elite actually rules the country.

Their response to the latter charge is that this phenomenon does not lend itself to the establishment of solid proofs but that a host of secondary evidence lends credence to the the-ory.

raised. It seems natural for the members to look for a leader. They look for this leader among their most outstanding members. What do such people think? What do they suggest? This kind of tradition in small communities has existed as far back as the ancient cities of the Middle East, where the people looked to the Elders seated by gates for guidance and governance.

If a community is functioning well, its outstanding individuals will not disappoint the general membership's expectations. Building upon the legitimacy that has become theirs through tradition, they will advo-cate new programs and solutions, and the community's life will move on. There is one important condition: the outstanding individuals, for all of their accumulated influence over the years, must not outrage their followers. If their conduct is thought bizarre, if their proposals appear inane, grotesque, or utterly foreign to the traditions and expectations of the group, the influentials will be influential no more. Power, to be granted, must be legitimated. It can also be withdrawn, that is, delegitimated, sometimes gradually and only incompletely, sometimes wholly and virtually overnight. As with the sergeant and his men in our first example, ideas and thoughts of groups about who is to lead and how are contained within a shared framework of mutual expectations.

People who make it their business to accumulate power know these facts, or soon learn them as the price of staying powerful. They will seek to enhance and harden their power by steadily, and probably slowly,

**Legitimacy, a Requisite
for Power**

arranging to have their possession of it specifically recognized and defined. The usual and most obvious way of doing this is to obtain public
office, which institutionalizes power into authority. To emphasize this
further they may associate various distinctive symbols of office with
their persons. They may insist on having a large desk in an imposing
office, surround themselves with a uniformed retinue, or wear distinctive clothing. Adolf Hitler changed his rather ordinary appearance with
a distinctive hairstyle and a small mustache. Such moves seem to be
especially effective in winning the attention of the populace at large.

Throughout history, rulers of every sort have expended great efforts
on this kind of thing. Ironically, those whose rule has been most dictatorial often made the greatest efforts of this kind. Despotic rule is one of
the most difficult forms of government for which to gain legitimation,
even when the blandishments of imposing symbols are backed by systematic terror and repression. Terror and violence are really signs of
political weakness. The most powerful regimes in history, the ones able
to demand heroic sacrifices as well as sustained cooperation from their
peoples, have been those able to engender loyal, even joyful, responsiveness and acceptance. They have obtained such support because they
succeeded in setting up a persuasive identity between themselves and
the deep-seated traditions, aspirations, memories, and expectations of
the societies they ruled. This sort of identity between government and
people is what prompted Dwight Eisenhower to say of America and
Great Britain in the depths of World War II that "an aroused democracy" is the most powerful kind of nation known to history.

National and Political Culture

The acquisition and exercise of power, once again, is a dialogue, but it is
one in which both the rulers and the ruled must draw upon profound
understandings of each other in order to perform their respective roles.
A number of terms can help put this matter into perspective.

The first term, national culture, is such a simple and familiar concept
that we could easily overlook it. Whether in a moment of crisis or day-
to-day living, people share experience as they go about their various
tasks and carry out the work that makes life meaningful and productive.
The activity of any given moment goes on against a backdrop of shared
memory and shared expectations. Our history gives meaning to the
present. The national culture that history creates is a great reservoir of
everything from a shared national language (or languages) and the
treasured books written in it, the great events and heroes of those
events, and our commonly understood values concerning politics, economics, and religion. Our national culture is a total social pattern by
which we interpret our present and face our future.

Political culture is abstracted from the national culture. It is a selection of ideas, values, theories, and constructions from the national culture with specific relevance to political life. The connection between the

A view of the political system sometimes regarded as an attempt to synthesize the pluralist and power elite views is the decision-making classification scheme established by Theodore Lowi.

According to Lowi, there are three distinct arenas in which political issues are settled: the distributive, regulatory, and redistributive. Distributive questions usually involve relatively small groups of people, and the settlement of these bears some resemblance to the pluralist model. There is a relatively small amount of conflict, and the distributive issue is resolved by allocating the resources in question often on a remarkably equal basis. A good example of a distributive matter is the rivers and harbors bills passed from time to time by Congress. Also known as "pork barrel bills" because they provide a "piece of pork" for everyone, this kind of legislation sets up lucrative projects for almost every section of the country. Historically, few members of Congress have opposed the rivers and harbors bills.

Regulatory issues are those in which the conduct of one group is restricted because of the demands of another group. Utility rates, for example, are governed by various commissions, both federal and state, because consumer groups believe that the natural monopoly necessary in utilities industries makes public control of rates necessary. A vast array of issues fits under this category—environmental laws, public health and safety, labor laws, rent control, and transportation are among the examples.

Issues of the redistributive arena call for large-scale transfers of resources from one large group in society to another. A host of welfare-state measures fit into this category, including various tax measures, Social Security, aid programs for the handicapped, minimum wage laws, and farm price supports. These issues tend to produce a high degree of conflict, often fought along economic class lines.

Lowi's scheme seems to work if the purpose is merely a classification of issues; but it does not tell us (nor is it supposed to) very much about power relationships within and between groups, or why one particular measure is adopted rather than another.

BOX 2–4
The Division of Political Power in America: The Decision-making Classifications of Theodore Lowi

national culture and the political culture must be intimate if political life is to be meaningful, vibrant, and enduring; but this also means that a nation's political life is, in a sense, trapped within its cultural inheritance. Political culture supplies the shared field of meaning within which specific patterns of dialogue can develop, the patterns concerned with the creation and exercise of power. If in the course of time the patterns of power dialogue develop smoothly, they can not only be deepened and enriched, but also conventionalized, institutionalized, and standardized. By a kind of shorthand involving generally understood conventions and meanings, they can also be richly symbolized to aid our debates and arguments about rules and legitimation.

Myth and Ideology

The political system is the actual, specific, institutionalized pattern or sets of patterns that a nation has evolved in its history to govern itself. The terms "myth" and "ideology," the central concepts in this book, represent the two major aspects of the political system, the legitimation side and the governance side, the side by which power is created, amassed, defined, and reaffirmed, and the side by which power is distributed, implemented, applied, and obeyed. The full meaning of these terms will become clear as we apply them to the American context of politics and government, but certain points need to be stressed here.

First, both myth and ideology are, in the academic phrase, value-laden and both refer to, and are deeply involved in, practice. More specifically, both terms refer to sets of ideals about how certain procedures, processes, and evaluations should be carried out and why. At the same time these terms closely determine the actual practice of politics.

Thus myth proclaims what America is and should be. At the same time, myth clearly determines how, for example, election campaigns should be run, the kinds of speeches that are appropriate to them, the kinds of media appeals that are made, the kinds of issues to be discussed, and, above all, who should have the right to vote and why. Myth also determines when, where, and how national emblems should be displayed, what the nation's capital should look like, what tourists should see and do when visiting national shrines, and even what those tourists should think and feel when making their pilgrimages there. Myth even determines how especially the president should talk and act in public, and it sets the standards by which the general populace determines whether a particular president is a success or a failure.

Meanwhile, ideology is just as effectively determining how laws and public policy should be made, by whom, and for whose benefit. Like myth, it is a vision of what ought to be. And also like myth, it translates this vision into practice, but not the practice of patriotic citizens, hopeful candidates for public office, and awe struck tourists, but of workaday legislators, bureaucrats, judges, and, of course, ordinary citizens when they pay taxes, obey laws, appear in court, or otherwise work for, or bear the burdens of, government.

Myth and ideology not only serve different political purposes—legitimation and governance—but they are also qualitatively different in highly characteristic ways. The most important of these differences may be listed as follows:

Myth of Legitimation	Ideology of Governance
Broad in scope	Narrow in scope
Aimed at citizens generally	Aimed at governors and those they immediately govern
Amorphous terms richly symbolized	Precise terms exactly defined
Philosophical and religious	Legal and bureaucratic
Excitement, challenge, and response	Negotiations, directives, agreements, compliance

The talk of myth and the talk of ideology are certainly different and have different goals but the same people, in the main, carry out both kinds of talk: sometimes they are talking one way, sometimes another.

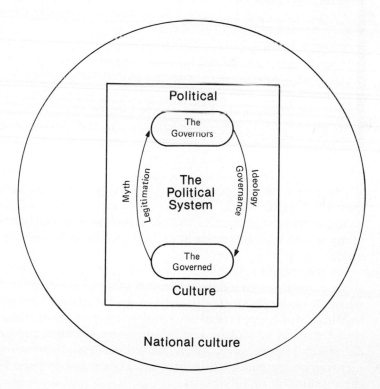

Figure 2–4.
A nation.

**BOX 2–5
Power and the
People: James
Madison Writes in
Federalist 10**

"To secure the public good, and private right, against the danger of . . . faction, and at the same time to preserve the spirit and form of popular government, is then the great object to which our enquiries are directed.

". . . The most frivolous and fanciful distinctions have been sufficient to kindle . . . unfriendly passions and excite their most violent conflicts. But the most common and durable size of factions has been the various and unequal distribution of property. Those who hold and those who are without property have ever formed distinct interests in society.

"Complaints are everywhere heard from our most considerate and virtuous citizens, . . . that our governments are too unstable, that the public good is disregarded in the conflicts of rival parties, and that measures are too often decided, not according to the rules of justice and the rights of the minor party, but by the superior force of an interested and overwhelming majority. However anxiously we may wish that these complaints had no foundation, the evidence of known facts will not permit us to deny that they are in some degree true.

". . . democracies have ever been spectacles of turbulence and contention; have ever been found incompatible with personal security or the rights of property; and have in general been as short in their lives as they have been violent in their deaths. . . . A republic . . . opens a different prospect and promises the cure for which we are seeking."

When governors and governed seek legitimation, they talk myth; when they want governance, they talk ideology. The possibilities for confusion are abundant in all this talk, which undoubtedly helps to explain many of the misunderstandings that plague political life and government.

We may summarize these points in terms of formal definitions. *Myth* is the conventionalized, routinized tradition of values and practices by which a nation historically defines and declares its identity and the legitimacy of its government. *Ideology* is the conventionalized, routinized tradition of values and practices by which a nation historically defines and operates its governmental processes for making and implementing policy and settling disputes. Figure 2–4 on page 49 connects all these points in one diagram.

James Madison.

The final general point about myth and ideology is perhaps the most important. The acceptance and acknowledgment of governmental authority and, equally, the exercise of that authority must be repeated many times a day as the government carries out its functions. In time, often enough by deliberate decision, sometimes simply by habit, these processes of legitimation and governance become conventionalized and routinized. They draw more and more upon the historically available resources of the political culture and, beyond that, of the national culture. Over the years, the legitimation process becomes mythic and, then, the national mythic tradition; correspondingly, governance becomes ideology and then the national ideological tradition. Each becomes institutionalized.

Myth in America

Myth and Patriotism

The definitions of myth and ideology as the conventionalized patterns of legitimation and governance, respectively, in a national community are highly formal. These definitions are easily enlivened, however, by referring to situations in real life, especially the political life of the American people.

First, as to myth, we can refer to our flag, the stars and stripes ("... forever!"), flying in every part of the nation, celebrated in song and story, hung in schools, churches, and sports stadiums, and draped over the coffins of our fallen heroes. What does the flag, our most prominent political symbol, express? It proclaims the primary myth: America is a nation, united and distinctive, a nation among nations deserving re-

**BOX 2–6
Patriotism—It's
Back in Style**

Old-time patriotism—almost rejected as a virtue a decade ago—is making a flag-waving comeback.

What was deemed corny, old-fashioned or tainted by politics only a few years back now is acceptable and even in style for more and more Americans.

Across the land, people are turning out in record numbers for holidays such as Flag Day and the Fourth of July.

On campuses where not long ago American flags were sewed on blue jeans in protest against U.S. military actions in Vietnam, students are asking for the return of Reserve Officer Training Corps programs they once scorned.

Military recruiters who sweated and failed to fill their quotas only a year ago are starting to turn away volunteers.

Membership in veterans' groups is up for the first time in years, and service organizations report that more youths than ever are entering their patriotic essay contests.

How deep does the fresh vein of patriotism run? A new Gallup Poll finds that 81 percent of teen-agers surveyed say they are "very proud" to be Americans, while an additional 17 percent are "fairly proud."

The rise of patriotism was triggered by the Bicentennial celebrations of 1976, which followed a period of natural trauma stemming from Vietnam and the Watergate scandals. Americans drew closer together when Iran took 66 of their countrymen hostage in 1979. Concern over national security rose when the Soviets invaded Afghanistan and threatened Poland. Pent-up pride burst forth when the U.S. hockey team upset the Russians in the 1980 Winter Olympics, even more so early this year when the hostages were freed.

Whatever the reasons, the burst of nationalism is making President Reagan's job easier. His plan to spend a whopping 1.5 trillion dollars for defense over the next five years is sailing through Congress with scant debate. . . .

—*U.S. News and World Report*, July 8, 1981, pp. 41–43.

The U.S. Government provides a booklet on the care of the flag.

spect at home and abroad (see box 2–6). Is this myth true? It is if we believe it is true. When we wave the flag, salute it, or pledge allegiance to it, or take any other oaths for our country, we declare ourselves by these acts to be a people—and thereby we do become a people. The declaration makes the fact.

Political myth is a strange mixture of fact and aspiration; as we believe it, we become what we believe. That is why politicians and other national leaders of all kinds so often call on us to respect our national emblem. As they initiate the legitimation dialogues of the political system, what better way do they have than to "wave the flag"? The technical name for this process is "symbol manipulation."

The flag is the premier symbol of our primary myth, and it is associated with a host of other symbols that all proclaim the same message that we are a distinctive and unified community, the American nation. Along with the flag, we have the Founding Fathers, great presidents, and war heroes from our past. Memorials are built to these larger-than-life figures not only to remind us of historical events, persons, deeds, and words, but also to teach us who we are as a people. America works hard at this process of legitimation, harder than many nations do. It is said that Canada, for example, has never sought to instill a Canadian identity in its citizens, whether they are native-born or immigrants, to the extent that the United States does. We seem to excel at this, or at least we make the effort to excel.

Myth and the Gettysburg Address

Traditional patriotism with endless repetition through the years, especially on national holidays like the Fourth of July or special occasions like the Bicentennial, has given a specific content to our broad, primary myth of a distinctive nationhood. Nothing sums up this specific content as well as Abraham Lincoln's Gettysburg Address.

Any attempt to read the address objectively must take into account the circumstances under which it was delivered. The South had rebelled against the authority of the federal government and launched a terrible and nearly successful effort to break the concept that we were one nation. Lincoln's task as head of the federal government and leader of the massive effort to preserve the Union was to reassert the nation's primary myth, to establish at the most fundamental level a relegitimation of America's nationhood. His words were nearly lost at the time.

**BOX 2–7
Duty and Patriotism: The Rifle Creed of the U.S. Marine Corps**

This is my rifle. There are many like it, but this one is mine. My rifle is my best friend. It is my life. My rifle without me is useless. Without my rifle I am useless. I must fire my rifle true. I must shoot straighter than my enemy who is trying to kill me. I must shoot him before he shoots me. I will.

My rifle and myself know that what counts in war is not the rounds we fire, the noise of our burst, nor the smoke we make. We know that it is the hits that count. We will hit.

My rifle is human, even as I, because it is my life. Thus, I will learn it as a brother. I will learn its weaknesses, its strength, its parts, its accessories, its sights, and its barrel. I will ever guard it against the ravages of weather and damage. I will keep my rifle clean and ready, even as I am clean and ready. We will become part of each other. We will.

Before God I swear this Creed. My rifle and myself are the defenders of my country. We are the masters of our enemy. We are the saviors of my life. So be it, until there is no enemy, but peace!

—*Marine Corps Recruit Depot* (San Diego: U.S. Marine Corps, undated).

**BOX 2–8
Regenerating Our
National Myth: The
Gettysburg
Address**

Delivered by Abraham Lincoln, November 19, 1863

Four score and seven years ago our fathers brought forth on this continent, a new nation, conceived in Liberty, and dedicated to the proposition that all men are created equal.

Now we are engaged in a great civil war, testing whether that nation, or any nation so conceived and so dedicated, can long endure. We are met on a great battlefield of that war. We have come to dedicate a portion of that field, as a final resting place for those who here gave their lives that this nation might live. It is altogether fitting and proper that we should do this.

But, in a larger sense, we cannot dedicate—we cannot consecrate—we cannot hallow—this ground. The brave men, living and dead, who struggled here, have consecrated it, far above our poor power to add or detract. The world will little note, nor long remember what we say here, but it can never forget what they did here. It is for us the living, rather, to be dedicated here to the unfinished work which they who fought here have thus far so nobly advanced. It is rather for us to be here dedicated to the great task remaining before us—that from these honored dead we take increased devotion to that cause for which they gave the last full measure of devotion—that we here highly resolve that these dead shall not have died in vain—that this nation, under God, shall have a new birth of freedom—and that government of the people, by the people, for the people, shall not perish from the earth.

They have rung clearly ever since. One reason for this is probably because the address is short enough for school children to memorize it. But the most important reason is that time has shown again and again that Lincoln's clear, simple language exactly caught the emerging faith that the American people held about themselves (see Box 2–8).

Lincoln's language is biblical through and through. This means much more than his use of the phrase "under God" at the end. He begins the address the way the Bible does its accounts of the nation Israel, by going back to the day of the nation's founding and saying that on that day the nation was both born and dedicated. It is as if Lincoln was saying that in the plans of the Creator, we are a "chosen" people, a burdened people that must carry out an historic mission. This mission was given to us by our founding and our past. The Civil War was a test of ourselves and of our faith. The future would test us severely to see whether we could carry out this mission for all nations. The mission Lincoln saw for America is encapsulated in the proposition that all men are created equal, the challenge of the Declaration of Independence. To fulfill this mission, Lincoln's final paragraph asserts, we have been organized into a popular democracy—a government of, by, and for the people. Fulfilling the promise of these great phrases is the task that many nations have looked to America to perform.

A final point about America's national myth as summed up in the Gettysburg Address lies in the remembrance that Lincoln personally wrote and delivered the Address. In our mythic consciousness, the American people look back, especially in times of crisis, to Lincoln's tenure of office; but the myth stays with the presidency up to the present day. People look to the White House and indeed to the sanctified Oval Office for meaning, assurance, and leadership. The myth says there has been greatness in the presidency, and in it, too, there is hope.

Our Primary Myth: A Single People

We can now summarize the nation's primary myth about our historic identity as a people: (1) we are a people, united and proud; (2) as a united people, we have been chosen by history, largely because we are dedicated to the proposition of universal equality; (3) to this end, we have organized ourselves into a system of popular government, a democracy of, by, and for the people; and (4) in times of stress, triumph, or tragedy, our popular democracy has been and will be led by great presidents who are virtual messiah figures.

Far more is Protestant in this myth than its overt references to biblical concepts such as chosen people and messiahs. It is profoundly Protestant in at least two senses. First, it rests upon a call to individual dedication in faith to social ideals. Second, it is laced with the hope that through these acts of personal dedication we will become a single people, a true community of "saints" bound by a single faith and hope about ourselves and our national future.

Protestant individualism issues through love and faith into a crusading community. This is the very essence of American nationalism as symbolized by the flag and expressed in such historical documents as the Gettysburg Address. This nationalism, this mythic hope and faith we have in ourselves as Americans, can be an awesome historical force. When it fades, when the myth seems thin and uncommanding to many of us, the American nation weakens and we become divided as a people, groping for national leadership and ordered purpose. When it is strong it is expressed through the full array of national symbols, speeches, parades, rallies, songfests, publications of all kinds, and in the electronic media.

The most important vehicle for the generation and reiteration of the nation's primary myth, however, is the political system's recurrent pop-

*Parade in support of
Lincoln, 1864.*

ular elections to fill the huge number of offices from the presidency to
the local coroner. These elections are the formal and obvious means by
which citizens select and legitimate their political leadership. But the
extraordinary range of offices filled by elections in this country, the
frequency of elections, and the emotional fervor they sometimes provide gives us a good clue that elections do more for the political system
than provide a leadership and policy selection process. As our later
chapters show, elections in America are only secondarily important for
their policymaking implications. Their primary function is the opportunity they afford ordinary citizens to involve themselves in the legitimation of the nation and its government, especially in presidential campaigns with their endless primaries.

Ideology in America

The Dialogues and
Practice of Governance

What is this government that we Americans in our Protestant individualism legitimate? It is something quite different from the humane, egalitarian, popular democracy we dream about in our national myth.

There is an important difference in the character of the dialogues
carried out on the two sides of America's power configuration. Legitimation dialogues are typically initiated by power holders and seekers
and are addressed to the broad reaches of the population. These dia-

logues are therefore couched in the traditional terms that the whole population can understand and respond to, the old, vague, but evocative symbols that everyone has known since school days. They are filled with sweeping promises that tend to boost our national pride and confidence.

The dialogues of governance, however, are typically of a narrow and certainly less inspiring character. They are welded to a day-to-day practicality, directed most often to specific individuals or groups rather than the general public, and they call upon these individuals and groups to perform in specified manners and modes. Governance dialogues are the business talk that actually carries forward the stuff of politics—barter and brokerage, carrot and stick, bureaucratic directive and staffing arrangement. Rather than worry about speeches and recitations, governance dialogue is filled with bureaucratic forms, memoranda, legal work, court decisions and opinions, and above all, the mostly private negotiations and hard-won understandings about policies and programs among active politicians, lobbyists, and their clients.

In legitimation dialogues, as we have seen, governors proclaim what we as a nation will do. Our mythic legends and hopes are declared. In governance dialogues, the principals proceed with the work of doing those things alluded to in our hopes and many other things as well. Legitimation dialogues leave all sorts of room for vagueness and exaggeration. Governance dialogues, on the other hand, put pressure on individuals to be practical and specific. In consequence, the separateness of function between the two kinds of talk inevitably causes misunderstandings, failures to live up to promises, and on occasion even some measure of deliberate subterfuge and misrepresentation. And just as the mythic dialogues of legitimation have been cast in Protestant terms, so the ideology of our conventionalized governance dialogues has been cast in the terms of the Bourgeois individualism of English Liberalism.

The Founders' View of Government and Society

The core of this Bourgeois individualism, as pointed out in Chapter 1, is a radical self-aggrandizing ego bent exclusively on obtaining personal security and gain. Instead of a goal of national love and solidarity characterized by a dedication of all to community effort, the assumption is one of a community permanently factionalized into a myriad of self-contained, constantly competing units. In the Bourgeois scheme of things, the functions of government are the protection of individuals in their rights and the preservation of domestic peace, a process sometimes called "conflict management." The liberal assumption, as pointed out in Chapter 1, is that it is necessary to frame everyone within a rigid "cage" of law to eliminate excesses and keep everyone within narrowly defined bounds. The American Founding Fathers and their political heirs learned the lessons of English Liberalism quite literally and then took them several steps further.

First, while retaining all the essentials of the Hobbesian conception of a society (aggressive individuals who must be tamed by some kind of authority), they rejected out of hand Hobbes's belief that authority of sufficient power could be guaranteed only by concentrating it in a single spot, a single person, or a single assembly. Influenced in part by their unhappy experience with George III, the Founders thought of concentrations of power as utterly dangerous. Instead, they insisted on a partitioning and dispersal of governmental authority. Federalism and separation of powers are the two main devices they used for institutionalizing this belief (see Chapter 3). Their hope was that by these techniques power would be so fractured and dispersed that no one group or combination of groups could ever be able to amass enough strength to tyrannize the rest of society.

Second, the greatest fear of the Founding Fathers was not an American version of George III tyrannizing the country, but the developing democratic enthusiasm for pure majority rule. Again and again they asked, what is to become of minority rights? To forestall the development of an unbridled majority, their system of partitioned and dispersed authority came to be governed by what we now call the "doctrine of concurrent majority."

The doctrine of concurrent majority is an implicit imperative in any political system in which power is completely and deliberately fractionalized, as it is in America. It was first propounded by John C. Calhoun. Though he is more often remembered as a spokesman for the South in the pre-Civil War days, he should be better remembered as a defender of minority interests and for having formulated the procedural rules still dominant in the American policymaking process. These rules guarantee protection of the vital needs of minority interests. The doctrine of concurrent majority insists that every recognizable interest in a political system must be given access to a position in the system from which it can veto the proposals of other interests even if these other interests constitute a majority of all those present and voting. Moreover, Calhoun saw that in any ordinary system of voting, whether in an electoral college or a legislature, a dissenting minority might well be overwhelmed and simply never heard. He insisted that a vetoing minority could be heard only if voting proceeded sequentially, that is, in any poll, each interest involved must be heard individually, one after the next.

The doctrine of concurrent majority, by garrisoning individual interests into their separate power positions throughout the political system, runs directly counter to the faith and hope of America's national myth. The doctrine does not undermine individualism, of course; it is an extreme extension of radical individualism. The contrast between the individualism in American myth and the individualism in the American

Minority Rights to Be Protected: Calhoun

**BOX 2—9
John C. Calhoun's
Concurrent
Majority**

John C. Calhoun, one of the dominant figures in American government over the first half of the nineteenth century, served as senator, representative, secretary of state, secretary of war, and vice-president. At times he hoped to win the presidency, though he never attained it. Calhoun regarded his doctrine of the "concurrent majority" as the superior of two modes of taking the sense of the community.

"One regards numbers only, and considers the whole community as a unit, having but one common interest throughout; and collects the sense of the greater number of the whole as that of the community. The other, on the contrary, regards interests as well as numbers, considering the community as made up of differing and conflicting interests, as far as the action of the government is concerned; and takes the sense of each, through its majority or appropriate organ, and the united sense of all, as the sense of the entire community. The former of these I shall call the numerical or absolute majority; and the latter, the concurrent, or constitutional majority. I call it the constitutional majority, because it is an essential element in every constitutional government—be its form what it may."

—August O. Spain, *The Political Theory of John C. Calhoun* (New York: Octagon, 1968), p. 129.

ideology of governance is seen in the way priorities of individuals become reversed. America's Protestant national myth orders each person to lead a life of love and sacrifice *in* community; America's governance ideology, as expressed in the doctrine of concurrent majority, urges each individual to look out for himself or herself first, and never mind the rest.

**Ideologically, a System
of Elite Rule**
The national myth longs for community and a spirit of fellowship. Ideology, our dialogue of governance, insists that community progress, if it comes at all, will result from unleashing a spirit of competition based on the realities of self-interest.

By devising a political system that entrenches separated interests to a degree that made government by concurrent majority inevitable, the Founders and their immediate descendants set in train a development that some of them privately welcomed but few of them expected and none cared to acknowledge: elitism. All government is inevitably practiced by the few over the many. In a sense, therefore, there are elites in

John C. Calhoun.

all nations. There are divisions between those who hold and seek power and those who grant power or who simply have no power. American elitism, however, is special in a variety of ways.

The American power elite is relatively large. It is composed of people who by one route or another have personal access to the ideological levers operating the political system. In a radically fragmented system, these levers are remarkably numerous. Correspondingly, the elite making use of them will also be quite numerous.

These same considerations mean that the governing class in the United States exhibits a good deal of fluidity, or what is often called "elite circulation," with individuals readily moving into and out of the governing class. The process is somewhat like an unending game of musical chairs, though some well-placed individuals and families seem to win more often than other players. More importantly, this high dispersal means that for certain periods, individuals and groups can con-

trol a part of the political system but no one individual or group can
control all of it. This condition has sometimes been called "elite pluralism." A more descriptive phrase is that in America there is a "non-
congruence of elites," meaning there are many elites and their areas of
influence only partially overlap.

These qualifications and special characteristics do not in any way
change the thesis that America has, on its ideological side, a system of
government by an elite. The American political system is notoriously
difficult to operate. It has many points of access and influence, but these
are hard to reach and use very effectively. Reaching and using them
requires skill, persistence, organization and, most often, money in considerable quantity. A well-known California politician, State Treasurer
Jess Unruh, has said that "money is the mother's milk of politics." Most
of us do not possess the resources adequate to the task. As a result, we
are powerless or relatively powerless, and there is a clear line between
us and the elite that has access to positions of power.

Thus there is an elite governance class on the American political system's ideological side, which is broad in size and scope. There are wide
variations in the kind and amount of power its various members can
wield. There are no dictators or monarchs among them. They are a
group of barons, some big, many small, but each of them has some
power, far more than those of us who do not have any.

On the ideological side of American politics, the overriding ethical imperative of Anglo-American Liberalism is that all barons, great and small, must work on behalf of their own interests, whatever these may be, and in the interests of their friends and supporters. However, the barons must change their tune when they turn to the mythic channels and seek legitimation for their power. In myth, America is a popular democracy in which leaders are responsible to the people, *all* of the

In Myth, a System of Popular Democracy

**BOX 2–10
The American
Establishment**

To some, the Establishment means a set of influential institutions that shape and govern our life as a nation. Included among these are large corporations, banking interests, important media such as network television and *The New York Times*, the largest foundations, a number of elite universities, and a number of other institutions, most of them centered in New York City and Washington, D.C. What is the role of this Establishment? Here is one opinion.

"Prestige counts. An echo chamber seems to exist out there in the country for what the Establishment says. Whether right or wrong, it matters.

For the Establishment is more than a collection of worthy and visible institutions; it is a spirit, a ghost, a force which draws others to it, especially in times of national crisis.

But the Establishment is influential not just because of its prestige or knowlege or moral principle, but because it, too, is "political." It listens to what the nation wants and it reacts, adapts, to meet changing national demands. Indeed the hallmark of the Establishment is its adaptability. This has enabled it to survive great lurches in public opinion and revolutions in economic and social conditions.

Adaptability, however, can also be a vice. The danger is that one day the Establishment might adapt itself out of existence, lose a secure sense of its moral and leadership role, see its institutions abridge their special character and become mere forums, or chameleons for every shifting color in the political jungle.

Should that happen, the Establishment would lose its strength as a unifying national force as mediator between rich and poor, black and white, management and labor, industrialists and environmentalists, hawks and doves."

—Leonard Silk and Mark Silk, *The American Establishment* (New York: Basic Books, 1980), p. 326.

people. Strain is thereby imposed on the minds of America's powerful. There is a conflict in their minds between the necessities of selfishness and selflessness, between the needs of the elite and the needs of the country as a whole.

This conflict in the minds of our leaders can spread to the entire country. When ordinary citizens find out what their leaders have been doing in their ideological pursuits, they can become angry and insist that the standards and promises of myth be met. But even this anger can become confused and self-defeating as ordinary citizens reflect on their own interests and wonder how these are to be serviced.

The strain between the imperatives of legitimating myth and the imperatives of the governance ideology is the root tension of American politics. Throughout the history of the American people, this conflict has been embedded in the very nature of the power relationships that make up the core of their political system. In consequence, the tension in the political culture can be traced through every pattern and institution of the system, the presidency, the Congress, the courts, the system of state and local government. Ultimately the tension comes to sharpest focus in the electoral system, the jewel sometimes held up as the most

BOX 2–11
Workplace Governance and the Support of Democratic Values

A leading sociologist, Carole Pateman, has pointed out that most work experiences involve living under a dictatorship for eight hours a day, five days a week—a big part of our lives. With few exceptions, orders are given in the business world, government agencies, and the like from the "top" to those who hold inferior positions. And this latter group is most of us.

What are the political consequences of this situation?

According to Pateman it means that a large part of our lives is spent in an environment in which most democratic values—choice, participation, perhaps equality—are put aside in the name of efficiency and the traditions of commercial and administrative practice.

Which is bad enough; but according to Pateman, it also tends to make us validate and support undemocratic principles and practices when we leave the work place. Many or most of us cannot probably adjust very well to employing one set of governance principles at work and another on our free time.

—(See Carole Pateman, *Participation and Democratic Theory* (London: Cambridge University Press, 1970.)

precious possession of the ordinary citizen. But in light of the argument now being advanced, it can be seen that the primary function of the American system of elections is to resolve the unresolvable, to overcome the tension between the egalitarianism of myth in which every vote counts and the elitism of ideology in which only powerful interests matter. Elections blur the line between the powerful and the powerless, while leaving that line in place.

FOR FURTHER READING

BACHRACH, PETER, and MORTON S. BARATZ. *Power and Poverty: Theory and Practice.* New York: Oxford University Press, 1970. Basing their thesis on a Baltimore study, these writers develop the insight that nondecisions can be as important as decisions in assessing power.

CONNOLLY, WILLIAM E., ed. *The Bias of Pluralism.* New York: Atherton, 1969. Readings that develop a critique of pluralism from a variety of stances.

CRENSON, MATTHEW A. *The Un-Politics of Air Pollution: A Study of Non-Decision-making in the Cities.* Baltimore: Johns Hopkins University Press, 1971. Uniquely successful application of elitist theory to a policy question.

DAHL, ROBERT A. *Who Governs?* New Haven: Yale University Press, 1961. The classic decision-making study that proved to be a landmark in the development of the pluralist thesis.

DE GRAZIA, ALFRED. *Eight Bads, Eight Goods: The American Contradictions.* Garden City: Doubleday, 1975. Interesting attempt to explore strengths and weaknesses of the American system, based on author's perception of various power configurations.

DE TOCQUEVILLE, ALEXIS. *Democracy in America,* 2 vols. New York: Knopf, 1945. Originally published in 1835. One of the first studies of the interplay among power, politics, and the American people.

DOMHOFF, G. WILLIAM. *Who Rules America?* Englewood Cliffs, N.J.: Prentice-Hall, 1967. Highly readable study that asserts American political life is dominated by elite-run institutions and a governing class.

GOLDWIN, ROBERT A., and WILLIAM A. SCHAMBRA, eds. *How Democratic is the Constitution?* Washington: American Enterprise Institute, 1980. Various viewpoints on the constitutional system and the citizen's place in it.

HAWLEY, WILLIS D., and FREDERICK M. WIRT, eds. *The Search for Community Power,* 2nd ed. Englewood Cliffs, N.J.: Prentice-Hall, 1974. Readings that, taken together, provide a fairly thorough introduction to the methods of measuring and assessing community power.

HUNTER, FLOYD. *Community Power Structure: A Study of Decision-Makers.* Chapel Hill: University of North Carolina Press, 1953. Perhaps the classic study of power based on a "reputational" approach.

HUNTER, FLOYD. *Community Power Succession: Atlanta's Policy-Makers Revisited.* Chapel Hill: University of North Carolina Press, 1980. An update of the earlier work that confirms its findings.

LUNDBERG, FERDINAND. *The Rich and the Super-Rich: A Study in the Power of Money Today.* New York: Lyle Stuart, 1968. A journalistic but fact-laden treatment of the subject.

MILLS, C. WRIGHT. *The Power Elite.* New York: Oxford University Press, 1956. The elitist case that a military-industrial complex rules America without reference to accountability or democratic ideals.

PARRY, GARAINT. *Political Elites*. New York: Praeger, 1969. An introduction to and summary of the literature on power.

PATEMAN, CAROLE. *Participation and Democratic Theory*. Cambridge: Cambridge University Press, 1970. Demonstrates the relationships between democracy and the need for participation and the problems caused for these by our work and life-styles.

RICCI, DAVID. *Community Power and Democratic Theory: The Logic of Political Analysis*. New York: Random House, 1971. Not only a good introduction to various studies of power, but also an excellent treatise on the impasse in social science wrought by problems and failures of analysis.

ROSE, ARNOLD M. *The Power Structure: Political Process in American Society*. New York: Oxford University Press, 1967. Discussion of groups that influence the policy process, taking an optimistic approach to citizen participation.

SCHATTSCHNEIDER, ELMER E. *The Semisovereign People: A Realist's View of Democracy in America*. Hinsdale: Dryden Press, 1975. First published in 1960. Conflict and change in the system and their position vis-à-vis what the author regards as a flexible power configuration.

The Partitioning of Authority: Federalism and the Separation of Powers

3

On election night, November 4, 1980, Americans followed the results of the presidential race on their television screens. They did not have long to wait. Ronald Reagan, former actor, governor of California, and propagandist for the General Electric Company, won in an electoral college, though not a popular vote, sweep (see Chapter 14), leaving incumbent Jimmy Carter with only six states and the District of Columbia. Two of the three networks charting the results used the graphic device of a very large United States election map to depict the election story. "Story," of course, is the term network journalists use to describe what is not a story at all but a quite random accumulation of voting totals. Little blue and red lights across the map came on as the evening progressed, showing that Connecticut was voting this way, Maryland that way, while some states were still to report.

Those blue and red lights representing the states underscored the appearance that this was an election by the several states. During the broadcasts, commentators would mention the shape of the party organizations in Illinois, Texas, Arizona, and other states, acknowledging that the party system follows the pattern of America as a union of states.

The division of America into a collection of states is called "federalism." Federalism is one of the two important ways in which authority is partitioned in the American governmental system. The other is the separation of powers, which is used to organize the interior workings of the federal government, each of the state governments, and, with some variations in detail, virtually all local governments. The operation of this latter principle is underscored by the fact that the presidential election was not the only contest being settled on that November night in 1980. While Ronald Reagan was winning, a host of other politicians at the national, state, and local levels were also being elected. To emphasize the independence of all these other races from the presidential election—and from each other—we point out that many officials are

(RCA Corporation)

elected at various times and to various terms depending on state and local laws. In the case of governors, for example, California and New York elect theirs every four years in the even-numbered years in which the presidential election does not take place. Indiana elects its governor in the presidential year, while Iowa elects its governor every two years. There are many other arrangements for elections to the thousands of offices that are filled in the country.[1]

Separation of powers *in* the organization of governments and the federal division of powers *between* the national and state governments are integral to the power patterns created by American individualism. Individualism, from its earliest beginnings in Europe, has been hostile to governmental power and has sought a variety of ways to control it. American individualism, more radical than most, has carried forward this basic antagonism toward government and sought to control government by forcing upon its very construction an unusually thorough partitioning of all authority between and within governments.

Federalism partitions power between governments. Federalism is concerned with the establishment of governments, with determining how many governments, national and state, there will be, how much and what kind of powers each shall have, and what the relationships among these governments should be.

Separation of powers, on the other hand, partitions power within governments. It is concerned with the organization of each of the governments, with laying out the internal patterns by which these various governments are assembled and determining what the respective powers of, and relationships between, their various parts should be.

Both the mythic and the ideological sides of the power patterns created by America's individualism call for these two devices for partitioning authority, but they make use of them in different ways. The mythic

---

[1] The Senate elects one third of its membership every two years for six-year terms. At one time, Maine voted for president and vice-president in September while the rest of the country voted in November.

In the compound republic of America, the power surrendered by the people is first divided between two distinct governments, and then the portion allotted to each subdivided among distinct and separate departments. Hence a double security arises to the rights of the people. The different governments will control each other, at the same time that each will be controlled by itself.

**BOX 3–1
Federalism and the
Separation of
Powers: James
Madison Writes in
Federalist 51**

legitimation side of American government defines federalism in one way, whereas the ideological governance side defines it another way. Likewise, separation of powers, in the legitimating language of American political myth, has one meaning and carries a particular vision of the political process. On the other side, in the practical language of America's operative political ideology, separation of powers implies something much different, a vision of the political process so much at variance with the mythic version that once we have isolated it for analysis, it will be necessary to call it not separation of powers at all, but "mixed government" theory.

The same terms meaning different things under different circumstances has long caused confusion in the study of American government. This confusion abounds in textbooks, in the press, and even in the minds of the politicians and governmental leaders who are called upon to operate the American political system. To sort out this confusion, this chapter considers the basic terms of federalism and separation of powers in a relatively formal way. The discussion of each of them begins with a brief, general definition followed by a more detailed discussion of what each term means in myth and in ideology. The next chapter sets these definitions in motion to show how the actual life of the American political system causes them to split into conflicting visions of democracy.

Federalism: A General Description

Purpose and Arrangements for Dividing Power

We must first define federalism to include not only the federation of states that we know as the United States but also the Soviet Union, West Germany, Australia, Canada, and many other nations ancient and modern. In this general sense, federalism is a form of government halfway between confederation and unitary government.

Great Britain, France, Italy, and a majority of the countries of the modern world have unitary governments. Whether by constitution, tradition, or otherwise, these countries have one government that has been established as the central and unified ruling authority in the country; it exercises, directly or indirectly, all of the power allowed by the system. These countries have local governments, too; but their local governments are established and assigned powers and functions by the central government. Local governments in countries governed by a unitary system are not much more than the servants of the central government.

A confederation, at the opposite extreme from unitary government, is a league or alliance of existing nations, such as the United Nations or the North Atlantic Treaty Organization (NATO), that have banded together to charter and organize an agency that, at their collective direction, will carry out certain assigned functions for them all. These are loose unions; each member nation is free to terminate its membership whenever it chooses. Before the American Civil War, the South was of the opinion that the United States was a confederation, as it certainly had been at the time of the Revolution and before the adoption of the Constitution in 1789. The South, therefore, held that each state, if it so chose, could nullify acts of the federal government in Washington and even secede from the Union if it wished.

President Lincoln and other Northern authorities believed that the United States was a federation, a much stronger entity than a confederation though certainly weaker than a unitary government. This ultimately prevailing point of view held that the United States is a single nation within which the Constitution, once adopted, brought the federal government into existence while maintaining the continued existence of the state governments and making provision for new ones as time went on. It is the Constitution that divides powers between the federal and state governments, not, as the South thought, the state governments that create and then delegate certain powers to the federal government.

In formal terms, federalism is a system for the *division* of powers. Political scientists do not use the word "separation" here, reserving that term for use only in connection with the doctrine of the "separation of powers" (see below). Federalism may technically be defined as a system for establishing governments in which, within a single nation, a fundamental law or constitution divides the powers of government between the central government and two or more provincial, state, or otherwise named regional governments.

Figure 3–1 illustrates the three concepts: unitary government, federation, and confederation.

Notice that in a confederation, the nations come first; they create the charter or other treaty that establishes the central agency. In a federation, the fundamental law comes first and is supreme. This fundamental law, or constitution, creates or authorizes the existence of the central and provincial, or state, governments. Also notice that in a federation the central government and the state governments are legally on an equal footing, both having the same source for their authority and neither having any formal authority over the other. This is very different from unitary government, in which the local governments are mere legal creatures, or agents, of the central government.

To return to our most important point, federalism is a division of governmental powers. One way of looking at this concept is to think of the Constitution as a pool of power, with the law ladling out some powers to the states and others to the central government. This division of power creates a kind of "dual citizenship" in which people are at the same time citizens of the central government for some purposes and citizens of their state for other purposes.

Another way of looking at the division of powers in federalism—one

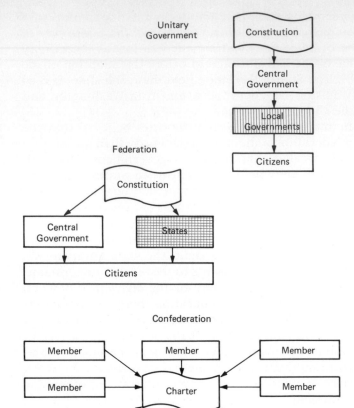

Figure 3–1.
Unitary government,
federation, and
confederation.

that allows us to see more of the complexities—is by imagining a pie without a rim, which is sliced as in Figure 3–2.

This figure shows us that under federalism, the state and federal governments each have their own powers, share others, and are both denied still others. For example, the federal government of the United

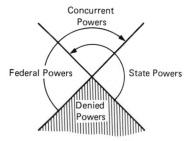

Figure 3–2.
The division of power.

States has exclusive jurisdiction over foreign policy and national defense; the state governments have jurisdiction over most personal or family law problems—property, marriages, death—and over most law enforcement and education policy; but both federal and state governments are denied authority in significant ways over the rights of free speech, assembly, and religion. But they share powers in such matters as welfare administration, the regulation of commerce, and standards for consumer protection.

Figure 3–2 also indicates that a major problem in the operation of any federation is maintaining the various areas of jurisdiction. In the United States, final determination of disagreements in this area is assigned to the Supreme Court in Washington. Some have said that this is like asking one of the players on the biggest team to act as umpire. The jurisdictional problem, however, is probably exaggerated. Over the years the federal government has greatly widened its jurisdiction at the expense of the states, most notably in the regulation of commerce. Nevertheless the most significant change has not been in the area of expanding jurisdiction. Instead the federal government has greatly expanded its activities by exercising, much more vigorously than in the past, the powers that no one ever questioned it had all along. The states have also increased their activities, though not on such a large scale. In consequence, there has been a significant shift in the simple preponderance between the federal government and the states, but it is a shift in relative budgetary sizes more than any major redefinition of the federal relationship.

Operating the System

Federalism has advantages and disadvantages. It has generally been adopted by nations that sought a degree of national unity in the face of powerful regional, ethnic, or religious differences. It can be characterized as a way of trying to achieve unity and diversity at the same time. Like all compromises, especially those in the political world, it tends to be slippery over time. Federations tend either to fall apart into confederations (or even to disintegrate altogether) or to coalesce into unitary governments in everything but name. Yet some federations have had relatively long histories of reconciling the conflicting demands for central control against the claims for local diversity and freedom. Among these, the United States is one of the most successful experiments. Even this successful example, however, has shown that federalism is essentially a device by which individualistic demands for local freedom and respect can be subjected to a sustained challenge by the need for a central authority.

In the American individualistic experience, both mythic and ideological, federalism has not only been taken seriously and even literally, but

Prescription drugs are a concern at several levels of government. The Food and Drug Administration, a federal agency, regulates their use and distribution while local law enforcement agencies seek to insure that they are neither the subject of drug abuse nor obtained illegally. (Fort Wayne Journal–Gazette photo.)

it has also been extended in political practice far beyond its strict legal requirements.

In law, American federalism means that the political system has established a central government under the Constitution, the federal government in Washington, and the various state governments. Each of the states is technically a unitary government that in turn has created, as agencies and legal creatures of itself, local governments. These are found in profusion—cities, townships, counties, and all sorts of special districts, the single-purpose governments that run schools or libraries or mosquito control programs. Almost all of these nearly 80,000 governments have taxing powers of some kind to guarantee their fiscal survival. And, once again, these units of government are by law directly under the control of the states in which they are found.

Unfortunately for those of us who study politics and government, no scheme is ever as simple as this. The spirit of federalism is a powerful force in America, springing from both sides of the nation's basic individualism. This spirit deeply affects the perceptions and actions not only of all the fifty states but also of their local governmental units as well. Local governments, however strongly tied in law to their respective state governments, often behave as if they were equal partners in the federal system in the same way that the states are; this is true of their relations with their parent state government and with the federal government as well. In fact, there is some similarity between the conduct and behavior of the liaison offices maintained by the states and many major cities in Washington and the conduct and behavior of foreign embassies. These states and major cities are represented by able lobbyists who seek favored status in the passage and application of federal legislation and the largesse offered by such federal departments as Housing and Urban Development, Education, and Transportation.

Neal R. Peirce, the well-known journalist who specializes in state and local government affairs, lists the goals developed by a consensus of delegates at a November 1980 conference of the National Municipal League. He reports: ". . . there was a strong unanimity of sentiment: toward a better ordering, a sorting out of functions within the federal system; toward assumption by state and local governments of clear *programmatic* responsibility for many of the areas of government activity into which the federal government has entered in recent years; but a concern . . . that state and local governments be fully prepared for their added responsibilities. . . . Toward a return at least as it may be feasible, of taxing authority to the state and local levels—to fuse the money-raising and money-spending functions as much as we can over time."

—Neal R. Peirce, "The Civic Agenda for the 1980s," *National Civic Review*, **70:**7 (January 1981).

How realistic are these goals? Will governors, state legislatures, and local governments be willing and able to enact new taxes for the many programs they may be asked to take on?

**BOX 3–2
The National
Municipal League
Speaks out on
Federalism**

Appalachia has been specially targeted for federal funds and assistance since the 1960's.

It is also true that in the past decade regional governments have come to the fore as powerful planning authorities with a great deal to say, often the most to say, about an area's land use, environmental, transportation, spending, and other policies. They are found in the form of councils of elected and appointed officials drawn from local governments in the area—cities, townships, counties, special districts, or other taxing authorities. It is occasionally claimed by political conservatives that these regional bodies, established in the era since the Lyndon Johnson presidency, are both unconstitutional and unresponsive to the people. Still another kind of government that may not come under the control of any state is that created by interstate compact; it exists through agreement of two or more states. One of the most famous examples of this is the Port of New York Authority. Brought into existence by a compact between New York and New Jersey, it has become, many allege, unresponsive to either state as an unaccountable collector of tolls, builder of buildings, and transportation administrator.

In sum, the American experience with federalism has extended it far beyond any formal legal requirements. From time to time state governments have drawn in the reins on local governments, particularly on cities that foundered on a financial crisis of some sort; but in the main, the spirit of federalism pervades the whole American political system, fragmenting it not just into fifty units but into tens of thousands, all claiming a distinctive and individual respect.

In the light of this pervasive federalism, the differences between its mythic and ideological interpretations, though not very broad, are important.

The Mythic Interpretation of Federalism

In myth, that legitimizing language by which American citizens and their leaders discuss their federal union and then applaud its virtues and actions, federalism emphasizes the uniqueness of individual local governments and state governments. It also emphasizes the need for a harmonious relationship between them. The significance of the federal government is de-emphasized. "Home rule" and "states' rights" are often the cry. The claim is that people, in their own communities and neighborhoods in a spirit of "grass roots" democracy know what is best for themselves and should be allowed to work out their own solutions to their problems. The tide of public opinion in recent years, as well as some election results, indicate that this point of view has a new strength. There is a feeling that "big government," which usually means the federal government, does not work well. For example, there are problems and disillusion with the Medicare program. We do not have solutions for the growing problem of financing the Social Security System. Yet local ideas and initiatives sometimes seem promising. The resulting diversities in the ways and means of providing such things as welfare services, far from being a cost, are seen as a tribute to the inventiveness, imagination, and spirit of experiment of local communities in America.[2]

Probably one of the most vivid tributes to this mythic conception of federalism occurs at the presidential nominating conventions of the two major parties during the roll call votes of the states. "Virginia!" calls out the convention secretary in full view of television screens across the country. "Madame Secretary!" comes the reply, and the cameras quickly zoom in on the appropriate rows of seats on the floor. A face appears and in broad regional accent intones, "The great State of Virginia, birthplace of Presidents and home of the greatest apples grown in

[2] On this diversity and its empirical importance, see some of the works of Daniel J. Elazar, including *Federalism: A View from the States* (New York: Crowell, 1972).

the world . . ." Anyone listening to this brilliant spectacle must carry away an abiding impression of America as almost a confederation, a loose alliance of sovereign states, each of which cherishes its separate identity. A more local example of this same mythic "federal" spirit can be seen in a small town's Fourth of July parade. Although these are no longer the gala affairs they used to be, they are still spirited assemblages of the volunteer fire departments, American Legion posts, high school bands, and clubs of sundry sorts from the towns in the area, each brandishing its distinctive colors and symbols of grass roots identity and membership. The impression, again, is of an aggregation of communities, each separate and stressing its uniqueness, outweighing any common identity that they all might share.

There is a trace of paradox in this, because alongside the emphasis on distinctiveness is also an explicit willingness of the various groups and communities to work together harmoniously in a common cause. At the national conventions of the parties, all the state delegations in the end seem to support the selected presidential nominee in a roar of unanimity. And at the village level, every town's fire department stands ready to aid any other nearby town in an emergency. In America, mythic federalism, like the mythic Protestant individualism on which it is based, combines separatist distinctiveness and communal cooperation.

The Ideological Interpretation of Federalism

In ideology, American federalism, like the Bourgeois individualism upon which it is based, emphasizes not only the separateness of units of government, whether state, city, or otherwise, but also the need of each unit to take care of its own interests. Major cities maintain liaison offices in Washington to get their share from the federal government's largesse. Quite suddenly, the cultural, regional, and historical distinctiveness that make Maine seem so different from Texas and New York City so different from San Francisco vanishes from view. In ideology, all the units of America's federalism are qualitatively much the same. Their differences lie in their political clout, the size and economic position of a given Standard Metropolitan Statistical Area (SMSA), and their social conditions and needs.

The federal government has responded to demands for money from state and local governments, so much so that many commentators on American federalism believe its chief characteristic today is its fiscal organization. Although this view overlooks the mythic symbolism of federalism, the financial relationships are very important, whether we speak of grants-in-aid programs, revenue-sharing, or projects such as Army Corps of Engineers construction of a dam (see Box 3–3 and Chapter 8).

The great size of some of these programs—in New York City, for example, one out of every six residents is on welfare—means that local and state governments depend heavily on the continuance of federal aid

**BOX 3–3
How the States
Divide Up Federal
Dollars**

Some states fare much better than others in obtaining a share of the federal largesse. The figures below show that whereas the South, West, and New England received $32.2 billion more in federal monies in 1980 than they paid in federal taxes, the Midwest and Middle Atlantic regions received $32.4 billion less.

Federal Expenditures Per $1 of Revenue		Federal Expenditures Per $1 of Revenue	
New Mexico	$1.72	Colorado	$1.02
Alaska	$1.58	Rhode Island	$1.02
Maine	$1.58	Oklahoma	$1.01
Mississippi	$1.48	California	$1.00
Virginia	$1.42	Nebraska	$1.00
Hawaii	$1.36	North Carolina	$ .98
Tennessee	$1.35	Connecticut	$ .97
Alabama	$1.32	Louisiana	$ .97
South Dakota	$1.29	New Hampshire	$ .95
Maryland	$1.24	New York	$ .95
North Dakota	$1.23	Kansas	$ .94
Missouri	$1.22	Pennsylvania	$ .93
Arkansas	$1.21	Nevada	$ .90
South Carolina	$1.20	Texas	$ .90
Utah	$1.20	Delaware	$ .86
Idaho	$1.15	Minnesota	$ .86
Washington	$1.14	Oregon	$ .85
Arizona	$1.13	Wyoming	$ .83
Montana	$1.13	Iowa	$ .79
Florida	$1.11	Ohio	$ .77
Georgia	$1.11	Illinois	$ .74
Massachusetts	$1.11	Indiana	$ .73
Vermont	$1.11	New Jersey	$ .71
West Virginia	$1.10	Wisconsin	$ .71
Kentucky	$1.07	Michigan	$ .68

—*U.S. News and World Report*, June 15, 1981, p. 12.

programs. This is just as true of the dependence of local authorities on certain federal "presences"—an army base, a veterans hospital, or a prison. The closing of such a facility can spell economic disaster for a small community. All of this is to emphasize that in ideology, the actual operations of American federalism, the involvement of the federal government in state and local government and economies is ongoing, intimate, and quite often indispensable. Moreover, this involvement is

BOX 3—4
Intergovernmental
Relations and
Dysfunctional
Federalism

During the past two decades, drastic changes have occurred in the American federal system. These changes, when combined with some standpat political attitudes and practices, have produced neither a dual nor cooperative brand of federalism (and certainly no "New Partnership"), but an increasingly dysfunctional federalism. [Today] intergovernmental relations . . . have become more pervasive, more intrusive, more unmanageable, more ineffective, more costly and, above all, more unaccountable, and chiefly because of the expansion of the federal role over the past 15 years.

. . . The prime symptom of this deepening dysfunctionalism is the continuing tendency to "intergovernmentalize" seemingly everything that becomes a public issue . . . [and these things have happened]:

—The old line between private and public concerns has been obliterated;

—The very real distinctions between federal and state—local matters of the early sixties have been lost;

—State and local budgets have become ever more fiscally dependent on grant revenues;

—State and local programs are involved in intergovernmental fiscal transfers, conditions and court orders;

—State and local regulatory processes are circumscribed by federal statutory and court sanctioned constraints;

—State and local policies and administrative processes have been affected by the Supreme Court's extraordinary expansion of what is "absorbed" within the orbit of the Fourteenth Amendment;

—Federal grants-in-aid have been "used" to serve national regulatory—not promotional, supportive, or additive—purposes;

—State and local governments have been "used" to implement wholly national policies; and

BOX 3–4
Intergovernmental
Relations and
Dysfunctional
Federalism
(Continued)

—The federal government has been "used" to further what not so long ago would have been a wholly local or, at best, a state concern.

. . . It has been the collapse of certain basic constraints in the constitutional, fiscal and political arena that has nurtured these troublesome trends, along with the rise of relatively unfettered individual policy entrepreneurs—usually in Congress—each pushing his or her own favorite program initiative from conception to enactment that has spurred federal growth . . .

—David B. Walker, *National Civic Review*, **70** 68–69 (February 1981).

often marked by strong concerns for self-interest and individual aggrandizement (see box 3–4). No matter what the region or the distinctiveness of local concerns, all the states and nearly all local governments wish to share in federal monies and in the political benefits which these can bring.

The strong preference of states and local governments now seems to be to receive these monies and benefits with as few strings attached as possible (see boxes 3–2 and 3–4). President Ronald Reagan probably suited many state and local leaders well when he stated during his presidential campaign:

The federal government has taken on functions it was never intended to perform, and which it does not perform well. There should be a planned, orderly transfer of such functions to states and localities, and a transfer with them of the sources of taxation to pay for them.[3]

America's governors, meeting in a conference at Denver in August, 1980, seemed more indignant than ever about the hundreds of federal programs with tight rules and regulations they allege put them in a bind when setting their own priorities and managing their own states. Separate federal aid programs, the governors complained, have mushroomed to 500 in number on every issue from dams to fire ant eradication, from jellyfish control to pothole repair. The annual cost of these programs has skyrocketed from $7 billion in 1960 to $88 billion in 1980. Many federal programs, moreover, are mandated—in other words, re-

[3] Quoted by Neal R. Peirce column circulated by Washington Post News Service, November 16, 1980.

quired—by the federal government, but often few funds (and even no funds, in some cases) are provided to carry out the mandate. Administrative costs of most federal aid programs chew up 12 to 17 percent of the program budgets. A great deal of confusion also accompanies the administration of many of these programs, and this confusion is most evident and frustrating at the local level.[4] Nevertheless, President Reagan's efforts to shift the burden of these programs from the federal government to the states has not met with much success.

There is solid evidence that criticism of federal aid programs and the understanding upon which they are based is shared by all shades of political opinion. It seems likely that the 1980s will see further attempts to free monies and program discretion, as well as administrative discretion, for state and local governments. A problem to be faced in such a set of changes will be to maintain the integrity and capability of the various health, housing, social welfare, education, environmental, and other programs involved. There is some evidence that these programs might be crippled badly or done away with altogether if transferred too abruptly to the states.

Whatever happens, the controversy over these programs shows that alongside the mythic view of America as almost a confederal union of sovereign, separate units with a weak central government, there is a more practical view of the United States as a tight union of heterogenous but highly interdependent units in which the federal government plays a dominant role. That is the ideological view of federalism, and the differences between it and the mythic view parallel the differences we will find in the American understanding of separation of powers.

Separation of Powers: A General Description

When we turn from American federalism in its mythic-cooperative and its ideological–self-serving senses to the patterns by which American governmental units are organized internally, the picture appears at first glance still quite simple. Almost all American governmental units are organized on a pattern that calls for separate legislative, executive, and judicial branches, even though the branches' names vary. The House of Representatives at the federal level often becomes an assembly, alongside a state senate, at the state level, and cities and counties have councils and boards. The president's counterparts are governors, mayors, town supervisors, and county executives. The nomenclature of the courts is even more varied. The New York Supreme Court is not the highest court in that state, for example, and the country's justice system is replete with magistrates courts, police courts, circuit courts, appeals

[4] Neal Peirce column, November 16, 1980.

BOX 3–5
The Separation of Powers

Many commentators on American politics and many political science textbooks have been influenced by what can be called the "civics" approach to the separation of powers. The well-known three-pronged diagram that underlies this approach is presented here.

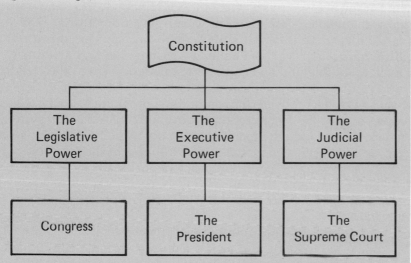

This diagram illustrates one central idea in American government: separation of powers theory. But as a complete explanation, it left much to be desired. Its separation of governmental entities into neat boxes tended to create the impression that government is static, when it is really dynamic, ever changing and subject to the ebb and flow of processes and personalities. Worse still, the "civics" approach was simply inaccurate. American government is neither by the Constitution nor by practice and tradition separated nearly so neatly as the three boxes suggest.

courts, and county superior courts. Whatever we call our institutions, law-making bodies are generally separated from law-executing bodies and these in turn from law-adjudicating bodies.

The standard pattern for the organization of American governments has often been illustrated in the more conventional texts (see Box 3–5). This traditional diagram emphasizes the core idea of separation of powers theory: it is not so much "powers" as "functions" that are separated by the different branches of government. Each branch performs a distinct task that is not to be performed by the other branches. This is an important idea, but it raises many difficulties.

The Parliamentary System: A Contrast

Before turning to these difficulties, we should first note how surprising it is that American government at least appears to conform to this three-branch pattern. Outside of the United States and its areas of immediate influence such as Latin America, South Korea, and Taiwan, virtually the whole of the modern world—even dictatorial regimes—has opted for a very different system of government organization, the so-called "parliamentary" or "cabinet" system. The parliamentary system evolved in England and came to its modern form in the middle of the nineteenth century, not quite a century after the American Constitution went into effect. The parliamentary system, though composed from principles almost the reverse of those built into the American system, is nevertheless often used in America, especially by political scientists and other commentators, as a model and as a source of the vocabulary and concepts for how a democratic politics ought to work. It is therefore worthwhile to examine this alternative system.

This is easily done because the whole intent of the parliamentary system is to be as simple as possible. All governmental power is assigned in the first instance to a popular elected legislative body. This body, known in Great Britain as the House of Commons, retains ultimate responsibility and law-making powers, but it delegates executive power and the primary initiative to decide what laws should be passed to a committee drawn from its members called the cabinet or council of ministers, led by the prime minister or premier. Notice, however, that because the cabinet is only an executive committee of the legislature, there is a tight union of the legislative and executive powers. The cabinet can therefore be dismissed or reconstituted by its parent legislative body at any time. That is to say—and this is the language of parliamentary government so often borrowed, however misleadingly, to describe our own systems—the cabinet is "responsible" to the legislature. If the legislature "loses confidence" in the cabinet, the cabinet "falls" and must be replaced. Usually, in parliamentary regimes, cabinets attempt to ensure steady support from a majority in the legislature by organizing a party of followers (sometimes a single political party, at other times a coalition of several parties) who are in turn supported by a national party working in the electorate at large. If this is done, the party backing the cabinet is said to "control" the "government." Other parties are said to be "in opposition." Figure 3–3 provides an outline of cabinet government.

Saying the cabinet is "responsible" to the legislature, and through it to the electorate at large, that the cabinet must command the "confidence" of the legislature or that it will "fall," that the majority party

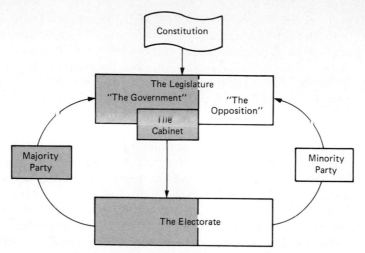

Figure 3–3.
Cabinet government.

"controls" the government, and that the minority party is the opposition party is meaningful talk within the context of a parliamentary system. These terms are meaningful only in the context of that system. That they are so often borrowed by Americans for use in general discussions about democratic government and even sometimes applied without understanding to the American political system is a source of great confusion. How many times have we heard such statements as "The Democratic Party won the election and now *controls* the government," or "In our system of government, our elected officials are *responsible* to the electorate."

These are technical terms, and the American political system, it must be reiterated, is not a system of "responsible" government. It has few if any effective mechanisms for holding elected officials "responsible" to the electorate in any constant or effective ways. Our primary means for holding government officials in line is our system of checks and balances. Yet this points to an even greater source of confusion in Americans' understanding of their government, made worse because it is so seldom discussed. In dealing with "what everybody knows" about the American system of government, and in fitting this common knowledge to the traditional diagram depicting legislative, executive, and judicial branches, we immediately need to modify our terms. The diagram tells us very little by its form. The systematic application of checks and balances to the three boxes can, of course, yield much more useful information—the presidential veto power, the ability of the Supreme Court to declare a law unconstitutional, the control of the budget by Congress. But there is a problem.

Most of us know about checks and balances. The problem is, how can we show this kind of information in the traditional, three-pronged dia-

American Government: Not "Responsible"

gram of the federal government? This is a much more serious problem than mere draftsmanship. We could conjure up images of arrows showing how each branch checks and in turn is checked by the other two. The result would be a messy diagram, but the real problem is, what happens to the inner logic of the diagram? Its original logic depended on a set of functional distinctions among the branches. Only the legislature was to make laws, only the executive was to execute them, only the courts were to adjudicate disputes. Indeed, a perusal of the Constitution in Articles I, II, and III shows that it uses language such as "All legislative Powers . . ." What are we to do with the fact that the system of checks and balances actually *dilutes* the functional differences upon which the separation of powers is based?

Stating the problem even more directly, how do we reconcile the facts that Congress is constituted as a law-making body but is also called upon to act regularly and forcefully as an executive? How can we explain and justify a presidency occupied by a single executive when so much of his work is formulating legislation? Or how can we defend the Supreme Court as an agency of adjudication above the pitched battles of politics when many of its decisions amount to legislation?

Separation of Powers and Checks and Balances

There is only one possible general explanation for this. Somehow in some little-noticed way, two theories about how governments are to be organized have been worked into the Constitution. One has to do with the separation of powers and the other with checks and balances. The two theories are mutually contradictory in their implications and have not been combined so much as simply superimposed on each other.

Once we make this admission about the self-contradictory, thoroughly confused character of the organization of American government, two clarifying steps become possible. One is to identify and analyze

BOX 3—6
Separation of Powers: James Madison Writes in *Federalist* **51**

[It is] essential to the preservation of liberty . . . that each department should have a will of its own; and consequently should be so constituted that the members of each should have as little agency as possible in the appointment of the members of the other.

. . . the great security against a gradual concentration of the several powers in the same department consists in giving to those who administer each department the necessary constitutional means and personal motives to resist encroachments of the others. . . . Ambition must be made to counteract ambition.

each of the theories separately. The other is to show how the two theories, rather than meeting head on, conflict only tangentially because they are used to perform different tasks. Taking these two steps will confirm that what can be called the "pure" theory of separation of powers largely describes what the federal government appears to be in legitimating myth, and that the checks and balances system derives from another theory—the theory of mixed government—which determines, at the ideological level, the day-to-day operations of the government.

The "Pure" Theory of Separation of Powers

The legitimizing appearance of the federal government is set out in the opening sentences of Articles I, II, and III of the Constitution (see Appendix). This appearance can be "seen" if we look at the buildings in Washington. Like temples in their magnificence, the White House, the Capitol with its House and Senate wings, and the Supreme Court building overshadow all else in the city's architecture. By spacing these buildings well away from one another, the planners of the city of Washington emphasized the distinctiveness of the functions carried out by each of these branches of government. The theory behind this appearance can be clearly identified if we are careful not to confuse it with checks and balances considerations. The "pure theory" rendered by these appearances was first popularized by French philosopher Baron de Montesquieu (1689–1755). Montesquieu thought he saw his theory actually working in the British government of his day. The theory can be defined by asserting two propositions: first, the functions of government are three—legislative, executive and judicial—and second, the performance of these tasks should be entrusted to individuals who have as little to do with each other as possible. This helps to explain, incidentally, why the Constitution forbids members of Congress to hold positions in the executive branch and vice versa.

The history of the theory is important to an understanding of it. It grew up as a protest against the tyrannical government of monarchs. Tyranny, as John Locke defined it, is when all the powers of government are concentrated in one pair of hands. The historical purpose of separation of powers doctrine was to take away from the king certain of his powers, namely the legislative and judicial, and to place these elsewhere in the governmental system where he could not get them back or otherwise tamper with them.

The assumption behind the theory is important: governments have a tendency to be bad. Power, a later observer would declare, corrupts and absolute power corrupts absolutely. The obvious solution is to divide up the power and keep it well-separated.

Thomas Jefferson, a leader in the cause of states' rights.

There is another assumption: not only is the concentration of power dangerous, but any power held without limit is absolute within its scope and is therefore corrupting. Power must therefore be divided, but it must also be assigned only for limited periods of time. This second limitation depends on the idea that the people, from whom all power stems, are virtuous and harmonious. The pure doctrine of separation of powers, then, is both a theory for the partitioning of authority within governments *and* a theory for mandating frequent elections of those wielding authority.

The pure theory of the separation of powers fits neatly into the innate tendencies of America's Protestant individualism and egalitarian humanism. It was highly popular during the Revolutionary period, especially with those elements that later went on to make up the Jeffersonian tradition in American politics. John Taylor of Caroline County, Virginia, was its most ardent philosophical spokesman. But it was also popular with the constitution makers in the various states, and its requirements dominated the writing of Pennsylvania's constitution, the most democratic of state constitutions, written in 1776. The Pennsylvania Constitution held that the executive branch should be headed by a series of officials, all independently elected; at the same time, it called for judges to be elected, which is still the case in most state constitutions today.

With such a popular theory it was natural that the Founding Fathers, gathered in Philadelphia at the Constitutional Convention of 1787, should set out a frame of government drawn to its terms. However, the content which they applied to this frame was actually drawn from another source, mixed government theory.

The Theory of Mixed Government

The theory of mixed government is ancient, dating from Greek and Roman times. It was first comprehensively stated by Aristotle and was much popularized by Polybius and Cicero. We can suppose that James Madison, the chief author of the American Constitution, became familiar with it directly from these authors.

Like the pure doctrine of the separation of powers, mixed government theory is concerned with the partitioning of authority. But it differs from separation of powers theory over both how and to whom the partitioning of authority should be affected. Its innate elitist tendencies also causes it to differ sharply from separation of powers theory on the question of why the partitioning of authority should be affected. And it should be stated, finally, that checks and balances are integral to mixed government theory, and their presence in the American Constitution is proof that mixed government theory determines the logic of the Constitution's operative clauses.

The primary division posited by mixed government theory is not between the branches of government, but within the legislature between its two houses. Bicameralism, or two-house legislatures, are the mark of mixed government theory.

Bicameralism

Whereas separation of powers theory assumes the possibility of tyrannical government within a virtuous and democratically inclined society, mixed government theory assumes that society is divided against itself. Its vision is that within every community there is a great division between the rich and the poor, one fearful, the other envious, and that the war between them is perpetual and dangerous to the liberty, persons, and prosperity of all. Thus, whereas separation of powers theory tries to take away from the king the powers that are to be granted to separate legislative and judicial branches rooted in the people, mixed government theory seeks to catch and cage the class war inherent in the nature of almost every society, then place it within the legal framework of a two-house legislature.

It must be admitted that American political experience has not confirmed the assumption that the Senate, with its qualifications for membership, and the House, with its requirements, would represent radically different elements in the society at large. But that fact does not

**BOX 3–7
Bicameralism and
Separation: From
the Very Beginning**

It is a strange fact that when the Founding Fathers set to work in Philadelphia in the summer of 1787, they had before them as their basic working paper a resolution introduced by Randolph of Virginia but largely written by Madison. The Randolph Resolution underwent many alterations as the convention proceeded, many of them hotly debated. Most of these issues were settled by compromises that the participants, and most historians since, have thought to be of major importance. But the Randolph Resolution assumed two matters from the very beginning: that the government would have three branches (and that the Constitution would therefore have three central articles), and that the legislature would be divided into two houses. These two central points were never seriously questioned by the Founders as practical men of affairs.

alter the essential principles involved. These principles are that each house must be, in its own way, representative, and that each must represent sets of competing interests in society at large. This the two houses have always done. That they represent a multiplicity of clashing interests—rather than just the interests of the two principal combinations in the war between the classes—is a distinction of practical but not of theoretical importance.

Notice the harsh assumption in mixed government theory that throughout society people are basically self-concerned and little moved by appeals to public-spiritedness. Calls for the common interest are fine

**BOX 3–8
Bicameralism:
Madison Writes in
Federalist 51**

. . . it is not possible to give to each department an equal power. . . . In republican government, the legislative authority necessarily predominates. The remedy for this incoveniency is to divide the legislature into two different branches; and to render them, by different modes of election and different principles of action, as little connected with each other as the nature of their common functions and their common dependence on the society will admit.

in rhetoric, but it is individual material interest that really matters. If people are rich, their first concern is to protect their property. If they are poor, their first concerns are leniency about debts and opportunities to earn. In this view, the Senate was designed to protect property whereas the House of Representatives was designed to assure easy credit and be jealous about taxation. John Adams, who did not attend the Constitutional Convention but whose books were widely read and appreciated by those who did, became the spokesman for these views. His cardinal assumption, which he boldly stated without qualification, was that self-interest would move rich and poor alike to action.

Mixed government theory places an extraordinary reliance on law. The seeds of social faction—self-interest—are planted deep in human nature and cannot be eliminated. But they can be contained. That is the function of law. Adams—and again, he made the point repeatedly—wanted what he called "an empire of laws." Reliance upon the law as a cage for factions carries with it a powerful bias in favor not only of constitutionalism but also of constitutional review by the courts. Constitutionalism is the belief that the fundamental laws should be sovereign in any society, that a true republic is a government "of laws and not of men." Constitutional review is the process by which judges, in the guaranteed independence of a sequestered system of courts, review the work of the other branches of government to ensure that their activities stay within the limits established by the fundamental laws. Both constitutionalism and constitutional review were prominent features of the thinking of Adams and also of John Marshall, the great chief justice of the Supreme Court.

*Mixed Government
Theory and Devotion
to Law*

Finally, the concept of checks and balances is inherent in mixed government theory. Ironically, the central check and balance with which this theory is concerned is hardly ever mentioned in popular discussions of checks and balances in the Constitution. This check is the absolute check and balance that the Senate and the House have on each other. This check and balance ensures that neither the "house of the rich" nor the "house of the poor" can act on significant legislation without the agreement of the other. It was believed that this balancing of the houses would make it possible for the classes in society to live at least in a state of truce if not in harmony.

The centrality of this check and balance that mixed government theory puts into the legislative arena determines both the need for, and the character of, the other checks and balances that the theory includes. We have just noticed how the emphasis upon law that characterizes mixed government theory implies a power by the courts of constitutional review. This check can now be seen as essentially a means by which the "war between the classes" remains caged within the institutional legal framework created by the two legislative houses.

Presidential Veto

A further check and balance about which proponents of mixed government such as John Adams were adamant was the power of presidential veto, or "negative" as they called it, over legislation. For these people the veto was the presidential office's most important power. They understood the president primarily in terms of his function as a guide and moderator of the strife in Congress. If you read the disproportionately long clause outlining the power and process of presidential veto in the Constitution, you will find that its language is permeated with a vision of the president as a dispassionate, apolitical, almost Godlike figure who from some distant height could calm the hearts of ordinary citizens and steer them into ways benefiting all society.

This picture sharply contrasts with what the doctrine of the separation of powers implied about the presidency. There the vision is of a kinglike figure who, while no doubt stripped of legislative and judicial powers, is still a leader of the populace and a steady advocate of their needs and ambitions. In this separation of powers vision, the president is to be, as he is in myth to this day, a tribune of the people. In mixed government theory, on the other hand, he is godlike but in a much more restricted and distant way, and his primary concern is with the management of conflict.

Elitism and the "Democratic Element"

This contrast between the mythic and ideological conceptions of the presidency built into the Constitution by its conflicting theoretical bases leads us to notice the elitist bias of mixed government theory. This bias is not immediately apparent. John Adams and the other enthusiasts at the time of the Philadelphia convention were all men of aristocratic bias. They acknowledged that in America there neither was nor should be a titled nobility. They did talk a great deal, all the same, about the "natural aristocracy" and believed that government should be mostly in the hands of people drawn from that class. That is why they gave the Senate significantly more power than the House in such matters as foreign policy and government appointments. They insisted, nevertheless, that the House be included in the design of the Constitution and that it be given real and not just window-dressing powers. They were emphatic that the House should have the primary responsibility of representing "the democratic element" in the populace at large.

Adams and his friends did not like this democratic element. They saw its power in the radicalism of the government of Rhode Island and even more plainly in the ranks of those who joined Shays' rebellion in western Massachusetts. But their supposition was that it was more dangerous to exclude this element from the Constitution than to tame it by fitting it into the system and giving it a partial responsibility for running the government.

Pointing out this bias, however, does not establish the limits of the elitism of mixed government. That bias is fully exposed only when we consider what kinds of people did Adams and his aristocratic friends have in mind when they talked about this "democratic element"? The obvious answer is "the poor," but who in their eyes were "the poor"? In general, these were poor farmers, small businessmen, and artisans sufficiently prosperous to take an interest in politics who also possessed the property required by the restrictions on the franchise then in force that entitled them to vote. In other words, the poor in the eyes of mixed government theorists did not include women, slaves, children, Indians, indentured servants, or the propertyless; that is, the *really* poor. A class of political invisibles clearly existed in the age of the Founding Fathers that constituted an overwhelming majority of the total population. They were cut out of the operation of the Constitution because they did not have an "interest," individually or collectively, that in the minds of the Founders enabled, allowed, or required them to participate.

This is the basis of the elitist bias of the American Constitution on its ideological, operative side. It persists to this day. Ideologically, the Constitution is designed from the inside out to serve the interests of those powerful enough to make trouble for the stability of the political system if their demands are not heeded. Persons in the population who do not have or who cannot with others muster such interests for whatever reason are simply left out of the political system. Ideologically, they remain in the class of the politically invisible.

We can sum up all that we have said about mixed government theory in the American Constitution with Figure 3–4, which can be compared with the separation of powers diagram in Box 3–5.

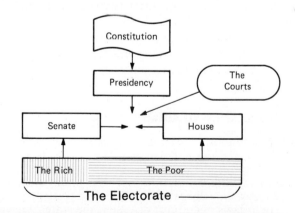

*Figure 3–4.
Mixed government.*

A "Bifocal" Vision of American Government

We began this chapter by asserting that America's bifurcated individualism expressed itself in the institutional structure of the political system in contradictory ways. The two main principles of the system, federalism as a way of establishing governments and separation of powers as a way of organizing them, has each been given double meanings, one for myth, one for ideology. It is as if we are looking at the American political system through bifocal lenses. Through one part of the lenses we see the broad horizons of mythic celebrations; through the other, we look at the system close up to see how it works in ideological practice.

Such a bifocal vision of American government allows us to see each of its principles in double images. Federalism is both a loose system of distinctive but cooperative units and a relatively tight system in which a huge central government spawns a multiplicity of qualitatively indistinguishable local and regional units. More important, the definitions supplied by the "pure" doctrine of separation of powers and by the theory of mixed government give us the following significant insights:

Congress is in myth the democratically elected, supreme legislative body of the political system and in ideology a rigid legal framework for containing within its two houses the perpetual strife between the important and self-serving elite "interests" of the community at large.

The president is simultaneously the democratically elected mythic tribune of all the people and an ideologically aloof figure whose important function is conflict management among competing groups.

The Supreme Court is at one and the same time a judicial body sensitive to the mythic needs and moods of all the people and a remote group of nine judges policing the political system to keep all inside it (especially the powerful) who might stray beyond its encaging limits.

FOR FURTHER READING

ARNOLD, VICTOR L., ed. *Alternatives to Confrontation: A National Policy Toward Regional Change.* Lexington, Mass.: D.C. Heath, 1980. Features articles that seek to resolve problems of present-day interstate rivalries.

ELAZAR, DANIEL J. *Federalism: A View from the States.* New York: Crowell, 1972. Elazar, an acknowledged expert on the subject, reviews federalism through the prisms of cultural diversity, the states' viewpoint, and the idea of a federal-state partnership.

GLENDENING, PARRIS N., and MAVIS M. REEVES. *Pragmatic Federalism.* Pacific Palisades, Calif.: Palisades Publishers, 1977. An examination of American government from the standpoint of the processes of intergovernmental relations.

GOLDWIN, ROBERT E., ed. *A Nation of States*. Chicago: Rand McNally, 1963. Essays that are still current and that examine the history, motives, and perennial issues of federalism.

HALE, GEORGE E., and MARIAN L. PALLEY. *Politics of Federal Grants*. Washington: Congressional Quarterly, 1981. A remarkably informative summary of the politics and problems of "who gets what" of the federal largesse.

PRITCHETT, C. HERMAN. *The Federal System in Constitutional Law*. Englewood Cliffs, N.J.: Prentice-Hall, 1978. An excellent and concise as possible introduction to the legal and constitutional status of federalism in various policy areas.

REAGAN, MICHAEL D., and JOHN SANZONE. *The New Federalism*, 2nd ed. New York: Oxford University Press, 1981. "New" federalism specifically refers to the last decade or so—the era of revenue sharing and regional government.

RIKER, WILLIAM H. *Federalism: Origin, Operation, Significance*. Boston: Little, Brown, 1964. A biting, provocative treatment of the subject that uses cross-national comparisons.

WRIGHT, DEIL S. *Understanding Intergovernmental Relations*. Cambridge: Duxbury, 1978. Descriptive treatment specially geared toward issues of finance and the fiscal organization of federalism.

4 The Processes of the American Political System

America's political actors, who operate the political system for the rest of us, are a diverse lot. Candidates for the office of district attorney have been known to campaign on the number of convictions they have obtained or will obtain. County coroners have been known to make claims about the high quality of the autopsies they perform. Some years ago, a county assessor's race in southern California took an odd turn when the assessor seeking re-election argued that his opponent, a Communist, would be a dangerous person to be given access to local property records. The Communist candidate rebutted this with the simple statement that as a citizen of Los Angeles County, she was already entitled to such access.

Officeholders and candidates are the most visible actors in our political system. They include chief executives—the president, governors, mayors, county executives—and other executives, legislators, both major and minor, and many judges. To these elected officials must be added members of the military and civil services, engineers, postal clerks, police, space scientists, accountants, and a vast corps of others. In all their diversity, the actors in the American political system reveal the diversity of the system itself and the work of every description that the system is called upon to perform.

We may classify these actors in a number of ways. The usual method is to follow the separation of powers patterns of the political system and talk about legislators, executives, judges, and, from what is sometimes called the "fourth branch," the civilian and military services who do the actual day-to-day work of government.

Political Actors and the Political Process

Our scheme of classifying political actors is somewhat different from that of conventional texts, because it is based on whether the actors work mostly at the system's mythic level or are more concerned with its day-to-day ideological operation and maintenance. This scheme yields three basic types of political actors.

First, there are the "heroes," mostly chief executives but also some of the better-known legislators who work mainly through the electoral system and the mass media to generate mythic legitimation from the general public for themselves and for the regime.

Next, there are the "barons." These are mostly legislators and secondary executives, but this category also includes many nonelected officials and the staff aides of major politicians. The baron category even includes some major figures from the private sector who work closely with the government. Barons work the ideological levers of American government back and forth among themselves in a way that satisfies their interests and those of their special constituencies.

Last, there are the "rational professionals," mainly civil servants of all sorts but also most judges, and personnel in the military services. These are the specialized personnel working for the government right down the scale to typists, janitors, and infantry soldiers, who, defined by their particular job competence, carry out the work of the government's multitude of programs.

The distinctions between these three actor-personality types are not hard and fast. Congress members, for example, usually fit the role of "barons" as they vigilantly seek to protect and enhance their interests and the interests of the groups they represent. In a time of national excitement, however, or under duress of a hard election campaign,

**Political Actors:
A Classification**

*Feminist groups such as the National
Organization of Women distribute these
buttons to emphasize that the average
woman in the U.S. makes only 59¢ for
each dollar earned by a man.*

members of Congress can rise quickly to "heroic" heights to defend the nation's honor, values, and destiny. At other times, individual members of Congress, especially when they are chairing a committee investigating a specialized area of activity in the executive branch, may don the rational-professional garb and work assiduously to uphold the law or define and defend the propriety and efficiency of the government.

The president can also be schizophrenic in these matters and in fact usually is. Day after day, he is called upon to be the foremost heroic leader of all the people. But he must also be a busy baron, managing the powers of his office to ensure the survival of himself, his allies, and his most favored programs. On the one hand he is expected to proclaim broad goals and in every way to act "presidential." On the other hand, he is expected to "solve" political problems that will help both himself and his loyal supporters.

Even the full-time rational professionals can get caught up in the confusion. The majority of them go through their routinized, often humdrum tasks as best they can, only engaging in office politics and other maneuvers from time to time in order to gain job security, a promotion, or other short-run objectives. At other times, though, government workers, especially the ambitious and highly ranked, are compelled not only to further their careers but also to push forward those programs to which they have made deep commitments. This requires them to lobby, wheel and deal, and negotiate as narrow-mindedly and as self-interestedly as the best of the barons.

Stages of the Political Process

The reason for these confusions in roles—why Congress members, presidents, and bureaucrats must shift personality types from time to time—lies in the different ways in which the political system reacts to stress. There are three stages involved.

The "normal" stage—the barons of the system go about their business of pursuing their interests, the bureaucrats do their jobs, and the only heroes are the politicians here or there who are mostly running for *re*-election without much of a contest. The newspapers make for dull reading during such periods.

The "stress" stage—something goes wrong or an unavoidable challenge to government policymaking and authority appears. Barons are called upon to act for the common good, and civil servants begin to worry about the adequacy of their programs. Elections loom ominously down the road. Two-line headlines appear in the press, perhaps with photographs of earnest legislators in conference or the president consulting with important advisors or national leaders.

The "crisis" stage—this is primarily marked by the appearance, for all to see, of a gap between the promises of myth and the performances

BOX 4–1
The Potential
Strength of Some
of the Groups That
Seek to Influence
Policy In
Washington

Catholics	49,836,000
Social Security recipients	35,300,000
Blacks	25,863,000
Union members	23,307,000
Hispanics	12,040,000
Persons receiving aid to families with dependent children	10,579,000
Jews	5,776,000
Federal and military retirees	3,020,000
Physicians	438,000

—*U. S. News and World Report,* September 29, 1980, p. 26

of ideology. The core problem at this time is trust. Politicians are found to have been doing one thing while saying another; there may have been a cover-up, or government programs are discovered to be not what they seemed. More fundamentally, the legitimacy of the government itself, at least in some important aspect, may be thrown into doubt. The political system has failed to perform as advertised. The underlying disjunction between myth and ideology in America comes into the open. And the newspaper articles become more strident, sometimes even panicked, while their editorial pages take on a worried, hand-wringing tone.

These different stages in the dynamics of the American political process and the swings back and forth between them are surprisingly distinct. A sharp switch of roles is forced by these stages on various political actors. A sudden crisis can cause a "heroic" president to start grubbing for allies, for example, or can cause others to desert him (see Box 4–2). That these different stages are so distinct is what makes it possible to find well-informed citizens who are deeply cynical about American politics, to find others who are unabashedly enthusiastic, and still others who are alarmed or confused. Over the years in a wide variety of ways and in sundry parts of the system, the American political process has supplied ample evidence to support all these views of its operations.

Let us examine each of the dynamic levels of the American political process to see how this can be so.

BOX 4–2
Watergate: A Crisis
Period in American
Government

Washington—Citing at least 370 legal and constitutional violations by President Nixon's administration and reelection committee, Senator Lowell P. Weicker, Jr., Rep.-Conn., said . . . that "we almost lost America . . . to subversives, terrorists and extremists of the White House." . . .

"Several years ago many Americans were willing to silently tolerate illegal government activity against militants, terrorists or subversives as an expeditious way to circumvent the precise processes of our justice system," he said. "Though quick, it also proved to be only a short step to using such illegal tactics against any dissenting Americans. . . ."

"Evidence presented to this [Watergate] committee can and will demonstrate every major substantive part of the Constitution was violated, abused and undermined during the Watergate period," Weicker said.

Weicker's staff said the report listed at least 370 violations of the law and the Constitution by President Nixon's administration and reelection committee. . . .

Weicker said no adminstration in his lifetime had a worse record of convictions in relation to indictment.

"Why?" Weicker asked. "Because it tried to achieve law and order by lawlessness. It was the courts that said no, not the Justice Department."

Weicker said it was difficult for him as a Republican to say what he was saying.

"But speaking out is a patriotism far better suited to 1974 than 1972's wearing of flag lapel pins by White House and CRP [Committee to Re-elect the President] employees while they advocated burglary, wiretapping, committed perjury, politicized justice, impugned the patriotism of those who disagreed with them and threw due process in the shredder," he said.

—UPI News Dispatch of June 30, 1974.

The "Normal" Stage—Liberal Democracy

Questions of legitimacy hardly arise when the American political system is not placed under much pressure. Myth, under these circumstances, is both conventionalized and routinized and thoroughly so.

Children recite matter-of-factly their pledges of allegiance and the Fourth of July celebrations are as awash with beer as they are with patriotism. Behind it all, ideology, the Bourgeois pursuit of private interests and gain, is the name of the game.

In this mood America defines itself unself-consciously as a Liberal Democracy. A *Liberal Democracy* is a society in which, within a framework of law, individuals pursue their private interests with maximum possible freedom. Liberal Democracy is not to be confused with Social Democracy, which is what America is in its mythic moods and will be discussed later in this chapter. Much less is Liberal Democracy to be confused with utopian visions of Participatory Democracy, in which all citizens of every sort and capacity are enabled to participate directly and fully in the common life of the social good.[1]

The Baronial Elite

In its Liberal Democratic operations, the American body politic is systematically elitist, not only in its original biases but also in its various institutions and processes. This aspect will be explored, but for now it suffices to point out that we are *not* saying that America as a Liberal Democracy is not democratic.

A Liberal Democracy is a framework of law in which *all* citizens are entitled to protection by the law so they may pursue their private interests as best they can. In these pursuits, some, whether by luck, talent, or effort, will manage to do well; others will fail more or less badly. But all are free to compete. To a remarkable degree, America has actualized the ideal of a personal freedom under law. This is especially evident when comparisons are made with other nations or when we consider the span of history. In a world and historical perspective, America is quite truly the land of opportunity; within its borders more people, both relatively and absolutely, have pursued and found wealth and personal comfort than anywhere else. If personal freedom is the test of democracy, there is no question that America as a Liberal Democracy passes it.

The meaning of Liberal Democracy as personal freedom in the operation of our political institutions depends on the narrow, ideological view of federalism outlined in the preceding chapter. It also depends on the view that mixed government theory organizes the operations of all the authorities established by the federal system and its extensions to the local level. The impact of these institutional principles upon Ameri-

---

[1] Nomenclature again is a problem. Calling one aspect of American politics "Liberal Democracy" will not disturb many readers, nor will the definitions given in the text. But calling the other principal aspect of American politics "Social Democracy" may have too European a connotation for some readers. The authors can do no more than admit this possibility, argue that other possibilities ("Progressive Democracy" was the most likely alternative) raise even more difficulties, and ask that the definition of "Social Democracy" given below be observed with care. "Participatory Democracy," it is assumed, will be understood in a strong Rousseauean sense that has little relevance to American Protestant-Bourgeois politics.

ca's Liberal Democratic politics has been to fragment governmental power into a vast array of highly individualized offices. But radical individualism has a consequence of making every one of these offices endlessly dependent on one another. Because power is so fragmented, no individual officeholder can do very much without the cooperation of a host of others. It is this double effect of individualized offices that are nevertheless highly dependent on each other that creates the race of barons for America's Liberal Democratic life.

Because power is so thoroughly fragmented in American Liberal Democracy, great numbers of people have some power, but no one has it all or even very much of it. There are many barons but no one is king, not even the president. The president, as it turns out, is simply the most prominent (or perhaps the most widely heard) of the barons, with little direct power to control the activities of anyone else.

Individual barons holding on to their fragments of power can nevertheless with skill and patience make the advantages of their particular office work for themselves and their friends, supporters, and allies. With such advantages, even a widely unpopular baron can ensure personal survival for extended periods of time. It is no accident that incumbents, that is, persons already holding office, succeed most of the time when they run for re-election.

The secret of baronial success and survival is the deal. The deal is the baronial way of life. Barons' fragments of power cause them to be independent; but by having only a fragment of power, they become dependent on what they can beg, borrow, or arrange—in a word, deal—from and with other barons with whom they are associated. Generally, a skillful baron is a sophisticated dealer, a calculating operator. Most barons seem to have a genial, easygoing personality despite what we have all been told about the ego problems of politicians. To survive, barons learn early in their careers the truth of the late House Speaker Sam Rayburn's oft-quoted advice, "If you want to get along, go along." Barons know how to go with the tide, how to test the winds of sentiment, and how to talk as good a game as they play.

Most barons hold some kind of governmental position. Around this position coalesces their personal entourage of aides, hangers-on, and followers. From this position a style and pattern emerge over the years, branching out to networks of old friends, useful allies, and grateful recipients of favors. Every baron keeps a record, sometimes mental but often actually written, of favors given and received, alliances made and kept, and others made but broken. Barons who are ambitious and unusually successful may climb the political ladder, carrying much of their network of support with them. But no matter how high or how far one may climb the ladder of success, from local council member to state legislator to governor, U.S. senator, or even the presidency, the essential patterns of combining independence and dependence remain the same.

These are the public barons we have described. There are also private barons of considerable significance to the political system. Sometimes they are people of enormous private wealth who are interested in politics. More often, they are people who hold positions of power and influence in major corporations, labor unions, and other organizations with strong involvements in political activities and governmental programs. We must stress that talk about these private barons, even in conjunction with discussion of the public barons with whom they may be closely allied from time to time, in terms of the "power elite" or the "military-industrial complex" can be highly misleading. Certainly private barons, like their public counterparts, often hold tremendous power. All the same, they, like their public counterparts, hold their power in terms of their individual positions; and these, while not as thoroughly scattered as the power positions in the political system, are still fragmented into separate domains with rather clearly defined limits. There is no single power elite in America, neither in the government nor in the private sphere. Instead, there is a plurality of elites, a broad and various class of individuals who have secured some kind of power position from which they can move to deal with others. The fundamental pattern of independence-dependence holds true for all barons, public and private.

This is the basic pattern of America's ideological Liberal Democracy, a framework of law within which baronial operatives pursue their interests and the interests of their friends and allies through an endless process of give and take, compromise, and dealing.

The system has its advantages. It is remarkably stable and has a strong record of harmonizing the diverse claims of all the competing interests. Perhaps even more important, it can harmonize the demands of the ambitious and skillful men and women who lead these interests. There are, nevertheless, outstanding weaknesses in this basic pattern of America's Liberal Democracy that set the stage for calls for alternatives.

Corruption

As must be obvious, the patterns of America's Liberal Democracy are exceptionally prone to what is ordinarily considered corruption. The definition of corruption is usually set in moral terms: the use of public office for personal benefit. However, this is precisely the imperative that Liberal Democracy places upon all officeholders. As the most famous and many would say the most important book on the American presidency points out:

> When we inaugurate a President of the United States we give a man [sic!] the powers of our highest public office. From the moment he is sworn the man confronts a personal problem: how to make those powers work for *him*.[2]

[2] Richard E. Neustadt, *Presidential Power: The Politics of Leadership* (New York: Wiley, 1976), p. vii.

The italics of that last word are in the original, without qualification or comment. The author of these words believed he was enunciating a little-noticed but fundamental truth of American Liberal Democratic politics: our number one politician, like everyone else in the system, had best look out for number one—first.

None of this, obviously, is a call for our presidents to be corrupt. It merely means that in a system of fragmented powers, any president worth his salt must worry constantly about whether his actions and proposals will enhance or weaken his power. All the same, the moral ambiguity is there. Pursuit of self-interest is the logical core of Liberal Democracy in America, for the presidency and every other office in the system. The line that distinguishes proper from improper pursuit of self-interest is not found in the moral qualities of this pursuit but in the laws that more or less mark off, rather arbitrarily, how much is too much. We know that the race for success can be hot and that in the heat of competition, it is understandable that many will read the law finely (see Box 4–2 for an extreme example). It is also understandable that the streetwise will in the end conclude that the only crime is not in committing it but in getting caught at it.

This matter will be taken up again. For now, the point to remember is that the ubiquitous tendency toward corruption in Liberal Democracy arises not merely from the frailties of peoples' souls but from the fundamental characteristics of the system itself. This is much the same point made earlier about the other major difficulty in Liberal Democracy, its tendency toward elitism. In America's Liberal Democracy, all are equally free to become as unequal as time, chance, talent—and the law—will allow. Neither accident, history, nor "human nature" dictates this result. It is the system's underlying Liberal Democratic imperatives that set men and women of the greatest good will for the common good in hot pursuit of goals that contradict their premises.

Public Policy and the "Public Interest"

The problem that most plagues Liberal Democracy and leaves it most vulnerable to criticism from alternative perspectives is its inability to be concerned about, much less to make "public policy" that is in any genuine sense either "public" or "policy."

Preoccupied with the furtherance and protection of private interests and rooted in the belief that the pursuit of private interest is the only morally sanctioned motive, America in its Liberal Democratic moods has difficulty conceiving of any public interest except in the narrowest terms. It can conceive of the need for a legal framework, of the need for judges to be fair, or occasionally of "collective goods" like parks and highways that a large number of individuals can enjoy even while they pursue their own private ends. American Liberal Democracy's goal of the public good is to a great degree merely additive, taking what one

BOX 4–3
Attitudes Toward
Organizations and
Government
Agencies

FBI	1979	1975	1973	1970	1965
Highly favorable	37%	37%	52%	71%	85%
Total favorable	81	80	85	92	98
Highly unfavorable	5	5	4	2	
Total unfavorable	15	16	11	5	1
Don't know	4	4	4	3	1

CIA	1979	1975	1973
Highly favorable	17%	14%	23%
Total favorable	62	50	67
Highly unfavorable	8	16	7
Total unfavorable	24	39	19
Don't know	14	11	14

Ku Klux Klan	1979	1973	1970	1965
Highly favorable	3%	4%	3%	1%
Total favorable	10	9	8	6
Highly unfavorable	66	68	75	76
Total unfavorable	83	82	86	84
Don't know	7	9	6	10

AFL-CIO	1979
Highly favorable	20%
Total favorable	63
Highly unfavorable	9
Total unfavorable	24
Don't know	13

National Association of Manufacturers	1979
Highly favorable	10%
Total favorable	42
Highly unfavorable	3
Total unfavorable	9
Don't know	49

BOX 4–3
Attitudes Toward
Organizations and
Government
Agencies
(Continued)

American Civil Liberties Union	1979
Highly favorable	14%
Total favorable	43
Highly unfavorable	8
Total unfavorable	22
Don't know	35

These polls test public attitudes on some of the most visible bureaucracies and interest groups. What would the results be on polls on the Federal Renegotiation Board or the American Society for Quality Control?

—*Gallup Opinion Index* Report 172, November 1979.

group wants, combining it with what another group wants and adding it all up into a legislative or policy package.

There is also a reverse form of this kind of understanding of the public interest in Liberal Democracy. Suppose that you desire a certain policy result but others do not want this. Under many circumstances, some kind of arrangement can be worked out; everyone agrees to settle for less all around, which is sometimes the case in labor-management negotiations, for example; or perhaps one or more parties will finally settle for nothing at all. It is also possible that one side will prevail over all the others. The American Medical Association, to cite an instance of this, has managed to prevent the enactment of a comprehensive medical insurance system since President Truman first proposed it in 1949, despite fairly consistent support for this idea in opinion polls. But let us suppose that the victory of one side over the other will have grossly destructive results; that it will wipe out one side altogether by adversely affecting their vital interests. When push comes to shove in these circumstances, it is apparent that the tenets of Liberal Democracy include the preservation of private interests at all costs. If you insist on playing the game to the extent that it destroys the other side or threatens to do so, that side will find it in their interest to quit the game or perhaps resort to other means—often violent means—in order to survive.

This is a persuasive argument; at least it is persuasive within the confines of the private interest articulations of Liberal Democracy. Calhoun's doctrine of the concurrent majority is based precisely upon the

Calhounian
Incrementalism

argument that no mere numerical majority has the right to ride rough-shod over minorities. The doctrine's procedural requirements hold that each interest should be polled individually and separately, in a series of consultations, so that minorities can make it clear when they feel vitally threatened. This requirement is so exactly attuned to the inner logic of America's Liberal Democracy that it remains the implicit rule of America's operative ideological politics. It provides a pattern of "public policymaking" geared exclusively to the protection and enhancement of private interests. But at the same time, it loses almost any claim to producing anything that can be reasonably characterized as "policy," let alone "public policy."

Those who have observed the development of the Calhoun-engineered political processes of America's Liberal Democracy have labeled it "incrementalism." These observers know that a political process compelled to consult a large number of individually situated interests *in seriatim* is bound to move forward on the narrowest possible front. If you put into this process some broad, programmatic policy proposal, it will be dismembered into such bits and pieces as can collect an aggregate of broad support and avoid vetoes. What may have been a proposal for a comprehensive and coordinated program becomes instead a series of disconnected actions, only a few of which bear much relationship to the program's original general objectives but each of which will have a direct and supportive connection to some private interest. It is no wonder that in the United States there is no comprehensive program of health care, no broad program for improving the status of blacks across the nation, for broadly halting the pollution of the environment, or for dealing generally with the problems of urban decay and economic decline in the older cities of the Northeast and Midwest.

This is not to say that Americans fail to see the problems that call for attention. They do so with much discussion and ongoing concern. In ideological practice, however, America's Liberal Democratic institutions have been able to deal with these problems only with an incrementally spliced melange of programs predicated upon particular aspects of the problems. Confusion, duplication of effort, excessive regulation, ambitions, and inefficiency all combine to do some good, make some interest groups happy, and often enough leave the most serious sides of these difficulties unattended.

But look at this: we can put into this Calhoun-inspired, incrementally oriented system an enormous appropriations measure for developing armaments for national defense, and the system moves ahead as if well greased. Who could oppose such a proposal except our enemies? Meanwhile, such programs are loaded with opportunities to divide up all kinds of benefits—a contract here, a subcontract there, benefits across the board for virtually every well-established interest group in every

**BOX 4—4
The Diversity of
Claims and
Opinions Found in
the Political
System: The
Military**

MARK CLARK, GENERAL, U.S. ARMY, RETIRED:

At the risk of sounding like an old-fashioned flagwaver, it is evident that many of our young people have rebelled at a permissive society. It is one thing to question the politics of your country, but to actively plot its downfall and support its enemies is little less than treason.
—Alan R. Pater and James R. Pater, eds., *What They Said in 1970* (Beverly Hills: Monitor, 1971), p. 37.

THOMAS H. MOORER, ADMIRAL, CHIEF OF NAVAL OPERATIONS:

Lost in the shuffle somehow . . . are such ennobling factors as: the will to work; the will to serve; the will to sacrifice for just cause. So seldom is focus placed on these attributes . . . that they are all but forgotten, and those who abide by them are, in effect, secondclass citizens.
—*Vital Speeches*, April 15, 1970, p. 392.

HYMAN G. RICKOVER, ADMIRAL, U.S. NAVY:

[If the Navy still had a carrier-pigeon service,] the senior pigeon in the pecking order would, I suppose, be a line Admiral. What we must recognize is that the purpose of our military is to defend the country, and not to provide a place for comfortable careers.
—*Washington Post*, April 5, 1977.

part of the country. No wonder that legislation of this sort is referred to as "Christmas tree" legislation.

In summary, American Liberal Democracy's fragmented system of public policymaking, whereas it makes the barons who skillfully operate it individually successful, is not very good at confronting the broad social problems of immediate interest to the poor, the disadvantaged, or simply the ordinary and the disorganized. The barons tend to be proud of their ability to appease and satisfy the various claims of competing interests; but for those left out of the process, the system is long on concern for the inputs of special interests and short on outputs for the common good. The result is that American Liberal Democracy leaves in its wake a great deal of generalized discontent that is ripe for exploitation.

The "Stress" Stage—Social Democracy

The Rise of Discontent Discontent among the mass of the population is always just beneath the surface even during the most routine times. The seemingly tranquil 1950s, with the great father figure President Eisenhower presiding over the suburbanization of America, were producing the seeds of the civil rights movement of the 1960s. The first appearance of Martin Luther King, Jr., on the national stage occurred in 1957 with the bus boycott in Montgomery, Alabama. Shortly afterward, the women's rights movement and the antiwar demonstrations would have socially and politically wrenching effects. As technological developments and changes in economic organization have deepened the interdependence of ordinary citizens for even the simplest kinds of benefits, the political system's inability to deal systematically and humanely at the operational level with the social problems of our age causes increasing pain and discontent among the population. It does not take much to bring the simmering discontent of the polity's "normal" stage to a full boil.

There are reasons why this happens. Liberal Democracy's preoccupations with tending to private interests involve legislators at all levels of government, as we have seen, and secondary executives, especially at the state and local level, as well as a host of bureau and agency chiefs, their allies, and their clients in the private sector. The "heroes" of American politics—the president, governors, many big city mayors, and an occasional maverick senator or representative running his or her own show—are largely peripheral to the wheeling and dealing of the barons. Chief executives are neither well positioned to enter the endless negotiating processes of the barons nor are they immune to the public pressures that call for staying aloof from them. Instead they look to their own interests, exploiting to the fullest extent they can the public discontent caused by the social injustices of Liberal Democratic politics and its continual pursuit of private interests.

Three lines of attack are open to chief executives. First, they can directly exploit the discontent that arises from the failure of the system to deal effectively with social problems. Chief executives, none more vociferously than the president himself, can deplore the failure of legislators to act on bills designed to remedy this or that pressing need. In cases where such necessary bills have not even been formulated, chief executives are quick to jump in with their own proposals, though this is technically the task of the legislators.

Second, chief executives, and again none more loudly than the president, can rail against the "special interests" whose entrenchment with their legislative and bureaucratic allies has blocked the nation's progress toward its ideals of social justice and humanitarianism. This

Vietnam Veterans Against the War hold a rally at the Statue of Liberty.

charge becomes even more effective when the implicit elitism of the special interest can be dramatized vividly. A good example is the resentment aroused by huge gains in oil company profits that clearly seem to come from gouging consumers in times of oil and gas shortages. This kind of situation lends itself to persuasive argument, because the special interests, together with their well-established contacts in the legislatures and bureaucracies, do indeed largely control the allocation of resources—namely, who gets what and when.

This opens up the third line of attack. Chief executives can charge that elitism and a policy of special benefits to the few is fundamentally undemocratic, hence un-American. With this charge, the chief executives can conjure up a different vision of democracy for America, not that of Liberal Democracy but of Social Democracy.

The Social Democratic Vision

If Liberal Democracy is a framework of laws within which persons pursue their private interests with the maximum possible freedom, so Social Democracy is an aroused nation led by charismatic heroes toward goals of social justice and humanitarianism. If the primary political value of Liberal Democracy is freedom, the primary political value of Social Democracy is equality—equality of respect, equality of participation, and equality of benefit. Rooted in our national Protestant enthusiasms, Social Democratic visions of American political life are our hope and myth of what we *should* be and do. In these hopes and myths we find our legitimacy as a self-governing people.

The Social Democratic vision evoked by our chief executives depends on the confederal interpretation of our federal system. It sees our nation as a congregation of self-defining local communities, villages, cities, and states. The slogans of this vision speak of "sovereignty of the people," "home rule," and "states' rights." In this Social Democratic vision, America is a grass roots democracy.

It is also strongly communitarian. Each of America's primary communities, whether town or city, is viewed as possessing powerful neighborhood traditions of togetherness through the years of trouble and victory, depression and growth. These neighborly traditions reject outside interference and look to self-help and community effort for mutual support. Social Democracy's egalitarianism extends to all members of the group but with caution to strangers and newcomers, and not at all to "outside agitators." The mythical importance of this is evident in political campaigns when candidates point out that they have been life-long residents of the community, which adds powerfully to their legitimacy.

This communitarianism of Social Democracy can be summoned to a powerful nationalism—as we saw in Lincoln's Gettysburg Address—and it is in the spirit of such a "people's nationalism" that Social Democracy interprets the "pure" doctrine of separation of powers. In this Social Democratic view, each of the three branches of government can

**BOX 4–5
The Diversity of
Claims and
Opinions Found in
the Political
System: Labor
Leaders Speak**

WALTER P. REUTHER, PRESIDENT OF THE UNITED AUTO WORKERS:

We're going to say pollution is a matter for collective bargaining—because it is, if the auto industry continues its gross neglect as the world's biggest air polluter. If the industry does not accept responsibility for this, then society, as a matter of survival, will intervene, and our job security is involved.
—UAW Convention, Atlantic City, N.J., March 13, 1970—*What They Said in 1970*, p. 151.

GEORGE MEANY, PRESIDENT OF THE AFL-CIO:

. . . we need the statutory support of the federal government to carry out the unanimously adopted principles of our organization. . . . Why is this so? Primarily the labor movement is not what its enemies say it is—a monolithic dictatorial centralized body that imposes its will on helpless dues payers. We operate in a democratic way and cannot dictate even a good cause.
—Graham K. Wilson, *Unions in American National Politics* (New York: St. Martin's Press, 1979), p. 72.

WILLIAM W. WINPISINGER, PRESIDENT, INTERNATIONAL ASSOCIATION OF MACHINISTS:

I think we in the labor movement have to quit trying to be so pragmatic all the time, and decide there are a few principles around that we stand for. Sometimes, we give lip service to principles, such as our stand in favor of national health insurance, which we've been pushing . . . since 1948 in Truman's Administration. But we're not really out there on the firing line on a consistent basis. . . .
—*What They Said in 1977*, p. 172.

be given a strict functional definition because, in the spirit of national cooperation, each can be trusted to carry out its special assignment in the sure expectation that the others will be doing the same. Congress, for example, can truly become the people's supreme law-making body (and no more) because the presidency will confine itself to executing the law, and the courts will strictly conform their duties to adjudicating disputes.

Special attention must be given to the courts in the mythic Social Democratic tradition summoned up by America's embattled chief executives. This tradition is hostile to judges being appointed and/or serving long terms, and is even hostile to the Supreme Court as presently constituted. Social Democracy seems to prefer the way many of the states elect their judges because of the faith that it places in the people's legislative assemblies and its opposition to elitism, wherever it may be entrenched. According to the tenets of Social Democracy, courts, like all other organs of government, should be directly responsible to the people. Judges should be periodically elected and should confine themselves to settling disputes according to laws promulgated by duly elected legislators. In this tradition, the assignment of the power of "constitutional review" to the courts is regarded with deep suspicion.

But it is in the chief executive that Social Democracy's mythic hopes are most fully entrusted. These men and women are the charismatic heroes and heroines to whom the people look for "leadership," that wonderful power to "bring us together again" and take us forward to a "rendezvous with destiny" on the "new frontier" of the "great society." Mayors, governors, and, above all, presidents promise us these new beginnings and new affirmations of our mythic hopes.

This is especially so at election time. The fundamental purpose of elections is to permit the populace, acting through citizens casting their ballots, to relegitimize the regime and its current leaders. Elections, because they raise questions of legitimacy, put exactly the kind of stress on the political system that will bring the simmering discontents left by the "normal" stage of Liberal Democracy to the surface. This permits and even challenges the heroic chief executives to exploit for all their worth the visions of Social Democratic justice for all.

Unlike most other democratic nations, the United States holds its elections at periodic intervals on specified dates, whether or not there is any particular reason such as a great crisis for holding elections at those times. Most of these elections are for entrenched barons, great and small, and they proceed smoothly with little fanfare. Elections of chief executives, however, regularly create excitement and can dominate the headlines for months on end. (Again, it is necessary to point out that some of the system's heroes are also those senators and representatives who try to be involved in great causes and, of course, great election fights.) Elections do for us what they are designed to do: to create not only excitement but also enthusiasm for the nation's relegitimated governments and officeholders, whoever they may be.

The "stress" stage of Social Democracy yields in election years a three-part theory of political organization. The primary part of this theory is that America has a "popular" government that rests meaningfully and directly upon the will of the people as expressed through their votes

Elections and Social Democracy: Relegitimation

and other avenues of civic participation, such as letters to newspapers and attendance at civic meetings. The elitism of Liberal Democracy is wholly lost from view, for the rhetoric of Social Democracy obliterates any lines that divide the powerful from the powerless. The slogan applied is that the voice of the people is the voice of God and the doctrine applied is that of the sovereignty of the people. The thesis underlying these principles is that America's political institutions are fully capable of performing, through the electoral system, whatever the people demand.

The second part of the Social Democratic theory of political organization holds that public officials are "responsible" to the voters for their conduct in office. This assertion is a corollary of the idea of the sovereignty of the people. It attributes powers to officeholders to perform certain acts and then to be held accountable for having done them. Presidents, for example, take credit—or are assigned blame—during campaigns for the state of the nation, the state of the economy, the plight of farmers, and so on. Charges brought against officeholders, or accolades aimed at them, depend for their meaningfulness on whether the officeholders in question hold the powers they are supposed by this theory to possess. Social Democracy does not, however, examine questions of this order; it proceeds on the basis of positive assumptions. Proud officeholders and the candidates running against them rarely hesitate to advance their claims and propose programs that will show them, by some (usually vague) future date, to have cured inflation, stabilized world affairs, revitalized our depressed urban economies, completed highway projects, cleaned the streets of filth and grime, and through it all, saved the taxpayers untold amounts of money.

As the candidates for the most prominent public offices assert their stances on the issues, they tend to demonstrate quite transparently that elections are personality contests more than anything else. But they will also assert, in flagrant contradiction of this impression, the third element in the theory of political organization set out by American Social Democracy: that elections are not personality but "party" contests. This element gives us the claim that "the two-party system is the backbone of democracy."[3]

There is a mythic sense in which the appearance of two-party government is the backbone of American democracy. As will be seen, however, American political parties are so organizationally loose and so weak that, at the level of ideological practice, they can hardly be said to exist. Nevertheless, in the rhetoric of electoral debate the notion of "party government" plays an essential role.

[3] For a debunking of the two-party system, see Walter Karp, *Indispensable Enemies: The Politics of Misrule in America* (New York: Saturday Review Press, 1973) and Ted Becker and Paul Szep, *Un-Vote for a Better America* (Boston: Allyn and Bacon, 1976).

BOX 4–6
The Diversity of
Claims and
Opinions Found in
the Political
System: Voices
from the Arts

FEDERICO FELLINI, MOTION PICTURE DIRECTOR:

When walking around Rome, you ignore the ruins of the
past, the ancient monuments. . . . But . . . the past is in your
subconscious. . . . It makes you say deep down: 'Look how
futile life is. It comes and goes. Nothing is really important.'
And then you go to America, where maybe the oldest monument is a gasoline station erected five years ago, and suddenly you must come to terms with the future. . . . you live in
a world where the clock is backwards. . . . Yes, America . . . is
truly fantastic!
—*What They Said in 1970*, p. 38.

LILLIAN HELLMAN, AUTHOR AND PLAYWRIGHT:

Nobody can argue any longer about the rights of women.
It's like arguing about earthquakes.
—*Dictionary of Contemporary Quotations*, vol. 2 (Syracuse: Gaylord Publica-
tions, 1977), p. 23.

LEONARD BERNSTEIN, COMPOSER AND CONDUCTOR:

. . . even patriotism can be rescued from the flagwavers
and bigots.
—*The New York Times*, November 25, 1970.

GORE VIDAL, AUTHOR:

They [the Establishment and the network news media] get
very upset when we don't vote. But why should we vote?
—Television appearance, October 31, 1980.

The notion of personal government is anathema to this vision of Social Democracy. Social Democracy believes it is not possible to build
politics or a nation predicated upon candidates and personalities. It is
the parties, built upon a base of vast armies of volunteers, that define
and determine the fate of the republic. The parties are made up of public-spirited citizens pursuing the common good while joined in a selfless
competition with one another. It is the political parties, so this theory
goes, that recruit and nominate candidates for public offices and, in so
doing, help to define the great issues on which elections are supposed to

MORAL MAJORITY, INC.
420 C Street, N.E.
Washington, D.C. 20002
Jerry Falwell, President

MORAL MAJORITY

OCTOBER, 1979

· · CAPITOL REPORT · · · CAPITOL REPORT · · · CAPITOL REPORT · ·

Why The Moral Majority? By Dr. Jerry Falwell

Two years ago I was down in Dade County, Florida, joining hands with Anita Bryant to fight the militant homosexuals who were trying to force their degrading lifestyle on innocent children there.

And there, in the thick of battle, the message was really brought home to me—America, our beloved country, is sick.

For too long now we have witnessed the concerted attack waged by ultraliberals and so called "feminists" against the family structure in America.

For six long years we have stood by helplessly while 3 to 6 million babies were legally murdered through abortion-on-demand—each baby a precious living soul in the eyes of the Lord. Can you imagine what that means to Almighty God? We are a so called Christian nation and we are the first civilized nation to legalize abortion in the late months of pregnancy!

For too long we have watched pornography, homosexuality and godless humanism corrupt America's families, its schools and its communities.

And when a country becomes sick morally, it becomes sick in every other way. Socialism, which is a first cousin to communism, is taking over the Republic. Today, everything is geared to the state ...to give-away programs and welfareism...to the point where our country is nearly bankrupt.

Right now our country is talking about signing a Salt II treaty with the godless, not-to-be trusted Russian communists—who are committed to world conquest, and we can't even monitor it! How misled can our leaders be? How much longer will we allow our leaders to continue degrading the United States' position as a world leader?

Dr. Falwell in front of Capitol.

And here at home the public school system across our nation is in the last stages of corruption. God has been thrown out of the back door, and humanism—which is nothing more than atheism—has taken over. There are still some good teachers in the public school

system, but, by and large, the schools are steeped in humanistic philosophy, guided by atheistic and vulgar textbooks, rotten with drugs, sexual permissiveness and lack of discipline.

It doesn't take much to see the moral decay invading America everywhere. Look at the pornography readily available all around and you can understand why families are disintegrating at such a fast rate. And you don't have to go to New York or San Francisco to find the garbage and the dirt—it's right there, in every city, in every community...in your community.

Now is the time for moral Americans to stand up for what is right and decent in our country—and change what is vile and wrong.

I for one believe that God is not yet finished with America. I say this for these reasons:

INSIDE....

More on "Why the Moral Majority?" . . . . .page 2

The Commitment And Sacrifice of Our Founding Fathers . . . . .page 4

The Family Protection Act in the Senate. . . . . .page 4

The Moral Majority is one of the conservative activist groups that have received a great deal of attention in recent years.

be decided. Political parties organize campaigns, publicize the qualities of the candidates, and educate the public about the issues and the differences among the proposed policy solutions. Above all, it is the parties to which the citizenry can turn in anger or gratitude when officeholders come up for review.

The "Crisis" Stage

Elections are stress points in the American political system. At these times the system's normal Liberal Democratic procedures and consequences are dangerously vulnerable to exposure. Most of the time the magic of electoral excitement can be conjured up to blur this vulnerability. The myth of Social Democracy's reality can be invoked to mask ideological practice.

Nevertheless, a startlingly high proportion of Americans see behind this mask. The statistics on presidential elections, for example, show that a very large share of eligible voters do not choose to use this means of legitimating the regime. The reasons for this nonparticipation may vary from boredom to laziness to cynicism to apathy. It can even be interpreted as satisfaction with things as they are as E. E. Schattschneider has suggested; but in greatest measure, the failure to legitimate the regime expresses an alienation from it and all it represents. This is at least a potentially dangerous situation. Citizens not willing to legitimate their government are prone to be unsupportive of it in other ways as well, to disregard pleas for cooperation, whether these relate to the draft, wage-price guidelines, or the purchase of domestically produced rather than foreign-manufactured goods. Such people tend to be unconcerned about the broad objectives of their government and also have a greater tendency to violate the laws enacted by that government, such as cheating on their income taxes.

Ironically, America's all-pervasive individualism in both its Bourgeois and Protestant expressions reinforces the average citizen's propensity toward alienation from legitimate government authority. There are great temptations in the American environment to flout authority, strike out on one's own, or even take the law into one's own hands. The authorities know this only too well. Their overriding preoccupation often seems to be to defend their right to command, whether they be police officials, teachers, or leading figures in the national government.

It is understandable in this kind of atmosphere that the political system should experience recurring moments of stress punctuated often by more serious crises. It sometimes seems that American government lives from crisis to crisis. It is in these crises that the contrast between our mythic aspirations and our ideological practice is most vividly exposed. It becomes clear that we have not been or achieved what we have so proudly said we would. Trust, the essential mutual confidence that makes us a self-governing nation, threatens to vanish.

The Civil War is the prime example of crisis in the American political system. In that war, and in the periods just before and after it, we can see writ large the pattern that the crises of the system seem to take.

The Civil War, Slavery, and the Pattern of Crisis

BOX 4–7
The Diversity of Claims and Opinions Found in the Political System: Business Leaders Speak

WILLIAM C. BATTEN, CHAIRMAN, J. C. PENNEY:

There is a common misconception about business and businessmen. We are often looked upon as the Establishment—whatever that is—dedicated to the preservation of the status quo. In fact, we are revolutionaries. Business is in revolution. The concept of free enterprise is itself a very revolutionary idea. It is still not an accepted thought in most countries. It is not designed to preserve the status quo. It is designed for change. . . . It creates, directs and manages change.
—*What They Said in 1970* (Beverly Hills: Monitor, 1971) p. 37.

THOMAS F. BRADSHAW, PRESIDENT, ATLANTIC RICHFIELD:

There is a basic rule: Any [government] regulation must be followed by another regulation that tries to overcome the problems raised by the first.
—*Time*, April 25, 1976, p. 32.

JAMES SINCLAIR, STOCKBROKER:

"I don't believe in chaos, luck or chance. . . . everyone gets what they deserve." Much of Karl Marx's analysis of capitalism was correct, he contends, citing federal support for Chrysler as another bit of evidence that the country is well along in a transition from capitalism to socialistic "state capitalism," and that the big risk ahead "lies in hyper-inflation."
—*Wall Street Journal*, January 22, 1980.

REUVEN FRANK, PRESIDENT, NBC NEWS:

[The Constitution] has allowed for 200 years of rapid, revolutionary and often unexpected changes within American society. As it stands, the document does for Americans of the late twentieth-century world what it did for Americans of the late eighteenth-century world, by allowing change, but not changing.
—*Vital Speeches*, March 15, 1970, p. 333.

BERT LANCE, GEORGIA BANKER AND FORMER CARTER ADMINISTRATION OFFICIAL:

Folks are serious about three things—their religion, their family, and most of all, their money.
—*Time*, December 6, 1976, p. 20.

For all the talk of historians about the causes of the Civil War, there is no question that the issue which brought on the war was slavery and the inability of the political system to deal with it. In myth, slavery was a dreadful wrong and had been implicitly declared such by the phrases in the Declaration of Independence, "We hold these truths to be self-evident; that all men are created equal." Ideologically, however, slavery was seen as a highly profitable institution in the South that had also come to represent a large capital investment. (Studies of the economics of slavery have shown that its profitability was dubious, but the point is that it was perceived as profitable.) The elimination of slavery would have had a devastating effect on the vital interests of slaveholders. Ideologically, therefore, the political system could not move frontally against slavery, even though this was precisely what the system's myth advocated. The slavery issue represents the classic example of a myth-ideology bind in which the American people in their own terms assert that what they were allowing to happen was wrong; but, again in their own terms, they seemed powerless to do anything about it.

The result was virtually foreordained. On one side, tension, anger, and frustration mounted. On the other, meaningless compromise, delay, and inaction were advocated and followed. In this light it is not surprising that after decades of controversy Lincoln's election on the most moderate of platforms for doing something about slavery should have been enough to trigger disaster. The disaster was unparalleled not only in our history but also, for sheer bloodiness per population, in the history of modern nations.

But what did this heroic effort accomplish? Lincoln achieved his primary ideological aim, the preservation of the Union, a laudable goal but one that simply restored the status quo antebellum. Ideologically, however, the strongest symbol of the war's achievement was Lee's surrender to Grant at Appomattox. Grant's terms were that once Lee's army had been disarmed of all but side arms, "each officer and man will be allowed to return to their homes, not to be disturbed by United States authority so long as they observe their parole and the laws in force where they reside." These terms are generally interpreted as exceptionally unvindictive and generous. But what, we must ask, did these terms implicitly make of the war they concluded? Mainly, that the only issue in it was rebellion. Now that it had ended, the only thing left to do was to forgive and forget. In other words, Grant was not ideologically prepared to stand in any moral judgment upon Lee, the Confederacy, nor the slave-based way of life it represented.

The Aftermath of Crisis

Grant spoke for the nation. During the war, as a measure to ensure victory, slavery had been abolished by proclamation. Myth requires us to regard this as a positive step, but it was not necessarily a large step. After a disgraceful period of Reconstruction, blacks in the South—and in less obvious ways in the North, too—returned to their subservient social, economic, and political position, regardless of the law. The return to the white leadership of exclusive responsibility for managing the relationship between the races was signaled by the "separate but equal" decision handed down by the Supreme Court in *Plessy* v. *Ferguson* in 1896. Myth has continued to enunciate the ideals of egalitarianism time and again, most notably in the *Brown* v. *Board of Education* decision, which overturned the *Plessy* ruling in 1954. But on the ideological side, the mass of America's black population, as measured by most statistical indices, is increasingly worse off in comparison with whites.

In the pattern revealed by the slavery issue and the war that grew out of it, the central point is that America fails itself in such crises. Its performance does not necessarily fall short of ideals espoused by ancient philosophers or by abstract definitions of what good communities should be and do. The standards America does not meet are those it prescribes for itself in myth. It does not measure up to these because its historic, ideologically prescribed institutions are not designed to enable it to do so. Myth calls for social action in the public interest in order to achieve a humane egalitarianism. Ideology drives individual political actors, with the siren call of elite success, to strive within the legal framework for private goals. Unavoidable and recurrent crisis is the inevitable result. A build-up of tension, anger, and frustration leads to such eruptions. When everyone seems exhausted by it, there is a gradual slide back to the normalcy of where it all started.

All kinds of examples of this crisis pattern in American politics could be cited, along with a description of how each of them grew out of the conflict between America's Liberal Democratic and Social Democratic characteristics. Not only the Civil War, but the Red Scare of the early 1920s, the New Deal, the Vietnam War, and Watergate, and even the Revolution itself can be seen to have followed this pattern.

FOR FURTHER READING

BARRY, JEFFREY. *Lobbying for the People: The Political Behavior of Political Interest Groups.* Princeton: Princeton University Press, 1977. Focuses on a particularly important segment of the community of interest groups.

GALBRAITH, JOHN KENNETH. *The New Industrial State,* 3rd rev. ed. Boston: Houghton Mifflin, 1978. Holds that political power and bureaucratic considerations are more important to the corporate world than the balance sheet.

GREENWALD, CAROL S. *Group Power: Lobbying and Public Policy.* New York: Praeger, 1977. Fairly comprehensive overview of the subject.

KARP, WALTER. *Indispensable Enemies: The Politics of Misrule in America.* New York: Saturday Review Press, 1973. Debunks the two-party system and asserts that no real choices are offered to voters.

LOWI, THEODORE J. *The End of Liberalism: The Second Republic of the United States,* 2nd ed. New York: Norton, 1979. Thoughtful reassessment of the role of interest groups.

McConnell, Grant. *Private Power and American Democracy.* New York: Random House, 1970. Antipluralist thesis that emphasizes the blurred line between corporate and governmental power.

Neustadt, Richard E. *Presidential Power: The Politics of Leadership from FDR to Carter.* New York: Wiley, 1979. Perhaps the most important book on the presidency, especially from the standpoint of its relationship with interest groups.

Ornstein, Norman J., and Shirley Elder. *Interest Groups, Lobbying and Policy-Making.* Washington: Congressional Quarterly Press, 1978. Explores the interest group process by using the case method.

Peters, John G., and Susan Welch. "Political Corruption in America: A Search for Definitions and a Theory." *American Political Science Review,* **72** (September 1978), 974–984. A breakthrough in the systematic analysis of corruption.

Ranney, Austin. *The Doctrine of Responsible Party Government.* Urbana, Ill.: University of Illinois Press, 1962. Takes an historical view of the argument for the "responsible" party system in America.

CONSTITUTIONAL STRUCTURES   II

America's Liberal Democratic tradition gives us the basic legal framework of the nation's major political institutions—the court system, the Congress, the presidency, and state and local governments across the land. But these ideologically defined constitutional structures have all been cast in a contradictory light by America's Social Democratic myths in order to secure legitimation for each of them from the people. The manner and extent to which this has been done varies in each case.

In operative ideology, the courts have been given the fundamental task of maintaining the legal framework that encages political action. In legitimizing myth, the courts distribute justice in the interest of all.

In myth, Congress is America's supreme law-making body, harnessed directly to the will of the people. In operative ideology, Congress is, much more importantly, the political system's primary mechanism for harmonizing the diverse claims of competing interests. This activity involves some legislation but it also involves extensive if piecemeal preoccupation with administrative processes at every level of bureaucratic activity.

In myth, the president is the charismatic, larger-than-life leader of the nation. His primary mission is to maintain the myth of not only his own but also the nation's greatness and purpose. The president's ideological possibilities and responsibilities are much more limited and are largely concerned with creating opportunities for his mythic roles, especially in policymaking.

State and local governments extend and complete the patterns of the political system's central constitutional structures. On the one hand, this profusion of nearly 80,000 governments must verify Social Democracy's concerns for local identity and neighborhood self-government, or grass roots democracy. On the other hand, behind this mythic cover Liberal Democratic principles require these governments to be highly oligarchic and, with an abundance of inefficiency and confusion, to satisfy competing interests more than to serve any general public good.

The Courts 5

An actual courtroom scene in America always has a terrible sameness about it. Instead of high drama, it offers frustration and boredom. Instead of seeking out justice, the principals have a prevailing attitude of seeking out a "deal." Cynicism is abundant in Department 20, Los Angeles Municipal Court, in Courtroom 8 of the Detroit Criminal Court, and in hundreds of other such rooms across America. People mill about— defendants, their friends and relatives, lawyers, police, bailiffs, court clerks. Defendants are usually asked to appear at ten o'clock in the morning, as if all their cases were to be handled simultaneously, but most of them can expect to spend several hours waiting. When their turn arrives, defendants either receive a calendar date for their trial or plead "guilty" immediately. The majority of those who obtain a trial calendar date also end up pleading "guilty," not bothering the court system with the time and expense of juries and the procedures of an actual trial.

Some of the lawyers present have no offices. They simply use the local courtroom as a base for their operations. Their "case preparation" consists primarily of keeping track of dates, defendants, and arresting officers or assistant prosecutors. The lawyers bargain with these officers of the law. Juggling dozens of clients to keep them straight in their mind, lawyers try, or are said to try, to extract as many concessions as possible from the prosecution side in exchange for a "guilty" plea. This process is known as "plea bargaining," and in some states and federal jurisdictions it accounts for up to 90 percent of criminal case dispositions.[1] The price to the prosecution of winning a "guilty" plea is a reduced charge, an agreement to throw out some of the charges, or perhaps a recommendation for a suspended sentence. The great advantage

---

[1] Leonard Downie, Jr., *Justice Denied: The Case for Reform of the Courts* (New York: Praeger, 1971), p. 23.

of this for the judicial system is, of course, speed and a minimizing of expense. The disadvantages include the possibilities that innocent persons will go to jail for offenses they did not commit and that dangerous or unreformed criminals will be freed sooner than otherwise to cause trouble again for society. Whatever the result, America's overloaded criminal justice system has come to depend on this "sausage factory" approach in order to hold down costs and expedite the business of the courts.[2] Plea bargaining has become essential to the functioning of the

[2] Ibid., Chapter 2.

system and, because it involves the vast majority of criminal cases and their determination, it tells us a great deal about the quality of justice dispensed by the system.

Debates about America's justice are often caught up in great ethical or constitutional questions. As fine as these debates can be, and as important as constitutional and philosophical issues are to the judicial system, some perspective is necessary to understand the everyday working of that system. Fewer than two hundred decisions, all supposedly on the great questions, are settled by the Supreme Court every year. Half again as many cases may be processed in a single day in one of the "sausage factory" courtrooms.[3]

The routines and processes of plea bargaining involve no research with law books, no detailed planning of a defense, no pondering by anyone about great issues of defendants' rights and civil liberties. Certainly plea bargaining is far removed from the courtroom dramas served up by the lawyers of the television screen, but it serves well as an introduction to the judicial system.

The practice of plea bargaining has been challenged on many occasions by social scientists, journalists, political reformers, and bar organizations. The criticisms directed toward it, however, are usually answered by the argument that we cannot afford any other system. But if the purpose of a legal system is to dispense justice, can we afford plea bargaining?

---

[3] A huge number of cases are also decided by arbitrary release of defendants (i.e., a kind of administrative default); see Leonard Downie, Jr., *Justice Denied*, Chapter 2.

"Plea bargaining" expedites court business but can result in freedom for the guilty and jail for the innocent.

In the vision of America's Social Democratic myth, the courts are halls of justice. They dispense swift, sure, and above all fair settlements to both plaintiffs and defendants as well as to society at large. In this vision, the function of the courts is to ensure that America is a just society. By these standards plea bargaining and the sausage factory approach, which is an indispensable part of it, leave much to be desired.

But at another level, plea bargaining is not only a necessity; it is a reasonably efficient way of achieving defensible ends. By Liberal Democratic criteria, the ideological function of the courts is not, in any direct sense, to secure social justice but to enforce the law, to maintain the legal "cage" that contains society in a relatively peaceful community. Plea bargaining in this perspective may or may not be just, but it is orderly. It gets the job done, and it is legal.

In the American political system, the role of the courts is predominantly determined by Liberal Democracy's ideological needs. Above all else, these needs require the courts to uphold, in the face of every kind of dispute, the Constitution and the legal structures within which all other political actors play out their parts. To emphasize the overarching significance of this essential role, this chapter on the courts appears before those on Congress, the presidency, and state and local government. They act; the courts ensure that they do so within the law.

The courts, especially the U.S. Supreme Court, also have mythic roles that are indispensable both to the prestige of the courts themselves and to the legitimacy of the political system as a whole. But these mythic roles are clearly subsidiary to the ideological function of the courts.

The Judicial System

The English Legacy

The judicial system in America owes much to its English legacy: the tradition of an independant judiciary, patterns of court organization, rules of procedure, common law, reverence for precedent, and a general social orientation of the legal profession. The American law of landlord and tenant, for example, is derived from centuries of legal tradition in England in which landowners held a dominant position in politics and society. Evictions, paying rent and under what circumstances, repairs, contract rights, and the ownership of deeds, to cite some examples, are matters in which the landlord holds a dominant and advantageous position over tenants from a legal point of view. Interestingly, much of this body of law has been revised or set aside in modern-day England, but it remains on the books in most of the American states.

The adversary system is another English legacy. All American court processes and procedures rely on the adversary system, a two-sided process with the judge serving as an umpire-arbitrator. This approach rests on the belief that justice is most likely to be served when each side has an advocate to present the best of his or her case while the weaknesses and faults of the other side are picked apart and laid bare. Conceivably the truth can elude us even when we rely on such debates, and there may be a third or fourth point of view. (To some extent, the latter contingency can be met by *amicus curiae,* or "friend of the court" briefs filed in important cases by interested groups not directly parties to the suit.)

It has also been found that the adversary system does not work well in every kind of case. Divorce cases, for example, are sometimes more complicated and bitter than they might otherwise be because conflict is encouraged by the opposing advocates.

The alternative to the adversary system is the inquisitorial system widely used throughout Europe and elsewhere in the world. In this system judges, often working in teams ("en banc") and from files ("dossiers") prepared by the lawyers for both sides, actively direct the proceedings by calling witnesses, asking questions, and searching for the truth as best they can.

The adversary system has never been seriously challenged in America, principally because it exactly reproduces within the courtroom the situation that Liberal Democracy assumes is standard in society at large. Citizens in this view are parties pursuing and defending their own interests to the limit allowed by law. Until this underlying tenet of American ideology is changed or redefined, it is unlikely that anything revolutionary will be undertaken to redefine the nation's traditional courtroom procedures.

Civil and Criminal Law

In America the law is divided into two categories: civil and criminal. Civil law is a much broader category than criminal and comprises laws governing the behavior between individuals and groups (marriages, wills, contracts, property rights, and the like). It seeks to forestall disputes or at least provide regularized ways for settling them. A civil wrong is one committed against a person, group, association, or corporation by another for which the typical remedy is money damages. Criminal law covers those activities considered so serious that the state intervenes to prevent or punish the offender. A criminal act is a wrong committed against a person or group in a way thought to threaten the legal fabric of society. A typical remedy is a fine, imprisonment, probation, or some combination of these. A civil case, because it deals with individual wrongs, is brought by the individuals concerned and may be called *Smith* v. *Jones* or *Brown* v. *Green.* A criminal act, because it is brought to court by the state on behalf of all of society, is called *People* v. *Jones,* or *State of Florida* v. *Jones.* It is possible to face both criminal and civil actions for the same alleged wrong. Shooting someone with the

THE WIZARD OF ID   by Brant parker and Johnny hart

intent of killing or injuring is a criminal offense, but it can also be regarded as a civil wrong and be the basis of a lawsuit for money damages. (This does not violate the double jeopardy provision of the Fifth
Amendment, which prohibits criminally trying an individual twice for
the same offense.) The standards for evidence in the two kinds of cases
are different. In a civil case, only a *preponderance* of evidence is required
to award damages. In other words, the weight of the evidence must be
shown to be on one side even though some facts or considerations may
support the claim of the other side. In a criminal proceeding, a preponderance of evidence is not enough; the prosecution must prove its case
against a defendant beyond any "reasonable doubt." However, these
standards do not always obtain, particularly in the "sausage factory"
courtrooms.

An Independent Judiciary

The officers of the court—the judge and the two advocates—are all lawyers. The values of the legal profession are therefore of paramount importance in assessing judicial systems and processes. These include a
belief in the adversary system, the rule of law, and precedent. At the
same time, a bias is built into legal education in this country that emphasizes property rights, sometimes at the expense of other rights. The
law school curriculum accounts in part for the tendency of most lawyers to seek a practice with a corporation or a law firm rather than to go
into consumer law, poverty law, or other "social conscience" fields (see
Box 5–1).

   In both England and America, an independent judiciary has evolved.
Today, even though most American states elect their judges, the political system supposedly gives judges a measure of independence. The
idea is that judges should run their courts and make their decisions free
of fear or favor and without threat of outside interference, especially
from members of the executive and legislative branches.

   Judges have a mystique about them, sometimes referred to as the
"cult of the robe." It should hardly be surprising that people attach a
certain awe to judges who wear black robes and sit behind tall desks at
an elevation high above everyone else. Judges and their staffs work hard
to maintain the impression that they serve all of us with impartiality,

but their practical, ideological role is more mundane. By their conduct in court and the decisions they hand down, they must contain or restrain all other actors in the system, both public and private, including at times presidents and Congress. Judges thus fulfill their role by umpiring disputes between the parties that appear before them and settling them in ways that protect the rights and obligations—the legal limits—of all concerned.

To do their work well, judges must display at all times a "judicious temperament." When citizens go to court, they carry a set of expectations about what constitutes reasonable judicial behavior that are very different from what they might hold for a business leader or a politician.

What are these expectations? They are ambivalent. In the Social Democratic vision, judges are supposed to be wise, just and well-attuned to the needs and expectations of the people. Judges are community elders. On the other hand, in the Liberal Democratic tradition the good judge is expected to be firm and skillful in conducting the proceedings in the courtroom—a cold and rather remote figure. The good judge in this tradition disciplines the parties before the bench and expedites the resolution of disputes. Good judges must be learned in the law and also adept at applying it to specific situations. In the language of this

Chief Justice Warren Burger

**BOX 5–1
The Law School
Curriculum**

FIRST-YEAR COURSES

First Semester		Second Semester	
Course Name	**Credit Hours**	**Course Name**	**Credit Hours**
Required Courses			
Contracts I	2½	Contracts II	2½
Torts I	2½	Torts II	2½
Civil Procedure I	3	Constitutional Law I	4
Criminal Law	3		
Property	3	Elective I	3
		Criminal Process/ Formal Pro-ceedings	
		Estates and Trusts I	
		International Law	
		Real Estate Transactions	
		and	
		Elective II	3
		American Legal History	
		Economic Analysis of the Law	
		International Law	
		Law and Social Change	
Legal Writing	2	Legal Writing	1
Total first-year hours	16		16

BOX 5–1
**The Law School
Curriculum
(Continued)**

SECOND- AND THIRD-YEAR COURSES

First Semester		Second Semester	
Course Name	**Credit Hours**	**Course Name**	**Credit Hours**
Accounting	1	Administrative Law	3
Administrative Law	3	Advanced Securities	
Advanced Business		Regulation	2
Associations—		Advanced Torts	3
Partnerships	2	American Legal	
Antitrust Law	4	History	3
		Antitrust	
Civil Procedure I*	4	Enforcement	2
Clinical Practice	4	Antitrust Law	4
Commercial Paper	3		
Conflict of Laws	3	Business Planning	2
Constitutional			
Law II	2	Civil Procedure II	2
Corporations	3	Clinical Practice	4
Counseling,		Clinical Trial	
Negotiation, and		Advocacy	3
Litigation	3	Corporation	
		Finance	2
Deceptive Trade		Criminal Process/	
Practices	3	Formal Pro-	
		ceedings	3
Estates and Trusts I	3		
Evidence	3	Debtor-Creditor	
		Relations	3
Family Law	3		
Federal Corporate		Economic Analysis	
Income Tax	3	of the Law	3
Federal Estate and		Environmental Law	3
Gift Taxation	2	Estates and Trusts I	3
Federal Individual		Estates and Trusts II	3
Income Tax	3	Evidence	3
Federal Jurisdiction	2		
		Federal Corporate	
Labor Law	4	Income Tax	3
Law of Dangerous		Federal Estate and	
Products	3	Gift Taxation	2
Legal Ethics	2	Federal Individual	
		Income Tax	3
Police Practices and		Federal Jurisdiction	2
Exclusionary			
Principles	3		

BOX 5–1
The Law School
Curriculum
(Continued)

SECOND- AND THIRD-YEAR COURSES			
First Semester		**Second Semester**	
Course Name	**Credit Hours**	**Course Name**	**Credit Hours**
Public and Private Control of Land Use	3	International and Foreign Antitrust Law	2
Real Estate Transactions	3	International Law	3
Regulation of Broadcasting	2	International Trade	2
		Jurisprudence	3
State and Local Government	3	Labor Law	4
		Law and Accounting	2
Trademarks, Trade Identity, and Unfair Trade Practices	2	Law and Social Change	3
Trial Practice I	2	Patents and Copyrights	
Trial Practice I and II	3	Private International Law	3
		Real Estate Development	2
		Real Estate Transactions	3
		Regulated Industries	3
		Scientific Evidence	2
		Secured Transactions	3
		Securities Regulation	2
		Taxation of Foreign Income	2
		Trial Practice I	2
		Trial Practice II	1
		Trial Practice I and II	3
		Welfare Litigation	2
		Women and the Law	2

BOX 5–1
The Law School Curriculum
(Continued)

SECOND- AND THIRD-YEAR SEMINARS

First Semester		Second Semester	
Course Name	**Credit Hours**	**Course Name**	**Credit Hours**
Advanced Problems in Constitutional Law	2	Antitrust Law and Policy	2
Appellate Procedure and Judical Administration	2	Banking Law	2
Civil Liberties	2	Consumer Protection	2
Computers and the Law	2	Criminal Appellate Advocacy	2
Criminal Evidence	2	Criminal Evidence	2
Estate Planning	2	Employment Discrimination	2
		Estate Planning	2
Food and Drug Law	2	Introduction to Civil Law	2
International Protection of Human Rights	2	Labor Arbitration	2
		Law and Education	2
Juvenile Law	2	Law and Psychiatry	2
Urban Housing Problems	2	Public Sector Labor Law	2

These courses and seminars are offered at a prominent, nationally known law school that has a fairly typical curriculum. How many courses deal with property rights or legal procedure and strategy? How many deal with other human rights? What are the emphases of law school education?

book, good judges are rational professionals who know their job and perform it competently, without favor or thought of personal advancement. Most important in Liberal Democracy's operative ideological framework, good judges are expected to preserve the law, the fundamental framework this tradition sees as essential to the stability and tranquility of society.

**BOX 5–2
One Day in a
Brooklyn
Courtroom**

Mr. Levy (defense attorney): Do you understand that if she [the defendant] fails to take the stand, that that is no evidence at all?

Judge Lane: Mr. Levy, I am going to stop you. I already gave him what the law is, and don't ask him any more questions. They're taking the law from me . . . go on to something else.

Mr. Levy: I object under *People* v. *Preston Williams*.

Judge Lane: Don't give me no citations.
[A few minutes later . . .]

Mr. Levy: Let the record reflect that while the defendent [is] making the responses previously placed on the record, Judge Lane was looking at the jury with a broad smile on his face.

Judge Lane: You're asking for a mistrial? . . . Motion for mistrial is granted. . . . Put this on the record. I have just declared a mistrial, and Mr. Levy, I am directing my attention toward you. Don't you ever appear before me under any circumstances to try a case, because I won't permit you to try any case in front of me because of your conduct. Your total disregard of court and order.

Mr. Levy: Is it on the record?

Judge Lane: Yes. And I am directing you now, and I am telling you, don't you ever come before me to try any case because I won't permit you.

Mr. Levy: Yes, and I'd like to place on the record that I have appeared as an attorney for fourteen years, in courtrooms—

Judge Lane: Well, you won't appear before me. . . .

Mr. Levy: Let me say this, on the record. You're obviously not permitting me to say this. I have been in courtrooms for fourteen years, from the criminal courts, to the Court of Appeals, and into the Second Circuit. And I have hardly, if ever, been pleasured to see such a gross abuse of judicial authority. And I regard the judge's action in this case as thoroughly injudicious. Thank you, Your Honor.

Judge Lane: Get everything on the record. Get everything on the record. Mr. Levy, appear here tomorrow morning on a citation for contempt. . . .

Mr. Levy: I am sure that the Legal Aid Society will find an attorney to defend me. . . . I'd like it placed on the record that—

Judge Lane: Just a minute. Nothing—

Mr. Levy: I can't go on the record when you're holding me in contempt?

Judge Lane: There is nothing further on the record as of now. Appear here tomorrow morning. The proceedings today are over.

—Jack Newfield, "The Ten Worst Judges," in *Verdicts on Lawyers*, Ralph Nader and Mark Green, eds. (New York: Crowell, 1976), pp. 274–275.

In the day-to-day operations of the judicial system, the Liberal Democratic vision of the good judge predominates. This means that the good judge is the servant, not the master, of the law. In applying the law, judges rely very much on the principle of *stare decisis* (Latin for "let the decision stand"), which means they use precedent as much as possible in arriving at their decisions. The law changes and new precedents are established from time to time, but these changes come about through an evolutionary process. The law is treated respectfully because it represents the combined result of the Constitution, actions of legislative bodies, and precedents established through centuries of Anglo-Saxon case law. Through all of these considerations and applications of the law, good judges are pure rational professionals, disinterestedly performing their assigned job as well as possible. Judges do not, in other words, find out what the law is by magisterially inventing it or by consulting some superior wisdom.[4]

This understanding of the special qualities required of judges in the operative, ideological side of the judicial system was recognized by James Madison in *Federalist* 51:

In the constitution of the judiciary department in particular, it might be inexpedient to insist rigorously on the principle [of election, direct or indirect], first, because peculiar qualifications being essential in the mem-

---

[4] See Robert P. Wolff, ed., *The Rule of Law* (New York: Touchstone, 1971).

bers, the primary consideration ought to be to select that mode of choice, which best secures these qualifications; secondly, because the permanent tenure by which the appointments are held in that department, must soon destroy all sense of dependence on the authority conferring them.

Nevertheless, the two sides of what we have come to expect from judges fit together. The independence of the judiciary, the "cult of the robe," and other such accoutrements help give the court system its mythic quality, which in turn enables court disputants and most other citizens to respond to the judicial system in a way that legitimizes and sanctifies it. Courts generally work in ways that conform closely in outward appearance to the myth. More important, as seen in the discussion of plea bargaining but also running through the day-to-day work of the courts, judges and lawyers are guided not by the values of myth but by ideology. And in ideology, the courts seek mainly to know the law and apply it, with all its biases and limitations.

U. S. Supreme Court Building, Washington, D.C.

The Organization of Justice

The process of selecting and appointing judges varies from state to state and is different again in the federal judicial system. Even within the federal system there is a considerable difference between appointment procedures usual for the appeals and district courts and the selection process for the U.S. Supreme Court. All these differences stem from the underlying ambiguities in the political system about what courts and judges are supposed to do.

There are two basic methods of judicial selection—election and appointment. Judges are elected only in state and local judicial systems. Even though there is a trend today against electing judges, more than two thirds of state and local judges are still chosen by election. Elections reflect the tendency of some state and local governments to be more concerned than the federal government about staying close, at least in form, to the Social Democratic requirements that judges be of, by, and for the people. Judicial elections vary as to term—judges may be elected for four, six, or twelve years, or even for life—as well as to type of ballot (party-affiliated versus nonpartisan). They may be elected by legislatures rather than by the people. Some state and local elections set up no opposing candidates for incumbent judges but merely ask on the ballot whether a judge should be returned to office for another term. In almost all cases, the voters say "yes." State and local appointment procedures, like elections, make it necessary for any candidate for judge to have a political background and connections, either with a local or state party organization or the local or state bar association, or with both groups.

Some states have established variations on the appointment process. Rather than simply having a judicial candidate nominated by the governor (or attorney general in some states) and approved by one or both houses of the state legislature, these variations seek to add a measure of popular control over the process while encouraging the professional involvement of state bar associations. The best-known and most widely acclaimed of these variations are those used in California and Missouri.

At the federal level, reflecting Madison's original Liberal Democratic bias for judges who are essentially legal technicians maintaining the constitutional framework, all judicial positions are filled by appointment for life on good behavior. Appointments to the Supreme Court and all other federal courts, when vacancies occur, are by the president with the advice and consent of the Senate (Article II, Section 2 of the Constitution).

For all the supposed professionalism of the federal selection process, politics has been a constant factor in it. The Senate has not proved to be

The U. S. Supreme Court, 1982: Standing, from left to right, are Justices Stevens, Powell, Rehnquist and O'Connor; seated, Justices Marshall, Brennan, Chief Justice Burger, and Justices White and Blackmun.

a "rubber stamp" for Supreme Court nominations by the president. Since 1789, the Supreme Court has been served by 102 members, but in the same period the Senate has denied confirmation of appointment to many nominees. In the early years of the Nixon administration, for example, the Senate turned down two nominees, Clement Haynsworth and G. Harold Carswell. Both men had segregationist records, and Carswell had associated himself with blatant racism early in his career. President Nixon had made it clear that he was paying a political debt to the South with these appointments because it had played an important role in his 1968 election victory. This was not unusual, because presidents often look at regional balance, party affiliation, and political viewpoint of individuals before nominating them. They sometimes look for ethnic and religious representation. The court has had Catholic, Protestant, and Jewish justices. The first and only black on the court, Thurgood Marshall, was appointed by Lyndon Johnson in 1967. The first woman to serve on the Court is Sandra Day O'Connor, picked by Ronald Reagan in 1981.

But none of this is to suggest that competence and experience are not also important criteria. The standard of competence seems to be the motivation for the American Bar Association's demand for a bigger voice in the Supreme Court selection process, but it remains conjectural whether the ABA will ever attain the level of influence it seems to exercise in staffing lower-level federal courts. This may not even be desirable, for that matter; one of the greatest legal minds to serve on the court by all accounts was Louis J. Brandeis, whom President Woodrow Wilson would not have appointed had he listened to the ABA.[5] In view of the ambiguities concerning the court's functions, it remains questionable whether it should be made up entirely of lawyers. The late Justice Hugo Black, for one, thought that it should not.[6]

Whomever the president appoints, the process itself assures a long-lasting indirect influence of his presidency. At any time the court is made up of appointees who represent several presidential tenures. In 1982, for example, the court contained Justice Brennan, appointed by President Eisenhower; Justice White, appointed by President Kennedy; Justice Marshall, appointed by President Johnson; Justice Stevens, appointed by President Ford; Justice O'Connor, appointed by President Reagan; and four appointees of President Nixon—Justices Blackmun, Powell, and Rehnquist and Chief Justice Burger. This Burger Court, sometimes referred to as "the Nixon Court" by unfriendly critics, will be with us for some time. If Justice Rehnquist, for example, serves as long as the late Justice Black, he will be on the court until 2005.

Federal Appeals and District Court Appointments

As with the Supreme Court, judges named to the Federal District Courts, the "trial courts" of the federal system, and to the Federal Circuit Courts of Appeals are nominated by the president and confirmed by the Senate. Because many more of these appointments are made than to the Supreme Court, the political machinations of the selection process are much less exposed to public view. Prominent politicians, some of them officeholders and some not, play a role. Aspiring judges have a hand in the various negotiations and bargaining that take place. The ABA is consulted and offers its opinion in a competency rating of potential nominees and, unlike its role in the Supreme Court selection process, it seems to have a great deal of influence at these district and appeals levels. Most important, senators of the president's party are consulted and have a great deal to say, especially with respect to the appointments made in their own states. If a senator of the president's party opposes a nominee, the rest of the Senate invariably goes along with the senator and rejects the nominee. This extra-constitutional custom is called "senatorial courtesy." The power to veto appointments does not mean that the senator has the affirmative power to name the

[5] Henry J. Abraham, *The Judicial Process*, 4th ed. (New York: Oxford University Press, 1980), p. 27.
[6] Ibid., p. 167.

**BOX 5–3
How to Find the
Law**

It is often impossible to learn all the facts, rulings, and circumstances of a case just by reading a press report or other second-hand account of it; and so it is convenient to know how to find a Supreme Court case. Often such cases are listed with their legal citation, like this: *Cantwell* v. *Connecticut*, 310 U.S. 296 (1940).

This makes it easy to find the case. The "310" stands for *volume* 310, *United States* (Supreme Court) *Reports*. The "296" is the first page number in the *United States Reports* in which the case is found. The date supplies further information that will be of aid in your search. When you find the case, you will have a full text of the majority opinion and of any concurring or dissenting opinions, the name of the justice who wrote the opinion, the dates of argument and decision, the names of the attorneys for each side, and the history of the case through the appeals process. The most important rules of law set out in the case will be emphasized in boldface type above the majority opinion. Occasionally a citation names two other unofficial sources of the same opinion—the *Supreme Court Reporter*, published by West, and the *Supreme Court Reports, Lawyers Edition*, published by the Lawyers Cooperative Publishing Company. The *Lawyers Edition* also includes commentaries on the cases. The citation that employs all three of these sources may then look like this: *Cantwell* v. *Connecticut*, 310 U.S. 296, 60 S.Ct. 900, 84 L.Ed. 1213 (1940). This makes it possible to find the case in any of the three sources. If, for example, your library should have the *Supreme Court Reporter* only, you can immediately find this case in volume 60, p. 900. All three of these reporters list the official citation (in this case, 310 U.S. 296) as well, so that you can find the case in any of them with just an official citation. A relatively new publication, *U.S. Law Week*, published by the Bureau of National Affairs, also contains Supreme Court opinions. Supreme Court cases are only a small fraction of the body of law that has developed in America. To learn how to find statutes, state court cases, legal definitions, and administrative rulings, for example, it is necessary to review a source such as Morris L. Cohen, *How to Find the Law*, 7th ed. (St. Paul: West Publishing Co., 1976).

successful nominee in all circumstances, but individual senators can bring a lot of pressure to bear on the process. Presidents nearly always name members of their own party to the bench. President Carter had more opportunities to make these coveted life-term appointments than most presidents because the federal judiciary was expanded during his term of office. He was not able, however, to make a Supreme Court appointment.

A final consideration when analyzing judicial selection is recognizing that the system is staffed from an exceedingly narrow base—middle-class lawyers (including blacks and women) with all the biases of their profession and education, who are politically active and sometimes (but not invariably) meet the standards and credentials set by their peers and their political friends. It must be admitted, however, that these people have generally served the divergent needs of the system well.

Powers and Jurisdiction of the Judicial Branch

The powers of the judicial branch are set out in Article III of the Constitution, which establishes two kinds of Supreme Court jurisdiction—original and appellate. The court has original jurisdiction over certain kinds of cases and controversies, including those affecting ambassadors and diplomats of foreign countries, cases between two or more states, cases between the United States and a state or states, cases between states and a foreign country, cases involving the high seas, and treaties. "Original jurisdiction" simply means that such cases come in the first instance to the Supreme Court rather than on appeal from decisions of lower federal or state courts. However, the Supreme Court's "original jurisdiction" does not necessarily mean *exclusive* jurisdiction. The requirement of Article III is satisfied if such cases are handled by district-

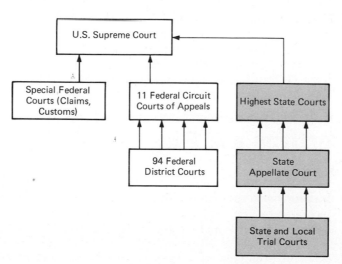

Figure 5–1. Organization of the courts.

level federal courts under a congressionally mandated power of *concurrent* original jurisdiction. The Supreme Court's appellate jurisdiction, which represents most of the cases that come before it, is over matters brought on appeal from lower-level federal courts, from special federal courts such as the customs and claims courts, and from the highest-level state courts, usually called the "State Supreme Court." An appeal brought from a state court system, however, usually must involve a "substantial federal question," such as a denial of rights guaranteed by the U.S. Constitution, federal law, or treaty.

It is important to point out that the appellate jurisdiction of the Supreme Court is established by statute, not by the Constitution. Article III leaves to Congress the matter of how broad the court's jurisdiction is to be. The appellate authority of the court therefore rests upon the Judiciary Act of 1789 and its amendments. In the late 1950's, public outcry against the supposedly "liberal" and "permissive" policies of the Warren Court led to an attempt by Congress to limit the appellate jurisdiction of the court. This attempt nearly succeeded. It it had, it would have altered radically the Supreme Court's role at the apex of the judicial system in maintaining a comprehensive, unified, legal framework for the whole nation.[7] Today we once again hear of proposals to remove Supreme Court control over its appellate jurisdiction, especially on the issues of busing, abortion, school prayer, and education.

The lower-level federal courts are the circuit courts of appeals and the district courts, which are the "trial courts" of the federal judiciary system. There are eleven appeals courts, or "circuits," divided geographically, and there are ninety-four district courts. Although it is sometimes possible to choose whether to initiate legal action in a federal or state court, a federal case is jurisdictionally defined by Article III, as noted above. The most common ways to get a case into federal court are to show either the involvement of a "federal question" or "diversity of citizenship," that is, an action in which a person or corporation in one state is suing the citizen of another. Most of America's case load is handled by state courts because of these federal jurisdictional limitations (see Figure 5–1 on page 143).

The Special Functions and Purposes of the Supreme Court

Ideology, Myth and the Supreme Court

Ideology and myth stand in stark relief in the Supreme Court more than in any other court. In terms of myth, the court has all the advantages enjoyed by any court—the mystique of the law and impartial decisions

[7] C. Herman Pritchett, *Congress Versus the Supreme Court, 1957–1960* (Minneapolis: University of Minnesota Press, 1960).

*Spiral staircase, U. S.
Supreme Court Building,
Washington, D. C.*

and settlements, the "cult of the robe," the independence of the judiciary—plus the awesome and splendiferous position of being at the pinnacle of the appellate system. In addition, the power of judicial review, the authority of the judicial branch to declare unconstitutional the acts of Congress, the executive branch, the lower courts, and the states, has a mythic as well as practical dimension. Judicial review seems at times to elevate the Supreme Court justices to the level of gods who declare finally what our revered Constitution really means.

The mythic nature of the Supreme Court is easy to document. It can be directly experienced at ten o'clock on Mondays through Wednesdays when the court is in session. At that hour, the nine privileged and powerful justices walk in their black robes from behind a curtain to their places at the great bench that dominates the Supreme Court chamber. A crier bangs down the gavel, requests the attention of all present, and asks for God's blessing on the court. The lawyers standing before this ceremony are understandably nervous.

Almost all close observers of the court agree that its power rests on its prestige, and prestige is only attainable through the development and maintenance of myth. The court's reliance on myth is therefore heavy. It has virtually no enforcement machinery, a fact of which Andrew Jackson was well aware when he said the Supreme Court had made the law (in a United States Bank case), so let them enforce it. Abner Mikva, a court of appeals judge and former congress member, has noted that at the time of the Supreme Court's famous *Brown* v. *Board of Education* desegregation decision in 1954, the coercive apparatus to enforce the decision consisted of a single federal marshal who was "getting on in years."[8]

The myth-based prestige of the Court is evidenced mainly by its historical ability to withstand bitter criticism at various times and by its ability to survive its own decisions such as the *Dred Scott* ruling, which fanned the fires of Civil War, and *Korematsu* v. *U.S.*, which placed a stamp of approval on large-scale imprisonment of a single minority group, the Japanese-Americans, during World War II. The court has survived the embarrassment of reversing itself within less than a year regarding the New Deal reforms of President Franklin Roosevelt in 1937. The court also easily withstood the comparatively minor scandal of the furtive Woodward-Armstrong best-seller, *The Brethren*, in 1979. This book provided new but undocumented insights into the personal behavior of the justices and displayed some of them as petty, egocentric, and unversed in the law.

In practice, it is well-recognized that the court, behind its mythical qualities and trappings, acts more as a political body (see Box 5–4). It has been said that the Supreme Court justices know how to read election returns even though they themselves, with their life-term appointments, do not have to stand for re-election. This is an oversimplification, for the court has taken any number of decisions that have not met with popular approval. History does show, however, that it has seldom seemed to overplay its hand. Its gauging of its prestige and power has been accurate enough so that it does not often get "ahead of its time." Indeed, the history of the court in a broad perspective tends to underscore that it has been no great mechanism for social and political change. It has been led much more often than it has chosen to lead. It tends always to conserve existing situations, and the "radical" or "revolutionary" aspects and effects of its decisions are regularly exaggerated, especially in the short run.

Judicial Review

The Supreme Court's strength in the ideological operation of the American political system rests upon its power of judicial review. This power was not directly given to the judicial branch by the Constitution, but there is a specific allusion to the need for judicial review in *Federalist* 78,

---

[8] Bennett Murphy, "Mikva Reflects on Judges, Politics," *Harvard Law Record*, **69**: 4 (November 20, 1979).

**BOX 5—4
The Myth of a
Perfect Judiciary
Perfectly
Administering a
Perfect
Constitution**

. . . there are . . . limitations implied by the fact that the Supreme Court is expected to be both a "court" in the orthodox sense of the word and something very much more as well. A full account of the confusions fostered by this seeming contradiction would almost involve a recapitulation of Supreme Court history. Legions of judges and their devotees have believed, or professed to believe, that constitutional law was a technical mystery revealing itself in terms of unmistakable precision to those who had the key, that the Constitution was the record and the judges merely the impartial phonograph that played it, a group of men who somehow managed to stop being men when they put on their robes and would not dream of letting their subjective value judgments affect their understanding of the Constitution. No court was ever like this, no system of law was ever so sure a guide to its interpreters. And the myth of a perfect judiciary perfectly adminstering a perfect Constitution was therefore deeply impaired in the twentieth century by writers who pointed out what some perceptive observers had always known—that judges are mortal. Like senators and presidents, it was said, judges may have prejudices, and those prejudices may affect their understanding of the Constitution. In fact, the critics went on, the American Supreme Court, so far from merely and imperturbably reflecting eternal constitutional verities, is a willing policy-making, *political* body.

—Robert McCloskey, *The American Supreme Court* (Chicago: University of Chicago Press, 1960), p. 19.

written by Alexander Hamilton in support of adoption and ratification of the Constitution; it was clearly in keeping with the thinking of such "Liberal Democrats" as John Adams; and such a process of review by the courts of the acts of other branches of the government was not unknown in Anglo-Saxon law. The most famous early use of judicial review in America was the landmark case of *Marbury* v. *Madison* (1803), considered the court's source of power of final constitutional interpretation.

The political background of the case is simple enough. President John Adams was leaving office and wished to make some last-minute judicial appointments of deserving Federalists. But some of these appointments, though they had been approved by the Senate and the outgoing president, were not delivered to the appointees by the time the new Anti-Federalist president, Thomas Jefferson, took office. One of the disappointed judicial office-seekers, William Marbury, along with several others sued James Madison, the secretary of state, whose duties allegedly included the delivery of these appointments. The focus of Washington politics then as now was on the narrow question of whether the appointees would get their jobs. Speculation centered on whether the Federalist-dominated court would support them. It did not, but Chief Justice John Marshall took advantage of the occasion to carve out, with extraordinary skill and care, the doctrine of judicial review.

Marbury's plea had been for a writ of mandamus, a court order requiring a public official to carry out a duty that had been ignored or refused. Marbury's plea for this writ was based on a section of the Judiciary Act of 1789 that spelled out the Supreme Court's appellate jurisdiction. But this particular section, Marshall ruled, actually sought to establish original, not appellate, jurisdiction, and the original jurisdiction of the court, he pointed out, had already been set out in Article III of the Constitution. Because the Constitution is supreme in the law, it cannot be amended by a mere act of Congress. Marbury was therefore seeking relief, Marshall concluded, under an unconstitutional provision of the law, and he could not be appointed. Thus the court itself set out its power of judicial review.

Jefferson and the Anti-Federalists were delighted with the "political" thrust of the decision, because they did not want Marbury to be given his job. They were quick to see, however, that Marshall had cunningly lost a battle to win a war. The Jeffersonians were appalled at the portents of the decision, with its implications for the powers of the federal government and, more important, of its nonelected, profoundly elitist (some would say oligarchic) judicial branch. The court rode out the storm of Anti-Federalist protest, although it had to endure the impeachment but not the conviction of one of its justices. And judicial review remained. The court's recognition of the symbolic and substantive importance of *Marbury* is emphasized by William Marbury's portrait, the only portrait of a person other than a Supreme Court justice on display in the Supreme Court Building today.

Judicial review has been accepted over the years as though it were spelled out in the text of the Constitution itself. Occasional arguments have been made, such as by the South in the 1950s and 1960s, that the court does not have the right to declare laws unconstitutional because this power is not listed in the Constitution. But nothing has come of these arguments. Marshall's decision had considerable logical force as well as cunning. But what has placed this power of judicial review into the very bedrock of the American political system, cementing it there with the weight of unchallengeable tradition? It is its exact conformity with the Liberal Democratic requirement that the nation be governed

John Marshall, Chief Justice of the Supreme Court from 1801 to 1835 and architect of judicial review.

by its laws and that the courts alone are in a position to perform this function impartially, case by case.

Marshall led the court into other significant expansions of its power and of federal power generally. In 1816, the court's power to declare a state law unconstitutional was established; state sovereignty was held to be inferior to the provision of Article III that the judicial power extends to all cases arising under the Constitution. National power over the states reached a more exalted level in the 1819 case of *McCulloch* v. *Maryland*, often regarded as Marshall's greatest judicial opinion. Citing Article VI,

Federal Supremacy and the Commerce Clause

the federal supremacy section of the Constitution, he argued that this must be construed generously so that the central government can function within its sphere of powers. Citing Article I, Section 8, which gives Congress the right to pass all laws "necessary and proper" to carry its enumerated powers into effect, Marshall went on to hold that the phrase "necessary and proper" must also be broadly interpreted. One effect of these arguments was to characterize the Constitution as a document carrying *implied*, as well as express, powers. This case completed the argument of *Marbury* by making it clear so far as the courts were concerned that the Constitution was the supreme law of the land, authorizing the powers of all governments, federal and state. The American nation thus became in law a single federal union rather than a confederation of states.

Article I, Section 8 of the Constitution also gives the federal government the authority "to regulate commerce with foreign nations, and among the several states." In 1824 Marshall applied this provision—the interstate commerce clause—in *Gibbons* v. *Ogden*. His order that this clause must be interpreted broadly was the genesis of the federal government's involvement in the regulation of economic activity. The authority of the government to do this has remained essentially unquestioned, and certainly since the New Deal, arguments about it now revolve around the type, extent, and desirability of regulation rather than whether it is constitutional.

Limitations on the Court's Power

Despite the legacies of judicial review and the Supreme Court's ability to define the nature of the federal union, there are limitations on the court's authority. In making its decisions the court apparently takes public opinion into account and, perhaps more important, the political resources of litigants and the branches of government affected by its decisions. The court is prudent, in keeping with its commitment to the Liberal Democratic vision of itself as custodian of the laws rather than an instrument of the people's will, as in the Social Democratic view. Prudent restraint is also forced on the court by a series of other guidelines, some of which are self-imposed.

Certain doctrines relating to the "justiciability" of cases impose restrictions on the court. Justiciability refers to whether the court is competent to act upon a case or controversy presented to it. The doctrines that have grown up around the concept of justiciability are based on Article III, which requires the court to look at "cases and controversies." One of the most important of these doctrines is the prohibition against deciding "political questions." The court has held that it cannot order other branches of government to settle such questions or do so itself. The court's essential purpose, it argued, is settling particular rather than general policy grievances. The court refused in 1946, for example, to order the state of Illinois to reapportion its legislature so that cities could obtain a fairer share of representation based on population. The court said this was a political question and it refused to get involved. But as is often the case, the court demonstrated its flexibility about what is a "political question" by reversing itself on this issue in a series of decisions in the early 1960s. Today both houses of various state legislatures must be apportioned according to population as a result of this reversal.[9]

Then there is the question of a principal's standing in a "case or controversy." Two cases illustrate this point. In a 1943 decision, the court considered the case of a Connecticut druggist who wished to challenge his state's ban on contraceptive drugs and devices, arguing that his inability to provide these items endangered the health and lives of three clients. The druggist invoked the Constitution's Fourteenth Amendment provision that protects the "life, liberty and property" of persons. But the court found that no justiciable claim was presented, because the druggist was not saying that any of his own rights or liberties were being infringed by the state's law, and the clients about whom he was concerned were not parties to the case. They had filed no briefs and made no claims.[10]

The 1975 decision *Warth* v. *Seldin* is an excellent example of the court's seeming to bend over backward to avoid making a judgment.[11] A group of low-income citizens in Rochester, New York, demanded the removal of zoning restrictions set up by the suburban city of Penfield, so that they could reside in the suburb. (The zoning established economic barriers that effectively barred poor people from Penfield.[12]) Joining in this suit against the zoning restrictions were a builders' group seeking construction work, a fair housing group in Rochester seeking to promote housing access for the poor of the entire metropolitan area, a Rochester taxpayers' group believing that social welfare costs of the area should be more equally distributed, and a group of citizens from another zoned suburb. None of these five groups was accorded standing to sue by the court, and each group was eliminated on different grounds. In addition, the Burger Court has taken a strong position against "class-action" suits that seek to generalize the effects of a settlement to include all persons who might be situated in the same "class" as the parties directly involved.[13]

The court's power is further limited because it will render judgments only on cases brought to it and will not issue advisory opinions re-

[9] *Baker* v. *Carr*, 369 U.S. 186 (1962); *Reynolds* v. *Sims*, 377 U.S. 533 (1964); *Wesberry* v. *Sanders*, 376 U.S. 1 (1963).
[10] *Tileston* v. *Ullman*, 318 U.S. 44 (1943).
[11] 422 U.S. 490 (1975).
[12] Gerald L. Houseman, *The Right of Mobility* (Port Washington: Kennikat, 1979), Chapter 4.
[13] See Karen Orren, "Standing to Sue: Interest Group Conflict in the Federal Courts," *American Political Science Review*, **70**: 723–741 (September 1976).

BOX 5–5
The *Harvard Law*
***Review* Reviews**
the Work of a
Supreme Court
Justice

From the appearance of his first opinion in March 1972 to the close of the 1975 term in July 1976, Justice William Rehnquist has written 164 signed opinions and participated in the disposition of at least 1,200 cases. His work . . . probably represents only the beginning of a long judicial career. But . . . [it is] not too early for a preliminary consideration of Justice Rehnquist's work. My conclusion, based on a study of his opinions and of his votes in cases in which he did not write, is that while he is a man of considerable intellectual power and independence of mind, the unyielding character of his [belief system] has had a substantial adverse effect on his judicial product.

A review of all the cases in which Justice Rehnquist has taken part indicates that his votes are guided by three basic propositions:

1. Conflicts between an individual and the government should, whenever possible, be resolved against the individual;

2. Conflicts between state and federal authority, whether on an executive, legislative or judicial level, should, whenever possible, be resolved in favor of the states; and

3. Questions of the exercise of federal jurisdiction, whether on the district court, appellate, or Supreme Court level, should, whenever possible, be resolved against such exercise.

These three propositions . . . are not unrelated . . . . and it is not at all unusual for more than one to be implicated in a single case. . . . The phrase, "whenever possible," appearing in each proposition, serves to state the obvious. No such proposition can be absolute in its application. . . .

It is . . . significant that only thirteen instances have been found in which Justice Rehnquist, in his vote, has evidenced less of a commitment to these propositions than one or more of the other Justices. This number represents an average of only . . . two or three cases per Term, and that average is virtually de minimis when one considers that hundreds of cases are disposed of . . . each Term, that the overwhelming majority present an opportunity for applying one or more of the three propositions, and that there is almost always some division on the Court when the case is a difficult one. . . .

[In] twenty-four cases . . . Justice Rehnquist, in dissent, evidenced his greater commitment to these propositions than did any of his colleagues. The frequency of lone dissent is especially impressive when it is remembered that several other members of the Court have themselves shown considerable . . . support for one or more of these same propositions. Finally, an analysis of the thirteen cases reveals that they do not in fact constitute significant departures from the Justice's commitments. . . .

It is unrealistic to expect that a newly appointed judge will come to the job without some established values and ideas, though they may well develop and change during the years on the bench. . . . But there should be sufficient flexibility to allow the development of a workable and coherent approach to the judicial function as well as the free exercise of intellectual capacity and full utilization of the lawyer's skills. Thus far, Justice Rehnquist has lacked that flexibility, and his judicial product has suffered as a result.

—David L. Shapiro, "Justice Rehnquist: A Preliminary View," *HLR*, 90: 293–357 (December 1976).

quested by even the highest authorities. It is also unlikely because of precedents, procedure, and the workings of the rational-professional mind that the court will give any parties to a case more than they ask for. The orders of the court are limited in their effects because they legally obligate only the parties to a suit. Even in class actions, the court's ruling binds only the actual litigants. A ruling affecting the operations of a state government—its judicial procedure, legislative apportionment, prisons, mental health centers, or whatever—also applies legally only to the state that is the subject of the case. If another state is apparently carrying out policies that are unconstitutional by logic of a new court ruling, it may choose to alter those policies to avoid suits and perhaps to be in a fair measure of conformity and consonance with the court and the Constitution, but it is not legally obliged to do this. The attorney-general of Indiana, for example, has announced his policy to persist in the Indiana way of doing things until the state is specifically brought to court and ordered to do otherwise. This may be imprudent and costly, but it is legally possible.

The court's discretion is limited by its rule that at least four justices must vote to hear a case. Lacking that number, an appeal is denied. This is not a legal rule but a custom that the court follows. The literature on the Supreme Court also tells us that its members may choose to hear a case because they have become interested in settling a point of law or legal doctrine for which the case may serve as a good vehicle for this clarification or change. In 1963, the court wished to determine whether it should require the states, under the Sixth and Fourteenth Amendments, to provide a lawyer for poor defendants in felony cases. It decided to establish this requirement because, in part, it had found a case that looked like a good opportunity for expounding this principle.[14]

The Supreme Court, as an appellate tribunal, is limited to making determinations of law; it is not supposed to make findings of fact. Fact finding is exclusively the function of trial courts, or courts of first hearing, whether they be Federal District Courts or local courts that serve state court systems. The division between fact and law, however, is not always a tidy one, and the circumstances of a case may cause it to blur.

The Ideological Limitation

In the final analysis the role of the Supreme Court is most limited in its discretion and policymaking by its dominant commitment to the ideological requirements of Liberal Democracy. Judges feel considerably inhibited about acting in any way other than what would win approval from their rational-professional colleagues in the legal process. All justices have had a legal education, with all its benefits and limitations. This career pattern signals a certain kind of predictability about attitudes toward the law and its traditions. Also the law to which the vast majority of judges are committed incorporates the powerful biases of Liberal Democracy toward social policy, economics and economic groups, and above all, the sanctity of property rights as identical to or more important than individual rights.

The history of the court bears witness to its strong Liberal Democratic bias. We have already seen how the Marshall Court defined, built, and expanded federal power and also established the rationale in *Gibbons* v. *Ogden* for government involvement in economic affairs. These policy directions were lauded and promoted by the country's propertied elite at the time. Yet this expansion of the federal government's economic involvement was not based on ideals of equality or the promotion of social welfare. Measures to further goals of this kind did not come into broad prominence, generally speaking, until the 1930s.

The rational-professional mode, method, and purposes of the court stand out in the most obvious ways in the period extending roughly from the aftermath of the Civil War to the Great Depression of the 1930s.

[14] Anthony Lewis, *Gideon's Trumpet* (New York: Random House, 1964).

In this period the court found a major justification for its property orientation in the doctrine of "substantive due process," which relied on the Fourteenth Amendment's and occasionally the Fifth Amendment's proscription against the government taking "life, liberty or property, without due process of law." "Due process" means that actions against individuals are legal only if carried out with strict regard for all required procedures. But in a series of decisions, the Supreme Court expanded this literal meaning so that it could hold "due process" protections had been violated if an individual's property right had been denied in any substantive way, regardless of the procedural correctness of the process in question.

This doctrine was applied in such a manner as to prevent a variety of social reforms—restrictions on child labor, wages and hours laws, health and safety acts, and legislation designed to correct some of the greater abuses of corporations and corporate barons. This kind of legislation was seen as an unconstitutional deprivation of the property rights of corporations.[15] Modern welfare state laws became possible only when the court reversed the doctrine of "substantive due process" in 1937 and began to approve enactments such as Social Security, minimum wages, and the legal recognition of labor unions.

Such doctrines as "substantive due process" do not die easily.[16] Up to New Deal days, the court was so suffused with a concern for property rights that it extended them into areas that did not logically have any connection with them. In 1928, for example, it refused to see any illegality in electronic eavesdropping, or wiretapping, unless a trespass was committed. Law enforcement officials listening in to a conversation violated no rights of property under the Fourth Amendment's "unlawful search and seizure" provision as long as they listened outside, or away from, the locale of the conversation.[17] Had the listening taken place inside the premises or a listening device actually protruded through an inner wall, it would have been a trespass. Trespass is a property concept representing a violation of property rights; yet this narrow concept was held by the court to be the foremost consideration in such eavesdropping cases until it overruled itself in 1967.[18]

The rational-professional mind that Liberal Democracy's ideological precepts require of judges as guardians of the legal cage around us all is not infallible. Reason can sometimes become a trap, as it proved to be with "substantive due process" doctrine. Yet it is reason that we expect

[15] *Lochner* v. *New York*, 198 U.S. 45 (1905); *Hammer* v. *Dagenhart*, 247 U.S. 251 (1918).
[16] In a different but significant way, the doctrine of "substantive due process" has now been revived in court decisions dealing with privacy and abortion.
[17] *Olmstead* v. *U.S.*, 277 U.S. 438 (1928).
[18] *Katz* v. *U.S.*, 389 U.S. 347 (1967).

(In 1962, the Supreme Court ruled, in *Engel* v. *Vitale*, 370 U.S. 421, that "Under the First Amendment's prohibition against governmental establishment of religion, as reinforced by the provisions of the Fourteenth Amendment, government in this country, be it state or federal, is without power to prescribe by law any particular form of prayer which is to be used as an official prayer in carrying on any program of governmentally sponsored religious activity." States and officials cannot constitutionally prescribe prayers in schools, although there is nothing to restrain individuals from praying while in the public schools.)

There is no recent national survey of observance of prayer [in schools], but in 1973 Richard Dierenfield, head of the education department at Macalester College . . . polled school superintendents. Of the 830 who responded, 10 per cent said prayer was offered in morning assemblies despite the Supreme Court ban. In the South the figure was 27.7 per cent, compared with less than 1 per cent in the East. Professor Diernenfield said he thought the figures today would probably be higher. "Prayer is creeping back into public schools rather sporadically," he said. "We can't identify it exactly, but it seems to me they're trying it more and more." Leo Pfeffer, special counsel to the American Jewish Congress, . . . said the issue is "chronic, persistent, and it heats up every time it gets into the paper." . . . One ardent supporter of class prayer is Katherine Jolley, who has been teaching . . . for 31 years. "I've found the best way to solve discipline problems with children is to make them repeat a little prayer after me," she said recently. "I know I'm not supposed to," she continued, "but there are so many evil things I've seen in the schools, violence and drugs. . . ." School-prayer observance is a constant issue in the courts. In New York . . . , parents . . . in . . . suburban Albany . . . sued their school district for refusing to allow prayer before classes begin. . . . California court [has] concluded it was unconstitutional to have any kind of religious gathering on school property during non-school hours. In 1978 the same issue came up in a Buffalo high school, and a Federal appellate court said children could not pray in the public schools. However, in 1965 a Federal court in Michigan had said prayer before or after school was permissible. In St. Louis a Federal appeals court is being

BOX 5–6
Can the Court's
Edicts be
Enforced? The Case
of School Prayer
(Continued)

asked to decide whether Christmas carols can be sung in public schools. The same issue has also been taken to a Federal court in Texas. In Chattanooga a Federal judge is considering a case involving Bible studies in the school. The Tennessee case followed a decision in which the Federal court said Bible study was permissible as long as it was totally neutral. . . . Last July the Mississippi legislature passed a school prayer law . . . to "permit voluntary participation of students or others in prayer." The Mississippi Civil Liberties Union filed suit against . . . [a] school board when it found a case where prayer was being broadcast over the school loudspeaker system and a teacher called any child refusing to participate a "devil." The state temporarily rescinded the law, but the issue is now before the . . . District Court of Appeals. . . .
—*The New York Times*, April, 20, 1978.

to find informing the law and the lawgivers, and it is reason that the Founders expected to reign in the courts. Madison argued that

the mild voice of reason, pleading the cause of an enlarged and permanent interest, is but too often drowned before public bodies, as well as individuals, by the clamors of an impatient avidity for immediate and immoderate gain.[19]

Court observers generally seem to believe that the Supreme Court displays its commitment to rationality in Madison's sense through its methods and traditions. These include a deep respect for the words of the Constitution as a constant reference point; a general awareness of political and social trends, particularly those that are palatable to elites; an avoidance of broad interpretations of laws, whether they be cases or statutes, so that it leaves itself maneuvering room in the future; the adherence to precedent and *stare decisis;* and a careful cultivation of the majesty and authority that give the court its mythic appearance in the American political system. The result is an image of the court as precise, distant, and unfailingly concerned for maintaining respect for the law.

Exceptional circumstances can cause the court to abandon some of its Liberal Democratic methods and traditions. This is the case with *Brown* v. *Board of Education,* the 1954 desegregation decision in which

[19] *Federalist* 42.

the court overturned its "separate but equal" doctrine used since 1896 to justify separate schools for blacks and whites, mostly in the Southern states. With the criteria of America's Social Democratic myth, it can be cogently argued that the time had finally arrived when America was ready for this change. But justified as it may have been in these terms, *Brown* was more of a political than a legal decision. In making its new pronouncement, the court overturned a host of precedents and relied instead on broad philosophical premises, as well as sociological data and advice. By Social Democratic standards, *Brown* was an historic decision, a milestone along the nation's march toward social justice. By Liberal Democratic standards, it was "bad law." It should also be noted that blacks had come to exert significant voting power in some key Northern states by the time the *Brown* decision came to pass.

Since *Brown*, the court has steadfastly and unanimously upheld the principles of that case, striking down what had once been legal segregation. But it has been much less consistent in dealing with *de facto* segregation, or segregation based on residential patterns, in the North as well as the South. It has supported busing edicts ordered by lower courts, but it has refused to order integration of metropolitan area schools when school district lines between central city and suburbs must be crossed.[20] The controversial *Bakke* decision of 1978 and the *Weber* decision of 1979 also show that the court has not made up its mind on the related questions of affirmative action, "quotas," and minority rights.[21] The Supreme Court's commitment to being a force for the realization of America's mythic values is a sometime thing. Its commitment to Liberal Democratic values and to maintaining the law is much more unswerving.

FOR FURTHER READING

ABRAHAM, HENRY J. *The Judicial Process*, 4th ed. New York: Oxford University Press, 1980. Compares the judicial systems of the United States, Great Britain, and France with informative insights.

ABRAHAM, HENRY J. *Justices and Presidents: A Political History of the Appointments to the Supreme Court*. Baltimore: Penguin, 1975. Describes this important appointment process with a comparative approach to various instances of controversy.

AUERBACH, JEROLD S. *Unequal Justice: Lawyers and Social Change in Modern America*. New York: Oxford University Press, 1976. Looks at the legal profession from a number of standpoints relating to its involvement and non-involvement in the cause of social change.

BALL, HOWARD. *Constitutional Powers: Cases on the Separation of Powers and Federalism*. St. Paul: West, 1980. With selections from cases and accompanying

---

[20] *Milliken* v. *Bradley*, 418 U.S. 717 (1974).
[21] *Regents of the University of California* v. *Bakke* (1978); *Weber* v. *Kaiser Aluminum* (1979).

commentary, this work makes its way through the thicket of tough constitutional issues on these subjects and ponders their development to the understandings we have of these concepts today.

BARTH, ALAN. *Prophets with Honor: Great Dissents and Great Dissenters in America*. New York: Random House, 1974. Presents great dissents of various Supreme Court justices and demonstrates how and why these became majority opinions at a later time.

BLUMBERG, ABRAHAM S., ed. *The Scales of Justice*, 2nd ed. New Brunswick, N.J.: Transaction Books, 1973. Set of readings that introduces the features and failures of the criminal justice system.

CARDOZO, BENJAMIN N. *The Nature of the Judicial Process*. New Haven: Yale University Press, 1921. Written by the author well before his appointment to the Supreme Court, this account describes the processes that govern judicial thought.

DOWNIE, LEONARD JR. *Justice Denied: The Case for Reform of the Courts*. New York: Praeger, 1971. Journalistic and highly readable introduction to the administration of justice in America; descriptions of conditions are, unfortunately, not dated.

GLICK, HENRY R., and Kenneth N. Vines. *State Court Systems*. Englewood Cliffs, N.J.: Prentice-Hall, 1973. One of the few available introductory texts devoted to this topic.

McCLOSKEY, ROBERT. *The American Supreme Court*. Chicago: University of Chicago Press, 1960. Now regarded as a classic, this history of the Supreme Court ties closely together its analysis of cases, court politics, and sociological considerations.

MURPHY, WALTER, and C. Herman Pritchett, eds. *Courts, Judges and Politics*, 3rd ed. New York: Random House, 1979. Major considerations of judicial selection, court administration, discretion of judges and courts, and other political ramifications of the judicial process.

ORREN, KAREN. "Standing to Sue: Interest Group Conflict in the Federal Courts." *American Political Science Review*, **70** (September 1976), 723–741. Describes and analyzes the problems of interest groups in obtaining standing in class-action suits; also introduces the reader to issues surrounding the question of standing.

PORTER, MARY CORNELIA. "Rodriguez, the 'Poor,' and the Burger Court: A Prudent Prognosis." *Baylor Law Review*, **29** (Spring 1977), 199–241. Prize-winning study that casts an important Supreme Court decision in light of political and social factors that brought the issue of educational financing into focus.

PRITCHETT, C. HERMAN. *Congress Versus the Supreme Court, 1957–1960*. Minneapolis: University of Minnesota Press, 1960. Analyzes the constitutional crisis nearly wrought by Congress's attempt to limit appellate jurisdiction of the Supreme Court.

SCHMIDHAUSER, JOHN R. *Judges and Justices: The Federal Appellate Judiciary*. Boston: Little, Brown, 1979. Explains social background characteristics, behavior, and viewpoints of this important level of the federal bench.

WHITE, G. EDWARD. *The American Judicial Tradition: Profiles of Leading American Judges*. New York: Oxford University Press, 1976. Brief, informative introduction to Justices Marshall, Taney, and others, providing a history of the court through biographies.

6 The Congress

The air was crisp near the Tidal Basin in Washington, D.C., one October evening. The statue of Thomas Jefferson, well-lighted and dramatic, stood in the memorial that bears his name. Suddenly, the U.S. Park Service patrol officers on duty saw a car speeding down the streets without its lights on. They gave chase and brought it to a stop, but before they could ask any questions, a woman in the car jumped out and leaped into the Tidal Basin. She was rescued and was later identified as a local striptease dancer named Fanny Foxe, "the Argentine firecracker." A much better-known person was identified in the group that remained in the car—Representative Wilbur Mills of Arkansas, the powerful and venerable chairman of the House Ways and Means Committee. Mills, like all of the car's occupants, appeared to have been drinking.

This fateful night of October 7, 1974, proved to be the beginning of the end of Mills's career in Congress. He did win a hard re-election fight in November, the first real challenge he had faced in thirty-six years. But he soon resigned his chairmanship, admitted that he was an alcoholic, and did not seek another term in 1978.

The facts concerning Mills's evening at the Tidal Basin were given more publicity than the political consequences of his demise. Mills was one of the great oligarchs of Congress. Perhaps only the speaker of the House possessed more power in that chamber. The Ways and Means Committee that Mills chaired is the revenue-raising committee of the House of Representatives, the chamber in which, according to the Constitution, all revenue measures must originate. Mills had jealously guarded his power. If he did not want a bill considered by his committee, he did not call up the matter for consideration. He carefully set his committee's agenda, and unlike other committee heads, he shared no power with subcommittees or their chairmen. Ways and Means simply had no subcommittees during his reign. All Social Security legislation had to cross his desk. All health bills tied to the Social Security System, such as Medicare or National Health Insurance, were within his province. Unemployment compensation, on-the-job injury compensation, and a host of welfare measures depended on his sanction. Most important, the nation's tax legislation was guided by Mills through Congress. If he believed that a certain industry deserved an investment credit or an accelerated depreciation schedule, there was a good chance that these lucrative favors would be passed. And Mills had a reputation for legislative skill: no member of Congress, it was claimed, knew the complexities and idiosyncracies of the tax code better than he. After all, he and the expert staff he had assembled in his office had written much of it over the past third of a century.

The Tidal Basin incident was doubly shocking because it just did not fit Mills's reputation. The folks in Kensett, Arkansas, his home constituency, were perhaps the most upset of all. He had been their member of Congress all these years, bringing home to his district government contracts, military spending, dams and other river projects, new post offices, and help in obtaining federal jobs and favors. He had sent many of them packets of Agriculture Department seed samples, and new parents in the district were sure to receive copies of *Infant Care*, one of the government's most popular publications. And the people had obliged Mills, re-electing him eighteen times. Only once or twice in his incumbency had Mills had to face any opponent at all, either in primary or general

The Capitol Building, Washington, D.C.

Former Congressman Wilbur Mills of Arkansas, pictured here in the days when he served as Chairman of the House Ways and Means Committee.

elections. Republicans were scarce in the district, and the few who were around did not relish wasting time in futile efforts to unseat him. Now, with Mills's sudden political demise, the constituency around Kensett—and perhaps more significantly, Congress—had come to the end of an era. Much of what Congress does that is politically significant is dominated by barons of Mills's sort. Often the greatest of these barons survive for long periods, decades in fact. When one of these fixtures passes on, it is natural to think of it as the end of an era. But then a new one begins.

Congress in Myth and Ideology

Congress, like all our institutions, functions at two levels, the mythic and the ideological. This chapter shows that at the mythic level Congress, true to the visions of Social Democracy and its principles of the pure doctrine of separation of powers, is a legislative body that, under the leadership of the president and organized along party lines, is harnessed directly to the will of the people. At this mythic level, Congress is essentially an instrument of *responsible* government.

On the ideological level, however, we show that in the tradition of Liberal Democracy, Congress and its members are up to a very different business. At this level the function of Congress is to provide *representative* government. Congress represents and harmonizes the conflicting demands of interest groups both inside and outside government. The Departments of Defense and Agriculture, for example, make demands on Congress just as do the American Farm Bureau Federation, the AFL-CIO, and the sugar industry. The influence and importance of the president and the political parties are peripheral to these concerns. Lobbyists and government bureaucracies, on the other hand, are an indispensable part of this representative process. Also, Congress is highly fragmented at this ideological level into committees, subcommittees, and very small groups that sometimes are not much more than a single legislator and the members of his or her staff.

Some popular impressions about Congress have changed very little over the years, but others are fast disappearing. Any number of polls show that the public holds our national legislature in low esteem,[1] lower than that of most other institutions, though there is some evidence that we tend to like individual members of Congress. Citizens who actually visit the Capitol in Washington are quickly shorn of any preconceptions about Congress serving as a great forum for national debate. On most occasions, a visitor sees largely empty chambers even when Congress is in session. Someone will be sitting in the chair of the House though it may not be the speaker nor, in the case of the Senate, the vice-president. Someone will be speaking in the "well," and the other people on the floor are likely to be the two floor leaders, a few clerks, and members who are soon scheduled to speak. Congress members may be seen dozing or reading newspapers at their desks. Many of the "speeches" are not speeches at all but are nonetheless published in full in the *Congressional Record* even though the Congress member reads only the first and last sentences of the prepared text. Only a vote or a quorum call—taking the roll of attendance—will bring many members to the floor. There are, of course, those occasions that occur two or three times a year when the president gives a State of the Union or similar address to a well-attended joint session of the two houses. If visitors to Congress should arrive on a Monday or Friday, they can assume that no important business will be transacted on the floor or in any committee sessions because of the Tuesday to Thursday club tradition. Most members of Congress, especially those living within range of a short flight home, are in their constituencies on those days, meeting the voters, conferring with major supporters, or perhaps working in their law practice.

[1]"Public Confidence in Key Institutions," *Gallup Opinion Index* Report 166 (May 1979).

Such scenes may not please the visitor, for the essential myth of Congress that all citizens are led to believe is that law-making is its function. In every appearance, Congress is organized and works as a party-divided legislative body. For the individual senator or representative, however, the ideological role assigned to Congress is both more time-consuming and also more personally significant. In this role, the Senate and the House of Representatives are an aggregation of constituent and interest representatives, and as such they are Washington's most important means by which private groups gain access to policy-making and the bureaucracy. Congress at this level sees itself as pluralist in character, an arena in which interests collide, bargain, negotiate, and engage in the brokerage of power. At this level, Congress does make laws, although not quite in the way that the public expects; but just as important, Congress also seeks at this level, on a highly individualized and piecemeal basis, to represent the needs of constituents and the interests in the major departments and other agencies that make up the vast Washington bureaucracy.

Congress as a Legislature

The Constitutional Mandate

That Congress is a legislature, a law-making body, is laid out in Article I of the Constitution, which states that "All legislative Powers herein granted shall be vested in a Congress . . . , which shall consist of a Senate and a House of Representatives." Section 8 of this article empowers Congress to make laws for a number of purposes that may be summarized under the following titles:

lay and collect taxes	organize armed forces
regulate commerce	borrow money
define bankruptcy	define naturalization
fix standard weights and measures	coin money
build a postal system	punish counterfeiting
build post roads	define piracy
define copyrights and patents	build a court system
declare war	

This list represents a typical eighteenth-century understanding of the matters to which government should give its attention. These citations of authority in Article I appear to give to Congress alone the power to do all these things, but this is not necessarily true. The president, through the assignment of the veto power and from other sources, has very important legislative functions. Also, a huge body of rules and regulations that all have the effect of law are promulgated by administrative agencies and also by the courts in ways often only distantly related to authorizations by Congress. This list of Congress's powers has also been subject to considerable expansion through judicial interpretation, both of individual items on it and of the clause at its end that reads, "To make all Laws which shall be necessary and proper for the carrying into Execution the foregoing . . ."

Scattered through the Constitution are assignments of other powers to Congress, especially to the Senate. These powers chiefly concern the approval of appointments and of treaties. In addition, both houses have certain powers in the impeachment and trial of public officials. But the point of Article I, Sections 1 and 8 is that it constitutes Congress as a legislative body and then assigns it a specific set of legislative responsibilities.

Today there is a consensus that the following list of powers and duties of Congress are the pre-eminent ones.

1. *Taxing and Spending Powers.* Article I, Section 8 grants Congress the power "to lay and collect taxes" and to administer our debts. This important power is given to Congress because this was the tradition in colonial legislatures and in the British Parliament. In general, Congress has been permitted broad latitude by Supreme Court decisions in carrying out this power.

2. *Regulation of Commerce.* Article I, Section 8 also contains the commerce clause, which says that Congress is "to regulate commerce with foreign nations, and among the several states, and with the Indian tribes." The scope of this power has been interpreted broadly by the Supreme Court, so that Congress has established a great array of economic and business regulation, particularly since the 1930s. Minimum wage and maximum hours laws, occupational safety, agriculture, health, Social Security and pension regulation, railroad freight rates, consumer protection laws, trade restrictions, and a host of other concerns have been made the subject of legislation under the aegis of the interstate commerce power. Even the Civil Rights Act of 1964, which prevents racial discrimination in public accommodations, was written under the broad authority of the commerce power rather than the Fourteenth Amendment's equal protection of the laws clause. The rationale is that this type of discrimination adversely affects interstate commerce more decisively than it does persons. The breadth of the commerce power is underscored by the welter of regulations required of virtually every business in the country, by the close supervision of such concerns as labor-management relations, and by the fact that the government can legally and very effectively tell farmers, if it wishes, how many crops they can plant, what crops can be planted, and what uses can be made of those crops.[2] In many instances, Congress has delegated its regulatory authority to

---

[2]*Wickard* v. *Filburn,* 317 U.S. 111 (1942).

**BOX 6–1
Theodore Becker:
When It Comes to
Choosing Members
of Congress, There
Must Be a Better
Way**

What this comes down to is whether the American people are going to keep swallowing the line that 50 to 60 percent lawyers, 20 percent millionaires, and a clique of professional pols really grasp these problems better than the average American. It's high time for the worm to turn. We believe, along with Alvin Toffler, that "you don't have to be an expert to know what you want." We believe that somewhere between 50 and 60 percent of the American Congress should be chosen at random from the American people in much the same way they are pressed into military service through drafts when they are deemed necessary.

Right now, with about 20 percent of the American population being black, Puerto Rican, and Chicano, only 4 percent of the House of Representatives and 1 percent of the Senate is nonwhite. With more than 50 percent of America's citizenry being female, 96 percent of the House and 100 percent of the Senate is male. Another very large proportion of the U.S.A. is under thirty-five. A very small number of Congresspeople are in that age group. Probably a majority of Americans are poor. No one in Congress is. Do you really believe that these peoples' viewpoints are the same as those of a group of wealthy, white men in their late forties or older, whose entire careers have been devoted to making money or representing large industrial, agricultural, and financial interests? Of course they're not. But no changes will be made within the presently operating system to make it possible to elect workers, housewives, students, welfare recipients, etc., into Congress. *No way!*

[We should] . . . alter our Constitution and adopt the Half a Random House System, at least *half* a Random House. Only then will the legislature represent the people to any close degree. Only then will America move quickly in the direction of becoming a much truer democracy.

The remaining 40 or 50 percent of Congress would still be elected. This would allow the Elite to maintain an important say in what policies emanate from the national legislature. Phase II of the Continuing American Revolution will be a transitional stage from elitism to democracy, purer democracy, sometime in the future. The elite will still have far more economic power than the people and they should have a large say in the relevant policies of the government at this stage of

**BOX 6–1
Theodore Becker:
When It Comes to
Choosing Members
of Congress, There
Must Be a Better
Way
(Continued)**

development of the American polity. They may even wield greater power than their numbers and "win" on almost all major issues for a while. But the people will have a strong presence; one that is felt; one that must at least be compromised—something no longer possible under the present system. Finally, to forestall the growth of a new class of politicians, all Congressional terms ought not exceed six years. Six years in public legislative office are enough. Those drafted into the Random House ought not have their names resubmitted into the national lottery. Those elected cannot run for re-election. We might also stagger both processes like we do at present in the Senate so that one-third of the random half and one-third of the elected half are chosen every two years. To help guarantee their incorruptibility, our new Congresspeople ought to be paid very well, more than the present salary schedule permits. Moreover, there should be a one-year pre-office period for on-the-job study and training. The newcomers can take courses, sit in on various committees of their interest, and get to know their way around the bureaucracy in Washington before assuming their new roles.

—Theodore Becker et al., *Un-Vote for a Better America* (Boston: Allyn and Bacon, 1976), pp. 184–185.

commissions established for specialized purposes such as the Federal Communications Commission, the National Labor Relations Board, the Federal Trade Commission, the Federal Aviation Agency, and the Federal Power Commission. Although these are often regarded as a part of the executive branch of the government, they are technically and legally agents of Congress and have considerable administrative independence.

3. *Confirmation or Denial of Appointments.* The commissioners who staff such regulatory agencies as the FCC and the NLRB, as well as Cabinet officials, department heads and subheads, diplomatic appointees, and all federal judges are appointed by the president. But these appointments must be confirmed (or denied) by the Senate. In most instances, the president is able to make his choice with little Senate opposition, even when the Senate is controlled by the opposition party. On occasion, presidents are grievously reminded of the Senate's power to withhold its approval.

4. *Congressional Role in Foreign Policy and National Security.* Although most foreign policy initiatives and certainly actions of an emergency

BOX 6–2
Length of
Congressional
Terms: What the
Polls Show

A law has been proposed which would limit a senator to two terms, or a total of 12 years in office. Would you favor or oppose such a law?

	1978	1971
Favor	60%	48%
Oppose	30	39
No Opinion	10	13

A law has been proposed which would limit a member of the House of Representatives to three terms of four years apiece, or a total of 12 years. Would you favor or oppose such a law?

	1978 (Only Poll)
Favor	59%
Oppose	31
No Opinion	10

—*Gallup Opinion Index* Report 156 (July 1978).

nature lie essentially with the president and the executive departments, Congress does have a role in foreign affairs and national security policy. Control of the government's purse strings gives Congress a big say on such matters as foreign aid, major weapons systems, and appropriations for the Defense and State departments and other national security and foreign policy-related agencies. The Constitution gives Congress the power to regulate foreign commerce, as we have seen, and the power to declare war, although this power was not exercised in the Korean and Vietnam wars. The Senate has the power to affirm or deny foreign policy and defense-related appointments; and all treaties negotiated by the president and the executive departments must obtain a two-thirds vote of assent from the Senate to take effect. The president can sometimes get around this latter requirement by negotiating an executive agreement with another nation, which does not need Senate approval, but this is difficult to manage for sensitive issues like the Panama Canal Treaty or the Strategic Arms Limitations treaties. The realities of this nuclear and electronic age give a great deal of discretion and initiative to the president, but Congress still plays an important role in foreign policy and national security.

5. *Impeachment.* The Constitution gives Congress the power to impeach and try federal officials. A majority vote of the House can bring about a resolution of impeachment. A two-thirds vote of the Senate, acting as a trial court, is required to convict an official, who is then removed from office if the vote is affirmative. Congress has impeached but failed to convict a Supreme Court Justice as well as one president, Andrew Johnson. The Watergate scandal of 1973–1974 brought Congress close to impeaching and removing from office President Richard Nixon. Three articles of impeachment were approved by the House Judiciary Committee, but Nixon resigned before any further action was taken.

6. *Constitutional Amendment.* Article V outlines two ways for amending the Constitution. The only way this has ever been done is through a two-thirds vote of Congress followed by ratification of the amendment by three fourths of the states. It is possible, however, for two thirds of the states to apply to Congress for a new constitutional convention, and this process is currently being pushed by a variety of groups interested in amending the Constitution's provisions on the budget and other matters. But there is no predicting what such a convention might do once convened.

7. *Electing the President and Vice-President.* If no single candidate receives a majority in the Electoral College (see Chapter 14 and Amendment 12 of the Constitution in the Appendix), the House of Representatives elects the president of the United States by casting one vote for each state delegation. The Senate, under these circumstances, elects the vice-president.

The Capitol building, one of the world's most impressive legislative halls, with chambers at each end and a magnificent domed lobby in between, is virtually overwhelming physical evidence of Congress's status as a legislature. But besides being constituted, assigned powers, and looking like a legislature, Congress is also organized and works like one.

    Legislative bodies in most modern countries follow procedures for enacting laws that are modeled roughly on the procedure in the Mother of Parliaments, the British House of Commons. These formal procedures for legislative bodies of all sorts enact a bill into law through the following steps:

The Legislative Process in Myth

First Reading: The bill is accepted by the house as an item of business and is printed and distributed to members; this is a necessary formality.

Second Reading: A substantive, wide-ranging debate about the bill's outstanding features ends with a vote to accept it in principle.

Committee Stage: A detailed consideration of the bill's particulars and all proposed amendments is undertaken by a committee of the house.

Report Stage: Guided by the work of its committee, the house debates and votes on any proposed changes in the bill.

Third Reading: A final debate is held on the bill as a whole and as amended, with passage leading either to the bill being sent to the legislature's second chamber for consideration there or to an executive authority for official signing and promulgation as law.

Some of this procedure is followed in the American Congress. Committees hold "mark up" sessions in which amendments, language changes, budget amount changes, and other alterations are made; first readings are formally taken care of; and bills are voted up or down on the floor.

But the British pattern is built upon hidden assumptions about legislative supremacy, the dominant role of the Cabinet in organizing and managing the work of the Commons, and the purely formal role of the monarch. In adapting the traditional British procedure to American conditions and especially to the requirements of mixed government ideology, major (if not always immediately obvious) changes have to be made. In the American system, for example, the committee stage has been moved so that it precedes the second reading; the president's role, unlike the Cabinet's, in the legislative process, is ambiguous although important; and the process itself is more than doubled in complexity and time consumption because for a bill to become law it has to pass through two houses of roughly equal legislative powers.

Important as these changes are, it remains the case that to all outward appearances the legislative processes of the U.S. Congress are much like those accepted as standard around the world. This appearance is reinforced even further by the semicircular layout of the two houses, after the European model, with a table for clerks down front and a recessed dias behind for the presiding officer. But mention of the presiding officers of the houses provides one more example of how, when laying out the mythic appearance of the Congress as a legislative body, we keep encountering ideological facts that point another way. The presiding officer of the Senate is, by constitutional assignment, the vice-president. Because of frequent and extended absences, his place is filled by some senator who has been elected by his fellows as president *pro tem*, and on most occasions even this person is replaced by a temporary presiding officer, usually a low-seniority senator. The Senate's presiding officer is just that, a figure who seems to apply impartially and impersonally the rules of the chamber to its processes. In the House, on the other hand, the speaker is to all appearances an impartial figure applying without favor the rules of the lower house to its activities. But the speaker is also the leader of the majority party in the House. His position makes him the most influential figure in that body as well as

*Speaker of the House
Thomas P. (Tip) O'Neill.*

one of the two or three most powerful figures in the entire national government.

The mythic appearance of the speaker above politics not only contributes to the appearance of the House as a true legislative body; it also lends considerable legitimacy to the speaker's personal standing as one of Washington's most powerful barons. But the most important contribution of the speakership is the edge it gives to the person who holds it in the effort that must be made to organize the House along party lines.

Party Organization in Congress

This is a very difficult business. As we shall see, the ideological situation runs against it. But the notion of party responsibility, which requires the appearance of party organization, is a core feature of the Social Democratic vision of responsible government. Paradoxically, the supposedly nonpolitical office of the speaker has been forced to become political in order to maintain the appearance of a House organized on party lines.

We are describing only appearances, but these are necessary for mythic legitimation. As we shall see, party does not count for very much at the level of ideological operations in the work of Congress. But in appearance both houses of Congress are organized on party lines, and in the House of Representatives the speaker labors mightily to maintain this appearance. In both houses, there are majority party leaders known officially as "majority floor leaders." In the Senate this is the principal majority party position; in the House it ranks just behind the speaker. These positions are supplemented by junior leadership positions called assistant floor leaders or "whips." The minority party has parallel positions. These leadership positions organize the party memberships in the two houses both on and off the floor—at least in appearance. Off the floor, both parties maintain caucus groups for each house that seek, even if often unsuccessfully, to adopt party positions on most legislative measures.

Party coherence is important to the myth of Congress. But ideologically, party discipline is a fairly futile exercise, not only because senators and representatives can go their own way on any issue they choose, but also because there are all kinds of specialized caucuses organized within and between the parties that undermine leadership positions. During the 1980–1981 sessions, Democratic House members known as the "boll weevils" (probably because of their Southern origins) and moderate Republicans from the Northeast known as the "gypsy moths" proved likely to bolt their respective parties on major issues. President Reagan's first budget and tax cut victories, for example, would not have been possible without "boll weevil" support. Later on, he was weakened by "gypsy moth" defections.

The most important evidence of party organization in the two houses, however, is the assignment of the (ideologically very powerful) committee and subcommittee chairmanships to the senior and influential members of the majority party. Special standing is also given by tradition to the ranking minority party member on these committees. The automatic assignment of these positions to the senior party person present on the committee is called the seniority rule. The automatic nature of this rule helps to solve two problems. First, it helps give the appearance of a Congress organized along strict party lines. This is good for the myth. Second, the parties in Congress are in fact so weak that to throw numerous powerful committee chairmanships up for grabs would set off personal infighting so intense and prolonged that Congress would have little time or energy for anything else.

And so we have our mythic picture of Congress: it is constituted and empowered as a legislative body; it looks like one; and it seems to work like one. By being organized for action along party lines, it is set to act like one. We can now add the final mythic touch, the role of the presidency in the affairs of Congress.

As the next chapter makes clear, the president is primarily a mythic figure. In developing that role, nothing is more important than his legislative involvements, which are grounded in the president's constitutional power to sign legislation into law, or to withhold his signature and return bills to Congress for further consideration, thereby vetoing them. He can also pocket veto a measure by doing nothing to it when Congress is not in session. The immediate impact of the presidential veto on Congress is to make its members alert to what the president may veto. In a sense, the veto power makes the president almost a third

The President and Congress

President Ronald Reagan addressing Congress, February 1981 (Copyright © 1981 by Time, Inc.).

house of Congress. But building on this power, and also on the fact that they are the only nationally elected figure in the government other than the vice-president, presidents since the time of Woodrow Wilson have been able to use the constitutional requirement that an annual report be given on the State of the Union to appear in person before Congress. The State of the Union address is an event of considerable moment; it is delivered by the president to a joint session of the two houses with members of the Supreme Court, the Cabinet, the diplomatic corps, the president's family, and the press in attendance. In this address the president sets the agenda for Congress and the nation. He claims to speak for the people. He lists, defines, and defends a broad set of proposals to meet the needs of the times, promises to send Congress detailed proposals one by one during the coming months, and urges one and all to get down to work. Presidential leadership in the legislative process is the final confirmation of the myth of Congress as a legislative body harnessed directly to the will of the sovereign people.

The Courts and Congress

The relationship of Congress and the court system does not contribute as significantly to our mythic perceptions of Congress. In fact, it may be that the Supreme Court and the lesser courts operate against these myths. They strike down legislation as unconstitutional, they have been known to reseat expelled members of Congress, they have occasionally limited Congress's investigative powers, and they have their own myths to protect, such as the cult of the robe and the independent judiciary. In the late 1950s and early 1980s, Congress has assaulted the courts with threats to withdraw some of their appellate jurisdiction, but this kind of action is viewed by many observers in and out of government as an attack on the separation of powers doctrine.

Representative Government

The Position and Privileges of Congress Members

Ideologically, the place to begin an analysis of the Congress and its day-by-day contribution to the functioning of the national government is with individual representatives and senators. The tenets of Liberal Democracy require that great respect be given to the representatives of individual interests, whether of particular groups or individuals. Through deference to and empowerment of individual senators and representatives, Congress meets this Liberal Democratic requirement squarely.

No legislative body in the world enjoys such lavish perquisites and privileges as members of the U.S. Congress. The salary is $60,663 a year, with generous tax breaks, but the staff assistance, travel allowances, free mail privileges, and generous expense accounts are more significant than the salary (see Box 6–3A). Capitol Hill is a beehive of nearly

20,000 employees (see Box 6–3B) housed in a complex of seven main buildings (see Figure 6–1), a huge factory of politics, policymaking, deal cutting, favors processing, and ego stroking. Observers of legislatures in other countries are hard put to find resemblances of Congress in their respective national legislatures.

A comparison with the British House of Commons is nonetheless instructive for purposes of perspective. The ordinary member of Parliament, or MP, is granted neither office space in Westminster nor staff. There are no assigned seats in the Commons, although the two front benches on either side of the speaker are reserved for the leaders of the government and opposition parties. The ordinary MP's salary is modest, and allowances and other benefits are minimal. It is not unusual for an MP to write a longhand reply to a constituent's letter. Perhaps the single most important MP privilege is access to the House of Commons dining room.

The chief reason for this relative austerity is that the ordinary MP does not have great need for an office or staff because the major job in the House is to support the party's leadership. That means perhaps listening to their speeches, maybe making one from time to time, and above all showing up for every vote. Without the votes of its followers, the government will lose power. Without the votes of its followers, the opposition party's leaders will look weak. The House of Commons is clearly organized on party lines, and the MP's first commitment is to be a good party member.

In contrast, the American Congress is organized along party lines only in myth, for these houses are grounded finally on their individual memberships. Each house, ideologically, is an aggregation of individually situated political barons. These barons gained membership in Congress through elections they fought virtually single-handedly. Each wears a party label but party labels are worn lightly in America and few candidates pay consistent attention to any political fate other than their own. Tactical alliances are made to assure personal victory in their particular district. Only if carrying the party banner high contributes to their own victory is it carried high. Often it does not. The first requirement, especially in a tightly fought race that may have included a hard primary battle, is to ensure voter recognition of the candidate's own name and personality.

The job of constituency service is also much greater in America than in Great Britain. No ordinary MP has the staff resources of an American member of Congress, who handles complaints about veterans' benefits, personal problems with immigration authorities, Social Security foul-ups, and hundreds of other matters. And the activities of lobbyists in the two countries also makes much more work for members of Congress. In Britain, lobbyists know that the Cabinet and the department heads make new policies, not individual MPs; thus they focus their pressure

**BOX 6—3A
The Benefits
Taxpayers Lavish
on Lawmakers**

Besides their $60,663-a-year salaries, members of Congress qualify for a vast array of perquisites that cost taxpayers hundreds of thousands of dollars yearly per lawmaker—

Liberal allowances for staff salaries. For senators, the amount ranges from $592,608 to $1,190,724, depending on their state's population. House members receive a flat yearly allowance of $336,384 for salaries.

Rent-free offices at the Capitol and in home districts, with liberal allowances for furniture and office equipment. Members also may lease mobile offices at public expense.

Sizable expense allowances for travel, telephones, telegrams, newsletters, field-office costs and official expenses outside Washington. House members may even charge off food and beverage costs incurred in connection with official duties. House members' expense accounts, including a $43,000 basic allowance, plus additional amounts for specific items, average more than $80,000 a year. Senators' allowances range from $37,000 to $143,000 yearly, depending on the number of constituents, distance from Washington and other factors. Each member also is allowed an additional free trip to Washington at the start of each session of Congress and a return trip at the end.

Opportunity for overseas travel on official business.

Unlimited free long-distance telephone service through the government's own Federal Telecommunications System daily between 5 p.m. and 9 a.m. on weekdays and any time on weekends and holidays.

Frequent time off for vacationing or campaigning.

Liberal retirement benefits after five years' service. Top pension after 32 years' service is $48,530, with automatic cost-of-living increases twice a year.

A $63,000 life-insurance policy for $418 a year.

Government-subsidized health-insurance plan.

Free emergency medical care.

For their exclusive use, free swimming pools, gymnasiums with steam rooms, masseurs and masseuses and physiotherapy specialists.

Haircuts for $3.50 for male members and aides at Capitol barbershops operated by public employees. Low-cost beauty services for female members and staff.

Reduced-rate meals in private dining rooms, with no sales taxes.

Low rates at radio-TV studios, maintained at public expense, for members to make recordings for political use back home.

Publicly paid photographers to provide free pictures of members for news, publicity or other use.

Free help from the Library of Congress on speeches and answering constituents' inquiries.

Reserved garage parking for members and most staff employees. Lawmakers also have free, reserved parking in preferred locations at nearby National and Dulles airports.

A package of special items to give constituents, such as subscriptions to government publications, calendars, maps and pamphlets valued at more than $10,000 a year.

—*U.S. NEWS & WORLD REPORT*, May 4, 1981, p. 25

Employees

	Senate	House
Personal staffs of members of Congress	4,000	7,700
Committee staffs	1,500	2,000
Service and Support	1,300	2,800
Totals	6,800	12,500
Total Congressional Employees	19,300	

Congressional Budget

(Fiscal Year 1982)   Approximately $1.5 billion

Figures supplied and rounded to hundreds by clerk of the House and secretary of the Senate; figures are as of April 30, 1982, and do not include other parts of the Legislative branch such as the Library of Congress, the General Accounting Office, or the Office of Technology Assessment.

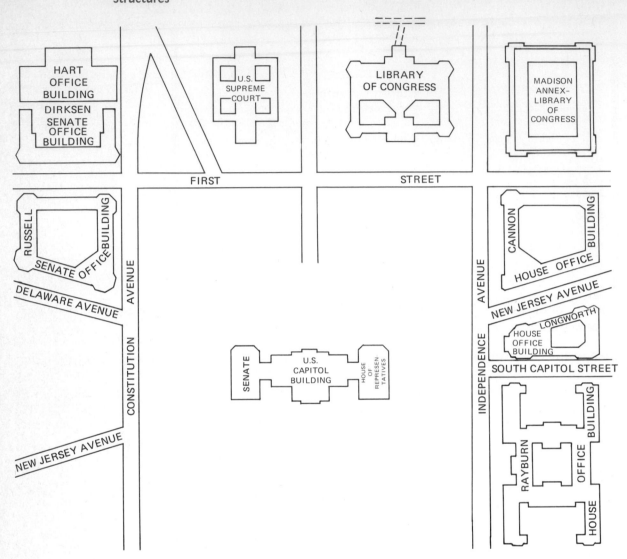

Figure 6–1.
The Capitol Hill area.

on these people. But in the fragmented, undisciplined politics of Congress, the favor of each individual legislator can be important. Congress members are therefore constantly buttonholed by lobbyists, which contributes to the beehive atmosphere of Capitol Hill.

The real reason then for the great differences in the position and perquisites of Congress and the British Parliament is that they are very different institutions performing very different jobs. An MP is a legislator, but a member of Congress is a legislator and much more as well.

The first concern of each Congress member is to ensure re-election. In the House, that is never more than two years away. Senators have six-year terms, but re-election is a concern for them as well. Members of Congress are known as incumbents when they seek re-election, and they can take some comfort in the fact that most incumbents are re-elected—about nine times out of ten is the national average. This percentage is exceeded in the House. To use the advantages of incumbency is hard work, and most members of Congress do work hard.

The first advantage of incumbency is the direct attention that members of Congress and their staff, both in the Washington office and in the home office, can give to the needs of constituents. Answering the mail is the biggest job for any congressional office. The attentive Congress member, as we have pointed out, can become an effective ombudsman—a dealer in complaints and their remedies—for constituents, intervening on their behalf in the government bureaucracy. Much of this work has to do with being adept with the bureaucracy, but two points should be stressed. First, because the federal government's modern programs impinge upon, and get caught up in, the work of state and local governments, Congress members frequently find themselves involved in matters having as much or more to do with those authorities as with Washington. Second, the overwhelming share of this work has little or nothing to do with a Congress member's legislative responsibilities but deals with the application of programs to specific and sometimes unique situations—locating the field office of a welfare program in one place rather than another, getting someone admitted to a training program, or helping a local transit authority in its request for aid. This kind of work is congressional involvement in administration at its most basic level. Such work is regarded as so unexceptional that executive departments and agencies, when letting a contract or initiating a new program in a particular part of the country, routinely allow the local Congress member to make the announcement through his or her office, thus taking the credit for it.

Tending to one's constituency is only the first advantage of incumbency. Other advantages include the free mail privilege, which enables members of Congress to saturate their state or district with newsletters, polls of constituents, and other information that tells the voters their senator or representative is doing a great job for them. Most important, the access to media provided by the capacity to produce videotapes and press releases in great abundance means that members are off to a running start in the race for re-election months and sometimes years before the names of opponents are even announced.

The infrequency of a test at the polls may be a minor disadvantage for senators in keeping abreast of political currents in their states. In any event, the political trends in a state are usually more difficult to calibrate and more diverse than those in a House district. A supposedly "safe" margin of victory in a senatorial contest can wither away completely within six years.

House members have a good idea of where they stand with the voters every two years. Incumbents who consistently win with 60 percent or more of the vote are ordinarily considered "safe." In this case, which is the situation in most House districts in most election years, incumbents can usually count on certain fortunate nonevents: they will have little or no primary election opposition, the opposing party will not marshal its resources for the House race but will concentrate on other opportunities, and national groups—labor, conservative political action committees, corporate political action committees, or the parties' congressional campaign committees—will not "target" the seat for special attention. These national groups will instead concentrate on the closer races in the relatively few marginal districts. In any election year, roughly one third of all House races involve only nominal opposition (or no opposition) to the incumbent. What is more, according to political analyst Michael Barone, "Fewer than one in 20 congressional districts have regular, two-party contests. . . ."[3] Extraordinary circumstances, of

[3]*Wall Street Journal*, October 7, 1980.

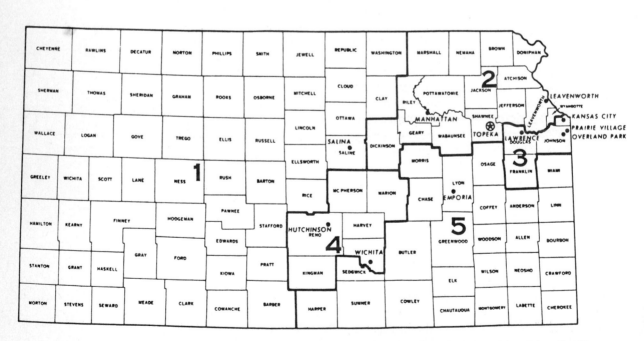

The five congressional districts of Kansas. The House member from the First District obviously represents a more sparsely-scattered constituency. The boundaries of congressional districts are drawn by state legislatures.

course, such as a scandal involving the incumbent, can suddenly produce a competitive situation. In the vast majority of House districts, which are not marginal, a key election usually occurs only when an incumbent does not seek another term. This key election can be hotly contested, although often only in the primary of the district's dominant political party.

We should point out, however, that members of Congress retire from office today much more so than in the past. The pension is good, and some of the frustrations of the job are great. This increase in retirements has affected the turnover rate considerably.

Woodrow Wilson wrote this famous phrase in the nineteenth century in his first book: "Congress in committee is Congress at work." Although this is a slight oversimplification, most of the work of Congress today could be described by amending this to read, "Congress in *sub*committee is Congress at work."

The Committee System and the Seniority System

Ideologically, Congress is structured around the committee system and the seniority system. Committees do most of the thorough work and consideration that is given to legislation, and long service on these committees is the key to chairing them. Chairing a committee, in turn, requires re-election over and over again to achieve a major share of influence. It also means that closely contested Senate seats and House districts are less likely to see their incumbents achieving this kind of power, because seniority requires staying power. Traditionally, a disproportionate share of chairmanships has gone to Southern Democratic senators and representatives because of their one-party states and constituencies; but this situation has changed so that in the Democratic Party the system now tends to favor moderate-to-liberal members from the North and West. The 1980 elections gave Republicans the hope that they may now share in these chairmanships more often. The seniority system seems to promote a cohesiveness—some might say "clubbiness" —among the more powerful members of Congress. In such an atmosphere the barons have wide latitude in governing the matters of their province of concern. Remedies are available against committees, such as petitioning a bill out of a committee and onto the floor, but this is seldom done because the committee and its chairman are so respected that such an action might be considered an insult.

Some efforts have been made over the years to share power in Congress through decentralizing responsibility and jurisdiction. In the 1950s, for example, Lyndon Johnson, then the Senate Democratic majority leader, set up a system of more evenly shared responsibility by ensuring that every Democratic senator receive at least one major committee assignment. In the House, the Democrats, because they are typically the majority party, have been the impetus for the establishment of many new subcommittees, providing more opportunities for leadership positions. Unfortunately, some members of the House may be stuck on a relatively unimportant committee—such as Administration, District of Columbia, or Post Office and Civil Service—for their entire political career.

Because members of Congress are free to introduce as many bills as they like, more than 10,000 legislative items can be introduced in a year. The only way to handle this mass of material is to divide up the work among a relatively large number of specialized committees with responsibility for determining what should come up for full debate.

To this end the House has organized twenty-one standing (permanent) committees and the Senate fifteen. Each of these committees jealously guards its specialized area of jurisdiction. Which committee receives a bill after it is introduced can be a matter of some significance, but the real import of the committee system is the way it fragments the Congress. The Constitution divides Congress into two branches, following mixed government theory; the committee system extends this principle, splitting Congress into thirty-six specialized fiefdoms. Nor is this all. Congress regularly creates select and special committees to consider immediately important problems not falling within the jurisdiction of one of the standing committees. An example is the Senate committee designated to investigate the Watergate scandals. There are also a few specialized joint committees of Senate and House members. And on top of all this, the proliferation of droves of subcommittees continues. In 1975 Congress had splintered itself into 268 subcommittees; by 1978 this number had grown to 299, 268 of which were attached to the standing committees and thirty-one to special committees.

The immediate effect of all this subdivision of the Congress is to ensure a very high proportion of its members each have, besides a suite of offices, personal staff, generous allowances, and so forth, a nearly personal piece of the committee system. This is what makes senators and representatives truly barons, persons to be seriously and individually reckoned with in Washington politics.

Customs, Folkways, and Reciprocity

Major studies of the two houses of Congress show that a set of norms and folkways have developed in these bodies over the years that can be related in a number of ways to the seniority and committee systems. These norms and folkways include specialization, courtesy, apprenticeship (though this is less important than it used to be), legislative work in which a regular work load is undertaken and accomplished, institutional patriotism, and, above all, reciprocity.[4] The reciprocity that develops in Congress depends upon experience and reliability. In other

---

[4]Donald R. Mathews, *U.S. Senators and Their World* (Chapel Hill: University of North Carolina Press, 1960), pp. 92–117; Herbert B. Asher, "The Learning of Legislative Norms," *American Political Science Review* **67:** 499–513 (June 1973).

words, the specialists in one committee rely on, bargain with, and respect the specialists in another, if only to ensure that they receive the same respect in return. Reciprocity means adherence to jurisdictional boundaries based on the understanding, "You respect my subcommittee's work and needs and I'll respect yours. That way we both win." A direct parallel to the reciprocity between committees is the tradition of senatorial courtesy discussed in the previous chapter in connection with judicial appointments.

"Do your homework" is one of the first lessons learned by new members of Congress, who are expected to do a certain share of the work load of their committee or subcommittee. This involves poring over bills, reports, and staff findings. An intelligent, productive piece of work earns the gratitude of colleagues and the committee chairman, and the Congress member will acquire a reputation for reliability, perhaps becoming an expert in some area of specialization.

Some Congress members do not heed this advice. They may prefer a maverick role, not care about specialization, and in fact may care little for any of the work of Congress. They may eschew membership in the inner club of the Senate or House. They may be politically hurt by these attitudes, but they may not suffer very much. (They will not, of course, be chosen for leadership positions.) Any number of nonconformists have managed to be re-elected, and displeasing their legislative leaders and colleagues may not be crucial to their personal ambitions. The Senate has more flamboyant individualists than the House. The Senate, after all, is looked upon by many as a jumping-off point for the presidency; senators are also more likely to be national figures, with access to greater publicity. House members are more likely to fit into the routines of legislative business, working toward becoming a committee chairman.

It should not be surprising that the atmosphere created at the ideological level by the committee system, the seniority system, and the norms and folkways of Congress is often bipartisan or nonpartisan cooperation and accommodation. Television and the press are often misleading in their coverage of Congress. Their tendency to focus on controversy or a particularly fierce debate at the mythic level obscures the frequency of members' crossing party lines not only in voting but in accomplishing the enormous legislative task.

We have already shown that our national legislature does not depend as heavily on partisanship as, for example, the British system. But many Americans persist in believing that party is an all-important dividing line in Congress. The myth of Democrats and Republicans fighting it out to advance their partisan positions was at least partially dissipated for a group of Indiana voters who visited their Democratic representative in his Washington office in the summer of 1974. Noting that the Watergate crisis was hurting the Republicans, one of these visi-

**BOX 6–4
The Conventional
View of Congress
and Congress
Today**

So much political science and journalistic literature is devoted to Congress and its power structure that a number of false assumptions and stereotypes have persisted in the face of important changes that have occurred in Congress during the 1970s. Professor Larry M. Schwab has provided a useful list of these contrasts in his book, *Changing Patterns of Congressional Politics* (New York: Van Nostrand, 1980, p. 5):

Old View of Congress	New Congress
Predominance of older, male white Anglo-Saxon Protestants from small towns and rural areas	Greater representation of other groups
Overrepresentation of rural areas	Increase in the representation of metropolitan areas
Dominance of committee chairpersons	Less power given to committee chairpersons
Control of committee leadership positions by rural conservatives	Control of committee leadership positions by metropolitan moderates and liberals
Southern dominance of Congress	Enormous decline of Southern influence
Little power wielded by party caucuses	Greater influence of party caucuses
Rural factions strong in both parties	Decline in the power of rural factions within both parties
Strong influence held by the Conservative Coalition	Decline in the effectiveness of the Conservative Coalition
Little power given to new members	Greater influence exercised by new members
Dominance of Congress by the Presidency	Greater defense of congressional power
Dependence on the executive branch for information and research	More research capacity within Congress
Development of most public policy by the president and the executive branch	Greater role of Congress in formulating public policy

BOX 6—4
The Conventional
View of Congress
and Congress
Today
(Continued)

Conservative control of the House Rules Committee hindered liberal legislation	House Rules Committee generally follows the wishes of the moderate-to-liberal House Democratic leadership
Senate filibuster was a major tool of conservatives	New cloture rule makes it more difficult to use a filibuster

We generally agree with the observations made on this list, though we believe that the demise of the Conservative Coalition is overstated by Schwab and many other observers of Congress. This Conservative Coalition, which came into existence in the 1930s, is made up of Republicans and Southern Democrats, and this coalition has often held sway in Congress. Alan I. Abramowitz notes:

"In the 95th Congress (elected in 1976), as in the 88th Congress, Southern Democrats, regardless of seniority, continued to vote against their party almost as often as they voted with it. . . . it appears . . . that reports of the demise of the Southern Democratic revolt in Congress have been greatly exaggerated."

—"Is the Revolt Fading? A Note on Party Loyalty Among Southern Democratic Congressmen," *Journal of Politics*, **42**: 572 (May 1980).

tors told the congressman that he expected the GOP to lose quite a large number of House seats in the fall. "Yes," answered the congressman, "It's very sad. We are going to lose some very good and experienced men." It was obvious that the congressman was more concerned about this large-scale loss of what he termed "good friends" than he was about the rising fortunes of his own party. Some members of Congress manage to keep their partisanship in low profile. Senator Mike Mansfield of Montana, the Democratic majority leader who succeeded Lyndon Johnson, was generally regarded as too gracious and accommodating to give partisanship more than pro forma attention. In the post-World War II period, Republican Senator Arthur Vandenberg of Michigan initiated a bipartisan approach to foreign policy that greatly affected Congress's foreign policy debates for thirty years. None of this is to say that party is not important; it remains, after all, as the most important predictor of a legislator's voting record. It does mean, however, that much of the partisan wrangling that supposedly goes on in Congress does not take place, and that to a great extent, partisanship is a myth.

"Representative" Congress

The enhancement that reciprocity, folkways, and absence of partisanship give to the ideological stature and influence of congressional fragments such as subcommittees and even individual members can be multiplied, with skill and hard work, by contacts with the bureaucracy and affected clientele. The fragmentation of Congress tends to mirror the fragmented Washington bureaucracy so that every committee and subcommittee gets tied into corresponding bits of the bureaucracy. Clientele groups serviced by Congress and the bureaucracy fit hand in glove with them in establishing patterns of influence. The result is that much of the Washington scene is dominated at the ideological level by "iron triangles," closely knit, long-standing, mutually supporting triple alliances among members of Congress and their staffs and committees, segments of the bureaucracy, and relevant interests in the private sector. The solidity and durability of these triangular relationships shows that Congress is truly a "representative" body at this ideological level, working to ensure that interests strong and organized enough to penetrate the Washington labyrinth will consistently be heard. These triangular relationships, by their prevalence and strength, also must typify the centrifugal forces that diffuse and scatter power in Washington. They work constantly against the mythic image, which pictures power in Washington as heaped up in the leadership of Congress and the presidency. The special interests of these triangles vary greatly, but they are often concerned with issues and favors that do not excite most citizens, such as shoe imports, the needs of sugar beet farmers, or the State Department's approach to a country in which American entrepreneurs have an interest. On the other hand, some of the most powerful of these triangular relationships dominate issues that affect all of us, for example, the selection of hugely expensive weapons systems for the military.

Law-making, though it is the heart of Congress's mythic role, is not the essence of its representative, ideological functions. At this level, representing the claims of the interest groups mainly in the administrative processes of the government is what matters most. Crucial to the discharge of this function are two other important powers of Congress, the investigatory power and the oversight function.

The Investigatory Power and the Oversight Function

The power to investigate is often regarded as an executive, not a legislative power, and the Constitution gives Congress no specific right to investigate. All the same, Congress has conducted investigations throughout its history. The rationale for this investigatory power is simple: Congress must find out the facts if it is to legislate intelligently. This need and ability to investigate carries with it the power to subpoena witnesses to testify before congressional committees. More important,

Congress has acquired the judicial-like power to hold individuals in contempt of Congress who have been uncooperative in investigations. This can result in the jailing of a witness.

Some congressional investigations appear to be valid and necessary attempts to build a factual base for the enactment of legislation or other legitimate purposes. Congress investigates the state of the economy, the status of antitrust legislation, drug problems, the quality of consumer products, and proposed educational reforms, for example. Any such investigation could be wide-ranging and result in specific legislative proposals. It could also have the practical effect of reinforcing Congress' concern and control over relevant administrative areas, another traditional and proper Congressional interest.

From time to time, however, individual members of Congress, working mostly through committees they have dominated, have clearly abused Congress's powers of investigation in order to promote their own careers. Many important rights of private citizens, like the right of association, the right to one's own political and philosophical beliefs, and the right against self-incrimination have been threatened by such units as the Senate Permanent Investigations Subcommittee and the House Un-American Activities Committee (HUAC). The careers of many famous politicians, including Senator Joe McCarthy, Congressman Richard Nixon, and Robert Kennedy when he was a staff aide, were built on the rather dubious foundations of work on these committees.

The "oversight" function of Congress is based on its investigatory power, but this function works rather differently and has slightly different purposes. The oversight function does not anticipate legislation on most occasions, as the investigatory power does, but seeks to monitor how legislation is administered by the bureaucracy. A close watch over the bureaucracy is allegedly maintained by Congress in this way. Specialization is said to be the key: the staffs of the congressional committees dealing with space programs follow the operations of NASA; the House Ways and Means Committee and its Senate counterpart, the Finance Committee, oversee the Internal Revenue Service; and the Agriculture Committees check the massive bureaucracy of the Department of Agriculture. A great deal of the literature on oversight, particularly in the press, seems to stress an adversary relationship between Congress and the various bureaucratic agencies. But the oversight function of Congress is not usually a cause of conflict. On the contrary, it is here that the iron triangle relationships produce an almost unchallengeable agglomeration of interests and expertise from the specialized congressional staff people, important administrators, and the lobbyists who represent the interest groups. In case after case—tobacco legislation, highway financing, maritime concerns, and all kinds of defense-related issues—it has been shown that an iron triangle holds sway on important policy questions.

BOX 6–5
The Investigatory
Power of Congress:
The Case of HUAC

Congress's power of investigation is broad, because it can be shown that investigation is often necessary to produce legislation. Perhaps the best example of this is HUAC, the House Un-American Activities Committee, which existed from 1938 to 1974. During this entire period it produced only four pieces of legislation, three of which were later declared unconstitutional, even though it was generously funded throughout this period. A 1957 Supreme Court decision, *Watkins* v. *U.S.*, requires questions of witnesses called before congressional committees to be related to a legislative purpose; this is a direct result of the excesses of HUAC. But the HUAC experience amply testifies to the dangers of the abuse of this power of Congress. Here are some examples:

"Mr. Velde (Republican of Illinois) asks a witness . . . 'Which side are you on in the revolt, Soviet Union's or the rebels?'

The witness replies, 'I am on the rebels' side.'

But Velde is not satisfied with the witness' answers . . . , so he concludes, 'From the witness' appearance and demeanor before this Committee, I am satisfied that he bears watching by the duly constituted authorities. I do not think he is on the side of the rebels. I think he is on the side of Moscow, the Soviets.'

The late Tom O'Connor, a liberal newspaper man, was interrogated in 1952 about a charge that he had been a Communist in 1938. Congressman Velde asked him:

'Are you a member of the Communist Party now?'

'No, sir,' O'Connor replied.

'Were you a year ago?'

'No, sir.'

'Were you five years ago?'

'No, sir.'

'Were you ten years ago?'

'No, sir.'

Velde . . . [then] made the following comment: 'I personally can draw only one inference, that you are not only a past member of the Communist Party, but that you continue to be a member of the Communist Party and that you are an extreme danger to the country as the managing editor of a large New York newspaper.' . . .

BOX 6–5
The Investigatory
Power of Congress:
The Case of HUAC
(Continued)

[Another] witness is asked to state her occupation. She answers, 'If I state my occupation, I will be fired. I prefer to withhold that. . . .''

Mr. Willis and Mr. Velde assure the witness that she will not lose her job, if she answers the questions.

Mr. Arens: What do you do at the place where you are employed?

Witness: I am a social worker. . . .

Mr. Arens: And among whom do you work?

The witness again begs the Committee not to force her out of her job. . . . Arens offers her [a] bargain: If the Committee doesn't require an answer to the employment question, will she talk about other organizations. She is asked about those and again about the Communist Party. The witness declines to answer on constitutional grounds. . . .

Mr. Arens: Did you have a discussion with your employers respecting your membership in the Communist Party when you accepted this position with this private social agency?

This last question is the standard question used to cue the employer to fire a witness and . . . Arens was beginning to weary of the cat-and-mouse game he was playing with the witness. . . . After taunting the witness a little more and permitting her to thrash about as the net was being drawn tighter, Arens asked, 'Are you presently employed at the Jenny E. Clarkson Home for Girls at Valhalla, N. Y.?'''

Careers, reputations, and livelihoods were destroyed by HUAC. But HUAC also made the careers of some people, including that of one of its earliest stars, a young congressman named Richard Nixon.

Today HUAC-type investigations have been revived by a new Senate Subcommittee on Terrorism and Subversion.

—Excerpts from Frank J. Donner, *The Un-Americans* (New York: Ballantine, 1961), pp. 77–79, 92–93.

Nevertheless, Congress is sometimes frustrated in carrying out its oversight function. This frustration has led to measures aimed at closer supervision of administrators and their budgets. Congress has sought to limit impoundment of funds, for example, a familiar tactic of the Nixon administration. (Impoundment is the refusal of the president to spend funds that Congress has allocated for particular programs or projects.)

Congress has also established some control over the bureaucracy by setting up a variety of legislative vetoes. These vetoes include "coming into agreement" sections of bills, which require the consent of a congressional committee before a specified action can be taken by administrators. Other kinds of legislation allow Congress to nullify certain actions of the bureaucracy by a majority vote in one or both houses. A kind of legislative veto was set up in the War Powers Act of 1973, which permits the president to send troops abroad if he deems necessary but requires withdrawal of these troops after thirty days if Congress has not given its assent for them to stay longer. Some government reorganization laws also have legislative vetoes built into them. Typically, these allow a president's reorganization plan to go into effect unless one or both houses vote against the plan within a specified period of sixty or ninety days.

Congress has also established institutional aids that help to carry out its oversight function. Two of these are committees it has created—the House Government Operations Committee and the Senate Governmental Affairs Committee. The General Accounting Office (GAO) is the agency of Congress that performs audits of administrative departments and agencies, evaluates programs, and reports its findings to the relevant congressional committee. The Office of Technology Assessment provides Congress with information on technical matters that affect oversight.

Some of the more zealous, perhaps publicity-hungry members of Congress also lead individual crusades and forays into bureaucratic activities. Senator William Proxmire, Democrat of Wisconsin, has long benefited politically from his "golden fleece" award, which he hands out for the biggest "boondoggle" he finds each month.

Congress's continuing preoccupation with the activities of the bureaucracy, for all its fragmented, piecemeal qualities, is intense and influential. The whole process, ranging from an individual representative seeking a favor for a constituent to a major committee holding a public hearing reviewing the work of an agency, is sometimes summed up by the phrase "lateral penetration"; that is, instead of simply the top-down flow of authority from cabinet officers to government departments, there is a penetration and influence "from the side" by congressional personnel. This is not to suggest that Congress exercises anything approaching total supervision of the bureaucracy. Congress is too fragmented for that. However, Congress through the work of its committees and individual members does influence powerfully if on a piecemeal basis the questions of who gets what from whom—which in Liberal Democratic theory is what politics is all about.

The Legislative Process in Ideology

In myth, Congress makes laws under presidential leadership and according to the will of the people as interpreted by the political parties

**BOX 6–6
Why Do People Run
for Congress? A
Senator Gives His
Reason**

Among the many reasons and motivations given by various people on why they decided to run for Congress, one of the most interesting is explained by Senator Donald Riegle, Democrat of Michigan. Reflecting on his experience with his first job after receiving his master's degree in business, he writes:

"On one occasion I was sent home for wearing a blue shirt instead of a white one to work. But the incident that finished my IBM career occurred in November 1963. I was on the telephone when word rippled through the building that President Kennedy had been shot. People dashed out of their cubicles, but nobody could get any information. There were no radios or TV sets in the building and the IBM intercom hadn't said a thing.

I ran out to the parking lot and turned on the radio in my car. I was facing this long, low, modern building with all the windows on one side and I could see people continuing to work inside. What struck me was how few of them left the building to find out what was happening. I was dumbfounded and I thought: 'Why aren't more people concerned enough to turn on their car radios? Why doesn't the need to know just shove them out that door? How can they be content with fragments of information? . . .

Minutes later the word came through: Kennedy was dead. I didn't want to believe it. I looked back at the building and it was business as usual. . . .

By some crazy distortion of events and relationships, IBM had removed itself from what was really important in the world. The world was at a crisis point, but IBM continued to roll along. It was one of those rare moments when you suddenly realize that what you're a part of is very different from what you really are. . . . That experience made me realize that I simply wasn't cut out to be that kind of organization man. The problems I cared about were on the public side. . . ."

—Donald Riegle, *O Congress* (New York: Popular Library, 1972), pp. 47–49.

Although Riegle was not "that kind of organization man," it can be asked whether he must be some kind of organization man in Congress; and, if so, what kind? Could it be that the IBM employees knew something about the American system that Riegle did not know?

and as mandated by their victories at the polls. In ideology, Congress goes through many of the same motions but with a different purpose. As aggregations of representatives of private interests, the two houses of Congress use the legislative process to register and harmonize as best they can the competing claims of these interests. This central ideological function of Congress makes it indispensable to the political system. The underlying principle by which Congress does this work is, as we have noted, Calhoun's doctrine of the concurrent majority (see Chapter 2). The legislative process through which bills pass is a maze in which interests can make their influence felt at an extraordinary number of points and, if need be, act to kill legislative moves that might adversely affect their vital interests. The committee system is essential to creating this situation, but there is more to it than that, as we shall see.

Congress members can adopt various strategies to further the interests they represent. Actual strategies are almost always a blend that may shift and change direction as a bill progresses through the legislature. Three basic strategies characterize Congress's legislative process:

1. Advance the narrowest possible bill to avoid stirring up unnecessary opposition and count heavily on reciprocity for support that can be "paid for" later.
2. Advance a "package" bill that bundles, sometimes in very odd ways, a number of objectives to build a coalition of interested support. In its extreme form, this used to be called "pork barrel" or "log rolling" legislation; a more modern term is "Christmas tree" legislation. The aim is a bill that accumulates, often through a process of continuous amendment at various stages, broad support by offering something to almost everyone. Defense appropriations acts, with their many clauses authorizing monies for weapons to be produced here, subcontracted there, and for refurbishing facilities somewhere else, are good examples of this kind of bill.
3. Advance a "nothing" bill that, filled with platitudes, has no bite or loses what it may have started with as it picks up support through the legislative process. Both the Employment Act of 1946 and the more recently passed Humphrey-Hawkins Act, each of which call for a policy of full employment, fit into this category.

These general observations should be borne in mind as we look more closely at the mechanics of the legislative process.

How a Bill Becomes a Law

The chances of eventual passage are quite slim for most bills introduced in Congress. In a remarkable number of cases, this may be what the senator or representative originally introducing the measure assumes. Members of Congress may know that the bill is bad public policy or that it will not accomplish what it is purportedly intended to do. But the constituents back home may want this measure, and their representative may want to give the appearance of carrying out their will.

Even if a bill has general support, the odds are often against it. The path it must wend is long and tortuous. The legislative process works, in fact, to the advantage of those who wish to kill legislation rather than to those who wish to pass it. When a bill is first introduced in either chamber of Congress, for example, its fate can be sealed almost immediately by referral to an unfriendly committee for consideration. Many bills can conceivably fall under the jurisdiction of any number of committees; thus when a bill is introduced in the House, for example, the speaker can refer it to any one of these committees. Where the bill ends up can therefore depend on the speaker's attitude toward it or toward the representative who introduced it. The committee assignment can also be determined by the speaker's need to mollify competing claims of jurisdiction made by different committees and their chairmen. On occasion, important pieces of legislation are referred to two or more committees.

When a committee receives a bill, the chairman has to make a number of choices about what to do with it. He may give it top priority, assign it to an unfriendly subcommittee, or try to stall action on it in various ways. In most instances, however, the latitude of the chairman is not great. Chairmen are watched more closely today by other members of Congress (and their staffs) than they were in the pre-1965 days of broader discretion. If the proposed legislation concerns complex matters, the committee staff may be asked to carry out extended research on it.

A subcommittee may hold hearings, "mark up" the bill with changes or amendments, or "report out" the bill, favorably or unfavorably, to the full committee. Favorable treatment by a subcommittee, however, does not guarantee such treatment by the full committee. This larger committee may vote to kill the bill or make it less likely to pass by burdening it with unpalatable amendments. Committee members may also weaken a bill's enforcement provisions or reduce the money allocated for its purpose.

If a bill is considered favorably by the full committee, it is "reported out" and, in the House, goes to the Rules Committee. The Rules Committee usually assigns a "rule" (a calendar date for floor consideration and sometimes a set of debate rules concerning the floor time for the bill). In the past, the Rules Committee has been used by party leaders to bottle up bills so that they never reached the floor. Today, the Democrats on the committee are regarded as a friendly arm of the speaker and provide scheduling times as he requires. Presumably a similar relationship will obtain if the Republicans win control of the House.

When a bill is given a "rule," it proceeds to the floor for debate. It usually can be amended on the floor. It can also be defeated on the floor vote, although the leadership of the House—the speaker, the majority floor leader, the assistant leader, and the chairman whose committee considered the bill in the first place—usually know whether the legislation has "the numbers" to win. If the bill obtains passage on the floor, it then proceeds to the Senate for consideration.

Bills, excluding money bills, may originate, of course, in the Senate rather than in the House. Important legislation is often simultaneously introduced in both chambers to expedite it. These identical measures often become known by the names of their respective Senate and House sponsors: the Taft-Hartley Law, the Magnuson-Lesinski maritime bill, or the Humphrey-Hawkins Act. Recently, Congress considered the Kennedy-Waxman health bill. Asked at a news conference about the "Waxman-Kennedy bill," Congressman Henry Waxman of California said, "It's the Kennedy-Waxman bill. Only my mother calls it the Waxman-Kennedy bill."

A bill proceeds through the Senate in much the same way as it does through the House—introduction, committee assignment, subcommittee consideration, full committee, and floor votes. There are two major differences, however. The Senate has a Rules Committee, just as the House has, but it does not have the general legislative role that the House unit enjoys. Calendar dates and debate rules are negotiated and set up by the Senate leaders and are formalized by "unanimous con-

Congressman Henry Waxman of California.

sent" agreements. The second difference is in the rules on the length of floor debates. The Senate has no general limitation on debate. In the House, the usual rule is a one-hour limitation on any House speech. But the Senate, with 100 members compared with 435 in the House, regards itself as the more select chamber and allows legislation to be debated for very long times, sometimes for days or weeks. It also does not require that these extended debates be germane to the subject matter of the bill under consideration. Senators occasionally try to talk a bill to death, holding up legislative business until the bill's backers agree to withdraw it or radically alter its contents. Senate Rule 22 permits a cloture vote to shut off debate. But a successful cloture vote must have the support of three fifths of the total membership of the Senate. It is not easy to win such a vote because of the absence of senators on other business, and because some senators never vote for cloture on principle. Talking a bill to death is called a "filibuster." This technique proved for decades to be effective in killing civil rights legislation, to cite the most important example. A filibuster can be effective when carried out by as few as half a dozen senators, especially if they are given to such heroic gestures.

Another pitfall for legislation can occur when the two houses pass differing versions of the same bill. There may be a $200 million difference in the money called for, or one chamber may pass an amendment not passed in the other. In these circumstances, the differences are ironed out in a conference committee, which is a joint Senate-House committee whose membership is determined by the Senate and House leaders and is drawn from the committees that originally considered the bill in question and other particularly interested members. Traditionally, conference committees have wide powers to revise bills in order to reach a compromise version. If they report out a compromise version, both houses will usually pass it. But there is always the chance that no compromise will be reached, or if it is, that one house will reject it.

The legislative process is thus a minefield for most bills. Most vanish into one or another subcommittee. Those who wish to kill a measure that shows signs of life or force substantial amendments to it can take advantage of any number of what are called "access points": the subcommittee that first considers it, the full committee to which it is then sent, the committees of the other house that may have very different attitudes toward it, the House Rules Committee, a conference committee, even an ad hoc clustering of senators to start a filibuster. And in all this, we have not even mentioned the quirks, detours, and dead ends that can be thrown into a bill's legislative journey by individual senators and representatives skilled and alert to the intricacies of parliamentary procedure. On the other hand, those who wish to see a bill passed must successfully guide it past every one of these obstacles.

Even when a bill passes both houses, it can still be vetoed by the president (see Chapter 7). Passage is then possible only if the two houses pass it over his head, obtaining a two-thirds vote in each body. The president, of course, may sign a bill into law or not sign it and let it become law, the latter being an option seldom exercised.

Lobbyists

The lobbyists of Washington seem almost always to labor under the public's suspicion that they are up to something nefarious. The standard civics text answer to such doubts is that lobbyists are vital to the legislative process. They supply lawmakers with necessary facts and arguments that help them make up their minds about issues. How, for example, can the ordinary member of Congress know whether one proposed weapons system is superior to another? How can Congress discern what *really* has to be done for the elderly in America? How can Congress deal with technical subjects like energy conservation? The lobbyists or their adversaries—other lobbyists—will tell them. This kind of argument does not mute the criticisms of lobbyists made by such groups as Common Cause and Ralph Nader's Public Citizen, who believe that most lobbyists do not flout the law but bias legislation in favor of those who can afford their services, and that the laws regulating lobbyist behavior are too weak and administered in a lax fashion.

Congress is almost perfectly organized for penetration by lobbyists. The committee system breaks down Congress into small, specialized units whose subject matter corresponds neatly with lobbyist interests. Banking groups, for example, are sure to gravitate toward the Senate Committee on Banking, Housing and Urban Affairs and the House Committee on Banking, Finance and Urban Affairs. With a few side trips to the tax writing committees, House Ways and Means and Senate Finance, the banking interests can take care of their legislative needs on most occasions by knowing the key people in these four committees. Agricultural commodities representatives, whether looking out for the interests of corn, sugar, or peanuts, deal with the two Agriculture committees and their subcommittees, which are conveniently broken up into various commodity specializations. It has long been said that the crops Congress pays the most attention to are not necessarily the most important from a nutritional standpoint; they are the most important from a political standpoint. Dairy products, for example, were denied government price supports for many years while peanuts, arguably a less important commodity, were given support. (The dairy interests have strongly come into their own today.) Civil rights groups are particularly interested in the work of the two Judiciary committees. The education lobby looks to the House Education and Labor Committee and the Senate Committee on Human Resources. And all the interests watch closely the work of the Appropriations Committees and their subcommittees.

Lobbyists represent a diverse set of political forces, not all of which could be called powerful. They include labor, farm, and business groups, all of which are subdivided into various categories. But business interests include many small business associations and also the powerful oil lobby. Labor is divided into independent unions such as the Teamsters and the AFL-CIO federation and its various affiliates. There are single-issue groups such as Right-to-Life, but there are also broad-based issues groups such as the liberal Americans for Democratic Action, the conservative Americans for Constitutional Action, the pacifist Friends Committee on Legislation, and the reformist Common Cause. There are powerful professional groups like the American Medical Association and such disparate organizations as the National League of Cities, the American Legion, the National Rifle Association, the Sierra Club, NewYork City, the government of Spain, the Zionist Organization of America, and the American Library Association.

Lobbyist strategies and tactics are just as diverse as the variety of organizations that carry them out. They include buying expensive lunches and throwing elegant parties, taking Congressmembers to sumptuous hunting lodges for a relaxing weekend, contributing or withholding campaign funds, setting up testimonial dinners and press conferences back in the home state or district, publishing lists of votes on issues considered crucial by the lobby group and "rating" the Congressmember accordingly, and, of course, moral suasion and intellectual persuasion.

Lobbying is sometimes associated with bribery in the minds of the public, and the so-called ABSCAM trials and scandals of 1980 have contributed to this perception. The ABSCAM trials involved bribes to members of Congress offered by FBI agents who posed as wealthy Arabs supposedly seeking immigration favors for their relatives. In most circumstances, however, bribery in the legal sense of the term does not take place; in fact, many Congressmembers and lobbyists know there is usually no need for bribery, for many of the ends that might be served by bribery can be accomplished quite legally.

An illustrative story by a congressional staffer makes the point. A lobbyist concerned about the vote on a given bill tells a member of Congress that it is very important to be present for the vote. The Congressman replies that he regrets that he has planned a visit to his home district on that day to speak at a convention of a teenage boys' organization. It is a longstanding commitment, and he must be there. Besides, he will receive a handsome fee for the speech, which is necessary to supplement his congressional pay. After a few more words are exchanged, the lobbyist asks the congressman what it is worth to be sure he is present for the vote. The congressman points out, first of all, that he must consider his speaking fee. The lobbyist offers to cover the fee in an immediate campaign contribution. The congressman points out that the group

**BOX 6–7
Cash Buys
"Personal
Relationships"
with Congress—
and Perhaps More**

. . . the notion of purchasing access—or the illusion of access—to power isn't new in Washington.

The current crop of fund-raising endeavors is illustrative. Sen. [John] Heinz [chairman of the Republican Senatorial Campaign Committee] is offering "personal relationships" with Republican Senators to donors of at least $1,000. These contributors are promised "give and take" meetings at private buffets; dinners and cocktail parties; a "confidential" telephone number providing a "clear channel" of communication to every GOP Senator, and "substantive information" about what is going on in Congress.

Sen. Heinz says his fund-raising is entirely proper. People donate not in quest of political favors, he says, but because they want to elect Republicans. "I'm happy to say that our committee has an exemplary record of compliance with the federal election laws," he says, "and since our contributions are pooled, no candidate or senator is beholden" to any donor.

Mr. Heinz might be right. The language of political solicitation is alive with hints of influential access—but lacking in promises of tangible results. For instance, $1,000 contributors to the GOP senatorial campaign become members of the Inner Circle, a new organization designed—rather vaguely— "to give members access on a face-to-face basis with every Republican in the U.S. Senate."

Inner Circle membership includes the right to "advise us about important issues," promises Mr. Heinz. Bigger donors get bigger access. Donors pledging $5,000 a year already have dined at the homes of five GOP senators. The lesser contributors, down to $10 or $100, may have to content themselves with periodic newsletters from the senatorial committee. . . .

—*Wall Street Journal*, August 6, 1980.

is also paying his first-class travel expenses, and that this trip is not one of those allotted to him each year by Congress to return to his constituency. The lobbyist will also include this amount, and perhaps a little more, in the campaign contribution. "Well, I don't know," replies the congressman. "Those boys mean an awful lot to me and they've been counting on this . . ." By the time the conversation ends, of course, the congressman has agreed to be present for the vote. The conversation may have taken several other turns; the congressman might point out that he expects a hard re-election fight. Yet no bribery has taken place;

only a legal campaign contribution has been made. One question remains: Did the congressman actually have a speaking engagement?[5]

A major goal of lobbyists is to make Congress members feel indebted to them. Charles Peters writes about one of the more convincing tactics with this aim:

> Suppose you are elected to Congress and you are invited to dinner by a clever lobbyist. You will find that as soon as you walk into his living room and the introductions begin, you are meeting one person after another who can be valuable to your career. Because you are also likely to be valuable to them, friendships will develop. And in the long run the friendships formed in these social situations can be a powerful force in decision making. . . .[6]

None of these explanations of lobbying, unfortunately, can convey the multitude of subtleties and nuances found in this art; but a skilled lobbyist—and many of them are former members of Congress or former government officials knowledgeable in the ways of Washington—can have a profound effect on the ebb and flow of legislation. Even the most innocent of favors provided by such people can touch upon important law- and policymaking processes.

FOR FURTHER READING

BARONE, MICHAEL J., et al. *Almanac of American Politics 1982.* New York: Dutton, 1981. Detailed guide to Congress published every two years.

DODD, LAWRENCE C., and BRUCE I. OPPENHEIMER, eds. *Congress Reconsidered,* 2nd ed. Washington: Congressional Quarterly Press, 1981. Up-to-date set of readings on various aspects of Congress.

DONNER, FRANK J. *The Un-Americans.* New York: Ballantine Books, 1961. Traces early history of, and problems with, the House Un-American Activities Committee.

FENNO, RICHARD F., JR., *Congressmen in Committees.* Boston: Little, Brown, 1973. A detailed look at the functioning of the committee system and the seniority system.

FENNO, RICHARD F., JR., *Home Style: House Members in Their Districts.* Boston: Little, Brown, 1978. A treatment of this vital aspect of a Congress member's political life.

GREEN, MARK J., JAMES M. FALLOWS, and DAVID R. ZWICK. *Who Runs Congress? The President, Big Business, or You?* New York: Bantam, 1972. Naderite view of Congress; very critical of its operations and makes some telling points.

JACOBSON, GARY C. *Money in Congressional Elections.* New Haven: Yale University Press, 1980. Up-to-date treatment of an all-important factor.

JEWELL, MALCOLM E., and SAMUEL C. PATTERSON. *The Legislative Process in the United States,* 3rd ed. New York: Random House, 1977. Derives generalizations from comparative study of the U.S. Congress with state legislatures.

[5]Conversation with a member of the staff of Congress, August 1980.
[6]Charles Peters, *How Washington Really Works* (Reading, Mass. Addison-Wesley, 1980), p. 6.

KINGDOM, JOHN W. *Congressmen's Voting Decisions*. New York: Harper & Row, 1981. Uses interviews to analyze the impact of interest groups, parties, and various political actors.

MAYHEW, DAVID R. *Congress: The Electoral Connection*. New Haven: Yale University Press, 1976. Makes effective use of comparisons with the British Parliament as well as use of both behavioral and phenomenological approaches.

OLESZEK, WALTER J. *Congressional Procedures and the Policy Process*. Washington: Congressional Quarterly Press, 1978. Detailed examination of procedural aspects of congressional action.

ORFIELD, GARY. *Congressional Power: Congress and Social Change*. New York: Harcourt Brace Jovanovich, 1975. Argues that the "passing of Congress" as a powerful force in government is a premature assessment.

RIEGLE, DONALD. *O Congress*. New York: Popular Library, 1972. Many members of Congress decide to write about their experiences; of this genre, this is one of the better and more interesting books.

SCHWAB, LARRY M. *Changing Patterns of Congressional Politics*. New York: Van Nostrand, 1980. Descriptive treatment that emphasizes great changes in Congress in the 1970s.

TAYLOR, TELFORD. *Grand Inquest*. New York: Da Capo, 1974. First published 1955. Underscores problems and dangers of congressional investigations.

WILSON, WOODROW. *Congressional Government*. New York: Meridian Books, 1956. Originally published 1855. Landmark in the study of Congress that is of important historical interest.

The Presidency 7

President Jimmy Carter saw a mouse running across the floor of his study one evening in 1977. The General Services Administration, which is charged with the care of federal buildings, was informed and the mouse was removed. Several weeks later, a second mouse was discovered, but this one had climbed inside a wall of the Oval Office and died there. The president, who was scheduled to greet some foreign dignitaries in his office, found the smell distressing. Once again the General Services Administration was notified and asked to act quickly. The GSA explained that it had exterminated all of the White House mice after the first call and, therefore, the new mouse must have originated on the grounds outside. This mouse, said the GSA, was the responsibility of the Interior Department, which had jurisdiction over the grounds. The Interior Department disagreed. Because the dead mouse was actually found *inside* the White House, it explained, it was clearly the GSA's problem. The angry president summoned officials from both agencies and complained that he could not "even get a damn mouse out of my office." An interagency task force was then established to remove the mouse.[1]

This incident, though surely amusing, underscores the schizophrenic quality of the American presidency. The office commands the most awe in the American system, perhaps in the Western world. It is to all appearances at the top of the pyramid of American power. It is the center of our national security and strategic planning. The president is described by the Constitution, statutes, textbooks, and the mass media as the Head of State, Commander in Chief, Chief Diplomat, Voice of the People, Chief Executive, and Number One News Maker. But he has trouble ridding his office of mice.

[1] Philippa Strum, *Presidential Power and American Democracy*, 2nd ed. (Santa Monica, Calif.: Goodyear, 1979), p. 80.

More seriously, the presidency is the American political system's central institutional paradox, the point at which all its most crucial contradictions come together. Whereas the courts participate in important ways in the national myth, their ideological function is clear and overriding: to maintain the legal framework that contains us all. And whereas Congress also participates in the national myth, especially in the Social Democratic vision of articulating the will of the people, its ideological function is clear and overriding: to harmonize the diverse claims of competing interests. But with the presidency, myth and ideology meet head-on, creating both paradox and ambiguity. At every turn the nation's highest office is bound up in the myth of America's greatness, vitality, and forward thrust. All presidents, but especially those who have just taken office, talk of purpose, growth, and progress. Every occupant of the office, even when first setting out on the long campaign trail toward achieving it, is overwhelmed by a national need to have him celebrate the myth, regenerate it, and proclaim it anew. The national myth imputes responsibilities, powers, and every kind of hope to the lonely occupant of the presidential office. Then in ideological practice, much of this mythic power drains away. In the day-to-day cut and thrust, deal and wheel, of Washington's politics, the president must scramble constantly from a position of real political weakness to maintain his stature and authority (see Box 7–1). Beneath the façade of his mythic power, his control over the bureaucracy is loosened, his relations with Congress become episodic and competitive, and he must pick and pursue his objectives with care. Even then, he may not be successful. In historical perspective, the record of almost every American president contains a sense of limitation and incompleteness, if not tragedy and failure. The presidency of Lyndon Johnson is a case in point. Taking office in an atmosphere of goodwill because of the assassination of President Kennedy, his early tenure in the White House was marked by reports and articles lauding his grasp of power realities (see Box 7–2). By 1968, the great disruptions produced by the Vietnam War in America's political life had taken their toll, causing him to forgo seeking another term.

In the language we have been developing in this book, the paradox of the American presidency can be stated in these terms:

In the nation's legitimizing Social Democratic myth, and especially in its doctrine of separation of powers, the president is a heroic leader of the whole people and the chief articulator of their will and their needs. In this role, the president appears to be a locus of power.

In the ideological practice of the nation's Liberal Democratic traditions, the president is but one baron among many, assigned by mixed government theory to the special and limited functions of representing

BOX 7–1
On the Presidency

The President must possess a wide range of abilities: to lead, to persuade, to inspire trust, to attract men of talent, to unite. These abilities must reflect a wide range of characteristics: courage, vision, integrity, intelligence, warmth, openness, personality, tenacity, energy, determination, drive, perspicacity, idealism, thirst for information, penchant for fact, presence of conscience, comprehension of people, and enjoyment of life—plus all the other, nobler virtues ascribed to George Washington under God.

—Nelson A. Rockefeller, quoted by Thomas E. Cronin, *The State of the Presidency* (Boston: Little, Brown, 1975), p. 31.

At both a ceremonial and a political level, we treat our President like a King; in so doing, we have destroyed something basic in the American democratic ideal. . . .

—Philippa Strum, "A Symbiotic Attack on the Imperial Presidency," in *The Presidency Reappraised,* Thomas E. Cronin and Rexford G. Tugwell, eds. (New York: Praeger, 1977), p. 249.

Those who cherish Gilbert and Sullivan will remember Pooh-Bah, the "particularly haughty and exclusive person" in *The Mikado* who filled the offices of "First Lord of the Treasury, Lord Chief Justice, Commander-in-Chief, Lord High Admiral, Master of the Buckhounds, Groom of the Back Stairs, Archbishop of Titipu, and Lord Mayor, both acting and elect." We chuckle at the fictitious Pooh-Bah; we can only wonder at the real one that history has made of the American President. He has at least three jobs for every one of Pooh-Bah's, and they are not performed at the flick of a lacquered fan.

—Clinton Rossiter, *The American Presidency* (New York: Time Books, 1960), p. 2.

the nation abroad, wielding the power of commander in chief of the armed forces, and contributing as best he can to managing the conflicts between the interests represented in Congress. In these roles, the president seems almost always destined to watch his mythic powers drift away and become fragmented among other centers of power and influence in Washington and the country at large.

**BOX 7–2
Presidential
Strength—Asset or
Liability?**

Lyndon Johnson seemed in those first few months to be always in motion, running, doing, persuading; if later much of the nation, bitter over its seemingly unscheduled and unchartered journey into Southeast Asia, turned on him and remembered his years with distaste, it was grateful for him then, and with good reason. His mandate seemed to be to hold the country together, to continue to exhort from those around him their best, to heal wounds and divisions. Kennedy had been the man who experimented, who ventured into new areas, civil rights, and in so doing caused division and pain. He had jarred our nerves in taking us places we had not intended to go; now Johnson would heal not just the pain caused by the assassination but the tensions caused in the venturesome days of some of the Kennedy policies. The healer. If later one of the Johnson qualities which caused doubts among the nation's critics was his force, the very *abundance* of it—the great capacity to plead, to bully, to beg, to implore, the capacity to manipulate them to what he considered his interest and the nation's interest—in those early days he was much hailed for it. He was not berated for being a manipulator then, that term would come later. His ability to drive men to a program and policy beyond what they themselves considered wise was considered a national asset, since the men he was manipulating were largely old tired conservative Southern congressmen who headed committees and thus blocked progress. A powerful Presidency was still considered very desirable in those days; the problem was seen as too much power in the Congress and too little in the executive branch, which was exactly the way that man of the Congress recently transferred to the executive office, Lyndon B. Johnson, felt.

—David Halberstam, *The Best and the Brightest* (New York: Random House, 1969), p. 369.

The Presidency: Tradition and Constitutional Position

The constitutionally assigned powers of the president are slim indeed. Article II states that the "executive Power" of the government "shall be vested" in the president and charges that "he shall take Care that the Laws be faithfully executed," but these general assignments are not detailed. This same article names the president commander in chief of the

BOX 7–3
**A Minority Always
Elects Our
Presidents**

The electoral college system sets up an indirect method of electing our presidents. It is therefore criticized on the ground that we should have a "popular" (direct) election. Never, however, has a majority of U.S. citizens elected a president. Here is the record since 1828:

Year	Winning Candidate	Percentage of Total Vote	Percentage of Voting-Age Population
1828	Andrew Jackson	56.0	12.4
1832	Andrew Jackson	56.5	11.6
1836	Martin Van Buren	50.8	11.4
1840	William Henry Harrison	52.9	16.9
1844	James Polk	49.5	15.1
1848	Zachary Taylor	47.3	13.5
1852	Franklin Pierce	50.6	13.8
1856	James Buchanan	45.3	13.8
1860	Abraham Lincoln	39.8	12.5
1864	Abraham Lincoln	55.0	13.4
1868	Ulysses Grant	52.8	16.7
1872	Ulysses Grant	55.7	17.8
1876	Rutherford Hayes	47.9	17.8
1880	James Garfield	48.3	17.5
1884	Grover Cleveland	48.5	17.3
1888	Benjamin Harrison	47.9	17.4
1892	Grover Cleveland	46.1	16.1
1896	William McKinley	51.1	18.8
1900	William McKinley	51.7	17.6
1904	Theodore Roosevelt	56.4	16.8
1908	William Taft	51.6	15.4
1912	Woodrow Wilson	41.9	11.7
1916	Woodrow Wilson	49.3	15.8
1920	Warren Harding	60.4	25.6
1924	Calvin Coolidge	54.0	23.7
1928	Herbert Hoover	58.1	30.1
1932	Franklin Roosevelt	57.4	30.1
1936	Franklin Roosevelt	60.8	34.6
1940	Franklin Roosevelt	54.7	32.2
1944	Franklin Roosevelt	53.4	29.9
1948	Harry Truman	49.6	25.3
1952	Dwight Eisenhower	55.1	34.0
1956	Dwight Eisenhower	57.4	34.1
1960	John Kennedy	49.7	31.2
1964	Lyndon Johnson	61.1	37.8
1968	Richard Nixon	43.4	26.4
1972	Richard Nixon	60.7	33.7
1976	Jimmy Carter	50.1	27.2
1980	Ronald Reagan	52.4	27.2

armed forces, ostensibly grants him the role of the nation's chief diplomat, gives him a measure of control over the major executive departments, and allows him ("as he shall judge necessary and expedient") a leadership role in the affairs of Congress. But even when the last of these powers is buttressed by the veto power granted him in Article I, Section 7, what the Constitution assigns him does not add up to anything approaching the powers of Congress, for example.

Tradition growing out of the continuous experience of the political process has made the presidency what it is today. The process began with the inauguration of George Washington, whom the Founders assumed would be the first president, with his great dignity and glacial deportment. What they did not foresee was that when Washington attempted to govern through the Senate, regarding that body almost as an executive council, he was rebuffed and forced to operate the presidency as a wholly separate entity in the government. This independence of the presidency from especially the Senate was continued by John Adams and then enormously reinforced by Thomas Jefferson, who became a political power in his own right on the basis of what was at least the semblance of a personal political party. By the time of Andrew Jackson's "democratic revolution," the presidency was a far larger political presence in the American system of government than its constitutional mandate had seemed to imply. Abraham Lincoln demonstrated what that political presence could become in a time of crisis, but it was Woodrow Wilson who reflected that the presidential office can be as big as the man in it wants to make it.

Institutionalization of the Presidency

Personal qualities—personality, talent, energy—are important in determining the stamp each president puts on the office. But those qualities can grow only on the expectations that the American people have invested in the office. Once it became clear that the Electoral College was an anachronism and that the president was to be elected in a popu-

BOX 7–4
A Cynical View of Presidential Leadership?

If our system does not choose "the best man," its winnowings tend to produce an *appropriate* man to lead us, one amenable to the merchandizing trends of the moment; one who, if not really answering the needs of popular symbolism, can nevertheless be given the requisite garb of relevance. He becomes our "man of the moment" by accomodating the moment.

—Garry Wills, *Nixon Agonistes: The Crisis of the Self-Made Man* (Boston: Houghton Mifflin, 1969), p. 535.

lar state-by-state contest, the presidency became the focal point of America's Social Democratic enthusiasms as the only nationally elected office of the government (save the vice-presidency).

The modern presidential election campaign with its paraphernalia of television, endless primaries, and national conventions, and the long trek through the summer and into the fall of speeches, rallies, debates, and "media events," is the embodiment of America's Social Democratic myth. But the myth of presidential greatness has also developed over the years through a steadily enlarged and increasingly complex set of staff operations, including those of the White House and the much larger unit of which it is a part, the Executive Office of the President.

This process has been called the "institutionalization of the presidency." Washington started out with a private secretary whom he paid out of his own pocket. Later presidents took to surrounding themselves with a group of private aides and advisers. From the time it was built, the White House has served both as a home for the president and his family and as the headquarters of presidential operations. In the twentieth century, this process of institutionalization has been formally organized in a series of steps authorized and generously financed by Congress. Now housed not only in the East and West wings and subterranean depths of the White House itself but also in the two massive Executive Office buildings nearby, the Executive Office of the President has become virtually a government within the government, with tens of thousands of employees. The most important units of the Executive Office of the President include the following.

The White House Office. Established in 1939 in the wake of the huge government expansion under Franklin Roosevelt's New Deal, it includes half a dozen or more assistants to the president who are hired and assigned functions at the discretion of the president. These usually include a chief of staff, press secretary, national security adviser, congressional liaison officer, appointments secretary, and other officials. Each of these persons has a staff of assistants and secretaries. The total personnel for the White House office usually exceeds 1,500. These people are indispensable for organizing the president's work and managing the flow of information, visitors, and meetings. Many observers have noted that the White House office has a built-in tendency to insulate the president and create for him an unreal sense of his own significance and that of his policies and program. This natural tendency of all large staff organizations seems to be particularly reinforced when a new arrival enters the Oval Office without a background of Washington experience. The staff, under these circumstances, is often as out of touch with political realities as their leader. The Carter administration is perhaps the most notable recent example of this, but the Reagan administration is affected by it as well.

President Ronald Reagan's White House staff chiefs: James Baker, Edwin Meese III, and Michael Deaver (Photo by Bill Fitz-patrick, The White House).

The Office of Management and Budget (OMB).   Originally the Bureau of the Budget, this office was inspired by British practice. Its job is to collect, collate, and tailor the spending plans of all government departments in a single, coherent "executive budget" for presentation to Congress. The OMB was given its present title and expanded functions in 1970 by President Nixon, who believed that harnessing all the departments to a single budget plan was not enough; he sought through this office to gain control over how the departments and bureaus actually spent the money they were allocated. But the history of the OMB is not one of thorough control of the budget process; experienced bureaucrats know how to deal with the OMB and to achieve their budget goals in spite of this appearance of close coordination.[2]

[2] See Chapter 9.

The National Security Council.   This body was created in 1947 in the wake of World War II and the difficulties encountered in trying to coordinate the policies and operations of the diplomatic and military services and their intelligence gathering departments. The debacle at Pearl Harbor seemed a symbol of all this. The National Security Council seeks to coordinate defense and foreign policies in light of the best information gathered by the State and Defense Departments and the specialized intelligence agencies. Two of these specialized agencies, the Central Intelligence Agency (CIA) and the National Security Agency (NSA), are attached to and serve under the direction of the NSC. Formally, the NSC is composed of the president, vice-president, secretary of state, secretary of defense, secretary of treasury, and other officials whom the president may invite. These regularly include the chairman of the Joint Chiefs of Staff of the Armed Forces and the director of the CIA. As a matter of practice, the president's national security adviser also attends because he effectively runs the NSC with a large staff of advisers and assistants working out of the White House basement. This staff also runs the White House Situation Room, the emergency control headquarters equipped with advanced communications gear. This is the president's control center in times of crisis.

The Council of Economic Advisers.   Like the National Security Council, this body dates to the period just after World War II. Composed of three professional economists and their staffs, it was created by the Employment Act of 1946 to provide the president at all times with expert advice on the state of the economy and on long-term plans for ensuring steady prosperity. Over the years, its importance has varied considerably as its personnel changed, crises arose and subsided, and presidents heeded (or ignored) its suggestions. It seems to be relied upon as a professional perspective on the health of the economy, even though it is strongly biased toward the president's economic philosophy. And it is not the president's only source of economic advice. He also consults well-known private economists and officials of the Treasury, the Federal Reserve Board, and other agencies.

The Cabinet.   Often included in discussions of the Executive Office of the President, the Cabinet has no formal status. It is simply a meeting of the president and the heads of the major "line" departments—State, Treasury, Defense, Agriculture, Labor, Interior, and so forth—and such other presidential appointees as may by law have been accorded Cabinet status, such as the White House Chief of Staff, the Ambassador to the United Nations, and the OMB director. This body's existence and name is one more bit of evidence of the misplaced fascination of Americans with British procedures. The British Cabinet as a collective body is the central executive agency of that nation's government. The American

**BOX 7–5
A Day in the Life of
the President**

4:30 a.m. The President, having trouble sleeping, gets up and does some paper work. Goes back to bed about 6.

8 a.m. Reagan receives wake-up call from White House switchboard.

8:41 a.m. Senior aides James Baker, Edwin Meese and Michael Deaver join the President in the family quarters to discuss the day's schedule.

9:08 a.m. Reagan walks from second-floor residence down to the State Dining Room for breakfast with 38 Democratic lawmakers who backed his budget cuts.

10:15 a.m. The President goes to the Oval Office for daily national-security briefing. Among those attending are Vice President Bush and National-Security Adviser Richard Allen. Meeting concludes at 10:34.

10:37 a.m. At his desk, Reagan is briefed on the day's developments by sides Baker, Meese, Deaver, Max Friedersdorf, David Gergen and Larry Speakes. At 10:46, the meeting ends.

10:50 a.m. *U.S. News & World Report* editors interview the President.

11:09 a.m. White House advisers Melvin Bradley and Thaddeus Garrett enter Oval Office to prepare Reagan for meeting with NAACP officials Benjamin Hooks and Margaret Bush Wilson.

11:13 a.m. Hooks and Wilson begin discussions with the President. Also present are Vice President Bush and White House aide Elizabeth Dole. Meeting ends at 11:59.

12:01 p.m. Reagan poses for photographs in Oval Office with new U.S. Ambassadors Arthur Burns, Maxwell Rabb and Ernest Preeg and their families.

12:15 p.m. Ocean explorer Jacques Cousteau enters for lunch with Reagan, Deaver and White House aide Richard Darman on patio outside the Oval Office.

1:31 p.m. Treasury Secretary Donald Regan briefs the President in the Oval Office on tax developments in Congress.

1:39 p.m. Reagan walks across the hall to the Roosevelt Room to meet with 11 Republican members of the Senate Finance Committee. Meeting ends at 2:01.

2:08 p.m. The President enters the Cabinet Room for meeting with the cabinet council on commerce and trade. Session ends at 2:27.

BOX 7–5
A Day in the Life of
the President
(Continued)

2:34 p.m. The Chief Executive convenes a meeting of the entire cabinet. It concludes at 3:38.

3:46 p.m. The President goes to the State Dining Room for meeting with the Presidential Advisory Committee on Federalism. Session ends at 4:24 and Reagan returns to the Oval Office.

4:33 p.m. Personnel Adviser E. Pendleton James enters Oval Office to discuss presidential appointments.

4:48 p.m. CIA Director William Casey enters for meeting with the President.

5:09 p.m. Reagan goes to Rose Garden reception for 175 teenage Republicans.

5:16 p.m. The President returns to the Oval Office to do some paper work.

5:51 p.m. Reagan enters the East Room for a reception in honor of 190 House Republicans.

6:12 p.m. The President goes back to the family quarters, has dinner alone, telephones Mrs. Reagan in California, catches up on some reading and retires at 11:15 p.m.

—*U.S. News and World Report,* July 6, 1981, p. 14–20.

Cabinet plays no such role. Newly installed presidents, with a fanfare of talk about "collective leadership" and "team management," begin their term with regularly scheduled meetings with their Cabinet. With surprisingly rapid adaptation to the realities of Washington's fragmented government, however, presidents soon dispense with these regular meetings (see Box 7–6). Presidents quickly become embroiled in particular problems or crises that affect only one or another aspect of their administration while the several secretaries become increasingly testy about having to listen to the other secretaries talk about problems that do not concern them. With no constitutionally supported function and with little political rationale, Cabinet meetings soon become hardly more than infrequently held ceremonial events.

In addition to the formal units listed above, the Executive Office of the President contains a variety of other offices, councils, and interagency committees, some of them temporary and some more or less permanent. The Domestic Council seeks to parallel the concerns of the National Security Council but on domestic issues. The Council on Environmental Quality, the Office of Emergency Preparedness, and

**BOX 7–6
Prime Minister
Reagan?**

WASHINGTON—. . . One morning last week, a visiting British member of Parliament remarked that Ronald Reagan struck him, not as the "king of Capitol Hill," perhaps, but at least as prime minister. Barely three hours later, Rep. Tony Coelho, D-Calif., told the House Democratic caucus that the main reason for their miseries in the first eight months of the year was that "the Republicans basically have moved to a parliamentary system, with all the discipline that involves."

If both a visiting parliamentarian and a leader of the opposition . . . can see Reagan in prime ministerial guise, then it might behoove even the dullest columnist to examine the proposition.

I have done so, and my conclusion is that thinking of Reagan's government in parliamentary terms does give you some interesting insights—but it is basically a mischievous notion.

The distinction between a presidential and a prime ministerial system of leadership is simple. . . . The prime minister is first among equals in a Cabinet system, sharing collective responsibility with cabinet colleagues for the formulation of national policy. Cabinet policy becomes government policy through the ratification device of a disciplined party majority in the Parliament; if discipline fails, the government fails, and everyone faces the voters. It is that simple.

The president, on the other hand, has sole responsibility for the formulation of executive branch policy. But his ability to make his policy government policy depends entirely on his political skills in persuading the independent legislators and the often recalcitrant interest group-bureaucratic alliances to go along with his plans.

In those stark and oversimplified terms, it is easy to see why both the British M.P. and Coelho might independently remark on the "prime ministerial quality" of Reagan's presidency. Clearly, he is sharing the responsibility for basic policy formulation with this Cabinet. He said he would have "Cabinet government," and he is doing so. . . .

. . . the House Republican party-unity score this year was an extraordinary 79 per cent, higher than in any year in the 1960s or 1970s and 10 points higher than the GOP average for those two decades.

So both Coelho and the British M.P. are right—in one way.

BOX 7–6
Prime Minister
Reagan?
(Continued)

But they are also fundamentally wrong because the Reagan-Republican, prime ministerial-parliamentary system is purely a political artifact, with nothing to sustain it in the written or unwritten constitution of this land, as there is in Great Britain. . . .

[The] bonds to his cabinet and his party in Congress . . . can be sustained only if his economic program surmounts the current wave of skepticism and his leadership continues to be proved in the budget and foreign-policy tests that lie . . . ahead. . . .

—David Broder, *Washington Post*, September 22, 1981.

other agencies round out the EOP, completing the image of it as virtually a government within a government.

A Presidential Perspective

The significance of the Executive Office of the President is twofold. First, its physical presence, size, and complexity has shifted the view of American government held by most scholars, the media, and the textbooks to a decisively presidential perspective. However important the courts, Congress, or political parties may be, virtually all observers appear to agree that the president and the office he occupies are the heart of American politics and government. This perspective is illustrated by Figure 7–1. Notice how the presidential mythic magnetism attracts a vast aura of power and responsibility from the electorate through the figure's concentric rings. But also notice how this power gravitates outward to what on the ideological side are the many power centers of American politics—the interest and other clientele groups on the figure's periphery. In this way, we seek to illustrate both the mythic and ideological dimensions of the presidential perspective of American politics and government that all of us seem to share.

The second general significance of the Executive Office of the President is the way in which it illustrates the ambiguous quality of presidential power. Viewed in one way, the office is a monument to presidential authority and responsibility. But looked at more broadly as an element in the totality of the political process, it becomes strangely paradoxical. Appearances of great strength become evidence of sustained weakness. New presidents dominate the TV screens, but usually in a short time, their press secretaries develop sharply confrontational relations with reporters. It has become almost routine for the secretary of state to develop an acrimoniously competitive relationship with the president's national security adviser or the secretary of defense. The

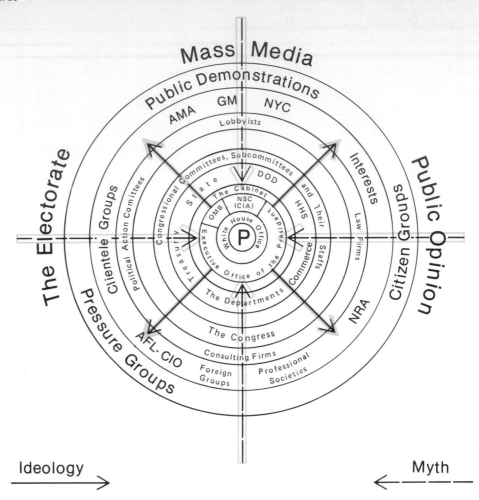

*Figure 7–1.
American government in
presidential perspective.*

Ideology →

Myth ←

director of the Office of Management and Budget, after perhaps a string of initial successes with Congress and the departments, finds that he has lost control of his spending goals. These are not just the normal troubles of any power holder in any political system coming to grips with the realities of office work. They go well beyond this to deepseated tendencies of the presidential office in the context of American political life.

The various units of the Executive Office are not only monuments to presidential authority. More immediately, they symbolize the nation's expectations about what its mythic hero, the American president, can and should do. Over the years, he has been given all the pieces of the Executive Office one by one, because the nation, wanting certain objectives achieved, looks to him to achieve them. But the very fact that he needs all this help points to the underlying possibility that even with this assistance, the goals may still be beyond his reach.

The Executive Office of the President and its accompanying bureaucracy represents not only the institutionalization of the presidency but also the institutionalization of the nation's *expectations* for the presidency. In this light, what it appears to do is more important than what it does—or even what it tries and fails to do.

The Mythic Role of the President

**Presidential
Personalities and
Styles**

Myth legitimizes and, in its most general dimensions, the mythic role of the presidency in the American political system is to persuade the American people to believe in themselves and in their government, to give them a sense of unity, identity, purpose, and strength. To a very considerable degree, the president undertakes this role through the force of his own personality and the symbols with which he can surround himself.

In the mass media age, presidents seek to project a personal image. Even before television, Franklin D. Roosevelt, considered by many scholars to have been America's most talented and accomplished president, cultivated a powerful and charismatic image, thereby setting a pattern for his successors (see Box 7–7). With unusual skill, FDR identified himself with both sides of the power equation, the aristocratic and the plebeian. As a Roosevelt he was born to the aristocratic manner and emphasized this by sporting a long cigarette holder, pince-nez glasses, a distinctly upper-class accent, and a waggish smile. At the same time he was warm and familiar to millions, associated himself with the concerns of the poor, and made no secret of the pain and disability he suffered from a bout with infantile paralysis in his early manhood in which he permanently lost the use of his legs.

None of FDR's successors seem to have matched his artistry, but not for lack of trying or lack of professional help. Truman was plain-speaking, earthy and blunt, and took famous morning constitutionals. Eisenhower was a father image with a towering war record and a broad appeal. Kennedy had his war record, too, but also an interest in the arts and a beautiful, aristocratic wife. Johnson cultivated his Texas mannerisms and his reputation as an effective politician. It is perhaps significant that neither Nixon nor Carter was able to project such distinctive images. In Ronald Reagan, the American people have a professional actor trained in television, grade B movies, and promotional films to project himself as an amiable, trustworthy fellow whom we can trust to think and feel "just like you and me."

In the end, the key to presidential leadership is popular trust. Nixon's days as a commanding figure in the White House were clearly numbered when the storm against him forced him to protest, "I am not a

**BOX 7–7
Our "Show Biz"
Presidency**

Patricia Roberts Harris, former Secretary of Health and Human Services and former Secretary of Housing and Urban Development, made these remarks in a 1979 address to the John F. Kennedy School of Government in Cambridge, Massachusetts:

"I was once asked by a European prime minister why Americans now seem bent upon destroying their Presidents. I replied, 'Because Clark Gable is dead!'

Perhaps you consider that response frivolous, but an argument can be made that whatever may have defined the American national character prior to the Depression of the 1930s, films made in the United States during and immediately after the Depression provided heroes and heroines through whom personal frustration could be vented and individual hopes, aspirations and fantasies realized. . . .

The nation was its movie stars and we defined ourselves by our matinee idols. We projected onto them our fantasies—our needs—our aspirations. They were larger than life, and they communicated the individualization of values that we seemed to need.

Concurrently, Franklin Roosevelt, my selection as the best intuitive politician ever to reside at 1600 Pennsylvania Avenue, used the newsreel and the radio to enter our mind space along with Gable and Lombard. . . .

I can see it now. Show biz and politics. On the same screen; on the same playbill—larger than life. Bigger than dreams. Before your eyes. So very real, yet so far away. How inspired, how classic it seems to me now in this Age of Video Excesses. . . .

But it was Jack Kennedy who moved the screamers from the spotlighted movie premieres and Frank Sinatra concerts to the political campaign trail.

With Jack Kennedy, Hollywood came to Washington, and Hollywood came because Kennedy was the star.

The process started by Roosevelt was completed.

We no longer needed to look toward the cinema to project our fantasies. Instead, we could expect the miracles of our fantasies to be accomplished by the leaders of public life—especially the occupant of the White House."

—*Wall Street Journal*, November 18, 1980.

crook." The mythic demand is that the president must radiate trust-worthiness so the people will join together in one nationhood.

This personal appeal to the people in their nationhood is magnified by the symbols that the president can gather around himself. These include not just the seal of the office, the protocols, and the White House itself, but also the mythic aspects of many of his official duties, especially his functions as commander in chief, chief diplomat, and head of state. The last of these is almost purely ceremonial, but it shows the president speaking and acting for the whole nation, even when he is only greeting delegations of Girl Scouts, lending his name to a Red Cross drive, or attending the funeral of a foreign statesman. The roles of commander in chief and chief diplomat have considerable substantive content, as we will see, but when the president flies to some distant capital in Air Force One, his personal plane, or is seen reviewing troops or inspecting a federal facility, his stature as mythic leader of the people cannot fail to increase. Knowing this well, presidents in recent decades—especially when other matters are not going well—have surrounded themselves with the panoply of military aides and advisers, parades, and trips abroad.

The Symbols of the Presidency

President Ronald Reagan visits flood-fighters in Fort Wayne, Indiana, March, 1982 (The Journal-Gazette, Fort Wayne, Indiana).

BOX 7–8
The Revised View
of Eisenhower:
New Myths for
Old?

Dwight D. Eisenhower has never been a favorite president of political scientists. If they have discussed his presidency at all they have generally used it as an example of how the job ought not be done. The standard scholarly view has been that the Eisenhower years were an era in which the United States "marked time" and in which the president was, at best, an aging, avuncular hero who, in the words of one political scientist, "reigned more than he ruled." In fact, . . . many political scientists have treated Eisenhower as someone who had "nothing between his ears but golf balls." Now, however, an era of Eisenhower revisionism may have begun. Fred I. Greenstein . . . of . . . Princeton University [has said] that several factors have contributed to a revised and less negative view of the Eisenhower presidency. Among them:

—Nostalgia for the 1950's as a pleasant, uncomplicated era.

—The increasing difficulty that scholars and others are having in finding anything to "celebrate about the five presidents who have succeeded Eisenhower."

—The neo-conservative movement, which has reexamined and generally praised substantive aspects of the Eisenhower Presidency.

In addition to the general reasons, Mr. Greenstein said that his research at the Eisenhower Library in Abilene, Kan., had produced a more scholarly basis for a revisionist view of the Eisenhower Presidency. "Great volumes of primary source material have become available since the mid-1970's," Mr. Greenstein said. That material . . . shows Eisenhower not simply as the hero of World War II, but as a "skilled political actor" who engaged in abstract thinking about presidential leadership. . . . for instance, Eisenhower regularly dictated "intricate memoranda to himself in an effort to think through issues." "In this disposition to express himself on paper, Eisenhower did evoke general propositions. One cannot say that he had a wholly integrated view of the presidency," Mr. Greenstein said, but he did propound coherent theories of leadership. These theories stressed a style of leadership that relied upon "deliberation and patience, and on achieving political goals through existing institutions." . . . Eisenhower did not believe that there were "universal principles of leadership, applicable in all circumstances." Instead, Eisenhower

BOX 7–8
The Revised View
of Eisenhower:
New Myths for
Old?
(Continued)

adopted an "interactionist" approach which recognized that specific rules require different leadership styles and that specific individuals have different capacities for leadership. . . . Eisenhower's theories led him to follow a "hidden-hand approach" to leadership in which he worked through intermediaries and played down his "direct influence on events." . . . As an example, Mr. Greenstein noted that during the McCarthy era, Eisenhower never mentioned the Communist-hunting senator from Wisconsin by name, but "pulled many strings which contributed to his censure."

—Malcolm G. Scully, *Chronicle of Higher Education*, **19**, 1, 13 (September 10, 1979).

There is a grandeur in the presidential office, the man and his retinue in near-Byzantine splendor. What does it all cost? Unfortunately, we cannot be sure (see Box 7–9). Ultimately, all this grandeur rests upon two facts we have already mentioned: the president's powers are more political than constitutional; and he is the only nationally elected official except for the vice-president. In consequence, every president, however reluctant he may be, is compelled to move forward from his symbolic, or mythic, base and lead, or appear to lead, the nation in full view of the electorate. Whatever "leadership" may mean, presidents are expected to lead, and their failure to do this convincingly and consistently has often proved, in recent decades, to be their undoing.

The presidency, according to Theodore Roosevelt, is a "bully pulpit." The mantle of greatness from the past is in many ways a burden upon the shoulders of every modern president, urging him to speak out, to lead, to point the way for the rest of us. Washington, Jefferson, Lincoln, and Teddy Roosevelt pointed the way; that is why their heads have been carved into the side of a mountain in South Dakota. Beyond symbolizing national unity, modern presidents have sought to define the national purpose, to give the people a sense of dedication and zeal, to set the national agenda. Win or lose, presidents must fight in this mythic role. So FDR said we have a rendezvous with destiny and gave us the New Deal, Harry Truman gave us a Fair Deal, Eisenhower a Crusade for Freedom, Kennedy a New Frontier, and Johnson the Great Society. Even Richard Nixon talked for a while of the New American Revolution and Ronald Reagan of a New Beginning.

These are broadly stated dimensions of political leadership, but presidents are also expected to detail their objectives in the specific terms of legislative proposals to Congress. Though it is not well-recognized as

**BOX 7–9
The President's
Secret Fund**

WASHINGTON, June 13, 1981—A White House official has confirmed that Ronald Reagan has access to a secret military fund, reportedly used for years to finance Presidential perquisites, but the official says he swears that the President will not misuse it.

"My assurance is that there will be no abuse of the fund and that it will remain secret," said the aide, Edward V. Hickey, Jr., director of the White House military office.

In a book, "Breaking Cover," Bill Gulley, former director of the military office, said the multimillion-dollar fund was established in 1957 to build and maintain secret sites where the President could take cover during a military attack. The fund is controlled by the military office.

Mr. Gulley said several Presidents had used the fund to hide the use of taxpayer money to build such things as swimming pools and movie theaters.

Mr. Gulley maintained that because the fund was classified, Presidents could use it any way they wished and never be discovered.

"There were lots of reasons Presidents [used to] abused [sic] the fund," Mr. Gulley said. "In some cases it was a simple matter of getting the military to do and pay for something a President wanted, like the work that was done at the LBJ Ranch. In others, it was also a way of keeping what was being done and the extravagance of it a secret from Congress and the people.

"The temptation of a ready source of money with no strings attached—no questions to answer or explanations to make—is tremendous. Things you'd hesitate to do, or would never do if you had to account for them, seem OK when no one is looking."

But Mr. Hickey contended that during the Reagan Administration the fund would be used only for its official purpose. . . .

—Associated Press Report in *The New York Times*, June 14, 1981.

such, it seems clear that the president's involvement with the legislative process is as much a mythic role as anything else. The modern practice, spelled out in some instances by law, calls for the president, in the wake of his State of the Union address, to send Congress not only an executive budget but also a series of other messages and proposals for legislation ranging from sweeping changes in social policy to detailed requests for the sale of certain weapons to particular countries. These issues, in fact, were major concerns of the Reagan administration in its first years in office.

The executive budget is the most important item the president submits to Congress. Composing it consumes the time of the OMB's six hundred staff members throughout the year. Work on a new fiscal year budget begins as soon as the current one is completed, and budget planning regularly runs two or even three years in advance. Advised by the Council of Economic Advisers and other economic consultants, and guided by overall presidential philosophies and directives, the OMB lays down limits for the various departments, bureaus, and agencies and receives from them a constant flow of information about their financial plans and needs. This monumental effort culminates in the president's presentation of the budget to Congress each January. Although it is only a proposal that Congress will dispose of in its usual piecemeal fashion, it still goes to Capitol Hill with considerable fanfare backed by all the prestige the president can muster for the occasion. The budget is important because government spending, both in its overall amount and in its detailed characteristics, has a decisive impact on the economy: on the general level of employment, business activity, rate of inflation, and interest rates; on the shifting patterns of development among the various regions; and on various industries, labor forces, and economic classes of people. The budget presentation is, therefore, a signal oppor-

The Budget Process

**BOX 7–10
The President
Rallies the Country**

Hoover

Kennedy

Johnson

Nixon

BOX 7–10
**The President
Rallies the Country
(Continued)**

Herbert Hoover, State of the Union Message, December 2, 1930:

Economic depression cannot be cured by legislative action or executive pronouncement. Economic wounds must be healed by the action of the cells of the economic body—the producers and consumers themselves. Recovery can be expedited . . . by cooperative action. . . . cooperation requires that every individual should sustain faith and courage; that each shall maintain his self-reliance; that each and every one should search for methods of improving his business or service; that the vast majority whose income is unimpaired should not hoard. . . . that each should seek to assist his neighbors who may be less fortunate; that each industry should assist its own employees; that each community and each state should assume its full responsibilities for organization of employment and relief of distress with that sturdiness and independence which built a great nation.

John F. Kennedy, Yale Commencement Address, June 11, 1962:

There is a show in England called "Stop the World, I Want to Get Off." You have not chosen to exercise that option. You are part of the world and you must participate in these days of our years in the solution of the problems that pour upon us, requiring the most sophisticated and technical judgment; and as we work in consonance to meet the authentic problems of our times, we will generate a vision and an energy which will demonstrate anew to the world the superior vitality and the strength of the free society.

Lyndon B. Johnson on the Vietnam War, AFL-CIO Convention, December 12, 1967:

. . . I want all America to know that I am not going to be deterred. I am not going to be influenced. I am not going to be inflamed by a bunch of political, selfish men who want to advance their own interests. I am going to continue down the center of the road, doing my duty as I see it . . . regardless of my polls or regardless of the election. . . . Peace will come—I

**BOX 7–10
The President
Rallies the Country
(Continued)**

am convinced of that. But until peace does come, I will continue, with the support of our loyal, determined people, to hold the line that we have drawn against aggression—and to hold it firm and to hold it steady. In all that I do, I will be strengthened by the powerful testimony for freedom that you sons of labor have given here in this hall. You courageous men of labor have supported our fighting men every time they needed you. You have spoken as free men under fire must speak. Now, may all the world hear you. And may God bless you for what you have said and what you have done. . . .

Richard M. Nixon, Speech in San Clemente, California, August 24, 1972:

. . . He got up to the microphone and he said that he and his group were honored to play in the White House. Then he went on to say, "You know, I never thought it would happen." He said, "It's a long way from Watts to the White House." You know, he was right. But then I got up and I said, "You know you are right. It is a long way from Watts to the White House, but it is also a long way from Whittier to the White House." I just want to say, let's build a country in which our young people can grow up in peace. Let's build a country in which any young person, a boy or a girl, if he is an American, an American citizen, whatever his background, has a chance to go to the top. That is what America is all about. The American dream can never come true unless it has a possibility to come true in the lives of anyone who is an American citizen. That is what we believe in. That is what that "Four More Years" [Nixon's campaign slogan] is all about.

tunity for the president to display national leadership, and it is understandable that every modern president has accompanied his presentation with television broadcasts to the country, extended press conferences, and public urgings to Congress to follow his lead.

In 1974, Congress formally responded to presidential budget-making initiatives by establishing its own Budget Office to study and evaluate the assumptions and recommendations of the OMB. It also set up special budget committees in both houses to receive the president's most general proposals and to respond to them by accepting them, modifying them, or formulating broad new budgetary outlines. More significantly, it set deadlines by which it should have accepted general resolutions for budgetary limitations within which its various appropriations committees and subcommittees would have to work when creating or continuing programs and providing funds for them.

For some years, this effort of Congress to follow the president's lead in a comprehensive approach to the federal budget was something of a chimera. The whole exercise smacked strongly, both on the part of the president and the Congress, of mythic politics being played out primarily for symbolic effect. At the ideological level in Congress, various committees proved able to sidestep or ignore the requirement that they "reconcile" their figures with the general budget resolutions initiated by the special budget committees. They argued that their specialized jurisdictions were primary and they would not be dictated to by anyone—neither the president nor any "super" committees. As a result, Congress regularly had to amend its original budget resolutions, sometimes several times over.

Congress has also continued to make use of two other practices that play havoc with comprehensive efforts at budget-making. One is passing "continuing resolutions." When agreement cannot be reached on a new appropriations measure for a particular set of departments before the next fiscal year begins, Congress enables them to operate by passing a resolution continuing their previous budget in force. When the holdup is caused by an acutely sensitive issue such as federal funding for abortions, continuing resolutions can be strung out for several years.

Congress also makes periodic use of "supplementary" spending bills. After a fiscal year is underway, departments sometimes find themselves spending more rapidly than their original plans called for. Urged on by their affected clients and actively supported by especially interested members of Congress, these departments go begging to the relevant appropriations committees for more funds. As these supplementary funding bills come up at odd times and mostly one by one, they rarely receive much public attention and presidents as rarely are politically positioned to veto them.

In 1981, in an extraordinary display of presidential dominance of Congress built upon seemingly solid public support, a marvelously effective TV and press performance by the president, adroit maneuvering by his zealous OMB director, and direct lobbying by the president and his staff, President Reagan forced Congress to adopt a single comprehensive budget. This feat was all the more extraordinary because this package sharply reduced the growth rate in government spending and curtailed or eliminated programs in every sector of government save defense. All this was accomplished while President Reagan was in the midst of pushing for, and getting, a tax reduction program from Congress as comprehensive and wide-ranging as his budget. The mythic aspect of these victories must be borne in mind as well as their prag-

President Gerald Ford rings a bell to mark the 200th anniversary of the United States Government.

matic results. President Reagan was clearly a "winner," even though the Democratic version of the tax cut bill, for example, was not very different in its terms or substance.

It now appears clear that President Reagan and his allies had to pay a heavy ideological price for these mythic victories in the form of protection for special programs and tax breaks favored by powerful interest groups. The oil industry, for example, received major concessions, as did tobacco, sugar, and banking interests.

This remarkable experience underscored two general features of presidential leadership in the budget process. The broad agreement that President Reagan's 1981 victories were extraordinary made it clear that in the *normal* course of events, presidents present a single, comprehensive budget to Congress but then Congress, in its own time and in a piecemeal way, disposes of that budget as it chooses with the help of allies in the bureaucracy and the interest groups. More directly, President Reagan's early, impressive victories demonstrated how, on extraordinary occasions, an especially effective and newly elected (as well as media-sensitive) president can sway Congress into his mythic train for at least a period of time. In the past, Presidents Woodrow Wilson, Franklin Roosevelt, and Lyndon Johnson had similar periods of triumph. They unraveled soon enough, and President Reagan's budget policy was in serious trouble with Congress less than a year after his initial triumphs.

The president's primacy in foreign policy is rooted in the constitutional mandates that he has the power to make treaties, by and with the advice and consent of the Senate, and to send and receive ambassadors. These powers are buttressed by his role as commander in chief of the armed forces. We have already noticed at the institutional level the pairing of these two roles in the president's National Security Council. In pursuing these roles, presidents have acted vigorously, albeit often controversially. FDR maneuvered successfully to align American efforts decisively on the British side well before we entered World War II. When Lyndon Johnson wanted a free hand for his Vietnam policy, he engineered, drafted, received, and pocketed (to show personally to numerous subsequent visitors) the Gulf of Tonkin Resolution supporting his use of force, passed by the Senate in 1964. When Richard Nixon wished to open the door to relations with the People's Republic of China, after building much of his early career on his opposition to such

The Presidency and Foreign Policy

SANTA BARBARA, Calif., May 28—Calling the Federal budget process "the most irresponsible, Mickey Mouse arrangement that any governmental body ever practiced," President Reagan suggested today that it be abolished.

He offered no specific plan with which to replace the budget process, saying, "I think that some real solid thinking should be given now to a budgetary process that befits the great Government of a great nation. . . . It's called the President's budget, and yet there is nothing binding about it."

"It is submitted to the Congress and they don't even have to consider it," he continued. He added that Congress would "finally come up with a budget resolution which the President has no ability to veto."

—John Herbers, *The New York Times*, May 29, 1982.

**BOX 7–11
President
Denounces Budget
Process**

a move, he prepared in deepest secrecy and then undertook his dramatic visit to Peking. Perhaps the broadest definition of a foreign policy mandate ever set out by any president is in the inauguration speech of John F. Kennedy in 1961:

> Let every nation know, whether it wishes us well or ill, that we shall pay any price, bear any burden, meet any hardship, support any friend, oppose any foe to assure the survival and the success of liberty. This we pledge—and more.

This commitment, of course, is heavily larded with elements of myth.

In between these spectacular doings, American citizens see accounts and photographs in the press of their president journeying to foreign conferences, receiving visiting dignitaries, announcing executive agreements, and supervising the negotiation of treaties. All these stridings across the world stage are convincing demonstrations of a president in charge of the nation's international destiny. Obviously, these performances also contribute to the president's mythic stature as heroic leader of all the people.

The President's Ideological Role

The president is a hero in myth, but in the operative ideology of daily governance, the president is a much weaker figure, one of many barons. As a baron, his powers are essentially personal, episodic, and dependent upon the cooperation he can obtain from a host of other actors, most of whom are as independently situated as he is.

Richard Neustadt, who worked in the White House office, tells this anecdote about the last days of the Truman administration when it seemed apparent that General Dwight D. Eisenhower would win the upcoming election:

> In the early summer of 1952, before the heat of the campaign, President Truman used to contemplate the problems of the General-become-President should Eisenhower win the forthcoming election. "He'll sit here," Truman would remark (tapping his desk for emphasis), "and he'll say, 'Do this. Do that!' *And nothing will happen.* Poor Ike—it won't be a bit like the Army. He'll find it very frustrating."[3]

Most frustrating to Eisenhower, as well as Kennedy, Johnson, Nixon, Ford, and Carter, not to mention Reagan, is the perennial tendency of American government, at the ideological level of mixed government

---

[3] Richard E. Neustadt, *Presidential Power: The Politics of Leadership from FDR to Carter* (New York: Wiley, 1979), p. 9.

and federalism, to fragment and disperse power. This problem is so pervasive—and so at odds with mythic requirements of presidential leadership—that it afflicts the president's own staff. More than one president has complained bitterly that he could not find out what was going on in his own Executive Office. Many examples from the history of the presidency show this; one of the most pertinent is that President Kennedy was not kept fully informed about the planning of the CIA's Bay of Pigs invasion of Cuba in early 1961.

Special factors are at work in each situation, but in the Bay of Pigs invasion example, it is clear that the CIA itself suffers from the secrecy requirements that inhibit the flow of information even to people who are supposed to have it. All bureaucracies, for that matter, develop an exclusive sense of their mission with a momentum that tends to resist outside control; they become a law unto themselves. The CIA is but one example of this; the FBI, the Army Corps of Engineers, and the Internal Revenue Service also exhibit this tendency.

The underlying, controlling source of fragmentation of power in Washington is the division of authority over the bureaucracy between the president and Congress, and the further fragmentation of authority in Congress between the two houses, between the committees and sub-committees of these, and, finally, between all the members of these bodies. With this many masters, it is not remarkable that in Washington the rule is often every bureau or agency for itself.

Budget-Making

In our perspective it is easy to see how the power that myth heaps upon the president to lead Congress and dominate the bureaucracy does not exist in practice. This is especially obvious in the two most important areas in which the president is supposed by myth to provide forceful leadership—budget making and foreign policy. The OMB depends on the departments and various agencies and bureaus for the information from which it prepares the executive budget for the president. On many or most occasions, these departments and agencies seem to cooperate with the OMB, at least outwardly. However, when hard decisions have to be made—decisions to cut budget items, for example—relations between the OMB and the bureaus and agencies can become confrontational and the president and his staff may have to intervene. Such intervention can sway the policy process and bureaucrats know this, but those who feel they have been adversely affected by the course of bureaucratic events know also that, over the long haul, it is Congress (more specifically, its committees and subcommittees) that makes the final decisions about who gets what, how much, and for what purposes. They also know that cut programs have a way of reappearing later, sometimes under a new name. Most important, they know that the interests served by their bureau may be more than willing to make their views known to legislators. The iron triangle of lobbyists, Congress

**BOX 7–12
Are Our Presidents
Simply a Reflection
of Ourselves?**

To the Editor:

It's rather curious how Richard Nixon cannot be mentioned these days without provoking controversy, vilification or humor.

Since Watergate, Americans have cast him as our national disgrace, a monster who once wore Presidential clothing. The Republican Party is so embarrassed by him that not a soul dared mention his name at its 1980 national convention.

Indeed, Americans now seem to partake of a peculiarly vindictive spirit in kicking around our former President. Little wonder, then, that the proposed Nixon Presidential library at Duke University has created such a stir. . . .

Perhaps, though, this profound rage stems from deeper causes than Mr. Nixon's abuse of Presidential power.

Put simply, Nixon, throughout his career, merely acted out some of the most subterranean—and sordid—desires of established postwar American society. It is much easier to heap all the blame on a disgraced President than to question those underlying cultural assumptions from which Mr. Nixon acted. Examples abound.

President Nixon's personal war against perceived enemies reflected a culture paranoiacally intolerant of dissent, most blatantly exhibited in McCarthyism as well as in the physical assault of civil rights and antiwar demonstrators.

President Nixon's secret bombing of Cambodia falls in the tradition of an American arrogance and insensitivity in international affairs which proclaims that might makes right and which can consider the possibility of a "winnable" nuclear war.

Finally, is Mr. Nixon's disdain for the Constitution and lust for power really any different from the spirit behind the American corporate mentality, which places profits before people and success before scruples?

It would be well here to consider comments by the philosopher Hannah Arendt on the Nazi war criminal Adolf Eichmann. Eichmann, according to Arendt, was no monster.

"The trouble with Eichmann," she wrote, "was precisely that so many were like him, and that the many were neither perverted nor sadistic; that they were, and still are, terribly and terrifyingly normal." Arendt concludes that "this normality was much more terrifying than all the atrocities put together."

Yes, Richard Nixon deserves repudiation. But he, too, is no monster. His ideas and character differ little from the people who voted him into the highest office of our land.

Perhaps we isolate and blame him because we fear finding the same impulses and thoughts in ourselves. If so, we must come to our senses and begin to re-examine our nation's fundamental values and assumptions.

Please, before it's too late.

LEONARD STEINHORN
Washington, Sept. 2, 1981

The writer is an instructor in the American Studies Program at American University.

—*The New York Times*, September 13, 1981.

**BOX 7–12
Are Our Presidents
Simply a Reflection
of Ourselves?
(Continued)**

members, and agencies is an established fact of Washington life that presidents often fail to appreciate.

Therefore the president's control of the budget process is often tenuous at best. MX missile programs, neutron bombs, Social Security revisions, food stamp programs, the Clinch River breeder reactor project, detailed and narrowly focused tax bills, and many other matters have a way of coming up again and again despite their previous rejection, or partial rejection by various presidents.

Mythically, the president is supposed to be a grand manager of the economy. Thus control over the budget alone would not be enough. Tax policy would also have to be managed, as well as interest rates and the money supply.[4] Control of the spending and taxing carried out by state and local governments would likewise be necessary. Western European governments typically have control over all these activities as a matter of course. In the United States, the president, who would have to have access to such controls if he was to be ideologically what myth demands, does not possess more than a fraction of them.

In foreign policy, where mythic expectations of presidential performance are even higher than they are in budgetary matters, the president's practical capabilities are even less substantial. Much of his ineffectualness is due to the complexity and intractability of world problems,

Foreign Policy

[4] See Chapter 11.

but there are also fundamental weaknesses in the president's ideological position hidden behind its mythic facade. These weaknesses stem from the same problems that afflict the president's position generally—the overall fragmentation of power in American government and the consequent difficulty of the president in controlling any program, situation, or individual beyond the threshhold of the Oval Office.

Presidents often have an awkward time with their secretary of state, though there are exceptions. Eisenhower worked well with John Foster Dulles, mostly by giving him a free hand. Ford and Henry A. Kissinger worked together well for the same reason. But most presidents are highly aware of their constitutional authority to conduct foreign relations personally. It is the president who sends and receives ambassadors, who supervises the negotiation of treaties, who meets with foreign leaders from all over the world and concludes "executive agreements" with them. And it is the president who must appear to be in charge when crises arise and who must make those crucial first decisions to send in troops or whatever else must be done. In consequence, most modern presidents have been jealous about sharing their stature in foreign affairs with the secretary of state. The appearance of being master of the nation's destiny on the world stage is simply too precious an asset to any president's mythic image. On the other hand, the president's opportunities in this area are mostly for dramatic initiatives and are always colored by his need to appear, as the press has put it, "presidential." Managing things over the humdrum of the long haul is not his style and is much better left to the secretary of state and the professionals in his department. With this much difference in perspective, it is understandable that the relationship between the president and his secretary of state is so often distant.

The president's difficulties with the secretary of state and the rivalries that seem to crop up inevitably between the secretary and the president's national security adviser are compounded by the Defense Department and its leadership. The Defense Department is a major presence in foreign affairs if only because of the military power it maintains with troops stationed in Europe, Korea, and elsewhere, with ships and submarines in the oceans, and with military aid missions in countries in all parts of the world. This presence overseas is backed by enormous political influence at home. Domestically the Pentagon has become essentially a weapons development and consumption mechanism of monumental proportions. As such it is both creature and master of a vast industrial and technological base spread through the nation's economy, and defense contracts and facilities have become indispensable to the welfare of millions of individuals and thousands of communities across the nation. Because of these facts, and quite apart from the deep divergences between diplomatic and military mentalities and perceptions,

President Lyndon B. Johnson signs a civil rights bill.

the needs, concerns, and capabilities of the Defense Department are bound to be very different from those of the State Department.

All these factors ensure that there are many occasions when the two departments are working at cross-purposes in many areas of foreign affairs and that an intense personal rivalry will develop between their chiefs. As we have seen, the president's national security adviser, working through the National Security Council and its staff, is supposed to ride herd on these rivalries, but his prospects for consistent success are never bright. They are dimmed even more by the probability that the secretary of state and the secretary of defense have come from different walks of life, may well have never met before going to work in Washington, and almost certainly have had no experience working together as a team.

Finally, the president has a problem in managing the Defense Department itself. The Pentagon, with its vast clientele in industry and entrenched allies in Congress, is a juggernaut that moves forward mostly under the weight of its own momentum and the gratitude of the millions of Americans whose livelihoods are based on providing the goods and services it consumes. What can a president do to control it? Not much. He can slow this process, perhaps speed up that one, from time to time intervene to steady a course between the extremes of caution and foolhardiness, and mostly let it run itself.

Philosophical Limitations

The restraints on presidential performance that we have been examining are mainly institutional and, in a narrow sense, political. There are more profound restraints as well. Philosophically, the men who have made it up the road to the White House do not come equipped with the intellectual qualities required for the grand, forward-looking roles that myth calls for. They may know the words and they can make the necessary gestures—they can play the part. But that is different from having the philosophical capacity to translate mythic hopes into substantive programs for political action and social change. Any presidential aspirant who may have started political life with that kind of wide-ranging intellect and imagination would have had it long since trained out of him by the compromises, deals, and coalition building necessary to become a candidate, secure the nomination, and raise the funds for a successful campaign. That process is a lifetime education in ideological limitation, in the smallness of Liberal Democratic visions about the purposes and possibilities of politics. Myth calls on presidents to be lions, to appear proud and bold; ideology cautions them to be foxes, to act shrewdly and for short-term personal gains. By such formulas revolutions are not won; they cannot even be envisioned.

What, ideologically, can a president hope to accomplish? If he understands the mythic nature of his call to greatness and is able to pair it to the weaknesses and limitations on his ideological position, and if he is skillful and prudent, he will make the powers of his office work for *him*. He will recognize that these powers adhere to him personally but that he can utilize and extend them only episodically. Like any good baron, he will therefore pick his shots with care. He will concentrate his attention on only a few issues at a time. On behalf of these he will work hard, twisting arms and nudging ribs with whatever ideological arguments of persuasion he may command at the moment, all the while appealing to the people at large with broad mythic calls to support his mandate for greatness and change.

The best kind of issue for presidents to select is the sort that allows them to use their relatively scant ideological powers to enhance and substantiate their mythic functions. Many presidents err in picking their issues. Ronald Reagan's charge of illegality against striking air traffic controllers in 1981 as his basis for firing them may not have yielded political dividends at all. Certainly Jimmy Carter chose a long, protracted, complex, "no win" matter when he took a stance on energy and ended up endorsing a program at odds with his own simply because Congress passed it.

On the other hand, most observers agree that Eisenhower made a master stroke during the election campaign of 1952, with the Korean

BOX 7–13
**The Presidential
Assault upon
Language**

From one point of view, and not an insubstantial one, the crowning evil of Watergate is the language which, as the tapes have made forever evident, clothed the thoughts and decisions of the principles. The vulgarity, the primitivism, the lack of meaning or referent, the groping for expression of the simplest ideas, quite apart from the monotony of the most unimaginative obscenity are all fit accompaniment to the political and moral substance of Watergate—accompaniment and also vehicle. Such is the symbiotic relation of idea and word that it is almost possible to believe that vulgarity and primitivism of native language in the White House helped generate the fact of Watergate. Here again, though, we are obliged to consider background. It is of course possible that had tapes covered all conversations in the White House and Executive Office Building by Presidents Kennedy and Johnson, their language would be more precise, expressive and lucid, and also free of the dreadful overtones of banality and vulgarity in the Nixon tapes. It is possible, but, on evidence that keeps increasing all the time, supplied by intimates . . . , hardly likely. The fact is, degradation of language in White House and government generally has been an almost constant process for the last three decades. Nor is the profanity or vulgarity the worst part of the degradation of official language. I rank obfuscation, whether deliberate or from carelessness and cynicism, as by far the greater evil. And who today, studying the speeches of Kennedy and Johnson on the whole complex of domestic and foreign matters that concerned them, can doubt that the art—if that is the word—of obfuscation was reaching consistently new heights in Washington prior to Nixon and Watergate. But very little of this would be possible in a culture that did not widely embody, in its ordinary speech and in its writing, most of the same qualities. The plain, unblinkable fact is that language in our culture has receded considerably from the position it once held.

—Robert Nisbet, *The Twilight of Authority* (New York: Oxford University Press, 1975), pp. 130–131.

War dragging to a bloody stalemate amid fitful peace negotiations, when he announced: "I shall go to Korea." He had the power to represent America overseas and to go anywhere he saw fit by any means he chose. Ideologically, the announcement tied him to no commitments

*The official residence of
the Vice President,
Washington, D.C.*

whose unfulfillment could not be blamed on the intransigence of the
other side. The trip actually accomplished little that staying at home
could not have done as well. But the announcement conjured up visions
of the fabled war hero riding chariots through the sky to bring peace on
earth. It inspired the American people in the midst of a depressing war,
and it probably played a significant part in Eisenhower's subsequent
election victory.

The Assassination Threat

Nothing brings into sharper relief what their presidents mean to the
American people than an assassin's attempt to take a president's life.
For a nation that thinks of itself as highly civilized and politically developed, attempts on the lives of our presidents have been surprisingly
frequent. Abraham Lincoln and John Kennedy are only the most cele-

brated instances; Garfield and McKinley also fell, and Presidents Franklin Roosevelt, Truman, Ford, and Reagan all had close calls. Assassination and the fear of it has cast a macabre shadow over the modern presidency. Security arrangements to protect the lives of the president and past presidents still living, leading presidential candidates, and the families of all these people are elaborate, cumbersome, and often more stringent than the persons involved like.

The consternation of the mass media and the public when an attempt is made on a president's life underlines the mythic meaning of the presidency and the extraordinary need of the American people to believe through it in themselves, their nation, and their government. Should the occupant of that office die violently, the belief it supports can be badly shaken.

But more is at stake in the assassination of a president than national identity and legitimization of the government. The myth of the presidency itself, of its grandness and power, is also put into question, and this myth has a special set of functions in the American political system. By persuading us that we are being greatly led toward distant horizons of social progress, the myth of the presidency masks underlying frailties in the political system. It masks ideological weakness in the office itself. It masks governmental fragmentation and confusion in which competing elites pursuing their own interests are the principal winners. Above all, it masks our ideological disunity.

The grief Americans experience over a fallen president is thus profound. Leaderless, at least for the moment, they are lost, and grieve as much for themselves as for their slain hero. Listen to the lines of Walt Whitman written on the death of Abraham Lincoln:

> O Captain! My Captain! Our fearful trip is done,
> The ship has weather'd every rack, the prize we sought is won,
> The port is near, the bells I hear, the people all exulting,
> While follow eyes the steady keel, the vessel grim and daring;
>
> But O heart! heart! heart!
> O the bleeding drops of red,
> Where on the deck my Captain lies,
> Fallen cold and dead.

Beyond all his other titles—head of state, commander in chief, chief executive, chief diplomat, even leader of the free world—the president of the United States is Keeper of the Myth.

FOR FURTHER READING

BRODIE, FAWN. *Richard Nixon: The Shaping of His Character*. New York: Norton, 1981. A thoroughly researched look into the background and personality of the only president ever to resign in disgrace.

CRONIN, THOMAS E. *The State of the Presidency*, 2nd ed. Boston: Little, Brown, 1980. One of the most important and comprehensive recent treatments, based on interviews with White House and Cabinet officials.

CRONIN, THOMAS E., and REXFORD G. TUGWELL, eds. *The Presidency Reappraised*. New York: Praeger, 1977. A variety of essays; the most important is C. Herman Pritchett's explanation of the constitutional position of the presidency.

GLAD, BETTY. *Jimmy Carter: From Plains to the White House*. New York: Norton, 1980. A recent president's personality and background explored by a specialist on these subjects.

HALBERSTAM, DAVID. *The Best and the Brightest*. New York: Random House, 1969. A well-written chronicle of the Kennedy and Johnson years, with many insights on Vietnam and other issues.

HODGSON, GEOFFREY. *All Things to All Men: The False Promise of the Modern American Presidency*. New York: Simon and Schuster, 1980. Charts the decline of the presidency in the face of bureaucratic entanglements; stresses the need for a reorganization of the office in light of this reality.

KEARNS, DORIS. *Lyndon Johnson and the American Dream*. New York: Harper & Row, 1976. Somewhat analytical biography; though weak in several places, it reveals many of the motivations behind Great Society and Vietnam policies.

KOENIG, LOUIS W. *The Chief Executive*, 4th ed. New York: Harcourt Brace Jovanovich, 1981. Comprehensive treatment; devotes a chapter to each of the major functions of the presidency and uses historical perspective to great advantage.

NEUSTADT, RICHARD E. *Presidential Power: The Politics of Leadership from FDR to Carter*. New York: Wiley, 1979. Almost regarded as a classic, this book searches for the sources of presidential power and finds that this "grand clerkship" relies primarily on persuasion.

PIOUS, RICHARD. *The American Presidency*. New York: Basic Books, 1979. A new look at the subject that is comprehensive and rests on the strength of its many incisive examples.

Presidential Studies Quarterly. New York: Center for the Study of the Presidency, New York University. Provocative articles, book reviews, insights, historical studies, and comparisons of the presidency with executive offices of other countries.

ROSSITER, CLINTON. *The American Presidency*, 2nd ed. New York: Harcourt, Brace and World, 1960. Though somewhat dated, Rossiter provides a classification scheme of presidential functions still greatly relied upon; his thesis holds that a good president is one who strengthens the powers of the office.

STRUM, PHILIPPA. *Presidential Power and American Democracy*, 2nd ed. Santa Monica, Calif.: Goodyear, 1979. Well-written treatment that raises, among other issues, the threats to democratic government posed by some of the powers we have invested in the White House.

State and Local Government 8

It was a perfect opening day for a weekend rock festival. The sun was shining brightly, as it nearly always does in West Palm Beach, Florida. A crowd of several hundred young people had gathered for the music and other "happenings" of this spectacular social event. At the edge of the festival area was a squad car, which had brought the county sheriff and a few deputies to the scene. The car of Governor Claude Kirk, Jr., appeared rather suddenly, and the governor walked into the crowd. He stopped to interview a long-haired young man. Governor Kirk asked him how he felt. "Pretty good," replied the youth. Then he asked him where he was from. The young man refused to answer. "Take him," shouted Kirk, gesturing to the sheriff. Two deputies grabbed the young man, dragged him to the squad car, and drove him away as a group of more than two hundred youths shouted obscenities at the governor. The deputies refused to say what charges would be brought against the youth, who looked to be about fifteen years old. "These kids think they can play in Florida," Governor Kirk declared to reporters. "Well, they are wrong. You can't play anywhere in this state or in Palm Beach County."[1]

We do not know the outcome of this young man's encounter with the governor, but the situation he found himself in, however unjust, involved the exercise of state governmental power. If he was formally charged with anything, the charge would have been brought against him in the name of the State of Florida, and the arrest procedures would have been carried out by the sheriff's deputies, who are officials of Palm Beach County, a local government authority created by the State of Florida. Although we hear a great deal about the power and authority of the central government and how it decides many matters we might bet-

---

[1] *The New York Times*, November 29, 1969; reprinted in *Government Lawlessness in America*, Theodore Becker and Vernon Murray, eds. (New York: Oxford University Press, 1971), p. 327.

ter decide locally for ourselves, the states and their agents—the 80,000 local governments of America—are important repositories of political power. The great bulk of criminal justice work, for example, is carried out by state and local governments, and most educational policymaking is a state and local government concern. In addition, state and local governments control most of the public services that seem to touch our lives directly: water and sewer, police, fire, sanitation, library, street and road maintenance, and emergency medical services. And we cannot overlook the role played by state and local governments in administering programs funded by the federal government through revenue sharing, grants in aid, and other arrangements.

State and Local Government in the Constitutional System

In the discussion of federalism in Chapter 3, it has been shown that the Founders, especially Madison, saw the American political system as divided into separate spheres: the federal government in Washington and the various state governments. Thirteen of these states, after all, existed in their own right prior to the formation of the federal union. They could not be expected to give up all their sovereignty, and the Tenth Amendment—a part of the Bill of Rights adopted by the First Congress—reserves all nonenumerated governmental powers to the states. The course of constitutional history has affected this arrangement from the Marshall court's decision in *McCulloch* v. *Maryland* (1819)[2] through the application of a "dual federalism" doctrine and the Civil War to the "new federalism" and "partnership" slogans of the present day. But to a great extent, Madison and the other Founders seem to have succeeded, though in ways different from what they imagined, in maintaining a mix of state political subcultures and policy arrangements, on the one hand, and the federal government on the other.

Despite the sometimes bewildering variations among states and their diverse characteristics, a number of broad uniformities also exist. They can be summed up in two major themes. First, state and local governments are integral to the totality of the political system. All of the myriad units of government—school districts, counties, cities, villages, fire protection districts, and of course the states themselves—are tied together administratively, legally, and politically within the unity of the American political system. This broad integration occurs even though these 80,000 units of government regard themselves as independent, each making its own rules, raising its own revenues, and planning programs and living up to the responsibilities of its particular jurisdiction.

[2] See Chapter 5.

*Oregon State Capitol
Building, Salem, Oregon.
(Oregon State Highway
Department)*

Second, all these governments display the same paradoxical tendencies toward Liberal and Social Democracy that we have seen in the
federal government, especially in the conflict between popular and representative government. One of the most distinctive features of American state and local government, in fact, is that their tendencies toward
the contradictions between Liberal (representative) and Social (popular) Democracy are often carried to extremes.

Ideology, Myth, and State and Local Government

Our practice and our perception of state and local government have been substantially conditioned by the national ideology and myth.

In ideology, the courts, especially the U.S. Supreme Court, strongly affected by the experience of the Civil War, have ruled that the Constitution is the supreme law of the land, and that in nearly all contests between Washington and the states preference should be given to the federal position. This legal and ideological foundation has been powerfully reinforced by the domestic crises of the past several generations and in the dominant role the federal government can play in revenue raising and program direction. The scope of these activities is so far-reaching that it has had the political effect of turning the American federal union at the level of ideological practice into a tight network of dependent units, with Washington making nearly all the important decisions in wide areas of governmental activity.

At the same time national myth de-emphasizes the federal role. States' rights and grass roots traditions hold that America is more like a confederation of loosely associated communities, each of which claims its unique identity. It would be hard to exaggerate this myth, which contains and constrains federal activities at the state and local level. It also provides much of the rhetoric of electoral campaigns both at the federal and the state and local levels. This confederal myth makes nearly impossible comprehensive governmental attacks on such problems as land use and development, crime, educational quality and opportunity, and environmental protection. The results of such efforts are often piecemeal and incomplete.

Intergovernmental Relations

As one might expect, myth provides a strong localist bias to federal policies. The Department of Agriculture cannot afford to enrage too many farmers with its policies. Housing and Urban Development must pay close attention to alliances linking mayors with local building contractors. Even the Pentagon, supposedly concentrating on national security, must take into account the concerns of its local supplier-contractors and of the people who live near its many bases and installations. Shutting down one of these installations or canceling a contract usually causes ripples and waves that are felt in Washington.

These considerations apply with even more force to elected officials in the national government. President Jimmy Carter learned this when he tried to do away with some Western water projects as a budget-cutting device during his first year in office. In 1976, President Gerald Ford flatly opposed aiding New York City at the height of its financial crisis. A New York City tabloid, the *Daily News*, headlined this development with a front-page headline reading "Ford to NYC: 'Drop Dead!'" A number of analysts have said that Ford might have carried New York State in the subsequent election had he not lost in the city by such an outsized margin, and this would have changed the result of the presi-

**BOX 8–1
How Does Your
State Rank in
Educational
Spending?**

Does more spending mean better education? As some politicians say, is it a matter of quality more than money? Or does money really make a difference?

Per Pupil Spending —State Rankings	Average Spending per Pupil	Per Pupil Spending —State Rankings	Average Spending per Pupil
1. Alaska	$3,341	27. Vermont	$1,550
2. New York	$2,527	28. Nebraska	$1,526
3. District of		29. Nevada	$1,526
Columbia	$2,368	30. Maine	$1,522
4. New Jersey	$2,333	31. North Dakota	$1,518
5. Wisconsin	$2,150	32. Louisiana	$1,481
6. Delaware	$2,138	33. New Mexico	$1,476
7. Massachusetts	$2,137	34. Oklahoma	$1,461
8. Maryland	$2,100	35. Indiana	$1,449
9. Pennsylvania	$2,079	36. Arizona	$1,436
10. Illinois	$2,058	37. Missouri	$1,425
11. Wyoming	$2,007	38. South Dakota	$1,385
12. Iowa	$2,002	39. West Virginia	$1,374
13. Michigan	$1,975	40. New Hampshire	$1,366
14. Hawaii	$1,963	41. Utah	$1,363
15. Minnesota	$1,962	42. Texas	$1,352
16. Washington	$1,951	43. North Carolina	$1,343
17. Oregon	$1,929	44. South Carolina	$1,340
18. Connecticut	$1,914	45. Kentucky	$1,294
19. Montana	$1,906	46. Alabama	$1,281
20. Rhode Island	$1,840	47. Mississippi	$1,209
21. Kansas	$1,682	48. Tennessee	$1,209
22. California	$1,674	49. Idaho	$1,206
23. Colorado	$1,649	50. Arkansas	$1,189
24. Florida	$1,594	51. Georgia	$1,189
25. Ohio	$1,581		
26. Virginia	$1,560	U.S. average	$1,739

—Based on average daily attendance. Figures are for 1977–1978 school year—latest available. *U.S. News and World Report,* March 10, 1980, p. 75, based on U.S. Department of Education statistics.

dential election. As Chapter 6 shows, local concerns and interests are vital to members of Congress, who must not only heed the demands of constituents but also protect their state or district from shutdowns of federal installations and other kinds of losses and "bring home the bacon" with contracts and other "goodies." David Stockman, President Reagan's director of the Office of Management and Budget, who has served in Congress himself, has said of his difficulties in getting Congress to agree to his budget-cutting proposals that no Congress member is a conservative in his own district. Speaker of the House Thomas P. (Tip) O'Neill alludes to the same set of factors when he says that politics is local, not national.

The relationship between the federal government and the state and local governments is a close, two-way relationship. All the factors that make this true also apply to the state-local relationship. In myth, this relationship is supposed to be loose, emphasizing the diversity and uniqueness of cities, towns, counties, and school districts. In ideological fact, the daily operation of state governments and local authorities they have spawned shows a high degree of interdependence. Local governments are not as self-governing as they may wish to be; school districts, for example, are usually supervised and scrutinized by state departments of education, and transit systems receive funds and directions from state transportation departments. Historically, "Dillon's rule," which gives the states a tight rein on local government, has been held to be operative (see Box 8–2), although today many states have replaced it with "home rule," which is more flexible. Home rule permits cities and localities to carry out policies on any matter that can conceivably and reasonably be afforded to local discretion and jurisdiction *unless* the state specifically forbids it.

**BOX 8–2
Dillon's Rule**

This rule has been historically important in state and local government relationships, and to some extent it still defines them today.

"It is a general and undisputed proposition of law that a municipal corporation possesses and can exercise the following powers, and no others: first, those granted in express words; second, those necessarily or fairly implied in or incident to the powers expressly granted; third, those essential to the accomplishment of the declared objects and purposes of the corporation—not simply convenient, but indispensable. Any fair, reasonable, substantial doubt concerning the existence of power is resolved by courts against a (municipal) corporation, and the power is denied."

Many states have now replaced "Dillon's rule" with a much more flexible "home rule" arrangement.

—*Commentaries on the Law of Municipal Corporations*, 5th ed., quoted by Jay S. Goodman, *The Dynamics of Urban Government and Politics*, 2nd ed. (New York: Macmillan, 1980), p. 48.

Legally, however, no structural analogy can be set up between federal-state and state-local relations. The first is based on an association of sovereign entities, with the states constitutionally retaining their Tenth Amendment residual powers. Local governments, on the other hand, are mere agents of their states from a legal standpoint and, unlike the states, are not considered sovereign. Politically, however, close analogies can be made. Mayors and county executives and others are constantly looking for aid and support from the state; and this is a two-way street, for governors and legislators in their turn seek out these local officials and local citizens when they make their re-election bids.

The relationships among the various states also deserve comment. They can vary between the extremes of costly litigation on water rights or air pollution to the achievement of interstate compacts that set up multistate authorities for administering bridges, transportation systems, or pollution control. The Port of New York Authority is one of the best known of these. Many other activities of the states demonstrate their cooperation with the federal government, such as the operation of the electoral system that, though it is constitutionally mandated, depends on more than a modicum of compliance to function properly. Many potential conflicts among the states are supposedly resolved by the full faith and credit clause of the Constitution (Article IV, Section 1), which implies that the legal acts of every state shall be given the same status by the courts of every other state. Suspected criminals are therefore usually (though not invariably) extradited from a state in which they are apprehended to the state where they allegedly committed a crime. Marriages and divorces that have legally taken place in one state, to cite another example, are recognized by all the other states. And many other activities, such as the exercise of the right to travel, depend on interstate cooperation.

The Structure of State Governments

State governments are all organized on the federal model. The doctrine of separation of powers dictates their outward appearance while mixed government theory provides the logic of their internal workings.

Each state, like the federal government, has a written constitution, even though these documents tend to be longer, sometimes very much longer, than their national counterpart. California's constitution, which has the greatest length at more than 300,000 words, deals with such matters as the shape and size of fruit boxes. Despite these variations in length and subject matter of their constitutions, the basic governmental format is the same for all the states except Nebraska, with its one-house legislature. The states also tend to restrict the powers of their governments in ways unknown at the federal level. States may limit the time their legislatures may meet, strictly enumerate what the state (and sometimes local) governments are not allowed to do, and restrict financial operations and indebtedness.

Popular Control of Government

These various state constitutional provisions tend to reinforce the myth of popular control of government at the state and local levels. But another set of constitutional provisions that establishes the initiative, the referendum, and the recall of officials contributes even more to this idea of popular control.

The initiative is often regarded as a pure form of direct democracy. It is permitted in one form or another in a majority of the states. It allows the people to initiate and pass laws through the petition process, whereby any interested person or group can devise a proposal, circulate it to obtain a required number of signatures, have it printed on the ballot, and campaign for its passage. In some states and localities a simple majority turns an initiative into law; in others, an extraordinary majority such as 60 percent or two thirds may be required.

The referendum also constitutes direct election on public policy questions. It differs from the initiative, which bypasses the legislature, by being placed on the ballot by the legislature, a city or county council, or other officials. Some states have established the compulsory referendum, the automatic placing of an issue on the ballot if it deals with certain types of laws or policy questions. All school-support tax increases, for example, must be referred to the residents of the school district in Ohio. Referendum by petition, another variant worth noting, occurs when the public challenges a new legislative proposal and places it on the ballot by force of numbers of signatures.

The recall of public officials promotes sensitivity to public opinion between elections. A dissatisfied citizenry has the right under this procedure to ask an official to resign from office or, most often, to hold a special election to decide whether the official should remain in office. Usually a very brief time period is permitted for obtaining signatures because it is recognized that recall is an extraordinary procedure.

All three of these innovations received a great impetus from the Progressive "good government" movement of the first three decades of this century, and all are vivid illustrations of the Social Democratic myth of popular government in operation at the state and local level.

The Governor

The myth of popular government strongly affects the executive branch of state governments. As in the federal government, governors as chief executives have opportunities to become mythic heroes even if on a smaller scale than the president. But in many states this tendency has been weakened by another popular government tradition that insists on plurality in the executive. Under this system not only is the governor elected with a partner, usually called the lieutenant-governor, but also with a number of other important state executives—secretary of state, comptroller, and attorney general, for example. All these other executives, however much they may be billed at election time with the governor as a "team" running together on a single ticket, must in the end look out for themselves. And many times voters will pick and choose among the candidates for these sundry offices, taking one from one party and another from a different party. In consequence, they often select a crew with wide divergencies on policy outlooks, ethnic backgrounds, and clientele affiliations.

Governors in the "unreformed" states—the states that were relatively untouched by the Progressives and the "good government" movements of the early part of this century—generally have more appointments to award to job seekers than do governors in the "reformed" states. A direct effect of this reduction in patronage is that party organizations tend to be weaker in the reformed states. But the appointment powers of governors are considered to be only one index of the strength of their office. The formal powers of governors are also weighed by their degree of control over the state budget process, their ability to veto legislation, and their "tenure potential" (the length of their term and whether they are permitted to seek re-election by the state constitution).

Most states now have an executive budget. The governor and an appointed staff are expected to prepare an annual budget and submit it to the legislature for consideration. This gives the governor's office, after reviewing the budget requests of the state's departments and agencies, the power of setting most of the terms of the budget debate. The veto powers of governors vary from state to state, but most governors enjoy the authority of an item veto. This authority, which the president of the United States does not possess, permits a governor to accept some items in a package passed by the legislature and to reject others. The item veto insures that governors do not have to be faced with an "all or none" choice on bills that come to their desks.

The term of office of a governor can be politically significant as well, because politicians and others will tend to ignore, or wait for the departure of, a public official whose tenure is coming to an end. Forty-six of the states give a four-year term to their governor. Twenty of these permit but one re-election, six permit no second term at all, and only nineteen permit an unlimited number of terms. Four states have two-year terms for their governors, but none of these restricts the number of terms.

With these criteria of appointment powers, budget powers, the veto, and the terms of office, it is possible to estimate roughly the powers of one governor in comparison with those of other governors.[3] Remember, however, that the formal powers of governors have a mythic aspect. We must ask how much governors actually immerse themselves in the sometimes uninteresting policy questions of state government. The huge percentage of state spending that comes from federal programs, such as grants-in-aid projects, also raises questions about gubernatorial discretion in policymaking.

It should also be borne in mind that governors are politicians more than anything else. Their ambitions may be centered on re-election, a Senate seat, or perhaps the White House. This brings us to a different set of powers wielded by governors to promote and enhance their political position. These are (1) patronage, (2) publicity, (3) the promise of (or threat of withholding) campaign support for other politicians, (4) control over the flow of information, both political and governmental, (5) influence over the scheduling of local-interest bills, and (6) the promise of advancement within the governor's political party or among his or her supporters in the legislature.[4] These powers may tell us more about what governors actually do than any index of state consitutional powers, for there is a real question as to how much governing governors do. If these political powers are the most important ones they have, then governors are in a relatively weak position. In myth, like presidents, governors are expected to be heroic. But in ideology they must share their supposed preeminence with a wide assortment of other power centers, the legislative chambers and their committees and leaders, the bureaucracy and its entrenched leadership, local government figures with a handle on one piece or another of state politics, and, last but not least, interest group leaders.

The Legislature

The same general question can be asked about state legislatures. How far in ideological practice do they fulfill their mythic calling? Do they govern?

The involvement of most legislators in state government is, first of all, brief. Legislatures have a high turnover. Richard Cory, who quit the Texas legislature in 1970, said, "There are only three ways a man can stay in the legislature and spend the time the job needs—be rich, have an angel, or be on the make."[5] At any given time, more than a third of all state legislators in America are new entrants who will depart from the

[3] Joseph A. Schlesinger, "The Power of the Executive," in Herbert Jacob and Kenneth N. Vines, eds., *Politics in the American States*, 2nd ed. (Boston: Little, Brown, 1972), pp. 220–234.

[4] Sarah M. Morehouse, "The Governor as Political Leader," in *Politics in the American States*, pp. 221–222.

[5] *Texas Observer* January 2, 1970, quoted by George E. Berkley and Douglas M. Fox, *80,000 Governments: The Politics of Sub-national America* (Boston: Allyn and Bacon, 1978), pp. 81–82.

political scene sooner than a member of Congress.[6] Some reasons for this are low pay, low prestige, high travel time and expense, disruption of family life, and the imposed neglect of a law practice or other business. Many state legislatures are part-time places of employment and are often designated with the misnomer "citizen legislatures" to emphasize their supposed "nonpolitical" character. They are of course political bodies as much as any other similar institution in American government, and it can be argued that "citizen legislatures" are simply inadequate in terms of pay, staff support, and other benefits. Some citizens' "good government" groups, heirs to the Progressive and reformist traditions, urge the establishment of full-time, professional, well-staffed, and well-paid legislatures. Their arguments have been supported by a famous study of state legislatures that rated each of them on the basis of how functional, informed, accountable, independent, and representative it was. The results showed the "sometime governments" scoring significantly lower than the rest.[7] However, because tradition and cost will prevent any great conversion to full-time legislatures, this problem is likely to persist. Alan Rosenthal of the Eagleton Institute of Politics believes that "Part-time legislators are worth keeping. They are closer to the community. They really have something at home—a job, or a business—unlike congressmen who don't have anything more than trying to get votes."[8]

New York legislators conduct a hearing on a proposed labor bill. (United Electrical Workers)

[6] George E. Berkley and Douglas M. Fox, *80,000 Governments*, p. 82.
[7] Citizens Conference on State Legislatures, *The Sometime Governments* (Kansas City: Citizens Conference, 1971).
[8] *Newsweek*, May 26, 1980, p. 90.

**BOX 8–3
The Rules of the
Game in State
Legislatures**

Observers of state legislatures have come up with the follow-ing sets of rules for their members:

RULES WHICH PROMOTE GROUP COHESION AND SOLIDARITY:

Support another member's local bill if it doesn't affect you or your district.

Don't steal another member's bill.

Accept the author's amendments to a bill.

Don't make personal attacks on other members.

Oppose the bill, not the man or woman.

Don't be a prima donna, an individualist, an extremist, or a publicity hound.

Don't be overambitious.

Defend the legislature and its members against outsiders.

Don't divulge confidential information.

RULES WHICH PROMOTE PREDICTABILITY OF BEHAVIOR WITHIN THE SYSTEM:

Keep your word.

Abide by commitments.

Don't conceal the real purpose of bills or amendments.

Don't engage in parliamentary chicanery.

Notify in advance if you can't keep a commitment.

RULES WHICH CHANNEL AND LIMIT CONFLICT:

Be willing to compromise; accept "half a loaf."

Go along with the majority of the party.

Respect older members and the seniority system.

Don't try to accomplish too much too soon.

Respect committee jurisdiction.

Don't vote to remove (discharge) a bill from a committee.

BOX 8–3
The Rules of the
Game in State
Legislatures
(Continued)

RULES DESIGNED TO EXPEDITE LEGISLATIVE BUSINESS:

Don't talk too much.

Don't fight unnecessarily.

Don't introduce too many bills and amendments.

Be punctual and regular.

Take the job seriously.

Don't be too political.

Don't call attention to the absence of a quorum.

—John C. Wahlke et al., *The Legislative Process* (New York: Wiley, 1962),
pp. 146–161.

State legislative processes are very similar to those of Congress, with introduction and committee assignment procedures for each bill, mechanisms for reporting bills out of committees to the floor of each house, and similar leadership roles such as speaker of the house and majority leader. Typically, the lieutenant-governor presides over the Senate or upper house. Conference committees are established to iron out differing versions of bills coming out of the two houses, and governors usually respond to a bill with their signature or, on occasion, a veto.

Legislatures seem to have little visibility with the public, and media coverage of their activities is scanty in many states. The only big news to come out of state capitols is usually a tax or budget matter, including passage of the budget, a ratification fight over a proposed amendment to the U.S. Constitution such as the Equal Rights Amendment, or, all too often, a scandal.

Legislatures are often criticized for their failure to regulate lobbying activities. Most states do not monitor lobbyists as closely as the federal government does in Washington, even though federal regulation is not stringent. Many state legislative lobbyists, unlike the legislators themselves, are full-time employees for their cause, whether they represent labor unions, church groups, banks, liquor interests, real estate agents, insurance companies (which are regulated by state laws), or internationally known firms. Chrysler Corporation, for example, obtained loans from several states as well as Washington, and oil companies are active in promoting their positions on regulation, pricing, taxation, and environmental issues. One of the most blatant lobbyists of the post-World War II era was Artie Samish of California, who funneled special

BOX 8–4
Some Notes on a
Day in the Life of a
State Legislator

An announcer on the radio was reading wire copy: "The House Finance Committee . . . public hearings today . . . take the sales tax off food. . . ." I chuckled. Hell, the food tax removal was dead this year. But the leaders who had already decided to engineer the bill's funeral would make a big deal out of the public hearings on it anyway. Sincere witnesses would testify. A forum would be provided. And the bill would die. Why bother? Well, I thought, the Legislature is part theater. Hold a hearing and people think you're doing something. A well-run hearing enables a politician to take a stand on principle while avoiding the necessity of a floor vote, which is perilously closer to meaningful action. The Legislature, I had learned, is chock full of neat tricks for avoiding commitment. . . .

I had put in my share of so-called "grandstand" bills, noble ideas with great purpose but a snowball's chance in hell of passing. . . . Other grandstand bills were less pretentious than mine. . . . Duplicate bills, too, ate up dozens of hours in staff time. Perennials were tax relief and "sock it to the utilities" measures, which ended up being introduced separately by half a dozen delegates who distinguished their versions from each others' by changing a nonsubstantive word or two among their proposals. . . .

A lobbyist approached me and asked me where I stood on a certain bill. I told him. Another delegate, who had heard me explain my position, stopped me as I headed into the chamber. "Why did you tell him where you stood?" he asked. "You could have kept him guessing and gotten a steak dinner out of him." . . .

After [my] radio show [appearance], I was leaving the hotel when an older member, who, it is fair to say, had had a few, approached me with a warm, kindly smile. "I was like you boys once," he beamed "Hell, I know you're right. You just go about it the wrong way. You'll learn when you get my age." "If you agree with us, why don't you vote with us?" I asked him. "How you vote don't matter, really, in the long run," he said. "You'll learn that, too, when you get my age." . . .

—Larry Sonis, former member of the West Virginia House of Delegates, in *Washington Monthly*, 11: 21–28 (June 1979).

interest money into one superfund controlled by him. In a famous statement, he said, "I'm the Governor of the Legislature. To hell with the
Governor of the State."[9]

The relationship of legislators and lobbyists more than anything else
fills out the understanding of legislatures as centers of Liberal Democracy's practice of representative government. It is known that legislators receive campaign contributions from special interests regularly,
and that some of these contributions are pledged during legislative sessions; that legislators fight bills to prevent them from coming to a floor
vote and then, if they fail, often vote for them, producing a public record
that contrasts with their less well-known activity; that legislators "load
up" bills they oppose with heavy budget authorizations to diminish
their chances of passage; and that some legislators are plied with favors
or even outright bribes.

The public seems generally unaware of these maneuvers and does not
seem to care much. It harbors a cynicism that state politicians are
mostly corrupt and nothing can be done about it, reforms are merely a
shuffling of symbols, and economic elites always prevail. Most people,
in addition, do not know who represents them in the legislature.[10]

Given the factors militating against legislative innovation, policymaking, and power—the dominance of the federal government in
grants-in-aid and other programs, the executive budget that gives so
much of the initiative to the governor and the bureaucracy, the part-
time nature of the job, the high turnover in personnel, and the relative
absence of public concern and support—legislatures, at the ideological
level, cannot be said to actually govern their states. Their impact is
marginal and episodic, considerably more so than is the case with Congress. Obviously, they can make a difference on one or another issue,
which is why they attract the attention of the lobbyists. But with the
governor also relatively weak, it is clear that political control of the
states at the ideological level is scattered through the bureaucracy, both
federal and state, among the directors and commissioners of the boards
of independent agencies, and, once again, the leadership and representatives of the client groups that feed off state government programs.

[9] *California Politics* (Stockton, Calif.: Relevant Instructional Materials, 1972), not
paginated.
[10] This is inferred from the lower visibility of state legislators in relation to Congressmembers, based on publicity impact, the greater amount of turnover in legislatures, and
hard data which show that a bare majority of the public can identify their representative
in Congress while only 20 percent or so can identify their Congressmember's position on a
single issue; these 1970 polls are in *The Gallup Poll: Public Opinion, 1935–1971*, vol. 3
(New York: Random House, 1972), p. 2264. Only a minority of the public knows anything
about their representative, according to Warren E. Miller and Donald Stokes, "Constituency Influence in Congress," *American Political Science Review*, **57**: 45–46 (March 1963).

BOX 8–5
Gerrymandering: Maximizing Seats for the Party

In this hypothetical apportionment model, it is assumed that four legislative seats are to be apportioned among twenty voters, ten of whom are Democrats and ten Republicans. Let us assume that the voters reside in the districts in this pattern:

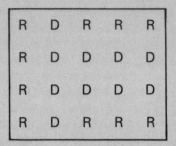

To maximize the number of Democratic seats, the legislature could draw this apportionment map:

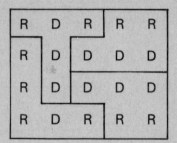

To give a three-to-one edge to the Republicans, this map could be drawn by the legislature:

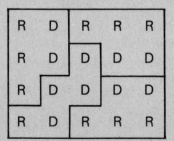

In the 1960s and 1970s, there was much excitement and dissension about reapportionment. The issue arose from the fact that state legislatures are the primary agents for drawing the boundaries of the districts from which their own members are elected and also those of the districts electing members to the House of Representatives in Washington. (Local government councils are comparably responsible for their electoral districts.) The issue attracted attention because it ultimately impinges on the relative value of the citizen's ballot, a matter, as we shall see in Chapter 14, of transcendent mythic significance. But because legislatures draw these boundaries with a sharp eye for party and personal advantage, ideological considerations can become paramount.

For many years, legislatures drew these boundaries pretty much as they chose. Often they would not redraw them for years, preferring to preserve the status quo (and their seats) regardless of how populations grew or shifted across existing constituency lines. Or they would flagrantly "gerrymander" district boundaries to favor the dominant group of incumbent legislators and/or to minimize the representation of voters favoring the minority party or those of some particular ethnic or racial group (see Box 8–5). A special problem arose in connection with the state senates, which were often designed, following what was called "the federal analogy," to represent territory, that is, counties, as the United States Senate does the states.

In consequence, malapportionment of districts was common and sometimes extreme. For example, a citizen of Los Angeles County in California had only one eighty-seventh of the voting strength of citizens of some low-population counties in the north of the state. A state senator from Inyo, Mono, and Alpine counties represented 13,000 people, while the senator from Los Angeles County represented 6 million.

In a series of cases, most notably *Baker v. Carr* in 1962 and *Reynolds v. Sims* in 1964, the Supreme Court made three points: the issue of where constituency boundaries are drawn is not exclusively a "political" issue and affected citizens can appeal to the courts for redress; apportionment of districts should adhere as closely as administratively possible to the principle of "one man, one vote"; and districts should be relatively contiguous and compact. Specifically, the court held that these principles applied to state senates as well as assemblies.

These decisions set off a flurry of reapportionment activity in the legislatures, with successive appeals and counterappeals for review to the courts. Argument over the validity of the Supreme Court decisions also continued for some time, especially over the contention that state senates should represent people—not areas, trees, or cows. A Michigan legislator argued that sparsely populated rural areas deserved greater representation because they have a better quality of citizen than cities have. A constitutional amendment was introduced to permit state upper chambers to be modeled on the U.S. Senate. Much of this argu-

Transportation planning has been increasingly recognized as a responsibility of regional governments.

ment has died away. It was pointed out that whereas the states which the Senate represents are sovereign entities, counties are not. More to the point was that members of the reapportioned legislatures had no personal interest in going back to the old system. On the other hand, gerrymandering continues to be a problem, with cases involving it clogging the courts.

In sum, what did the "reapportionment revolution" accomplish? In myth, the results are impressive although not always quite as expected. It was assumed that cities, especially the major ones, would show a significant increase of voting strength in state legislatures. Cities did gain—but their suburbs gained even more.[11] Also many citizens experienced the satisfaction of knowing that their votes counted for no less than anybody else's. Yet it is also true that at the ideological level, careful studies of actual legislative output discerned only a few and very slight changes in policy initiatives and budgetary allocations.[12]

The Structure of Local Governments

The most striking feature of local government in America is its variety, and concomitant with this variety, its fragmentation. At the same time, there is a great deal of replication of the patterns of myth and ideology found in the national and state governments. Mayors, for example, often try to assume a heroic role. Legislative bodies, such as county commissions and city councils, usually reflect and articulate the interests that are locally organized and concerned with local questions. Developers, construction companies, realtors, and environmentalists are some of the interests represented. Building trades unions are attentive to such matters as zoning laws and building codes, just as transit unions have an interest in matters affecting bus and subway systems. And in the same way that state governments were structurally changed early in this century by reform movements, cities and other local governments reflect this influence in many areas of the country.

City Governments

Whether reform-style institutions have benefited the structure and responsiveness of city governments is an open question. Some people applaud the initiative and referendum processes, though these are often manipulated by well-heeled interest groups for their own purposes. Among city governments there also seems to be a preference for home rule over Dillon's rule.

The council-manager form of city government, a reformist invention found most often in the states that experienced the "Progressive revolution," is today often criticized for centralizing control of policymaking in the hands of a single person. Under this system, the council is usually small and works part-time, elected on a nonpartisan ballot. The council sets policy for the city, and the city manager, a professional appointed by the council, carries out policy and supervises the budget, personnel, and administration of the city. The manager is presumed to be a nonpolitical technician, but the realities of the council-manager system show that this is rarely the case. In the council-manager system the position of mayor may be nothing more than an honorary title; a typical practice

[11] Gordon Baker, *The Reapportionment Revolution: Representation, Political Power, and the Supreme Court* (New York: Random House, 1966).

[12] Roger A. Hanson and Robert E. Crew, Jr., "The Policy Impact of Reapportionment," *Law and Society Review*, **8**: 69–94 (Fall 1973).

is for the council to select the mayor from its own ranks. The key person is the city manager, who can often adroitly develop his or her powers and prerogatives so that council actions are mere ratifications.

Two other common systems of city government in America are the mayor-council, or "strong mayor," system and the commission system. In the mayor-council system, politics can be overt and partisan. The mayor and council are separate entities, roughly dividing executive and legislative functions between them. The mayor has appointment powers and proposes legislation to the council. The mayor also has extensive control over the budget. Administration may be carried out by political appointees, although mayors are beginning to use professionals in a variety of policy areas—housing, finance, planning, traffic control, federal grants administration, and community development. The "strong mayor" system also provides for a full-time mayor and a part-time council, although the council may work full-time in larger cities. The mayor-council system is often found in the unreformed states, and it is often associated in the minds of political scientists and other observers with strong political machines such as those in Chicago or Albany, New York. Some observers argue that such machines have provided a fair quality of government. They have the power to act on important matters, they pay attention to ethnic and poor groups, and it is said that they represented a more humane and caring system of providing for these needs merely in exchange for votes in the days before social welfare laws came into being. Such machines have often proved to be, on the other hand, brutal and arrogant and nearly always have shown a strong tendency to corruption.

The commission form of government is the least common of the three systems. Approximately one hundred cities use it. Unlike the other two systems, it is decentralized. A board of commissioners is elected by the people (five seems to be a favorite number), and these commissions are the city's legislative body. But they also serve executive functions, because each commissioner is placed in charge of one or more city departments. Commissioner A, for example, may be in charge of the public safety departments—fire, police, and emergency medical services—whereas Commissioner B handles parks, recreation, and street repair. Commissioners become a kind of expert in the fields they administer and help guide other commissioners in setting overall policy in these areas. The commission system is usually found in reform states.

Counties

Counties are as important as city governments for most Americans, and they are especially significant in rural areas and small towns. County government tends to defy generalizations, but in the main it provides such services as record keeping, law enforcement, county courts, road maintenance, parks, health, and sanitation services, and in large urban areas, land use planning. The chief governing body is usually a board of commissioners or supervisors. This arrangement strongly parallels the commission system of city government.

Special districts are single-purpose units of local government. They are found in virtually every state and in all large metropolitan areas. Special districts usually have governing boards, taxing authority, and a staff or work force that reports to the board. Quite often the boards are elected, but they may be appointed by state or local officials or by a combination of representatives from other governmental units. School districts are the best-known type of special district government, but there are many others, including sanitary districts, fire protection districts, library districts, parks districts, and scores of others. Property taxes are often the financial base of special districts. In most localities, these taxes are added to the county and city property tax bills so that the taxpayer pays for all government services at one time. Special districts are low profile governments. Citizen participation and the democratic dream do not figure largely in the total picture. But special districts can be very powerful agencies, running schools, airports, port facilities, or transportation systems.

Special Districts

A 1978 CBS-New York Times poll asked a national sample: "If taxes were reduced in your community, would you be willing to have services cut back a lot or only a little or not at all?"

	Cut a Lot	Cut Only a Little or Not at All
Police services	6%	94%
Library hours	18	82
Fire protection	3	97
Garbage collection	7	93
Public transportation	16	84
Street repair-improvements	9	91
Welfare and social services	43	57
Park maintenance	21	79
Schools	7	93

People seem to want (1) lower or less taxation, (2) a continuation of most services, and (3) greater efficiency.

—Everett C. Ladd et al., "The Polls: Taxing and Spending," *Public Opinion Quarterly*, **43**: 126–135. (Spring 1979).

**BOX 8–6
Balancing Taxes
and Services: A
Poll**

Regional Government   Regional planning councils, sometimes called "coordinating councils," came into being with the Great Society programs of the Lyndon Johnson administration. These councils, organized at the suggestion of the federal government, are made up of officials from the various local governments in the area. The "area" usually consists of a number of city and county governments. A staff is hired whose job is to implement, with the consent of the council, coordinated planning schemes for such areawide problems as air pollution, solid waste management, land use, and transportation. Such planning limits the options of local governments, but their participation (which is not required) is encouraged by the benefits of attacking problems on an areawide basis and by the lure of federal grants, many of which are contingent upon areawide planning programs. The Reagan administration has announced its intention of reducing the role and importance of regional governments.

Financing State and Local Governments

The Cost of State and Local Government   State government has grown rapidly in recent decades, and its bureaucracies have expanded in terms of personnel if not budget much more than the federal bureaucracy in the past twenty years. Typically, the states and their supporters have said that Washington has put them into a bind by requiring costly programs that the states must support and administer, but at the same time the federal government has soaked up too many revenue sources so that the states must be reluctant to add to the tax burdens of their citizens. The Reagan administration, by trying to cut aid to the states drastically, has put even more of a burden on their programs of welfare, law enforcement, corrections, mental health, education, and highways. It argues that ultimately this shifting of the burden of taxes and services to the states will result in decentralization, economies, and a greater measure of popular control.

Although the United States is the least taxed of any major industrial society, its citizens claim that their tax burdens have brought them to their financial limit. A series of Harris Polls taken from 1969 to 1978 show that the number of people who believe their taxes have reached the "breaking point" increased from 61 to 69 percent. Also, 80 percent of the people in the United States feel their taxes have reached an unreasonable level.[13] A good part of this resentment is vented against the three taxes relied on by most states for their revenues—the property, sales, and state income tax.

The year 1978 saw the beginning of a nationwide tax revolt against state and local government. As seems to be so often the case, California

---

[13] Everett C. Ladd et al., "The Polls: Taxing and Spending," *Public Opinion Quarterly*, **43**: 126–135 (Spring 1979).

was the pacesetter. Its voters passed Proposition 13, a ballot referendum that cut property taxes by an average of 40 percent. Sixty-five percent of the state's voters approved this measure, which gained a great deal of national attention. Similar ballot referenda were passed in Idaho, Michigan, and other states, and state legislatures also moved to cut taxes. Even states that saw no tax cuts saw legislatures holding the line on state expenditures.

Types of State and Local Taxes

The property tax is particularly unpopular with Americans. It has been steeply increased in a number of states in recent years, and it is seen as a threat of homelessness for the elderly, who cannot always afford to pay it. A number of critics have denounced it as a primitive "head tax" that bears no relationship to income, ability to pay, or any other reasonable economic criterion. On the other hand, some experts have argued that the property tax, properly administered, is the fairest tax of all. It is, after all, a tax on wealth, and these defenders say it reflects both income and wealth even better than the income tax does.[14] Administration of the property tax is the real catch. Assessment procedures, favoritism, and the location of industries and businesses outside of taxing districts either in unincorporated areas or small towns that serve as tax shelters are some of the problems of property tax administration and enforcement that kindle public displeasure with it.

State sales taxes are generally agreed to be regressive taxes that hurt the poor the most, especially in states that charge the sales tax on food and other necessities such as prescription drugs. Because the sales tax is a levy on purchases and the poor spend all, or nearly all, their incomes, the burden of the tax is not related to ability to pay it.

The state income tax is regarded as a fairer tax than property and sales taxes by many observers because it is usually graduated so that proportionally higher rates are paid by those most able to pay. Certain exemptions for the wealthy, and in some cases, a flat rather than graduated rate schedule can make the income tax less fair than it seems. The income tax does not appear to be as unpopular as the property tax. In the midst of the tax revolt of recent years, for example, California voters rejected a halving of the state income tax in a 1980 referendum.

Inequities: The Case of School Financing

It is obvious that a number of inequities exist in state tax systems. Schools, for example, are often financed by property tax levies, but some school districts are not as wealthy as others. This has brought a demand that states establish equalization schemes so that a great part, or even all, of school financing is done at the state level rather than locally. Some states have established equalization, although no state

[14] Mason Gaffney, "In Praise of the Property Tax," *Washington Monthly*, **4**: 2–6 (February 1973).

has managed to equalize school financing completely from district to district. Court challenges have also demanded equalization policies and asserted that the poverty of some school districts assures unequal access to education and unequal treatment under the law in violation of the Fourteenth Amendment's requirement of equal protection. The Burger Court effectively blocked such challenges, however, in its 1973 ruling in *San Antonio Independent School District* v. *Rodriguez*. Such disparities in income as are found, according to the court, are not so irrational as to be invidiously discriminating. A cherished American belief in a good education for all does not necessarily extend to the ideological management of school systems.

**BOX 8–7
The Low-Tax
Auction: Which
State Will Charge
Industry the Least?**

The Southern and Southwestern states, it is widely believed, are gaining in both population and industrial development faster than other regions of the country because they impose lower taxes. Southern and Southwestern legislatures, local governments, and chambers of commerce have used this advantage for years.

The importance of this low-tax advantage is demonstrated by a study conducted by the Southern Regional Education Board. It shows that Sun Belt states and localities are collecting only about four of every five available tax dollars. They used only 82.5 percent of their tax "potential" in 1975, the most recent year for which figures are available. This revenue loss of about $7 billion is mostly accounted for by property and income taxes, the two most sensitive taxes for industry and new settlers.

No other region of the country so underutilizes its tax potential. The New England, Mid-Atlantic, and Pacific Coast regions, in fact, are overutilizing tax potential. New York led the country in 1975 in overutilization by 34.8 percent collecting $18.6 billion. Had it collected what the study showed to be the average national collecting rate, it would have taken in $13.8 billion. By contrast, Alabama, a state rapidly gaining industry and population, underutilized its tax potential by 24.6 percent.

What can be done about this problem? Surely the Northern states cannot compete with the Southerners in climate, but, it has been occasionally suggested, a minimum federal tax, returnable to the states, could eliminate some of the regional tax incentives.

One effect of the tax revolt of recent years has been to force governments to rely increasingly on user fees to pay for the costs of government services, tuition for educational programs, admissions to zoos and public concerts, and various licenses. The effect of this is similar to that of the sales tax because it is a kind of tax on purchases that falls unequally on the poor. Gasoline taxes whose revenues are earmarked for highway construction and maintenance are another example of inequality. As higher prices drove "pleasure drivers" off the roads, those who had to use their cars to get to work had to put up with badly maintained roads.

Federal Grants in Aid

More than 20 percent of state revenues come from the federal government in the forms of grants-in-aid and revenue sharing. The range of grants-in-aid programs is broad and complex. They may include assistance for educational projects, rental subsidies, community redevelopment, public transportation, highways, law enforcement, environmental protection, and any number of other concerns. Some grants-in-aid programs are mandated; that is, every state must participate in them. Many others are simply available on a "matching funds" basis, with the strong sweetener of federal dollars providing an attraction. A typical arrangement is for two dollars of federal money to be allotted for every dollar of state participation, but there are a number of exceptions to this. Capital expenditures for public transportation, mainly bus purchases, are financed with a 4:1 ratio of federal to state dollars. The most generous ratio of all has been the interstate highway program, with its 9:1 arrangement proving to be difficult to resist unless the highways are to go through cities. A frequent requirement of grants-in-aid programs is that the states have to pick up all or a major share of administrative expenses. In some cases, a contract arrangement is established in which a state agency provides a service in exchange for federal dollars. In the 1960s, the Johnson administration greatly expanded grants-in-aid, focusing many new programs on the poor (the War on Poverty) and on cities. Urban renewal and redevelopment programs were undertaken with brave words and high hopes, but poverty and urban decay remain as stubborn as ever. The outlook now is bleak, given the extensive grants-in-aid cutbacks of the Reagan administration.

Revenue Sharing

Revenue sharing was set up by the Nixon administration after Congress provided an authorization in 1972. The idea of revenue sharing is to provide discretionary funds to states and local governments above the specific categorical programs tied to grants. The alleged lack of state revenue sources because of federal growth and the need to avoid federal bureaucracy and red tape are often cited as reasons for having revenue sharing. Until the cuts of 1981, one third of these funds, which had grown to a total of $7 billion a year, went directly to the states, with the remainder going to local governments. Revenue sharing funds are not completely free of strings, but broad discretion in their use has remained a principle of the program.

A broad mix of programs and funding schemes has developed among the federal, state, and local levels of government. Many of the programs have their basis in myth. Revenue sharing was seen as a way of restoring the "sovereignty" of the states. The War on Poverty was aimed at helping the poor and disadvantaged. Grants-in-aid grew out of a demand by social planners and politicians for uniform or nearly uniform urban and welfare programs to be developed across the country. At the ideological level, however, the result has been a patchwork of hundreds of different confusing and sometimes overlapping programs that often work at cross-purposes and mostly benefit the people who run and supply them.

State and Local Government in Social Democratic Myth

Citizenship Participation Amid Fragmented Government and Fragmented Hopes

Local government in America has evolved since colonial times in a piecemeal fashion. Many New England towns still hold town meetings, an institution of direct democracy. But throughout the country "citizen input" (an unfortunate term) is heard today from the lips of mayors, county executives, and others who seek, or merely appear to seek, the views and ideas of "the people." Social Democratic myth retains a unique strength at the level of local government, and it also affects the states. The variety of structures that has evolved into local government in America is not necessarily amenable to citizen involvement, however, and the response of many people is confusion and frustration.

A meeting in the summer of 1980 in a medium-sized Midwestern city illustrates this confusion and frustration. A local antihighway group called TAB (The Truth About the By-pass) was meeting with a director of the Regional Coordinating Council. The director was presenting the case for the highway and emphasized that the meeting was held for informational purposes, not to solicit opinions. Opinions were offered anyway, but they were not taken down and, in fact, seemed to be generally ignored. Late in the meeting, a questioner asked to whom a protest could be directed. The director answered, after much hesitation, that it could be lodged with the Coordinating Council (in practical terms, himself), the County Council (to some extent, also himself), the State Highway Commission (which was pushing for the project), and the Federal Highway Administration. He could have added the state's two senators, a Congress member, eight state legislators, the secretary of transportation in Washington, the regional office of the Department of Transportation, and a local transportation planning consortium. Asked about maintenance of existing roads, he referred the citizen to the state and

A citizens' gathering opposite the County Court House in Spokane, Washington

county highway departments. Asked about public transportation alternatives, he cited the local bus company, a separate taxing authority. When the safety of children crossing the new highway was brought up, the school boards involved were cited as supporters of the highway, and the citizen was referred to them. During the course of the evening's questions and discussions, an assortment of other governmental units were mentioned in connection with the project—a county plan commission, which was concerned with the preservation of agricultural land, two cities and their mayors and councils, state and federal environmental agencies, township governments, and the governments of adjacent counties.

Most Americans are confronted with a similar welter of local governments that make decisions, or supposedly make decisions, affecting their lives and that tax them to support their bureaucracies and programs. The community affected by the highway project is fairly typical. The multiplicity of local governments can be even greater than this example demonstrates. The New York metropolitan area, spread over New York, New Jersey, and Connecticut, has more than 1,500 governments servicing it, often found on opposite sides of state boundaries. A notable trend toward consolidation of governments in the past two decades—in Miami, Nashville, Indianapolis, Minneapolis-St. Paul, and other areas—has hardly made a dent in reducing or amalgamating the total number of local government units. At a distant point in the future, it has been predicted, such consolidation will be mandated by the federal government, but there are immense political, legal, and constitutional problems to resolve if this is ever to occur.[15] Some believe that regional government (see above) is the first step down this path.

At the same time, many believe that such a development would be undesirable because there are advantages to fragmented government not obvious at first impression, and that local governments can be responsive to the wishes of the people. Whether this is true is conjectural, but there is no doubt that the demands for greater autonomy for neighborhoods, and even the establishment of neighborhood-level governments, have gained momentum at various times, such as the late 1960s and early 1970s.[16]

Social Democratic Myth and the Spirit of Reform

The spirit of reform is closely linked with Social Democratic myth in our history, and this has had broad effects on state and local government and our perception of them. Knowing the background of the Progressive movement, a major reform effort that swept through many states and localities in the 1910s and 1920s, helps to explain a great deal about the varieties of structural and institutional characteristics we encounter.

The "Progressive revolution" succeeded in reshaping state governments, mostly in the West and upper Midwest, but its effects were sometimes felt—and are still felt today—in many states that did not encounter the full sweep of this movement. Largely a reaction to widescale corruption and undemocratic practices of the two major political parties, this reform movement gained its major impetus from the Progressive Party, a group that formed within the Republican Party but later left it and gained new adherents who shared its liberal, reformist, antipolitician, antiparty sentiments. The changes wrought by these reformers placed party machines at a disadvantage. They introduced primary elections for state offices, replacing state conventions that had per-

---

[15] Congressmember Henry S. Reuss, "The Year 2000: State and Local Government," in *The Future of the U.S. Government: Toward the Year 2000*, Harvey S. Perloff, ed. (Englewood Cliffs, N.J.: Prentice-Hall, 1971), pp. 351–361.

[16] David Morris and Karl Hess, *Neighborhood Power: The New Localism* (Boston: Beacon Press, 1975); Milton Kotler, *Neighborhood Government: The Local Foundations of Political Life* (Indianapolis: Bobbs-Merrill, 1969).

formed the task of choosing party nominees and that, not incidentally, were easier to control and manipulate than primaries have proved to be. They abolished party labels for some offices and even for two entire legislatures. Most important, at least from the standpoint of the party organizations and the reformers themselves, they established merit systems for public employment, sometimes referred to as the "state civil service." Instead of parties naming employees to their jobs based on party service, the reformers established continuity of personnel (and, to some extent, of policy) and a measure of professionalism and efficiency in government by insulating employees insofar as possible from party pressures and influences. The thrust of such changes is obvious: reduce the influence and importance of political parties by removing them from their sources of power, namely the ability to nominate candidates and to closely control this process, and the ability to reward the faithful through jobs supplied by the spoils system.

At the local government level, the Progressive reformers usually set up nonpartisan ballots for all, or at least most, offices—mayor, county sheriff, county clerk, and so forth. They also established local merit systems for career service, rather than party service, in local government, and perhaps most significantly, they established city manager systems. Running local government, they argued, was a matter of efficiency and dedication to sound principles of management. It was typical of reform groups to say that there is no Democratic or Republican way to fix the street. Professionally trained city managers were therefore given most of the prerogatives of initiating policies, administering finances, hiring and promoting personnel, and organizing city departments. The mayor and city council in this system serve largely as overseers with a veto power, but they are not expected to be as involved as the city manager in the day-to-day affairs of government. Just as the parties were hurt by all these reforms at the state level, they suffered a similar loss of power at the local level.

The effects of these reforms can be seen in the states today, and it is comparatively easy to contrast the party systems and state employment systems of "reformed" states such as Michigan, Wisconsin, Minnesota, California, Oregon, and Washington with states that the reform movement bypassed or failed to affect such as Ohio, Indiana, and Illinois. A few states, such as New York and Connecticut, achieved some of the Progressive-type reforms at a much later date and in an incomplete way. Some of the contrasts between the two systems are striking. A governor of New Jersey, Pennsylvania, or Indiana has 40,000 to 50,000 jobs to fill with patronage appointments (party-sponsored appointments) upon election. The governor of California, the nation's most populous state, can make 600 appointments. Until recently, the lower house of the Illinois legislature was apportioned to insure the victory of the

Effects of Reform

BOX 8–8
The Archetypes:
The "Patronage
Politician" and the
"Merit System
Politician"

It is sometimes a good idea to look at archetypes—people who represent a certain tendency or type to the nth degree. In patronage politics, the most famous name of recent decades is the late Richard J. Daley, mayor of Chicago from 1955 until 1976. Daley ruled both his city and its Democratic machine as a not-always-benign despot. In "merit system" politics, the civil servant who undoubtedly changed the face and shape of a city the most is Robert Moses, who welded various New York "public authority" enterprises into an unelected but nearly omnipotent center of power. Though they achieved power in different ways through different kinds of systems, the results of their efforts were reasonably similar and their policies were much the same. Both men were builders as well as acute managers of favors and public purse strings. Both men knew how to obtain and retain power for themselves, and both knew how to work with local elites and interest groups.

Daley's base was partisan politics. Holding the position of mayor and county chairman of the party simultaneously, he was able to exert firm control over jobs, appointments, construction contracts, building and zoning laws, and the policies of city departments. Though the newspapers were almost always full of news of indictments, arrests, trials, disappearances, embezzlement, and other scandals—including alleged murders—the majority of the people of Chicago always apparently felt satisfied that the mayor's firm control over the city was good for it. One of the myths most ardently believed was that the machine might be corrupt, but it was efficient on its own terms, the city was financially sound, and Daley had been able to give the city prosperity while resisting urban decay. But tens of thousands of Chicagoans were thrown out of their homes by urban renewal schemes, police scandal was piled upon police scandal, and good race relations always seemed to take a back seat at City Hall. Mayor Jane Byrne, Daley's successor after a brief caretaking interval, has found that the schools are out of money, the city's finances were badly managed, the city is as scandal-ridden as ever, and unemployment is a growing problem since more than 500 firms left the city during Daley's reign. And urban decay can be seen all over Chicago.

Robert Moses took advantage of reform-type institutions to build his power in New York City. He became much more powerful than any mayor, council, or county government. At one time or another, he controlled more than thirty separate "authorities," including the Triborough Bridge Authority, the New York City Tunnel Authority, the Long Island State Park Commission, Jones Beach, and Marine Parkway. Moses served simultaneously on many of these boards and commissions, so that he was able to levy taxes and tolls, issue bonds, and construct parks, beaches, buildings, and other public projects, including even a World's Fair in 1964. He was the principal planner for all of the major expressways, save one, which now exist in the New York metropolitan area. His projects displaced more than 200,000 people, because he believed in having a park here, or a bridge or highway there. He believed, and tried to prove, that New York City could be made convenient for auto traffic, even though this was a patent impossibility. Most of his projects were opposed by various neighborhood or environmental groups, and so many of them wound up in court. When this happened, Moses would sometimes simply bulldoze the homes out of existence during the night and claim a mistake had been made. He strongly believed that if he could get the first shovel-full of dirt dug, no judge would stop the project. And he was right. Today, New York is faced with Moses's concrete achievements on every hand.

Looking at these archetypes of the patronage, or "unreformed," system and of the merit, or "reformed," system, is there any difference in policy results? Would we find any difference in policy results if we picked less well-known persons, perhaps some other mayor in an "unreformed" city and a city manager in a "reformed" city? For further reading, see Mike Royko, *Boss: Richard J. Daley of Chicago* (New York: New American Library, 1971), and Robert A. Caro, *The Power Broker: Robert Moses and the Fall of New York* (New York: Random House, 1975).

**BOX 8–8
The Archetypes:
The "Patronage
Politician" and the
"Merit System
Politician"
(Continued)**

Women have increasingly been elected to the position of Mayor in recent years, in such cities as Houston, San Francisco and Phoenix. Pictured here are Chicago's Mayor Jane Byrne and San Jose's Mayor Janet Gray Hayes.

incumbents in the strongest party of a given district. This assured complete party control of its members when they got to the state capitol. In Washington State, by contrast, voters are permitted to cast ballots in the primary of either party as long as they choose only one candidate for each office, and the parties have virtually no control over the nominating process. In Michigan and Wisconsin, local officeholders are chosen without party designation on the ballot, but in Indiana it is apparently important whether autopsies are performed by a Democratic or a Republican coroner.

But does reform really matter? Has it given some states better government while unreformed states have measurably worse government? Are the policies of reformed states different from those of unreformed states? Has the Social Democratic dream of popular government produced concrete results for the citizens of state and local governments? A debate still goes on, but the best evidence seems to indicate that the policies of states are not appreciably affected by reform, that government in the reformed states does not do a demonstrably better job for its citizens, and that the quality of life in the various states has very little to do with the presence or absence of a patronage system or a nonpartisan ballot.[17] Reform, then, appears to be essentially a myth. This does not exonerate unreformed states as exemplary systems; the evidence seems to indicate that the charges brought against them by the reformers are often true. State government proceeds, however, in much the same way from state to state, although there are apparent differences in the ways decisions are made and by whom—parties do it in Illinois whereas various politicians and interests may see to this in Oregon. There is evidence that some of the states tend to be policy innovators more than others[18]; and unquestionably, America has a diversity of political cultures, premises, emphases, and myths within which political functions are carried out in the various states. The Madisonian vision of diversity within the federal system has been realized.

State and Local Government in Liberal Democratic Ideology

However powerful the myth of grass roots democracy and reform may be, it is still true that for most Americans the ongoing operations of their state and local governments remain remote. One indicator of this is participation levels in elections, which has been low in recent years, but another is found in public opinion data on attitudes and perceptions of the citizenry.

The states seem to be held in low esteem. A Gallup Poll of January 1978 gives state political officeholders an exceptionally low "confidence" rating; in fact, only two occupational groups—car salesmen and advertising practitioners—had lower ratings.[19] A batch of other polls, some relating to general attitudes toward state government and others related to specific actions of state government, also show public discontent with the states, including their police tactics, court orders to ban rock concerts, and long jail sentences for marijuana possession.[20]

Not all of the polls on the states are negative. Governors, for example, seem to have increased in popularity in recent years. The reason for this

[17] Leonard G. Ritt, "State Legislative Reform: Does It Matter?" *American Politics Quarterly*, **1**: 499–510 (October 1973) is a convincing example that one aspect of reform has had no measurable effect upon policymaking; see also Robert L. Lineberry and Edmund P. Fowler, "Reformism and Public Policies in American Cites," *American Political Science Revew*, **61**: 701–716 (September 1967).

[18] Jack L. Walker, "The Diffusion of Innovations Among the American States," *American Political Science Review* **63**: 880–899 (September 1969).

[19] *Gallup Opinion Index*, Report 150 (January 1978).

[20] Gerald L. Houseman, "The Credibility of State Government," *Proceedings of the Indiana Academy of Social Science 1974* (Muncie: Ball State University, 1974), pp. 121–133.

slight advance in public support may be because of contrasts with public officials at other levels of government, and this may have especially been the case during the Watergate period.[21] The remoteness of state government could even contribute to this; not knowing much about a public official also means that one might not know much that is bad about the individual. A Harris Poll of December 1973 underscores this point. When asked how state government changed their lives, 27 percent of the respondents said it had improved theirs, 14 percent thought it had made their lives worse, and 52 percent thought there had been "no change for good or ill."[22] We cannot be certain why state government seems to be so far removed from the people. It does receive less attention in both print and electronic media than the federal government. Most certainly, it is less accessible to most people than local government is. It is easy enough to take a petition or complaint to city hall, the court house, or to the school board, but most state residents do not live in the capital city of their state. This inaccessibility and lack of media attention perhaps combine to add to the aura of remoteness of state government.

Over the years, state governments also have acquired reputations for corruption, which could account for public apathy and/or chagrin. Illinois has seen twelve of its state legislators convicted of bribery, tax evasion, or extortion in the period 1975–1980.[23] Deserved or not, the states of Illinois, Texas, Maryland, and Massachusetts seem to frequently serve as examples of corrupt state government. Arizona and New Mexico are infamous for their land sale scandals, a failure of regulation. Indiana requires all patronage workers (virtually all state and local government employees) to contribute 2 percent of their pay to the political party responsible for their appointment, despite a federal court ban on the practice. A governor of Tennessee recently handed out pardons to convicted felons of political importance on the eve of his departure from office. Despite these and many other malfeasances, a number of experts on state government maintain they are no worse, and may in fact be better, than other governments on this score.[24]

The Problem of "Representative" Government

Corruption and other forms of overt malfeasance, common as they may be, are not the real source of the difficulties of state and local governments in America. The real problem is that these governments, scattered and fragmented beyond counting and little exposed to continuous

[21] Frederick T. Steeper of Market Opinion Research, Inc., quoted in "1974 Primaries: Ominous Signs for Republicans," *Congressional Quarterly Weekly Report*, **32**: 1813 (July 13, 1974).

[22] "What America Thinks of Itself," *Newsweek*, December 10, 1973, p. 45.

[23] *Newsweek*, May 26, 1980, p. 90.

[24] Daniel J. Elazar, "Can the States Be Trusted?" *The Public Interest*, **35**: 89–102 (Spring 1974); Ira Sharkansky, *The Maligned States*, 2nd ed. (New York: McGraw-Hill, 1978).

public scrutiny, are especially prone to the shortcomings of Liberal Democracy. Ideologically, these governments carry the principles of "representative" government to extremes—and to head-on collisions with the Social Democratic mythic principles of "popular" government when, in any sudden glare of publicity, these are brought into view.

The difficulties of state and local governing units with "representative" government are primarily two: an ingrown tendency toward elitism and a persistent inability to mount adequate social programs.

The tendency toward elitism in American state and local governments at the ideological level is inherent and irreversible and even more powerful than the comparable tendency at the federal level. But this elitism must not be confused with any penchant for European aristocracy. It is much more a matter of "insiders versus outsiders," of people who through talent, hard work, and an assiduous concern for making and maintaining connections have gained access to the inside workings of the particular government with which they have long associated themselves.

In other words, the elite of America's state and local governments are quite ordinary people who, for a variety of reasons, are on the inside track. They constitute no social or economic "class" in the Marxian sense. As a class, they are as fragmented and dispersed as the governments they tend to dominate. Although they may be genial and cooperative, both among themselves and toward outsiders with whom they have to do business from time to time, they are highly individualistic. Their well-cultivated spirit of camaraderie does not extend to working for themselves as a group against all the rest, for these are the barons of America's state and local politics. By the dictates of Liberal Democratic ideology, they are in the game for themselves. Their genius is to know more, know it sooner, work harder at it, and then use what they know always for their personal advantage. Their surface geniality is simply to ease the way.

Many of these barons work for state and local governments in one capacity or another, full-time or often only part-time. They serve in legislatures, both as members and as aides and counselors to members; as elected officeholders and as appointed officials in the executive departments; as board members and commissioners of state and local regulatory agencies and commissions; and as agency heads and bureau chiefs scattered all through the upper reaches of the civil service. Many judges must be counted among their number. Paired with them are all those people from the private sector with whom the barons in government work on a daily basis: contractors, developers, suppliers, legions of lawyers and other professional people, and ordinary business men and women.

We must reiterate two factors that most account for the elite status of this group. The first is that nonelite citizens—that is to say, the rest of

**BOX 8—9
Tom Wicker on
State Repression:
The Case of Attica**

. . . Thirty-nine prisoners and guards were killed that day [September 13, 1971], and more than 80 wounded, all during 15 minutes of state police gunfire. More than two years later, 60 inmates have been indicted on about 1,300 charges, but not a single state trooper, corrections officer or state official has been indicted for anything. . . .

The state troopers' assault on Attica's D-yard (which on the morning of Sept. 13, 1971, was held by about 1,300 inmates), as well as the aftermath of the assault, the McKay Commission said, was "marred by excesses." These included "much unnecessary shooting" by the assault forces, which had been equipped by their superiors with "shotguns, loaded with '00' buckshot pellets which would spread at distances exceeding 30 yards and hit unintended targets," thus creating "a high risk of injury and death to unresisting inmates and hostages."

The "excesses" of the assault also included gunfire by corrections officers, all of whom had been specifically ordered by Gov. Nelson A. Rockefeller not to take part in the assault; nevertheless, said the McKay Commission, "their gunfire killed at least one inmate and one hostage."

Then, in the aftermath of the assault, "hundreds of inmates, stripped of their clothing, were brutalized by correction officers, troopers and sheriff's deputies. In addition, the suffering of the wounded was needlessly prolonged by an inexcusable failure to make adequate prior arrangements for medical attention." In fact, when the shooting finally stopped "leaving over 120 inmates and hostages dead or wounded, there were only 10 medical personnel inside the walls, and only two of them were doctors"—although the prison rebellion had been going on for five days, providing ample time for medical as well as military planning. It was four hours after the last shot was fired before "emergency surgical procedures began." "But that was not all," said the McKay Commission. "Corrections officers and, to a lesser extent, state troopers and sheriffs' deputies, engaged in frequent and systematic acts of retribution against inmates." Numerous witnesses "confirmed the almost universal inmate descriptions of widespread beatings, proddings, kickings and verbal abuse of the vilest nature." . . .

It is clear by now that the state of New York does not intend to prosecute any of its own, whether they are high ranking or low. . . .

—Tom Wicker column issued by New York Times News Service, November 23, 1973.

us, who are often termed "the powerless"—are powerless largely because we are busy with other matters and do not know much about who is in charge or how the system works or why. Our concerns are mostly aroused only by situations of personal involvement. In addition, the instruments available to us for popular control of state and local governments are, as we have seen, complicated and mostly ineffectual. In this light, the elite hold their positions of dominant influence because of a combination of citizen default and institutional isolation.

The other factor that drives the elite to seek and keep power and use it to their private advantage is, once again, the fact that the system in which they operate is one of "representative" government whose ideological imperatives are defined and sustained at every level of the American political system. These barons of state and local governments are all "representatives" of themselves, their friends and allies, and the client and interest groups that support them. As such, they are expected by a powerful moral tradition to hear, heed, and service—in a word, to "represent"—the interests of all these individuals at whatever level and place in government they happen to work.[25] On the whole, they do this job well, even if sometimes to excess.

In sum, the elite of America's state and local governments are an elite because they are doing ideologically what they are supposed to do. It is only in myth that this is not enough.

In myth, the call is for comprehensive programs of governmental action to deal with broad social and economic problems. But the baronial elite lacks both motive and technique to come to grips with social needs of this sort, if only because they are too busy servicing the private, narrow needs of themselves and their supporters.

Even if there were a will, is there a way? Take any large metropolitan region, criss-crossed by state, county, city, town, and suburban boundaries. If the region has a crime problem, where is the authority to coordi-

**Social Program
Inadequacy**

[25] James Phelan and Robert Pozen, *The Company State* (New York: Grossman, 1973); Robert C. Fellmeth, *Politics of Land* (New York: Grossman, 1973); Toby Moffett, *Nobody's Business: The Political Intruder's Guide to Everyone's State Legislature* (Riverside, Conn. Chatham, 1974).

nate the attack on it? If land use and development is a problem, with valuable resources and their preservation for future generations at stake, who in the area could finance, develop, coordinate, and apply a comprehensive, long-term plan for it? It is a wonder, given the nature and structure of state and local government in America, that problems of this sort are tackled at all.[26] In truth, these problems are tackled and with great effort—as myth demands—but generally with very poor results, which is all that ideology allows. Waters are polluted, cooperation between police forces is minimal, and land use assignments are all too frequently inane by any realistic social standard. But in all this activity, state and local governments are only carrying to extreme the tendencies of the political system as a whole.

FOR FURTHER READING

BAKER, GORDON. *The Reapportionment Revolution: Representation, Political Power, and the Supreme Court.* New York: Random House, 1966. Covers in a complete way the ramifications of this important change in state government.

CARO, ROBERT A. *The Power Broker: Robert Moses and the Fall of New York.* New York: Random House, 1975. Pulitzer Prize-winning study of the use and abuse of power in local government by a political master.

Citizens Conference on State Legislatures. *The Sometime Governments.* Kansas City: Citizens Conference, 1971. Interesting both for its substantive content on the reform of legislatures and for the view it provides of the Social Democratic reformist tradition.

KEMP, ROGER L. *Coping with Proposition 13.* Lexington: D.C. Heath, 1980. Timely assessment of what governments can do in light of reduced revenues in the 1980s.

KOTLER, MILTON. *Neighborhood Government: The Local Foundations of Political Life.* Indianapolis: Bobbs-Merrill, 1969. One of the first and most successful descriptions of the motivations of the community control movement.

MOFFETT, TOBY. *Nobody's Business: The Political Intruder's Guide to Everyone's State Legislature.* Riverside, Conn.: Chatham, 1973. The author, now a member of Congress, takes a caustic view of legislatures in this Nader-sponsored study, a rarity in state government literature.

MORRIS, DAVID, and KARL HESS. *Neighborhood Power: The New Localism.* Boston: Beacon Press, 1975. Impassioned plea for neighborhood government and community control of services.

NORWOOD, CHRISTOPHER. *About Paterson: The Making and Unmaking of an American City.* New York: Harper & Row, 1974. Traces the decline of a city through the corruption and inattentiveness of its local government; a superb case study.

PALLEY, MARIAN L., and HOWARD A. PALLEY. *Urban America and Public Policies,* 2nd ed. Lexington: D.C. Heath, 1981. An introduction to, and analysis of, several important urban concerns, including finances, transportation, welfare, education, housing, and the environment.

[26] Citizens Conference on State Legislatures, *The Sometime Governments* (Kansas City: Citizens Conference, 1971); *The Report of the President's Commission on Campus Unrest* (Scranton Report), (New York: Avon, 1971); *Attica: The Official Report of the New York State Commission* (New York: Bantam, 1972).

RITT, LEONARD G. "State Legislative Reform: Does It Matter?" *American Politics Quarterly,* **1** (October 1973), 499–510. Measures the impact of reform devices on state legislatures.

ROYKO, MIKE. *Boss: Richard J. Daley of Chicago.* New York: E.P. Dutton, 1971. One of several studies of His Honor, well written and provocative.

SCHNEIDER, MARK. *Suburban Growth: Policy and Process.* Brunswick, Ohio: King's Court, 1980. Surveys the problems of growth, provides a brief history of suburbanization, and briefly analyzes the need to provide public services for these areas.

SHARKANSKY, IRA. *The Maligned States,* 2nd ed. New York: McGraw-Hill, 1978. Holds a brief for the states, defending them against social science and journalistic critics.

WALKER, JACK L. "The Diffusion of Innovations Among the American States." *American Political Science Review,* **63** (September 1969), 880–899. Landmark study of an important comparative topic.

WINTER, WILLIAM O. *State and Local Government in a Decentralized Republic.* New York: Macmillan, 1981. Comprehensive introduction to state and local government that is up-to-date.

THE ADMINISTRATIVE STATE

We have so far discussed who governs America, how, and why. This discussion examined government—whether federal, state, or local—from the top.

We now turn our attention to the people who actually do the work of the government under the leadership of the people at the top, the members of the bureaucracy who administer welfare programs, build dams, enforce tax policies, staff courts and jails, collect and interpret statistics, keep records of births and deaths, make foreign policy studies, and a host of other tasks. Five million people carry out this work for the federal government, including one million in military service, and millions more work in state and local government.

Our treatment of these people begins with Chapter 9, which is general and descriptive. The next three chapters deal with especially important policy areas—foreign policy, economic management, and the welfare state. In these chapters, we mostly focus on the federal bureaucracy but we notice other bureaucracies as well.

Three themes are central to these chapters. First, the civil and military servants of American government are very different from their political masters even though they are closely connected to them. Rather than pursuing Protestant-Bourgeois individualistic interests and goals, governmental servants are trained to fulfill their roles in the most reasonable and professional way they know how. That is why in this book we call these people "rational professionals."

Second, in myth the bureaucracy is organized into neat, hierarchical pyramids clustered under the executive heads of the nation's federal, state, and local governments. In this way, myth holds, Social Democracy's vision of popular government can be made to work. The people, choosing among policies, elect legislators and executives. The legislators enact the chosen policies into law, and the executives see to it that the bureaucracy administers them.

Third, the ideological practice of this policymaking and administering process is anything but neat. As we have seen, legislators in America make few comprehensive, programmatic decisions. Instead, in continuous tension with chief executives, they produce a patchwork of dispersed, overlapping, incremental policy detail, compounded by an ongoing competition for control over bits and pieces of the administrative process. Thus, at the ideological level, the leadership element in the policy process is thoroughly fragmented. In consequence, the operative picture of the American administrative state is of a vast amount of work done usually to fairly consistent levels of competence but also marred at every turn by confusion, misdirection, inefficiency, and, often enough, outright failure. More poignant are the widespread feelings of frustration and harassment experienced especially at managerial levels. These are the inevitable effects of rational professionals trying to do their work according to their technical standards of trained competence within the context of America's schizoid politics.

The Bureaucracy 9

The reminiscences of former employees of the federal government are a continuous source of interesting reading. In 1979, this story appeared:

> The first day I went to work as an economist for the Agriculture Department, I was assigned to a nine-by-twelve cubicle, to be shared with my immediate supervisor. Bob . . . had a Ph.D. in economics, but he was prouder of a pin he had just been awarded marking his 20 years of government service. [Bob] . . . showed me the ropes . . . [he] laid out his philosophy of how to succeed in the bureaucracy: please your boss, cover your ass, and always be cautious. . . . I would never get away with challenging my superiors. Patience was the greatest virtue, not performance. The way to get ahead was not to outshine everyone else, but to do precisely what your superiors wanted, prove your absolute loyalty and meanwhile get to know everything you could about the bureaucracy's inner workings. . . .[1]

This is not an unusual story. It fits with the preconceptions many of us have about the people who work in the federal bureaucracy. These are the civil and military employees who, unlike elected and appointed political officials, are on the job year in and year out, surviving all kinds of administrations—passive, active, expansion-minded, penurious, Democratic, Republican, liberal, conservative.

A conventional view of the bureaucracy that may not be far from the truth is that it is always in power. Presidents and their appointees down the line, in this view, are transients who have very little effect on the government or its policymaking processes in the long run. For these transients, learning the procedures and folkways of bureaucracy is not an easy task. It is also the case that government bureaucracy as much as any other is often run on informal organizational patterns based on networks of old friends and associates accustomed to working together

---

[1] James North, "My Brief Career as a Bureaucrat," in Marc Holzer and Ellen D. Rosen, eds., *Current Cases in Public Administration* (New York: Harper & Row, 1981), p. 172.

over the years, special relationships that have developed between agencies or bureaucrats having a common interest in a certain type of program or policy, and communications patterns that involve contacts outside of normal channels (see Box 9–1). These informal routines and understandings may be especially difficult for new policymaking political appointees to grasp, and they may not have learned much about such matters until they are about to leave government service. Unfortu-

**BOX 9–1
The Informal
Organizational
System Found in
Government and
in All Other
Bureaucracies**

"The informal system for any organization will not be found on an organization chart. It is not written down. No single designer sketched it out; it is the product of many actors over an extended period of time. And although informal systems do demonstrate remarkable stability they do change over time (after all this is one of their virtues) and the changes are recorded nowhere but in the minds of the actors involved. Perhaps more importantly, the people who do know the contours of the informal system will try to keep them hidden, for . . . the value of informal channels decreases . . . [with] public exposure. Further, since informal power is less often based on positional authority than personal competence, formal titles are of little more than vague help. It is therefore expensive and time-consuming to discover the informal system. . . . [A formal] management system and the informal system operate on different logics. The former demands a strict order of value preference, hierarchical control, command, and deductive rationality. . . . The informal system tends to work through the building of coalitions on the basis of agreement on values . . . but does not demand agreement on all values. It functions on principles of bargaining, reciprocity, and mutual trust."

—Donald Chisholm, "The Informal Organization: Phantasm, Obstruction or Instrument?" Paper delivered to the American Political Science Association, Washington, D.C., August 28–30, 1980.

Would it be in the interest of the president and his staff to know about such informal channels and patterns? Would it be in a lobbyist's interest? Which would be more likely to know about these? A rational-professional approach to policymaking typifies the thinking and work of both the formal and informal organizational systems.

nately, they leave with a pattern of continuing frequency. The average assistant secretary, who, below the level of cabinet secretary, is said to really administer the line departments such as Agriculture, Interior, or Transportation, has stayed with the government for an average of twenty-one months in the years since World War II.[2] This is hardly enough time to become acquainted with even the basic responsibilities of the job. Perhaps the permanent bureaucracy does indeed reign over all of us.

This is an important problem for any vision of democracy, Liberal or Social. To say that bureaucracy is the systematic organization of a work force is to state only half of the theory. Not much is added by embellishing that original statement with talk about routinization, rationalization, and professionalization. Essential to a complete theory of bureaucracy is the notion that once a systematically organized work force has been established, it should be responsive to direction from the top, from a master. This is true whether the work force is the department of foreign affairs for a whole nation, an army in the field, or a one-room schoolhouse.

Control of a systematically organized work force is the essence of bureaucracy, and nowhere is it more important to emphasize this than in a democratic community. In a democracy, the people decide what is to be done and then the bureaucracy does it.

The difficulty in the American political system is that our conflicting visions of democracy send our federal, state, and local bureaucracies conflicting signals. In Social Democratic myth, these bureaucracies are massive, monolithic administrative units each constituting a unified "executive branch" under the leadership of a single executive head, president, governor, or mayor. Moreover, Social Democratic myth holds that this executive branch carries out policy as enunciated by the legislature, which in turn is directly responsible to the will of the people.

In Liberal Democratic ideology, however, this leadership is fragmented to an extreme. In consequence, to talk about an "executive branch" as a monolithic entity at the ideological level of American government is seriously misleading. The picture is rather of a melange of bureaucratic bits and pieces pulled in a variety of directions. Far from these bits and pieces being "responsible" in any realistic sense to the "will of the people," they are busy representing the interests of their client personnel in all their diversity.

The general situation of American bureaucracy is that it is caught in a three-way tug of war. It tries hard to be a bureaucracy in the classic sense—rational, professional, competent, and efficient. It tries hard to

---

[2] Charles Peters, *How Washington Really Works* (Reading, Mass.: Addison-Wesley, 1980), p. 49.

service the needs of all the people in pursuit of their mythic traditions of social justice and egalitarianism. And it works, sometimes feverishly, to service the ideological needs of the competing interests.

In this chapter, we observe many of the consequences of this three-way tug of war. Some are simply exaggerations of tendencies in all bureaucratic organizations. Others are indigenous to the American situation. But all are inescapable features of the American administrative state.

Another focus of this chapter is on the kind of mentality that bureaucracy most encourages, what we have called the "rational-professional" mentality. Rational professionalism, with its emphasis on impersonal efficiency, trained competence, and devotion to the public good in the most general terms, is very different from the Protestant-Bourgeois mentality characteristic of elected politicians and other barons and is frequently at odds with it.

Bureaucratic Organization

The Size and Shape of the Federal Government

Although many of us tend to think of the federal bureaucracy as situated in Washington, 85 percent of its 5 million employees are located in places outside the capital—in foreign posts with the State Department, the military, the CIA, the Peace Corps, the foreign aid programs, for example, or in regional offices and headquarters, defense installations, Indian reservations, national parks and forests, post offices, and other places in this country. Many are clerks and typists, a great many are soldiers or sailors, and there are lawyers, economists, pharmacists, doctors, researchers, pilots, urban planners, janitors, cooks, railroad engineers, computer programmers, and vast numbers of other occupations. Titles include Schemes Routing Specialist, Suggestions Awards Administrator, Fringe Benefit Specialist, and Confidential Assistant to the Confidential Assistant (all real titles and all, as we shall see, very rational-professional.)[3] Government has grown a great deal since Thomas Jefferson's presidency, when there were about 3,000 federal employees. Even one of the smaller Cabinet departments such as State operates today with a budget that approaches $2.5 billion (see Box 9–2).

Two categories of agencies are usually identified in a way that stresses their relationship to other governmental units and to the "outside world." Those that deal with the latter are line agencies, whereas those that work mostly on an intragovernmental level are called "staff" agencies. A line agency like the U.S. Forest Service, for example, concerns itself with such policy matters as conservation of forests and wildlife, preservation of watersheds, limiting the activities of lumber com-

---

[3] Charles Peters, *How Washington Really Works*, pp. 35–36.

**BOX 9–2
Growth of the
Budget of the
State Department,
1781–1980**

1781	$	57,309
1800		294,894
1850		716,521
1880		1,343,242
1900		3,356,174
1920		13,590,289
1940		24,003,329
1950		350,855,774
1960		246,625,627
1970		447,753,720
1980		2,354,139,276

—*A Short History of the Department of State, 1781–1981* (Washington, D.C.: Department of State Bureau of Public Affairs, 1981), p. 37.

Water management in the dry Western states is one of the jobs of the Department of the Interior.

BOX 9–3
The Reagan
Cabinet Appointed
in 1981

Secretary of State	Alexander Haig	NATO Commander; President, United Technologies; White House Chief of Staff under Nixon
Secretary of Defense	Caspar W. Weinberger	Secretary of HEW and Director of OMB under Nixon; General Counsel, Bechtel Corporation; state official under Reagan
Secretary of Treasury	Donald T. Regan	Chairman, Wall St. firm, Merrill Lynch; former Vice-Chairman, New York Stock Exchange
Attorney General	William F. Smith	Reagan's lawyer; Director, Pacific Telephone, Pullman, Crocker Bank, Pacific Mutual Life
Secretary of Health and Human Services	Richard Schweiker	Former senator, official with National Gypsum
Secretary of Commerce	Malcolm Baldridge	Director, Scovill, IBM, AMF, Bendix, Uniroyal, Connecticut Mutual Life
Secretary of Labor	Raymond J. Donovan	Construction firm owner
Secretary of Agriculture	John R. Block	Illinois farmer
Secretary of Transportation	Drew Lewis	Management consultant; former official, National Gypsum, Simplex Wire

Secretary of Energy	James B. Edwards	Former governor of South Carolina; dentist
Secretary of Education	Terrill Bell	Utah educator
Secretary of Housing and Urban Development	Samuel R. Pierce	Director, General Electric, International Paper, Prudential Insurance, First National Boston Corporation
Secretary of Interior	James G. Watt	Head of Mountain States Legal Foundation, an anti-environmental group

**BOX 9–3
The Reagan
Cabinet Appointed
in 1981
(Continued)**

panies in the national forests, road construction and servicing, and recreation. A "staff" agency provides support for government operations in various ways and sets some overall policies and guidelines on matters like personnel recruitment and promotion, travel, buildings, office equipment, and accountability procedures. The Office of Management and Budget, for example, is charged with overseeing the spending plans of all government bureaus and agencies and seeks to coordinate these within the framework of the annual administrative budget. This same line and staff distinction is recognized within organizations as well. Thus the finance officer in a major department, for example, obviously fills a line position, whereas the secretary working for this person is clearly carrying out a staff function.

Cabinet Departments

The Cabinet departments are the federal government's major line departments. These departments are made up of various subunits called agencies and bureaus. The Federal Highway Administration, for example, is affiliated with the Department of Transportation, the Bureau of Labor Statistics with the Department of Labor, and the U.S. Fish and Wildlife Service with the Department of the Interior. The line departments are, formally, directly responsible to the president through the Cabinet secretaries who head them (see Box 9–3). The departments and their subunits are staffed mostly with career civil servants but are headed by political appointees responsible to the Cabinet secretaries whose leadership is temporary.

At least three of these departments—Agriculture, Commerce, and Labor—can be broadly defined as "clientele agencies" that look directly after the interests of a certain group as if these were coincident with the broad, general interests of the public. A study carried out by the Labor Department, for example, may be undertaken because the United Auto Workers wants it. The task of protecting a domestic industry against lower-priced imported goods might well be a concern of Commerce. Framing a new law aimed at helping sugar producers or tobacco farmers is the kind of activity that might go on at Agriculture. It is fairly certain, of course, that not all the actions of these departments will please all sectors of a client interest group. It can also be assumed that some of the other line departments—Housing and Urban Development, for example, or Health and Human Services or most certainly Defense—also serve much of the time the interests of particular client groups, as do some of the independent agencies and regulatory commissions. In myth, all these departments and agencies serve the public interest; in ideological practice, they often serve a more narrow interest or set of interests.

Some of the departments—Transportation, Energy, Education, Housing and Urban Development, and Health and Human Services— have been created since World War II in response to crises in our cities, our welfare state system, and the provision of energy. In all these cases, the Cabinet departments incorporated previously existing government units. The giant Social Security Administration is with Health and Human Services, to cite one.

The Justice Department, headed by the attorney general, carries out civil and criminal investigations, provides legal advice to other departments and agencies, and concerns itself with such matters as antitrust prosecutions. The Department of the Interior administers federally owned lands, mostly in the Western states, and enforces such matters as mine safety and Indian protection. The Department of the Treasury pays the government's bills, administers its debt, enforces narcotics laws, and collects taxes through the Internal Revenue Service. The Department of Defense, with almost a million civilian employees and a million in the military services, is the largest of the line departments. (By contrast, the independent Arms Control and Disarmament Agency has barely 200 employees.) Finally, the Department of State formulates foreign policy and carries out the day-to-day operations of the 250 U.S. embassies, consulates, and trade missions abroad.

Independent Agencies   In addition to the line departments, the bureaucracy includes a number of independent agencies not subsumed under any department. These include the National Aeronautics and Space Administration (NASA), famous for its moon shots, its voyages to the planets, and the space shuttle. Other important independent agencies include the Environ-

	Executive Branch	Legislative	Judicial	Total
1980	2,822,000	40,000	13,000	2,875,000
1970	2,891,000	30,000	7,000	2,928,000
1955	2,876,000	22,000	4,000	2,402,000

—Bureau of the Census, *Statistical Abstract of the United States, 1979–80* (Washington, D.C.: U.S. Government Printing Office, 1979); pp. 460–464.

**BOX 9–4
Federal Civilian
Employment**

mental Protection Agency and the Veterans Administration, the largest of these, with over 200,000 employees.

A variety of industries, public utilities, and areas of public concern are the administrative domain of the independent regulatory commissions. Some of the best known of these commissions are the Interstate Commerce Commission (ICC), the Federal Reserve Board (see Chapter 11),

**Independent
Regulatory
Commissions**

The National Aeronautics and Space Administration, famous for its moon trips and the space shuttle program, is an independent agency. (NASA)

**BOX 9–5
A New Political
Appointee Can
Shake Up an
Agency . . . But
There Are
Consequences**

WASHINGTON—Shortly after Anne Gorsuch took over last May [1981] as head of the Environmental Protection Agency, her staff hit upon a bold plan to help President Reagan in his battle against federal regulations.

By quickly scaling back certain hazardous waste rules and giving states greater authority to control disposal sites, aides figured, Mrs. Gorsuch could establish her credentials as a no-nonsense administrator. But the carefully conceived strategy backfired.

The new EPA chief had to relent on some of her cutbacks after lobbyists for several chemical companies and trade groups protested that the proposed changes would go far beyond what they wanted. Parts of the plan, these business people complained, could create additional delays for licensing new dumps and expose many companies to conflicts among various states' requirements.

"Nobody from the administrator's office bothered to check with all the parties they were trying to help," recalls one industry executive. "We had to convince them to ease up and go a little slower."

The episode illustrates how Anne McGill Gorsuch's effort to bring swift, dramatic changes at the EPA is running into harsh political realities. The former Colorado state legislator was expected to emulate the confrontational style of her political mentor, Interior Secretary James Watt. "She came in like a whirlwind, itching to shake up the agency," says a former EPA official who worked with her until last month. "Now, she's out there trying to test the political winds to see what's possible" to accomplish. . . .

Mrs. Gorsuch's supporters still praise her knowledge of the issues and her desire to rein in the bureaucracy. But now, barely five months after sweeping into office, . . . [she] appears increasingly isolated and much of her staff is in turmoil—two of her own top appointees quit abruptly last month. . . .

The EPA Administrator and a "close-knit group of aides have developed a white-knuckles approach to running the agency," says a veteran career official who agrees with many

of her goals. "There's a sense of lurching from one issue to the next, without much control," he says. . . .
—*Wall Street Journal*, October 20, 1981.

Is it possible, then, to make sweeping, immediate changes within the bureaucracy and the policymaking apparatus? Mrs. Gorsuch's experience makes this doubtful.

BOX 9–5
A New Political Appointee Can Shake Up an Agency . . . But There Are Consequences (Continued)

the Federal Communications Commission (FCC), and the National Labor Relations Board (NLRB). In the most technical sense, these commissions are agents of Congress, created by the legislative branch in order to attend to specialized rule-making that would require too much time and expertise for a legislature to consider. An additional rationale for their creation is the belief that the activities to be regulated should, if possible, be insulated from politics. In myth, the independence of the independent regulatory commissions is supposed to guarantee that they each will work exclusively "in the public interest," however vague and undefinable that term may be.

The president appoints members to these commissions with the consent of the Senate. Members of the commissions' controlling boards receive terms of appointment ranging from three to fourteen years. Their terms are staggered so that no board or commission has to operate with all new personnel. This is to assure continuity, a rational-professional goal, and is said to cast the commissions into a bipartisan mold because their members are appointed by various presidents. The regulated industries include natural monopolies such as public utilities or those in which totally free market competition is considered undesirable as with, until very recently, the airlines and trucking industries.

The independent regulatory commissions often make controversial rulings—for example, on labor matters in the case of the NLRB, on consumer matters by the Federal Trade Commission, on the stock market and the securities industry by the Securities and Exchange Commission, and on radio and television broadcasting by the FCC. The controversy stems in part from the subject matter of the rulings—whether a company president can address employees on the subject of unions on company time and expense without permitting the union to have equal time and facilities, for example, or how many cockroach feet can be legally permitted in a can of tuna fish (nothing is perfect, after all). But controversy also arises because of the strong ideological tendency for these commissions to become dominated by the very corporations they are supposed to be regulating, largely because the people appointed to these commissions and their staffs are supposed to be "experts" with broad personal experience in the field. They therefore often come from the industries or corporations they are supposed to regulate and they bring their built-in biases with them. Lawyers who work for the Securities and Exchange Commission quit after gaining valuable experience to work for a brokerage house, one of the stock exchanges, or a major corporation. Public utilities lawyers sometimes become members later in their career of a federal or state utilities regulation board. To prevent this career pattern from occurring and to protect the public from this "revolving door" relationship between regulators and regulated, it has occasionally been argued that a period of time such as five years should be required to elapse before an individual can move from a position with a commission to a regulated company and vice versa.

The work of the independent regulatory commissions is also controversial because of their quasi-legislative power. Their regulations, handed down and published on a continuing basis, are sometimes resented by business firms or other interest groups. Sometimes rulings are criticized by ardent conservatives who feel that such matters should be determined by Congress alone or, perhaps even more desirable, determined by no one at all.

The independent regulatory commissions also have quasi-judicial powers. They can make rulings on freight rate disputes, broadcast li-

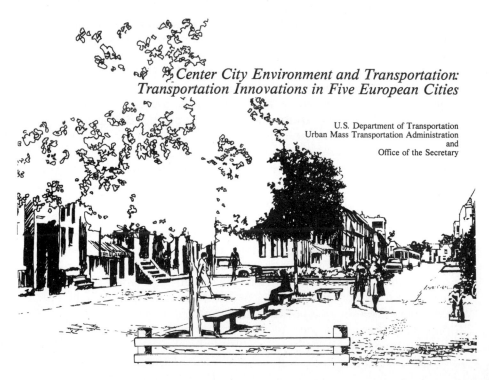

Center City Environment and Transportation:
Transportation Innovations in Five European Cities

U.S. Department of Transportation
Urban Mass Transportation Administration
and
Office of the Secretary

One of the thousands of government reports issued every year.

cense applications, labor conflicts, advertising practices, and other matters of important economic concern. Generally, their hearings have a more informal atmosphere than court proceedings. The courts, incidentally, will not hear a case that involves regulatory jurisdiction unless it is an appeal from the final ruling of one of these boards or commissions.

The independent regulatory commissions are a uniquely American solution to the problem of controlling private economic activity in the public interest. Developed extensively at the federal level, they have been widely imitated at the state and local levels where power commissions, insurance commissions, railroad commissions, and zoning commissions are organized and work in ways that closely resemble the federal model.

The total power and responsibility assigned to these commissions is enormous and directly affects the safety, health, and welfare of every one of us. These commissions can determine or at least shape the fares we will pay when we travel, the procedures we must follow when we buy stocks, the quality and quantity of TV and radio programming we can tune to, and so forth.

But overall these commissions are a classic example of the three-way tug of war afflicting bureaucracies in the American administrative state. Their staffs over the years have developed enviable reputations for competence and professionalism, and commission members themselves are generally known to work hard and with technical competence. Yet the jurisdictions of the various commissions frequently overlap and as often leave wide gaps where no one is responsible. Moreover, there is virtually no institutional apparatus for ensuring coordination among them, and their lauded independence precludes much being done to get them to work together on an informal basis. Finally, the absence of a clear definition of the "public interest," which in myth and by their charters they are told to serve, leaves them continuously vulnerable to special interests pleading for the right to define that term in the light of their particular bias.

Another category of independent agency in the federal bureaucracy is the government corporation. Examples of this include the U.S. Postal Service, the Federal Deposit Insurance Corporation, and the Tennessee Valley Authority. The organizational rationale of these agencies is somewhat analogous to that of corporations in private enterprise. A service or product is marketed with some attention to the techniques of the private firm, and the performance of the agency is measured to some extent by private sector standards.

In addition to these various kinds of units, the bureaucracy contains a number of coordinating agencies of a staff character. The General Services Administration is in charge of all government buildings and

Government Corporations and Coordinating Agencies

grounds, furniture, office equipment, motor pools, telecommunications facilities, and record keeping equipment and standards. The Office of Personnel Management, which emerged out of the old Civil Service Commission in 1978, defines the level, character, and quality of standards expected in each of the skills and occupations required by government jobs. It supervises the testing of these skills for hiring and promotion purposes and represents rational professionalism *par excellence*. The GAO's top official, the comptroller general, is appointed to a fifteen-year term by the president. This long tenure tends to insulate the office from political pressures.

At the pinnacle of the mythically termed executive branch beneath the president is the Executive Office of the President. This massive unit was described and evaluated in Chapter 7, although we can note here that its Office of Management and Budget, National Security Council, Council of Economic Advisers, and White House Office are the most important examples of coordinating agencies in the federal government. It is also worth noting that the White House Office was the only nondefense unit to be given an increase, rather than a cut, in the budget proposals that President Reagan outlined in early 1981.[4]

Making and Administering Laws and Regulations

Most of the federal bureaucracy is involved with formulating and administering laws. The bureaucracy, in fact, can be said to be involved mostly in the tasks of writing legislation for congressional consideration, transforming legislation passed by Congress into rules and guidelines, and applying and implementing the resulting laws, rules, directives, and regulations.

Writing and proposing legislation to Congress is an obvious interest of the departments and agencies because new laws can result in expanded roles or mandates, increased budgets, and perhaps progress in resolving some perceived economic, social, or political problem. A friendly member of Congress, or a gaggle of influential Congress members, can be found to introduce such laws and maneuver them through the legislative process. The mere passage of a measure seldom establishes a means of executing it, however; this requires the transformation of various sections of the new law into detailed rules and guidelines. This is done under the authority of the Administrative Procedures Act of 1946. On occasion, this process of developing what is known as administrative law derived from congressional statutes is criticized on the ground that the bureaucracies tamper with, and sometimes reshape, the original legislative intent. Most of the time, however, the particular agencies involved develop and apply their rules, occasionally rescinding or amending them with little sustained opposition. The *Federal Register*, published daily, lists these various rules and guidelines

[4] *Wall Street Journal*, March 17, 1981.

BOX 9—6
Your Hamburger:
41,000 Regulations

A recent three-volume study produced at Colorado State University revealed that America's staple sandwich, the hamburger, is the subject of 41,000 federal and state regulations, most of which are carried out in accordance with 200 statutes and 111,000 court cases. These regulations affect every phase of meat production—wholesaling, retailing, grazing, and fast-food operations. Collectively, these regulations are said to add 8 to 11 cents per pound to the price of hamburger. These regulations include:

Bun—Enriched bun must contain at least 1.8 milligrams of thiamine, 1.1 milligrams of riboflavin and at least 8 but not more than 12.5 milligrams of iron.

Cheese—Must contain at least 50 per cent milk fat and, if made with milk that is not pasteurized, must be cured for 60 or more days at a temperature of at least 35 degrees Fahrenheit.

Content—It must be fresh or frozen chopped beef and not contain added water, binders or extenders.

Fat—No more than 30 per cent fat content.

Growth Promoters—Use of growth-stimulating drugs must end two weeks before slaughter.

Inspections—As many as six inspections under Federal Meat Inspection Act can occur as meat is checked before and after slaughter and at boning, grinding, fabrication and packaging stages.

Ketchup—To be considered Grade A fancy, it must flow no more than 9 centimeters in 30 seconds at 69 degrees Fahrenheit.

Lettuce—Must be fresh, not soft, overgrown, burst or "ribby."

Mayonnaise—May be seasoned or flavored as long as the substances do not color it to look like egg yolk.

Pesticides—No more than 5 parts of the pesticide DDT per million parts of fat in the meat.

Pickle—Slices must be between $\frac{1}{8}$ and $\frac{3}{8}$ inches thick.

Tomato—Must be mature but not overripe or soft.

—*U.S. News and World Report;* February 11, 1980, p. 64.

along with other important laws—presidential executive orders, statutes, rulings of the independent regulatory commissions—at a rate now approaching 100,000 pages per year. President Reagan has been especially critical of this volume of laws, rules, and regulations and has vowed that his administration will see a reduction in the number of pages printed in the *Register*.

The *Register* first prints proposed rules and asks for comments on them or announces where and when a hearing on these matters will be held. After the final rule is adopted, it is placed in the *Code of Federal Regulations* and becomes a part of the great body of administrative law used to govern this country.

Rational Professionalism and Organizational Behavior

An important and indeed dominant factor in the bureaucracy is the rational-professional mentality. Rational professionalism suffuses the bureaucracy, because the task of running the government—whether it be budget administration, law enforcement, gathering health statistics, or supervising agricultural aid programs—requires certain general skills and standards of performance. The ideal mental type to perform these tasks well is the rational professional.

In the bureaucracy, rational professionalism seems continually tempted to go its own way. Nevertheless, the American political system maintains an overall stability. In the end, it seems able at least to defuse and contain the bureaucracy in certain ways. It is clear, for example, that the overall growth of the bureaucracy has been limited for some years (see Box 9–4). In addition, the elected policymakers in Congress and the presidency can determine whether a given program or policy shall continue to exist. Congress, the president, policy appointees, or even the courts may eliminate an entire agency. The Subversive Activities Control Board, for example, ultimately died in the 1960s because it had no duties to perform that the Supreme Court regarded as constitutional. The early days of the Reagan administration also made it clear that some programs would be severely cut, if not done away with, because the president and his policymakers favored these moves.

Rational professionalism is found in the courts, in state and local government bureaucracies and in the congressional staffs. It strongly affects wide areas of the private sector economy too. Rational professionalism is endemic whenever and wherever work is highly organized and bureaucratized.

The contrasts between rational professionalism and the Bourgeois and Protestant traditions that dominate the thinking of American politicians is of decisive importance. Most noticeable is that the rational-professional mentality is not linked with these two traditions in the way these partners are linked to each other. Protestant myth and Bourgeois ideology have a common history and a shared attachment to individualism. But the rational-professional mentality is different from either one of them and is forced to contradict them. The rational-professional mentality is also unlike the Protestant-Bourgeois tradition in that it suffers from few schizoid tendencies. Internally it is a unified way of understanding and acting in the political world. The overall vision and goals of public servants are clear, self-assured, and uncomplicated. They generally know what to do, how to do it, and why they must do it. As professionals, they neither experience nor empathize with the ambitions, doubts, or guilts that wrack the Protestant-Bourgeois barons who are their nominal masters, nor with the ordinary Americans whom they serve in theory.

The rational professional's unity of outlook stems from its general "objectivity." Rational professionals achieve a sense of selfhood through no assertion of ego. They do not pursue an "interest." Selfhood comes instead through demonstrated and acknowledged professional competence. This competence is recognized in terms of admission to a professional status through training, examination, or, quite often, holding an appropriate job. In the federal bureaucracy, this process is elaborately structured and codified in terms of admission, promotion, tenure, and, most important, the written job description. The rational-professional mind therefore has a self-understanding that is objective rather than subjective. It comes from recognition by others rather than an inner experience. This recognition, in turn, makes the rational-professional bureaucrat one of a class of people—economist, tax lawyer, oceanic hydrographer—who can perform to a set standard of competence. The performance is invariably expected to be rational, impersonal, and tailored to the techniques and canons of the bureaucracy and of that unit and profession to which public servants give their loyalty.

> **The Rational-Professional Mind**

Even the vocabulary of the rational professional is different from that of most citizens or the politically self-conscious Protestant-Bourgeois (see Box 9–7). A good case in point is Special Prosecutor Archibald Cox, whose task was to track down the corruption and violations of civil liberties of the Watergate scandal in 1974. President Nixon, the quintessential Protestant-Bourgeois baron, resisted the efforts of Cox and his staff, knowing full well the disasters in store were Cox to proceed in his rational-professional way, and in the end moved to have Cox fired. Just hours before Cox was to be formally discharged for doing his job too well, he held a news conference. The atmosphere was one of tension, but Cox conducted the conference calmly, with traces of dry wit and unfeigned self-effacement. He began the press session by noting a headline, "Cox Defiant," in one of the morning papers. Cox insisted that he was not defiant, that he held the greatest respect for his superior, the

BOX 9–7
The Battle Against
Bureaucratese

"DOT maximizes its phase-out performance in deregulatory obligations . . ." Wha-a-a . .?

A Letter Is Better
In English

The Commerce Department's Wang word processor . . . beeps at "viable," "to optimize," "bottom line," and 60 other words and phrases culled from Washington's native language—bureaucratese.

Then the Wang flashes on its bright green screen: "Do not use this word" or "Unacceptable phrase."

The Wang was programmed to search out and destroy bureaucratese as part of Commerce Secretary Malcolm Baldridge's continuing war on wordiness in memos, letters and reports.

The secretary launched his offensive with a memo in March telling employees to write in "plain English." He fol-

BOX 9–7
The Battle Against
Bureaucratese
(Continued)

lowed up with a meeting in June at which he told 600 letter writers that "clarity and brevity are key factors when preparing a letter for the secretary or deputy secretary." . . .

The Wang will not automatically beep at the offending words and phrases. It has to be asked to check the list.

"If it's just a little memo to someone on the same level, they might not check," [an aide] said. "But for major items that are going upstairs or out of the department, they check."

The list [includes] "viable," followed by "input," and such other bureaucratese classics as "ongoing," "specifically," "effectuated," "prioritize," and "hereinafter."

Forbidden phrases include "mutually beneficial," "contingent upon," "management regime," and "I regret I cannot be more responsive."

There is also a list of verboten verbs, among them "to impact," "to maximize," "to finalize," and "to interface." . . .

[Baldridge said:] "The only reason I could see for talking that kind of talk was a subconscious urge to cover oneself. There is a kind of protection in . . . a recommendation so vague that it can be interpreted two or three ways on a single issue." . . .

Although the bureaucrats are trying, it is hard for them to kick the habit. Letters and reports are still mired in bureaucratese.

One letter written to be sent out over Baldridge's signature ended with: "Please be assured that the comments you have submitted will receive due consideration as the Department of Commerce works with the Congress on the 1981 and 1982 budget proposals and subsequently moves to implement administration policy and congressional mandate."

—Chicago *Tribune*, September 6, 1981.

attorney general, and that he understood the need for loyalty. He insisted that he was not defying anyone and that he was trying to do a job as best he could. If this was not satisfactory, he would be happy to return to teaching law. Which is exactly what happened.

Conventional Norms, Terms, and Roles

The rational-professional mode of thinking incorporates terms and understandings conventionally accepted as features of any bureaucracy. "Chain of command" is one of the most important of these concepts. A hierarchy is in place in all units and subunits of a bureaucracy, and the

point of command contact for any person in this hierarchy is supposed
to be only with the strata immediately above and below one's own position. (There are lateral contacts, too, of course, but these are cooperative, not command.) No one is supposed to go up "over the head" of
anyone or by pass anyone below with problems or suggestions, and the
jurisdiction of each supervisor within the chain is to be carefully respected. "Division of labor" is another feature of bureaucracies. Specialization is brought to most tasks so that workers and their efforts are
deployed in the most rational, efficient way. Scientists and engineers
provide technical advice and perform technical tasks; lawyers handle
the legal aspects of problems; clerks and secretaries do typing and fil-
ing; staff units provide support and assistance. "Routine" is closely related to the division of labor. Established norms, forms, and procedures
are followed to accomplish tasks, and matters that do not lend themselves to routinization almost invariably cause problems.

Another important concept for the organization of bureaucratic
structures—one that is especially important in understanding the ra-

*The Occupational Safety and Health Administration is one of the government's
most controversial agencies. Business interests and employers claim it hampers
their operations; labor, on the other hand, supports OSHA. The Reagan
Administration has sought to remove and simplify some of its regulations.*

tionality demanded by the bureaucratic mind—is "span of control." This concept refers to the number of inferiors in a chain of command reporting to a single supervisor. The width of any span of control should be directly related to the volume and complexity of the orders that the supervisor must pass down and also the volume and complexities of the responses expected to be received. Thus the chief of an intelligence gathering unit should be given a narrow span of control because of the complexity and detail of the reports that are expected from the work of the staff. On the other hand, the supervisor of a typing pool could oversee the work of a large number of typists.

There is little doubt that putting into practice such concepts as chain of command, division of labor, span of control, and routinization can have stifling effects on creativity and lead to a general expectation that everyone is to follow orders and do little else. This makes radical change or even mild reform from within bureaucratic organizations improbable. On the other hand, without the rigorous application of these concepts, the development of systematically organized work forces would also be out of the question. The comprehensive organization of work forces in which the division of labor is efficiently routinized and organized hierarchically through effective chains of command is essential to seeing that jobs get done.

This observation brings us back again to the central problem for any democratic theory of public administration—the problem of control. The cornerstone of any solution to this problem is the policy-administration dichotomy. In one sense, the dichotomy of policy and administration is merely a division of labor, but it is also much more than that. It is a belief that decisions can be made in relatively broad terms, then carried out on a more narrow administrative basis. The big decisions are made at the policy level and are executed at the administrative level. In government the policy level is supposed to be the domain of political officers, whether elected or appointed, whereas administration is handled by the career civil servants. A great deal of confusion surrounds this dichotomy. Here is an example:

> What this country needs is not so much a higher class of politicians as a better-trained professional class of civil servants at the topmost level, to carry on the necessary functions of government despite the changes in administration.[5]

This statement, whether its author realizes it or not, ignores the policy side of the policy-administration dichotomy and demonstrates a belief that civil servants and skillful administration are all that is required for good government. No administration can be better than the policies it is directed to carry out. On the other hand, the notion that civil servants

[5] Sydney Harris, "Thoughts at Large," Fort Wayne *Journal-Gazette*, November 5, 1981.

do not have any voice in policymaking is misleading. And this is the problem with the policy-administration dichotomy. In myth, it holds to a neat separation of these functions, but in ideological practice, a blending of the two inevitably takes place.

The bureaucracy, then, reflects the rational-professional mentality by being hierarchical, professionalized, specialized, and impersonal. Its impersonal nature also makes the bureaucracy tend to establish equality of treatment for American citizens in the absence of external pressures. When pressures are applied, for example, by a member of Congress in favor of a friend or constituent, if the bureaucracy responds to such pressures, it merely moves the matter of concern to the top of the pile of things to do, then resumes its work.

This contrasts with the conventional wisdom of the public on the subject of the bureaucracy, which it frequently regards as uncaring, inefficient, and faceless: a burden to one's plans or business, meddlesome, highly routinized, unimaginative, and unnecessarily expensive. The bureaucracy is a favorite target of politician and citizen alike. Letters to the editor of newspapers often contain unflattering descriptions of bureaucrats. The relationship between citizen and bureaucrat is often seen as one of adversaries (see Box 9–8). Politicians, of course, rely on the bureaucracy to do the work of government, and there is usually a great difference between politicians' working attitude toward the bureaucracy at the ideological level and the attitudes displayed in the mythic tones of their public speeches.

There are reasons for the politicians' public attitudes. Despite a professional tradition of disinterestedness, the bureaucrats soon learn that in America's ideological environment they, too, have interests to protect. Foremost among these is the life of the bureau or agency itself, a life defined by its budget and by such factors as whether the budget is to be expanded or cut. Many observers believe that no activity in a government agency has as high a priority as securing and enlarging its budget. Agency heads and bureau chiefs frequently visit Capitol Hill for formal presentations to appropriations committees, for informal lobbying, and for other related activities. Among these other activities may be shoring up the strength of the iron triangle uniting them with the lobbyists and members of Congress committed to the same specialized interest. All these activities are aimed at preserving or expanding the agency and its functions. Given the unpredictability of the American ideological environment and the effort required to survive in it, bureaucrats have always a double objective, to do their job and to keep it.

Bureaucratic Practices   These ideological realities easily account for a range of bureaucratic practices common in the federal government that run counter to both rational-professional standards and mythic expectations. Let us examine some of them.

BOX 9–8
Jack Anderson's Rules for Outsmarting the Bureaucrats

On those occasions when the citizen is embroiled in a controversy or is merely seeking action on a problem, columnist Jack Anderson offers the following advice:

1. "Remember who the sovereign is. The people are the source of the power that the bureaucrats wield. . . . you don't have to take 'no' for an answer. Find out and follow the appeal procedure.

2. "Don't let the bureaucrat hide behind his anonymity. . . . identify and isolate the civil servant responsible for your case.

3. "Fight paper with paper . . . keep detailed records—letters, forms, receipts, memos. Put into writing any verbal promises you extract. . . .

4. "Don't start at the top. It's useless to go over the heads of . . . bureaucrats. . . .

5. "Keep it cool . . . the right [approach] can persuade him to be helpful.

6. "A word on paper is worth two on the phone.

7. "If at once you don't succeed . . . try, try again; then raise hell. . . . the hardcore bureaucrat in his heart of hearts is at odds with democracy. He dislikes controversy, which disrupts the smooth implementation of plans and procedures. . . . Complain to . . . superiors; write to your Congressman. . . .

8. "Seek legal help. . . . You will be better off . . . if you can afford a lawyer. . . . For those who cannot afford the law fee, there are legal aid societies. . . .

9. ". . . it . . . help[s] to write your Congressman."

—Jack Anderson, "How to Outsmart the Bureaucrats," *Parade*, July 27, 1980, pp. 6–8.

Overestimating Budget Demands. It is generally assumed that once tough budget negotiations get underway, especially with Congress, one can always adjust demands downward but never upward. In addition, a cutting process takes place in stages that include review by the Office of Management and Budget, the president, and a variety of procedures in

**BOX 9–9
Three Mile Island:
A Portrait of
Regulatory Failure**

The Three Mile Island nuclear plant in central Pennsylvania was "out of control" for several days in March 1979, and the regulatory agency responsible for administering this catastrophe is the Nuclear Regulatory Commission (NRC), which is composed of five members. The following narrative describes the commission and its actions during this time of crisis and panic:

Transcripts of the commissioners' meetings depict, on the third day of the accident, an agency in utter confusion, with only rudimentary and unreliable communication with Met Ed [Metropolitan Edison, the utility in charge of the nuclear plant], Pennsylvania state authorities, and its own people at the site. The immediate question facing the commission at the beginning of the transcripts was whether to recommend to Pennsylvania Governor Richard Thornburgh that he order an evacuation of the more than one million people within 20 miles of TMI. An uncontrolled release of radiation . . . that was much larger than previous emissions heightened the alarm. The following are quotes from official transcripts:

Mr. Joseph Fouchard (NRC information officer): This is Joe, Mr. Chairman, I just had a call from my guy in the governor's office and he says the governor says the information he is getting from the plant is ambiguous, that he needs some recommendations from the NRC.

Mr. Harold Denton (director of reactor regulation for NRC): It is really difficult to get the data. We seem to get it after the fact. They opened the valves this morning, or the let-down, and were releasing at a six curie per second rate before anyone knew about it. By the time we got fully up to speed, apparently they had stopped, there was a possible release on the order of an hour and a half. . . .

We calculate doses of 170 millirems per hour at one mile, about half that at two miles and at five miles about 17. Apparently, it is stopped now, though I'd say there is a puff release cloud going in the northeast direction and we'll just have to see. We did advise the state police to evacuate out to five miles but whether that has really gotten pulled off, we'll just have to—

Mr. Fouchard: Well, the governor has to authorize that, and he is waiting for a recommendation from us. . . .

Chairman Hendrie: Harold, where is—For a puff release, what you have got is an oblong plume headed out. Where it is now, would you guess, that is, if we go ahead and suggest to the governor that the evacuation in that direction out to five miles be carried out, is it going to be after the fact of the passage of the cloud?

Mr. Denton: Well, if they haven't gotten it cranked up, it might well be after passage. There are people living fairly close to the northeast direction. I guess the plume has already passed there. . . .

Yes, I think the important thing for evacuation to get ahead of the plume is to get a start rather than sitting here waiting to die. Even if we can't minimize the individual dose, there might still be a chance to limit the population dose. . . .

It just seems like we are always second, third hand; second-guessing them. We almost ought to consider the Chairman talking to the owner of the shop up there and get somebody from the company who is going to inform us about these things in advance if he can and then what he is doing about it if he can't. We seem not to have that contact.

Commissioner Gilinsky: Well, it seems to me we better think about getting better data. . . .

Mr. Fouchard: Don't you think as a precautionary measure there should be some evacuation?

Chairman Hendrie: Probably, but I must say, it is operating totally in the blind and I don't have any confidence at all that if we order an evacuation of people from a place where they have already gotten a . . . dose they are going to get into an area where they will have had .0 of what they were going to get and now they move someplace and get 1.0.

Commissioner Gilinsky: Does it make sense that they have to continue recurrent releases at this time . . .?

Mr. Denton: I don't have any basis for believing that it might not happen—is not likely to happen again.
    I don't understand the reason for this one yet. . . .

Chairman Hendrie: Now, Joe, it seems to me I have got to call the governor—

Mr. Fouchard: I do. I think you have got to talk to him immediately.

Chairman Hendrie: —to do it immediately. We are operating almost totally in the blind, his information is ambiguous, mine is nonexistent and—I don't know, it's like a couple of blind men staggering around making decisions.

—Ellyn R. Weiss, "Three Mile Island: The Loss of Innocence," in *Accidents Will Happen: The Case Against Nuclear Power*, Lee Stephenson and George R. Zachar, eds. (New York: Perennial Library, 1979), pp. 31–34.

Congress—hearings, committee actions, floor actions, authorizations, and appropriations. Any agency realistic about its ultimate budget goal surely takes these processes into account as it estimates its initial demands.

Underestimating Funds for Vital Programs.   This is a ploy usually carried out by a Cabinet-level department or multifaceted independent agency. The overall budget request may not look very different from that of previous years, but reallocations have taken place that shortchange some vital or politically sensitive benefit. The agency will have to ask for supplemental money later in the fiscal year (the budget year, which begins October 1), and it will receive its initial request too. Next year it will again want both and will have a case for budgetary expansion.

Spending All Appropriated Money by the End of the Year.   This is one of the most hard-and-fast traditions. How can an agency or bureau justify its current budget or a bigger one if it fails to spend all its money in a budget year? The fear is that someone in Congress or elsewhere will cut next year's budget accordingly. The result is that a lot of offices are painted, a lot of contracts are authorized that might not be, a lot of stationery is ordered or restocked, and such things as travel sometimes increase considerably as the last months of the fiscal year run out to be sure all funds are spent.

Empire-building.   A famous saying known as Parkinson's Law charges that there is "little or no relationship between the work to be done and the size of the staff to which it may be assigned."[6] Some bureaucrats and agencies are more adept at building their empires than others, and some simply have more opportunities than others. If the Soviets should achieve a new breakthrough in space, for example, it is probable that NASA would benefit in terms of increased personnel, budget, and responsibilities. Untoward events can likewise result in setbacks. The Nuclear Regulatory Commission, it is generally agreed, was hurt by the Three Mile Island incident of April 1979 (see Box 9–9). In the absence of such external events, the political ability of a particular agency can carry it far. No one doubts that the Federal Bureau of Investigation was successful in its growth goals during the four decades when it was led by J. Edgar Hoover. Empire-building is characteristic not only of government bureaucracy but of large corporations as well. Increasing the budget, staff, and tasks of a unit brings rewards in salary, prestige, and perquisites.

Memoranda, Meetings and Travel.   These things demonstrate to Congress and the public that the work of government is busily getting done. At times, these activities are considered excessive and a lot of them are thought unnecessary. The production of memoranda can lead to an excessive amount of rule-making and can often be pointless.

Other practices and activities also cause public disenchantment with the bureaucracy. Yet to be fair, we must ponder the massive results of the rational-professional bureaucrats: millions of Social Security and veterans checks mailed on time each month, a tax collection system considered to be without parallel anywhere in the world, an awesome destructive force that can be unleashed at the press of a button, and an individual in the Department of Agriculture whose task is to count, and keep track of, all the snakes in the United States.

In recent years presidents, top political appointees, and Congress have made special efforts to understand the bureaucracy, its perceived growth (as Box 9–4 shows, this perception is inaccurate), and its apparent ability to operate the government with minimal or no supervision by the transient politicians in command of it. One of their problems may be failure to understand the rational-professional mind. Another problem may simply be the organizational complexities of the bureaucracy, both in their formal and informal structures. But there is the undeniable fact, especially obvious to anyone living and working in Washington, that the federal bureaucracy is huge, confused, entrenched, and

Reorganizing the Bureaucracy

[6] Quoted by Bertram M. Gross, *The Managing of Organizations: The Administrative Struggle*, vol. 1 (New York: Free Press, 1964), p. 42.

BOX 9–10
Some Unrepresentative Memoranda From Your Government

CHIEF OF STAFF
Commander Amphibious Force
U.S. Atlantic Fleet
Norfolk, Virginia 23520

01: jrr
10 September 1971

MEMORANDUM FOR ALL PHIBLANT COMMANDING OFFICERS

Subj: Refreshments in wardroom

1. For your information and action as you see fit, I have personally overheard Admiral Bell say many times that he does not like to see kool aid served in the wardrooms of ships. Over to you.

Respectfully,

J. E. McCauley
Captain, U. S. Navy

STATUS OF APPLICATION FOR EEOC EMPLOYMENT

Tunley, Tracer F.
APPLICANT *(Last Name, First, Middle Initial)*

☐ YES ☒ NO
SF 171 ATTACHED

170-73
VACANCY ANNC. NO. OR TYPE POSITION DESIRED AND GRADE

As you know, you recently applied for consideration for the above vacancy under the Merit Promotion.

☒ A review of your application indicates that you are not qualified because:
☐ Minimum qualification requirements are not met.
☐ Special qualification requirements are not met.
☐ Time in grade requirements are not met.
☒ Other. *You were not selected*

☐ Your application is returned for the following reasons(s):
☐ There are no present or anticipated vacancies commensurate with your qualifications. Acceptance of application is limited to the line of work in which a turnover is expected.
☐ You do not appear to have Federal Civil Service status. Position in which you are interested require eligibility from a U.S. Civil Service examination or a reinstatemnet of a former Federal employee with competitive status. You are advised to contact your local Civil Service Commission Area Office for examination announcement for which you might file.

| EEOC *(Personal Division)* 1800 C Street, N.W. Washington, D.C. 20506 | QUALIFYING OFFICIAL *(Signature)* *Ronald B. Krueger* | DATE 7/24/73 |

ADMINISTRATIVE MEMORANDUM   12¾
OFFICE OF THE LEGAL ADVISER   12½
ADMINISTRATIVE

ADMINISTRATIVE MEMORANDUM
OFFICE OF THE LEGAL ADVISER

Number 5B
June 13, 1977

SUBJECT: Additional Responsibilities of the L Duty Officer

Effective immediately, in addition to the responsibilities listed in the earlier memoranda identifying the responsibilities of the L duty officer, upon arriving in the office on Saturday mornings the duty officer should get a copy of the NEW YORK TIMES for the Legal Adviser's Office.

The following procedure should be used in order to get a copy of the NEW YORK TIMES:

Take the freight elevator closest to the Office of the Legal Adviser (next door to L/PM, Room 6429) down to the basement. Turn left through closed double doors and follow corridor to the left until you reach Room B-528. Ask the attendant for the Legal Adviser's copy of the NEW YORK TIMES.

If you have any difficulty in obtaining a copy of the NEW YORK TIMES following this procedure, inform L/EX of this fact the following Monday morning.

**BOX 9–10
Some Unrepresentative Memoranda From Your Government (Continued)**

much in need of redefinition and reorganization at nearly every level.

To deal with such problems, Congress since 1949 has given the president the power to reorganize the federal bureaucracy, retaining for itself the right to veto within sixty days any proposed plan. If neither of the two houses takes action within this period, the reorganization scheme stands. (This arrangement had existed earlier, during the Franklin Roosevelt administration, for example, but had been rescinded.) The president is not permitted under this procedure to create new Cabinet-level line departments. The president's reorganizing discretion, all the same, is substantial, and Presidents Carter and Nixon, among others, made use of it.

Reorganization is regarded as one of the most important methods of dealing with bureaucratic growth, but it has limits. One case suffices to show this: the establishment, with congressional authorization and presidential support, of the Department of Energy in October 1977. Energy policies of the government, it was argued, should be integrated. Regulation of various types of energy sources—coal, oil, nuclear—was dispersed among a variety of bureaus, agencies, and commissions, as was energy research. Put all these elements into one department, it was said, and a comprehensive, rational energy policy would soon emerge. Such a policy did not emerge, and President Carter spent much of his four years in office trying to obtain some kind of energy program from the Department of Energy and through Congress. The only result was a set of laws bearing scant resemblance to Carter's original proposals and a measure of public resentment against the new department. Ronald Reagan believed that it was in his interest to make abolition of the Department of Energy one of his positions in his successful 1980 campaign. As president, he still vows to do this, but whether he succeeds remains to be seen. If Reagan is successful, it will be a break with many past presidential experiences. Abolishing a department once established is not easy in Washington politics.

It should also be noted that a president can *cause* bureaucratic disorganization, especially if this is part of a design to wreck or weaken a program. A 1970 policy memorandum of the Nixon administration stated, "The goal of an organizational structure is the implementation of policy, not efficiency."[7] Taking this cue, the administration deliberately set out to tangle some welfare programs into an administrative morass in order to discredit them. According to former Senator James Abourezk, this included three strategies:

1. binding programs to administrative regulations that are too rigid and unworkable;
2. reorganizing operations to remove career bureaucrats—loyal to their programs—from the center of action within agencies, and often to replace them with political appointees;
3. decentralizing programs to fragment accountability and frustrate efforts to coordinate and oversee them.[8]

A demoralization of the bureaucracy can ensue from this, along with administrative confusion and an atmosphere of greatly pronounced struggle between the executive and legislative branches, which leaves the program or programs vulnerable to political attack. This is precisely what occurred, and Nixon proved, not for the first time, that a determined political baron can thwart and disorient the rational-professional bureaucracy.

Reform of Bureaucratic Budgeting   Probably the best evidence of the limitations of the president, Congress, and the OMB in dealing with the bureaucracy is the pervasiveness of incrementalism in the budget process. Incrementalism is the approach

---

[7] Quoted by William L. Morrow, *Public Administration: Politics, Policy, and the Political System* (New York: Random House, 1980), p. 207.
[8] William L. Morrow, *Public Administration*, pp. 207–208.

BOX 9–11
The Bureaucracies
of the States—and
Their Payrolls

Some 11 million people work for state and local governments, an increase of 1 percent from 1970 to 1980. This is only one third of the growth rate of the 1970s. Here is a state-by-state look at the work forces and their pay:

	Employee Per 10,000 Population	Average Yearly Salary		Employee Per 10,000 Population	Average Yearly Salary
Alabama	504	$13,176	Montana	556	$14,892
Alaska	803	$26,136	Nebraska	590	$14,292
Arizona	506	$17,352	Nevada	501	$17,148
Arkansas	465	$11,832	New Hampshire	450	$13,596
California	468	$20,292	New Jersey	502	$16,896
Colorado	515	$16,704	New Mexico	589	$14,280
Connecticut	445	$16,404	New York	539	$17,748
Delaware	526	$14,772	North Carolina	508	$13,812
Dist. of Columbia	762	$21,300	North Dakota	502	$15,768
Florida	471	$14,292	Ohio	438	$15,648
Georgia	563	$12,588	Oklahoma	524	$13,008
Hawaii	503	$16,812	Oregon	514	$16,812
Idaho	481	$14,244	Pennsylvania	401	$16,140
Illinois	446	$17,724	Rhode Island	471	$16,692
Indiana	451	$14,316	South Carolina	515	$12,900
Iowa	508	$15,180	South Dakota	500	$12,996
Kansas	536	$13,872	Tennessee	490	$13,308
Kentucky	423	$13,632	Texas	488	$14,316
Louisiana	532	$12,876	Utah	463	$15,852
Maine	458	$13,764	Vermont	481	$13,776
Maryland	547	$16,632	Virginia	503	$14,484
Massachusetts	500	$16,644	Washington	495	$18,540
Michigan	470	$19,260	West Virginia	511	$12,972
Minnesota	498	$17,376	Wisconsin	480	$17,364
Mississippi	514	$11,388	Wyoming	643	$16,104
Missouri	465	$13,740	United States	488	$16,044

—*U.S. News and World Report*, August 17, 1981.

that starts with a current figure for a budgeted program (or "line") and adds a marginal variation to it, usually upward, for the next year's request. Inflation is commonly cited as one reason for this upward adjustment; but whatever the reason, the purpose is to avoid disruptive changes in either direction, growth or reduction. New and unusual cir-

**BOX 9–12
How to Obtain
Your FBI File: A
Sample Letter**

It is conceivable that a great many people would like to obtain their FBI file. It is not necessary, of course, to have a criminal record in order to have such a file. Merely applying for a job with the Federal Government could result in having one. The American Civil Liberties Union suggests the following letter for requesting your file.

Your address
Your phone number
Date

Mr. William Webster, Director
Federal Bureau of Investigation
10th and Pennsylvania Avenue, N.W.
Washington, DC 20535

Dear Sir:

This is a request under the Freedom of Information Act as amended (5 U.S.C. 552).

I write to request a copy of all files in the Federal Bureau of Investigation indexed or maintained under my name and all documents returnable by a search for documents containing my name. To assist you in your search, I have indicated my Social Security number and place of birth below my signature.

As you know, the amended Act provides that if some parts of a file are exempt from release that "reasonably segregable" portions shall be provided. I therefore request that, if you determine that some portions of the requested information are exempt, you provide me immediately with a copy of the remainder of the file. I, of course, reserve my right to appeal any such decisions.

If you determine that some or all of the requested information is exempt from release, I would appreciate your advising me as to which exemption(s) you believe covers the information which you are not releasing.

I am prepared to pay costs specified in your regulations for locating the requested files and reproducing them.

As you know, the amended Act permits you to reduce or waive the fees if that "is in the public interest because furnishing the information can be considered as primarily bene-

**BOX 9–12
How to Obtain
Your FBI File: A
Sample Letter
(Continued)**

fiting the public." I believe that this request plainly fits that category and ask you to waive my fees.

If you have any questions regarding this request, please telephone me at the above number.

As provided for in the amended Act, I will expect a reply within ten working days.

> Sincerely yours,
> Name (notarized)
> Social Security Number
> Date of Birth
> Place of Birth

(Write: "Attention: Freedom of Information Act Unit" on envelope)

—*How to Get Your Personal File* (New York: ACLU, undated).

cumstances can cause radical and significant program changes, but the usual approach, all the same, is incrementalism.

Incrementalism has its share of critics, mostly because of its almost mindless tendency to perpetuate whatever programs and policies are already in place. Some new approaches have therefore been advocated to promote rethinking of goals, efficiency, and, above all, cost reductions. These include such ideas as zero-based budgeting and sunset legislation. None of these has proved to be wholly successful in curbing the bureaucracy's inertial tendencies or any of the other practices we have mentioned in this chapter. But they are widely discussed and several have been put into at least partial effect.

Zero-based budgeting, a campaign topic (but little more than that) of President Carter in 1976 purportedly does away with the incrementalism of using current spending as a base. Under this arrangement, agencies are asked to rank the importance of all their activities. The budget request that follows only after this ranking has been done is then linked to these priorities. The result sought is that the agencies will be required to justify all their activities every year. This strikes at the heart of the rationale of incrementalism. In practice, however, zero-based budgeting seems to have foundered on the extreme difficulty of long-term planning, its tendency to isolate programs too much from one another, and political and bureaucratic objections to the rejustification of programs every year.

Sunset laws are based on the principle that many government programs, after some period of time, no longer serve any purpose. In several states, sunset laws automatically end an agency, law, or program after a set period of years *unless* the legislative branch re-enacts it. The assumption is that this process will require a review of the reasons for having a particular program or agency. This process does not always happen in the states with sunset laws; moreover, some agencies are exempt from automatic termination. There appears to be a good chance at the federal level that Congress would be overwhelmed by the reviews a sunset law calls for because of the complexity of the government. In any event, sunset laws have not yet been tried at the federal level.

Other attempts to control the bureaucracy include crackdowns on unnecessary paperwork and travel, which never seem to be very successful, hiring freezes, which seem to have only temporary effects, and across-the-board budget cuts, which rest on the logic that all government programs are inherently equal.

**Freedom of
Information Act**

How can the average citizen deal with the bureaucracy if the efforts of Congress, the president, and other official agencies meet so often with only partial success? All the departments and agencies that deal with the public provide ways for determined citizens unhappy with the treatment they have received to appeal for review and changes. And it is always possible, even if usually prohibitively expensive, to take a department to court. Even so, the scales are tipped heavily against the citizen.

A partial correction on the citizens' behalf came into being with the Freedom of Information Act, first passed in 1966 but strengthened considerably in 1974 and 1976. This law gives individuals the right to find out whether government records kept on them are correct. Because many agencies are likely to keep records on individuals—Social Security, the FBI, the Defense Department, the IRS, the Commerce Department, the Passport Division of the State Department—a great deal of personal information is gathered about people, some of it unverified. These raw data sometime stay in files for years after they could have been checked. The civil liberties implications of these data banks are obvious and, unfortunately, even a request to see one's own file can prompt another file entry (see Box 9–12).

The Freedom of Information Act imposes some restrictions. Certain kinds of information are not made available because they are classified or involve government investigations of particular sorts. President Reagan has indicated that he would like to see the access rules tightened. But the Act has served as a partial control of one of the more dangerous aspects of bureaucratic prerogative, and Congress has shown little inclination to tamper with it.

FOR FURTHER READING

Downs, Anthony. *Inside Bureaucracy*. Boston: Little, Brown, 1967. An interesting economist's approach to the subject; some of the examples may be dated but the theoretical approach is fresh.

Greider, William. "The Education of David Stockman." *Atlantic Monthly*, **248** (December 1981), 27–54. These revelations about the bureaucracy and the limited revenue sent shock waves through the Reagan Administration.

Holzer, Marc, and Ellen D. Rosen, eds. *Current Cases in Public Administration*. New York: Harper & Row, 1981. Fast, entertaining articles on the bureaucracy based almost entirely on journalistic sources.

Jones, Charles O. *An Introduction to the Study of Public Policy*, 2nd ed. North Scituate, Mass.: Duxbury, 1977. Public policy text that introduces the student to bureaucratic and governmental decision-making processes.

Lowi, Theodore J. *The End of Liberalism*, 2nd ed. New York: Norton, 1979. Plea for a stronger measure of congressional control of bureaucracy and administration.

Morrow, William L. *Public Administration: Politics, Policy, and the Political System*. New York: Random House, 1980. Closely ties the bureaucracy to the political process and discusses the various ways in which they interact.

Ripley, Randall, and Grace Franklin. *Congress, the Bureaucracy, and Public Policy*. Homewood, Ill.: Dorsey Press, 1980. Formation of policy through the interactions of Congress and the bureaucracy and, again, the question of Congressional control of administration.

Rourke, Francis E. *Bureaucracy, Politics and Public Policy*, 3rd ed. Boston: Little, Brown, 1978. One of the standard texts written by a distinguished public administration analyst.

Ruttenberg, Ruth. "Regulation is the Mother of Invention." *Working Papers for a New Society* (May-June 1981), pp. 42–47. Argues the case that regulation can promote and enhance the economic welfare and personal health of all; uses environmental and occupational safety regulation as examples.

Vidich, Arthur, and Joseph Bensman. "The Bureaucratic Ethos," in Herbert G. Reid, ed. *Up the Mainstream*. New York: McKay, 1974, pp. 315–319. Humorous but also serious examination of bureaucratic language and euphemisms, demonstrating both apparent and operative meanings.

10 Foreign Policy and National Security

On January 17, 1966, a U.S. B-52 bomber collided in midair with a refueling plane and exploded over a village in Spain, losing the four twenty-five megtaton hydrogen bombs it was carrying. A major international crisis could have ensued had this incident occurred near the Soviet or East German borders, for example, and the American people certainly were understandably curious about what kinds of risks their government was taking. But for days thereafter the Air Force information officer in charge led the public to believe that the hundreds of men, planes, ships, and special equipment brought into the area were searching only for "parts of the planes." Even as Spanish troops were being taken to hospitals with radioactivity burns, the officer responded with a "no comment." Two reporters, however, had managed to get the real story out of a sergeant who told them that three of the bombs had been recovered but "there's still one bomb missing, probably in the sea off the coast." The information officer chose, all the same, to be mysteriously ambiguous:

Q. How many ships are offshore today, Colonel?

A. Ships? All I can say is that certain elements of the U.S. Navy are here.

Q. Has the missing bomb been found yet?

A. I know absolutely nothing about a lost bomb.

Q. When will the recovery submarines arrive, Colonel?

A. No comment. Do you really think you're going to see them? . . . They don't fly.

Q. Is there any risk of radiation, or are you merely taking precautions?

A. No comment.

Q. Where can we get information, Colonel?

A. From me. I have no comment to make about anything, and I cannot comment on why I have to say no comment.[1]

Obviously, it was the intention of the Defense Department to supply as little information as possible about this dangerous and embarassing situation. This was not because the Soviet Union would have learned some important fact about our national security apparatus; it was because the officials felt that their policies involving incidents of this sort should not be subject to public scrutiny. Beyond this, it is normal for bureaucracies to be secretive, especially the defense, foreign policy, and national security bureaucracies. Should the American people be told what their government is doing in such foreign policy matters? Should public opinion be a factor in deciding whether, as in this instance, America should have "nuclear flights"?

One could argue that if the Spanish government knew about this incident (and it did), and that if the Soviet government knew about it (and it surely did—its surveillance ships were operating just off the coast), the American people should likewise be privy to such information. But whether or not they should, this issue points up the problem of maintaining an ostensibly democratic society in the face of an historically unprecedented fact of our national life: for a period of more than three decades, we have devoted a high proportion of our national wealth, research activities, economic capacity, creative inventiveness, and political resources to the ultimately unprofitable task of war or preparation for it.

Many people born since 1945 have come to accept this state of affairs as "natural." Compared with the rest of American history, however, it is quite unnatural. The United States has historically kept its military forces and weaponry at fairly low levels during peacetime. It has relied on such factors as rapid mobilization of the population in a national emergency and the great distances that separate the United States from other parts of the globe. This distance advantage is now much less important than it once was, and the United States has accepted the role— some call it the responsibility—of being a "great power" on the world scene.

Acceptance of this role has meant that America is regarded by friend, foe, and neutral alike as the Soviet Union's principal rival in the world, and perhaps more important than this, as a "mover and shaker" of other nations. The commitment to this role has involved us in two wars, one in Korea, the other in Vietnam, and in many other military actions such as the 1960 Bay of Pigs invasion of Cuba. It has also brought in its

[1] Sidney Lens, *The Military-Industrial Complex* (Philadelphia: Pilgrim Press, 1970), pp. 68–69.

wake the formation of military alliances, a huge annual outlay for weapons and military personnel, foreign aid, intervention in the domestic political affairs of countries such as Iran, Guatemala, Chile, Vietnam, and Cambodia, and the dispatching of military personnel to such places as the Dominican Republic, El Salvador, Lebanon, Japan, and Thailand.

The foreign policy of the United States, despite its seeming remoteness from the concerns of most Americans (how many of us know, for example, what *did* occur in Spain in 1966?), is intimately bound up with the country's traditions of political thought, both mythic and ideological.

This chapter has three themes:

1. In myth, America has traditionally viewed itself as having a major, and rather glorified, international role: to be a leader in the causes of social justice and human rights. For much of our history, we pursued this role passively simply as an example to other peoples. Beginning with the Spanish-American War in 1898, we have pursued this role, sometimes referred to as our "destiny," with an increasing aggressiveness and through a wide variety of means.

2. To back up this mythic international role America has set for itself, the country has developed, at the ideological level, a vast and expensive diplomatic and military establishment supported by a virtually permanent industrial and technological base of enormous size and power. This ideological process has been particularly emphasized since the end of World War II.

3. There is poor fit, a low level of compatibility, between the nation's lofty mythic goals and the ideological propensities and capabilities of its diplomatic-military establishment. This was clearly and tragically revealed in Vietnam, but it underlies just as essentially the whole structure of America's involvement in foreign affairs.

Imperial Crusades

Myth and Ideology in Foreign and Defense Policy

The mythical view of American foreign policy is comforting. The United States seeks no selfish advantage, no territorial expansion, and no military involvement with any other country for such malign purposes. We want to be left alone to pursue our lives and goals peacefully. Conflict in the world is not the result of American actions; it arises because some other country—the Soviet Union, Cuba, China, Vietnam—has decided to menace another, and our interests are affected by this menace, at least in the long range. At the same time, America's international conduct is almost unprecedentedly humane and generous. We helped to put Europe back on its feet in the aftermath of two great conflicts. We have given generous assistance to the poor nations of Asia, Africa, and Latin America, providing them with food, low-interest credit, technical assistance, and Peace Corps volunteers. We have defended a variety of countries against would-be aggressors. And in Latin America our unilateral declaration of hemispheric leadership, the Monroe Doctrine, has served as a basis for interventions that have presumably been necessary to ensure stability if not promote the forces of democracy. In this view, America is a benevolent presence and spirit in the world, protecting the peace and territorial integrity of many nations while also showing them the path of development to modernity and progress.

On the other hand, we have to be practical. Ideologically, our foreign policy appears in a quite different light. The U.S. economy is a large industrial and technological machine that must be fed and maintained with resources. Some resources are abundant in our own country, but many others are not. We need to import oil, for example, as well as nickel, copper, magnesium, bauxite, and cobalt. This means that we must maintain a certain political—and often military—presence in the world. It also means that we must be willing to meet threats to our access to these raw materials and block any adventures or initiatives of our rivals, even when these are directed at a seemingly insignificant country. Vietnam, for example, has never seriously been considered an important supplier of raw materials for America, but our commitment to a large-scale war there was made all the same, in part as a demonstration of our power. Moreover, making war and manufacturing the weapons of war has become a vast economic enterprise in which major corporations can develop and huge fortunes can be made.

As a great power, the United States often sees itself as having a mythic justification for intervention into the affairs of other nations. When this occurs, it is undoubtedly also for an ideological reason—to help the International Telephone and Telegraph Corporation (ITT) when its branch in Chile was nationalized, or to install friendly regimes in power in Iran or Guatemala.

These imperial crusades are dressed up in the language of myth. It has been said that America has a "rendezvous with destiny," that it must "make the world safe for democracy," that it must "walk softly but carry a big stick," and that it must "roll back the tides of barbarism." We must be ready at all times to respond to calls for help from independent nations threatened by Communist aggression. Our success in installing the Shah of Iran in power in place of the nationalist Mohammed Mossadegh in 1954 has been described in the noblest of terms. But policies such as these have not always proved prudent. The Iranian reaction to the Shah's rule resulted eventually in a new government in 1979 that has been hostile to United States in every conceivable way.

These examples, along with many others—Guatemala in 1954, Zaire in 1960, Chile in 1970, Angola in the late 1970's—demonstrate the difficulty of separating myth and ideology in American foreign policy. Many times during the Vietnam War debates, the opponents of the war were hooted down for their lack of "realism." But the question of who is realistic can be a tricky one, and it still animates many of the discussions concerning our proper response to world events (see Boxes 10–1 and 10–2).

Historical Roots of Our Foreign Policy

Whatever realism may be, it is certain that American foreign policy reflects the nature and characteristics of the Bourgeois-Protestant, ideology/myth split in our political consciousness. Occasionally this schism shows up within the confines of a single explanation of our foreign policy aims. Look, for example, at the recital of the Monroe Doctrine set out by Secretary of State Richard Olney just prior to the Spanish-American War of 1898:

> The United States is practically sovereign on this continent and its fiat is law upon the subjects to which it confines its interposition. Why? It is not because of the pure friendship or good-will felt for it. It is not simply by reason of its high character as a civilized state, nor because wisdom and equity are the invariable characteristics of the dealings of the United States. It is because in addition to all other grounds its infinite resources combined with its isolated position render it master of the situation and practically invulnerable against any and all other powers.[2]

[2] Quoted by Walter Millis, *The Martial Spirit: A Study of Our War with Spain* (New York: Literary Guild of America, 1931), p. 33.

**BOX 10–1
Five Principles of
"Great Power"
Foreign Policy for
the U.S. to Follow**

a. In general, it is both wrong and self-defeating for a great power to intervene in the purely domestic affairs of a smaller nation. However, there are some exceptions to this rule which quickly come to mind.

b. A great power has the right to intervene in the affairs of a small nation in order to counter the intervention of another power.

c. A great power has the right to intervene in the affairs of a small nation in those cases—fortunately rare—in which the government of that nation behaves in so barbarous a way that it . . . [offends] civilized opinion. The systematic practice of genocide would be an instance of such barbarism.

d. A great power has the right to intervene when a smaller nation insists in pursuing policies that are [contrary] to the vital interests, economic or strategic, of that great power or its allies.

e. The right to intervene, for whatever good reason, should always be subordinated to prudential considerations. . . . Having a right is one thing, exercising it is another.

—Irving Kristol, *Wall Street Journal*, January 13, 1981.

Should the United States as a great power apply these principles? Does item d. give too much latitude to a great power for intervention? Is this a "might makes right" view? Would this set of principles justify many of the activities of the Soviet Union, such as its invasion of Afghanistan?

**BOX 10–2
American
Imperialism: Is It
Unrealistic?**

The imperial persuasion in American foreign policy toward the Third World [the underdeveloped nations] is not open to question only on moral, legal, and humanitarian grounds. In long-term perspective interventions do not serve the political, economic, and strategic interests that are usually cited to justify them. It is . . . in the interest of the United States . . . to make nonintervention the keystone of U.S. policy.

In the first place, interventions against nationalism confirm suspicions of, and hostility toward, the United States . . ., thus limiting American access and influence in the Third World. . . . American behavior in the Third World has conformed to the descriptions of it proferred by Moscow and Peking. The United States would today have far greater diplomatic latitude and economic opportunities abroad than it now enjoys had it chosen not to intervene against radical movements and governments.

Where the United States has . . . intervene[d] against revolutionary movements, moreover, it has often become entangled in commitments to governments that are inefficient, corrupt, lacking in popular authority, and oppressive. . . . Should such regimes be overthrown, the American capacity to disengage its support and re-align with a successor revolutionary government is weakened if not eliminated for years to come.

Intervention against radical governments does more than assure their lasting hostility toward the United States. . . . these governments are bound to move closer toward the socialist world, and may become politically and economically dependent on it . . . (Cuba is one example). . . .

Intervention, often carried out in parts of the world that are as remote from the United States politically and strategically as they are geographically, makes defense of the "national interest" a world-wide responsibility. The arenas in which a direct confrontation of the major powers may occur become ever wider; the chance of war brought on by the momentum of conflict or miscalculation increases. . . .

Another long-term disadvantage of interventionism is that it confirms radical stereotypes, increases racial hatreds, and thus enhances the possibility of race conflict.

—Melvin Gurtov, *The United States Against the Third World: Anti-Nationalism and Intervention* (New York: Praeger, 1974), pp. 210–211.

It is the perceived nature of the Reagan revolution—radical, cumulative, and wholesale—which promotes allied anxiety. Fundamentals which have long underlain Western confidence in American policy suddenly have become subject to extremes of emphasis and extremes of de-emphasis: defense without detente; arms without arms control; stretchouts leading to abandonment of international economic commitments with little apparent empathy for the human consequences, a palpable militarization of attitude approaching doomsday chic with little apparent interest in America's traditional liberal values, or awareness of their universal appeal.

—Thomas L. Hughes, "Up From Reaganism," *Foreign Policy*, **44**:13 (Fall 1981).

Here we have an allusion to high purposes and the belief that the United States, a "civilized state," has the "invariable characteristics" of "wisdom and equity." The Protestant ideal is very much in evidence; simultaneously, there is the assertion that the will of the United States is "law" in the western hemisphere because, in the operational, Bourgeois spirit, this country is an invulnerable "master of the situation" (see Box 10–4).

Sentiments and language of this sort are historically important. They reflect the way the Americans view themselves. One seldom hears such terms as "master," "invulnerable," or "infinite resources" anymore. Statements today tend to reflect the interdependence of nations, the scarcity of resources, and the vulnerabilities wrought by the technology of modern warfare. Yet certainly the Reagan administration had to learn that it was not the master of many situations and came painfully through the process of toning down its original bellicosity.

The mythic and ideological traditions persist all the same. For many Americans, including some policymakers, the flexing of our muscles through military or economic threats is not a sufficient cornerstone for foreign policy. There must be a framework of moral propositions as well as common decency, which will prove to be to our practical advantage in the long run (see Box 10–2). These people like to think of the United States in terms of its unprecedented, generous foreign aid program, the Peace Corps volunteers, the U.S. role in the development of the United Nations, and the oft-repeated American insistence that all countries should respect human rights.

The ideological view, once again, in its purest form eschews such a stance and insists that we be thoroughly practical in our goals. A great

Button which symbolized Canadian resentment of U.S. water and resources policies.

In 1973, the number one best-selling novel in Canada was Richard Rohmer's *Ultimatum*. Its plot was concerned with Canada's needs to preserve its natural resources and its political independence, needs which cause it to place an embargo upon all oil and mineral exports to the resource-hungry United States. The following is the novel's finale, in which the president of the United States, an aggressive Texan, is making a speech that is broadcast to Canada:

" . . . I have decided on a completely different course of action, one which will avoid the effects of a disastrous confrontation by sanction and counter-sanction. It is a course of action which should be of direct and welcome benefit to all Canadians.

"My decision has been made with the concurrence of all the members of my Cabinet and that of the leaders of both parties in the Senate and the House of Representatives. It will provide all the Canadian people with a better opportunity to share their massive resources with us, and in exchange to participate in the high standard of living and superior citizenship enjoyed by the people of the United States.

"As of this moment, Canada will become part of the United States of America. The Government of Canada is hereby dissolved. The provinces will become full member states of the Union. All necessary legislation will be presented to Congress to implement this decision.

"To ensure that this transfer of power takes place smoothly and without incident, transport aircraft and helicopters of the United States Air Force carrying troops and equipment are now landing at airports in all major Canadian cities and at all Canadian Armed Forces bases.

"I hereby instruct the Governor-General of Canada, as Commander-in-Chief of the Canadian Armed Forces, to instruct the Chief of the Defence Staff to order his forces to lay down their arms and to co-operate fully with our troops.

"The citizens of Canada are now citizens of the proudest, finest, greatest nation in the world. To all of you we give the gift of citizenship in the United States of America. I want every one of you to be proud of this new gift, and I bid each of you welcome, my fellow Americans. . . . "

—Richard Rohmer, *Ultimatum* (Toronto: Clarke-Irwin, 1973), pp. 221–222.

**BOX 10–4
America Viewed by
a Friendly Nation:
An *Ultimatum* for
Canada?
(Continued)**

Note the mythic and ideological elements in the "president's" statement. Do you believe that the popularity of such a book in Canada signifies genuine fears of an *Ultimatum* situation developing, or do Canadians just like a good story? Is the *Ultimatum* scenario very likely? Why or why not? Is it possible? If it occurred, what would be the U.S. public's reaction?

power should be aware of the realities of power. It should be willing to build up and demonstrate its military power but not be hesitant in threatening to use its power. At the same time, it should avail itself of other options—diplomatic initiatives, economic aid, economic coercion, and, from time to time as circumstances permit, the use of the Central Intelligence Agency (CIA) and other clandestine instruments to promote chaos or subversion in another country. Human rights are to be respected if possible, but as the Reagan administration's ambassador to the United Nations, Jeane Kirkpatrick, argues, this may not be possible, and it may prove to be in our interest to support and align ourselves with such governments as those of South Korea, South Africa, Chile, Argentina, or the Philippines, whose human rights records range from negligent to deplorable. This ideological view tends to support America's great imperial forays such as Vietnam, large defense outlays, an emphasis on military goods in foreign aid programs, and wide latitude for agencies such as the CIA. This ideological view can also be said to have carried the day for much of the past two decades.

The Foreign Policy Establishment

Foreign policy is really a plural term, for it represents the many decisions, processes, initiatives, and actions that govern the relations of a nation with other nations. But how is it developed and carried out? The short and incomplete answer is that the nation's foreign policy establishment, both diplomatic and military, sets policy goals and objectives and then utilizes any number of resources to implement them.

These resources are varied and are used as deemed appropriate. If the goal, for example, is to stop North Korean aggression against South Korea, the response is military. If the aim is to conciliate Arab-Israeli differences, the response may be diplomatic. President Jimmy Carter, for example, sought to reconcile differences between Egypt and Israel in the 1978 talks at Camp David, and he achieved a modicum of success. If a small power is giving the United States trouble, the response may be economic—either in the "carrot" form of inducements such as loans, aid, or tarriff concessions, or in the "stick" form of economic coercion. Reducing cocoa imports from a country whose economy is heavily dependent upon sales of this commodity is one possibility. Responses may combine diplomatic, military, or economic initiatives. And responses may take other forms—clandestine activity of the CIA, for example, or using another government to further our aims. It has been alleged, though not proved, that the United States considered asking Israel to send a strike force into Iran to rescue our embassy personnel who were taken as hostages in 1979.

The Constitutional Mandate: President and Congress

As Chapters 6 and 7 make clear, the ultimate constitutional authority in foreign policymaking is the president, who carries out these duties with the advice and consent of the Senate (Article II, Section 2). This authority is combined with the president's national security policy role as commander-in-chief of the armed forces (also Article II, Section 2). The day-to-day management of foreign policy and national security policy is in practice the concern of specialists and bureaucrats of the foreign policy establishment, while the president is more likely to be involved with crisis management, major current policy concerns, and such matters as meetings with ambassadors and foreign dignitaries. We have seen that the foreign policy and national security tasks of Congress center on appropriations, the investigatory power, and, in the Senate only, confirmations of officials to be appointed, and treaty ratification.

These formal distinctions between foreign policy and national security policy, between big issues and day-to-day concerns and to a more limited extent between concerns of the executive and legislative branches of government, are much neater than the actual divisions that take place in the foreign policy apparatus. Bureaucrats and specialists have considerable autonomy. Various units of the apparatus—military policymakers, embassies, policy-planning staffs, and clandestine operations are examples—are often split on policy matters and these splits are made more serious by a confusion of roles and agencies, and fragmentation of leadership. This organizational confusion is in turn a mirror of the nation's mythic and ideological strains in foreign and national security policy.

Whatever the policy response to any given situation, particular officials and agencies are designated as sources and executors of American foreign and national security policies: the State and Defense departments, the National Security Council, the Central Intelligence Agency, and a variety of other bureaus and agencies. But these sources also include research institutes, universities, defense contractors, lobby groups interested in one or another aspect of policy, and a variety of other nongovernmental interests and associations. Also included are such influential institutions as the press and prestigious foreign policy journals like *The New York Times* and *Foreign Affairs* (see Boxes 10–5 and 10–6). Together all these institutions amount to a foreign policy establishment; and although "establishment" is sometimes regarded as an amorphous term we regard it as appropriate for defining the diverse institutions and individuals who have a substantial impact on the policymaking process, whether they be the secretary of state, a professor of international relations at a prestigious university who is a policy consultant, or a member of the Israeli lobby group.

We have pointed out that the foreign policy apparatus of the United States resides in part in the Executive Office of the President. This office

The NSC, NSA, and the CIA

**BOX 10–5
A Foreign Policy
Lobby Group**

**BOX 10–6
The Top Twenty
Universities in
Military Research**

University	Fiscal Year 1979 ($ million)	Fiscal Year 1980 ($ million)
1. Johns Hopkins University	$155.8	$163.3
2. Massachusetts Institute of Technology	123.7	154.6
3. University of California System	24.2	29.7
4. Illinois Institute of Technology	23.4	26.3
5. Stanford University	10.7	18.1
6. University of Texas	15.1	15.8
7. University of Rochester	12.8	15.5
8. Georgia Tech Research Institute	8.4	14.8
9. University of Dayton	13.6	13.9
10. Pennsylvania State University	14.6	12.2
11. University of Southern California	11.9	10.3
12. University of Washington	8.7	10.1
13. University of Alaska	9.3	8.1
14. Carnegie-Mellon University	4.5	7.3
15. University of Illinois	3.7	6.8
16. University of New Mexico	5.4	5.5
17. California Institute of Technology	3.3	5.4
18. Harvard University	1.4	4.9
19. University of Pennsylvania	3.1	4.9
20. Columbia University	4.1	4.8

—*Society*, **19**:4 (November/December 1981).

includes the National Security Council (NSC) and the agencies it officially administers—the National Security Agency (NSA) and the Central Intelligence Agency (CIA). Membership on the NSC includes the president, the vice-president, and the secretaries of state and defense. The NSC has its own staff whose duty is to provide advice to the president on the national security implications of any important foreign or domestic policy development.

The two agencies that operate under the authority of the NSC are supersecret in nature. The NSA deals primarily with coding and electronic espionage. The CIA, which is the better known of the two, is in charge of research and data gathering on matters relating to the operations of foreign governments, particularly unfriendly ones. It also conducts "covert operations," a term it seems to prefer to "spying" and "foreign espionage." Its charter limits its operations to foreign countries; it is not supposed to work within the United States. But the CIA has violated its charter on any number of occasions, and the Reagan administration is seeking legal authorization for domestic operations (see Box 10–7).

Old hands and young ones alike throughout the intelligence community endure common frustrations. Their social lives are constricted by their involvement in intelligence. Many drink just a little too much, and some, if they have the good sense, seek the help of psychiatrists; CIA has an "approved" list. The phenomenon of the "burned-out" intelligence officer, or the spy who has come in from the cold, is a real one. It is accepted blandly as part of the game. It is "understood" at CIA. The agency takes care of these guys whether their collapse came about from a series of hard tours overseas or from too long on the firing line of current intelligence and the endless paper wars of Washington. Jobs and high-sounding titles are created for them to await their retirement.

[This is] a harsh reality . . . men beaten to a moral pulp by their profession. The operational chief of the base in Central America from which the [unsuccessful] Bay of Pigs invasion [of Cuba] was launched was relegated to the CIA training facility afterwards. I ran into him during my training there. He couldn't make it through the day without a half-pint. By early evening he could be found standing at the bar in the CIA club silently staring into his glass. He wouldn't join bar conversations. He'd simply stand till he fell. The bartender was thoroughly familiar with his nightly ritual and used to come from behind the bar at about ten-thirty and guide Ray to the door, where he'd call a jeep to take him back to his quarters. His wife had divorced him, and he spent all of his time on the CIA training facility, either drinking or instructing us on amphibious landings. Whenever the question of the Bay of Pigs came up during a lecture, and it invariably did, he refused to answer it. Most of the time he'd be fighting back tears; some of the time he got so worked up at the mere mention of the Bay of Pigs that he'd have to dismiss the class.

—Patrick J. McGarvey, *CIA: The Myth and the Madness* (New York: Saturday Review Press, 1972), pp. 7–8.

The major difficulties with the NSC and the CIA in terms of policy-making stem from their penchant for working autonomously from time to time, creating confusion and embarrassment. Autonomy is not considered a desirable bureaucratic goal within the foreign policy establishment nor in the minds of such officials as the president, the secretary of state, and the secretary of defense. But this problem also surfaces at lower rungs of authority. Many ambassadors have had their advice ignored, policies abandoned, or hopes dashed because of the seizing of an initiative by the CIA. On occasion this has taken the form of a "revolution" or coup d'état, a change of government in which a pro-Western, but often dictatorial, leader is installed with covert CIA backing. On occasion an ambassador and other embassy personnel learn that the CIA representative attached to their particular embassy has more policy-making authority than they have. There are perhaps many reasons why this occurs, but the basis for it probably resides in a syndrome called "the banishment of expertise." One ex-official of the State Department who recalls many Cuba, Vietnam, and other decisions of the 1960's speaks of "the replacement of the experts, who were generally and increasingly pessimistic, by men described as 'can-do' guys, loyal and energetic fixers unsoured by expertise."[3]

The State Department

The State Department is expected to carry out the detailed, day-to-day operations of American foreign policy. It supplies expert advice and information to the secretary of state, the White House, and other government agencies. It has a tremendous resource in its more than 250 embassies, consulates, and trade missions around the world, which serve among other functions as sensitive "listening posts." In Washington, its "country desks" serve as a counterpart and liaison office for each post. It operates a training center, the Foreign Service Institute, for its career officials in the Foreign Service, which operates separately from other civil service units of the government. It administers cultural exchange programs, conducts seminars for visiting scholars, has a congressional liaison unit, and serves as the nation's representative not only in the United Nations but in a myriad of other international organizations. It has its own intelligence-gathering unit (see Figure 10–1).

The traditional role of foreign policy formulator, spokesman, and administrator has been carried out by the secretary of state. There can be little doubt that some of the holders of this office have established policies with lasting effects. John Foster Dulles (1953–1959), who served under President Eisenhower, devised many of the mutual security treaties to which the United States is still tied today. Henry Kissinger (1973–1977) revamped our China policy, an abrupt change from the

[3] John F. Campbell, *The Foreign Affairs Fudge Factory* (New York: Basic Books, 1971), p. 54.

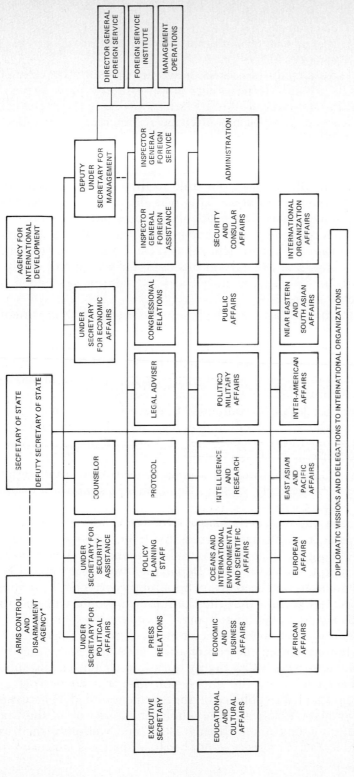

Figure 10–1.
Organization chart of the State Department.

* A separate agency with the director reporting directly to the Secretary and serving as principal adviser
to the Secretary and the President on Arms Control and Disarmament.

post-1949 insistence on no diplomatic or trade relations with mainland China.

As we have already indicated, however, the State Department has often lost its primacy in the foreign policy establishment. In part this is because it has not fared well in its battles with other agencies. The CIA with its "can-do" outlook has often been preferred by presidents and important White House officials. The Defense Department is much larger and has a powerful political constituency. The president's own national security adviser, the special assistant to the president for national security affairs, has from time to time overshadowed the influence of the secretary of state. This was the case in the Kennedy and Nixon administrations, and probably in some others as well.

It has also been suggested that unlike other Cabinet departments, State has no natural constituency that it can count on for support in the way that Commerce can call on business, Labor can call on the labor movement, or Defense can utilize defense contractors and a host of closely related interests.

This may be the case, but the history of the State Department since 1945 may provide even more compelling reasons for its decline. State took a terrible hammering from its critics in Congress in the early 1950s, especially from Senator Joe McCarthy of Wisconsin. McCarthy alleged Communist subversion was taking place in the department and used his Senate floor immunity (thus averting lawsuits) to label various career diplomats as disloyal. He contended that various numbers—he changed the numbers often—of Communists had worked to bring about territorial concessions to the Soviet Union in Eastern Europe and Asia at the end of World War II. Among many other charges, McCarthy and his followers said that the United States had "lost China," as though it were ours to lose, because of the State Department's support of Communist revolutionaries there.

The China policy issue is instructive. The Communist revolution in China was a great military success by 1949, driving the Nationalist forces of Chiang Kai-skek off the mainland to the island of Taiwan. What had in fact occurred at the State Department was that some advice and recommendations had been given, apparently correctly, by a number of China experts who said that the Communists would win and that the Nationalists lacked popular support. This advice was not heeded by the department. It never took the recommended stance of neutrality in the struggle but supported the Nationalist cause. McCarthy and his congressional supporters, using highly questionable but hardly subtle tactics, managed to create the impression that treasonous voices in the department had led to policies of appeasement and abject surrender to the Communists. Practically the whole China section of the State Department, including many distinguished and well-published experts, were fired as "security risks"—not because any treasonous activity was shown to have occurred but because these officials merely had their security classifications "revised." In the end, McCarthy never found or caught a single Communist at State, despite all the clamor of his investigations. Perhaps it is significant that McCarthy's downfall came about only when he attacked the Defense Department later on. Defense had the strength and resources to combat him and his followers.[4]

One of the more interesting sidelights of the China episode is the question of whether we would have become as involved in Vietnam as we did had we still had the expertise of the old China hands available to us. This cannot be answered, but we do know that McCarthyism virtually wiped out the State Department's experts on China. And it is no great consolation that one of the politicians who built his early career on the chant of "treason" and the "loss of China," Richard Nixon, was heralded as a statesman for reversing our China policy, a trend he himself helped set in motion with McCarthy.

The State Department was badly riddled and shocked by its experiences with McCarthyism. Career foreign service people became more cautious than even their usual rational-professionalism called for; they had seen promising careers suddenly dashed upon the shoals of right-wing politics.

Has State ever recovered from this great trauma? Certainly the times have changed. McCarthy later fell into disgrace, censured by the Senate for his conduct before his death in 1956. But many observers doubt that the fearsome memories will go away for some time to come, and the timidity and indecisiveness of State, as noted by many presidents, is undoubtedly rooted in its past.

The Department of Defense must also be considered a preeminent factor in the foreign policy establishment. Part of the rationale of America's great power role in the world is based on its immense destructive capacity. The Pentagon spends roughly one quarter of the entire federal budget and is expected to spend one third by 1984. Some 40 percent of the 5 million government personnel work for it. Not even these figures tell the entire story, however; some estimates suggest, for example, that up to one third of the NASA budget is used for military applications. The size of the CIA budget is an official secret. Military aid is an important share of the foreign aid budget. And costs such as those imposed by the Veterans Administration are certainly defense-related.

There are strong indications that defense spending will become an ever worsening problem. The Reagan administration has drawn up plans for Defense to spend more than $1.5 trillion in this decade. Defense equipment costs are currently increasing at twice the inflation

**The Defense
Department**

---

[4] Alan D. Harper, *The Politics of Loyalty* (Westport, Conn.: Greenwood Press, 1969); Athan Theoharis, *Seeds of Repression* (Chicago: Quadrangle, 1971).

rate, which raises the question as to the kind and quality of defense that we are purchasing as well as the question of how long this can continue.[5] There is also the matter of relative shares of defense spending in the West. The United States is the dominant military power in this group of nations, but it has fallen to tenth place in the world in terms of per capita gross national product. United States living standards are also falling with its declining productivity. Its productivity is lower than that of almost any other Western nation (it suffered a net decline in 1980). Whether Americans will continue to be willing to pay for the defense of nations that are per capita wealthier than we is doubtful.[6]

Many of the reasons usually given for having a large defense budget and a military presence in the world involve the need to react to aggression, particularly by the Soviet Union. Just as important a rationale for the defense establishment is the often stated need of avoiding war or smaller-scale conflicts. This reasoning overall says that a strong military posture will deter aggressors large and small. The logic extends, however, mostly to the nuclear "balance of terror" between the United States and the Soviet Union. This balance supposedly prevents nuclear war because of both sides' fear of assured retaliation. This reasoning presupposes our ability to anticipate the reactions and perceptions of the Soviets (see Box 10–8).

Critics of this reasoning claim that nuclear arms provide no security, and that the continued production and emplacement of nuclear weapons—in a triad of planes, submarines, and land silos—will assure only mutual destruction. Weapons built usually become weapons used; no amount of assurances about how secure we are nor any statements about the possibility of "winning" in a nuclear confrontation are capable of convincing the public that it can take a relaxed attitude toward the nuclear buildup. Also, nuclear armaments complicate conventional arms clashes and diplomacy because there is always the threat of a progression from these flashpoints to all-out warfare. And there is always the possibility in our technological and computerized age that nuclear war could be set off by accident. Two computer malfunctions in 1980 underscored this threat when the computers falsely reported that Soviet missiles had been launched.

The rationale of deterrence—the belief that we fend off nuclear terror by creating our own credible threat—rests ultimately on the "triad," a three-pronged approach to nuclear capability that has been sustained by the United States over the past two decades. The triad presupposes that the failure of one nuclear delivery system will mean two others are still intact. The triad consists of manned bombers, missiles placed in

---

[5] *Wall Street Journal,* April 10, 1981.
[6] Lester Thurow, "The Moral Equivalent of Defeat," *Foreign Policy,* **42**: 114–124 (Spring 1981).

hardened ground silos, and Polaris submarines, which can deliver missiles from their underwater locations to a target more than 1,200 miles away. Defense Department officials stress that the manned bombers are needed because they introduce a manual delivery threat into the triad system. The land missiles are necessary because they are much less

> Questioned on whether the computer false alarm that showed Soviet missiles on the way to destroy the U.S. could have led to a world war, the Defense Dept. spokesman said, "I'm going to duck that question." He may duck the question, but no one would be able to duck the missiles turned loose by the robots in the Defense Dept.
> —*UE News*, June 16, 1980, p. 1.
>
> The following exchange is from an interview with [Vice President] George Bush by Robert Scheer of the *Los Angeles Times*:
>
> **Q.** Don't we reach a point with these strategic weapons where we can wipe each other out so many times that it really doesn't matter whether we're 10 percent or 2 percent lower or higher?
>
> **A.** Yes, if you believe there is no such thing as a winner in a nuclear exchange, that argument makes a little sense. I don't believe that.
>
> **Q.** How do you win a nuclear exchange?
>
> **A.** You have survivability of command in control, survivability of industrial potential, protection of a percentage of your citizens, and you have a capability that inflicts more damage on the opposition than it can inflict upon you. That's the way you can have a winner, and the Soviets' planning is based on the ugly concept of a winner in a nuclear exchange.
>
> **Q.** Do you mean like five percent would survive? Two percent?
>
> **A.** More than that—if everybody fired everything he had, you'd have more than that survive.
> —*UAW Washington Report*, October 3, 1980, p. 3.

BOX 10–8
The Government Speaks on the Ultimate Conflict

vulnerable than aircraft to defensive weapons. The submarines offer the advantage of a mobile force. They are so difficult to track, that no known defense against them has been devised.

Congress and the Reagan administration have authorized a revamping of the triad to modernize it and purportedly make it less vulnerable. An MX missile will replace the present arsenal. A B–1 bomber will replace the B–52s that many claim are now obsolete, and the B–1 will in turn be replaced in 1989 or 1990 by the Stealth bomber, which cannot be tracked by radar. Finally, the Trident submarine, after years of delay and cost overruns, appears to be nearing completion so that it can replace the present fleet. All this weaponry is very expensive, of course; the Stealth project alone is set minimally at $21 billion, and cost overruns are likely.

A fleeting look at the triad nuclear defense system might mislead a novice into thinking that national security policies are smoothly devised and coordinated. It is quite likely, however, that the Pentagon is the least manageable and least well-managed department in the government. Its sheer size is by itself a challenge to management, but it is also clearly a center of waste, occasional corruption, and service rivalries among the Army, Navy, Air Force, and Marine Corps. A joint chiefs of staff arrangement has been in effect throughout the post-World War II period to promote cooperation among the services, coordination of policy, and divisions of responsibility, but this does not appear to have solved the problem.

Service rivalries were recently investigated by the General Accounting Office, and the GAO's findings were not good news for the economy-minded. All of the services, for example, strive mightily to maintain their own logistics and training systems, even though a consolidation of these appears to be practical. The Army and the Navy were each found to be running helicopter-training schools at a cost of $63 million per year more than the expense of a combined school. The four separate air forces require excess repair depot expenses of $250 million to $400 million annually. The failure to standardize ground repair gear for military aircraft results in a waste of $300 million a year. The independent supply functions, which could be consolidated to provide common services to all, results in an extra expense of $100 million a year.[7] And defense logistics and training represents only one small area of defense operations. Despite this and the great waste in many other areas of the defense effort, President Reagan's stance has been to enlarge, rather than cut, the defense budget.

Defense often appears incapable of quickly putting together new plans or policies to meet new situations. A recent example is the devel-

[7] "Billions Down the Pentagon Drain," *U.S. News and World Report,* April 27, 1981, pp. 25–28.

opment of the Rapid Deployment Force (RDF), described officially as "a four-service reservoir of forces suitable for use in a wide range of non-NATO contingencies."[8] Middle East instability and crises have combined with our petroleum needs to give a new policy emphasis to that area of the world. Defense planners therefore believe it is necessary to develop a force that can be quickly sent from as far away as the continental United States to protect the oil fields and shiekdoms of the Persian Gulf. Unfortunately, the Defense Department admits, it took three years of elaborate manuevers and exercises to test RDF capabilities, and strong doubt remains whether even an agreed command structure has been established for the force.[9]

There is no doubt, however, about the political influence of the Defense Department. Its far-flung operations, bases, installations, and contracts reach into every state and congressional district. The result of this widespread influence of Defense is reassuring for those who like to see large defense budgets and often politically indispensable even to those who do not.

[8] U.S. Government, *Department of Defense—Annual Report, Fiscal Year 1982*, p. 189.
[9] *Ibid.*, Chapter 6 and p. vii.

There still are some concerns that . . . the Stealth [bomber project] is a bubble, inflated by still-unconfirmed reports of the program's massive size. Northrop [Corporation] and the Pentagon aren't talking about spending projections for the bomber, which is designed to be undetectable by radar. But *Aviation Week* magazine, which is well-respected on such matters, places the total value at $21.9 billion, and says Northrop's work will be more than $7 billion by 1990.

"One hates to invest on press reports and rumor," says Mr. [Wolfgang] Demisch, although it's "faintly reassuring" to have a confirmation from the company that the program will have a material effect. Still, he believes Wall Street is correct in believing the reported potential huge sums involved in Stealth.

Even if the program is as big as it seems to be, "remember that the B1 program was solid once, too," cautions Mr. [John] Simon. And a Carter-like cutting of the project isn't the only possible devastating blow.

"Peace could break out between now and 1990," says Mr. Demisch.

—*Wall Street Journal*, October 22, 1981.

**BOX 10–9
The Risk of
Investing in
Defense Industries**

AID and ICA

In addition to the president, the State and Defense departments, the NSC, the national security advisers in the White House, and the intelligence agencies, there are other programs and agencies that play a role in foreign policymaking and policy development. These include the Agency for International Development (AID), which dispenses grants and loans, much of it in the form of military aid, to various countries. The International Communications Agency (ICA), technically part of the State Department, assumes an important role as the propaganda arm of the United States abroad. Most embassies have an ICA information or cultural officer attached to them. In many cities around the globe, ICA cultural centers provide libraries, film showings, art exhibits, and other presentations. ICA also runs the Voice of America broadcasts heard around the world. Such departments as Commerce, Agriculture, and Labor also commonly provide an attaché at the larger embassies and present the U.S. view at various international meetings. Finally, the Peace Corps is claimed by some observers to have peripheral effects on the international position of the United States because of the work its volunteers carry out in poor countries.

**BOX 10–10
The Pentagon
Budget is
Increased for
Planes, for
Missiles—and for
Tubas**

Military spending is going up. So spending for military bands is going up. What could be more natural?

It isn't fair, say outraged partisans of the arts, to spend more money on Sousa oom-pahs when spending for genuine classical music is being cut. They note balefully that the National Endowment for the Arts has been targeted for a 50% budget cut . . . while the Army, Navy, Air Force and Marine bands are in line for a 2% increase. . . .

The discrepancy has arts hawks in Congress seething. "There are three full [military] bands in the Washington area, and each of them has a larger budget than the National Symphony Orchestra," says Rep. Fred Richmond, a New York Democrat. . . . "I don't think it's fair. . . ."

"It looks like everybody's trying to chop our heads off," complains an Army band official, Sgt. Major Donald Young. The bands "wave the flag" and "stir patriotism," he says. A Pentagon spokesman says the 5,335 military-band members are needed to help lure recruits, preserve morale at foreign bases and burnish the military image. . . .

—*Wall Street Journal,* November 9, 1981.

BOX 10–11
Mrs. Kirkpatrick
Calls U.S. Impotent
in U.N.

Jeane J. Kirkpatrick said yesterday that the United States was impotent in the United Nations because "we simply have behaved like a bunch of amateurs."

The American delegate, speaking in New York at a meeting of the Heritage Foundation, a conservative research group, said she had come to her conclusions after months of reflection. . . .

She said American influence had declined because of "a persistent ineptitude in international relations, an ineptitude that has persisted through several decades, several administrations."

One problem, she said, is that the United States has been unable to express a cohesive national purpose, instead "stumbling from issue to issue almost on a Mad Hatter basis."

—*The New York Times*, June 8, 1982, p. 1.

Policy Coordination

The problems of coordinating the work of all these agencies and maintaining a semblance of policy consistency are immense. Leadership is supposed to come from the president and his advisers, especially his national security adviser and the National Security Council and its not inconsiderable staff. This staff, in particular, is supposed to maintain a complete file of up-to-date and approved "position papers" outlining American policy in various areas of the world and laying down the responsibilities of each of the units of the government in the event of possible developments. Commendable as all these efforts may be, history often seems to outrun them, and American foreign policy regularly appears to be mainly reactive—responses and reactions to a scattering of developments as news about them crowds in, a propaganda statement by some foreign power here, an invasion there, the revocation of treaty-imposed economic obligations somewhere else.

Part of the problem lies in the variety of roles America feels compelled to play in the world. It may aim to develop a "strategic consensus" across the Middle East to resist Soviet influence in the area but find itself also bound to play the role of peacemaker between Israel and its neighbors while at the same time trying to prop up near-feudal Arab regimes in the face of dangerous (to our oil supplies) revolutionary ferment. It may find that cooperation with and support of our traditional allies, the European democracies, conflicts with our hope of developing working relationships with South American military regimes. And in region after region of the world, we find that our concern to be friendly

Food is shipped abroad under the auspices of an AID program.

and helpful to governments is in conflict with our traditional role of supporting and promoting the activities of our own business community overseas.

A world as chaotic as this is bound to strain the most coherent of governments. The fragmented character of American government is singularly ill-positioned to confront in a unified way that kind of confusion overseas. Each of our major national security units and their internal divisions has its own way of looking at the world and its own political needs and goals, all intensified by the ongoing rivalries among them. The political needs of the presidency, in particular, may well be at cross

purposes with its responsibilities for coordinating the work of the foreign policy establishment. At best, its leadership will be episodic. We
should also remember that Congress is a part of this picture. Especially
through its committees and subcommittees, not to mention a senator
off on a junket, Congress plays an important if sporadic role in foreign
policymaking and implementation. Quite apart from its vestigial constitutional mandate to declare war, Congress authorizes all expenditures, conducts investigations of major developments, helps in all kinds
of ways to mold public opinion, and, in the Senate, reviews treaties and
important personnel appointments. And as we have seen, Congress is no
model of internal coherence and consistency.

Beyond these problems of policy coordination is the fundamental
problem of the contradictions between the hopes of myth and the mundane practices of ideology. These run through every level of American
foreign policymaking and implementation and often infect the internal
operations of agencies such as AID and ICA. We give foreign aid because
we are a generous people anxious to support the democratic forces of
the "free world." It is also true that, with callous disregard for the suffering of others, we give aid to certain of our allies simply because it is
in our immediate political interest to do so, or in the interest of some of
our giant corporations. We tell highly embarrassing truths about ourselves because we believe a proud nation should not fear the truth; at
the same time, we order the Voice of America to portray the United
States in the mostly favorable light.

In the light of these complexities, it is not surprising that in Washington and in our embassies and other overseas stations, rational professionalism is the dominant mode in the absence of consistent political
leadership. As leadership vacuums develop here and there, some of the
more aggressive officials take charge, not of all foreign policymaking
but those bits and pieces of it for which they have immediate responsibility. In routine situations this may be acceptable, but as we saw in
Chapter 9, the rational-professional mentality is geared to executing
policy, not making it. Left to their own devices, rational professionals
tend to let commitment to their particular skills take charge, as the Bay
of Pigs adventure, frequent incidents in Vietnam, and many other examples testify.

The Military-Industrial Complex

Since the end of World War II, large defense budgets and an immense
arsenal of weapons have become features not only of the nation's security posture but also of our domestic economy. The expenses of wars,
rearmament, and massive allocations to research and weapons development have warped other national processes and goals. Myth and ideol-

ogy are both present here in graphic relief. Myth proclaims that our vast security establishment is necessary to deter the spread of tyranny in the world; ideology promotes keeping the nation on a continuous war footing. But these factors can get thoroughly mixed together when officials seek to justify their policies and actions. In the Vietnam War, it was never clear whether we were involved for the noble reasons of defending democracy, stopping the spread of communism, and correcting violations of international law, or for the mundane reasons of protecting our economic interests in the region, proving we could fight and win, and preserving the Southeast Asia Treaty Organization (SEATO).

What keeps America in a continuous state of war or preparation for war? Is it solely because of the threat of aggression by the Soviet Union? No, say some observers; we have a "permanent warfare state" because this is the result—perhaps even the goal—of the military-industrial complex. But the military-industrial complex is a hard term to define. How can we know that it exists? And if it exists, how does it operate?

**BOX 10–12
U.S. Military Treaty
Obligations**

The United States is committed by treaty alliances to the military defense of dozens of nations around the world. Some of these major commitments are:

North Atlantic Treaty (NATO)	Nearly all Western European countries plus Greece, Turkey, Iceland, and Canada
Rio Treaty (OAS—Organization of American States)	Nineteen Latin American countries
Anzus Treaty	Australia and New Zealand
Southeast Asia Treaty (SEATO)	Australia, Great Britain, France, New Zealand, Pakistan, Philippines, and Thailand
Republic of Korea Treaty	South Korea
Republic of China Treaty	Taiwan
Japanese Treaty	Japan

All these treaties were signed in the 1940's and 1950's, reflecting the "pactomania" that existed in the early postwar period.

In the first place, no serious observer of this phenomenon believes that a plot exists in which the complex plans ways to thwart the public concern over the costs and threat of war. This complex includes a variety of "private" institutions—banks, universities, defense suppliers, the scientific and research communities, foundations, Washington consulting firms, and privately organized defense lobbies, to name a few. Military and foreign policy matters may not even be the most important concerns of some of these institutions. The Boeing Company, for example, is generally regarded as a major defense contractor; but in recent years, the bulk of its business has been devoted to the sale of aircraft for civilian uses.

The military-industrial complex has a shadowy, amorphous character, but it seems to exist all the same. The influence of its major elements is brought to bear upon the budget and other policy processes of Congress and the bureaucracy. Its ability to mobilize a large segment of the public is felt when base closings, military construction projects, or defense contracts are at issue. Most importantly, the top officials of the government, whether holding office currently or in the past, believe that it exists. Not only did President Eisenhower warn of its dangers in his Farewell Address; Supreme Court Justice William O. Douglas believed that its existence is uncritically accepted by the American public.[10] The prominent conservative economist and former chairman of the Federal Reserve Board, Arthur Burns, says that

> The defense establishment has left its mark on both the structure and functioning of the economy. The effects are all around us. . . . , defense oriented industries—notably the aerospace group, electronics and communications—have become a major factor in the economy, and their development has favored many communities . . . .[11]

Professor Burns notes that other communities have suffered retarded growth because skilled workers have moved to defense-heavy areas.[12] And sociologist C. Wright Mills also gave us a compelling version of the idea of the military-industrial complex in his book *The Power Elite*.[13]

The military-industrial complex is also characterized by certain routines that show up in career patterns. A great many generals, admirals, and colonels join the corporate boards of defense contractors when they leave the military. And quite often, they reverse the pattern and return to the military fold after serving on some corporate boards. It is obvious there is a close institutional relationship between the foreign policy and defense agencies and the corporate world, as shown in many of the ca-

[10] William O. Douglas, *International Dissent: Six Steps Toward World Peace* (New York: Vintage, 1971), pp. 14–15.

[11] Quoted by James A. Donovan, *Militarism, U.S.A.* (New York: Scribners, 1970), p. 46.

[12] James A. Donovan, *Militarism, U.S.A.,p. 46.*

[13] C. Wright Mills, *The Power Elite* (New York: Oxford University Press, 1956).

**BOX 10–13
A Soviet View of
U.S. Foreign Policy**

Pravda, February 1, 1981—In his first press conference as U.S. Secretary of State . . . A. Haig accused the Soviet Union of "training, funding and equipping international terrorism." . . . Washington is starting a new propaganda campaign. . . .

In switching to the problem of "international terrorism" at this time, Washington is pursuing at least the following goals:

First, to try to discredit the peace-loving policy of the Soviet Union and to ascribe to it features that it lacks altogether, since our country has always consistently opposed terrorism and continues to oppose it;

Second, to distort the essence of national-liberation movements and label these "international terrorism," so that, having done so, it can then "prove" that the progressive states' aid to national-liberation movements is the same thing as support for "international terrorism"; and

Third, under the pretext of combatting "international terrorism," to untie its hands for imperialist interference in the internal affairs of other states, primarily those with shaky reactionary or fascist regimes. . . .

The main element in this whole undertaking of the Reagan Administration is an attempt to jeopardize the processes of international detente and to justify America's negative position with respect to strategic arms limitation and other measures aimed at lessening international tension.

The campaign that Washington has undertaken, which involves lies and hypocrisy, cannot help but raise anxious questions among the international public, which perceives it as a game that poses a great danger to the cause of peace. The peoples expect something else from the American administration—an end to Carter's policy, which was in every way dragging the world into a cold war situation. So far, the first steps of the Republican administration in Washington indicate otherwise.

—*Current Digest of the Soviet Press*, **33**:1–2 (March 4, 1981)

reers of the famous names of the post-World War II years—Robert S. McNamara of Ford Motor Company, the Defense Department, and the World Bank; General Douglas MacArthur of the Army and Remington Rand; General Maxwell Taylor of the Army, several corporations, and the State Department; and General Alexander Haig of the Army, the White House, NATO, the State Department and United Technologies.

Research carried out by Senator William Proxmire several years ago showed that Lockheed, General Dynamics, North American Rockwell, and other big defense contractors employed large numbers of retired military personnel.[14]

The military-industrial complex is not a monolithic entity. Corporate rivalries are obvious in the quest for defense contracts. Competition also plays a role in the decision making about locations for military facilities and projects. Georgia and South Carolina, for example, are fairly bristling with military installations because of the long-term and well-placed influence of some of their members of Congress. Important rivalries also exist among the separate military services. All of them

[14] William Proxmire, *Report from Wasteland* (New York: Praeger, 1970).

**BOX 10–14
Women Vote for
Peace**

Women do not recognize it, [but] they have voted as a bloc on one crucial issue: opposition to war. Since 1950, foreign policy, far more than any other issue, has divided men and women. This tendency, reflected in the womens' vote, results from shared political attitudes, not political organization. Public opinion survey data abundantly describe women as more opposed than men to American involvement in Korea and Southeast Asia.

In 1969, a Gallup Poll found that 64 percent of women respondents declared themselves "doves," as against 48 percent of the men. In 1972, Gallup found that 70 percent of women questioned, and 54 percent of the men, favored a troop withdrawal from Vietnam by the year's end. In 1980, this pattern holds true.

In January [1980], Gallup found that 43 percent of the men questioned and 30 percent of the women favored the use of force if the hostages in Iran were harmed. In a February poll, Gallup found that 50 percent of the men questioned felt there was too little defense spending, as compared with 41 percent of the women; 66 percent of the men, and 53 percent of the women, favored a return to the draft; 65 percent of the men and 55 percent of the women felt that the president was not tough enough in dealing with the Soviet Union.

The message is clear: in foreign policy, women as a group are more peace-oriented than men.

—Marjorie Lansing of Eastern Michigan University, *New York Times* column reprinted in the Fort Wayne, Indiana, *Journal-Gazette*, October 6, 1980.

have pet projects that they wish to see developed, and often Congress and the bureaucracy pick and choose among these projects using political as well as other criteria. There is overall agreement within the military-industrial complex, however, on the need for large defense budgets and all of the premises and accoutrements of warfare that accompany them.

Perhaps the most dangerous effect of an ongoing and dominant military-industrial complex is the automatic belief that any Soviet military development represents a new superiority that must be offset by a new counterweapon. This kind of belief produces a corresponding reaction by the Soviets, and the arms race escalates.[15]

What seems surprising to many is that Americans manage to live with the threat of a nuclear holocaust. The "survivalist" movement, whose adherents take to the hills, store food and water, and arm themselves heavily for any eventuality, live with their plans built around it. For many years, though not so much today, there was a ready market for G.I. dolls, war toys, and children's versions of military uniforms. A letter to the editor of *Life* magazine published in 1969 demonstrates the socialization of the public that sometimes prevails:

> I grew up on a diet of Hollywood war films. The heroism, the romance, the adventure and even the death excited my interest. For these were men. When I entered the service I was astonished that no Fredric Marches, Clark Gables [or] Humphrey Bogarts were to be found in my barracks. Only young kids like myself (17), half frightened, confused, immature kids stumbling through the senselessness of combat.[16]

However we may choose to deal with the threat of nuclear war—ignoring it, romanticizing it, or like the survivalists, expecting it—the possibility of the annihilation of the human race is the great and melancholy fact of our age. We have learned that the U.S. government has not only used the nuclear threat as a "credible deterrent," but that it secretly has considered the use of such weapons at various times against opponents in Southeast Asia, Korea, and China.[17] Whether the use of such weapons can ever be justified, it is clear that the myth of our international goodness and responsibility for ensuring international peace and justice clashes with our operational ideological modes of thinking about money, might, and power. As long as this conflict persists, the future is unpredictable and neither America nor the world is secure.

---

[15] Ralph Lapp, *The Weapons Culture* (Baltimore: Penguin, 1969), pp. 183–184.
[16] Quoted by James Donovan, *Militarism, U.S.A.*, p. 198.
[17] John W. Dower, "Asia and the Nixon Doctrine: the New Face of Power," in *Open Secret: The Kissinger-Nixon Doctrine in Asia*, Virginia Brodine and Mark Selden, eds. (New York: Harper Perennial Library, 1972), pp. 182–187.

FOR FURTHER READING

ACHESON, DEAN. *Present at the Creation*. New York: Norton, 1969. Memoirs of the
secretary of state who had a great deal to do with formulating many of the
Cold War and containment assumptions of the post-1945 period.

GALBRAITH, JOHN KENNETH. *Ambassador's Journal: A Personal Account of the Kennedy Years*. Boston: Houghton Mifflin, 1969. Galbraith's years as ambassador
to India provide insights into policy at this level.

KENNEDY, ROBERT F. *Thirteen Days: A Memoir of the Cuban Crisis*. New York:
Norton, 1971. Firsthand account of the eyeball-to-eyeball Cuban missile
crisis of 1962.

KISSINGER, HENRY F. *White House Years*. Boston: Little, Brown, 1979. Memoirs of
one of our most recent secretaries of state.

KOLKO, GABRIEL. *The Politics of War: The World and United States Foreign Policy*.
New York: Random House, 1968; and *The Roots of American Foreign Policy:
An Analysis of Power and Purpose*. Boston: Beacon Press, 1969. Kolko, a historian, should be read; his "radical" view of America as an imperialist power
and his survey of American political culture and its relationship to this are
highly instructive.

McGARVEY, PATRICK J. *CIA: The Myth and the Madness*. New York: Saturday Review Press, 1972. Of all the many good books on the CIA—Snepp, Marchetti,
Wise, or whomever—this one is probably the best introduction to the agency.

MILLS, C. WRIGHT. *The Power Elite*. New York: Oxford University Press, 1956.
Sets out the original thesis of the military-industrial complex.

MORGANTHAU, HANS J. *Politics Among Nations*, 5th ed. New York: Knopf, 1973.
Contends that international policies of a nation are dictated by self-interest,
which is extensively defined.

SPANIER, JOHN G. *American Foreign Policy Since World War II*, 8th ed. New York:
Holt, Rinehart and Winston, 1980. Primer on policymaking and the foreign
policy apparatus since 1945.

WILLIAMS, WILLIAM APPLEMAN. *The Tragedy of American Diplomacy*. Cleveland:
World, 1959. Traces the historical roots of foreign policymaking; a progressive view of history, society, and international politics.

Economic Management

On October 24, 1980, the focus of the nation was on the televised debate between presidential candidates Ronald Reagan and Jimmy Carter. Seeking to score a point, Carter said he believed that Reagan's plan to increase defense spending and cut taxes at the same time would lead to a woefully unbalanced federal budget. Reagan replied it was not only possible to balance the budget under these circumstances but that he would see this was done by the 1983 fiscal year and perhaps even by 1982.

On April 21, 1981, President Reagan announced that the budget would be balanced by 1984. Skepticism set in, however, especially among members of the press, after Reagan's defense and tax cut measures were passed in Congress. All the same, a determined Reagan was still saying as late as September 1981 that the budget would be balanced by 1984. In October, Treasury Secretary Donald Regan, testifying before a congressional committee, admitted that there would be no balanced budget by 1984. Finally, on November 10, 1981, Reagan himself called such a balancing an "unlikelihood."

As Reagan has found out, the problems of economic management often seem to be beyond solution. Yet the president and the various units of government are expected to find solutions and provide a measure of economic well-being for all of us.

Managing the nation's economy is a political problem. A large number of respected social scientists even regard politics and economics as parts of one indivisible discipline, for which they often use the term "political economy." This view has a great deal to commend it, especially when we remember that in America political myths and ideological practice are both well ensconced in economic thinking and policymaking.

The Reagan budget-balancing snafu illustrates the great differences between the hopes and realities of economic management. Many peo-

ple, apparently including Reagan himself, believed it was possible to
achieve all his contradictory goals and still have a balanced budget. But
prudent political action dictated a retreat when it became obvious that
the "real world" of economics was going to intrude on these plans.

Some simple policy decisions rooted in preferred economic values
will yield clear results. Early in 1981, the Reagan administration de-

*Government booklet on the
dangers of cotton dust.
President Reagan ordered
this book withdrawn and all
copies destroyed, stating that
the worker on the cover
looked "sick."*

cided that 100,000 government booklets on the dangers of cotton dust must be destroyed. Why? Might not textile workers and others have a legitimate interest in being warned of the dangers of cotton dust? Even if the booklet had limited value, should it not have been kept for those who might be interested in the subject? No, the publication did not fit in with the new administration's policy on occupational safety, which it considered primarily the responsibility of workers in their respective industries. Besides, administration officials pointed out, the worker in the picture on the cover of the booklet looked sick. So the booklets had to go, along with a number of films and slide-tape presentations on health hazards faced by American workers. Worker responsibility for their own health and safety means fewer intrusions into the economy by the Occupational Safety and Health Administration, and less intrusion was a primary goal of the Reagan presidency.[1]

[1] *UAW Washington Report,* **21**:2 (April 17, 1981).

**BOX 11–1
Economist Lester
C. Thurow on "Free
Enterprise" and
the Economy**

The standard conservative response is to advocate the "liberation of free enterprise" and a reduction in social expenditures. Yet this is not how any of these countries [that] have outperformed us [have worked things out]—quite the opposite. Sweden is famous for the most comprehensive social-welfare system in the world; West Germany insists that union leaders hold places on corporate boards of directors; the Japanese Government controls and plans the economy to a degree that makes the U.S. seem like rugged free enterprise.

"Liberating free enterprise" also runs into the facts about the U.S. economy. In the history of the United States our best decade in terms of growth in real per capita (gross national product) . . . was that of the 1940s when the economy was run as a command [socialist] wartime economy. The second best decade . . . was that of the 1960s with all of its social-welfare programs. . . . Real per capita growth since the advent of government intervention has been more than twice as high as it was in the days when government did not intervene or have social-welfare programs. . . .

. . . The lack of government planning, worker participation, and social spending may in fact be at the heart of our poor performance in recent decades.

—*Newsweek,* February 14, 1977, p. 11.

Models of Economic Management

The Reagan administration's position on occupational safety and health is cut from the Liberal Democratic cloth of "free enterprise." This position can be traced back to Adam Smith's economic doctrines as published in his *Wealth of Nations* in England in 1776.

Adam Smith and Free Enterprise

Reacting to a variety of monopolistic and governmental practices of his day, Smith argued for free markets and free trade. He opposed government controls on the economy and private businesses. The arbiter of the economy was to be the pricing system, which every member of the market can accept, reject, and affect through the pursuit of self-interest. Smith saw self-interest as the engine of the economy and the supply of and demand for goods as responses to it. The role of government in this free enterprise system is very limited. It provides for public safety, a legal system, the national defense, and public works such as bridges and roads. But it is not to interfere with the workings of the market.

Smith's laissez-faire economics (laissez-faire refers to government keeping its "hands off" economic matters) is the creed of the Reagan administration, although it has been redefined into modern "supply-side" terms, and the business community widely subscribes to it. However, it is common to hear laissez-faire, free enterprise, and Adam Smith praised by officials of corporations that indulge in pricing and marketing practices and relationships with the government that Smith would have abhorred. The truth is that Smith set out a model, not a working system that has ever existed.[2]

Smith's laissez-faire economics is deeply appealing to the American political tradition of resolute individualism, especially on its Bourgeois, Liberal Democratic side. An "invisible hand" operates the system, Smith tells us, so that each of us promotes the general welfare as we pursue our own selfish goals. Individual greed brings collective prosperity.

Unfortunately, in actual economic life, things have never worked out that simply. Capitalistic societies that tried to model themselves on Smith's principles have been plagued with major social and economic disruptions, including recurrent business slumps, widespread poverty and suffering among the population, and waste and misdirection in economic development.

---

[2] In his *Free to Choose* (New York: Harcourt Brace Jovanovich, 1980), p. 37, economist Milton Friedman suggests Hong Kong as a possible modern exemplar of a laissez-faire system; but laissez-faire is supposedly tied to a self-governing political system, and Hong Kong, as a British crown colony, is assuredly not one of these. See Duncan Campbell, "A Secret Plan for Dictatorship," *New Statesman*, **100:**8–9, 12 (December 2, 1980).

**BOX 11–2
The Public's
Understanding of
Economic Terms**

Question: People in the government and the media use a lot of words and phrases when they talk about economy. I'm going to read you some of them. For each one, would you tell me when you hear that word or phrase used, whether you have a pretty good idea of what the person is talking about, some idea, or not much of an idea what that person is talking about?

Item	Have Pretty Good Idea of the Meaning	Some Idea	Not Much of an Idea	Don't Know
Inflation	85%	12%	3%	1%
Depression	81	15	4	1
Recession	72	19	6	2
Depreciation	64	17	11	9
Deregulation	48	24	18	9
Investment Capital	46	23	17	15
Balance of Payments	45	22	18	15
Tight Monetary Policies	36	21	21	12
Stagflation	11	12	37	40
Supply-Side Economics	10	10	34	45

—*Public Opinion,*4:40 (October-November 1981).

Socialism

Because of these problems, the nineteenth century saw important changes in economic thinking. As industrialization and urbanization increased, two important economic schools of thought emerged in western Europe and America. One of these is socialism, which has never achieved much acceptance in the United States. The other is the "mixed economy," which incorporates the private enterprise system but seeks to temper it with economic planning and regulation by the government, and welfare state measures such as public housing programs, state health care assistance, minimum wage laws, and government-enforced occupational safety programs.

There is a strong tendency in America to equate socialism with the Soviet Union's system of government and command economy. But the Soviet model is only one form of socialism. Socialism can also be a kind of primitive communalism in which the members of a society agree to pool all their wealth and resources for a common life together. During

America's history, several small communities have been organized to experiment with this kind of socialism in different parts of the country. On the other hand, it is widely assumed especially in Western Europe that socialism means state ownership of major industries and rigorous state management of the economy, and there is a parallel tradition in America that describes degrees of government involvement in the economy as degrees of socialism. There is even one socialist tradition—guild socialism, which has had supporters in England and other countries— that advocates "small government," a limited role for the state in planning the economy, and worker-run arrangements in industry. Most socialist parties believe in the democratic process; that is, they give up power when they lose elections and they do not practice coercion against other political parties.

In the United States, the Socialist Party made some impact on state and national politics and the labor movement, and it won elections to Congress and state and local offices until World War I, when it was repressed by the government for its opposition to the war.[3] The socialist philosophy had some impact on the welfare state laws adopted in the 1930s and on the New Left student movements of the 1960s. And intellectually, socialism in America does not appear to be dead. It is widely discussed in some university circles and *Business Week* magazine recently stated that "Socialism is no longer a dirty word to [the] labor [movement]."[4] But it remains true that socialism, however defined, has been marginal to the American political experience.

[3] Gustavus Myers, *History of Bigotry in the U.S.* (New York: Capricorn, 1960).
[4] Quoted in *UAW Washington Report*, **19**:4 (September 21, 1979).

The test of our progress is not whether we add more to the abundance of those who have more; it is whether we provide enough for those who have too little.
—President Franklin D. Roosevelt, Second Inauguration, January 30, 1937.

I don't believe that there is any entitlement, any basic right to legal services or any other kinds of services, and the idea that's been established over the last ten years that almost every service that someone might need in life ought to be provided, financed by the government as a matter of basic right, is wrong. We challenge that. We reject that notion.
—David Stockman, Director of the Office of Management and Budget, on ABC-TV's "Issues and Answers," March 22, 1981.

**BOX 11–3
The "Mixed
Economy" Vs.
Laissez-Faire
Economics**

The Mixed Economy: A Response to the Demands of Ideology

The mixed economy has had much more impact in the United States than socialism. In fact, the nation has always had a mixed economy, with government involvement increasing at various times—with the rise of industrialism in the latter half of the nineteenth century, with the establishment of the Federal Reserve System under the Wilson administration, and with the much more substantial regulation of economic life by the government since the Great Depression of the 1930s. The mixed economy serves as a model for economic management just as the free enterprise system and socialism do, and it has many supporters.

The Eighteenth Century

At the Constitutional Convention of 1787, the Founding Fathers made sure that commercial interests would be both encouraged and protected by the new government. The powers that Article I, Section 8 gave Congress (to regulate commerce with foreign nations, among the states, and with Indian tribes; to lay and collect taxes; to coin money; and to establish government credit, standards of weights and measures, and a postal system) were all designed to facilitate commerce. Section 9 of Article I prevents the states from levying customs duties that would inhibit the free flow of commerce within the nation or hinder the development of a national economy. As the Constitution was being adopted, Alexander Hamilton, soon to be Secretary of the Treasury in George Washington's first administration, insisted with others on a sound international credit position for the United States by making sure that the new government honored its debts. Hamilton also authored a series of influential reports calling for active government assistance to fledgling businesses in the new country.

The government's active concern for the interests of business was made even more evident by the decisions of the early Supreme Court under Chief Justice John Marshall. In 1824, Marshall ruled in *Gibbons* v. *Ogden* that the commerce power established by Article I, Section 8 must be interpreted broadly. Any critics of "big government" interference in business today looking for a culprit might well be advised to study Marshall, for the commerce power, from that day to this, has been the cornerstone of all government involvement in the economy.

The Nineteenth Century

The nineteenth century, particularly after the Civil War, saw the rise of the American industrial system. The corporation became the dominant kind of business firm, and the government generally heeded the demands made on it by these enterprises. Industries received strong tariff protection from their infancy. Direct government assistance including cash subsidies was common and became a part of the mixed economy. Many of the Western railroads, for example, were built with the help of government financing and were given huge tracts of land, much of which was nowhere near the tracks but in rich mineral, forest, and agricultural areas. Federal government regulation of economic activities began in earnest in the 1880s, when the Interstate Commerce Commission (ICC) was established to regulate freight rates. Throughout this period laissez-faire doctrines served as a formal justification for all sorts of corporate activities; but the continuous interaction of government with the business community demonstrates beyond doubt that maintaining a "free market" was a secondary concern of government. "Competition is the death of trade" is a famous quote of railroad magnate Cornelius Vanderbilt, while "The public be damned" is one of the more famous statements of his son William.

Alexander Hamilton's statue in front of the Treasury Building, Washington, D.C.

**BOX 11–4
The United States
Has Lower Taxes
Than Most
Comparable
Nations**

TAX REVENUE AS A PERCENTAGE OF TOTAL OUTPUT OF GOODS AND SERVICES:

Country	1960	1979
Sweden	25.5%	52.9%
Netherlands	30.1	47.2
Norway	31.2	46.7
Denmark	25.4	45.0
Belgium	26.5	44.5
Austria	30.5	41.2
France	33.0	41.0
West Germany	31.3	37.2
Finland	28.1	35.1
Great Britain	28.5	33.8
Ireland	22.0	33.3
Italy	34.4	32.7
Switzerland	21.2	31.5
New Zealand	32.1	31.4
UNITED STATES	26.6	31.3
Canada	24.2	31.2
Australia	23.5	28.8
Portugal	16.3	25.9
Japan	18.2	24.1
Spain	16.0	22.8

—*US News and World Report,* March 2, 1981, p. 61 (based on OECD statistics).

The overall burden of regulation borne by industry and business, however, was relatively light through the first decade following World War I. Some antitrust laws had been legislated to protect the public against monopolies and price-fixing, though to little effect. Banking became regulated to some degree by the Federal Reserve System, set up in 1913. But a usually friendly Congress and a consistently friendly Supreme Court saw to it that business interests were given as free a rein as possible. Government could indeed involve itself in the economy, and it usually did so on the side of business interests.

The Great Depression   Demands for government action accelerated greatly in the wake of the Great Depression of the 1930s. Franklin D. Roosevelt's administration, first elected in 1932, initiated a broad range of government interventions and programs popularly known as the New Deal. It established government relief and employment programs such as the Works Progress Administration (WPA) and the Civilian Conservation Corps (CCC) to alleviate the economic hardships posed by widespread unemployment.

More lasting in their effects were the laws that established new agencies
and regulations to deal with a vast array of other economic problems:
aid to families with dependent children and other public welfare programs, the Social Security system, farm marketing and pricing controls, fair labor standards (minimum wages and maximum hours), a
variety of public health measures, housing programs, regulation of the
stock markets, loans and other forms of help for small businesses, and
programs aimed at providing work for artists and writers.

Many of these measures were responses to mythic concerns about
human suffering. However, almost all historians and observers agree
today that despite the controversial character of the Roosevelt administration and these New Deal programs at the time, no revolutionary
change was intended. The major aim was simply to keep the capitalist
system in operation by cleaning up and otherwise taking care of some of
its most unfortunate effects. In other words, for all its mythic, Social
Democratic enthusiasm for caring for the ill-fed, ill-housed, and unemployed, the New Deal was essentially an effort to conserve America's
ideological commitments to the business community through a time of
crisis.

To deal with the strictly economic aspects of the Depression, the Roosevelt administration adopted Keynesian economics in modified form,

"DON'T TELL ME IT ISN'T WORKING."

*The National Recovery Act
was one of the earliest
Keynesian measures of the
Roosevelt Administration.
Although it was declared
unconstitutional by the
Supreme Court, many of
its provisions were later
given clearance by the
Court so that minimum
wage laws, recognition of
unions, and other reforms
came into being.*

a set of economic management criteria that has influenced American government policies to this day. John Maynard Keynes (1883–1946) was a brilliant British economist and lecturer at Cambridge University. He advocated heavy government expenditures and publicly supported programs to revive the economy in the face of depression. This policy was called "pump-priming." He also urged the use of government deficits as an instrument of economic management, because pushing government expenditures in excess of revenues would inflate demand and stimulate production. This was only one side of Keynes's approach to government spending and taxing policies. The other side is that government should run up a budget surplus—that is, have more tax revenues than expenditures—in times of inflation and economic expansion. This piece of Keynes's advice, unlike his recommendations on deficits, has rarely been followed.

The conscious effort to plan government spending and taxation rates to counteract the swings from boom to bust in general economic activity is called "fiscal policy," which is largely the concern of the president and Congress. It is to be distinguished from "monetary policy," which has to do with interest rates and other factors affecting the supply of money and is largely the concern of the Federal Reserve Board (see below).

Economic Management Since World War II

A modicum of success in managing the economy was achieved under a variety of administrations in the post-World War II period using various Keynesian stratagems. It was generally believed by government leaders and their expert advisers that planning, fiscal controls, interest rate policy, and money supply management could be manipulated to trade off inflation against unemployment, and vice versa, whenever the need arose. Perhaps the principal accomplishment of Keynesian economics, or so it seemed at the time, was the avoidance of a large-scale business downturn at the end of World War II. Keynesian economics also rode high during the Kennedy and Johnson administrations, when economists were beginning to believe that they had perfected management of the nation's economic welfare to the point of fine tuning. The expansion of the economy after tax cuts were made—on business investment in 1962, on individual and corporate rates in 1964—tended to prove that stable prices and low unemployment were achievable. Even President Nixon, a critic of government spending and involvement in the economy, was later to describe himself as a Keynesian.

The term "fine tuning" is seldom heard today; and Keynesian economics is not embraced by the Reagan administration. Indeed, things have gone so badly for the U.S. economy in recent years that economists' judgments sometimes seem to be barely trusted. Unemployment has usually stayed well above the 6 percent level, with figures as high as 20 percent in some depressed areas and 40 percent among black youths.

**BOX 11–5
Ten Years' Erosion
of the Consumer
Dollar**

Imagine you had put aside $1,000 in cash in 1970 and that you now are ready to spend it. How much will it buy today? It depends, of course, on what you are buying. If it is gasoline, you can purchase only $280 worth. Other items:

Home fuel and utilities	$380 worth
Food	$460
Medical care	$460
Home purchase	$470
Average of all consumer prices	$470
Public transportation	$530
Used cars	$540
Public college Education	$560
Rent	$580
New cars	$600
Footwear	$620
Clothing	$660

TWENTY-FOUR PRICES AND HOW THEY HAVE CHANGED (NATIONAL AVERAGES)

	1970	1980	increase
Eggs (dozen)	$ .62	$ .81	31%
Man's dress shirt	6.97	$ 10.41	49%
Refrigerator	288.62	446.30	55%
Auto tire	33.84	52.69	56%
Bacon (lb.)	.97	1.56	61%
Pork chops (lb.)	1.19	1.91	61%
Washing machine	228.20	378.49	66%
Cigarettes	$ .43	$ .73	70%
Chicken (lb.)	.39	.67	72%
Movie ticket	2.02	3.49	73%
Tomatoes (lb.)	.30	.52	73%
Eyeglasses (with exam)	41.44	74.85	81%
Man's haircut	2.61	4.82	85%
Milk (half gal.)	.58	1.09	88%
Permanent wave	14.61	27.85	91%
White Bread (lb.)	.25	.49	96%
Potatoes (lb.)	.09	.18	100%
Hamburger (lb.)	.67	1.41	110%
Round steak	1.32	2.83	114%
Butter (lb.)	.87	1.89	117%
Bus fare	.35	.87	149%
Hospital room (semiprivate)	54.42	156.52	188%
Gasoline (prem. gal.)	.38	1.33	250%
Coffee (lb.)	.95	3.48	266%

—Government Statistics reported in *U.S. News and World Report,* September 8, 1980, p. 58.

The United States has now generally become a net importer rather than an exporter of goods, a historic reversal of our trading position. The dollar has frequently been weak against other currencies. High interest rates set by the Federal Reserve System to fight inflation have almost become the normal state of affairs, depressing housing markets and causing many small businesses to fail. Perhaps worse for the economy than any of these problems, inflation raced along at double-digit rates for years in a row, creating hardship, financial chaos, and a psychology of expectation that continued to add to its threatening strength (see box 11–5).

Supply-Side Economics   A new doctrine called "supply-side" economics has replaced Keynesian economics as the central economic tool of the Reagan administration. Although it is not clear how the major ideas behind supply-side thinking developed, it contains strong elements of the laissez-faire belief in allowing the private sector of the economy to work its will. It also contains the remnant of a Keynesian principle: that increasing investment will promote production, jobs, and strong anti-inflationary tendencies in the economy. It is presumably from this feature that supply-side economics gets its name. (Keynesian economics, by contrast, is often misperceived as being concerned only with stimulation of demand.) Lastly, but central to the whole structure of the supply-side scheme, the supply of money in the economy must be strictly controlled. Monetary growth must bear a close relationship to the levels of economic activity, particularly the production of goods and services, if it is not to be inflationary. This monetarist view, associated with Nobel Prize-winning economist Milton Friedman and others, holds that the only cause of inflation is the oversupply of money wrought by easy money policies and excessive government spending and budget deficits. Escalating demands by labor unions for wage increases and soaring profits for corporations are consequences, not causes, of inflation.

The view that monetary problems are the source of the nation's major economic difficulties combines with the political conservatism of the supply-side economists in the Reagan administration and prompts them to espouse three strong policy preferences: deregulation, tax cuts, and balanced budgets. Cutting back on government regulation of business (in their phrase, "Getting the government off our backs!"), will supposedly free initiative and inventiveness in the private sector, stimulating business growth. Cutting taxes, it is claimed, will leave more funds available for investment in that same sector. It will also dampen the fires of inflation on this supply-side of the economy by giving businesses better value in their plant, equipment, and other investments. Quite often, supply-siders point to the successes of the Kennedy and Johnson tax cuts in stimulating business expansion in the early 1960s, although these cuts were enacted at times of low inflation. Balancing budgets will have the effect of keeping the government from borrowing in the money markets, an activity that forces up interest rates and tends to be inflationary. It also holds down government spending, which is also considered inflationary.

The tax and budget positions of the supply-siders are influenced by conservative economist Arthur Laffer, whose Laffer curve shows that government can theoretically obtain as much or more in tax revenues when tax rates are low because of the increased economic activity generated by these lower rates.

A major commitment to Adam Smith's laissez-faire, a bit of Keynes, control of the money supply, deregulation, tax cuts, and balanced budgets—will it all work? The Reagan administration set out boldly in pursuit of these objectives and for a time made considerable progress toward them. But within months, although inflation seemed curbed, a deepening recession set in, bringing higher rates of business failures and unemployment than the nation had seen in decades. Skepticism became widespread about specific aspects of the Reagan program—for example, cuts in social services to reduce government spending—as well as its overall conception, especially the notion that major increases in military spending were possible in the wake of massive income tax reductions. President Reagan and his advisers soon began to accommodate themselves to the prospects of enormous budget deficits and the necessity of enacting "revenue enhancement measures" (their phrase for tax increases).

The predicaments of the Reagan administration suggest a conclusion about the art of economic management in a mixed economy such as that of the United States: it is a chancy business in which neither pure Keynesians nor ardent laissez-faire supply-siders can claim much success.

The Mixed Economy: The Reaction of Myth

The mixed economy is largely designed and fueled in ideological terms, and the efforts to have the government manage its levels of prosperity are also largely defined in ideological terms. The government's business, Calvin Coolidge is said to have remarked, is business. But as we have seen in connection especially with the New Deal, when things are going badly for business, mythic factors can come into play.

Mythic aspirations can lead politicians and policymakers to establish prosperity by decree. The Full Employment Act of 1946 and the Humphrey-Hawkins Act of 1978 are good examples of this. Both these laws commit the government to a policy of full employment over other economic goals such as balanced budgets or stable prices. Humphrey-Hawkins calls for the government itself to provide employment for those who are not hired by the private sector of the economy. Both these acts lack enforcement machinery, however, so that they amount to little more than statements of policy intentions.

It is instructive all the same to reflect upon the hard work that goes into the creation of our mythic hopes for economic management. Look at the preamble of the Full Employment Act of 1946:

It is the continuing policy and responsibility of the Federal Government to use all practicable means consistent with its needs and obligations and other essential considerations of national policy, with the assistance and cooperation of industry, agriculture, labor, and state and local governments, to coordinate and utilize all its plans, functions, and resources for the purpose of creating and maintaining, in a manner calculated to foster and promote free competitive enterprise and the general welfare, condi-

tions under which there will be afforded employment, for those able, willing, and seeking to work, and to promote maximum employment, production, and purchasing power.

Obviously, for any of these goals to be achieved, a very large number of people (from "industry, agriculture, labor, and state and local governments," not to mention all the branches and agencies of the federal government itself) would have to be consulted and induced to cooperate in terms of some common, broadly defined program. Mythically, that is a fine hope; ideologically, given the fragmented character of American politics, it is a most unlikely prospect. And it should also be pointed out that the goals this act calls for are not only full employment all across the nation and in every segment of the economy but also steady growth, a fair division of resources between military and civilian needs, and an equitable allocation of rewards and protections among all willing workers. Against the backdrop of that kind of aspiration, it should be counted among the act's accomplishments that it set up the three-member Council of Economic Advisers, thereby guaranteeing full employment for at least those three persons.

The point remains that American government is often motivated and mobilized for economic management by the most ambitious mythic hopes. This was certainly true in the Truman era, when the Full Employment Act was passed, and again more recently when the Humphrey-Hawkins guaranteed employment bill was passed. It was true during the Johnson administration, which proved overly ambitious in assuming that the economy could pay for both guns and butter—the

Despite the rising crescendo of criticism and disagreement dinning our ears today. I still believe we have a stronger, bipartisan agreement on our fundamental economic goals, including economic growth, than we have had for decades. . . .

Both parties have agreed on the need to encourage savings, risk-taking and investment in order to create productive jobs in the private sector. Evidence of this consensus can be found in the last two tax bills. There is, of course, a difference of opinion about details—about the best policies to achieve the goals—and that is normal in the political process. But the encouraging fact is the level of agreement on the basic goals of economic policy.

—William M. Batten, Chairman, New York Stock Exchange, *Wall Street Journal*, January 13, 1982.

**BOX 11–6
A Claim of
Consensus on
Economic
Management**

Vietnam War and domestic prosperity—while simultaneously waging "an unconditional war on poverty." And mythic hopes are no small part of the supply-side economics of the Reagan administration.

What limits these mythic aspirations are the ideological factors in the political system and the dispersed, self-seeking characteristics of the economic system itself. While mythic goals may be proclaimed, ideological demands are also being made upon the political system in forceful and subtle ways and must be met at least part of the time whether or not they contribute to the fulfillment of the mythic hopes. Again and again, objective constraints developing in the economy—unemployment rates, interest levels, inflation increases—distort the best laid plans for the government's programs and budget projections, and these combine with personal political needs of individual politicians to sway both decisions and intended results away from the broad mythic goals. As new administrations come in and struggle to put into place a whole range of new policies, everything appears to be changing, only to be followed by everything remaining much the same. The changes sought and, in part, wrought, with glee in some quarters, anger in others, by the Reagan administration appeared for the moment to be "revolutionary." But time will show that they were not so in fact, either in intent or in effect, any more than were the programs of the Johnson administration, the Franklin D. Roosevelt administration, or the Wilson administration. All proclaimed high hopes, often persuasively, but all in the end proved most effective in preserving and conserving what was already there.

As William S. Gilbert (of Gilbert and Sullivan fame) might say, what we have here is a most ingenious paradox. The most ardent (at the mythic level) supply-siders often (at the ideological level) approve and promote policies that on an individual basis call for the government to sustain interest groups and corporations in ways that find no justification in Adam Smith or any other philosopher of laissez-faire. And equally on the other side, many of the most pious in their protests against slashing programs for the poor actively campaign at the same time for subsidies for some of their favored supporters who are far from indigent. The actual record of the government's performance shows a vast patchwork of often contradictory economic policies extending back through virtually every presidential administration to the days when Alexander Hamilton and Thomas Jefferson fought out their conflicting interpretations of what the national interest required of the government. In that perspective, what is important is that for all the squabbling over techniques, details, and who should get what from whom, there is in the American tradition about economic policy an extraordinary undercurrent of agreement about long-term goals. The American dream, all seem to be saying, is of a prosperous mixed economy in which the government will ensure that all hardworking individuals can reap their just rewards, the whole business tempered by an undying and heartfelt concern for the plight of the truly needy. This kind of underlying if self-contradictory consensus threads its way not only through the rhetoric of politicians but also the commentaries of economists and financial leaders (see Box 11–6).

The Tools of Economic Management

It is generally accepted by all but the most narrow-minded free market advocates that some tools of economic management can be effective. These tools are variously utilized by the most influential economic policymakers of the government: the president and his advisers in the OMB and the Council of Economic Advisers, the Treasury Department, the Federal Reserve Board, and congressional committees and their staffs of experts. The principal tools of economic management can be listed as (1) fiscal policy, (2) monetary policy, (3) jawboning and guidelines on wages and prices, and (4) wage and price controls.

Fiscal policy, as we have noted, is largely set by the president and Congress and is an attempt to manage the economy through taxing and spending policies. Keynesian in its origins, it seeks to affect demand by increasing total government spending relative to taxes during recessions or economic downturns and by curbing spending during times of economic growth. In the latter case, the main concern is to curb infla-

Fiscal Policy

Every month the federal government measures the growth or decline of the U.S. economy by drawing up a composite of various economic indicators. This composite, called the Index of Leading Economic Indicators, is said to show how the economy fared over the previous month. A decline in the index for a period of three consecutive months is generally said to indicate that the economy is in recession. The ten indicators employed by the Commerce Department for the Index are

Average Workweek	Liquid Assets of Firms
Unemployment Rate	Plant and Equipment Orders
New Orders	Building Permits
Rate of Deliveries	Stock Prices
Producer Prices	Money Supply

**BOX 11–7
The Index of
Leading Economic
Indicators**

tion. In the case of a recession, unemployment is most likely to be the worry. A recession is presently defined by government economists as a three-month or longer period of decline in the index of leading economic indicators (see Box 11–7).

Taxation is related to government spending, but tax policies tend to be blunt economic instruments for two reasons. First, tax cuts or increases usually take a long time for Congress to enact. A president may propose a tax cut to promote consumer spending, but this proposal may precede the actual cut by as many as two years. Economic conditions can change a great deal between proposal and enactment. There is also some lag between enactment and the actual enforcement of new tax laws. Second, taxation has many purposes; tax laws are not always passed for their economic effects. There are three important reasons for taxes. (1) Taxes raise revenue to pay for government programs such as defense. (2) Taxes transfer wealth from one group in the population to another. Social Security benefits, for example, are distributed to recipients who may have contributed in the past to the fund from which they are drawn but now that fund is sustained mainly on a year-to-year basis by taxes on wage earners receiving no benefits at the present time. (3) Taxes can be used to regulate or promote economic activity. An investment tax credit, for example, may induce a company to purchase new computers whose cost can be partly written off against its taxes. For years generous tax allowances to oil producers have been justified on the grounds that they encourage oil exploration.

These are all reasonable grounds for taxes, but they may well be remote from or even contradictory to the goals of fiscal policy. Moreover, tax laws in the United States are an extreme example of incrementalism in public policymaking. Every level of government uses taxation for its own purposes, whatever they happen to be at a particular time, to raise revenue for public services, to encourage local industry, to discourage consumption of certain beverages, and so forth. Changes in the tax laws accumulate over the years; once enacted, they are difficult to repeal. The hope that this massive, complex body of tax laws could be manipulated to achieve fiscal policy goals is not reasonable. One level of government, most notably the federal government, might give its tax laws a new shape, as the Reagan administration induced Congress to do in 1981 with a series of across the board income tax reductions (at considerable cost in special tax breaks for favored groups). But the broad fiscal policy goals this action was designed to achieve not only may be slow in coming but also may be countered all along the line by taxation policies at the state and local levels.

Particular spending policies can likewise be more designed to achieve specific objectives than be geared to overall fiscal policy goals: the construction of military bases, dams, or public housing in particular parts

Behavior	Percentage of Respondents Who Would *Not* Be "Bothered a Lot" If They Participated in Behavior
Not declaring the value of a service that you traded with someone else	61.6%
Not declaring large gambling earnings	52.6
Padding business travel expenses	48.9
Overstating your medical expenses	46.4
Understating your income	42.2
Not filing a return on purpose	30.7
Claiming an extra dependent	29.0

—Internal Revenue Service Survey reported in *Public Opinion* 3:16 (August-September 1980).

**BOX 11–8
"Cutting Corners"
on Income Tax**

of the country, teaching programs for the handicapped, the production of certain crops, hiring of minorities, women, or veterans, or the mergers of libraries or school districts. Many of the effects of government spending are indirect: prosperity for a town near a new military base, intensification of farming on some land when the government is paying some farmers to allow their land to lie fallow, or the abandonment of public transportation because of highway modernization and improvement. The spending side of fiscal policy, like taxation, is riddled with value preferences, contradictory policies and economic signals, and noneconomic policy tests to such a degree that it too is an imprecise instrument for affecting economic change.

The need to enact new fiscal policy is often eased by the actions of some built-in responses the government makes to economic changes. Government tax revenues tend to increase automatically, for example, in times of economic prosperity, leading to a balanced budget or even a surplus, which is presumed to have an anti-inflationary effect. On the other hand, unemployment compensation payments rise in a recession, making up for some of the decline in private income but also automatically increasing government spending. Revenues also tend to decline in times of economic downturn, promoting the stimulus of deficit spending and government borrowing. These factors, called automatic stabilizers, help keep the economy on an even keel by producing government actions most economists agree are needed as times and conditions

BOX 11–9
The Public Views
Taxes and Public
Services

Question: Considering all government services on the one hand, and taxes on the other, which of the following statements comes closest to your view?

	Decrease Services and Taxes	Keep Taxes and Services Where They Are	Increase Services and Raise Taxes	No Opinion
1975	38%	45%	5%	12%
1976	30	51	5	14
1977	31	52	4	13
1979	39	46	6	9
1980	38	45	6	11

—Advisory Committee on Intergovernmental Relations Poll, *Public Opinion*, 3:17 (August-September 1980).

change. These automatic stabilizers, however, tend to underscore the blunt, imprecise, and often untimely nature of fiscal policy as an instrument of economic management.

As with taxation, it is important to include in this discussion the spending policies of state and local governments. These policies often run counter to the policies of the federal government. Times of prosperity increase state and local revenue and can easily lead to larger outlays by these governments. Hard times usually cause these units of government to engage in cost-cutting and belt-tightening measures. State and local governments also lack the freedom enjoyed by the federal government in matters of fiscal policy. Their indebtedness—and consequently their ability to spend—is regulated within stricter constitutional and statutory guidelines, and they have little access to such dynamic levers on the economy as monetary policy, which in theory can be used in Washington in harmony with fiscal policy. But the sheer volume of the total spending of state and local government is alone enough to affect seriously all federal efforts at fiscal policymaking.

Monetary Policy

Monetary policy is the second major tool of economic management available to the federal government; as we have seen, to some conservative economists it is the single most important tool. Through monetary policy, government authorities attempt to influence the growth of the economy by controlling the interest rates businesses must pay for their cash borrowings, regulating the availability of credit, and through these

BOX 11–10
Reagan's Director
of the Office of
Management and
Budget David
Stockman Speaks
Frankly on Fiscal
Policies

"None of us really understands what's going on with all these numbers," Stockman confessed when speaking of the budget process. ". . . People are getting from A to B and it's not clear how they are getting there."

"The pieces [of the process] were moving on independent tracks—the tax program, where we were going on spending, and the defense program which was just a bunch of numbers written on a piece of paper. And it didn't quite mesh. . . . But, you see, for about a month and a half we got away with that because of the novelty of all these budget reductions."

The Defense Department "got a blank check," said Mr. Stockman. ". . . they [the Defense Department] got so goddamned greedy that they got themselves strung way out there on a limb."

"The hard part of the supply-side tax cut is dropping the top rate [of taxes on investment income] from 70 to 50 per cent—the rest of it is a secondary matter," Stockman explained. ". . . the general argument was that, in order to make this palatable as a political matter, you had to bring down all the brackets. But . . . [it] was always a Trojan horse to bring down the top rate."

"It's kind of hard to sell 'trickle-down,'" he explained, "so the supply-side formula was the only way to get a tax policy that was really 'trickle-down.' Supply-side is 'trickle-down' theory."

". . . we [had] to get a program out fast. . . . We didn't add up all the numbers. We didn't make all the thorough, comprehensive calculations about where we really needed to come out and how much to put on the plate the first time, and so forth. . . . we ended up with a list that I'd always been carrying of things to be done, rather than starting the other way and asking, What is the overall fiscal policy required to reach the target?"

On the 1981 tax cut bill, Mr. Stockman said, "Do you realize the greed that came to the forefront? The hogs were really feeding." And one of his sad conclusions was simply that "The supply-siders have gone too far . . ."

—Based on William Greider, "The Education of David Stockman," *Atlantic Monthly*, **248**:27–54 (December 1981).

and other devices, controlling the total supply of money in the economy.

Monetary policy is largely effected through the Federal Reserve System created in 1913. Policy is set by a seven-member board of governors and implemented through the system's twelve regional banks that function as "bankers' banks" in the various sections of the country. All federally chartered banks must be affiliated with the Federal Reserve System, and many state banks also belong to it (see Box 11–11).

The Federal Reserve Board operates as one of Washington's most important independent regulatory commissions. Administratively, it is wholly independent of the president, other units of the executive bureaucracy such as the Treasury, and Congress and its committees. The members of the board, including its chairman, are appointed to fourteen-year terms by the president with the advice and consent of the Senate. Members serve staggered terms to ensure continuity of membership and preclude a president's appointing a majority of the board all at once. Once appointed, members cannot be removed except for cause.

The "Fed," as it is often called, can regulate the money supply in three different ways: (1) by buying and selling government securities, (2) by raising or lowering interest rates, and (3) by changing the reserve requirements of banks.

When the Fed sells securities—mostly to banks, insurance companies, investment fund companies, and other corporations—it causes a drying up of liquid funds because checking accounts at commercial banks (the biggest part of the money supply) are reduced. A corporation purchasing these securities draws from its bank balance to do so and its bank thus has fewer funds to loan. Total deposits and the total money supply are likewise enlarged when the Fed buys government securities. The sellers of these instruments deposit their proceeds in their banks, which then become available to be loaned by the bank. The Fed publishes money supply figures regularly, and sometimes the stock markets and other economic transactions—the sale of commodities, for example—are affected by these figures. But the more important, direct effect on the economy comes from the expansion or shrinkage of the money supply.

The Fed raises or lowers interest rates by fixing the discount rate, which is the rate paid by Federal Reserve member banks for the money they borrow from the Federal Reserve System. Banks are encouraged to borrow when the Fed offers them a favorable rate, and they in turn offer loans more readily and at more reasonable rates to the public. On the other hand, a high-interest or "tight money" policy discourages bank borrowing and also causes a relative scarcity of funds for the public to borrow. The movements of the discount rate tend to correlate with money supply policies; that is, high interest rates are likely when the

**BOX 11–11
The Federal
Reserve System:
The Hand on the
Tiller in Money
Supply**

THE "FED" STRUCTURE

Board of Governors—7 members, 14-year terms
12 regional Federal Reserve banks
5,420 member banks (as of August 1980)

THE "FED" PROCESS

1. *The Federal Open Market Committee decides monetary policy.*
Voting members are the seven governors, the president of the New York Fed, and presidents of four other regional banks, who serve rotating one-year terms. The seven other presidents attend but do not vote.

2. *The "morning call."*
A daily conference call links staff specialists in Washington with their counterparts at the New York Fed, which handles trading for all the regional banks and the System itself. The Federal Reserve chairman and the New York Fed president often take part. The daily instructions to the Fed's trading desk come out of this meeting.

3. *Federal Reserve Bank of New York.*
Its System Account, or trading desk, handles day-to-day buying and selling of securities. The department also prepares frequent estimates of commercial banks' reserves, a key indicator in carrying out monetary policy.

The Federal Reserve affects the supply of money by buying and selling government securities. It trades with about three dozen "primary" dealers. When the Fed buys securities, it pays the seller by adding to the seller's checking account at a commercial bank, thus increasing demand deposits (checking accounts), the largest component of the money supply. When the Fed sells, the buyer's payment comes from its bank account, thus reducing this component of the money supply.
—*The New York Times*, May 3, 1981.

money supply is curtailed and lower interest rates accompany the sale of securities by the Fed.

The setting of reserve requirements by the Fed affects the proportion of reserve assets compared with loans in member banks. If, for example, a reserve requirement is 20 percent, a bank must retain $1 on hand for every $5 loaned; raising or lowering this requirement affects the nation's level of economic activity because availability of loan funds is affected. As of 1980, banks were permitted for the first time to count some foreign currency deposits as a part of their reserves.

The Fed is not alone in this manipulation of interest rates, the money supply, economic growth and contraction, and banking policies. The Treasury Department, to raise cash for government programs, also issues government securities, often referred to as "T-bills." The Treasury's decisions on what interest rates to put on its T-bills and on whether to finance a particular issue on a long-term or short-term basis can strongly influence interest rates generally. But the Treasury's actions not only affect interest rates; they also have an impact on the money supply because of the activities of banks in these Treasury bond markets.

We have pointed out that the Fed is ostensibly independent of political pressures from the president and other agencies of the government. There is little doubt that the president can influence the board from time to time, however, mostly through exerting the prestige and suasion of his office. It has been suggested though not proved that the expansionary economic policies that often characterize the board's actions at the time of presidential re-election campaigns are not mere coincidence. The fact remains, all the same, that the Fed enjoys a real measure of independence. Although the president may feel the economy should be attuned to certain mythic needs, the Fed may believe that its particular policies fulfill certain ideological, "real world" needs of the banking community to which it is close. By the same token, the Treasury may often go its own way. The result can be a confusion of cross-purposes and a blurring of goals and needs.

Monetary policy is not viewed by all economists in the same way. Some conservatives see it as a potentially effective short-term instrument of economic management, but they are often quick to add that the Fed has not done its job well enough to achieve this potential. A range of economists from conservative former Fed Chairman Arthur Burns to liberal John Kenneth Galbraith are dubious about the ability of any government to define, much less control, the money supply.[5]

[5] *Wall Street Journal*, November 17, 1977; John Kenneth Galbraith, "The Conservative Onslaught," *New York Review of Books*, **27**:35 (January 22, 1981).

Wage-Price Guidelines and Jawboning

Wage-price guidelines and jawboning are another means of managing the economy. In this case, the objective is to control inflation. Jawboning is merely the use of persuasion by the president to induce corporations, and occasionally labor unions, to exercise restraint in setting wages and prices to keep inflation within bounds. Its effects are minimal at best, even in the short term; over the long run, this kind of exhortation carries no weight at all. President Lyndon Johnson is one of the many who used jawboning and in his case the immediate results sometimes looked good because he was a persuasive person. Jawboning does not necessarily take on a diplomatic tone, however; one of the most successful short-term examples of its use occurred in 1962, when President John F. Kennedy and the steel industry clashed over price increases. Kennedy's characterization of industry leaders as "S.O.B.'s" offended them, but steel price increases were temporarily held back.

Guidelines were developed by the Kennedy administration and continued by the Johnson administration for a time. Presidents Nixon and Carter also used them. Such guidelines usually consist of a figure related to the current inflation rate or less, which is supposed to represent the maximum annual price increase of a product or maximum wage increase settlement. But guidelines are little more than formalized jaw-

Strikes and labor contracts obviously affect attempts of presidents to establish wage and price guidelines or controls. (UE News)

boning, for they are strictly voluntary. A business firm or union may exceed them at will. Conceivably, the government could exact some form of retribution. President Carter threatened the loss of government contracts for such business firms, and this caused the business community to argue that this kind of coercive action removed the "voluntary" aspect from the guidelines. Occasionally the president tries to jawbone the entire nation, asking consumers not to buy high-priced items, urging them to save money, or asking union members to exercise restraint in their wage demands. The biggest effort of this kind in recent years was launched by President Gerald R. Ford, who advertised his campaign with "WIN" ("Whip Inflation Now") buttons he urged everyone to wear.

Jawboning and guidelines are akin in their effects to the antiunemployment laws of 1946 and 1978 discussed above. They have no enforcement machinery and attempt to create the illusion of economics by

**BOX 11–12
Disagreements on
Emphasis Within
"Reagonomics"—
Supply-Siders,
Monetarists,
Budget-Balancers**

The supply-siders fear that a low-growth, low-inflation forecast [will] increase pressure in Congress and the White House to delay or modify scheduled tax cuts in order to help balance the budget. They charge that the monetarists and the budget-balancers place too much emphasis on anti-inflation policies that . . . choke off economic growth.

The monetarists worry that impatience for faster growth will force the administration to demand an easier, more expansive monetary policy from the Fed. Their fears were fueled by Secretary [of the Treasury] Regan's . . . call for slightly faster money growth.

The budget-balancers complain that the supply-siders overlook the importance of a decisive reduction in the deficit as a way to reduce federal borrowing, a step that should boost financial-market confidence in the Reagan program and lead to lower interest rates.

Some monetarists and budget-balancers believe the administration damaged its credibility and aggravated nervousness in the financial markets early this year when it issued an economic forecast [in early 1981] that was too optimistic for many private forecasters to accept. They are campaigning to prevent the administration from making the same mistake again.

—*Wall Street Journal*, October 27, 1981.

decree. They are part of the American mythic temperament, but operationally their inevitable failure is due to our Bourgeois, self-seeking nature. Guidelines are ignored because they call for some de-emphasis of self-interest in the national interest, and such appeals are rarely heeded when economic self-interest is at stake.

Wage and price controls are mandatory guidelines. They were imposed during World War II, the Korean War, and by the Nixon administration, which faced high inflation owing to the Vietnam War. These controls are difficult to administer because of the complexities of the range of prices and commodities, because of enforcement problems, and because there always seems to be a need for exceptions and exemptions for economic or political reasons. Despite these problems, wage and price controls are a popular solution to inflation. Most opinion polls over the past several years indicate that the public believes wages and prices are controllable. And there is some evidence that they will work on a temporary basis or during an emergency period such as World War II, when a great national effort is supported by practically everyone. During the most recent attempt to use them from 1971 to 1974, controls had no great lasting effects. Yet they cannot be ignored as a tool of economic management. There are circumstances and events which can very well bring them into play. Their short-term success, for example, can help a presidential incumbent through a re-election campaign.

Wage and Price Controls

Conclusion

Although of doubtful ideological significance, the success or failure of economic management with its use of the various tools of fiscal policy, monetary policy, and guidelines can have important political consequences in myth. The party that has the presidency, for example, is held responsible for the economy's poor performance and may also receive credit for prosperity. There is also a correlation between economic conditions and election results for U.S. senator, with incumbents operating at a disadvantage in times of economic hardship. No similar correlation, however, can be discerned in races for the House of Representatives.[6] In terms of the parties' images, there is a clear tendency of voters to support the Democrats if they are worried about unemployment and a much more limited tendency to support Republican candidates if the concern is inflation.[7]

[6] James H. Kuklinski and Darrell M. West, "Economic Expectations and Voting Behavior in United States House and Senate Elections," *American Political Science Review*, **75**:436–447 (June 1981).

[7] D. Roderick Kiewiet, "Policy-Oriented Voting in Response to Economic Issues," *American Political Science Review*, **75**:448–459 (June 1981).

FOR FURTHER READING

BLAIR, JOHN. *The Control of Oil*. New York: Pantheon, 1976. The definitive work on the world oil crisis and how we got there.

CASTELLS, MANUEL. *The Economic Crisis and American Society*. Complex but significant treatment of the American economy's structural problems from a Marxist viewpoint.

CONNOLLY, WILLIAM E., and MICHAEL E. BEST. *The Politicized Economy*, 2nd ed. Lexington, Mass.: D.C. Heath, 1981. Primer on American economic history and contemporary problems.

FRIEDMAN, MILTON. *Free to Choose*. New York: Harcourt Brace Jovanovich, 1980. The conservative economist and Nobel Prize winner sets out his political and economic prescriptions.

GALBRAITH, JOHN KENNETH. *The Great Crash 1929*. Boston: Houghton Mifflin, 1979. Now regarded as a classic examination and explanation of this great event.

GREIDER, WILLIAM. "The Education of David Stockman." *Atlantic Monthly*, **248** (December 1981), 27–54. Revealing picture of economic management from the inside of the Reagan administration.

HARRINGTON, MICHAEL. *Decade of Decision: The Crisis of the American System*. New York: Simon and Schuster, 1981. An original analysis of the structure of the economy from a democratic socialist viewpoint.

SCHUMACHER, E. F. *Small Is Beautiful: Economics As If People Mattered*. New York: Harper & Row, 1973. Questions the commitment to economic growth and posits the theme of restructuring the economy through appropriate technology.

SCHWARTZ, GAIL G. and PAT CHOATE. *Being Number One: Rebuilding the U.S. Economy*. Lexington, Mass.: Lexington Books, 1981. One of the many treatises on reindustrialization and revitalization of the American economy.

SILK, LEONARD. *The Economists*. New York: Basic Books, 1976. Introduction to the thinking of five renowned economists—Galbraith, Samuelson, Friedman, Boulding, and Leontief.

STERN, PHILIP M. *The Rape of the Taxpayer*. New York: Random House, 1973. No longer current because of extensive tax law revisions, this is nevertheless an excellent window on the history of tax dodges and inequities.

WANNISKI, JUDE. *The Way the World Works: How Economics Fail—and Succeed*. New York: Basic Books, 1978. The supply-side thesis, with the addition of the advocacy of a gold standard.

The Welfare State 12

Joseph A. Califano, Jr., one of the most influential Democrats in Washington, has recently written:

> From the time I left my job at the White House as President Lyndon Johnson's staff assistant for domestic affairs in January 1969, I knew that if I ever returned to government service, I would like to be Secretary of Health, Education and Welfare.[1]

And he was, from the opening day of the Carter administration in 1977 until he was asked for his resignation in July 1979. By the time Califano left the office, Health, Education and Welfare (HEW) had been split up. The new Department of Education was established with more than 7,000 former HEW employees and a budget of more than $14 billion, and HEW was designated as the Department of Health and Human Services.

More significant than this name change, however, is the general assessment of Califano's reign; except for some broadening of the rights of the handicapped, which was merely enforcement of an already existing law, little changed during this period of thirty months. The department, Califano explained, got caught up in such controversial issues as busing and abortion (not to mention national health insurance, fair housing policies, welfare reform, and Social Security funding and reform) and was therefore not as effective as it might have been. In addition, a conservative shift was making itself felt in the country that culminated in the Reagan victory of 1980.

Califano cannot be faulted for wishing to lead HEW. After all, HEW was where much of the action in domestic policy took place. But the modern welfare state that has been constructed in this country and that

[1] Quoted by Nathan Glazer, "Democratic Difficulties," *The New York Times Book Review*, June 14, 1981, p. 1.

BOX 12–1
Disorder and Relief
Programs: Cycles
and Dynamics

The irony is simply this: that large-scale work relief—unlike direct relief which merely mutes the worst outbursts of discontent—tends to stabilize lower-class occupational, familial, and communal life, and by doing so diminishes . . . (the) disruptive behavior which give(s) rise to the expansion of relief in the first place. Once order is restored in this far more profound sense, *relief-giving can be virtually abolished,* as it has been so often in the past. And there is always pressure to abolish large-scale work relief, for it strains against the market ethos and interferes with the untrammeled operation of the marketplace. The point is not just that when a relief concession is offered up, peace and order reign; it is, rather, that when peace and order reign, the relief concession is withdrawn.

The restoration of work through the relief system, in other words, makes possible the eventual return to the most restrictive phase in the cycle of relief-giving. What begins as a great expansion of direct relief, and then turns into some form of work relief, ends finally with a sharp contraction of the rolls. . . .

—Frances Fox Piven and Richard A. Cloward, *Regulating the Poor: The Functions of Public Welfare* (New York: Vintage, 1971), pp. 347–348.

was centered in HEW is subjected to ebbs and flows. It does not receive consistent support from the American people nor from our political leaders (see Box 12–1).

One of the reasons for this ambivalent attitude toward welfare measures undoubtedly goes back to an earlier age in American history, the preindustrial time of the Founders. No welfare state existed anywhere then; and the work ethic, which seems to be its bane, was evident in the values and activities of almost everyone. To work hard even for its own sake was considered both virtuous and a matter of survival. The culture-defining era of settlement of the western frontier and the nation's new-found prosperity as an industrial economy reinforced this attitude through most of the nineteenth century.

The needs of an industrialized state eventually caught up with the outmoded idea that government could not intervene in economic matters. The Great Depression of the 1930s produced a tremendous reaction in the Roosevelt administration that brought the welfare state into being in America—a state that provides minimum benefits and guarantees of care for virtually all of the population suffering various forms of economic and personal adversity. These New Deal reforms, as they were called, established Social Security, unemployment compensation, minimum wages and maximum hours, payments to those injured on the job, and a variety of other benefits (see Box 12–2).

Over the years since the 1930s, these benefits and programs have been expanded and others added, such as Medicare, Medicaid, food stamps, Head Start, legal assistance for the poor, education grants, payments to workers displaced by competition from imports, day care, job training programs such as the Job Corps and those carried out under CETA (the Comprehensive Employment and Training Act), meals programs for the elderly, and assistance payments for fuel costs. The greatest period of expansion of these programs occurred during the administration of Lyndon B. Johnson (1963–1969) and have been referred to as Great Society programs. But new programs and innovations have been steadily added during the Nixon, Ford, and Carter years, some of them

BOX 12–2
FDR's "One-Third of a Nation" Speech: The Beginning of the Modern Welfare State

With his re-election to a second term, President Franklin D. Roosevelt turned his attention from recovery from the Great Depression to the building of the modern welfare state. Some measures such as Social Security and labor's right to organize and bargain collectively had been enacted in 1935. But it was on March 4, 1937, at the Democratic victory dinner in Washington, that FDR issued his clarion call for reform in his famous "one-third of a nation" speech:

"If we do not have the courage to lead the American people where they want to go, someone else will.

Here is one-third of a Nation ill-nourished, ill-clad, ill-housed—NOW!

Here are thousands upon thousands of farmers wondering whether next year's prices will meet their mortgage interest—NOW!

Here are thousands upon thousands of children who should be at school, working in mines and mills—NOW!

Here are strikes more far-reaching than we have ever known, costing millions of dollars—NOW!

Here are Spring floods threatening to roll again down our river valleys—NOW!

Here is the Dust Bowl beginning to blow again—NOW!

If we would keep faith with those who had faith in us, if we would make democracy succeed, I say we must act—NOW!"

Urban and rural housing programs have long been established as a part of the welfare state picture.

quite imaginative. The Reagan administration has sharply reduced or abandoned altogether many of these programs in what amounts to at least a temporary policy turnabout.

This turnabout, like all the important developments in the history of the welfare state, reflects once again the myth-ideology dichotomy, as well as the contradictions within each of these vital elements of American politics. In myth, America's Protestant conscience has assumed a generous spirit, deciding the government must provide for the poor, the sick, the elderly, the handicapped, and other less fortunate citizens. But in ideology, our Bourgeois nature often rebels against welfare assistance. Operationally, the welfare system is viewed as a burden, and it is often planned, implemented, and administered with a meanness of spirit or an eye toward benefiting these suppliers of these services—bureaucrats at all levels of government, government suppliers and contractors, the agricultural interests who promote food stamps—as much as those designated to receive them. Political speeches, the media, and public opinion polls regularly display a disdain for many or most welfare programs.

Welfare programs are divided into two broad categories—contributory and noncontributory. The latter, sometimes also called public assistance programs, involve no payments or contributions by those receiving such help. Among these are various training and employment assistance programs, child care, school lunches, housing assistance, food stamps, Medicaid, job counseling, Supplementary Security Income (which provides cash payments to the aged, the blind, and the disabled), and Aid to Families with Dependent Children (in popular parlance, AFDC is often referred to as "welfare"). The contributory system is built into the Social Security Act of 1935 and its various amendments. This includes Old Age, Survivors and Disability Insurance, Medicare, and Unemployment Compensation. Virtually all employed people pay a special (and often heavy) payroll deduction tax to support this system. A family of four, for example, pays more in Social Security taxes than in income tax if its annual income is $14,000 or less. The contributory, or Social Security, system is our major social insurance against the misfortunes of infirmity, old age, and unemployment.

Contributory Welfare Programs: The Social Security System

Although it endures a great amount of criticism and public misgivings, the Social Security System is a well-accepted part of American life. The American people recognize the need for it. Politicians who have attacked its foundations or premises—that all Americans should be provided with a measure of security—have found themselves caught up in a whirlwind of public opposition. President Lyndon B. Johnson used this issue effectively against Senator Barry Goldwater in the 1964 presidential election, which for this and other reasons resulted in a landslide for Johnson. President Ronald Reagan's first legislative defeat in 1981 came in the Senate on his proposal to reduce Social Security benefits for people in the 62–65 age bracket. The vote was 96 to 0 against the president's proposal.

But strong public support for a social insurance system does not necessarily translate into unqualified acceptance of all features of the system. Almost everyone who has studied the system recognizes that it has major problems.

The greatest problem is overhauling the financing of the system. According to a report issued by the trustees of the system, the trust fund account has shrunk drastically in recent years, losing $12,000 a minute. This dramatic figure is perhaps less important than the projection that the trust fund could run out of money by late 1982 or early 1983. These are the trust fund projections set by the trustees:

Year	Balance
1980	$26.5 billion
1981	21.8 billion
1982	3.2 billion
1983	−11.7 billion
1984	−19.6 billion

Increases in benefits, including cost-of-living adjustments that are raised in times of considerable inflation, and the increasing number of eligible recipients are among the principal causes of the deficit. Projections for the future of the Social Security System are also clouded by an increasingly adverse ratio of recipients to supporters. In 1950, for example, there was one Social Security recipient for each sixteen persons paying Social Security taxes. By 1960, this had dropped to one recipient per five taxpayers, and today it is one for three. By 2025, this ratio is expected to decline to one recipient for every two taxpayers.[2]

Solving the Funding Dilemma

The Reagan administration has sought to ease the funding burdens by reducing various benefits. Although its proposal to cut payments for the 62–65 age bracket appears to be dead, it has also sought to reduce survivors' benefits, cost-of-living increases, and the $122 minimum monthly payment. In addition, the administration has favored increasing Medicare premiums (Medicare is also financed by Social Security taxes) and a general tightening of eligibility requirements.

Many alternatives to the present funding could be adopted that seem equally effective. One is to require the vast army of federal workers, who now have a separate plan of their own, to participate. Another is to make up the shortfall from general taxation revenues. Social Security was never set up as an actuarially based program in the first place. Perhaps the most important of all proposals is the one that would require payments into the system by workers earning above the annual maximum wage of $29,700. Employees who make more than this amount per year are presently relieved of making any payments beyond this level. This proposal alone, if adopted, could wipe out the deficit.[3]

Social Security Financing: Not Based on Ability to Pay

The proposal to increase the wage level on which the tax must be paid touches on one of the sorest points about the Social Security tax: it is essentially a flat-rate tax; that is, it is not based on a graduated system

[2] "The Battle to Save Social Security," *U.S. News and World Report*, July 20, 1981, p. 41.
[3] "'Social Wage' Takeaways," *UE News*, June 22, 1981, p. 6.

Unemployment assistance programs are tied to the Social Security system.

of payments according to ability to pay (unlike the income tax, which is graduated despite various concessions and "loopholes"). All contributors pay the same proportion of their pay up to the $29,700 maximum, at which point the tax becomes regressive because its effect is to make lower-income workers pay proportionally more than workers in high-income brackets. Another unfair feature is the disparity between em-

**Box 12–3
The Innovative
Welfare State:
Wino Park**

San Francisco has long been toasted as one of the world's easiest places to get drunk and stay drunk. It has the requisite amenities: relatively cheap liquor, a temperate climate, and legions of tourists who are easy marks for a practiced panhandler. Now, to these attractions is added another: a park dedicated exclusively to winos.

Wino Park, officially called Sixth Street Park, is a transformed sandlot tucked amid the transient hotels, pawn shops and liquor stores of the city's tough South-of-Market area. There, a wino can recline with a bottle of Thunderbird or Night Train Express wine, build a bonfire, cook a meal, sleep, loiter or play a game of sodden volleyball without being arrested. A brass plaque commemorates famous people who liked their drink. The winos like to read it aloud, like a roll call of heroes: "Honoring: Winston Churchill, Ernest Hemingway, W. C. Fields, John Barrymore, Betty Ford, Janis Joplin, Dylan Thomas . . . ," they intone.

A $135,000 metamorphosis, incorporating a $20,000 federal grant, has turned the sandlot into a combination campsite and open-air lounge, complete with benches, toilets and trees. It is about the size of a small store. Its sponsor is the Gilde Memorial Church, an inner-city congregation. . . .

—*Wall Street Journal*, May 13, 1981

BOX 12–4
A Labor Unionist Computes Social Security Costs

When dealing with the costs of the present Social Security system, we are told that the funding is based on a payroll tax . . . paid equally by the employer and the worker. It looks like a fifty-fifty deal. What could be fairer? But that is not the true picture because the employer pays its [share] before taxes whereas the worker pays after taxes. Let us see how this works out for the average factory worker using . . . data of the Bureau of Labor Statistics. . . .

Average weekly wage	$ 170.05
Social Security tax (5.8%)	9.95
Federal tax paid on $9.95 (four dependents)	1.39
Illinois state tax (4% of 9.95)	.40
Total cost to worker per week	$ 11.74
Average annual wage	$8,842.60
Annual Social Security tax (52 x $9.95)	517.40
Annual net cost of Social Security to worker (52 x $11.74)	610.48
Federal corporate tax 48% withheld weekly (48% of $9.95)	4.78
Illinois state tax (4% of $9.95)	.40
Total tax withheld	5.18
Net cost of Social Security to employers per week ($9.95 — $5.18)	4.77
Average annual wage	$8,842.60
Annual Social Security payment @ 5.85%	517.40
Less taxes withheld (52 x $5.18)	269.36
Annual cost per worker of Social Security to the company	$ 248.04

—Ernest DeMaio, "Social Security: Who Pays?" *Labor Today*, **13**: 6 (May 1974).

ployee and employer contributions. Most people familiar with Social Security financing seem to assume that equal contributions are made by workers and their bosses; but the system requires employees to make their contribution *before* taxes, a considerably greater proportion of income, whereas employers contribute an *after-tax* figure (see Box 12–4). Moreover, this tax does not simply finance old-age benefits but also such important programs as Medicare and unemployment compensation.

BOX 12–5
**Social Security and
Illegal Aliens**

What about those who are poor but who do not legally qualify, for one reason or another, for the protections of Social Security, Medicaid, occupational health and safety measures, or minimum wages? The truth is that we know very little about the plight of such people. Illegal aliens do not have such protections because their contact with officialdom could result in arrest and/or deportation. Here is a comment on the lives they lead:

"Illegals live in a world of lies. They are not liars, but theirs is a world of lies. They have to live—to eat—and to eat they have to say things that others want to hear. If a boss asks if they are here legally, they say they are. But they know that the boss knows they are lying and that the boss is lying when he acts like he believes them. When the boss asks for a Social Security number, they give him one. It may be someone else's number or it may be their own or it may be just a made-up number. The boss doesn't care; he just wants a number. The *mojados* do care. They would like to escape the deceit and they would like the Social Security benefits. But that's a luxury that comes way after salary. They need the work. When they use someone else's Social Security card, they may also use that person's name, so they are frequently known by a half-dozen or more names to the people they work for and the people they work with. I was in a bar once with a bunch of people, and there was one guy at the table who knew everyone there, but they all called him by a different name."

—Farm worker interviewer, quoted by Paul R. Ehrlich, Loy Bilderback, and Anne H. Ehrlich, *The Golden Door: International Migration, Mexico and the United States* (New York: Ballantine, 1979), p. 242.

Noncontributory Programs

What is left out of our contributory welfare system should also be borne in mind: the provision of adequate medical care for all. The Medicare program, which is not comprehensive, covers only Social Security recipients. The noncontributory program of Medicaid administered jointly by the federal government and the states is only for welfare recipients or poverty cases. Since 1949 proposals have been brought forward every year to include a national health insurance system within

Although the Reagan Administration is generally seen as hostile to many welfare programs, it does seem to emphasize the development of minority-owned enterprises through a Commerce Department program.

the framework of the Social Security System. The American Medical Association and its allies in Congress have always thwarted any such program, however, even though national health insurance is a generally accepted part of the welfare system of almost all technologically advanced nations of the world.

This is a missed chance in more ways than one, for the skyrocketing costs of hospital stays, laboratory tests, and doctors' fees have created a nonsystem that is so expensive that it could bankrupt the government if it now assumed its costs. But even this set of circumstances does not prevent the proffering of innovative solutions to the health care problem.

Noncontributory programs are even more controversial than those financed through the Social Security System. Lacking the legitimacy of contributory programs, they run up against the work ethic, racial preju- dice, and the values of political practice that seem to overcome easily the generosity and charity that are imbedded in myth. Opinion polls demonstrate conclusively the low position of welfare programs on our list of national priorities and a low regard for welfare recipients (see Boxes 12–6 and 12–7). Not all noncontributory programs are intensely controversial—payments to the blind and the disabled, for example, are

---

Question: Where should cuts be made to balance the budget?

Welfare	54%
Defense	29
Health/Medicare/Medicaid	9
Education	8
Social Security	5
No opinion/no answer	16

—Total more than 100% due to multiple responses; *Gallup Opinion Index* Report 164 (March 1979).

**BOX 12–6
Welfare: A Low
Priority Item with
the People**

Question: It has been suggested that all able-bodied moth- ers of children thirteen and older who are on welfare be re- quired to register with state employment offices and to take any full-time work available. Would you favor or oppose such a plan?

Favor	79%
Oppose	17
No Opinion	4

The same question, except that "children between the ages of 6 and 13" is substituted:

Favor	68%
Oppose	28
No Opinion	4

—*Gallup Opinion Index* Report 166 (May 1979).

**BOX 12–7
Public Opinion on
Welfare Mothers
and Their Problems**

not usually the focus of tax cut protests—but many of them are bitterly resented by many middle-income taxpayers who bear the brunt of our tax burdens. Conservative economist Milton Friedman claims that noncontributory welfare programs are resented because they are the only programs of the federal government that really do benefit the poor at the expense of those who are better off. All other income transfers administered by the government, he claims, help those who are above the poverty level.

Many of the popular attitudes about welfare programs are simply not true—that they are essentially programs for blacks and other minorities, that welfare recipients refuse to look for jobs, that they are lazy, that they drive Cadillacs to the welfare offices to pick up their checks (according to a popular song), that several generations of one family pass down the welfare tradition to one another, and that the lives of such people are carefree, irresponsible, and savored for the freeloading opportunities they have managed to make for themselves (see Box 12–8).

The Reagan Cuts

Many of the noncontributory programs were slated for deep cuts by the Reagan Administration after it took office in 1981. Especially hard hit were CETA (Comprehensive Employment and Training Act) programs for job training, Aid to Families with Dependent Children, day

America's "work ethic" has been a traditional obstacle to non-contributory welfare programs.

VENERATE THE PLOUGH

care, nutrition, housing, and education. Allowances for food stamps were to be set without regard to unemployment or inflation rates, which was the practice at one time in the past, and all families were to be eliminated from the program if their yearly income exceeded 130 percent of the poverty line of $11,000 for a family of four. In addition, any household with a member on strike would be removed from food stamp eligibility. These and other cuts took place in the cause of lowered taxes, a balanced federal budget, and greatly escalated defense expenditures against a backdrop of high unemployment, a widening gap in the incomes of rich and poor, and inner-city decay. Unemployment among youths, especially black youths, has escalated over the years, as the accompanying table shows.[4]

[4] *Wall Street Journal*, September 8, 1980.

**Box 12–8
To Some, Welfare Is
Just a "Game"—or
Is It?**

New York—The creators of two controversial board games sued certain New York City officials for $5.5 million in damages, charging they interfered with marketing one of the games.

. . . inventors and marketers of games called "Public Assistance—Why Bother Working for a Living" and "Capital Punishment" filed their lawsuit in federal court here. [The action states that the city's Human Resources Administration wrote to retailers discouraging them from stocking the welfare game.]

A letter allegedly written . . . in November 1980 describes the welfare game as "not, as its inventors claim, a harmless spoof of welfare cheats and liberal government bureaucrats. It is an ugly and damaging slam at this society's poorest citizens. . . ."

. . . about 28,000 "Public Assistance" games have been sold nationally since last fall, when it was introduced. It sells for $15.95 and a related promotional brochure promises an experience in "government cake walkism, able-bodied loafism, Saturday night crimcism and jail jauntism." The brochure adds, "Avoid if you can: working person's rutism."

—*Wall Street Journal*, May 21,1981.

	White Youth Unemployment	Black Youth Unemployment
16–19 Years of Age		
1960	13%	24%
1980	17	37
20–24 Years of Age		
1960	4%	9%
1980	10	22%

Whether the Reagan policies and new alternative programs will work remains to be seen. There is no question that a gamble is involved (see Box 12–8).

Does the Welfare System Work?

Because the welfare system in America is so extensive and much of it is controversial, we must ask whether maintaining it is worth the cost. The argument that the social welfare programs of the United States are too broad today is made by critics who point out that other countries—Canada, Great Britain, the Netherlands, and even the great social laboratory, Sweden—have been cutting back their programs and commit-

**BOX 12–9
A Reagan
Alternative to
Welfare Programs:
"Enterprise Zones"**

Because it strongly dislikes most welfare state programs, the Reagan administration has sought to establish alternatives. One of these alternatives is the enterprise zone program. President Reagan has approved, in principle, the setting up of seventy-five enterprise zones in the country's depressed urban areas.

An "enterprise zone" is defined as an area established to attract industrial and commercial development in an economically depressed neighborhood. Taxes on these industries and businesses are greatly reduced or abolished altogether, as are some building and zoning regulations. Legislation may also be sought to reduce the minimum wage requirement of employers in enterprise zones. Businesses and industries are expected to be enticed to these locations rather than, say, the suburbs, even though there is considerable evidence that taxes are not a particularly important factor in location decisions. Will enterprise zones work? Only time will tell.

© 1982 Huck/Rothco

ments in recent years. Is this because social welfare programs are bad, or because they have not lived up to expectations? Both answers may be true, but it is also true that all Western countries have experienced some measure of economic difficulty in recent years and reduced commitments may merely reflect these conditions.

A major reassessment of the social welfare system in the United States has been undertaken in recent years by a group of loosely affiliated individuals known as "neoconservatives." These influential intellectuals were, generally speaking, committed at one time or another to the liberal welfare state, but they have come to feel that such programs are either too expensive, too wasteful, or both. They particularly single out the poverty programs, community action programs, and welfare state extensions enacted under Lyndon Johnson's Great Society as examples of overextended big government. In small-circulation journals such as *Public Interest* or *Commentary* and in a variety of books and articles, the neoconservatives have spent the past few years keeping up a drumfire of complaints against the welfare system.[5]

[5] Peter Steinfels, *The Neoconservatives* (New York: Simon and Schuster, 1979).

Is it possible to measure objectively the performance and cost of welfare programs? Isolated examples will not suffice. The antics of a famous welfare chiseler in Chicago (a story President Reagan often told) or the tale of a CETA-trained welfare mother who becomes a computer programmer at $21,000 a year after a relatively brief period of training (a true story) do not give us a complete picture. In recent years, some fairly sophisticated techniques have been devised that give us a well-detailed set of measurements by which we can evaluate specific programs and policies. A recent evaluation of the Job Corps program, for example, shows that the time, effort, and expenditures involved are apparently well worth it in terms of social results.[6]

Complicating such tasks is the overriding question of the purpose of welfare programs. If we cannot agree on the purposes of the welfare state, our assessments are likely to be in conflict with one another.

Social Needs and the Purposes of the Welfare State

If the misery of the poor be caused not by the laws of nature, but by our institutions, great is our sin.

—Charles Darwin
Voyage of the Beagle[7]

In assessing the purposes of the welfare state, it is important to measure the depth of the problems of the poor, the elderly, minorities, and others who need the services and programs provided. Any number of such measures are available to us because the government regularly prints statistics on the subject. The Census Bureau tells us that well over 20 million Americans are poor, living below the official poverty line. Blacks, Hispanic-Americans, and the elderly represent disproportionate numbers of poor according to these statistics, and consistent patterns of employment trends show quite conclusive evidence of racial discrimination. Labor Department joblessness figures, for example, show that among high school dropouts, blacks have an unemployment rate of 31.6 percent compared with 16.4 percent for whites; for high school graduates, the figures are 21.3 and 8.5 percent, respectively; and among college graduates, whites show an unemployment rate of only 4 percent while blacks are at an astronomical 17.1 percent. The tragedy told by these particular figures, according to employment experts, is that we seem to be creating a permanent class of unemployed blacks whose chances do not improve very much as they get older.[8]

[6] Charles D. Mallar, "A Comprehensive Evaluation of the Job Corps Program," *MPR* [Mathematics Policy Research] *Policy Newsletter*, 4–6 (Spring 1979).

[7] Quoted by June Goodfield, "A Mind Is Not Described by Numbers," *The New York Times Book Review*, November 1, 1981, p. 11.

[8] *Wall Street Journal*, September 8, 1980.

Statistics may simply not coincide with the perceptions of America's relatively well-off majority, however. The poor are a significant minority but they are a minority, all the same. Blacks may be out of work, but how many white suburbanites frequent inner-city ghettos to see whether this is really true? Hispanics, American Indians, the elderly, and other disadvantaged minorities are often "ghettoized" out of sight and out of mind of their more prosperous fellow citizens. Freeways and expressways help conceal the poor areas of our cities. The colors of clothing do not fade as fast as they once did and even the desperately poor do not dress in rags. In many ways, the poor are simply invisible to the great majority of Americans. Their invisibility makes their need for welfare less obvious to the people who provide the bulk of the revenues that pay for it.[9]

Another side of this problem is the failure or inability of the poor to air their grievances. An elderly woman of limited means riding a bus in Fort Wayne, Indiana, describes her worries of frequent increases in bus fares, telephone rates, and postage which give her the feeling that she is gradually being cut off from the rest of society. Her feeling is real, but to whom can she tell it? And, she asks, who would care? And what could they do if they did care?

The benefits of our welfare state are sometimes very good: childcare, employment opportunities, housing programs. Far too often, however, the welfare state produces or aggravates dependence, insecurity, or despair.

Welfare recipients are usually placed under some form of supervision by a social worker. A case in point is two women living in a northern California city who are recipients of Aid to Families with Dependent Children payments. The payments are just enough for these women to house, feed and clothe themselves and their children. They live together in order to share expenses. For whatever reason, they are fortunate enough to receive two small checks in the mail from their long-lost ex-husbands. After assessing their needs, they decide to spend the money on some new clothes for themselves. Then the social worker pays a visit. She tells the women to get rid of the new clothes because they are too "flashy" and will not help the two women in obtaining employment. They are also told that their house is clean except for the closets. These must be swept out before the social worker leaves. Some people would not mind being told to do these things, but it is unlikely most people want to be told what to wear and what to clean by someone who has the power to cut off their livelihood.

[9] This is a major point of Michael Harrington's *The Other America* (New York: Macmillan, 1962), which had a major influence in bringing some of the antipoverty programs of the Great Society into being.

**BOX 12–10
On Providing Job
Opportunities for
Minorities**

Question: Would you favor the Federal Government offering special educational or vocational courses, free of charge, to enable members of minority groups to do better in tests?

Favor	53%
Oppose	39
No Opinion	8

Question: Some people say that to make up for past discrimination, women and members of minority groups should be given preferential treatment in getting jobs and places in college. Others say that ability, as determined by test scores, should be the main consideration. Which point of view comes closest to how you feel on this matter?

Give preference	11%
Ability main consideration	81
No opinion	8

—*Gallup Opinion Index* Report 151 (February 1978).

Regulation of the Poor   Again we must ask, what is the purpose of the welfare system? A powerful thesis that has gained acceptance in recent years is that the welfare system provides an effective and efficient means of regulating the poor. Welfare, according to this view, should not be considered benign, institutionalized charity. Instead, it should be considered a means of coordinating the behavior of the poor and keeping this behavior narrowly channeled within the guidelines for the conduct of the poor formulated by those who "know better."[10]

Why must the poor be regulated? Both myth and ideology tell us why. Myth tells the American people that they are generous in spirit, at least generous enough to prevent the poor and other unfortunates from falling through the safety net established by the welfare system. The poor, it is often believed, are unable to discern their own best interests. They simply cannot be left to fend for themselves because they will not act responsibly.

At the ideological level, the welfare system is important because the aged need medical care, the physically limited need assistance, and the

[10] Frances Fox Piven and Richard A. Cloward, *Regulating the Poor: The Functions of Public Welfare* (New York: Pantheon, 1971).

poor must not be allowed to starve. Often these realizations do not move the government to provide more than a modicum of necessities and services, while some relatively simple aids like the removal of curbings to benefit wheelchair users are overlooked (see Box 12–10).

Yet another ideological aspect of the welfare system explains a great deal. The welfare system, after all, benefits more than its recipients. It also benefits the army of welfare administrators, medical personnel, social workers, counselors, teachers, and others who make their living in the welfare system. This is not to say that these are evil or pernicious people, nor that they do not do important work. But they do have a stake in the welfare system and are prone to support the status quo. Many people may feel that this army serves a nobler purpose than the Pentagon's legions of bureaucrats, but the fact remains that the welfare establishment operates in ways that are not dissimilar to those of the Pentagon. Budgets for various welfare programs are key points of applied political pressure for this bureaucracy, but preventing reform of the welfare system remains a primary goal. It is also clear that reform is generally viewed as undesirable by the many interest groups who supply the welfare system with services and goods, whether these are hospitals, agricultural interests, food companies, or profit-making vocational schools.

CETA worker helps to restore a historic building.

Reforming the Welfare System

Reforming the system is imperative if the nation is ever going to truly tend to the needs of the poor, the sick, the physically limited, and those whose fortunes have turned down through no fault of their own. The years since the mid-1960s have seen a variety of guaranteed income schemes presented by authors, planners, and academics concerned with the subject. The Nixon administration briefly considered a Family Assistance Plan (FAP), which would have guaranteed individual incomes at a level of $1,600 a year, but it abandoned even this modest beginning.

The most famous of all welfare reform plans is the Negative Income Tax (NIT) proposed by Milton Friedman, the Nobel Prize-winning conservative economist. Friedman sees the NIT plan as a replacement for Aid to Families with Dependent Children, food stamps, public service jobs, public housing, and many of the poverty remedies now wielded by the bureaucracy, including Social Security. In the long run, he asserts, it would also be less expensive because it would do away with the great overhead costs of welfare administration—reports, checking procedures, forms, eligibility tests, and invasions of recipients' privacy. The NIT plan offers cash payments directly to the poor, the kind of aid that many observers believe is the most helpful to them. Friedman also claimed that his plan would promote self-esteem among the poor, give them incentives to do things for themselves, and abolish many of the political factors now present in poverty programs and welfare adminis-

**BOX 12–11
The Rights of the
Physically Limited**

Bruce P. Hillam, a professor of mathematics at California State Polytechnic University at Pomona, who is paralyzed from the shoulders down, speaks out:

"The Declaration of Independence states that everyone has an inalienable right to life, liberty, and the pursuit of happiness. Medical science has provided life, but where is liberty if I cannot cross the street because of a man-made barrier, the curb? How is my pursuit of happiness compatible with society's preoccupation with what I *cannot* do? And how can I pursue happiness if I am excluded from many of our society's normal social and recreational functions? What is needed is a civil-rights bill for the physically limited."

—*Newsweek*, November 1, 1976.

In New York City, only 23% of doctors accept Medicaid patients, and 4% to 7% of the City's doctors—many of them practicing in its infamous "Medicaid mills"—collect up to 85% of all Medicaid fees; one doctor, William Triebel, received $451,156 in 1974 and $785,114 in 1975. 95% of New York City's Medicaid dental services are provided by 5% of the City's dentists. In Chicago, 73 of Cook County's 6,000 private doctors (another study puts these figures at 100 of 9,000) see over half of the County's 285,000 Medicaid recipients. This amounts to one doctor per 2,000 persons on Medicaid, and the ratio gets worse as these doctors, with their increased income from Medicaid fees, leave the poorer sections of the County. In New York City there are 280 doctors per 100,000 population, but in the impoverished South Bronx area the number has fallen to 10. In the nation's capital about 20 persons, most of them elderly poor, die each year in the process of transfer from private hospital *emergency* rooms, where they are not wanted, to the District of Columbia General Hospital. In 1970 in Chicago, 18,000 persons, again with a disproportion of elderly poor, were turned away from private hospital emergency rooms, and more than 50 of them died in the process of dismissal or transfer to Cook County Hospital, an overloaded facility which cares for half of Chicago's Medicaid patients (and half of the County's blacks). The turnaway, known in medical circles as patient dumping, generally consists of suggested use of a car or taxi, or simply pointing out the nearest bus stop.

—Howard Freeman, *Toward Socialism in America* (Cambridge: Schenkman, 1980), p. 7.

tration. Many experts in the social welfare field agree that a lot of the programs now in existence result in the demeaning and mistreatment of the poor (see Box 12–11).

The basic point of NIT is the provision of incentives to better oneself. At the present time, welfare recipients are penalized if they earn extra income. Under NIT, income level would be an explicit indicator of what an individual receives from a list of charted cash benefits. Most important, according to Friedman, NIT would meet the specific needs that all welfare programs must meet from a political standpoint—reasonable cost, strong incentives to work, and a decent level of support for the recipient.[11]

One major difficulty for the NIT plan as with the present welfare system is the reluctance of Americans, no matter how self-professed their generosity, to accept the idea of paying taxes to guarantee a certain income level, no matter how low, for others. The second difficulty is ideological: disestablishing the welfare establishment of poverty workers, big city mayors, social workers, and other bureaucrats through a system of guaranteed and automatic payments may be politically impossible.

Another frequently proposed reform is "workfare," which has the support of the Reagan administration. Workfare sets up jobs that are mandatory for welfare recipients to accept or lose their benefits. Penalties for refusing jobs already exist under current welfare laws, but workfare is based on the premise that the jobs offered to welfare recipients, which they must accept, will be so unattractive that they will provide an incentive to look for a better job. But workfare is a somewhat futile measure because over a quarter of all AFDC recipients already hold or are seeking jobs. Welfare policy specialists point out that useful, rewarding jobs created in a more ambitious and constructive workfare plan might prove to be valuable for both recipients and society at large, but that the present work-or-be-punished approach is ill-conceived and impractical. Workfare in this form is probably a questionable reform.[12]

Still another reform frequently proferred in recent years relates to financing the welfare state. This proposal, most often associated with various governors and local officials, calls for the "federalizing" of welfare expenditures. States and localities would be relieved of the burden of helping to pay for (and, presumably, administer) welfare programs. Because the Reagan administration favors a decentralization of authority over domestic programs, however, "federalizing" of welfare is unlikely to receive any attention in the near future.

The Clouded Future of the Welfare State

The 1980s will be years of trial for the welfare state. Social Security financing problems, cutbacks in food stamps, job training, AFDC, Medicare, and other programs and a growing disenchantment with welfare administration all contribute to a condition of malaise. In many ways the antiwelfare state reactions of politicians and the public are strange, because the United States has never developed its welfare state to the

[11] Milton Friedman and Rose Friedman, *Free to Choose* (New York: Harcourt Brace Jovanovich, 1980), pp. 120–127.

[12] See the letter of Thomas C. Joe, Director of the Center for Study of Welfare Policy, University of Chicago, *Wall Street Journal*, July 1, 1980.

extent of the various innovations in Europe: comprehensive medical care, as in Great Britain, very generous pension systems as in Denmark, the Netherlands, and Belgium, or extensive day-care programs and virtual job guarantees as in Sweden.

Some of the problems of the welfare state question may lie in our definitions. The term "welfare" is applied only to programs designed to aid the poor, minorities, the aged, the sick, or the physically limited. The term therefore invariably takes on a class dimension. Should it not be applied to corporate subsidies and tax concessions as well? Or to the cost overruns of big defense contracts? A few years ago, a Canadian politician, David Lewis, campaigned successfully in his country on a platform that castigated "corporate welfare bums." Lewis cited tax giveaways, government subsidies to various companies, and the privileged position of wealthy business executives to show that the term "welfare" should apply to them.

Analogous factors and circumstances seem to apply to the American political system. Frances Fox Piven, long recognized as an expert on social welfare matters, has noted that the Reagan administration, for example, has demonstrated a strong preference for sugar industry subsidies over food stamps in its budget negotiations with Congress. She points out further, "Nowhere is [the Reagan administration] proposing to reduce state intervention on behalf of" corporate interests.[13] One person's "welfare," then, may be another person's "subsidy."

We must ask, why does America have a welfare state at all, let alone the very costly and variegated one described in this chapter? Recall that the welfare state largely benefits the poor and the disadvantaged (though as we have shown, hardly exclusively). These people as a class are in an important sense invisible. However much they count in myth, they are in ideological terms an underclass far from the perimeter of policymaking and administration. Because of the weak position of this underclass, we should hardly expect America to have much more of a welfare state than, say, England had in the days of Adam Smith.

The system exists all the same, with its monumental inefficiency, poor planning and administration, and more than occasional outright failure. Four primary reasons point to why this is so.

First, America's mythic conscience genuinely cares about the plight of our less fortunate citizens and has increasingly turned to government to remedy it. This demand shifts in focus from time to time, both on the matters of quantity and quality of welfare programs, but it persists even so. Second, there is a practical view of the welfare state that says, "There but for the grace of God go I." The safety net provided by welfare programs is something we want for ourselves should we ever need it. Third, it is apparent that there are profits to be made from programs

[13] Quoted in *P.S.*, **14**: 787–788 (Fall 1981).

New public housing project in Brownsville, Texas.

for the poor. The poor may lack the political strength to defend the welfare state, but the interests and industries that provide goods and services for it do not. Last, and underlying these first three reasons for the welfare state, is the need of our political and economic systems to rectify or at least minimize the great social damage caused by our industries, our technology, and our government. Unemployment, health problems, poverty, inadequate housing, and lack of employment opportunity could create a breakdown in political legitimacy. The great advantage of the welfare state is that it ameliorates these problems without threatening to undo any part of the economic (that is, Liberal Democratic capitalist) structures that created them.

In this light the welfare state, in America as well as in other capitalist countries, can be seen as an essentially conservative device: with mythic (Protestant) enthusiasms, it is effective in preserving the ideological economic (Bourgeois) structures with which it would otherwise be at odds.

FOR FURTHER READING

CALIFANO, JOSEPH A., Jr. *Governing America: An Insider's Report from the White House and the Cabinet.* New York: Simon and Schuster, 1981. Memoirs of a recent secretary of Health, Education and Welfare that provide a view from the top of social welfare administration.

DERTHICK, MARTHA. *Policymaking for Social Security.* Washington: Brookings Institution, 1979. A serious attempt to grapple with the problem of the future of the Social Security system.

GAVENTA, JOHN P. *Power and Powerlessness: Quiesence and Rebellion in an Appalachian Valley.* Urbana: University of Illinois Press, 1980. Prize-winning case study of the responses of the poor to their plight.

GILDER, GEORGE. *Wealth and Poverty.* New York: Basic Books, 1980. Conservative guidelines on welfare policy are included in this influential book that has been read by top officials of the Reagan administration.

HARRINGTON, MICHAEL. *Decade of Decision.* New York: Simon and Schuster, 1980. An avowed American socialist seeks to chart the future of poverty policy as well as other policies related to the welfare state.

HARRINGTON, MICHAEL. *The Other America.* New York: Macmillan, 1962. Classic study of poverty in America that strongly influenced the development of the Great Society programs of President Lyndon Johnson.

HAYDEN, TOM. *The American Future: New Visions Beyond Old Frontiers.* Boston: South End Press, 1980. A radical of the 1960s assesses the future of the welfare state and related issues.

HOUSEMAN, GERALD L. *City of the Right: Urban Applications of American Conservative Thought.* Westport: Greenwood Press, 1982. Criticizes the views of five prominent conservatives, including Milton Friedman, on their assumptions about the welfare state.

HORWITZ, JULIUS. *Diary of A.N.* New York: Dell, 1971. Hard-hitting fictional work that effectively describes the life of welfare recipients.

JAMES, DOROTHY B. *Poverty, Politics and Change.* Englewood Cliffs, N.J.: Prentice-Hall, 1972. For a short book, this work does one of the most effective jobs of tying the problem of poverty in America to the country's political traditions and influences.

PIVEN, FRANCES FOX, and RICHARD A. CLOWARD. *Regulating the Poor: The Functions of Public Welfare.* New York: Pantheon, 1971. States the thesis that the function of the welfare system is to control the behavior and perceptions of the poor.

REDENIUS, CHARLES. *The American Ideal of Equality: From Jefferson's Declaration to the Burger Court.* Port Washington: Kennikat, 1981. Arrays traditional American support of the concept of equality against the reality of our economic history by making effective use of constitutional development and precedents.

SCHILLER, BRADLEY R. *The Economics of Poverty and Discrimination,* 3rd ed. Englewood Cliffs, N.J.: Prentice-Hall, 1980. Ties together racial discrimination and its economic and social effects using recent data.

STEINBERG, STEPHEN. *The Ethnic Myth: Race, Ethnicity and Class in America.* New York: Atheneum, 1981. Debunks ethnic stereotyping of the poor that has crept into American consciousness through pseudosophisticated "social science."

The Welfare State in Crisis. Washington: OECD Publications, 1981. An account of the OECD Conference on Social Policies in the 1980s, with essays by Nathan Glazer, Lester Thurow, and others.

THE PEOPLE IV

In their mythic, Social Democratic vision, Americans see themselves as politically united, active, and hopeful. In this sense, they are the People.

In their ideological, Liberal Democratic vision, Americans see themselves as individually protected by law to go about their personal business as they see fit. In this sense, they are simply people.

In the preceding parts of this book we have described the American political system in terms of its underlying principles, major constitutional structures, and administrative processes. Now that we know what the system is, we can study the involvement of the People (or simply people) in it.

Chapters 13 and 14 concentrate on the ways the People are prepared for and then actively participate in the system's mythic, Social Democratic aspects. Although these features have ideological aspects as well, we are primarily concerned in Chapter 13 with the ways in which the People collectively acquire their mythic beliefs, become knowledgeable about the nation's political symbols, and express themselves through public opinion. Then in Chapter 14 we see how the People are directly involved in the political process through participation in civic movements, parties, and elections. Our central theme here is that this participation is the means by which the People legitimize the political system.

The last two chapters have a largely ideological bent. By the most fundamental tenets of Liberal Democracy, all Americans are entitled to their civil rights and liberties, and to a degree that often surprises the rest of the world, America is by almost anyone's standards a relatively free society. All the same, many times the Bill of Rights and our other basic freedoms are ignored or capriciously administered. It is also the case that balancing the conflicting claims for specific kinds of freedom within the law in a modern, interdependent, technological society

raises many difficult problems of definition and application. Chapter 15 covers these issues.

It is also true that the system's powerful elitist tendencies on its ideological side work to the advantage of some people. Talent, diligence, and good luck also contribute to the heaping up of material benefits—and power—in the hands of a few. We study these people and their mores in Chapter 16, examining why this elite exists, its general composition, how it manages America's corporate wealth, and how, from their positions of privilege, its members manipulate the political system to their own purposes.

Opinion Research, a polling firm, recently reported on the results of an interesting experiment. Deciding that the impact of certain words may provide different responses to polling questions, the firm first asked a sample of citizens to choose government programs that might best be sacrificed in a severe budget squeeze. On the list of choices was an item called "aid to the needy." Only 7 percent of the respondents thought that money should be cut from such programs. Two months later, the same question was asked with one change made in the list of possible answers: the "needy" item was called "public welfare." This time, 39 percent decided that it was good to cut funds from this category.[1] The emotional response to the term "public welfare" appears to be substantially more negative than to "the needy."

This example illustrates one of the problems in measuring public opinion. Questions must be formulated with precision or the poll may not yield very useful information. This is one of the reasons the results of polls must be carefully scrutinized when they are cited as representing a particular trend in public opinion.

The polling firm's experiment also reveals a strong possibility that people are socialized to think in positive terms about helping "the needy." Such soft, broad terms appeal to our Social Democratic mythic aspirations. But Americans view public welfare negatively because it is regarded as antithetical to such Liberal Democratic values as the work ethic. As Liberal Democrats, the American people characteristically have an antigovernment, antibureaucratic bias and believe that public welfare is at best a necessary evil of the operational, ideological side of government.

Our mythic and ideological heritages blend with our personal experiences to produce socialization patterns that are relatively standard

[1] *Wall Street Journal*, February 23, 1982.

405

among the population but also prompt a variety of opinion and political action.

In Social Democratic myth Americans see themselves as a People united in pursuit of social justice at home and freedom and peace for all nations everywhere. This is a comforting vision, a proud and hopeful picture of ourselves. It is also a fuzzy vision, and in many respects it is dangerously untrue. It tempts us to grandiose gestures and adventures from which we have often emerged scalded, holding deepseated feelings of having been misled or betrayed.

By believing their Social Democratic myth Americans become *a* People, a nation unique among all other nations. The substance of the myth is that we are historically and institutionally a Social Democracy. This is often expressed in religious, often specifically biblical terms. Just as the Bible recounts the history of the Hebrew people, so the Social Democratic myth of America projects an account of our nation's origins, the crisis of our present, and our mission in the future. Only by becoming a People in the family of nations are Americans prepared to become the People within their own political system, playing their part in government.

That America treasures a mythic account of its past does not make it unique. All nations revere their histories with greater or lesser fidelity to the facts. What sets America apart from other nations is simply the particular detail of our past as we remember it and project it into our shared understandings about our present and future.

There is the added fact, stressed throughout this book, that Americans' mythic account of themselves is often at odds with their ideological practice. America is perhaps unique among modern nations in the intensity of the strains between its myth and its ideology.

Components of the Social Democratic Myth

We all know the high points of our nation's mythic self-understanding. The problem is to add them up, perceive them as a whole, and analyze what they mean.

The primary mythic understanding of our nation's history is that America was conceived in liberty and dedicated to the proposition that all men are created equal. Like the Israelites of old braving the waters of the Red Sea, America's early pilgrims ventured across the ocean to plant on these wild shores the first seeds of freedom. That pilgrimage was our first Exodus, and it was regarded by those early settlers very much in this way. But in form our original Exodus was repeated again and again as peoples from all over the globe made their way here to find freedom and opportunity. To this day Haitians, Mexicans, Vietnamese, and others continue to come. This initial conception of America as a haven for the oppressed has determined America's mythic self-understanding as perhaps no other historical process has; for peoples everywhere America has been the promised land, a haven of freedom and hope.

Nevertheless this is a mythic self-perception, partly true but also partly false. Quite apart from the problem of what happened to the immigrants after they arrived—we tend to hear mostly the individual success stories—how did the blacks get to this country? And what became of the Indians, who were already here? In myth these questions are not raised. What remains is that America is the first "new" nation, the land of hope. Blacks, women, and other groups find themselves mentioned in the myth only when they, too, begin to win their "freedom," such as after the Civil War or the passage of the Nineteenth Amendment in 1920.

The historical development in myth of America as a Social Democracy is punctuated by our wars. The Revolution was fought in the name of liberty and wrested our national freedom from a distant colonial power, although we might wonder whom the conflict freed who was not already free before it began. The Mexican wars gave Texas to the Texans. The Civil War is not noticed as a breakdown in our institutions or for their failure to resolve fundamental moral problems; rather, it is remembered as a test of our commitment to freedom and for the emancipation of the slaves. The Spanish American War set us on the world stage to bring the benefits of our civilization to distant peoples such as the Filipinos. We fought World War I to make the world safe for democracy, and World War II was supposed to do the job again against the hated Axis powers of Germany, Italy, and Japan. In all these wars myth tells us we were victorious in the cause of human liberation and social justice. The symbol of these victories is not only the stars and stripes but also the typical member of our armed forces embodied in G.I. Joe, tough but amiable, little given to discipline, and generous to a fault, especially to children.

Our wars were all conducted against a backdrop of national growth from a fledgling former colony to a great nation that expanded across a continent and then swelled to an economic colossus with the highest standard of living in the world and the military might of the leading superpower. As much as our military victories, this phenomenol growth is held in myth to be proof of our national moral, economic, and political virtue.

Our political virtue is expressed in those mythic principles and institutions we have encountered throughout this book: sovereignty of the people, federalism and separation of powers, and the vision of our government as a popular democracy seeking to express the People's will through a system of political parties led by heroic presidents.

Over the years our Social Democratic myths have generally sustained

BOX 13–1
American Public Opinion on Current Social Issues: What the Polls Show

Issue	Favor	Opposed
Favor death penalty for murder	66%	25%
Favor Equal Rights Amendment	63	32
Support Supreme Court abortion ruling of 1973	45	46

—*Gallup Opinion Index* 187 and 190 (April 1981 and July 1981).

us. In recent decades, however, the assassinations of national leaders, the Vietnam War, the domestic turmoil of the 1960s and early 1970s, the scandals of Watergate, and the severe difficulties of the Carter and Reagan administrations have unsettled our national self-assurance. The works and words that used to guide us so surely have become blurred. The call of myth has become a faltering trumpet.

Perhaps this always seems to be the case in any present age. Perhaps it is only when we look back that everything seems clear. But it is hard not to believe that the deepseated concerns we are now feeling over the profoundest matters of national direction and purpose are new.

When myth becomes uncertain and no longer leads us, it is not because myth has been proved false but because it no longer seems relevant, because it no longer answers important questions about who we are and where we should be heading. It is in that sense that stories about Washington cutting down cherry trees or Lincoln splitting rails can become "unbelievable." Whether factually true or false, the virtues these stories celebrate no longer seem part of the self-image we would have of ourselves.

Socialization

Political socialization is the process by which the values and aspirations of a society become absorbed by its individual members. Each of us has a pattern of political attitudes and beliefs acquired through the understandings and experiences we have gained from life. The major influences that shape this pattern are the family, peer groups, schools, churches, and the media. An individual's political value pattern tends to remain stable over long periods of time, but it may change in dramatic or subtle ways. Abrupt changes, which are relatively rare, are sometimes caused by a cataclysmic turn of events such as the Great Depression, a war, or a great personal tragedy or success. Most changes, however, occur gradually and undramatically.

Because it is not subject to great changes except in rare instances, the political socialization process ensures a certain stability in the body politic. Values and norms, once learned, are cherished. Attitudes, though they never seem to become permanently frozen, become durable regime supports. This process has never been truer than in America, where the mythic side of our national consciousness legitimates the system.

The family background of an individual is of great importance in the socialization process. We have long known that children seem to share the traditions and values of their parents, and that this carries over to voting preferences and behavior, modes of political participation or nonparticipation, and attitudes on a variety of social questions. In many cases, parental influence upon the political attitudes of offspring are brought about through imitation or simply immersion in a family atmosphere rather than through overt attempts of parents to inculcate political values in their children.

The Family

Studies of childrens' attitudes show that the political socialization process is well established by the age of ten. At this age children are learning to become little Democrats or Republicans (or neither). They are also developing an awareness of their family's place in the social and economic strata of their community. They know the religious preference, if any, of their parents, and they realize that other families may prefer different religions. Pluralism, at least in this area, is becoming acceptable. In many cases, they are aware of an ethnic identity. And it is possible that other family affiliations—social clubs, labor unions, veterans organizations—may affect socialization.

Children first learn about authority from their parents. It is probable that the lessons learned at, or over, the parental knee are of lifelong significance. If the parent is awesome and arbitrary, the child learns to fear and obey a Liberal Democratic authoritarian figure. On the other hand, a parental figure identified with strength and warmth may prepare the child to revere the father figures of Social Democracy

By the age of ten children are also well aware of political authority figures, such as the president and police officers. Children tend to view presidents, past and current, as performing a heroic role for the benefit of all the American people. We also know that attitudes of black and white children toward the police can be quite different and may depend on experiences of considerable contrast.[2] Power relationships also become understood. Children learn at an early age what people have authority over others and when those in authority can impose binding obligations, whether these are between parent and child, teacher and

---

[2] See for example Richard G. Niemi, *The Politics of Future Citizens* (San Francisco: Jossey-Bass, 1974).

pupil, employer and employee, or leader and member. The prevalence of power understandings in the political socialization patterns of children is often explained as necessary to increase the regularity of people's behavior. Whether this is a wholly justifiable reason for the existence of power hierarchies is open to doubt. It strikes some observers as unfortunate that childrens' first perceptions of people in government are of distant authority figures.

Religious affiliations, which come primarily out of family background and experience, can have significant effects on political socialization. Some of these effects are directly traceable to attitudes on issues like pacifism, refusal to salute the flag, or abortion. Or they may be indirect: for example, Catholic and Jewish voters support the Democratic Party and welfare state measures more strongly than Protestants do.

Ethnic identification is sometimes correlated with socialization patterns, and the interest of researchers and the general public in this area has picked up markedly with the "ethnic revival" since the 1960s. Unfortunately there is a tendency, especially in popular attitudes and literature, to make broad generalizations and to engage in stereotyping. Some generalizations about ethnic voting behavior and attitudes are verifiable and therefore valid. Black voters, for example, overwhelmingly favor Democratic candidates in presidential and most other elections. Cuban-Americans and recent immigrants from Eastern Europe tend to favor conservative, identifiably anticommunist candidates.

**BOX 13–2
Socialization and
Group Conformity**

Whether desirable or undesirable, conformity to community and group standards is, in any event, "natural." Few social science findings have been more firmly and repeatedly confirmed than those revealing man's vulnerability to group pressure and his responsiveness to group norms. Through association with family, peers, and other reference groups, and through the routine mechanisms of socialization (e.g., imitation, modelling, indoctrination, reinforcement) one learns which standards society prizes and one conforms to them, for the most part, without reflection.

—Giuseppe DiPalma and Herbert McCloskey, "Personality and Conformity: The Learning of Political Attitudes," in *A Source Book for the Study of Personality and Politics*, Fred I. Greenstein and Michael Lerner, eds. (Chicago: Markham, 1971), p. 279.

Friends, work associates, fellow students, and other peer groups have a marked effect on political socialization. It is difficult, however, to make many generalizations about the influence of peer groups because relatively little research has been done on the subject. Individuals tend to conform to group standards and values (see Box 13–2), but we are not sure to what extent this conformity takes place. We are not completely certain, to cite just one example, how peer group influence works—nor to what extent it works—against parental influence when the two are in conflict. Peer pressure may be stronger in adult years than in adolescence because of career pressures. There is a tendency to retain political party identification or affiliation even in the face of peer pressure. But individuals are less "issue resistant"—that is, they tend to change their views on issues—against peer pressure.[3]

In many cases, peer pressure and family background do not conflict, and friends and associates may merely reinforce positions. We choose our friends and sometimes our work associates, and these relationships are often born out of similar social and economic backgrounds. People tend to associate with others like themselves, even though politics and attitudes on social issues are seldom the basis of friendships.

Peer Groups

Much of the explicit content of America's Social Democratic myth is imparted by the schools, which are decisive instruments of political socialization. Primary, secondary, and college education are all involved in the process though in different ways.

At the primary level, the major emphasis is on the essential political symbols and the heroes and historical events that surround them. Traditionally, and in many schools today, classes begin with the pledge of allegiance to the flag. This act indoctrinates students with the meaning of the flag and makes it an object of reverence. But notice what else the pledge teaches: that we are (1) one nation under God, (2) indivisible, (3) with liberty, and (4) justice (5) for all. All five points are essential to the American mythic faith, even though in the schools the pledge is rarely presented in this way. The national anthem and other patriotic songs sung in the schools undoubtedly perform similar socializing functions.

Primary education introduces students to our great presidents, the myths surrounding them, and their various exploits. America's wars and military victories are often given special emphasis. Often it appears that the idea of a country and its people on the march toward great progress in social justice is taught as an explicit principle. Washington, Lincoln, and other presidents are used as examples to demonstrate the idea of the president as a tribune of the people, a myth that becomes familiar to every child.

Schools

[3] Robert S. Erikson, Norman R. Luttbeg, and Kent L. Tedin, *American Public Opinion: Its Origins, Content, and Impact* (New York: Wiley, 1980), pp. 126–127.

Civics education is undertaken in earnest, however, as secondary education begins. The basic tripartite diagram of the separation of powers is reproduced on chalkboards and, along with photos of the temple-like buildings that house the government, in textbooks. Alongside this is presented the system of checks and balances, usually with little or no mention of its contradictions and complications. Sustained emphasis is usually placed on the need to pay attention to political news, on the civic duty to vote, and on quite general definitions of freedom and democracy. Studies also show that there is a tendency to promote the idea of "voting for the man, not the party."[4] Almost all of this instruction is presented in forthright mythic terms with little regard for the ideological side of politics and government. Occasionally this emphasis is reinforced with class trips to the nation's capital, the state capital, or city hall.

Considerably more sophisticated civic education is continued at the college level. The ideological practices of American government are no secret, after all, to professional political scientists. But this newer sort of knowledge about politics in America is seldom analytically integrated with the old. It is admitted that problems are unsolved, that Congress is in trouble, or that we may be moving into an era of one-term presidents after the records of leadership established by Johnson, Nixon, Ford, Carter, and Reagan, with all that this may imply. Nevertheless the old values of the myth are often pressed—that our Constitution is "a living document," that Watergate actually proved the vitality of our institutional mechanisms, and that the first duty of the college-educated citizen is civic participation.

The function of schools in political socialization, then, is to teach good citizenship largely in terms of the myths of American politics. This is understandable. The essential cultural function of the schools is to preserve and perpetuate our nation's heritage. In politics this means the systematic development of students into citizens who will legitimize and relegitimize the regime, whatever the partisan or social currents may be at any given time (see Box 13–3).

Newspapers, television, radio, and magazines also have an important impact upon political socialization. From time to time the awareness of their effects causes a hailstorm of criticism against the "bias" of the mass media by both informed observers and those who cannot tell the difference between a news story and an editorial page. Not infrequently, politicians and bureaucrats decry the irresponsibility of electronic media and the press (see Box 13–4).

Mass Media

Recent studies of childrens' exposure to the news media and the effects on their socialization have found that (1) exposure does not correlate with support for any particular political party or support for the party system; and (2) children who become more knowledgeable about the party system feel more negatively about it.[5] These findings are not surprising when we remember that political parties in America tend to receive a low level of support from adults.[6]

[4] Robert S. Erikson et al., *American Public Opinion*, p. 117.
[5] M. Margaret Conway, Mikel L. Wyckoff, Eleanor Feldbaum, and David Ahern, "The News Media in Children's Political Socialization," *Public Opinion Quarterly*, **45:** 164–178 (Summer 1981).
[6] Ibid.

BOX 13–3
College Students are Increasingly Conservative and Materialistic, Say the Polls

A famous study of Bennington College students in the 1930s found that they moved from conservative to liberal (and even radical) orientations during their four college years. But the worry of some conservatives that this is because of professorial "indoctrination" is not well-founded. The Bennington study showed, quite to the contrary, that peer groups and overall environmental factors were the causes of change in political outlook rather than the work of leftish professors.

Interestingly, radical students are not found to be randomly or evenly distributed throughout higher education. They tend to be clustered in "prestige" universities where (it is claimed by some researchers) student bodies are diverse and faculties are disproportionately liberal. But we can also be reasonably certain that self-selection accounts for some of this clustering of radicals.

Recent survey data demonstrate that college students are seldom found to be radical today. They are increasingly conservative and materialistic. In 1967, 43.5 percent of the national freshman class said that "being well-off financially" is a very important personal goal. In 1982, this figure had risen to 65.2 percent. In 1971, less than half of the freshman class—49.9 percent—said that "to be able to make more money" was a very important reason for attending college. In 1982, this number had moved up to 67 percent. At the same time, these polls have measured declines in student interest in helping with the environment, in altruistic goals of helping others, or in helping "to promote racial understanding." Survey data of recent years also clearly indicate a growing conservatism of faculty, so that any impact they may have on values of students would not necessarily be liberal or radical at all.

—Sources: Poll reported in Fort Wayne, Indiana, *Journal-Gazette,* February 7, 1982; Theodore M. Newcomb, "Attitude Development as a Function of Reference Groups: The Bennington Study," in *Readings in Social Psychology*, Eleanor S. Maccoby et al., eds. (New York: Holt, Rinehart and Winston, 1958); Robert S. Erikson et al., *American Public Opinion: Its Origins, Content, and Impact* (New York: Wiley, 1980), p. 131.

BOX 13–4
On Politics and the
Media

Television *is* the political process; it's the playing field of politics. Today, the action is in the studios, not in the back rooms.

—Theodore H. White (Quoted in *Washington Journalism Review*, 2: 25, September 1980).

Every reporter knows that when you write the first word, you make an editorial judgment.

—Robert E. Kitner, former president of NBC, quoted in Robert Cirino, *Don't Blame the People: How the News Media Use Bias, Distortion and Censorship to Manipulate Public Opinion* (New York: Vintage, 1971), p. 198.

A newspaper or magazine reader can be his or her own editor in a vital sense. He can glance over it and decide what to read, what to pass by. The TV viewer is a restless prisoner, obliged to sit through what does not interest him to get to what may interest him.

—Eric Sevareid of CBS News, quoted in *Watching American Politics*, Dan Nimmo and William L. Rivers, eds. (New York: Longman, 1981), pp. 261–262.

Television.   It is difficult to overestimate the importance of television, the medium that is widely thought to have revolutionized political campaigns as well as many other political practices in our time. A 1977 Roper Poll shows that 64 percent of the public regards television as their major news source. Television is truly a mass medium whose influence cannot be doubted. It brings political figures and events right into the home. It has helped shape many political careers and the outcomes of many electoral contests. For Richard Nixon, television proved to be the means of his political salvation when he made his famous "Checkers speech" in 1952, forcing Dwight Eisenhower to keep him on the vice-presidential ticket despite questionable financial arrangements he had made as U.S. Senator from California. It was also television in 1973 and 1974 that helped bring Nixon's career to its inglorious end when it focused its relentless eye day after day on the unfolding Watergate scandal.

The unquestionable influence of television makes it all the more important for us to understand how it achieves its effects. Television is a slave of time; no news story, debate, campaign platform, or policy issue can be examined more than superficially. Television focuses on the glamour of personality. It is an action medium that cannot accommodate the subtleties or vagaries of political dialogue. The essential appeal of political advertisements is visceral rather than cerebral. Showmanship intrudes upon television journalism in a variety of ways that can lead to distortion—the choice of anchor men or women made on criteria other than journalistic capabilities or the choice of an "action story" of comparatively little consequence over a less graphic but more important item of reportage. Above all, television tries to provide excitement. Reporters seek to ask provocative questions. Campaign coverage pays most of its attention to the horse race aspects of an election contest—who is going to win, what the polls show, what so-and-so is predicting, whether a mistake was made by concentrating on the farm vote.

But what does television specifically contribute to the process of political socialization? In our myth-ideology perspective, let us list some of television's contributions. First, television has a severely limited capacity to portray the ideological side of American politics. It does not have the time or interest in digging into the tough questions of who gets what from whom over the long haul. Protracted negotiations of the sort that typically take place in Congress's routines—especially with its piecemeal, complex, and somewhat unspectacular conclusions—receive quick summaries at best.

Second, with extraordinary skill and effectiveness, TV contributes marvelously to the notion that the "real" world of American politics is its mythic side. It is nearly impossible to avoid the sustained hyperbole, after watching television coverage of any political event of consequence; even when reports involve insignificant or inconsequential events, the impression of importance is often created. Watergate may be the classic example of this. Caught up in the center of the drama provided by television, citizens could hardly fail to believe that Nixon's resignation signaled a new dawn in American politics and government. At the same time, it became difficult to remember during the excitement of Watergate that all the other problems of American politics were continuing, including the war in Vietnam. More routinely, TV coverage, more than that of any other medium, sustains the myth that elections, especially presidential elections, are grand party contests in which significant choices about policies and candidates are made. After watching this kind of elevation of the political process to new heights of significance, many observers including professional political scientists and journalists come to attribute a seriousness to mythic matters that no ideological analysis of how the operative choices of American government are made could possibly sustain.

This suggests that television for all its limitations will continue to play a prominent role in American political life. But future developments in TV's political role seem destined to be confined to technological improvements. For sustaining the myth of American political life, television has become indispensable. Yet it has not revolutionized

Earth Day, 1979

American politics; rather, it has raised to new levels of exaggeration tendencies as old as the political system itself.

Newspapers. Newspapers usually provide more in-depth coverage of politics and government than TV does, and they therefore remain important as socializing agents. Survey data from several studies indicate that regular newspaper readers are better informed than other citizens, and marketing data show advertisers that newspaper readers are the more affluent customers. Some of the national "prestige" newspapers, such as *The New York Times, Wall Street Journal, Washington Post,* and *Christian Science Monitor,* are regarded as influential opinion makers. This is also true of some of the regional dailies such as the *Boston Globe, Atlanta Constitution,* and *Los Angeles Times.* Most people do not read the "prestige" press but rely on one or more of the 2,000 other daily papers published in the nation.

   Diverse as these local newspapers are, however, most of them subscribe to the same wire services so that they provide the same "canned" reports to their readers. Even those papers with their own Washington bureaus are subject to the pack influence generated by the 1,000 plus members of the capital city press corps. And through mergers and acquisitions, newspaper ownership is now developing into large chains

**BOX 13–5
The Biggest
Newspaper Chains**

This list of twenty-three large newspaper publishers must be considered in the light of two facts: (1) most of them also own a number of television and radio stations, and (2) their boards of directors are acquainted with one another through direct and indirect corporate interlocks.

Press Group	Newspapers
Affiliated	Boston Globe, North Adams (Mass.) Transcript
Capital Cities Communications	Kansas City Star/Times, Fort Worth Star-Telegram, Wilkes-Barre Times-Leader
Central Newspapers	Indianapolis Star/News, Arizona Republic/Phoenix Gazette, Muncie Press/Star
Copley	San Diego Union/Tribune, Springfield State Journal-Register, Aurora (Ill.) Beacon News
Cox	Atlanta Constitution/Journal, Dayton Daily News/Journal Herald, Austin American-Statesman
Dow Jones	Wall Street Journal, Middletown (N.Y.) Times Herald-Record
Evening News	Detroit News, Palm Springs Desert Sun, Vineland (N.J.) Times Journal
Field	Chicago Sun-Times
Freedom	Santa Ana Register, Colorado Springs Gazette Telegraph, Fort Pierce (Fla.) News Tribune
Gannett	Cincinnati Enquirer, Oakland Tribune, Rochester Democrat and Chronicle/Times-Union, and others
Harte Hanks	Corpus Christi Caller/Times, Anderson (S.C.) Independent/Mail, South Middlesex (Mass.) News
Hearst	San Francisco Examiner, Los Angeles Herald-Examiner, Baltimore News-American
Independent Publications	Philadelphia Bulletin, Santa Barbara News-Press
Lee	Wisconsin State Journal, Quad City Times, Billings Gazette
Media General	Richmond Times-Dispatch/News-Leader, Tampa Tribune/Times, Winston-Salem Journal/Sentinel
Minneapolis Star/Tribune	Minneapolis Star/Tribune, Buffalo Courier-Express, Rapid City Journal

**BOX 13–5
The Biggest
Newspaper Chains
(Continued)**

Press Group	Newspapers
New York Times	New York Times, Lakeland (Fla.) Ledger, Gainesville (Fla.) Sun
Newhouse	Cleveland Plain Dealer, Newark Star-Ledger, New Orleans Times-Picayune/States-Item
News America	New York Post, San Antonio Express/News
E. W. Scripps	Pittsburgh Press, Memphis Commercial Appeal
Thomson	San Gabriel (Calif.) Valley Tribune, Canton Repository, Lafayette (La.) Advertiser
Times-Mirror	Los Angeles Times, Newsday (Long Island), Dallas Times Herald
Washington Post	Washington Post, Trenton Times, Everett (Wash.) Herald

that in most cases are unlikely to allow much local editorial latitude or innovation (see Box 13–5). In addition, most cities and towns have now become one-newspaper centers because of the daunting economics of the business. This puts a special responsibility on owners and editors to provide diversity of viewpoints, a responsibility they sometimes shirk.

Magazines.   Magazines also affect our political views and values. This point may be difficult to accept when the names of some of the largest circulation magazines are listed—*Reader's Digest, TV Guide, Cosmopolitan*—because they often have little or no political content. There is no question, on the other hand, that news magazines such as *Time, Newsweek,* and *U.S. News and World Report* have some effects on the country's political views. In their own way, the financial periodicals—*Business Week, Forbes,* and *Barron's* are examples—are also influential. Many political analysts feel that a number of relatively small circulation journals have an impact well beyond their readership. The *New York Review of Books, The Nation, New Republic,* and *Progressive* appeal to small bands of well-informed readers who like a liberal-to-left political orientation. *National Review* and *Conservative Digest* are considered thoughtfully rightist. *Public Interest* and *Commentary* are often regarded as fitting into a neoconservative cast of opinion. What makes such small journals as these influential is more a matter of *who* reads them—bureaucrats, academics, intellectuals, professionals, politicians—than how many readers they have.

A final category of socialization by the media is the variety of public relations programs of corporations, labor unions, and other interest groups. Companies like Mobil and General Electric spend great amounts of money to promote their political stance. Many people are familiar with the union label song of the International Ladies Garment Workers Union. The American Federation of Teachers pays for a weekly column by its president, Albert Shanker, that appears in *The New York Times*. Any of these efforts may pay off in influencing some segment of public opinion.

Cultural Rituals

Our mythic instruction continues throughout our adult lives by our participation, directly or vicariously, in various cultural rituals. The patriotic novels of John Jakes, for example, were very popular during and after the celebration of the nation's Bicentennial. Movies, television programs, holidays, and civic events all contribute to the socialization process. In many ways, voting too can be seen as participation in a ritual of socialization.

Other rituals may seem less obvious but are effective socializing agents all the same. There is that day in January, for example, when a huge percentage of the population sits in front of the television set to watch Super Bowl Sunday. This is not just a football contest between professional teams but a spectacle combining our national participation with the frenzied crowd, prancing cheerleaders, clergymen pronouncing an invocation, a folk celebrity who sings the national anthem, and perhaps a military aircraft fly-pass. All this activity is interspersed with camera shots of hefty bodies crushing flesh to flesh, shots of young women in the crowd, and swift running figures chasing each other across the fields of glory. It is possible to become so fascinated with the mythic accoutrements and their symbolic meanings in these scenes that one can forget a game is being played, so skillful is the blend of religion, sex, patriotism, and sadism, not to mention advertising. However we view them, the cultural and political effects of such events cannot be denied; they perceptibly deepen our experience as a people.

Varieties of Unbelief

The political socialization process does not always work, principally because in America it is too exclusively concerned with myth and the assumptions of Social Democracy. The ordinary citizen is therefore perpetually liable to discover the operative presence of Liberal Democracy in the political system and the consequent disillusion such a discovery causes.

Liberal Democracy's presence is easily detected in spite of the mask of Social Democratic interpretations and activities. Newspapers are usually full of items that are simply not consonant with myth. Perhaps there is a scandal or news of some special interest group receiving more than its fair share of our national largesse and achieving this in some legal but underhanded way; or there may be an article on some politician who has not kept his or her word. The "inside dopester" type of political column receives a ready audience. But the most persuasive teacher of the facts of Liberal Democracy in America is Liberal Democracy itself. Anyone who has to deal with government at the practical, day-to-day level is bound to discern the reality of its norms and processes. Anyone who has been through one of the "sausage factory" courts is not likely to forget the experience; and the same goes for anyone who has actively pressed for legislation through Congress or a state legislature. And at one time or another, most of us have had to deal with the bureaucracy. All these learning experiences tend to undo the civic education we acquired in school.

Unlearning the myth while simultaneously learning gradually about Liberal Democracy can be unsettling. Myth and ideology blend poorly. Yet people's reactions to this unsettling feeling are varied. Many people bury it, pretend that it does not matter, or insist they can live with it because they cannot do anything about it. Others deny they are disturbed because, they insist, there is nothing about the American political system that disturbs them. This latter group is usually well along the way toward becoming superpatriotic and chauvinistic. The first of these groups is the larger and may be a majority of Americans. Beyond this likely majority that accepts the contradictions of the system and the superpatriots is a third group, the citizens who are so unsettled by the system that they are politically disaffected. This group is not large and its actual size is difficult to estimate with precision. Whatever its size, it is neither large enough nor organized enough to be of much positive political significance. As individuals or small groups, these people may occasionally cause enough trouble to break into the headlines,

---

Question: Are you satisfied with the way things are going in the U.S. at this time?

        33% Yes   61% No

Are you satisfied with the way things are going in your personal life?

        81% Yes   16% No

—*Gallup Opinion Index* 189 (June 1981).

**BOX 13–6
Polls Show
Personal
Satisfaction, But
Unease About the
Country**

but their chance of forcing substantial changes in the system or decisively affecting the thinking of the rest of the population is almost nil.

Nevertheless this group of the disaffected is of extraordinary interest to observers of what is called "political pathology."[7] In the variety of its disaffection, this group reveals with great clarity the ways in which myth and ideology, as transmitted by all the agents of political socialization, reach into the minds of citizens, including the rebellious, resistant, and disaffected.

The ranks of the disaffected can be classified into the following categories.

The Apathetic

"Apathetic" calls to mind the lazy, the lethargic, and the ignorant; but apathetic people are really very much like the ordinary majority of citizens; from a political standpoint they are simply more depressed. They may be quite energetically involved in nonpolitical matters. But the contradictions they see and experience in the political system are so severe that they feel demoralized. Apathetics do not actively reject the system, but they are not able to speak or act out of any positive political attachments. Disregarding the blandishments of myth, they tend to ignore political news, rarely take sides on policy issues, and seldom vote.

Having rejected politics, the apathetics tend to turn to private solutions for their problems. Distress about crime in the streets, bad schools, or corrupt politicians may lead them to move to the suburbs. If they are unemployed and feel they have no chance to get a job, they may become drifters. An intensely personal religion or drug use may be their way of dealing with feelings of aimlessness and depression. All these twists and turns require action and may even demand a sustained form of hard work. In extreme cases, a life of crime may be necessary. From a political standpoint, these reactions all rest upon a disbelief in the effectiveness of politics in America.[8]

The Cynical

Cynicism is an extreme of disaffection with politics that lies beyond apathy. Cynicism, especially about our mythic values, is endemic in certain circles in America. Much as myth is decried in these circles, however, the principles of our national ideology are embraced with a vengeance. The public be damned and every man for himself are common attitudes, along with "to the victor goes the spoils" and "the devil will take the hindmost." Such views are nothing more than an extreme statement of the Bourgeois individualism that lies at the core of our Liberal Democratic politics.

[7] Harold Lasswell first forged theory in the field of political pathology; see for example Harold D. Lasswell, "The Politics of Prevention," in *A Source Book for the Study of Personality and Politics*, Fred I. Greenstein and Michael Lerner, eds. (Chicago: Markham, 1971), p. 540.

[8] See Philip Slater, *The Pursuit of Loneliness* (Boston: Beacon Press, 1976).

The cynic is thus revealed as both a disbeliever and a believer. While dismissing the mythic side of our politics as pitiful and silly, the stuff by which the gullible masses are kept in place, the cynic clings to the principles of personal endeavor and success. The operational half of American politics was made for the cynic, who will therefore exploit it whenever possible. American business is often pointed to as motivated by cynicism; it will argue that laborers in agribusiness, the corporate farms of this country, should not be protected or regulated by federal labor law but then changes its mind when these same laborers use the absence of federal regulation to mount effective product boycotts. Or it will argue for states' rights and local prerogatives until it decides it would be good to have a federal law denying federal housing moneys to cities that enact rent control programs. But business is not alone in practicing cynicism. Cynicism can also be seen in the childless couple that votes against school levy increases because they are not directly concerned about education, even though they might benefit indirectly from living in a better educated society. Piously intoning every tenet of our national myth, cynics turn the political system to their personal advantage with much success.

The Alienated

The spectacle of the cynics' ill-gotten gains is enough to make many people turn away from politics altogether and join the ranks of the apathetic. But the same spectacle also enrages some citizens, driving them toward a more direct form of disaffection from politics, namely, alienation. The estrangement of the alienated moves them away from the ideological side of political activity. It is noteworthy, however, that although they reject the ideological side of politics, they still embrace the values and ideals of the mythic side. In a sense, the alienated of American politics are the reverse of the cynics. Like the cynics, they are half disbelievers and half believers. Because they abandon ideology altogether, they can condemn and make demands with great consistency solely in terms of myth. They will stridently insist that only the dictates of myth be followed. Anything short of this they consider morally indefensible. At the same time, of course, it is virtually impossible within the confines of the American system to use myth consistently for operational purposes for any long-term policies or programs. America's practical political wisdom will intervene, bringing on negotiation and compromise. But the alienated will continue to insist passionately on the higher values of myth. The consequence is that for all their fervor, the alienated live in a state of sustained frustration.

The Anomic

The anomic are beyond apathy, cynicism, and alienation. They may never have made it to these earlier stages in the first place. The typical anomic individual was never socialized into citizenship. The schooling in politics just did not take. As a result, the anomic do not abide by the norms of politics because they hardly know what the norms are; at least, they have never internalized them into their social personality. As such, the politically anomic individual is a "lost" person for whom politics has no meaning.

The politically anomic—the word is derived from "anonymous," meaning nameless or unknown—are scattered throughout America though their absolute number is small. They are often the products of urban ghettos, barrios, or areas of abysmal rural poverty. They are unemployed and "unemployable." They may have a propensity to commit mindless crimes. There is a tendency to think of the anomic as predominantly young males, but many anomics—the poverty-stricken aged, derelicts, "bag" ladies—are elderly or prematurely "old." The existence of anomics in a society as rich and supposedly humane as America is a shocking comment about the fringes of our political life.[9]

Two final observations must be made about the disaffected in America. The first is that we have just described these people in terms of categories. Actual people cannot be grouped so neatly, and most of America's disaffected are only predominantly in one or another of the boxes we have set out. Individually, they may have characteristics of several of the categories.

Second, the disaffected darkly underline the seriousness of the problem of legitimacy for the political system. They may not pose an immediate threat to the system, but they do challenge its ability to solve its problems. For better or worse, the anomics, simply by existing, demand that the system show them it merits their trust. Their presence within the system is bound to make the supporters of the system uncomfortable. In bad times, the disaffected should be a source of considerable concern to those in authority.

Public Opinion

The political socialization process, as we have seen, is a set of ways by which the citizen is inculcated with basic political values and attitudes. The content of this process involves long-enduring attachments. Furthermore, it is concerned mostly with the principles of myth and is generally pervasive and standardized throughout the population, apart from the relatively small groups of the disaffected.

Now we turn to the phenomenon of public opinion, which we define as follows. First, it is a set of generalized sentiments and understandings about mostly current policies and personalities. Unlike the basic values associated with socialization, public opinion can be highly vola-

---

[9] To note that anomic people exist in society is not the same as building an entire theory of political life on this fact; for an attempt to do this, see Edward C. Banfield, *The Unheavenly City Revisited* (Boston: Little, Brown, 1974).

tile and sharply divided. In a polity as uniformly committed to an underlying national myth as America, it is safe to assume that virtually all public opinion about political issues is heavily influenced by, if not positively grounded upon, our common allegiance to Social Democratic norms. But public opinion is also greatly affected by the particular character of specific policy proposals and the personalities associated with them. Accordingly, all sorts of differentiating factors can come into play. The wealthy react differently to a tax proposal than do the poor; Irish Catholics respond differently to abortion legislation than do blacks or Jews. And there may well be differences within these groups between the opinions of old and young or women and men. Finally, public opinion can be influenced by deliberate efforts to manipulate it.

Measuring Public Opinion: The Polls

Polls designed to measure public opinion are well established as important reference points in the political process. Their results are greeted with skepticism by some citizens and analysts because they are certainly not perfect as pulse-takers of the public, as borne out by their erroneous forecast of the 1948 presidential election between Truman and Dewey, to cite one famous example.

The fact remains that polling organizations are accurate most of the time, and their track records are good enough so that an industry has grown up around opinion sampling (see Box 13–7). Most polls are privately conducted for business and industry, trade associations, interest groups, and political organizations. No serious candidate in a major race for public office fails to budget for polling; this expense is second only to advertising in campaign management today.

A poll is defined as a representative sampling of a few people that, with considerable accuracy, can tell us how everyone represented thinks about a given subject. Some polls may measure attitudes toward a candidate, a public figure or a foreign country rather than opinions on substantive issues. On occasion people may say that they doubt poll results because they themselves have never been interviewed. This is because a poll can be taken with only a tiny sample of each group represented. Many national polls use a sample composed of only 1,500 respondents.

Most polls pick their respondents on the basis of where they live; in many or most polls, the sample is randomly selected to produce a low probability of error. A random sample is usually generated by using computer-selected random numbers. In this way every individual in the population has an equal, or nearly equal, chance of being sampled.

Opinion sampling gives up-to-the-minute information on the "horse race" aspects of politics and provides politicians with some inkling of where they stand with voters. But polls have also provided social scientists with important data bases for deriving conclusions about public opinion at a given time. Linking poll results together over a period of

BOX 13–7
A Survey of
Surveys

Nine polling organizations take national samples on a regular basis and publish the results: the Gallup Poll, the ABC News/Harris Survey, the CBS News/*New York Times* Poll, the AP/NBC News Poll, the *Los Angeles Times* Poll, The *Washington Post* Poll, the *Time Magazine* Poll (administered by Yankelovich, Skelly, and White), the *Newsweek* Poll, and the *Wall Street Journal* Poll (administered by Gallup). Other newspaper chains and magazines (Gannett, Knight-Ridder, *U.S. News and World Report*) carry out and publish national polls on an occasional basis.

A number of private polling firms release the results of national polls when this is requested or authorized by the sponsoring organization. Thus, Louis Harris and Associates released the results of a nationwide poll on attitudes toward blacks, Jews, Catholics, and other minority groups that was commissioned in 1978 by the National Conference of Christians and Jews.

In addition, academic organizations, such as the National Opinion Research Center of the University of Chicago and the Survey Research Center of the University of Michigan, take regular nationwide polls. . . . The data are primarily intended for use by scholars in their research. A large number of national polls are carried out by private research organizations. . . . Several polling firms, including Harris, Yankelovich, Dresner, Roper, the Opinion Research Corporation, and Cambridge Survey Research (Patrick Caddell), administer national polls on a regular basis, and make the results available . . . to subscribing clients.

Finally, CBS News has compiled a list of some 140 state and local polls carried out and made public by local media and research organizations. . . . The CBS News list is admittedly incomplete, since new polls are springing up all the time (and a few become defunct). . . .

Most polls are administered by telephone. . . . So-called "exit polls," however, have become much more prominent in the past 12 years. These are polls taken of voters as they leave their polling places on the day of the election. . . .

ABC, NBC, CBS News/*New York Times*, and the *Los Angeles Times*, which conduct these exit polls, argue that they are reliable because only actual voters are surveyed.

> But the selection of random polling places makes exit polls—like all others—more of an art than a science. After the New York primary [of 1980], for example, CBS reported that 22 percent of the Democratic voters were Jewish, the *Los Angeles Times* put the figure at 29 percent, and NBC said 38 percent.
> —*Washington Journalism Review*, 2:45 (September 1980).

**BOX 13–7
A Survey of
Surveys
(Continued)**

time can enable us to chart past (but not future) political trends and changes, broadening our views of political and social history. The polls themselves cannot do this, of course, but we can interpret them to enable us to perceive the trends.

This leads us to the important point that polls cannot always be accepted at face value. How can we evaluate the accuracy of polls? There are some obvious questions to ask about any poll: who conducted it? for what purpose? what kind of sample was used? what is the margin of error? Is the poll merely an attempt to manipulate public opinion for the purpose of some interest group? Many members of Congress conduct polls of their constituents by mail, and some of these polls are suspect while others are quite straightforward. But these polls depend on the intensity of interest of the respondent to fill it out and mail it in without being prompted to do so.

The intensity of support for or opposition to a candidate or an issue is difficult to measure in polls. Most polls are not taken in such an in-depth way; therefore, polling organizations may make the mistake of weighing each opinion equally when the political facts of life say otherwise. Some polls try to take account of this when measuring voting intentions by discerning, through a variety of tests, whether a respondent is likely to vote. Another shortcoming of many polls is that they assume those questioned view the subject of the poll as important when this may not be the case. The subject becomes important perhaps only because the polling organization thinks it is important. Another assumption of many polls is that there is a roughly equal level of knowledge of political information held by the various respondents, and we know this is not the case for a variety of reasons—among them, the differences in socialization patterns. In addition, data from a variety of polls demonstrate that the level of political information can range from only 23 percent who can name their state legislators to much higher

**Evaluating
Polls**

percentages when it comes to naming the president, the vice-president, or other officials (see Box 13–8). In other words, polls do not account for variation in levels of political information among respondents, and this can skew our perceptions of poll results. Still another question on polls relates to the types of questions asked. At the outset of this chapter we showed that a question put one way can yield one response while putting it another way can lead to a different response. The science of form-

BOX 13–8
Level of Political Information Known by the Adult Public

	Year	Polling Source
94% Know the capital city of the U.S.	1945	AIPO
94% Know the president's term is 4 years	1951	AIPO
93% Recognize photo of current president	1948	AIPO
89% Can name governor of their state	1973	Harris
79% Can name the current vice-president	1947	AIPO
78% Know what initials "FBI" stand for	1949	AIPO
74% Know meaning of the term "wiretapping"	1969	AIPO
70% Can name their mayor	1967	AIPO
69% Know which party has most members in U.S. House of Representatives	1978	NORC
68% Know president is limited to two terms	1970	CPS
63% Know China to be Communist	1972	CPS
63% Have some understanding of term "conservative"	1960	SRC
58% Know meaning of term "open housing"	1967	AIPO
52% Know that there are two U.S. senators from their state	1978	NORC
46% Can name their congressman	1973	Harris
39% Can name both U.S. senators from their state	1973	Harris
38% Know Russia is not a NATO member	1964	AIPO
34% Can name the current Secretary of State	1978	NORC
30% Know term of U.S. House member is two years	1978	NORC
31% Know meaning of "no fault" insurance	1977	AIPO
28% Can name their state senator	1967	AIPO
23% Know which two nations are involved in SALT	1979	CBS/NYT

—Polls compiled by Robert S. Erikson, Norman R. Luttbeg, and Kent L. Tedin, *American Public Opinion: Its Origins, Content and Impact*, 2nd ed. (New York: Wiley, 1980), p. 19.

ulating questions and establishing interviewer procedures is still developing, and the occasional debates on such matters that appear in public opinion journals are good evidence that there is no consensus on the subject.

Some observers claim that polls distort the political process. Public officials, it is often asserted, should not be so sensitive to poll results because those polled may have little knowledge of what they are talking about. Polls taken during campaigns can create a bandwagon effect for the front-runner or they can create sympathy for the underdog, especially if it appears that the underdog may be catching up with the front-runner. Polls can also create effects of manipulation, according to some critics, because candidates inevitably gear their appeals and tactics to what their polls tell them. One public opinion specialist has written an article on this phenomenon entitled "The Voters are Telling the Pollsters to Tell the Candidates to Tell the Voters."[10]

Distorting the Political Process

Elite rule theorists, who believe that the political system is managed by a small, unrepresentative elite regardless of elections, often show a disdain for public opinion studies because they believe there is no strong tie between opinion and policy. They can point to many examples to buttress their case: national health insurance has been favored by a majority in nearly all polls since 1949, so why do we not have such a system? The Vietnam War was prosecuted by the government long after a plurality of citizens demonstrated their disapproval of the war and urged unilateral withdrawal. On the other hand, some correlations can be shown from one congressional district to another between public opinion preferences and the actions of a legislator representing the people who hold them. Whether public opinion is actually translated into public policy is a matter for debate. It must be conceded, however, that public opinion is at least an occasionally important variable in the political process and polls do seem to help us understand the American body politic a little better than we would otherwise.

Public Opinion and Public Policy

Public opinion polling is the most common means of measuring political attitudes. This is one of the reasons why readers find a great many polling results mentioned in the pages of this book. But political behavior can also be demonstrated in individual and collective conduct. The stock market, for example, can serve as a gauge of certain collective attitudes, as can bond prices, levels of savings, voting behavior, religious membership and attendance, gun ownership, abortions, membership in interest groups and voluntary associations, conformity to tax

Other Objective Indicators of Political Attitudes

[10] Adam Clymer, "The Voters are Telling the Pollsters to Tell the Candidates to Tell the Voters," in *Watching American Politics*, Dan Nimmo and William L. Rivers, eds. (New York: Longman, 1981), pp. 278–282.

laws, participation in the "underground economy," drug use, suicides, strikes, crime statistics (though many of these are unreliable), and housing patterns. The measure of such conduct is sometimes more valuable than the results of public opinion polling because people sometimes say one thing and do another.

FOR FURTHER READING

CIRINO, ROBERT. *Don't Blame the People: How the News Media Use Bias, Distortion and Censorship to Manipulate Public Opinion.* New York: Vintage, 1971. Interesting muckraking approach.

ERIKSON, ROBERT S., NORMAN R. LUTTBEG, and KENT L. TEDIN. *American Public Opinion: Its Origins, Content and Impact,* 2nd ed. New York: Wiley, 1980. Quite thorough coverage of the nuts and bolts of this subject.

GREENSTEIN, FRED I. *Children and Politics,* rev. ed. New Haven: Yale University Press, 1969. Landmark study of the political learning process.

HENNESSY, BERNARD. *Public Opinion,* 3rd ed. Belmont, Calif.: Brooks Cole, 1981. Especially useful in its description of polling techniques.

KRIEGHBAUM, HILLIER. *Pressures on the Press.* New York: CROWELL, 1972. A review of a variety of press issues during the Nixon era; still timely.

LUTTBEG, NORMAN R., ed. *Public Opinion and Public Policy,* 3rd ed. Itasca, Ill.: F. E. Peacock, 1981. A useful reader that presents a variety of issues and viewpoints.

PATTERSON, THOMAS E. *The Mass Media Election: How Americans Choose Their President.* New York: Praeger, 1980. Argues that presidential campaigns are now essentially mass media campaigns.

WRAY, J. HARRY, and ROBERT HOLSWORTH. *American Politics and Everyday Life.* New York: Wiley, 1982. An unusual, thought-provoking, and original look at the interaction of government and political attitudes.

Political Participation, Parties, and Elections

During the 1980 presidential campaign, candidates Ronald Reagan and Jimmy Carter were engaged in a television debate. Carter made a point, citing facts and figures. In an almost casual aside, Reagan put him down by inserting, "There you go again. . . ." It was a small thrust, but it had a devastating effect because Carter had been struggling to overcome a reputation for hiding an essential indecisiveness behind flurries of precise statements.

In a debate between Carter and Gerald Ford during the 1976 campaign, Ford insisted, to the shock and amazement of the press and the public, that Poland was not a Communist-dominated country. It was probably only a momentary mental lapse, but making it on TV hurt Ford a great deal because he already had a reputation for being slow and clumsy.

Early in the 1968 presidential campaign, George Romney, then governor of Michigan, was regarded as a significant challenger for the Republican nomination. But during the primary season, he told the press that while visiting Vietnam he had been "brainwashed" by the American military authorities so that he had developed a mistaken impression of the war there. This too candid admission finished him; the press and the public concluded anyone so easily "brainwashed" did not have what it takes to be president.

In 1960, the first debate between John F. Kennedy and Richard M. Nixon was widely assumed to have been "won" by Kennedy not because he was wiser or had a better command of the facts but because Nixon's heavy beard looked darker than usual on the TV screen, making him seem seedy and untrustworthy.

In 1944, Franklin D. Roosevelt devastated the Republicans when he effectively accused them of making an issue even of his little dog, Fala. "They can pick on my wife," said FDR in a national radio address, "they can pick on my children; but when they pick on my dog. . . ." This

BOX 14–1
An Interview with
a Campaign
Consultant

[David Garth of] Garth Associates has a staff of 22 ("We keep 90 per cent of them year-around," he maintains) and does public relations and advertising for nonpolitical as well as political clients. The New York Jets and Joffrey Ballet are on the account list, as well as the winning presidential candidate in Venezuela's December elections. But home-grown politicians are the firm's meal tickets. Garth's monthly fees run from $25,000 ("when we do everything") down to $10,000, plus commissions on advertising the firm places. . . .

Garth: You know, there's a cliche that somehow less information is given out about candidates now that there is television. But go back in history and look at how much information was passed on to the public before they had media. How many people in the United States heard the Lincoln-Douglas debates? One percent is the highest estimate.

Questioner: Doesn't that cliche refer to "packaging the candidate" for television, and using short 30- and 60-second commercials?

Garth: Well, we did 40 television spots with [New York Governor] Hugh Carey. If you took a tape and hung those 40 spots together, it would be a 36-minute presentation of Carey's accomplishments. All together, you get a total picture—far more than people ever knew about Roosevelt when he ran for governor, far more than they ever knew about Herbert Lehman. And the proof is that you find more cross-voting in this country today than you had 15 or 20 years ago. . . .

Questioner: . . . you told Carey to lose weight.

Garth: Losing weight is something . . . I am very big on. I don't care about the cosmetics as much as . . . the fact that campaigns have a physical side to them that is quite grueling. You look at the kind of campaign [New York City Mayor Edward] Koch had with 30, 40, 50 debates. Carey had 16 debates in three weeks. I believe you've got to be in condition to do it . . . getting in shape is an important thing. The cosmetic value, I couldn't care less about. . . . There is a part of this business that people don't under-

**BOX 14–1
An Interview with
a Campaign
Consultant
(Continued)**

stand, and that's the physical and mental effort. What happens at two o'clock in the morning when the guy gets tired? He makes a remark on the plane that takes the campaign into the crapper.

—"E.P.O. Interviews David Garth," *E.P.O.*, January-February 1979, pp. 52–57.

remark, skillfully delivered, brought gales of laughter from politicians and citizens alike across the country and succeeded in making the Republicans appear petty and pointless.

Thrusts and slips of this sort are what keep campaign managers awake at night. Their candidates may make an inadvertent remark that will by itself wreck months of planning and campaign effort, or, alternatively, demolish the opposition. But these terrible gaffes or master strokes also point to the degree to which campaigns and elections, in the era of electronic journalism, have become theatrical spectacles played out before audiences who expect to be entertained by charming personalities and dramatic events more than they hope to be informed by competing candidates and platforms (see Box 14–1).

This chapter focuses on that audience called the electorate, how it is organized, how it is appealed to, how it is delivered to the polls on election day, and why. The chapter's central thesis is that political participation in America by the electorate—the People—has more to do with legitimation of government than with public policy choices. In social science terminology, voting in America is primarily an expressive activity, giving people a chance to express their feelings about the government. It is only secondarily an instrumental activity, one that might allow people to influence directly the course of governmental decision making.

This is not to say that voting is meaningless or unimportant. Legitimation and relegitimation of the regime is of cardinal importance, and nowhere more so, because of the strains between myth and ideology, than in America. As we shall see, it is also time-consuming, complicated, expensive, and not wholly successful. Or in the language of this book, ideologically, the People, their parties and elections, do not play a central role in the political system. In myth, their role is of decisive importance, but it is rarely played with total success.

Civic Participation

Citizen involvement in politics and government can take any number of forms. It can range from purely personal efforts to obtain policy or administrative changes in the government (often called "citizen contact") to more or less organized participation in pressure and interest groups to full-scale membership in political parties and all their activities leading to election campaigns and voting.

A Profile of Political Participants

Studies of civic participation demonstrate that it correlates with certain sociological and demographic factors such as age, sex, race, religion, and socioeconomic status. The elderly tend to withdraw from participation, including voting, at a certain point. Historically, women have participated in the political process less than men have, although this may now be changing. Some of the polls on President Reagan's performance, for example, show a marked disillusionment with him on the part of women. Blacks and other minorities tend to participate less than most citizens do; however, blacks actually participate more relative to others of comparable income levels. Religious affiliation also is an important participation variable. Proportionally, Catholics and Jews tend to participate in the political process more than Protestants. Finally, those who are closer to the "center" of society in terms of income and status are more likely to participate in politics than those at the "periphery"—the destitute, the infirm, the poor, and the transient. Some variables, all the same, do not correlate with levels of participation. Urbanization, for example, has not been shown to be a factor promoting greater participation (see Box 14–4).[1]

Recent studies tend to confirm the popular impression that the less well-off participate less in the political process than others do. The participation of the poor in community organizations, for example, has declined notably since the heady days of the 1960s and 1970s, when such participation was not only encouraged but often required for local agencies and organizations to obtain federal grants of support.[2]

The legitimating nature of participation is important for filling out the profile of the participant citizen. By participating, citizens show themselves to be believers in the system, and the more they participate and the wider the range of their activities, the firmer they show their faith in the system to be. There may well be an element of cooptation at work here, too. The more citizens participate, the stronger their commitments to the system will become.

[1] Lester Milbrath and M. L. Goel, *Political Participation*, 2nd ed. (Chicago: Rand McNally, 1977), pp. 113–114, 128–130.

[2] Marilyn Gittell et al., *Limits to Citizen Participation: The Decline of Community Organizations* (Beverly Hills: Sage Publications, 1980).

The aim of all organizations that seek citizen involvement is to persuade citizens to translate their attitudes and opinions into action. This effort is generally supported by civic education in the schools and preachments by the mass media and civic leaders and is directly organized by all sorts of civic organizations. Many of these are exclusively political organizations; many, many more are businesses or other organizations intervening in politics only because of some special need.

Perhaps the simplest action citizens can be called upon to perform is signing their name to petitions. The sight of earnest men and women with clipboards gathering signatures or standing at makeshift quarters set up in shopping malls or on street corners has become increasingly common in recent decades. The petitions they ask citizens to sign may be simple statements asking particular public officials to take a stand

on such issues as abortion rights, nuclear disarmament, school bond proposals, or the building of an arterial highway through a residential area. Often the petitions are more formal. Initiative, referendum, and recall election measures often require the collection of signatures as one of their first steps. In many states, a certain number of signatures must be collected before minor parties can place the names of their nominees for public office on the ballot.

Closely allied to petition signing is letter writing. Citizens often write letters on political matters to the editors of their local newspapers, and political professionals, knowing that the editorial page is closely read, encourage this kind of activity. They also encourage systematic writing of letters to members of Congress, state legislators, city councilmembers, and to the president, governors, and mayors. Sample letters are often prepared and distributed or printed in the press. Individually composed letters from prominent citizens can be collected and published as brochures. And various interested organizations can be urged to direct

BOX 14–2
The Dimensions and Modes of Political Activity

Mode of Activity	Type of Influence	Scope of Outcome	Presence of Conflict	Initiative Required
Campaign activity	High pressure, low to high information	Collective	Conflictual	Some
Cooperative activity	Low to high pressure, high information	Collective	Maybe yes, usually no	Some or a lot
Voting	High pressure, low information	Collective	Conflictual	Little
Contacting officials on social issues	Low pressure, high information	Collective	Usually nonconflictual	A lot
Contacting officials on personal matters	Low pressure, high information	Particular	Nonconflictual	A lot

—Norman H. Nie and Sidney Verba, "Political Participation," in *Nongovernmental Politics*, Fred I. Greenstein and Nelson W. Polsby, eds. (Reading, Pa.: Addison-Wesley, 1975), p. 17.

their members to write letters, with clear instructions about what to say and to whom their letters should be addressed, for instance, to the chairmen of critically important committees or subcommittees.

Finally, individual citizens can be called on to turn out for rallies and demonstrations. Supporters can be urged to demonstrate at a construction site to preserve a landmark. Across the nation, citizens can be called by public-spirited groups to march along designated routes to show support for civil rights measures, world peace, and the like. During the Vietnam War, the antiwar movement organized some of the largest demonstrations the nation has ever seen. In New York City, as many as 250,000 people marched in a single parade, chanting slogans like "Stop the Bombing" and "Bring the Troops Home." And in 1982, more than 500,000 marched through New York City again to protest the nuclear arms race. As interesting are the much smaller but highly organized demonstrations that rally the faithful to swarm through government buildings to lobby intensively in the offices of legislators and other public officials.

Demonstrations can be massive; Congress members can be inundated with petitions and other mail; protesters practicing civil disobedience can be arrested by the hundreds; the White House switchboard can be swamped with calls. What is achieved?

In the short term, on a sharply focused issue, organized pressure of this sort can be effective. If enough citizens put themselves between a cherished landmark and the bulldozers, the landmark can be saved. If enough parents make life unpleasant for school board members at a public hearing, buses can be taken off the streets until repaired. Congress members can be induced to put back money into an appropriation measure for student loans if their mail starts running heavily against cutting it out.

Much more questionable is the effectiveness of this kind of activity on broad, longer-term issues. Mobilizing public sentiment to block an action in Congress takes time and resources of a sort not easily repeated. But we have seen that, at the ideological level, public policy in America is made incrementally, on scattered fronts. A huge public effort to halt legislative or administrative decisions and/or to promote others may deflect or give a desired forward push to a general policy process for a time but is unlikely to have a long-term effect on entrenched ideological factors. The hue and cry against nuclear power development has been intense, and remarkably sustained. But what has stalled the nuclear power program has been economic considerations. The outcry against the Vietnam War was broadly supported but the war dragged on for years until the costs in the field outweighed military and foreign policy considerations for continuing it. In the American political system, mythic mobilizations have little chance for long-term success unless by accident or design they coincide with ideological supports.

Organizing Groups

Learning this kind of truth about American politics, citizens wishing to have real impact on the policy process are driven to organize themselves in systematic and controlled ways. Huge demonstrations are expressive politics; they make their participants feel that they have made a point and done something about an issue. Instrumental politics requires moving sharply away from such mythic displays to more ideologically oriented actions.

The first step is organization. A headquarters must be established, preferably in Washington if the issue is a national one, and staffed with paid professionals. Mailing lists must be drawn up and funds raised in programs sparked by celebrity donors and backed by direct mail campaigns to masses of small contributors. Lobbyists are employed to identify relevant public officials and determine what arguments can sway their decisions. Newsletters and pamphlets must be researched, written, published, and distributed.

As important as the organizational effort is the plan to translate the group's broad goals into negotiable proposals. This almost certainly requires paring them down to specifics about what can be done by whom in particular situations. A concern as broad as halting the superpower arms race must be condensed into a call for specific legislative bodies to pass resolutions in support of a "freeze" on nuclear arms development. Demands for "women's liberation" must be translated into demands for an equal rights amendment to the Constitution. Even an

**BOX 14–3
Participation in
Interest Groups**

As many as 20 million Americans belong to, or contribute to, special interest groups of various kinds. A recent poll shows that 23 per cent of a national sample gave money to a group, held membership in a group, or both.

The most frequently mentioned and/or supported organizations are as follows:

	Gave money	Member	Either/ both
Wildlife protection	10%	4%	11%
Conservation/environment	6	2	7
Vietnam veterans	4	2	·4
Anti-abortion	3	1	4
Anti-gun control	3	2	4
Blacks' rights	3	1	4

—*Gallup Opinion Index* 191 (April 1981).

issue as initially specific as antiabortion, when it runs into heavy opposition, must be translated into efforts to unseat specific members of Congress or to knock funds for abortions for poor women out of appropriations measures.

Recent years have seen an extraordinary increase in citizen-based organizations of this sort pursuing carefully selected steps toward broad political goals. Technically, they can be called "pressure groups," and the kind of politics they spawn is termed "single-issue politics." Their growth has been associated with the often noted decline in the cohesion of political parties. But citizen mobilization of this sort has been around as long as the republic itself and so has single-issue politics. The abolitionists and the organizations promoting prohibition are early examples.

The effectiveness of this sort of organization can be measured by an example. The National Association for the Advancement of Colored People (NAACP) is one of the oldest American pressure groups. Its objectives are clear and confined to meeting the needs of a single, easily defined group. Its administration is professional. Its citizen base is broad and its financing, although often pressed, is sound. Finally, its tactics since its founding have been practical and realistic. Knowing that its chances for victories in statehouses and Congress were slim, the NAACP concentrated with considerable success on step-by-step challenges advanced principally through the courts. *Brown* v. *Board of Education* of 1954 was its most signal achievement.

This record brought down a torrent of criticism on the NAACP in the "revolutionary" 1960s. Younger members of the black community and liberals argued that the NAACP was too traditionalist to understand the social and economic problems of American blacks. What was needed was a frontal attack on the forces of repression and segregation. To answer this need the civil rights movement developed as a broad coalition of activists who staged sit-ins, bus boycotts, and street marches. These activities were central factors in the passage of civil rights legislation by Congress at the time.

But what is the situation a decade or so later? The civil rights movement is virtually dead. Its demise can be dated not just to the assassination of its most prominent leader, Martin Luther King, Jr., but to King's deliberate decision to link the issue of civil rights for blacks to more general problems of discrimination and poverty and the then still raging war in Vietnam. This decision failed to broaden the movement's base of support; even more important, it threw out of focus its core demands. Meanwhile, the NAACP, which had mostly tagged along during the heyday of the civil rights movement, still enjoys its record of moderate, continuing success.

This example points to a painful paradox of a form by now familiar to readers of this book: the civil rights movement made a powerful appeal

**BOX 14–4
Social Groups and
the Presidential
Vote, 1980 and
1976**

	1980			1976	
	Carter	Reagan	Ander-son	Carter	Ford
Party*					
Democrats (43%)	66	26	6	77	22
Independents (23%)	30	54	12	43	54
Republicans (28%)	11	84	4	9	90
Ideology					
Liberal (18%)	57	27	11	70	26
Moderates (51%)	42	48	8	51	48
Conservatives (31%)	23	71	4	29	70
Race					
Blacks (10%)	82	14	3	82	16
Hispanics (2%)	54	36	7	75	24
Whites (88%)	36	55	8	47	52
Sex					
Female (48%)	45	46	7	50	48
Male (52%)	37	54	7	50	48
Religion					
Protestant (46%)	37	56	6	44	55
White Protestant (41%)	31	62	6	43	57
Catholic (25%)	40	51	7	54	44
Jewish (5%)	45	39	14	64	34
Family Income					
Less than $10,000 (13%)	50	41	6	58	40
$10,000–$14,999 (15%)	47	42	8	55	43
$15,000–$24,999 (29%)	38	53	7	48	50
$25,000–$50,000 (24%)	32	58	8	36	62
Over $50,000 (5%)	25	65	8	—	—
Occupation					
Professional or manager (39%)	33	56	9	41	57
Clerical, sales, white collar (11%)	42	48	8	46	53
Blue-collar (17%)	46	47	5	57	41
Agriculture (3%)	29	66	3	—	—
Unemployed (3%)	55	35	7	65	34
Education					
Less than high school (11%)	50	45	3	58	41

BOX 14–4
Social Groups and
the Presidential
Vote, 1980 and
1976
(Continued)

High school graduate (28%)	43	51	4	54	46
Some college (28%)	35	55	8	51	49
College graduate (27%)	35	51	11	45	55
Union Membership					
Labor union household (28%)	47	44	7	59	39
No member of household in union (62%)	35	55	8	43	55
Age					
18–21 years old (6%)	44	43	11	48	50
22–29 years old (17%)	43	43	11	51	46
30–44 years old (31%)	37	54	7	49	49
45–59 years old (23%)	39	55	6	47	52
60 years or older (18%)	40	54	4	47	52
Region					
East (25%)	42	47	9	51	47
South (27%)	44	51	3	54	45
White South (22%)	35	60	3	46	52
Midwest (27%)	40	51	7	48	50
Far West (19%)	35	53	9	46	51
Community Size					
Cities over 250,000 (18%)	54	35	8	60	40
Suburbs-small cities (53%)	37	53	8	53	47
Rural and towns (29%)	39	54	5	47	53

*The figures in parentheses are the percentages of the 1980 voters belonging to each group. The table entries are percentages, which total approximately 100 percent in each row for 1980 or 1976. Missing data account for those categories that do not total 100 percent.

Source: CBS News/*New York Times* interviews with 12,782 voters as they left the polls, as reported in the *New York Times*, 9 November 1980, p. 28, and in further analysis. The 1976 data are from CBS News interviews. For that year, the large-city vote is for communities over 500,000 population.

—From Gerald Pomper et al., *The Election of 1980: Reports and Interpretations* (Chatham, N.J.: Chatham House, 1981), pp. 71–72.

to America's mythic understanding about equality and social justice but its tactics could bring only short-term triumphs. The more ideologically conditioned NAACP has always been sound on tactics, but the criticisms of its general philosophy have considerable merit. In other words, in America what citizens gain on goals they lose on tactics, and vice versa.

Political Parties

The major difference between citizen pressure groups and political parties is that parties do not just aim to influence government decision making; through the electoral system, they try to determine the people who make the decisions. Parties aim to put people into office. Interest groups, by contrast, tend to accept the current officers of government and influence them.

The role of parties in the American political system is hotly debated, both in terms of what they ought to be doing and what they in fact do. This is not surprising even though parties have been part of the political system for almost two hundred years. The trouble is partly because the Founding Fathers made no provision for parties in the constitutional system they designed because they had a negative impression of parties from what they knew of them. Yet for most observers and students of politics today, political parties have become indispensable agents— some would say the most important agents—for the mobilization and expression of citizen participation in the American political system.

That parties were given no role by the Constitution but are still held to be indispensable to its operation is a characteristic paradox of American political life. Political parties are central features of the Social Democratic myth by which citizens legitimize the regime; they are almost nonexistent, however, at the ideological level at which governance takes place in Liberal Democracy. Once again, this is not to say that parties are meaningless or unimportant. On the contrary, parties are of vital significance, but only to the practices and hopes of American myth.

The Mythic Role of Political Parties

In myth, the first function of political parties is to organize, nationwide, citizens who agree, at least in a general way, on the kinds of policies and programs that the nation's governments—federal, state, and local— should implement. Just to state this function is to challenge its realism for the American environment. But the stereotyped characterizations of our major parties persist, even so, in the minds of citizens and politicians. Republicans are said to be the party of the wealthy, the white, the Protestant, Main Street if not Wall Street, the business community, and sometimes the military. The Democrats are the party of the poor, Catholics, Jews, minorities, workers, intellectuals, and the rural South. There are other stereotypes of the parties and some of these are verified by poll results (see Box 14–6).

We will not question these stereotypes for the moment. Instead, let us point out that in myth the assumption is that not only do the two parties divide America into two groups of citizens, each like-minded and accommodating to their various elements, but also that they oppose

[There is a] legitimacy of . . . self-government in a Republic constituted for liberty and self-government. Beneath the feet of every citizen lies the foundations of the Republic. Beneath the party oligarchy [of both parties] lies nothing but unexposed mendacity and successful fraud. It is this which accounts for the peculiar condition of American politics, at once so puzzling and so infuriating to foreign observers; the existence of a public life polluted with lies yet virtually untainted by public cynicism. The true voice of political corruption has not yet been heard in this Republic—the voice of the usurper who openly claims that his might is his right, that power belongs to whoever can grasp it. The party oligarchs make self-government a sham, but they dare not call self-government a sham. They wield great power but they claim no right to such power; they are forced to deny its very existence.

Hypocrisy, it is said, is the respect vice pays to virtue, and so it is with the incredible hypocrisy of public life in America. It is impossible for party politicians to be candid about anything, for what they would soon have to admit in candor is that they stand opposed to self-government and the constitution of liberty. That they dare not do. That corrupted the Republic is not. The authority of a free constitution lived under for nearly two centuries has a weight and force in public life which is beyond human ken to measure and beyond the oligarchs' power to defy. It is the force and weight of that authority—and Americans recognize no other authority—which stands behind the cause of liberty and of every citizen who elects to fight for it. The party oligarchs wield innumerable weapons but one mighty weapon is denied them in any struggle to oppose . . . liberty. They cannot tell American citizens that they are unfit for self-rule. By an apparent paradox it is the adherents of liberty in this Republic who are free to speak and who speak with authority. It is the ruling dynasty which is gagged. . . . They know that liberty and self-government form a standard to which Americans will repair. That is what the ruling dynasty knows and fears, and their fears, as always, are identical with our hopes.

—Walter Karp, *Indispensable Enemies: The Politics of Misrule in America* (Baltimore: Penguin, 1973), pp. 315–317.

each other. The parties, it is believed, positively organize themselves for political action in competition with each other.

The two major parties have elaborate constitutions and rules for their internal government. These dictate delegate selection procedures for national conventions, national committee membership, financial management of the national party, and a myriad of other concerns. Both parties constitutionally lodge their highest governing authority in their quadrennial national conventions held principally to nominate candidates for the presidency and vice-presidency. Both parties have their headquarters in Washington, D.C., and staffs to run them. Loosely organized into what must best be called a confederational arrangement, the parties tie their national headquarters into organizations in each of the states, and, beyond these, to city, county, and local organizations.

As significant as these apparent institutional patterns is the claim of each party to a past and a future. Both parties look back with pride to past successes and heroes—the Republicans to Lincoln and Eisenhower and the Democrats to Jefferson and Franklin Roosevelt. With an elaborate display of energy, both parties put together platforms at their national conventions that contain "planks" that spell out the policy and program choices for the future with considerable specificity. Once adopted, these are printed, distributed, and widely analyzed in the press. It is rather amazing in light of this that the national chairmen of the respective parties seem hard put to describe their characteristics and uniqueness (see Box 14–7).

Again we choose not yet to assess the reality of these features of American political parties. For now, we are content simply to point out that to all appearances, the two major parties put on a convincing display of being national, relatively permanent organizations with competing views on public policies.

The second major mythic function of political parties is to recruit candidates for public office, nominate them, and organize, finance, and support their campaigns. The most prominent features of this process are the presidential nominating conventions, the months of primary campaigns that precede them, and the grueling presidential campaign that follows them. In myth, the supposition is that something like comparable processes take place in support of party candidates for seats in Congress and in state and local elections. The assumption is that in this process of leadership recruitment for the total political system from the presidency on down, party organization, financing, and support—not just party endorsement—is an important factor. The mythic assumption is that when a Republican runs for office this is done with more than just the blessing of the GOP; the assumption is that the party selected the candidate, provides her or him with aides, campaign literature, television time, and election day organization. This mythic view holds that parties are indispensable to democracy because only the par-

BOX 14–6
Polls on the
Parties

Which political party do you think would be more likely to keep the United States out of World War III—the Republican Party or the Democratic Party?

Republican	26%
Democratic	59
No difference	22
No opinion	13

Looking ahead for the next few years, which political party—the Republican or the Democratic—do you think will do the better job of keeping the country prosperous?

Republican	41%
Democratic	28
No difference	18
No opinion	13

What do you think is the most important problem facing this country today?

High cost of living, inflation	73%
Unemployment, recession	8
Energy problems	5
Defense; war	3
Moral decline	2
Foreign relations	2
Crime	2
Dissatisfaction with government	2
Government spending	1

Which political party do you think can do a better job of handling the problem you have just mentioned—the Republican Party or the Democratic Party?

Republican	39%
Democratic	20
No difference	30
No opinion	11

(Taken in April 1981)

—*Gallup Opinion Index*, Report 187 (April 1981).

BOX 14–7
What Do the
Parties Stand for?
The National
Chairmen Speak

Questioner: What do the Republicans stand for besides cutting the budget and reducing taxes?

Richard Richards (Chairman, Republican National Committee): We stand for values that we feel are important: Working for what we get; making the family an important institution in our lives; getting government out of places where it has no business; creating economic opportunity for everyone.

We've now got a great opportunity to show that our programs work. If we fail, those people who joined us in 1980 will say, "It really doesn't make any difference who is in charge; everything is going to come out the same." We're confident we can show it does make a difference.

. . .

Questioner: Aren't Democrats confused about what they stand for?

Charles Manatt (Chairman, Democratic National Committee): There's more consensus today on what the Democratic Party needs to be about than a year or two ago. We're focusing on job creation, development of a fuller economy, and we're not giving up on the social-justice concerns we've always had.

On taxes, we see the need for business and individual cuts to encourage investment. But we're opposing Reagan's enormous transfer of wealth to higher-income groups.

—*U.S. News and World Report*, May 25, 1981, p. 44.

ties can make the commitments of time, energy, and money that candidates require to run in the electoral system.

Again we will not challenge this assumption for the moment. The third mythic function of parties is to hold elected candidates responsible for their conduct in office. The parties, it is said, keep tabs on their officeholders, provide guidance and discipline when needed, and joyously support those who have stayed true to the cause. Like the first two functions, this one is said to be indispensable if democratic government is to have meaning. Why should anyone vote for a candidate if the promises and platforms surrounding the election are just so many words?

Linking these three mythic functions of parties is an underlying presupposition that politics in America is about issues. Issues imply alternatives. Voters make choices between alternative policies by selecting one set of candidates over another. The candidates then implement the choices or take the consequences at the next election. This is the Social Democratic mythic understanding of what parties contribute to the political process. They "make democracy work."

The situation in ideology is very different from myth. But this is not a case of practice falling short of theory, of performance being less than promise. At the ideological level, politicians play a very different game, the elitist game of Liberal Democratic interest group politics, in which parties, as they are mythically understood, have no place (see Boxes 14–8 and 14–9).

The Ideological Role of Parties

Let us contrast the ideological practice of parties point by point with the mythic perceptions of them.

At the level of daily practice, the major political parties are in no way mobilizations of like-minded persons sharing common views on policies and programs. Within the range of their respective labels are citizens of great diversity—conservative, liberal, radical rightist, pro-this, anti-that, all age levels and, despite the stereotypes of the parties, all minority groups. Despite occasional emphasis on political faith of the right or the left seen in campaigns in recent years, the parties remain organizationally loose, almost ramshackle coalitions of groups and interests. They must in fact have such a diverse membership if they are to survive, even at the mythic level, because of the political system's extensive fragmentation of power.

Institutionally the structure of the two major parties tends to dissolve upon ideological inspection. The national conventions, often described by analysts as the institutions that display parties so that one can see them "in action," are hardly in a position to manage their par-

**BOX 14–8
The "Educating" of
a Politician**

Speaking of Governor Jerry Brown of California, Tom Quinn, one of his political advisers, says:

"He learned to be more practical in his approach to the power structure. . . . You can attack the timber industry as environmentally unsound, you can go after the freeway lobby and the medical lobby. But at some point there has to be some detente. The financial side of politics is dominated by special interests. You have to have some ties to survive."

—Marguerite Michaels, "Can Fortune's Child Survive?" *Parade*, November 29, 1981, p. 13.

**BOX 14–9
A Politician Looks
Back on a Fifty-
Year Career**

Frank G. Rossetti's half-century of service with the Democratic Party is ending where it began—at the corner of First Avenue and 116th Street.

That block was his first constituency when he was an election district captain 50 years ago, and it is on that corner where his small, fading Kanawha Democratic Club occupies what was once a dentist's office. . . . "The district has changed and I'm getting on in years," said the 73-year-old Mr. Rossetti, who still looks like the boxer he once was.

His adult life has been totally identified with the Democratic Party. It gave him party and public offices and the financial and emotional rewards that lifted him from the poverty he had known as an orphaned immigrant. . . .

But the party of which Mr. Rosetti speaks no longer exists. Surrounded by the past—pictures of himself and various politicians covering the paneled walls of the Kanawha club—he spoke of a party which [used to have the habit of following the "leadoff"]. . . . When "the leadoff"—[a leader such as] Greenwich Village district leader Carmine G. DeSapio—voted, . . . all the other district leaders fell into line like sheep. . . .

"I went along with the party," said Mr. Rossetti. . . . The difference is loyalty and trust," he said, comparing the old and new Democratic Party. . . . "When you were a county leader or a district leader, you meant something—all the patronage cleared through you. . . . A leader needs power and there's nothing wrong with that power if it's used in the right way," said the man who was a district leader for 37 years and Tammany leader for 10 years. . . .

Mr. Rossetti blamed the decline of the parties on Mayors . . . who, he said, had tried to select party leaders and control patronage themselves, and on President Lyndon B. Johnson's Great Society, which set up community antipoverty organizations that rivaled political clubs for local allegiance but had the advantage of the Federal Treasury behind them.

"Why should someone join the club?" he asked. "I've got nothing to give them."

However, the party is still giving to Mr. Rossetti, even in his semiretirement. He holds a patronage job as a part-time labor consultant for the Assembly and is paid as much as $10,000 a year. . . .

**BOX 14—9
A Politician Looks
Back on a Fifty-
Year Career
(Continued)**

Mr. Rossetti left his Assembly seat in 1972 when he was reapportioned into a largely black district and now he is leaving as a district leader because only two of his 26 captains are white. Mr. Rossetti had already fended off several Hispanic challenges to his leadership and expected more.

He said that the Hispanic politicians "will be the same as us, looking for their rewards—they know it's there for them, they're entitled to it and they'll get it."

—*The New York Times*, September 6, 1981.

ties day by day or even year by year,[3] nor do they attempt such tasks. Their focus is almost exclusively devoted to nominating their national candidates with all the fanfare and unity they can generate. They have no particular interest in disciplining any other candidates running under their banner or on their party line. They have even been fairly hospitable to candidates who have castigated the party and its leadership from time to time. George Wallace has been courteously received at a Democratic national convention, for example, and "rebel" Republicans such as Congressman Paul McCloskey of California have been allowed to run their hopeless races against Republican favorites. The party platforms adopted at these conventions, which conceivably could be used as tools for disciplining leaders and members as is done by many Western European parties, are of only marginal interest to delegates and presidential candidates. These candidates usually chart their own courses in light of their own views, their particular political situations, and the needs and strategies of their own campaigns.

The national committees, national party chairmen, and headquarters staff of the parties, which are charged with the parties' day-to-day operations between conventions, are of little practical significance. These organizations do seek to plot national strategies, publish party organs, and collect some money—though in relative terms, not much—to donate to congressional and other candidates. But they have no control mechanisms—and often, it seems, not even any coordinating mechanisms—to provide guidance, discipline, or fealty to candidates, leaders, state party officials, or anyone else. It is not unusual to hear a state or local party leader react to the national office as though it were just a nuisance.

[3] The Democratic Party holds a convention every two years. The midterm convention, which is devoted to policy and party rules, receives relatively little attention in the press and is considered not nearly so important as the quadrennial nominating convention.

It's time for serious leadership.

Republican campaign brochure used in Illinois in 1968.

The clinching fact in this analysis of the ideological reality of party cohesion is that whatever organizational structure the parties do have is not grounded in any base of organized membership. Citizens of course give money to the party of their choice and they often work hard for this party. Neither the Democratic nor the Republican party has a systematic membership program, however. To be a "member" of either party, you need do no more than write the name of the party on a form when you register to vote. There are no dues, no statements of principle to sign, no meetings to attend, no duties to perform. There is a sense of attachment to a party we call "party identification," and we know that many persons consider this identification an important part of their political personality. But the major parties are organizationally and ideologically rooted in little more than a sea of voter preferences and subjective perceptions. Thus by the mythic criteria of parties as mobilizations of like-minded citizens, the Republican and Democratic parties are, ideologically speaking, virtually nonexistent. They could hardly be more in a political system fragmented by the constitutional principles of federalism and mixed government theory reinforced by the pervasive ethos of Bourgeois individualism.

The second major function of parties, in myth, is to recruit and nominate candidates and to support their electoral efforts. The facts of this matter begin with the majority of officeholders who are shoo-ins for renomination and often for re-election. No recruitment is necessary under these circumstances. Most members of the Senate and the House of Representatives, for example, are returned to office by the voters (see Box 14–10). For these officeholders, the party's recruitment role is perfunctory. For a variety of reasons, in recent years presidents have had to contest their renomination and cannot be sure of re-election. But even so, the advantage of incumbency is considerable, as Carter showed by winning renomination against the formidable opposition of Edward Kennedy in 1980. Incumbency—not party—was also a major factor in Nixon's landslide election victory in 1972.

What about the close contests for renomination and re-election? Not all incumbents are guaranteed a free ride, and close races often develop in those contests in which the incumbent is retiring from politics. For the most part, however, candidates fight for and gain nomination or election by their own efforts. Occasionally a party organization endorses one candidate over another in a primary election, but this does not always assure victory. Even when candidate selection takes place at a convention or a meeting of a local party committee, the usual practice is not so much for the party to seek out candidates but for those who want the office to contend for it.

Individual initiative by candidates also applies to questions of campaign staffing, planning, and finance. Local party organizations dominated by a mayor or party official may pick cipher candidates for some of the lesser offices, but certainly in all of the attention-getting elections that stir the media and the voters, candidates handle campaign matters by and for themselves. They surround themselves with personally loyal aides who are probably not party officials. They propound ideas and programs in their own name and not in the name of a party. Hardly any serious candidate relies on financial support from resources other than those he or she personally can tap; the party provides a relatively insignificant share of financial help.

It is also notable that in the arrangements for federal government

BOX 14–10
Getting Re-elected
is Easier Than
Getting Elected

		House		
Year	Seeking Re-election	Defeated Primary	Defeated General	Percent Re-elected*
1946	398	18	52	82.4
1948	400	15	68	79.2
1950	400	6	32	90.5
1952	389	9	26	91.0
1954	407	6	22	93.1
1956	411	6	16	94.6
1958	396	3	37	89.9
1960	405	5	25	92.6
1962	402	12	22	91.5
1964	397	8	45	86.6
1966	411	8	41	88.1
1968	409	4	9	96.8
1970	401	10	12	94.5
1972	390	12	13	93.6
1974	391	8	40	87.7
1976	384	3	13	95.8
1978	382	5	19	93.7
1980	398	6	31	90.7

		Senate		
Year	Seeking Re-election	Defeated Primary	Defeated General	Percent Re-elected*
1946	30	6	7	56.7
1948	25	2	8	60.0
1950	32	5	5	68.8
1952	31	2	9	64.5
1954	32	2	6	75.0
1956	29	0	4	86.2
1958	28	0	10	64.3
1960	29	0	1	96.6
1962	35	1	5	82.9
1964	33	1	4	84.8
1966	32	3	1	87.5
1968	28	4	4	71.4
1970	31	1	6	77.4
1972	27	2	5	74.1
1974	27	2	2	85.2

		Senate		
Year	**Seeking Re-election**	**Defeated Primary**	**General**	**Percent Re-elected***
1976	25	0	9	64.0
1978	25	3	7	60.0
1980	29	4	9	55.2

*Counting both primary and general election defeats.

Source: *Congressional Quarterly Weekly Report*, April 5, 1980, p. 908 and November 8, 1980, pp. 3302, 3320–3321.

—Chart appears in Barbara Hinckley, *Congressional Elections* (Washington: Congressional Quarterly Press, 1981), p. 39.

contributions to the financing of presidential elections, funds directed to the national party organizations are only for defraying the costs of the national conventions. The bulk of the funds now funneled from the government into these elections goes directly to the personal organizations of the candidates. Significantly, Congress has successfully resisted proposals to fund congressional races, not only because its members are unenthusiastic about voting funds for their opponents, but also because this would interfere with the fund-raising process they now personally control. Raising money is an effective method for cementing relationships with important clients and supporters.

Against the backdrop of these arguments we come to the third mythic function of political parties: holding candidates responsible for their conduct in office. This is almost pure myth; such an assignment is formally impossible in America because, as we have shown, the American political system is designed to conform to principles wholly different than those of "responsible government." At the day-to-day level, American parties have neither the power nor the machinery for holding officeholders to their platforms or commitments in any practical, ideological way. Officeholders of course get blamed for what goes wrong by virtually everyone from voters to commentators to editorialists. The point is that officeholders are blamed personally—not the party—and in most instances they are re-elected anyway. This is reasonable, for parties can hardly be responsible for what various officeholders do in their name. When it comes to plaudits, the same principles apply. Politicians gladly rise to accept credit personally for those things that have gone well, and their party affiliation is hardly mentioned. What we hear is that "The

president's program is working" or "Congressman Doe succeeded
. . . ." Party responsibility seems almost to vanish whether bouquets or
brickbats are being given out, and it reappears only when it is personally advantageous for someone to have it do so.

All these matters must be kept in perspective. At the mythic level
parties will remain important for the foreseeable future, and many political consequences flow from this. To cite one example from the 1980
presidential campaign, there was the independent candidacy of John
Anderson who ran third and received approximately 7 percent of the
vote (see Box 14–12). Anderson was apparently considered an intelligent and articulate candidate by a number of voters and certainly by a
large contingent of the press, and he made a national effort. But he had
no party affiliation, at least for purposes of the general election campaign, so he was never able to establish credibility as a serious candi-

**BOX 14–11
Total Costs
(Publicly and
Privately Financed)
of Campaigns in
Presidential
Election Years—
and Their
Escalation**

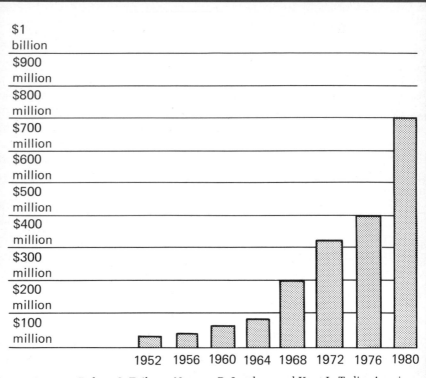

—Sources: Robert S. Erikson, Norman R. Luttbeg, and Kent L. Tedin, *American Public Opinion: Its Origins, Content, and Impact,* 2nd ed. (New York:
Wiley, 1980), p. 194; *U.S. News and World Report,* September 22, 1980, p.
22.

date. In particular, he was unable to stage a national convention to nominate him. He went down before the myth that the two-party system is the backbone of American democracy. Since the inauguration of that myth in the decades before the Civil War, this has been the fate of all candidates trying to operate outside the two parties.

Elections

You must register in order to vote, to participate in the myth. At the founding of this country the right to register to vote was restricted to white male citizens over twenty-one years of age, and most of these had also to meet literacy, property ownership, and other qualifications. The determination of suffrage qualifications for all elections—federal, state, and local—is a matter for the states to decide under the Constitution. Over the years the states have been increasingly required to meet standards laid down by the federal government. These include those imposed by constitutional amendments—the Fifteenth, adopted in 1870, which forbids discrimination on the basis of "race, color, or previous condition of servitude"; the Nineteenth (1920), which gave women the right to vote; the Twenty-Fourth (1964), which abolished the poll tax; and the Twenty-Sixth (1971), which lowered the voting age to 18.

Some states found ways to circumvent the intent of the Fifteenth Amendment in the latter decades of the nineteenth century and continued discriminatory practices well into this century. To prevent these practices, Congress passed the Voting Rights Act in 1965, providing for federal supervision of registration procedures. The Act accomplished massive increases in black voter participation in the South in the years since.

Voter registration laws vary from state to state, and there is a correlation between increasing registration opportunities and increased voter participation in elections. North Dakota requires no registration at all. Minnesota, Wisconsin, Maine, and Oregon permit election-day registration, which has very slightly increased voter turnout.[4]

District boundaries can also produce odd and unfair results in elections. A discussion of boundary and reapportionment problems can be found in Chapter 8.

The Electoral College

The Constitution provides for the election of the president and vice-president through the mechanism of the Electoral College. Most observers agree that this method is anachronistic and fraught with special problems, some of which have the potential of creating a constitutional crisis.

[4] John A. Crittenden, *Parties and Elections in the United States* (Englewood Cliffs, N.J.: Prentice-Hall, 1982), p. 186.

BOX 14–12
The 1980
Presidential Vote

State	Electoral Vote		Popular Vote		Percentage of Three-Candidate Vote			Percentage of Two-Party Vote	
	Carter	Reagan	Carter	Reagan	Carter	Reagan	Anderson	Carter	Reagan
Alabama		9	636,730	654,192	48.7	50.0	1.3	49.3	50.7
Alaska*		3	41,842	86,112	26.5	54.7	18.8	32.7	67.3
Arizona		6	246,843	529,688	28.9	62.1	9.0	31.8	68.2
Arkansas		6	398,041	403,164	48.3	49.0	2.7	49.7	50.3
California		45	3,083,652	4,524,835	36.9	54.2	8.9	40.5	59.5
Colorado		7	368,009	652,264	32.0	56.7	11.3	36.1	63.9
Connecticut		8	541,732	677,210	38.9	48.7	12.4	44.4	55.6
Delaware		3	105,754	111,252	45.3	47.7	7.0	48.7	51.3
District of Columbia	3		130,231	23,313	76.8	13.7	9.5	84.8	15.2
Florida		17	1,419,475	2,046,951	38.9	55.9	5.2	41.0	59.0
Georgia	12		890,955	654,168	56.4	41.4	2.2	57.6	42.4
Hawaii	4		135,879	130,112	45.6	43.6	10.8	51.1	48.9
Idaho		4	110,192	290,699	25.8	67.9	6.3	27.5	72.5
Illinois		26	1,981,413	2,358,094	42.2	50.4	7.4	45.6	54.4
Indiana		13	844,197	1,255,656	38.1	56.8	5.1	40.2	59.8
Iowa		8	508,672	676,026	39.1	52.0	8.9	42.9	57.1
Kansas		7	326,150	566,812	34.0	58.9	7.1	36.6	63.4
Kentucky		9	617,417	635,274	48.1	49.5	2.4	49.3	50.7
Louisiana		10	708,453	792,853	46.4	51.9	1.7	47.2	52.8
Maine		4	220,974	238,522	43.1	46.5	10.4	48.1	51.9
Maryland	10		726,161	680,606	47.5	44.6	7.9	51.6	48.4
Massachusetts		14	1,053,800	1,056,223	42.2	42.4	15.4	49.9	50.1
Michigan		21	1,661,532	1,915,225	43.2	49.7	7.1	46.4	53.6
Minnesota	10		954,173	873,268	47.6	43.7	8.7	52.2	47.8
Mississippi		7	429,281	441,089	48.6	50.0	1.4	49.3	50.7

Missouri	12		931,182	1,074,181	44.7	51.6	3.7	46.4	53.6
Montana	4		118,032	206,814	33.3	58.4	8.3	36.3	63.7
Nebraska	5		166,424	419,214	26.4	66.5	7.1	28.4	71.6
Nevada	3		66,666	155,017	27.9	64.8	7.3	30.1	69.9
New Hampshire	4		108,864	221,705	28.7	58.3	13.0	33.0	67.0
New Jersey	17		1,147,364	1,546,557	39.2	52.8	8.0	42.6	57.4
New Mexico	4		167,826	250,779	37.4	56.0	6.6	40.1	59.9
New York	41		2,728,372	2,893,831	44.8	47.6	7.6	48.5	51.5
North Carolina	13		875,635	915,018	47.5	49.6	2.9	48.9	51.1
North Dakota	3		79,189	193,695	26.8	65.3	7.9	29.1	70.9
Ohio	25		1,752,414	2,206,545	41.6	52.4	6.0	44.3	55.7
Oklahoma	8		402,026	695,570	35.4	61.2	3.4	36.6	63.4
Oregon	6		456,890	571,044	40.1	50.1	9.8	44.5	55.5
Pennsylvania	27		1,937,540	2,261,872	43.1	50.4	6.5	46.1	53.9
Rhode Island		4	198,342	154,793	48.0	37.5	14.5	56.2	43.8
South Carolina	8		430,385	441,841	48.6	49.8	1.6	49.4	50.6
South Dakota	4		103,855	198,343	32.1	61.3	6.6	34.4	65.6
Tennessee	10		783,051	787,761	48.8	49.0	2.2	49.8	50.2
Texas	26		1,881,147	2,510,705	41.7	55.8	2.5	42.8	57.2
Utah	4		124,266	439,687	20.9	74.0	5.1	22.0	78.0
Vermont	3		81,952	94,628	39.3	45.4	15.3	46.4	53.6
Virginia	12		752,174	989,609	40.9	53.9	5.2	43.2	56.8
Washington	9		650,193	865,244	38.2	50.9	10.9	42.9	57.1
West Virginia		6	367,462	334,206	50.1	45.6	4.3	52.4	47.6
Wisconsin	11		981,584	1,088,345	44.0	48.8	7.2	47.4	52.6
Wyoming	3		49,427	110,700	28.7	64.3	7.0	30.9	69.1
National Total	489	49	35,483,820	43,901,812	41.7	51.6	6.7	44.7	55.3

*Alaska third-party vote includes 18,479 votes for Ed Clark, Libertarian party, as well as 11,156 votes for Anderson.

—From Gerald Pomper et al., *The Election of 1980: Reports and Interpretations* (Chatham, N.J.: Chatham House, 1981), pp. 68–69.

In a technical sense, the voter in America does not vote for a particular candidate but chooses a slate of electors who in turn are committed to vote for one or another candidate. Each elector on a slate has one vote. Electoral votes are apportioned among the states on the basis of the size of their congressional delegations, counting senators and representatives, a total of 538 in all. Electoral votes are reapportioned among the states every ten years on the basis of the new census. Under this arrangement, there is a wide variation in the voting strength of the

George C. Wallace, Governor of Alabama, who carried five states in the 1968 presidential election. He had hoped to carry more so that the election would have been thrown into the House of Representatives.

several states. Currently, Vermont has only 3 votes, for example, while Georgia has 12, and California 47.

Tradition and law dictate that whichever candidate gains the most votes in the popular election within a state receives all of that state's electoral votes. Moreover, if there are more than two candidates, the winner does not need a majority, only a plurality. This means that a candidate can win the presidency without receiving a majority of the popular vote across the country, and this has in fact occurred many times—Richard Nixon in 1968, John F. Kennedy in 1960, Harry Truman in 1948, and Woodrow Wilson in 1912 are just a few examples.

A more remote possibility, but one that poses no small amount of constitutional uncertainty, is that one candidate can win the popular vote while the other wins a majority of the electoral vote. Under these circumstances the latter wins the election, and this actually occurred on one occasion.

Still another possibility is that when there are more than two leading candidates, as was the case in 1948, 1968, and 1980, the electoral vote could be divided so that no one receives a majority. Should this occur, the Twelfth Amendment of the Constitution requires the election be taken to the House of Representatives with each state delegation having a single vote. The results of such a procedure are uncertain not only because of the bartering and whims of Congress but because there would be a considerable delay between the time of the general election in November and the actual choosing of a president by Congress. The strategy of American Independent Party candidate George Wallace was aimed at such a result in 1968.

All these considerations point to an awkwardness inherent in the electoral college system. Of more immediate effect are the political consequences of the system in virtually every election, and two of these are worth noting. First, because of the "winner take all" rule operating in each state, candidates concentrate their efforts on those states they believe they have a chance of winning or losing by a small margin of popular votes. These anxieties are increased if these "close race" conditions appear in big states, as is often the case. In every campaign, consequently, states like California, New York, Texas, Illinois, Ohio, and Pennsylvania receive disproportionate shares of time, energy, and money in campaign plans and budgets (see Box 14–13). Thus the issues of special concern to the voters in these big either-or states dominate the campaign dialogue. National issues and issues of interest to only the smaller states tend to be downplayed.

Second, the winner take all nature of the electoral system in the states creates a false image of election "landslide" on many occasions. The 1980 election is a case in point. Reagan received 489 electoral votes because he carried 44 of the states, Carter received 49 electoral votes, and Anderson none. For many months after President Reagan took of-

BOX 14–13
Electoral Strength of States After 1980 Census

	Electoral Votes		Electoral Votes
East			
Connecticut	8	New Hampshire	4
Delaware	3	New Jersey	16
Dist. of Columbia	3	New York	35
Maine	4	Pennsylvania	25
Maryland	10	Rhode Island	4
Massachusetts	13	Vermont	3
Midwest			
Illinois	24	Nebraska	5
Indiana	12	North Dakota	3
Iowa	8	Ohio	23
Kansas	7	South Dakota	3
Michigan	20	Wisconsin	11
Minnesota	10		
South and Border			
Alabama	10	North Carolina	13
Arkansas	6	Oklahoma	8
Florida	21	South Carolina	8
Georgia	12	Tennessee	12
Kentucky	9	Texas	28
Louisiana	10	Virginia	12
Mississippi	7	West Virginia	6
Missouri	11		
West			
Alaska	3	Nevada	4
Arizona	7	New Mexico	5
California	47	Oregon	7
Colorado	8	Utah	5
Hawaii	4	Washington	10
Idaho	4	Wyoming	3
Montana	4		

With 270 electoral votes needed to win a presidential election, a candidate could conceivably be carried to victory by as few as twelve states. In recent years, population shifts from the East and Midwest toward the South and West have added electoral strength to the two latter regions.

fice, the White House and presidential supporters elsewhere trumpeted the supposed fact of a decisive and overwhelming Reagan victory and claimed unquestioned support for his programs and policies. Buried underneath these claims is the hard fact that Reagan received 52 percent of the popular vote. In light of this fact, it is not surprising that the president's polls and standing ran down as soon as they did; Reagan's "massive" mandate simply was never there in the first place.

Over the years a number of proposals have been made to abolish or reform the electoral college. Any of these would require a constitutional amendment. They include proposals to give one electoral vote to each congressional district rather than a proportion of the total to each state, to eliminate the rituals of the electoral college, and to abolish the electoral college system altogether, substituting a popular vote election.

Primary Elections

This is a complex topic because the laws governing primary elections vary from state to state and, because of frequent changes, from election to election. Generally speaking, a primary election is a way to involve voters in the candidate selection process of the parties prior to a general election. Two distinctions may amplify and also clarify this definition.

Primary elections can be direct or preferential. In the latter, voters choose delegates to a party nominating convention who in most cases have already announced their preference for a certain candidate. In the direct primary, voters directly choose the candidates for the party nomination.

Primaries may also be open or closed. Any registered voter may participate in an open primary, and the voter's choice of ballot is neither recorded nor disclosed by the officials administering the election. In a closed primary, only voters registered with a particular party are per-

		BOX 14–14
February 26	New Hampshire	**The Presidential**
March 4	Massachusetts, Vermont	**Primaries, 1980**
March 8	South Carolina (Republican only)	
March 11	Alabama, Florida, Georgia	
March 16	Puerto Rico (Democratic only)	
March 18	Illinois	
March 25	Connecticut, New York (Democratic only)	
April 1	Kansas, Wisconsin	
April 5	Louisiana	
April 22	Pennsylvania	
May 3	Texas	
May 6	Indiana, North Carolina, Tennessee	
May 13	Maryland, Nebraska	
May 20	Oregon, Michigan (Republican only)	
May 27	Idaho, Kentucky, Nevada, Arkansas (Democratic only)	
June 3	California, Montana, New Jersey, New Mexico, Ohio, Rhode Island, South Dakota, West Virginia	

mitted to choose the candidates of that party. Three states have a variant of the open primary known as the "blanket" primary. In this arrangement, a single ballot is used for a primary election, and voters are permitted to pick candidates for both parties so long as they vote for only one candidate for each office. All the states hold primary elections for at least some offices, and thirty-six states now run a presidential primary in presidential election years (see Box 14–14).

Primary elections for state and local offices tend not to be serious hurdles for incumbents seeking re-election. On many occasions incumbents have no primary opponent. The party that does not hold office may have a spirited primary or, if the general election race does not look too hopeful, may simply endorse the one candidate—sometimes known as a "sacrificial lamb"—who has agreed to run.

The states have increasingly used presidential primaries since the early 1970s. The rules governing these primaries are as varied as the states that use them: the date of the election, whether the delegates elected are tied to a specific presidential candidate, whether the vote for a presidential candidate is a vote for a delegate slate or merely a preference registered for the candidate, and the degree of fealty to a candidate required of elected delegates. Some states, for example, have required delegates to vote for the candidate they have pledged to support for at least one convention ballot.

The steady increase in the number of primary elections is a clear response to mythic demands to involve the People as directly as possible in the candidate selection process. Nevertheless, turnout in them is often low and their widespread use has brought a spate of criticism, especially of presidential primaries. Having to wade through up to three dozen of these contests enormously increases the expenses of serious candidates for the presidency. It also greatly exaggerates the character of presidential campaigns as personality contests between individually financed and organized candidacies. Concomitantly, the dependence of the candidates on their respective parties is reduced to virtually nil. Even the politicians have been disturbed by these developments. The Democratic Party in planning its 1984 convention decided to increase the number of delegates selected from the ranks of party members holding public office as governors, senators, and congress members, thereby decreasing the significance of delegates selected through the primary election process.

Campaigns

It is still possible for a campaign for county auditor or city council member to be run by amateurs. Brochures may be printed, the candidate may do some handshaking, and friends and supporters can be herded one by one to the polls on election day. Some of the routine and unexciting contests for higher offices, even a seat in the House of Representatives, may also be conducted in this way. But almost any statewide

**BOX 14–15
Our Poor
Presidential
Primary System Is
Fragmented and
Unrepresentative**

Presidential primaries were designed to take the nomination away from party bosses in the back room and to give the decisions to the voters. But they haven't worked out that way. Instead, the current version of primaries turns the decisions over to a new kind of boss. Today a small, unrepresentative handful of party activists, often concerned with only one issue, or with narrow, special interests, dominate the primaries. Because the broad center of moderate and independent voters seldom vote in party primaries, decisions are abdicated to tiny groups of motivated extremists of the left or the right. Current pressures push the Democrats to the left and the Republicans to the right. And the new sort of boss system may be worse than the old. . . .

For example, let us look at the current system by examining the 1976 primaries. New Hampshire [usually the first primary held in the nation] has 488,870 eligible voters; 336,000 voted in the general election. But in New Hampshire, only 82,381 voters participated in the multicandidate Democratic primary. The winner, Jimmy Carter, had 23,373 votes—or 28%. That is just about the same number of votes cast in the Presidential Primary in 1976 in only one of Chicago's 50 wards. President Carter's primary victory represented only 7% of the voters in the New Hampshire general election. Similarly, President Ford's 56,156 votes in the New Hampshire Republican primary represented only 17% of the vote in the New Hampshire general election. In some presidential primaries in 1976, as few as 11% of the voters actually voted. The average turnout is less than 40%.

Thus, our present system is way out of touch with the broad electoral center. The result is a process that tends to fragment rather than unify, and to confuse rather than enlighten. Well-qualified possibilities for President are not even considered. . . .

—Newton N. Minow, *Wall Street Journal*, August 13, 1979.

race and a lot of lesser races as well today require television appearances and commercials, expensive, targeted direct mail, and professional campaign managers and consultants. This is not just the case in states with big populations (see Box 14–15); it is also true in lightly populated states such as Wyoming.

Campaigns have both a mythic and an ideological side. The mythic appears on the television screen, on the radio, in newspaper ads, and in direct mail. The ideological side is found in the work that goes into creating the images that result from television, radio, newspapers, and direct mail.

A serious candidate for national, statewide, and often local elective office employs a professional firm at considerable expense. Sometimes

Buttons are still a part of political campaign efforts. How effective they are in serving a candidate's needs is an open question.

more than one firm is used; nearly always both consulting and managing personnel are involved. The following is a partial list of the types of professionals typically employed in such a campaign:

Management—public relations counselor, advance person, advertising agent, fund raiser, management scientist, industrial engineer, telephone campaigner, organizer;

Information—market researcher, public opinion pollster, political scientist, social psychologist, psychologist, computer programmer, demographer, statistician;

Media—journalist, media advance agent, radio and television writer, radio and television producer, film documentary producer, radio and television time buyer, television coach, radio and television actors, direct mail advertiser, computer printing specialist.[5]

The complexity of campaigns, the tremendous resources needed to finance them, and the sophistication of the skills necessary to run them often worry those who are immersed in the mythic beliefs about the political processes of this nation. They see harm in the evolution from the simpler days of handshaking campaigns to the semiscientific, manipulative efforts of today: the southern California firm that supposedly requires its client-candidates to leave the country until election day because they may say something to knock the campaign off its track; the apparent ability to create something akin to the "perfect candidate" (see Box 14–16); or the targeting of each citizen by direct mail experts intent on appeals to visceral reactions. There is also that plague of modern campaigns, the "media event" staged only for the wider audience that will see it in their living rooms. In Washington state, for example, Senator Henry "Scoop" Jackson appears at the Sons of Norway Hall not for the benefit of the people there but for the people watching him on television. But media politics and professional campaign management are so atuned to the mythic requirements of campaigns that they seem here to stay.

The Meaning of Elections

In conclusion, we must ask, what is the point of all this civic participation in politics within the context of the American political system?

We have seen that a large, perhaps major proportion of the elections in this country are hardly more than formalities in which incumbents are returned to offices they have long held. We have also seen that in close, hard fought elections parties are weak, emphasis is placed on

[5] Robert Agranoff, "The New Styles of Campaigning: The Decline of Parties and the Rise of Candidate-Centered Technology," in *The New Style of Election Campaigns*, Robert Agranoff, ed. (Boston: Holbrook Press, 1972), p. 17.

**BOX 14–16
Creating the
Perfect Candidate**

Normal, Ill.—. . . The creation of a phantom candidate was originally undertaken as a "satire" by two communications professors who developed a computerized speech-writing method to produce political oratory that—literally—can "play in Peoria." . . .

Believing that election to public office has become more a matter of manipulating symbols than dealing with substantive issues, [two professors] programmed an IBM 370/145 to write the "perfect" foreign policy speech.

The speech was judged on its ability to appeal to the most and offend the fewest in any given audience. . . .

"As long as people are writing speeches trying to appeal to what the majority of the people want to hear," [one of the professors] observed, "I'm convinced our machine will win." . . .

"For all I know, some candidates may well be doing [this] already, or very close to it. . . . They're employing high-powered marketing firms that develop the advertising for consumer products such as Virginia Slims for 'liberated women' or 7-Up for members of the counter-culture."

The professors' underlying theory is that to get elected, a politician need only recognize that voters generally hold one of three "dramatic" views of the world and then play to the most widespread view. . . . the foreign policy views can be described as cold-war, neoisolationist and power-politics attitudes. . . .

In order to program the computer to write the perfect speech, the professors first searched periodicals for months, jotting down quotations on 20 foreign policy issues that reflected all three world views.

The pair then asked 60 Peorians to indicate which of the statements most reflected and least reflected their own views. The ranked statements were keypunched onto cards which were processed . . . at Illinois State.

Using factor analysis and linear equation programs written by the two political observers, the system spewed out a short speech describing the hypothetical candidate's opinion on how best to handle U.S. foreign policy—that is, for the ears of Peorians.

**BOX 14–16
Creating the
Perfect Candidate
(Continued)**

"First of all," the speech began, "let me say that the United States is not a failure. I recognize that it's foolhardy to unilaterally disarm, but . . ."

While the computer's speeches are . . . bland, . . . the 1977 version received an ovation when it was presented before a Peoria audience. According to [one of the professors,] "The point is that you can take any idiot, parade him around the country for 12 months and get him elected.". . .

—Marguerite Zientara, *Computerworld*, September 24, 1979.

personalities rather than policies, and the consequences of electoral outcomes are not clear. However heralded in the press as new beginnings or radical changes, the actual consequences of such elections regularly are muffled by the weight of the business as usual and incremental emphases of the political system's ideological politics. In this perspective elections, especially the widely reported exciting ones, are not much more than television events (or nonevents). They are nevertheless expensive events; the 1980 elections for all offices cost nearly $1 billion.

Again we make the point that this activity is not meaningless. Quite apart from the mistaken notion that the American people would be willing to spend $1 billion on something that has no meaning, we have argued at length in this book that elections and similar activities are mythic in form and function and as such are critically important for the legitimation they give the political system.

Now let us put this assertion into specific terms. The reason elections are held, besides fulfilling constitutional requirements, is that the political system in America must be relegitimated over and over. This is an urgent requirement because of the vulnerability of the ideological processes of Liberal Democracy. It does not, indeed cannot, meet Social Democracy's mythic criteria and claims. The specific problem addressed by elections is the inherent elitism of Liberal Democracy—the constant, pervasive tendency on the ideological side of American politics to lodge power and privilege in the hands of a self-interested, self-protective group of well-placed individuals. Most of these individuals have economic baronies in the business world, but they also have access to and control over important aspects of government operations that are of signal importance to them. This control is in contradiction to what citizens have been taught in school and by politicians themselves about government and its democratic grassroots, its responsiveness to popular opinion, and its commitment to be "of, by and for" the people. America's political elitism must therefore be concealed.

Elections are wonderfully adapted to this task of concealment. Campaigns, though often viewed cynically, generate wide public interest and with this interest the recurrent notion that through the ballot box the People rule. Campaigns further suggest that voters' decisions are directly translated into public policies. The underlying, specific function of elections in the American political system, then, is to help mask the division between the powerful and the powerless and to propagate the myth that in this country all the people rule on more or less equal terms.

We must stress that the myth of the power of the People and the meaningfulness of elections is not brought about by some dark conspiracy of the national elite. Members of the elite certainly contribute generously to election campaigns and also to the socialization process by which myths are inculcated into citizens. It is probably true that key members of the elite are aware of the immediacy of their interest in doing this. But even the elite gets caught up in myth and in the excite-

BOX 14–17
Why the American People Vote

Why do citizens vote? The recent history of attempts by political scientists to answer this question reveals a growing recognition that [motivations assigned to self-interest] are inadequate and that ethical considerations must be introduced (even to explain voting in American elections). [Anthony] Downs tries to account for the fact that many people vote by suggesting that a rational citizen may be "willing to bear certain short-term costs he could avoid in order to do his share in providing long-run benefits." As [Brian] Barry points out, the notion of doing one's "share" smuggles in a moral argument and is inconsistent with Downs' model of rational self-interest. To avoid such inconsistencies, Riker and Ordeshook expand the idea of rationality to embrace the psychic satisfactions (a "duty factor") that citizens receive from voting. Ashenfleter and Kelley, in a recent . . . study of the decision to vote in Presidential elections, conclude that "a sense of duty or obligation" is the "primary motivation for voting." Citizens "go to the polls because they have been taught that it is the right thing to do and they believe it."
—Dennis F. Thompson, *Political Participation* (Washington, D.C.: American Political Science Association, 1977), pp. 45–46.

ment of the electoral process. Thus the unceasing efforts to make us all believe we share in governmental power converts the elite into believers as well. It is in fact the elite and those who do their bidding that most fervently preach that good citizenship requires us to vote and make us feel that failure to vote is a matter of moral turpitude (see Box 14–17).

That observation raises a question on which we end this chapter: who votes and why? Although the figures vary from election to election, the American people are relatively inactive as voters compared with other democratic peoples such as the British, the French, and the Swedes. Moreover, voter turnout for presidential elections has steadily declined since 1960. In the off-year elections, the years of congressional elections in which there is no presidential race, voting is often down by half in many states. Turnout in local elections is regularly even lower, and lower still in most primaries. Finally, studies show that between one fourth and one fifth of the adult population simply does not participate in the political process in any way.[6] They neither vote, sign petitions, write letters to their congress members, nor participate in demonstrations.

How can this state of affairs exist alongside a determinedly Social Democratic myth that places a premium on citizen involvement, particularly on voting? This phenomenon has attracted increasing attention from voting analysts in recent years, who have found some differences among the voting propensities of blacks, Catholics, Jews, women, ethnic groups, and the rest of the population, but hardly anything of stunning significance. The general proposition with the fullest empirical support is hardly more than a truism: people in higher socioeconomic and educational brackets tend to vote more than the poor, the aged, the young, the ill-educated, and the unemployed. In other words, those who are doing well in the system tend to legitimate it by voting. On the other hand, those who are doing poorly in the system see no reason to legitimate it—and don't.

This explanation depends on the assumption that, within limits, voters are rational—and nonvoters are too. But the rationality of voters has been a much disputed point among scholars in recent years (see Box 14–17). Some contend that the ordinary voter is neither rational nor informed, and it is certain that some campaign managers and media consultants proceed on this premise at least part of the time. Other observers claim they have found consistent evidence of fairly high levels of voter rationality. Still others hold that while levels of rationality and information are low, it is a plus for all of us that citizens in the relatively higher socioeconomic and educational brackets are the ones who participate the most in voting. The prospects for a democratic system, some observers assert, are improved by this fact.

[6] Lester Milbrath and M. L. Goel, *Political Participation*, pp. 18–19.

Our conclusions, proceeding from the lines of argument developed in this book, can be summarized simply. The voter is faced with two decisions, not one. The first of these permits a relatively high degree of rationality; the second, given the nature of the American context, does not.

The first decision a voter must make is whether to vote at all. If voting is a decision to legitimize the regime, then it is rational for those doing well within it to vote. It is equally rational for those not doing well to forget about voting. It does not take much street smarts for a young black male facing nearly permanent unemployment prospects to know that voting holds little meaning for his life.

The second decision for voters to make, if they decide to vote, is whom to vote for. Given the kinds of candidates the system has been offering voters and the way elections have been reduced to personality contests, it would be hard for even an advanced student of politics to make a rational choice on this second question. The fundamental characteristics of the political system combined with present-day campaign techniques and media exploitation prohibit rationality. In these circumstances choosing between Candidate A and Candidate B is akin to asking someone to choose to cheer for the New York Mets rather than the San Francisco Giants. The choice can be easy if you live in New York City or San Francisco. It is harder if you live in Milwaukee or Atlanta. In any event, the choice, like many election choices in America, is based more on emotional reflex than on rational distinctions.[7]

FOR FURTHER READING

AGRANOFF, ROBERT. *The Management of Election Campaigns.* Boston: Holbrook Press, 1976. In many ways a how-to book that describes modern campaign techniques in detail.

ALDRICH, JOHN H. *Before the Convention: Strategies and Choices in Presidential Nominating Campaigns.* Chicago: University of Chicago Press, 1980. Advances the theoretical treatment of nominating strategies, focusing on 1976 races.

CRITTENDEN, JOHN A. *Parties and Elections in the United States.* Englewood Cliffs, N.J.: Prentice-Hall, 1982. Introduction to parties, elections, and the electoral system; up-to-date and filled with useful and pointed anecdotes and examples.

FERGUSON, THOMAS, and JOEL ROGERS, eds. *The Hidden Election: Politics and Economics in the 1980 Presidential Campaign.* New York: Pantheon, 1981. Essays devoted not only to political economy but to a variety of interesting topics related to campaigns and elections.

[7] The argument of this and the preceding paragraphs is based on Kim Ezra Shienbaum, *Beyond The Electoral Connection: A Reassessment of the Role of Voting in Contemporary American Politics,* forthcoming, 1983.

Jacobson, Gary C. *Money in Congressional Elections*. New Haven: Yale University Press, 1980. Makes good use of newly available data on campaign finance to illuminate their impact on these races.

Karp, Walter. *Indispensable Enemies: The Politics of Misrule in America*. Baltimore: Penguin, 1973. Unconventional view of parties and elections in some ways consonant with the theme of this text.

LeBlanc, Hugh L. *American Political Parties*. New York: St. Martin's Press, 1982. Standard and readable introduction to this subject.

Lipset, Seymour M., ed. *Party Coalitions in the 1980s*. San Francisco. Institute for Contemporary Studies, 1981. Essays and articles that deal with images of the parties, the possibilities of realignment of factions of the public, and 1980 campaign strategies.

Milbrath, Lester W., and M. L. Goel. *Political Participation*, 2nd ed. Chicago: Rand McNally, 1977. Discusses the various factors affecting participation, using comparative data.

Pomper, Gerald, et al. *The Election of 1980: Reports and Interpretations*. Chatham, N.J.: Chatham House, 1981. Assesses this election from a variety of viewpoints and also provides a variety of interesting and useful statistics.

Sabato, Larry J. *The Rise of Political Consultants: New Ways of Winning Elections*. New York: Basic Books, 1982. Probably now the standard work on consultants, media people, pollsters, and direct mail techniques.

Verba, Sidney, and Norman H. Nie. *Participation in America*. New York: Harper & Row, 1972. Examines, among other things, the motivations for voter participation and the effects of participation.

15 Civil Liberties

High schools are not necessarily the best places in which to launch protests aimed at changing public policy. All the same, some high school and junior high school students in the Des Moines, Iowa school system decided to wear black arm bands to classes on a given day to show their disapproval of the Vietnam War. It was 1965, a time of deepening commitment to the war by President Lyndon B. Johnson and his foreign policy advisers.

Anticipating this protest, the school authorities adopted a policy whereby anyone wearing an arm band would be asked to remove it. Students who refused would be suspended until they agreed to return to school without the arm band. The students challenged this rule as a violation of their right to freedom of speech—in this case, symbolic freedom of speech—as guaranteed by the First Amendment of the Constitution. The case proceeded over a four-year period to the U.S. Supreme Court, where Justice Abe Fortas read the court's majority opinion:

> First Amendment rights, applied in light of the special characteristics of the school environment, are available to teachers and students. It can hardly be argued that either students or teachers shed their constitutional rights to freedom of speech or expression at the schoolhouse gate.[1]

But this was not the only consideration. As we have pointed out in Chapter 5, the courts, in the ideological context of Liberal Democracy, are charged with maintaining the framework, the "cage," of the law. This requires balancing interests, the rights and needs of some against the rights and needs of others. The Fortas opinion goes on:

[1] *Tinker* v. *Des Moines School District*, 393 U.S. 503 (1969).

On the other hand, the Court has repeatedly emphasized the need for affirming the comprehensive authority of the States and of school authorities, consistent with fundamental constitutional safeguards, to prescribe and control conduct in the schools. . . . Our problem lies in the area where students in the exercise of First Amendment rights collide with the rules of the school authorities.[2]

In this case, the balancing of interests resulted in a victory for the students and the cause of free speech. The court found that wearing arm bands did not interfere with the functions of work of the schools. The rules adopted by the school authorities, on the other hand, did impose a substantial detriment to the students' welfare, for they amounted to a denial of free expression.[3]

If you agree with the outcome of this case, you should be aware that the side arguing for its free speech rights is not invariably the winner. If you think, on the other hand, that the school authorities were justified in their actions, you can take heart because although they lost on this particular interpretation of the Bill of Rights, such authorities often prevail on other similar matters.

The case of the Des Moines students, like thousands of other cases, illustrates the tensions between freedom and order that exist in American society. Freedom and order are both important to the ideological practice of American government. The whole point of Liberal Democracy is to provide personal liberty within the ordering limits of the law. As a result, decisions to demark and resolve tensions between freedom and order are a vital part of the operational framework of American government. More to the point, the definition and support of individual freedoms—speech, religion, privacy, association, fair trial, and others—have been so frequently the subject of Supreme Court rulings and only less occasionally of legislation and executive edicts that the American political system is revealed as having an uncommon concern to secure and protect the legal rights of people to pursue their personal goals in their own ways with as little interference as possible.

Even so, the outcome and consequences of contests in America between freedom and order are never certain. None of the Bill of Rights freedoms is considered absolute by the great majority of those called upon to interpret their meaning. Supreme Court Justice Oliver Wendell Holmes, Jr., argued, for example, that the right of free speech does not extend to falsely shouting "Fire!" in a crowded theater. The right of privacy apparently does not preclude government eavesdropping in certain circumstances. And equal protection of the laws does not, in practical terms, mean equal access to the justice system. Legal costs, plea

[2] Ibid.
[3] Ibid.

bargaining (see Chapter 5), and a host of other considerations make equal protection more available on the basis of ability to hire good lawyers than equality of persons.

As is understandable in a complex and technologically advanced Liberal Democracy such as the United States, controversy over civil rights and liberties touches on a wide range of topics. But more is involved here than just technological problems. Alexis de Tocqueville said long ago, "There is hardly a political question in the United States which does not sooner or later turn into a judicial one." That statement is as true today as it was when it was written in the 1830s, and it also describes a process that has its costs. When courts start handling political problems, they get transformed in important ways.

In America, political questions, that is, the broad, substantive issues about how to make this nation a generous, forward-looking community, usually arise within the Social Democratic, mythic vision we maintain about ourselves. But when we turn from discussions about these mythic goals to talk about ways of accomplishing our objectives practically, we become Liberal Democrats mostly concerned with questions about who, within the "cage" of the all-encompassing laws, has the right to do what with which and to whom. And this means, especially when the pressure is on about some crisis or a proposal for action, that we end up in the courts, the final arbiters of these questions in a Liberal Democracy. By this process, the Social Democratic concerns of the People, expressed characteristically through their political parties and other civic mobilizations, are resolved again and again into Liberal Democratic questions about the rights and obligations of people as individuals.

What must be noticed about this process is that in it the substantive issues myth raises get defined away into simply procedural questions. In the Des Moines case, for example, as the controversy was resolved, the First Amendment right of free speech became the central issue in the dispute; questions about the wisdom and morality of the Vietnam War, which is where it all started, were all but forgotten.

The most celebrated example of this way of dealing with problems is the Civil War and the issue of the status of black people in America. In the decades preceding the war, executives and legislative bodies fumbled the issue first one way then another, mostly in terms of compromises. But even before the war started, a major piece of the issue ended up in the courts in the Dred Scott case. In that case, the courts guessed wrong, and the country had a political breakdown of catastrophic proportions. As we have already had occasion to notice, the war itself did little to settle the moral issue at its core. But the courts were back in the picture before long. In 1896, in the case of *Plessy* v. *Ferguson*, the Supreme Court held, on procedural grounds, that "separate," if "equal," was constitutional. Thus, on what was almost a procedural technicality,

The frailty of civil liberties in America has been demonstrated by the presidentially ordered and Supreme Court approved removal of tens of thousands of Japanese-Americans to detention camps, often referred to as "concentration camps" in government documents, during World War II.

the South was handed what it had fought the war to defend, not only the principle of segregation but also the right to govern the relationship between the races as it saw fit.

The final irony in all this is that when the issue of segregation was again confronted in *Brown* v. *Board of Education* more than a half century later, the courts were again the arena and the principle of resolution was again effectively procedural, the question of "equal protection of the laws." Even today, civil rights activists, although they may start from positions holding that racial oppression is both unwise and unjust, prefer to press their specific claims in terms of the rights and obligations of individuals. In the light of this, it is hardly surprising that progress on the substantive grievances of the black community in America about employment, health, housing, and education has been slow.

This chapter concentrates on what civil liberties in America are, what they amount to, the disputes that have arisen about them (see Box 15–1), and how the courts, especially the Supreme Court, have tried to reconcile these disputes. We begin with a description of the Bill of Rights, the original charter of the Liberal Democratic vision of the individual's rights within the law. Then we examine two areas of law that

**BOX 15–1
A Civil Liberties
Quiz**

The following statements represent various propositions involving civil liberties. They may or may not be statements of the law as presently interpreted. As an experiment, write your answer on a sheet of paper—yes, no, or qualified, specifying why you qualify your answer—for each of these propositions. Defend your position, either to yourself or to your fellow students. Remember, this quiz does not have any clearly "right" or "wrong" answers.

1. Wiretapping, or electronic eavesdropping, of the conversations of one person by another should never be permitted under any circumstances.

2. Books, films, or other materials that contain demeaning characterizations of ethnic or racial groups should be subject to censorship.

3. Determining what is "obscene" or "pornographic" requires such a highly subjective judgment that the authorities should not be enpowered to decide it.

4. Communists and Nazis have the right to teach in American universities and colleges in the same way and to the same extent that members of any other group have such a right.

5. Pickets in a labor dispute have the right to forcibly detain employees who seek to go to work in spite of the dispute.

6. Corporal punishment should be permitted in public schools.

7. Police should be required to inform suspects of their rights upon arrest.

8. Morning prayers should be required in all public schools.

9. Citizens should be given access to all public records and files that relate to them personally.

10. Members of the press and other media should be required to give their sources to police or other authorities if it is likely that this will result in the arrest and conviction of criminals.

have caused the courts a great deal of trouble in recent decades—the First Amendment freedoms and the "equal protection" clause of the Fourteenth Amendment. Finally, we look at the problem of privacy, an issue that lies at the heart of Liberal Democratic concerns but is ill-defined both in law and tradition.

The Bill Of Rights

The Bill of Rights, the great charter of individualism set out as the first ten amendments to the Constitution, was adopted by the First Congress in 1791. Many historians believe that the promise that these ten amendments would be added to the Constitution was the price of its ratification. But what the Bill of Rights spells out in detail was a philosophy that was already evident throughout the Constitution. The Constitution, as we have pointed out, fairly breathes the basic Liberal Democratic outlook. It regards the individual in a rational Enlightenment perspective, expecting each of us to pursue our own interests. The duty of the law, first and foremost, is to protect individuals as they go about their pursuits. Government must assist individuals where and when it can and protect and enhance the general peace and welfare of citizens.

In this light it is understandable that even the Constitution's greatest supporters were nevertheless willing, through adoption of the Bill of Rights, to set limits on how far the new government could go. As in the body of the Constitution itself, clause after clause of the Bill of Rights uses "no," "not," or "nor" as the operative word. Thus in many cases arising under the Bill of Rights, the central problems are procedural questions about rights and limits, rather than arguments about whether it is wise or wrong to do or not to do certain things.

The First Amendment is the one that most fully articulates the idea of individualism within the framework of the law of the land. This amendment reads:

The First Amendment: Freedom of Speech, Freedom of Religion, and Separation of Church and State

> Congress shall make no law respecting an establishment of religion, or prohibiting the free exercise thereof; or abridging the freedom of speech, or of the press; or the right of the people peaceably to assemble, and to petition the Government for a redress of grievances.

This list of what has come to be called the First Amendment freedoms has been the basis of enormous controversy. Although it refers only to Congress, the courts have, by easy extension, held that the other branches of government are similarly bound; and the wording of the Fourteenth Amendment has enabled many of the restrictions the First Amendment places on the federal government to be gradually extended to state and local governments as well. A great deal of confusion nevertheless exists about the precise meaning of these restrictions.

The language of the amendment is plain enough, and it conforms with the prejudices of the men who wrote the Constitution. These prejudices were essentially Hobbesian, regarding government as an absolute necessity but only for the maintenance of peace among warring individuals. However, unlike Hobbes, the early American statesmen had learned from bitter experience, both at home and abroad, that unrestrained government was unlikely to confine itself to keeping the peace.

**BOX 15–2
Does the
Fourteenth
Amendment
Incorporate the
Bill of Rights
Freedoms into the
Constitutions of
the States?**

The most comprehensive arguments supporting the total incorporation theory were made in *Adamson* v. *California* (1947). Here the Court's five-man majority refused to upset a state conviction where the appellant argued that the state procedure infringed the Fifth Amendment guarantee against compulsory self-incrimination, which was made applicable to the states through the Fourteenth Amendment. The four dissenters—Justices Hugo Black, William O. Douglas, Frank Murphy, and Wiley B. Rutledge—contended that all the specific guarantees of the first eight amendments should be read into the due process clause of the Fourteenth Amendment and made applicable to the states. Justice Black's dissenting opinion is most often cited in support of this thesis. He maintained that the legislative history of the Fourteenth Amendment, as well as the debates in the state legislatures ratifying it, clearly revealed that the Fourteenth Amendment was designed to make the Bill of Rights applicable to the states. . . . [H]is position was that the framers of the Fourteenth Amendment intended the due process clause to be a shorthand restatement of the specific guarantees of the Bill of Rights. . . . Justice Felix Frankfurter not only questioned Black's reading and interpretation of history but contended that incorporation of the specific guarantees of the Bill of Rights into the due process clause would impart to it a far more expansive meaning than intended in some cases and a more restricted meaning than intended in others. To him, such a construction would also do violence to the principle of federalism upon which the Republic was founded.

—Excerpted from Lucius J. Barker and Twiley W. Barker, Jr., *Civil Liberties and the Constitution: Cases and Commentaries*, 4th ed. (Englewood Cliffs, N.J.: Prentice-Hall, 1982), p. 15.

Governments are sorely tempted, for example, to suppress unfavorable comment about themselves and their policies, not for the sake of peace but merely to keep themselves in power. As a result, the First Amendment was added to the Constitution to guarantee, as absolutely as language will allow, freedom for individuals and the press to speak out against the government and to have such speech freely heard and heeded by others.

The same thing applied to the problem of controlling religion. Hobbes thought that peace could be secured by state establishment and control of one church, prohibiting all others. This solution did not seem to work even in England; but it did not stand a chance of being accepted in America. The Founders knew this and therefore decided in favor of an opposite conclusion—freedom for all faiths with a "wall of separation" (Thomas Jefferson's phrase) between church and state. The general aim was the same as in all the Founders' endeavors: if religion could be kept out of politics, and vice versa, public peace and tranquility, with the maximum personal freedom, would result.

Defining religious freedom and freedom of political expression is not a simple business. For example, traditionally churches and religious groups enjoy tax-exempt status, which means that the public provides them with a healthy subsidy. Churches, after all, use fire and police protection and other public services just as everyone else does. Should this tax exemption apply to profit-making ventures owned by churches as well? Many churches and religious organizations own publishing houses, factories, and motel chains that yield substantial revenue. The Internal Revenue Service has ruled, moreover, that tax exemptions are to be revoked if the church or religious group takes a specific stand on political issues or candidates. Is this reasonable? Should religious organizations or churches be barred from speaking out on such issues as religious education in the schools, abortion, disarmament, or the rights of minorities? Many other issues are raised by the separation clause that demarcates church and state, and these issues frequently arouse bitterness.

On the issues of freedom of speech and press and the right of peaceful assembly, complexities again abound. There must be some limits in even the most freedom-loving community. Libel and slander cannot be permitted, nor incitement to riot. Verbal harassment and obscenity are not protected by the First Amendment either. But who can define these terms with sufficient and lasting precision? Where are the lines to be drawn and how? The anomalies can be very great: we permit some of the most sadistic acts of violence to be seen in movies or on television, but comedian George Carlin is not permitted to utter his seven prohibited words on the radio.[4] Finally, an enormous and essential amount of

---

[4] *Federal Communications Commission* v. *Pacifica Foundation*, 438 U.S. 726 (1978).

public order enforcement is necessary to ensure that meaningful opportunities exist for individuals to speak, publish, and assemble, and only government can provide this.

The Second Amendment and Gun Control

The Second Amendment guarantees the right to keep and bear arms for state militias. There is considerable confusion on this issue because many people interpret the amendment as a guarantee for individuals personally to keep and bear arms. The Supreme Court has ruled that the amendment applies only to state militias and that no challenge can be made against gun control laws based on this constitutional provision (see Box 15–3).[5]

The Third Amendment: Quartering Troops Banned

The Third Amendment prevents the government from quartering soldiers in private homes. In modern times, this provision appears to be of relatively little consequence, although it did reflect a grievance that American colonists held against the British government. It also verifies, for those who would doubt it, that individuals' homes are their castles, and it has been suggested by the Supreme Court as one of the possible constitutional supports for the right of privacy.[6]

Amendments Four, Five, Six, Seven, and Eight: Due Process

The five amendments numbered four through eight most directly seek to restrain the government in its "work" of restraining individuals. These should be looked upon as almost inevitable rules of any highly individualistic society. At the critical point at which government seeks to apprehend persons on suspicion that their acts may have violated some law, the scales are supposed to be weighted against the government by these amendments. Individuals thus threatened are given a number of guarantees that we call "due process," which define how the government is to proceed in order to be fair and just. Although some judges and scholars such as the late Learned Hand would argue to the contrary, the system of legality built upon these five amendments places a high premium on keeping the innocent and unjustly accused free, a higher premium, in fact, than that placed on convicting and incarcerating the guilty.

The guarantees provided by these amendments include the right to be secure in one's own person, house, papers, and effects against unreasonable searches and seizures (the Fourth Amendment); a series of rights in criminal proceedings including the right against self-incrimination (see Box 15–4), the requirement of an indictment and information so that the accused can know what she or he is charged with, and a "double jeopardy" provision that holds that one cannot be accused and made to stand trial more than one time for a single cause (the Fifth

[5] *U.S.* v. *Cruikshank*, 92 U.S. 542 (1876); *U.S.* v. *Miller*, 307 U.S. 174 (1939).
[6] *Griswold* v. *Connecticut*, 381 U.S. 479 (1965).

**BOX 15–3
The Gun Control
Issue**

Humorist Art Buchwald has suggested that the right to keep and bear arms should be given to anyone, as long as he or she agrees to join the state militia. But gun control has been a deadly serious and emotional issue for some years, especially since the assassinations of President John F. Kennedy, Senator Robert F. Kennedy, and civil rights leader Martin Luther King, Jr., in the 1960s. A heightened interest in the issue came in the wake of the attempt on President Ronald Reagan's life in the spring of 1981.

Public opinion polls show some fairly consistent support for the idea of gun control, even though the lobbying efforts of the National Rifle Association have been able to thwart this. In January 1980, a Gallup survey asked whether the laws covering the sale of handguns should be made more strict, less strict, or kept as they are now. The results:

More strict	59%
Less strict	6
Same	29
No opinion	6

Even a National Rifle Association-commissioned poll shows that the public generally favors controls on handguns by 48 to 41 percent. Perhaps the strongest procontrol survey, however, is another January 1980 question asked by Gallup:

In Massachusetts, a law requires that a person who carries a gun outside his home must have a license to do so. Would you approve or disapprove of having such a law in your own state?

Approve	75%
Disapprove	20
No Opinion	5

In the American culture, possession of a gun is more than just having a deadly weapon. A gun is also a symbol, which is apparently important psychologically and philosophically to many individuals. Possession of a gun can be seen to be an important part of the claim that the power of ultimate violence against the state should reside with the individual.

Amendment); the right to a speedy and fair trial, a trial by jury if requested, and the right to confront witnesses and to obtain friendly witnesses (the Sixth Amendment). The Sixth Amendment, as presently interpreted by the Supreme Court, also establishes the right to have a lawyer represent you in criminal proceedings.[7] The right to a jury trial, if desired, in civil cases is insured by the Seventh Amendment, and as-

[7] *Gideon* v. *Wainwright*, 372 U.S. 335 (1963).

BOX 15–4
One of the Least
Understood
Freedoms—the
Fifth Amendment
Right to Silence

The principle of immunity from self-incrimination is expressed and accepted in the Jewish Talmud. The Code of Canon Law of the Catholic Church includes the principle. . . . In the earliest days of the common law, [it] was a recognized principle of law. It was against this background that the men who wrote the Constitution and the Bill of Rights realized the need for expression of the privilege against self-incrimination [and wrote] the Fifth Amendment, the amendment which has become the most maligned part of the Constitution. . . .

. . . the Fifth Amendment is widely regarded today as an obsolete obstacle to law and order. It has become almost indissolubly linked with the image of a guilty man parroting words he does not understand in order to avoid punishment he surely deserves: "I refuse to answer that question on the ground that the answer might tend to incriminate me."

. . . If our primary goal were the punishment of the guilty at all costs, it would be difficult to find . . . justification for this privilege. Without doubt it hinders the conviction of the guilty far more frequently than it protects the rights of the innocent.

. . . The justification for the privilege [rests] upon [the consideration that] it seems basically unfair and unfree to confront a suspect with conviction if he confesses guilt, perjury if he denies guilt, and contempt if he stands mute. Essentially, it is like telling a child that you suspect him of taking your loose change and that you intend to thrash him for stealing if he admits it, for lying if he denies it, and for disobedience if he refuses to tell you whether he took it or not. This is not the way to discipline children, and it is not the way to discipline a free society.

—Edward Bennett Williams, *One Man's Freedom* (New York: Atheneum, 1962), pp. 123–126.

surances against cruel and unusual punishments and excessive bail are established in the Eighth Amendment.

The Ninth Amendment, which has had little application in constitutional law except as a suggested source for the right of privacy, states that no rights listed in the Constitution shall be construed to disparage any other rights "retained by the people."[8] The Tenth Amendment reserves the powers not delegated to the federal government by the Constitution to the states and to the people. This is the famous (or infamous) "states' rights amendment," a provision much celebrated in political rhetoric even though it has lost much of its strength through the gradual encroachments of Washington's power over the past two centuries.

The Ninth and Tenth Amendments

Threats to the Bill of Rights Freedoms

The freedoms outlined in the Bill of Rights make individual living in our society much more tolerable than it might otherwise be. The most cursory review of the various countries of the world and of all the ages of history will show that freedom, in the form of the civil liberties set out in the Bill of Rights, is the exception to the norm, almost an oddity in the course of human events.

However, a variety of evidence from the American experience demonstrates an attachment to human rights that is less consistent in deed than it is in word. The United States has had recurring spasms of bigotry and attempted thought control—the Alien and Sedition Acts during the first Adams administration, the pre-Civil War "Know Nothing" Movement, which sought to close off America only to "natives," the Ku Klux Klan, which grew to significant strength in the early decades of the twentieth century and still persists here and there to this day, the great "Red Scare" after World War I, and the even more frightening specter of McCarthyism after World War II. McCarthyism is defined by the Seventh Merriam-Webster Dictionary as "the use of tactics involving personal attacks on individuals by means of widely publicized indiscriminate allegations . . . on the basis of unsubstantiated charges." In addition, American society has established an unenviable record of racial and sexual discrimination that gives pause to anyone contemplating the nation's commitment to civil liberties.

Psychologists and philosophers have also contributed a great deal of insight into questions of individual commitment to freedom. Erich Fromm's *The Fear of Freedom* tells us just what its title implies—that the choices given to some people by their legal freedoms prove to be discomfiting and even threatening.[9] Theodor Adorno's study *The Au-*

---

[8] Suggested as a basis for privacy in *Griswold* v. *Connecticut*, cited above.
[9] Erich Fromm, *The Fear of Freedom* (London: Kegan Paul, 1941).

thoritarian Personality demonstrates that there are personalities scattered through the population who respond to the cues and symbols of authoritarianism and who could be expected to support antilibertarian causes (see Box 15–5).[10] The controversial work of Stanley Milgram points out how ordinary citizens can be goaded quite easily into actions that are inhumane simply because of the directions issued by an "authority." The subjects of Milgram's experiments, according to his book *Obedience to Authority*, proved to be altogether willing to administer pain to paid actors who feigned being attached to electric shock machines.[11] Finally, Raul Hilberg, though he concentrates on German rather than American society, has come up with some startling findings. He was able to look into the minds of such people as civil servants and railroad employees to show how "ordinary" events such as the construction of signals to facilitate the movement of rail cars full of Jews and other victims to Hitler's death camps are viewed in an ordinary way by ordinary people. These people bowed to authority and never questioned its morality or its legitimacy. To believe that Americans are immune to such thoughts or conduct would be the height of folly. Poll after poll demonstrates, for example, that Bill of Rights freedoms in America are neither well-understood nor well-supported.[12]

The First Amendment Freedoms: Interpretations and Analyses

Free Speech

It is fair to say that the entire structure of the Bill of Rights freedoms ultimately rests upon the First Amendment, and especially on this amendment's protection of free speech. Without this basic framework, the other freedoms in the first ten amendments and in the post-Civil War additions—the thirteenth, fourteenth, and fifteenth amendments—would be meaningless.

Aside from making us all feel better and certainly more comfortable when talking, why should we support free expression? Seventeenth-century English poet John Milton, English philosopher John Stuart Mill, and Supreme Court Justice Oliver Wendell Holmes all provided a famous answer. There should be a competition of all ideas, a marketplace of ideas, that will enable us to discern, after a proper length of time and debate, which ones are valid and which are false. Of course,

---

[10] Theodor W. Adorno, *The Authoritarian Personality* (New York: Harper & Row, 1950).

[11] Stanley Milgram, *Obedience to Authority: An Experimental View* (New York: Harper & Row, 1974).

[12] Raul Hilberg, "German Railroads/Jewish Souls," *Society*, **14**:60–74 (November-December 1976); the Bill of Rights polls have been conducted on a more or less systematic basis over the years by Gallup, Harris, and other polling organizations. The first of these took place on the campus of Purdue University in 1948.

**BOX 15–5
Characteristics of
the Authoritarian
Personality**

1. Conventionalism. Rigid adherence to conventional middle-class values.

2. Authoritarian Submission. Submissive, uncritical attitude toward idealized moral authorities of the ingroup.

3. Authoritarian Aggression. Tendency to be on the lookout for, and to condemn, reject and punish people who violate conventional values.

4. Anti-intraception. Opposition to the subjective, the imaginative, the tender-minded.

5. Superstition and Stereotypy. The belief in mystical determinants of the individual's fate; the disposition to think in rigid categories.

6. Power and Toughness. Preoccupation with the dominance-submission, strong-weak, leader-follower dimension; identification with power figures; exaggerated assertion of strength and toughness.

7. Destructiveness and Cynicism. Generalized hostility, vilification of the human.

8. Projectivity. The disposition to believe that wild and dangerous things go on in the world; the projection outward of unconscious emotional impulses.

9. Sex. Ego-alien sexuality; exaggerated concern with sexual "goings on," and punitiveness toward violators of sex mores.

—Nevitt Sanford, "The Approach to 'The Authoritarian Personality,'" in *A Source Book for the Study of Personality and Politics*, Fred I. Greenstein and Michael Lerner, eds. (Reading, Mass: Addison-Wesley, 1976), p. 317.

there are problems with this proposition. Who is to police the marketplace? Is there any guarantee that truth will emerge victorious in time for urgent decisions to be made? Liberal Democrats believe that, more often than not, these questions can be answered positively. At all events, the alternatives to a free market of ideas look grim and unacceptable.

The most important test of free speech seems to occur when controversial ideas are presented or examined. Very few of us become upset about mundane issues of little or no controversy. Issues of great moment are another matter, however. The war in Vietnam, for example, the focus of the protest in the Des Moines schools case, was a matter of great controversy at the time.

As important as it is, free speech has not always prevailed in court tests. A number of factors and considerations—national security, public safety, the use of "fighting words," the dangers created by stirring up an audience, the use of allegedly obscene materials, libel, and conflict with other Bill of Rights freedoms—can curtail the exercise of speech. In one sense this is rather remarkable, because the language of the First Amendment—"Congress shall make no law . . . "—can be interpreted as clear and unqualified. It was indeed this very interpretation that was placed on free speech issues by Supreme Court Justice Hugo Black, who served on the bench from 1937 until 1971. Black read the Constitution in literal terms, and so he held that "no law" governing free speech meant precisely that. He rejected the idea of balancing free speech rights against any other considerations, even though the balancing view has been dominant throughout the history of the court's involvement with the First Amendment.

The "Clear and Present Danger" Test

The need to balance free speech against other considerations was formally recognized by the Supreme Court's decision in *Schenck* v. *United States* (1919).[13] In this case the court reviewed the conviction of a Socialist for passing out leaflets urging resistance to the World War I draft. It upheld Schenck's conviction, asserting with Justice Oliver Wendell Holmes, Jr., who wrote the majority opinion, that the applicable test to be used was one of "clear and present danger." The court felt that national security considerations overshadowed the First Amendment in this case because of the existence of a "clear and present danger" created by such activities.

Since the *Schenck* case, free speech has been subjected to both broadening and narrowing interpretations. The 1920s saw more restrictive tests applied than even the "clear and present danger" test called for[14]; the 1930s, on the other hand, saw Justice (later Chief Justice) Harlan Stone pronounce that free speech held a "preferred" position among all other rights.[15] But national security concerns have continued to clash with First Amendment protection. The Smith Act, passed by Congress in 1940 and upheld by the Supreme Court in a 1951 ruling,[16] made it illegal to advocate the overthrow of the government by force or violence, and this law was systematically used to prosecute Communist Party leaders and members. The effects of the Smith Act were essentially nullified, however, by a later decision (1957) in which the court

---

[13] 249 U.S. 47.
[14] *Gitlow* v. *New York*, 208 U.S. 652 (1925), *Whitney* v. *California*, 274 U.S. 357 (1927).
[15] *U.S.* v. *Carolene Products*, 304 U.S. 144 (1938).
[16] *Dennis* v. *U.S.*, 341 U.S. 494 (1951).

held that mere "abstract advocacy" of overthrowing the government, without being combined with some threatening action, could not be prosecuted under the First Amendment.[17] On this collision of national security considerations with the assertion of free speech, the present status of constitutional law is still found to be one of balancing interests in a manner akin to "clear and present danger." Free speech is not held by the court to apply to just any action claimed for it; publicly burning a draft card, for example, has not been held to be protected by a claim of symbolic free speech.[18] On the other hand, the Des Moines students prevailed with their arm bands intact, and an allegedly inflammatory

[17] *Yates* v. *U.S.*, 354 U.S. 298 (1957); also, *Brandenburg* v. *Ohio*, 395 U.S. 444 (1969).
[18] *U.S.* v. *O'Brien*, 391 U.S. 367 (1968).

> Corporations are a legal fiction that makes them into persons; but they are not real persons and have therefore never had Bill of Rights freedoms in the same way or to the same degree that real persons possess them. In recent years, however, the Supreme Court has moved to place corporations within the sphere of Bill of Rights protection. One of the many notable of these decisions, handed down in 1980, approved a public utility's practice of including inserts when it mailed bills to its customers. These inserts discussed issues of public policy, stressing the utility's point of view. Because utilities are granted monopoly status by the government in exchange for government regulation of their rates, a consumer group argued, the inclusion of this propaganda was at public expense. Free speech is all right, in other words, if another group does not have to pay for it. Justice Lewis Powell, who wrote the majority opinion, rejected this argument, stating that "Even if a short exposure to [these] views may offend the sensibilities of some customers, the ability of government to shut off discourse solely to protect others from hearing it [is] dependent upon a showing that substantial privacy interests are being invaded in an essentially intolerable manner."
> —*Consolidated Edison* v. *Public Service Commission*, 447 U. S.—(1980).
>
> Should consumers be required to finance the free expression of corporations in this way? One of the inserts stated that "independence is still a goal, and nuclear power is needed to win the battle." But is the *content* of the corporate message the issue?

**BOX 15–6
Do Corporations
Have Free Speech
Rights?**

(The Journal-Gazette,
Fort Wayne, Indiana.)

statement against the draft, written on a publicly displayed jacket, also
received Bill of Rights protection.[19]

**Public Safety and
"Fighting Words"**

Public safety considerations prevail over free speech advocacy in some
situations, particularly when public speakers, usually espousing an
unpopular cause, arouse a crowd to violence or the threat of violence;
quite often, this threat is directed against the speaker. One of the most
prominent speech-limiting doctrines of the Supreme Court has been the
"fighting words" rule, which holds that speech is not protected when it
can be shown to endanger public safety.[20] But this doctrine seems to
have had less applicability in the 1960s and 1970s than formerly. The

[19] *Cohen* v. *California,* 402 U.S. 15 (1971).
[20] *Chaplinsky* v. *New Hampshire,* 315 U.S. 568 (1942).

public safety balancing test often seems to be one of practical problems involved in law enforcement. It is much simpler for the police to arrest a controversial speaker or, say, a group of fifteen or twenty Nazis or Ku Klux Klan members than it is to deal with a crowd of several hundred people who are offended by the speaker or group. The civil rights "revolution" in the South in the 1960s showed, however, that the court was not going to tolerate overt and official actions against free speech in the name of public safety.[21] And even the argument of the right of privacy, which has sometimes been tied to the public safety objection, has not prevented the victory of free speech claimants who choose to picket and demonstrate in front of the homes of public officials.[22]

Obscenity questions are among the most difficult of free speech issues because of the daunting task of establishing objective standards. Censorship of books and motion pictures by local governments was at one time not unusual, and it still occurs today. The pace and frequency of such activities has in fact increased since 1980 (see Box 15–7). Movies appear to fare a little better, because the Supreme Court has established procedures for censorship that are so strict that it is not practical to use them.[23] A series of important cases in the late 1950s and early 1960s brought the Supreme Court to the point of declaring that whereas obscenity is not protected by the First Amendment, the proof of obscenity is that the item in question must have no socially redeeming importance, it must be "patently offensive," and, to the average person, applying community standards, the dominant theme of the material must appeal to a "prurient interest." The court also indicated that a book must fail all three of these tests to lose Bill of Rights protection.[24] In 1969, the court also ruled that a person has the right to possess and view pornographic materials in the privacy of the home, but this decision has had a narrow application in practice.[25]

All of these obscenity rulings were made by the Warren Court. The Burger Court, which came into existence in 1969, imposed a sharp change in the direction of policy on obscenity. In 1973 it held, in *Miller* v. *California*, that obscenity is found if the material in question *lacks* serious literary, artistic, political, or scientific value.[26] The "patent offensiveness" test has been retained, but the matter of community standards has been defined in terms of the local community. This definition and the lack of value test are expected to ease the task of prosecutors.

---

[21] *Edwards* v. *South Carolina*, 372 U.S. 229 (1963); *Cox* v. *Louisiana*, 379 U.S. 536 (1965).
[22] *Organization for a Better Austin* v. *Keefe*, 402 U.S. 15 (1971); *Gregory* v. *Chicago* 394 U.S. 111 (1969) also touches on this issue.
[23] *Freedman* v. *Maryland*, 380 U.S. 51 (1965).
[24] *Roth* v. *U.S.*, 354 U.S. 476 (1957); the *Fanny Hill* case, 383 U.S. 413 (1966).
[25] *Stanley* v. *Georgia*, 394 U.S. 557 (1969).
[26] 413 U.S. 15 (1973).

But whatever tests are applied, the question of obscenity seems a fairly elusive one.

Libel and Defamation   Libel and defamation cases are often in the news, and they supply dramatic headlines. One of the most celebrated cases of recent years involved the entertainer Carole Burnett, who sued a weekly newspaper, *National Enquirer*, and received a settlement in 1981 of $800,000, an uncommon and unusual victory. But what is the basic law of libel? In the first place, truth is always regarded as an absolute defense in a libel suit and has been so regarded for centuries as a legacy of English common law. But English and American law diverge greatly today on the question of libel. In England, public officials sue their critics on a fairly regular basis and often win. In the United States, this is nearly impossible to accomplish. Under the *New York Times* rule, a public official or public figure must show malice as motivation for the slander directed against her or him, which is very difficult to do.[27] This may be just as well, though it certainly imposes hardships, for it gives a breadth and depth to the definition of free speech that does not exist in other countries. This is why Ms. Burnett's victory was so unusual. She is obviously a public figure, but in her case she was able to prove malice to the satisfaction of the trial court.

The free exercise of religion is also protected by the First Amendment. Ordinarily, this has required the government to give religious activities and practices a wide berth. A number of practices in the Supreme Court's history, however, have been judged illegal by the court, including polygamy, inhumane administration of church-affiliated homes for youths and the elderly, and the use of poisonous snakes in religious services. The mass murders and suicides that took place at Jonestown, Guyana, in 1978 vividly raised the public question about claims of bizarre cults that they hold the status of a "religion." In addition, some tax-avoidance schemes involving large-scale certifications of "clergy" have failed to receive legal approval.

Free Exercise of Religion

Claims directed against state interference with religion are sometimes successful. A member of Jehovah's Witnesses whose children were expelled from school for refusing to salute the flag prevailed in a landmark 1943 case. In setting out the court's opinion, Justice Robert H. Jackson said:

> If there is any fixed star in our constitutional constellation, it is that no official, high or petty, can prescribe what shall be orthodox in politics, nationalism, religion or other matters of opinion, or force citizens to confess by word or act their faiths . . . [28]

The court has also permitted Amish parents to remove their children from the public schools after eighth grade despite the existence of a state law requiring ten years of education. This was done because the Amish faith stresses only the basic elements of education and regards any other exposure of children to worldly influences as detrimental to their religion and their way of life.[29]

[27] *New York Times* v. *Sullivan*, 376 U.S. 254 (1964).
[28] *West Virginia Board of Education* v. *Barnette*, 319 U.S. 624 (1943).
[29] *Wisconsin* v. *Yoder*, 406 U.S. 205 (1972).

The military draft is often regarded as a religious issue. In most cases, exemptions are now granted by Selective Service legislation to conscientious objectors to war by permitting them to render alternative service. But these laws did not appear to extend to objectors who lacked religious training or belief. This issue was joined by the Supreme Court in 1970 in *Welsh* v. *United States*,[30] when it held that sincere moral and ethical beliefs against war, even though they are not religiously based, permit exemption from the draft. This exemption does not apply, however to objectors to particular wars such as Vietnam.[31]

The federal government has regulated admissions policies of religious schools by denying tax-exempt status to those that discriminate on racial grounds. This has been done since 1974 because of an IRS ruling. Early in 1982, President Reagan had the ruling set aside. An almost instant protest of this governmental subsidizing of discrimination was heard, and the protest had a great impact on the media. As a result, the president asked Congress to pass a statute that would have the effect of reinstating the tax ruling. Reagan's explanation of his action, accepted only skeptically by the media representatives at a press conference, was that he really wanted a statute, not administrative law, to govern tax-exempt status. A bill has been introduced to effect this, but the tardiness of the president's explanation for his action hurt his credibility on the issue. The constitutionality of denying tax exemption for discrimination has been challenged, but the indirectness of the coercive aspects of such a law seems to answer this challenge.

The Separation Clause   The nonestablishment of religion clause, or separation clause, of the First Amendment is a perennial controversy. Religious liberty and nonestablishment are treated by the amendment and by the Supreme Court as two sides of the same coin. It is sometimes argued that the phrase "separation of church and state" is not actually found in the Constitution in those words, but then neither are such terms as "federalism," "freedom of association," "right to privacy," "self-incrimination," or "interstate commerce." Controversy has swirled about the nonestablishment clause, nonetheless, and continues to the present day. Moreover, the Supreme Court took its time in coming around to a definitive interpretation. Such a decision was made only in 1947, a century and a half after the Constitution came into existence.

The court chose to rely on the intentions of the Founders. The Constitutional Convention was clearly aware of the religious and philosophical differences among and within the various states. Colonial experience had provided the delegates with the Rhode Island example of tolerance and, more recently, the Virginia example of disestablishment

[30] 398 U.S. 333 (1970).
[31] *Gillette* v. *U.S.* 401 U.S. 437 (1971).

of the Anglican Church. More important, the delegates recognized the interdependence of the principles of religious freedom, freedom of thought and action, and separation of church and state. The Philadelphia Convention believed that a variety of evils would ensue from governmental meddling with religion, and among the proofs of this is the banning of religious tests for public office by Article VI. The intentions of the Founders, according to Thomas Jefferson in a statement made while he was president, was to build a "wall" between church and state. The court relies on this statement in *Everson* v. *Board of Education* (1947).[32] Justice Hugo Black, stating the court's opinion, held that

> Neither a state nor the Federal Government can set up a church. Neither can pass laws which aid one religion, aid all religions, or prefer one religion over another. Neither can force nor influence a person to go to or to remain away from a church against his will or force him to profess a belief or disbelief in any religion. No person can be punished for entertaining or professing religious beliefs or disbeliefs.[33]

The cases decided by the court since 1947 have been no less controversial than *Everson*. "Released time" programs that permit public school students to attend religious classes outside of school, but during school hours, have been upheld.[34] State aid to parochial schools is permitted, but only in severely limited forms such as the loan of textbooks or the administration of driver education or testing programs. Bible reading for devotional purposes and recitation of the Lord's Prayer in unison is not permitted in public schools by the ruling in *Abington School District* v. *Schempp*.[35] But perhaps the most controversial of all court rulings in favor of the nonestablishment clause is *Engel* v. *Vitale*, the 1962 "school prayer" decision.[36] This has brought on a concerted movement for legislation or a constitutional amendment, or both, to override the court. Many politicians have campaigned on this issue, decrying the judicial branch's denial of the right of children to pray in the public schools. But the court has never denied such a right, and children are quite free to pray in school. The *Engel* decision merely banned the practice of state-written and administered prayers, such as the New York State prayer that was the subject of the case. In the meantime, the nonestablishment clause seems to show clearly that governments, whether state or federal, can seek only secular (or civil, as opposed to ecclesiastical) ends and can achieve these only through secular means.

[32] 330 U.S. 1 (1947).
[33] 330 U.S. 1 (1947).
[34] *Zorach* v. *Clauson*, 343 U.S. 306 (1952).
[35] 374 U.S. 203 (1963).
[36] 370 U.S. 421 (1962).

**BOX 15–8
You Can Be Fired
for Your Political
Views**

A few years back, a private employer in New York fired one of his employees, whom he knew to be in favor of and working for the impeachment of President Nixon. There was no claim that the employee's political activity after hours was in any way affecting his performance on the job; rather he was fired simply because the employer didn't like his politics.

For the dismissed employee, the consequences were shattering, far more severe, for example, than an arrest by the police for taking part in a demonstration. [He came] to the New York Civil Liberties Union, but we couldn't help because the employer was private. No law—not the Constitution, nor any statute, not any regulation—limits the discretion of private employers to fire employees because of their politics.

. . . if a *public* employer like the post office or the police department or a public school had fired one of its employees for supporting the impeachment of President Nixon, it would have been possible to challenge the dismissal. . . . The Constitution, and, particularly, the Bill of Rights, limits *governmental* power.

But private employers are not agents of any government, and, therefore, are not limited by the Constitution. So . . . the employee has no legal recourse. . . . The ACLU has committed itself to work for the establishment of free speech in the work place.

—*Civil Liberties*, **327**: 8 (April 1979).

**Freedom of Assembly
and Freedom of
Association**

Freedom of assembly and of association are also valued First Amendment rights, as well as the right "to petition the Government for a redress of grievances." Most of the constitutional law cases that arise under these provisions involve challenges to governmental administration of parade permits, coercive activities in connection with demonstrations, marches, or rock concerts, and police practices. The freedom of association, though it is not explicitly spelled out in the First Amendment, is inferred because of the freedoms of speech, assembly, and petition. Some of the most important cases on association have involved the activities of the National Association for the Advancement of Colored People (NAACP) in the South, when it was faced with state demands for its membership lists. It successfully resisted these demands, with Supreme Court help, on the grounds that this could expose its members to social and economic coercion.[37]

[37] *NAACP* v. *Alabama*, 377 U.S. 288 (1964), *Gibson* v. *Florida Legislative Committee*, 372 U.S. 539 (1963).

Senator Jesse Helms, Republican of North Carolina, has introduced a bill that would remove Supreme Court jurisdiction from school prayer cases.

Equal Protection of the Laws

The second sentence of Section 1 of the Fourteenth Amendment, ratified in 1868, reads as follows:

The Due Process and Equal Protection Requirements of the Fourteenth Amendment

> No State shall make or enforce any law which shall abridge the privileges or immunities of citizens of the United States; nor shall any State deprive any person of life, liberty, or property, without due process of law, nor deny to any person within its jurisdiction the equal protection of the laws.

The original purpose of the Fourteenth Amendment as a whole was to guarantee the status of former slaves in the Southern states as citizens entitled to all the legal protections and assurances of Americans everywhere. But no sentence in the Constitution has been more utilized by lawyers and courts than the sentence of the amendment just quoted, and it has been applied to people and problems far beyond the concerns of its drafters. The "due process" clause in particular has been seized upon in a broad range of cases to protect the rights and properties of both individuals and business corporations against governments seeking to police their behavior on behalf of the public welfare. It has therefore been an especially fruitful source of legal opinion for those wishing to dissolve "political" questions about what does—or does not—promote the public good into procedural questions about whether governments have the right to restrict individual behavior with one or another measure. On these grounds the Supreme Court invalidated a host of social reform laws in the period between the turn of the century and the Great Depression of the 1930s. This approach came to a head especially in the Franklin Roosevelt administration, when the Court used it to thwart some of Roosevelt's aims of recovery and reform. Mythically perceiving these as remedies for the nation's economy and general welfare, Roosevelt ran into the court's ideological and Liberal Democratic attachment to personal due process rights.

Equality and Equal Protection

The Fourteenth Amendment can be seen to have taken its place alongside the Bill of Rights as a sanctuary of Liberal Democratic values. In recent decades this has become even more abundantly true because of the court's reliance on the next clause of the sentence we have quoted, the "equal protection" clause.

"Equal protection of the laws" is a nearly perfect rendering of the Liberal Democratic tradition's core value, and it is nearly a perfect bridge between the nation's mythic demands for equality of membership and status in the body politic and the procedural demands for equality of rights and treatment.

The idea of equality in America has had a variety of interpretations placed upon it. Some of these seek or assume equality of result while others seek or assume equality of treatment and equality of opportunity. Not everyone agrees that even the latter are desirable. The noted conservative columnist and editor William F. Buckley, Jr., reflecting on the admissions policies of Yale University, his alma mater, complains that a "son of an alumnus, who goes to private preparatory school, now has less of a chance of getting in than some boy from P.S. 109 somewhere."[38]

Even when it is assumed that social equality and equality before the law are desirable goals, it is not always clear what this means. The old saw tells us that both the rich and the poor are denied the right to sleep under bridges in the city of Paris, and many civil rights leaders have asked what good it does blacks to be finally admitted to hotels or restaurants that most blacks cannot afford. Many of the tests of the equal protection clause of the Fourteenth Amendment, which is the most

---

[38] Quoted in Charles L. Markmann, *The Buckleys: A Family Examined* (New York: William Morrow, 1973), p. 264.

likely basis for suits alleging discrimination or unequal treatment, are based on arguments that a law or its administration have created a "suspect classification" of certain people. If this can be proved, litigation may be successful. On the other hand, equality claims can be denied when government classifications make rationally designed distinctions between people (such as a law that says all residents of a county can vote after living there for six months but not until then) or make no distinctions at all.

The most important equal protection case of this century is *Brown* v. *Board of Education,* handed down by the Supreme Court in 1954.[39] This ruling invalidated school segregation laws by overturning the "separate but equal" doctrine sanctioned by the court in 1896. (See Chapter 5 for another discussion of this case.) The full effects of *Brown* were not felt until the passage of the 1964 Civil Rights Act, which withdrew federal funding support from any school system that practiced segregation. The 1964 act also provided for desegregation of interstate travel facilities including restaurants, hotels, and bus terminals, but this part of the law was based on the much stronger commerce clause of the Constitution rather than on any Bill of Rights or equal protection provision. The 1964 act has also been the basis for a great deal of the equal employment protection given to minorities today, because it bans discrimination in hiring and in other personnel policies.

Equal Protection and the Supreme Court

Much less successful have been the desegregation efforts aimed at housing patterns and at schools that remain segregated because of these patterns. Many, perhaps most of these patterns have involved Northern cities. Segregation based on residential patterns is commonly referred to as *de facto* segregation, as opposed to the *de jure,* or legally based, segregation that existed in the South. Federal and occasionally state courts have ordered crosstown busing as a remedy to the problem of inequality in education. Busing has proved to be very unpopular, however, and has often met massive resistance from parents who withdraw their children from the public school system affected. In some large cities, even busing is not seen as a cure by civil rights activists because minority students have become an overwhelmingly dominant percentage of the student population in the school system. Attempts to merge inner-city and suburban school districts have seldom proved successful as a remedy for this condition, and the Burger Court has ruled against equal protection claims aimed at crossdistrict busing that would involve suburban schools. The court has ruled that the suburbs cannot be shown to be responsible for the segregated character of central cities.[40]

Suburbs and other segregated areas thus continue to remain isolated

---

[39] 347 U.S. 483 (1954).
[40] *Milliken* v. *Bradley,* 418 U.S. 717 (1974).

through their own efforts and, to no small degree, with the help of the court. It has been difficult, as Chapter 5 points out, for civil rights litigants to obtain standing to sue in order to bring about changes in housing patterns in large metropolitan areas.[41] The singularly successful desegregation-in-housing suit in the Burger Court era, *Hills* v. *Gatreaux*, a 1976 case, saw a high standard of proof of discrimination required by the "affirmative action in housing" program that the *Hills* ruling helped to create in the Chicago area.[42] This establishes goals and recommended numbers of minority residents for certain suburban areas. It is the only program of its kind anywhere in the country, however. The Department of Housing and Urban Development (HUD) offers a program of assistance to metropolitan areas called the Housing Opportunity Plan, which is designed to break residential patterns of segregation. So far, the program has had no takers because no local government has applied for this assistance.[43] Once again, we see a great gap between mythic aspirations and the actual operation of the law.

Affirmative Action and Equal Employment Opportunity

When discrimination in hiring was outlawed by the 1964 Civil Rights Act, this law also made a special point that universities, federal contractors, and other recipients of federal aid could not discriminate in their hiring or personnel policies. But over the years, any number of private and government employers have established affirmative action programs that mandate a preferred position in hiring for minorities and for women. This has been done in spite of a provision in the act that is aimed specifically at *not* requiring any preferential treatment for minorities and also not requiring an adjustment of numbers in a work force to correct racial imbalance. Critics of affirmative action claim that it actually thwarts the intent of the 1964 act, which was to end discrimination on behalf of any person or group; affirmative action, they say, amounts to "discrimination in reverse." Proponents of affirmative action argue that many of these critics never worried about discrimination until it became a war cry of groups that have historically been privileged. And many American Jews, mindful of the discriminatory quota systems used against them in the past by universities, employers, and others, have pointed out the dangers of the "numbers game" of requiring so many of this group and so many of that to be hired or promoted.

The issue came to a head in two recent Supreme Court decisions. In the 1978 case of *Regents of the University of California* v. *Bakke*, a white male applicant to the University of California medical school at Davis,

---

[41] *Warth* v. *Seldin*, 422 U.S. 490 (1975).

[42] 425 U.S. 284 (1976); Gerald L. Houseman, "Access of Minorities to the Suburbs: An Inventory of Policy Approaches," *Urban and Social Change Review,* **14**: 11–20 (Winter 1981).

[43] Houseman, "Access of Minorities to the Suburbs."

who was refused admission even though his admission test scores were higher than those of some minority applicants who were admitted, charged that his refusal was unconstitutional under the Fourteenth Amendment's equal protection clause and illegal under the 1964 act. Sixteen of the one hundred available openings had been set aside by the University for minority applicants. The Supreme Court, by a 5–4 vote, ordered Bakke to be admitted. The decision is not a very clear one, because the court, while it condemned the use of specific numbers, said that universities could give preferential admissions to minorities as long as a rigid quota formula was not followed. The court also noted the important, or potentially important, fact that the medical school also set aside thirteen places for discretionary admissions. These admissions presumably worked to the advantage of the more privileged groups who have benefited from discrimination in the past, although there was no data on this.[44] In the 1979 case of *United Steelworkers of America* v. *Weber*, a white employee of Kaiser Aluminum challenged the company's training program, which was developed along affirmative action lines as a part of the union-management contract. The company had agreed to eliminate racial imbalance in its training program by reserving 50 percent of the training positions for black workers. Citing the antidiscrimination requirement of the 1964 act as Bakke had done but also focusing on the specifically stated nonrequirement of preferential treatment, Weber pointed out that he had more seniority than several blacks admitted to the program. In a 5–2 decision against Weber, the court pointed out that the training program was a private and voluntary arrangement that was not in conflict with the 1964 act's prohibition of preferential arrangements; and it was in harmony with the spirit of the act's intention, which is to erase racial discrimination from employment practices in America. The court also pointed out that Weber was not really penalized by the agreement because it did not call for him to be fired and replaced by a member of a minority group.[45] At the present time, affirmative action is considered constitutional as long as there are no rigid quotas established for its enforcement; at the same time, privately developed plans, even when they establish numbers, are beyond the reach of the act and are considered constitutional.

Debate will continue over equal employment, affirmative action, educational opportunity, and other Fourteenth Amendment issues. But is the Fourteenth Amendment adequate as a guarantor of equal protection? Certainly blacks and other minorities can argue that they have still to achieve the full benefits of equal protection, and civil libertarians have pointed out what they feel is a need to "federalize" fully the Bill of Rights through the Fourteenth Amendment.

Is The Fourteenth Amendment Adequate?

[44] 438 U.S. 265 (1978).
[45] 443 U.S. 193 (1979).

In addition to these dissatisfactions, it is apparent that the womens' movement in America does not regard the Fourteenth Amendment as an adequate guarantor or an adequate expression of the rights of women. The Equal Rights Amendment (ERA), introduced into every Congress since the early 1920s, was passed in 1972 and sent to the states for ratification. Its terse language reads: "Equality of rights under the law shall not be denied or abridged by the United States or by any State on account of sex." Although this language seems simple enough, no one can say with certainty what the course of statutory or case law developments would have been had the ERA been passed. It might have been symbolically important, however, for American women to have had this amendment written into the Constitution. Thirty-five states, three short of the necessary three fourths, ratified the amendment as of 1981; but resistance to the ERA from the political Right was too strong and a 1982 deadline to gain the final ratifications was not met.

Other groups in American society—the elderly and the physically handicapped, to cite just two examples—may also feel that the Constitution and our laws are inadequate in affording equal protection. Some gains have recently been registered by these groups, but they have been

Rights of the physically limited appear to be weakening as a result of Reagan Administration ideas for changing the Rehabilitation Act of 1973.

slow in coming. Achieving enforceability of the Rehabilitation Act of 1973 required a great deal of lobbying as well as some embarrassing demonstrations at the home of Joseph Califano, then secretary of Health, Education and Welfare (now Health and Human Services) in the early days of the Carter administration. Finally, in April 1977, Califano issued orders to implement the act, which states that "no otherwise qualified handicapped individual . . . shall, solely by reason of his handicap, be excluded from the participation in, be denied the benefits of, or be subjected to discrimination under any program or activity receiving federal financial assistance."[46] Much rebuilding, ramp-building, curb-smoothing, and other work has been carried out to comply with this

[46] Rehabilitation Act of 1973 (Public Law 93–112 as amended by Public Law 93–516).

BOX 15–9
The Coming Police State?

Plainly stated, my thesis is that the United States today possesses the intelligence apparatus of a police state. This apparatus is not something of the future; it exists today as a loose coalition of federal, state, municipal, and military agencies. Together, these law enforcement, counterintelligence, and internal security agencies have developed to the point where authoritarian government is now an operational possibility.

I do not mean to suggest that the emergency (sic) of this domestic intelligence community has turned the United States into a police state. On the contrary, I find it somewhat paradoxical that as this apparatus has proliferated, the civil liberties of most Americans have also grown. The reason for this apparent contradiction may be that the men who have developed these agencies are, by and large, decent and well-intentioned men. However, the fact that we may trust them is no guarantee that the apparatus which they have created will not someday come under the control of others for whom the investigatory power is a weapon to be wielded against political and personal foes. As . . . Justice Brandeis once wrote: "Experience should teach us to be most on our guard to protect liberty when the government's purposes are beneficient. . . . The greatest dangers to liberty lurk in the insidious encroachment by men of zeal, well-meaning, but without understanding". . . [*Olmstead* v. *U.S.* (1928)].

—Christopher H. Pyle, in Richard M. Pious, ed., *Civil Rights and Liberties in the 1970s* (New York: Random House, 1973), pp. 185–186.

**BOX 15-10
A Brief Guide to
the Law of Search
and Seizure**

To claim a violation of the Fourth Amendment, you must find evidence of *state action*—by a federal agent, a local police officer, a public servant. . . . Searches by private parties may invade your privacy but they do not violate your constitutional rights unless the action is taken in behalf of the state. Searches by the managers of a . . . sports arena, by an airline, by a hotel manager, by a landlord, or by a neighbor do not raise constitutional issues. . . . [Note—They could, of course, raise such issues as burglary or false imprisonment.]

Under the Fourth Amendment, a search may be conducted by a representative of the government only if it is reasonable or pursuant to a search warrant based on probable cause of criminal activity.

A police officer may always search your body or premises with your consent, as long as the consent is given freely, clearly, explicitly, without duress, and with the knowledge that you need not consent if you do not wish to. . . .

If an officer shows up at your front door and announces that he or she wants to look around and you agree, the courts often find that kind of consent invalid because it was by implication coercive.

An officer may search your person incident to an arrest (but) An arrest may not be used simply as an excuse for a general search, nor may the officer search for evidence of a crime different from the one for which the arrest was made.

The U.S. Supreme Court has permitted the search of the driver of an automobile stopped for a minor traffic offense. The search is allowed to protect the arresting officer, to prevent escape or suicide, or to prevent the destruction of evidence. The officer may use force if necessary and may seize just about anything. Officers are also permitted to "stop and frisk" a suspicious person on the street, only for purposes of "patting down" the person for possible weapons. If the officer comes across evidence of a crime—illegal drugs, for instance—the officer may seize the evidence.

An officer may search your premises if there is no time to get a warrant because there is an emergency, if he or she is in hot pursuit of a suspect, if there's reason to believe that evidence will be destroyed or removed, or if an arrest occurs within the premises. Viewing your premises by binoculars,

**BOX 15–10
A Brief Guide to
the Law of Search
and Seizure
(Continued)**

flashlights, or similar electronic devices is not a search, as long as there is no expectation of privacy where you are.

There is no need to get a warrant to search a vehicle, in most cases, because it can easily be moved beyond the reach of the officer.

In all cases of warrantless searches, there must be probable cause to believe that a person has committed, is committing, or is about to commit a crime.

All other searches must be conducted with a valid search warrant approved by a local or federal judge or magistrate, based on affadavits of facts. . . .

—Robert Ellis Smith, *Privacy: How to Protect What's Left of It* (Garden City: Anchor Press, Doubleday, 1979), pp. 309–310.

directive. But the Reagan administration has indicated that it wishes to ease these requirements, including one that calls for equal access to public transportation facilities. Perhaps just as depressing is the heavy blow suffered by some of the handicapped in *Southeastern Community College* v. *Davis,* handed down by the Supreme Court in 1979. After all the difficulty of obtaining Secretary Califano's agreement to enforce the Rehabilitation Act, the legal definition of "handicapped" turns out to be quite severely qualified. In this case, a person with a hearing disability was denied the opportunity to undertake an education as a registered nurse. Her deafness was held not to be a sufficient condition for her to qualify as a "handicapped individual" within the meaning of the act, and her denial of admission was therefore not considered discriminatory.[47]

Supreme Court decisions and the domain of public law, despite some rather obvious threads and guidelines that appear from time to time, still contain highly subjective elements that define what equal protection is and to whom it shall apply.

Privacy

**Privacy of the Home
and the Person**

The Constitution provides for privacy of the home only by virtue of the Fourth Amendment's prohibition of unlawful searches and seizures (see Box 15–10). As with many other areas of the law, however, the right to privacy of persons and their abodes has been outpaced by technological

[47] 47 *Law Week* 4689 (June 12, 1979).

developments. This trend was noticed as long ago as the 1890s, when a famous *Harvard Law Review* article by Charles Warren and (later Justice) Louis J. Brandeis urged judicial and constitutional protection of this right. It is found today in the concerns over data banks, the use of government, banking, medical, and credit information, the powers of police to search automobiles (which are much broader than the powers of home search), the cooperation of the telephone company with police and government authorities, illegal break-ins of homes and offices committed by the FBI in the recent past, and the increased sophistication of electronic surveillance.

Privacy lies at the heart of America's Liberal Democratic vision. It is surprising, in light of this, that its protection has been developed at such relatively late dates in our history as the 1960s and the years since. The tendency for the law to be outpaced by technology is only a partial explanation for this. We would speculate that the unconscious elitism of Liberal Democracy may have something to do with this lateness. Privacy is perhaps so precious that it is regarded as something that should be awarded to those who can most afford it—those who can buy homes built far back from the street or secluded in the country, limousines with darkened windows, private (even anonymous) bank accounts, and private guards.

Privacy of the person has been substantially hindered throughout the history of the Supreme Court and American constitutional law by its omission from the text of the Bill of Rights. It also suffered because of tendencies of the court to become occasionally sidetracked by other issues. We pointed out in Chapter 5 how the court's preoccupation with property rights and considerations led it to approve wiretapping in a 1928 case merely because the listeners had technically committed no trespass on the property in question.[48] But the textual omission was perhaps even more serious, for it gave the court no provision on which to hang this important protection. The court seemed to recognize this as it sidestepped the privacy issue, on technical grounds, for many years.

Griswold v. Connecticut: Finding the Right of Privacy in the Constitution

The Supreme Court finally decided to confront the issue in the landmark case of *Griswold* v. *Connecticut* in 1965.[49] The case presented the question of whether a married couple could be convicted and jailed under a state law for using birth control methods. Griswold, an officer of Planned Parenthood of Connecticut, together with the organization's physician, had been convicted as accessories to a crime for giving out information on contraception and prescribing the use of a contraceptive device. Most members of the court saw the difficulties or near impossibility of enforcement of such a statute, and the majority opinion by

[48] *Olmstead* v. *U.S.*, 277 U.S. 438 (1928).
[49] 381 U.S. 479 (1965).

Justice William O. Douglas, which overturned the convictions, noted that the court was dealing with "a right of privacy older than the Bill of Rights."[50] Not all the justices agreed. Hugo Black, a literalist on the First Amendment, was consistently literal when it came to privacy: because the right is not listed in the Constitution in so many words, it does not exist. Justice Arthur Goldberg, who agreed with the majority, imaginatively suggested that privacy could be placed under the Ninth Amendment, which states that the "enumeration in the Constitution of certain rights shall not be construed to deny or disparage others retained by the people." The Ninth Amendment is a seldom used provision, and Goldberg's idea, though interesting, died aborning.

Hard cases make bad law, it is said, and there is little doubt that *Griswold* proved to be a hard case for the court. Whether it is bad law depends on whether you think personal privacy should be protected and the way you are impressed by the court's method of finding that a right to privacy exists. Justice Douglas, speaking for the majority, found that it exists because a "zone of privacy" is created by the "penumbras" that come from a variety of human rights set out in the Constitution—the Ninth Amendment, to be sure, but also the First Amendment right of association, the Third Amendment prohibition against the quartering of troops in homes, the Fourth Amendment "secure in homes" provision, and the Fifth Amendment right against self-incrimination. And just what is a "penumbra"? It is a space of partial illumination located, as in an eclipse, between a shadowed object and a light. Perhaps this is a clear enough concept for some natural phenomena, but it is not an altogether clear concept of the law. Perhaps it is true that tough cases make bad law; but this may be bad law only in an artistic sense, not in a substantive sense. The right of privacy, most libertarians seem to agree, needs to be protected.

How far does the right to privacy extend? *Griswold* is the precedent for the controversial *Roe* v. *Wade* decision, which makes abortions legal during the first trimester (three months) of pregnancy and makes them legally possible during all but the last trimester.[51]

Griswold is essentially a civil law definition. The most important criminal law definition of privacy is set out in *Katz* v. *U.S.*, a 1967 ruling that rests on the Fourth Amendment prohibition against unlawful searches and seizures and that overturns the "trespass" test used in earlier cases.[52] This decision requires the authorities to obtain a court order to listen to private conversations; otherwise, a person's normal expectation of privacy is considered to prevail. (Katz had been prosecuted for

The Criminal Law Definition of Privacy

[50] 381 U.S. 479 (1965).
[51] *Roe* v. *Wade*, 410 U.S. 113 (1973).
[52] *Katz* v. *U.S.*, 389 U.S. 347 (1967).

conversations in a public phone booth dealing with gambling, a place in which, the court held, he had every right to expect privacy.) This normal expectation of privacy protects people and not just "areas" such as homes against unlawful searches and seizures.[53] The Burger Court has not been as consistent in upholding the *Katz* doctrine as many civil libertarians would like. In 1979, it approved break-ins by government agents for the purpose of planting court-authorized surveillance devices.[54]

A number of statutes have had some effect in strengthening the right to privacy. The Privacy Act of 1974 requires written consent from persons before the government can make available such of their records as those dealing with employment, medical history, or financial matters. The Freedom of Information Act of 1966 and its amendments (see the

[53] 389 U.S. 347 (1967).
[54] *Dalin* v. *U.S.*, 441 U.S. 238 (1979).

**BOX 15–11
The "National
Emergency"
Detention Plan**

From 1939 until 1975, the FBI kept a list of "potential detainees" who were to be incarcerated in detention camps in the event of a "national emergency." According to FBI documents obtained under the Freedom of Information Act, this list of potential detainees reached a high of 26,174 names in 1954, the height of the McCarthyism period of national hysteria, but it still had 1,294 names as late as August 1975. This detention plan was set into motion by President Franklin D. Roosevelt in 1939, but it obtained a greater measure of support and legitimacy when it was written into the McCarran Act of 1950. During the two decades before the Supreme Court invalidated this act, the U.S. Bureau of Prisons maintained six camps in stand-by condition—one each in California, Florida, Oklahoma, and Pennsylvania, and two in Arizona. These camps, which could be ready to receive detainees within hours if an "emergency" had been declared, would have been centers for keeping Ku Klux Klansmen, Minutemen, Marxists of every kind, New Leftists, and black and Puerto Rican nationalists under control. Although these camps have now been closed and the detention plan has been cancelled, there is always the chance that they could be activated again.

—Based on American Friends Service Committee, *J. Edgar Hoover's Detention Plan: The Politics of Repression in the United States, 1939–1976* (Philadelphia: AFSC, 1976).

discussion in Chapter 9) permits individuals to obtain copies of various government files kept on them and also provides for reviews of past classifications of persons made by various agencies.

The right to privacy has not had an easy road to legal and constitutional recognition, nor does it seem to be dependably guaranteed for the future. Privacy advocates fear the continued threat emanating from technological developments as well as from changes in government policies. They were not consoled by the 1981 pardon given by President Reagan to two FBI officials who had been convicted of authorizing illegal break-ins.

FOR FURTHER READING

ADORNO, THEODOR W. *The Authoritarian Personality.* New York: Harper, 1950. A psychological study that will give pause to any libertarian.

BARKER, LUCIUS J., and TWILEY W. BARKER, JR. *Civil Liberties and the Constitution,* 4th ed. Englewood Cliffs, N.J.: Prentice-Hall, 1982. An introduction to civil liberties cases and commentaries.

BELTH, NATHAN C. *A Promise to Keep: A Narrative of the American Encounter with Anti-Semitism.* New York: Times Books, 1979. History, description, and analysis not only of anti-semitism but of various forms of bigotry in America; because anti-Semitism is shown to correlate with other forms of bigotry, this book is instructive on several counts.

DIONISOPOULOS, P. ALLAN, and CRAIG R. DUCAT. *The Right to Privacy: Essays and Cases.* St. Paul: West, 1976. The only casebook devoted exclusively to the law of privacy.

FLATHMAN, RICHARD E. *The Practice of Political Authority.* Chicago: University of Chicago Press, 1980. Examines definitions of, approaches to, the need for, and the criticisms of authority.

GUNTHER, GERALD. *Cases and Materials on Individual Rights and Constitutional Law,* 3rd ed. Mineola, N.Y.: Foundation Press, 1981. Thorough and nearly comprehensive treatment of the Supreme Court and civil liberties.

HOUSEMAN, GERALD L. *The Right of Mobility.* Port Washington, N.Y.: Kennikat Press, 1979. Examines an important deficiency in the Bill of Rights and suggests how to remedy it.

JENSON, CAROL E. *The Network of Control: State Supreme Courts and State Security Statutes, 1920–1970.* Westport, Conn.: Greenwood Press, 1982. Examines First Amendment freedoms as they are challenged at the state level; new material never covered before.

KLUGER, RICHARD. *Simple Justice: The History of Brown v. Board of Education and Black America's Struggle for Equality.* New York: Knopf, 1976. Detailed and enlightening examination of the dynamics of this most significant of Fourteenth Amendment decisions.

MILGRAM, STANLEY. *Obedience to Authority: An Experimental View.* New York: Harper & Row, 1974. Chilling look at the possible motives for obedience to authority.

MURPHY, WALTER F., and C. HERMAN PRITCHETT, eds. *Courts, Judges and Politics: An Introduction to the Judicial Process,* 4th ed. New York: Random House, 1979. This excellent reader, generally devoted to studies of the judicial system, nevertheless contains a number of articles and studies that touch directly on civil liberties issues.

O'BRIEN, DAVID M. *Privacy, Law and Public Policy*. New York: Praeger, 1979. Comprehensive landmark study of the law of privacy.

SMITH, ROBERT ELLIS. *Privacy: How to Protect What's Left of It*. Garden City, N.Y.: Doubleday Anchor, 1979. Practical approach to the subject taken by the author of the popular *Privacy Newsletter*.

STOUFFER, SAMUEL. *Communism, Conformity and Civil Liberties: A Cross-Section of the Nation Speaks Its Mind*. Garden City, N.Y.: Doubleday, 1955. Presents polls and other information that present a frightening but apparently accurate picture of public opinion on civil liberties questions during the McCarthy period.

Corporate America   16

"Do you smell something in the halls here?" Joseph V. Reed asked a visitor to the plushly furnished seventeenth floor of One Chase Manhattan Plaza in New York City. Mr. Reed was the aide-de-camp of David Rockefeller, Chairman of the Chase Manhattan Bank until his retirement in 1981. "Do you know what it is?" he pressed. "It is the smell of power."[1]

Mr. Reed, like many of those who have worked near a center of influence and power, delighted in his position. "That man in there," he pronounced grandly, pointing toward Mr. Rockefeller's office, "is the equivalent of a head of state. He is the chairman of the board of the Eastern establishment."[2]

Few can doubt the accuracy of Mr. Reed's statements. David Rockefeller, and certainly his successor, Willard C. Butcher, hold a position of power equivalent to that of many heads of state. Chase Manhattan Bank has the power to accede to, or deny, the development plans of many a country. And it has a great deal to say about the economics, politics, and social direction of America. Its operations, as do those of many other large rich corporations, have widespread effects.

These effects concern us in this chapter; but we shall also take a look at the operational mode of America's large corporations, the corporate ideology that helps to determine so much of the nation's—and the world's—fate.

The Modern Business Corporation

What is a corporation? The term refers to a collective entity, and the lineage of the term, appropriately enough, is one that includes reference

[1] *Wall Street Journal*, April 3, 1981.
[2] Ibid.

(The Bank of New York.)

to institutions that enjoyed special privileges in medieval times—churches, guilds, and local governments, for example. These entities were usually given charters that referred to, or included, the title "corporation." But the modern corporation has evolved into an organization with three specific characteristics:

Limited Liability—The owners of a corporation, the stockholders, are not personally responsible for its debts. The assets of a corporation represent the limit of its total indebtedness.

Perpetuity—The corporation continues to exist even after its owners have died or sold out their interests. This privilege allows the corporation a virtually perpetual life.

Persona—The corporation is a legal person with a life of its own that is separate, under the law, from the lives and status of its shareholders. Because of this recognition as a legal entity, a corporation can contract, own property, sue and be sued, and do most of the things that individuals can do under the law. This status as a person is also a great convenience, for a corporation acts in its own name and not in the names of its thousands of shareholders (whose names, presumably, would all have to appear on its legal documents otherwise).

We typically think of corporations as privately owned and profit-making. It is possible, however, for corporations to be government-owned, as in the case of the Tennessee Valley Authority, and many non-profit corporations in America are devoted to educational, charitable, or foundation purposes. This chapter focuses on privately owned, profit-making firms that operate on a wide scale; in most cases, we are

An annual report of a corporation.

referring to the "Fortune 500" companies, the list drawn up by *Fortune* magazine every year of the American-based corporations possessing the largest profits, sales volume, and assets. The Fortune 500 firms are not only important in America. They are what we call "multinational corporations," which operate on a global scale as economic, political, and social forces.

The factor of private ownership can be misleading. Many commentators and other observers tend to see a strong line of demarcation between the spheres of government and large "private" corporations. The Fortune 500 companies, however, are private in only a narrow sense. Their policies and programs are today so enmeshed with those of government that it is difficult to separate corporate and government activities into neat categories. Instead of a strong line of demarcation, there is

BOX 16–1
The Pay of
Corporate Chiefs

Of 940 top officials in 350 of the largest U.S. companies in 1980—

60 earned $700,000 to $2,400,000
35 earned $600,000 to $700,000
89 earned $500,000 to $600,000
146 earned $400,000 to $500,000
208 earned $300,000 to $400,000
243 earned $200,000 to $300,000
147 earned $100,000 to $200,000
12 earned less than $100,000

Some selected examples (1980 figures):

	Salary	Bonus	Total
Rawleigh Warner, Jr., Chairman, Mobil	$498,350	$ 957,000	$1,455,350
Thomas H. Wyman, President,CBS	201,923	1,158,840	1,360,763
William Tavoulareas, President, Mobil	416,804	817,000	1,233,804
J. Paul Austin, Chairman, Coca-Cola	462,333	300,000	762,333
A. W. Clausen, President, Bankamerica	450,000	250,000	700,000

—*U.S. News and World Report*, May 18, 1981, pp. 81–83.

a blurred line that makes allowances for government contracts, favors, and subsidies on the one hand and for corporate influence, favors, and support on the other. But the distinction between government and "private" corporations is misleading in another way as well: we all concede that government acts have public policy effects, but some of us overlook the public results of corporate acts. These include important decisions on the economic fate of cities and entire countries, resource use, research and development, political support or non-support, public relations image-building and tactics, taxation, and the environment. Corporations have created ghost towns, worker migration patterns, and scarred landscapes. They have provided jobs, high standards of living (especially for their top executives; see Box 16–1), economic opportunities, and civic projects for many communities. And they are responsible for dangerous nuclear accidents and the overthrow of freely elected Third World governments. Although corporations are ostensibly "private" in terms of ownership, they are assuredly public and often quasi-governmental in their modes of operation, and in the effects of these.

One does not have to look far to find important political results stemming from corporate decisions. For example, McDonald's hamburger chain made a decision to sell its products to customers in small styrofoam boxes. Styrofoam is not biodegradable; it is not subject to decay in the same way that paper containers are. This poses a solid waste problem for every city that has one of this firm's restaurants. The "billions served" sign on the front of these restaurants underlines the seriousness of the problem.

The purpose of the modern corporation, it is generally assumed, is to provide a profit for its owners and jobs for its employees. It is often stated that another purpose is to provide good products at reasonable prices. In recent years, however, students of the corporation have demonstrated that the people who run them see other purposes to be just as important. These include providing a niche for the managerial class and the technocrats who are considered the dominant groups in the modern corporation. Political and social purposes are also sustaining forces, according to John Kenneth Galbraith and others.[3] According to this thesis, a corporation is more interested in sustaining itself politically and socially than it is in mere profit-making. In addition, organizational theorists tell us that bureaucratic behavior in the large corporation is really not very different from bureaucratic behavior in government. Most of the same tendencies—empire-building, budget feuding, and so forth—are found in both.

Although these observations about corporations seem to have a great deal of currency, it is only fair to point out that they amount to a far from unanimous view. Political conservatives, for example, may have a

---

[3] John Kenneth Galbraith, *The New Industrial State* (Boston: Houghton Mifflin, 1967).

**BOX 16–2
A Conservative
View: The
Entrepreneurial
Role of the
Corporation is
Misunderstood**

Financed more and more by their own cash flow and commercial paper, run by professional managers and technicians, largely beyond the control of stockholders or boards of directors, spreading their operations around the globe, modern corporations are seen as great multinational leviathans that require ever growing governmental power merely to keep them in line. The fabled entrepreneurs, cranky financiers, and small-scale inventors of early capitalism are regarded to be a dying breed, unimportant in the new world economy, the new industrial state.

This is the essential position propagated continually by John Kenneth Galbraith and his followers, and there is enough truth in it to disguise its essential falsity. Galbraith is right, for example, on the existence of a large commercial technostructure, somewhat divorced from the direct control of its owners. Modern corporations do have some sway over their own demands, are at least partly capable of fixing prices, and to some degree do give rise to countervailing powers and complementary services of government. Galbraith is also right that this sector of business, bestriding world markets and increasingly facing the subsidized competition of government firms abroad, is extraordinarily efficient and should not be broken up by the sweeping enforcement of antitrust laws against bigness itself. Galbraith's mistake is to [believe] that the technostructure would inevitably expand its sway over the economy and be assimilated by government in a socialist future. . . .

. . . Such a prediction has been made by some eminent pundit every five years or so since the Industrial Revolution. But the theory springs from an error so simple and familiar that any schoolboy should be able to avoid it. The prophets of socialism are making static observations of dynamic phenomena. At any time in the history of a reasonably mature economy, the largest businesses will tend to be the most efficient. That's how they became large. They benefit from economies of scale and specialization. But only someone viewing the economy as a system of statistical quantities could imagine that size is the crucial fact about successful companies. That is like supposing that the crucial fact about professional football teams is huge stadiums filled with people yelling and drinking beer. The crucial aspects of big companies are not quantitative but qualitative: the nature of the product and the mode of manufacture and marketing.

—George Gilder, *Wealth and Poverty* (New York: Basic Books, 1981), pp. 75–76.

**BOX 16–2
A Conservative View: The Entrepreneurial Role of the Corporation is Misunderstood (Continued)**

different set of explanations of the modern corporation and its behavior (see Box 16–2). In almost no instance, however, does anyone claim that the modern corporation has anywhere near the inventor spirit of people like Ford, Firestone, Carnegie, or Edison. The managerial class and spirit have long since preempted these except perhaps in the works of fiction by Ayn Rand.[4]

Roots and History of the Corporation in America

America has been a fertile seedbed for the modern corporation. We pointed out in Chapter 11 that the Founders assured a strong position for commercial interests by their adoption of Article I, Section 8 of the Constitution and their cue was shortly taken up by the Supreme Court, under the leadership of Chief Justice John Marshall, which gave this article, and specifically its interstate and foreign commerce clause, a generous interpretation.

The sharpest debates about America's future among the Founders were between Alexander Hamilton and Thomas Jefferson. Hamilton, an outstanding patron of the American Liberal Democratic tradition, argued for political liberty protected by a strong central government that would in turn foster the growth of a truly national economy. This centralized organization would require a selected and selective leadership that would be both aristocratic and meritocratic. This idea was anathema to Jefferson, who distrusted the kind of independence of leadership bound up in Hamilton's idea. This distrust was also a distrust of government, one of the most important features of American Social Democratic myth. Jefferson stood for the anticentralist doctrine of states' rights, which was closely linked to the experience of the frontier, and some measure of hostility to all organizations. From the standpoint of American myth, the Jeffersonian set of ideals won out. Today these

---

[4] See Gerald L. Houseman, *City of the Right: Urban Applications of American Conservative Thought* (Westport, Conn.: Greenwood Press, 1982), Chapter 6.

ideals are still expressed in corporate propaganda. There is a great deal of irony in this, for the Hamiltonian ideals won the ideological battle, the operational side of American corporate life as well as a great deal of American political life (see Box 16–3). American corporations talk of

BOX 16–3
The Constitutional Convention and the Dominance of a Property Rights Emphasis

It was Alexander Hamilton . . . who stated most clearly the prevailing conception of the natural rights philosophy. Early in the debates at the Constitutional Convention he declared: "It was certainly true that nothing like an equality of property existed; that an inequality would exist as long as liberty existed, and that it would unavoidably result from that very liberty itself. This inequality of property constituted the great and fundamental distinction in Society." Whereas Jefferson had struck "property" from Locke's phrase ["life, liberty and property"], Hamilton not only restored it, he also elevated it to a position of preeminence. . . . Both used the language of natural rights, but from that language they drew nearly opposite conclusions concerning the nature of man and the nature of civil society.

The results of the Constitutional Convention warrant the conclusion that Hamilton's shift in the natural rights philosophy to an emphasis on property was the dominant view at the convention. This conclusion is supported by at least three . . . considerations. First, the absence in the seven basic articles of any provisions which would enact in law . . . bulwarks against inequality attests to the dominance of property rights. Next, the absence of any serious consideration of a bill of rights . . . [until the First Congress] indicates a shift from concern with civil rights to a concern with property rights. Finally, . . . the Father of the Constitution, James Madison, argued at the convention that the government "ought to be so constituted as to protect the minority of the opulent against the majority." He stated essentially the same view in the *Federalist Papers*, although the need to be circumspect was greater than during the secret convention debates. In *Federalist* Number 10 Madison wrote: "The diversity in the faculties of men, from which the rights of property originate, is not less an insuperable obstacle to a uniformity of interests. The protection of these faculties is the first object of government. . . ."

—Charles Redenius, *The American Ideal of Equality: From Jefferson's Declaration to the Burger Court* (Port Washington: Kennikat Press, 1980), p. 19.

rugged individualism but they eschew it in practice; they much prefer to have the government look out for their interests. And they are meritocratic and privileged in a way not unlike the aristocrats of old.

Corporate Governance and Perquisites

The financing of corporate operations and growth with the sale of stock has a number of implications that are both politically and commercially important. In the first place, it establishes a kind of governance that is only remotely, if at all, connected with any principles of democracy. The stockholders have the right to vote at annual meetings on a variety of policy matters (usually not very many) and on the vital question of who shall run the company. They do this by voting their shares, and in the case of most stockholders these do not amount to very much. Note that shares, not people, are the measure for voting. In most cases the officials of the corporation own large blocks of stock themselves and are also able to vote the "proxies" of thousands of stockholders who have given them this permission. They can also buy and sell the company's stock with the advantages of insider knowledge that few members of the public have available to them. In a technical sense trading stock with inside knowledge is illegal if it is done in light of changes such as

The New York Stock Exchange.

[David Rockefeller retired as Chairman of the Board of Chase Manhattan Bank in 1981.]

Q: You've been criticized for having access to various heads of state that often seems better than that of U.S. governmental officials. Do you feel it's inappropriate for a businessman to become too involved in politics?

A: I don't see anything that is inappropriate about meeting with heads of state. In the first place, they have the choice as to whether they want to see me or not. I'm not imposing myself on them. And most of them, I think, feel an exchange of views with a businessman who travels a lot and knows a lot can be productive.

Q: What if business interests are at odds with the interests of the country?

A: I feel very strongly it would be improper to persuade any country to do anything that would be against the best interest of the United States. . . .

Q: How do you feel about repeatedly being attacked by fringe elements from both extremes of the political spectrum?

A: As long as it is from both sides it puts me right in the middle, which is where I like to feel I am. I wouldn't say I particularly enjoy being called names and having things thrown at me, but I think in the world we live in today this has come to be something we come to expect if you're going to take a position. . . .

Q: How did your parents teach you to manage your wealth?

A: I was always given an allowance—and quite a modest one right up through the time I graduated college. I would say that probably what I had to spend was less than that of my contemporaries. Also, father taught us—my generation—what he and his had been taught: not only to keep account of what we were given in the way of an allowance, but also to save 10 percent of it and to give away 10 percent. I think as time went on he didn't necessarily follow that as closely with us as he did in the early days, but I remember as a child that was a principle. Father would go over our ac-

**BOX 16—4
An Interview with
David Rockefeller
(Continued)**

counts with us each week to make sure they added up right. Quite often they didn't. Then we'd have to put "unaccounted for" in the margin of the ledger.

Q: How have you tried to pass along that same sense of responsibility to your own children?

A: I started for a time trying to do the same thing in terms of keeping accounts, but I'm afraid I was less good than my father was in the sense that I didn't keep on top of them as well as he did. Nevertheless, we did have the same principle of giving them an allowance, and it was also a modest amount in relation to what they might subsequently hope to have. . . .

Q: Have you ever wished you weren't a Rockefeller?

A: No, I really haven't. At times there are aspects of it that one isn't happy with, but on balance I think the advantages far outweigh the disadvantages.

—*Wall Street Journal*, March 27, 1981.

mergers or acquisitions; but most any corporate official, stock market analyst, or securities regulator will admit that it is impossible to regulate the use of "inside" information for personal financial advantage. Many corporate officials also have a "stock option" plan available to them and financed by the corporation. Most of these plans permit the official holding the option to buy stock at a set price at a future time. For example, the option may be to buy the stock at $15 a share even though it has appreciated to perhaps $35 or $40 a share.

The modern corporation has created a class of privileged officials and executives who may or may not be beneficial to the corporation and its stockholders. This class has some diversity within it, but possesses a general agreement on corporate myth and corporate ideology. The myth is described usually in terms of the competitive market, the glories of "free enterprise," and the Adam Smith legacy of laissez-faire (see Chapter 11). The ideology, or operational side, of corporate life is quite another matter, for corporations depend on government for all sorts of privileges and preferences. The opposition of corporate officials to government involvement in the economy is therefore largely myth. It is heard in its crassest form in statements like a recent one by silver manipulator and billionaire Nelson Bunker Hunt: "The most important thing to have is a spiritual environment in this country that will mean we can keep the money we can make."[5] Perhaps a franker expression of corporate privilege and power is found in a recent interview of David Rockefeller (see Box 16–4). Rockfeller acknowledged corporate ideology as he discussed his meetings with heads of state and his position of power and influence.

Socialization of the Public by Corporations

Corporate myth is for the masses. Mobil runs advertisements extolling its contribution to the solutions of our energy problems. It notably fails to mention its contribution to getting us into an energy crisis. Mobil also tells us of the need to provide it with tax incentives for energy exploration, but then it uses its resources to buy out Montgomery Ward or to try to buy out existing oil companies with existing energy sources.

Socialization of the public by corporations has been with us since the latter part of the nineteenth century. Some of this effort has been direct, such as campaigning against labor union organization. Less direct but no doubt equally effective efforts have been made to influence the education process so that the public is receptive to corporate blandishments (see Box 16–5). Corporations have often adopted a paternalistic attitude toward the public and their employees based not only on the corporation's economic goals but also on obtaining a measure of cooperation and assent to the corporate myth. In many ways corporate socialization efforts have been effective.

Perhaps the most successful corporate socializing efforts have been aimed at developing the consumer society. Trade has always been a part of civilization, but it has taken on a new centrality in the lives of people as they continuously test new products or variations on old ones. Cosmetics are urged on women while men are goaded to be "macho" in their choices of beer, cars, tobacco, and sports equipment. Children are told to ask their parents to buy the newest toy products ("batteries not included") or to provide them with chocolate-flavored breakfast cereal. Products are designed around such ideas as the creation of needs and planned obsolescence. Television is a particularly influential medium for this purpose, but the temple of consumption is the shopping mall, an institution that has truly changed our lives and social habits (see Box 16–6).

Conceivably it is possible to resist these imperatives that tell us to spend our money. Nutritious foods can be prepared without resort to the purchase of prepackaged, superprocessed convenience. Games can be played that require no electronics or batteries. Cars can be bought

---

[5] *Wall Street Journal,* July 30, 1981.

**BOX 16–5
The History of
Education and the
Corporate Order**

Cultural differences between urban immigrants and the schools were a . . . point of conflict. Industrialization attracted immigrants to the cities and held them there, producing a deluge of non-English-speaking families at the turn of the century, especially in the East. The response was twofold: efforts were made to use the schools as vehicles of intensive and rapid socialization—preparation for citizenship and work—and the movement to centralize urban school government was accelerated.

American educators had always assumed that the public school was essential to cultural unity, but at the turn of the century that idea received intensive application. Immigrants were inculcated with the values of the dominant culture through evening schools—often compulsory for the non-English-speaking—language instruction, civics, and American history, the celebration of patriotic holidays, and countless informal ways. Specially designed textbooks taught immigrants cleanliness, hard work, and how to apply for a job and naturalization papers, and informed them that rural, Protestant America epitomized the best in American life. Evening school teachers in Lawrence, Massachusetts, were told to convince the foreign-born of the efficacy of schooling: "Try to make them feel that they are coming to school not because they are obligated to, but because they wish to, because they know America means Opportunity . . . and the Opportunity now knocks at their door. . . ."

Americanization programs were also established outside the schools. In the International Harvester Company plants, immigrants learned English through such lessons as:

I hear the whistle, I must hurry.
I hear the five minute whistle.
It is time to go into the shop. . . .
I change my clothes and get ready to work. . . .
I work until the whistle blows to quit.
I leave my place nice and clean. . . .

—David K. Cohen and Marvin Lazerson, "Education and the Corporate Order," (Andover, Mass.: Warner Modular Publications, 1973), pp. 63–64, reprint 355.

with transportation in mind. This path of resistance is difficult to take, however. Corporate socialization and propaganda can also work in more subtle ways. During President Gerald Ford's administration, for example, government and industry decided to cooperate in a "Buy-a-Car" campaign. In this case the purchase of a car was not for the satisfaction of consumer wants as much as it was for the patriotic purpose of salvaging the auto industry. During World War II a great many industries could not advertise consumer products because no such products were being made; so corporations took out advertisements in magazines and on the radio telling about what they were doing for the war effort, in the hope that consumers would remember the company when its products became available again (see Box 16–7). Most of us have

Come to
Shell for answers

**BOX 16–6
Consumption: A
Major Form of
Recreation**

Going shopping has become a major form of recreation. The proliferation of shopping malls since World War II is ample evidence of this. It is a rare American who has not attempted to relieve a fit of the blues or a moment of boredom by heading to the nearby mall. Many of us have even advised friends who appear to be in low spirits that they ought to go out and buy a record or a dress. Visit a mall on Saturday afternoon and you will see how deep the consumer ethos is embedded in the fabric of American life. The most notable feature of these malls is the omnipresent invitation to purchase something. We are invited to buy in honor of Abe Lincoln and George Washington, in order to get ready for Easter, to celebrate summer, and to prepare for returning to school.

A visitor to the mall will also note that activities previously held at churches, schools and neighborhood gatherings are now located at shopping centers. On a random Saturday afternoon, the malls across America will have bake sales for the PTA, arts and crafts displays of local artists, fundraising drives for the high school band, a clown show, and an exhibition of dance aerobics by a Parents without Partners group. These activities do offer a welcome touch of variety to the monotonous urgings to consume. Yet the very fact that shopping centers have become the accepted locale for these activities indicates how traditional American culture has been entwined with the consumer ethos.

—Robert D. Holsworth and J. Harry Wray, *American Politics and Everyday Life* (New York: Wiley, 1982), p. 27.

**BOX 16–7
General Motors
Builds Patriotism**

". . . the country was split in the midst of the Vietnam conflict. . . . The country was, and still is, racked with racial conflict. The institutions of the United States, including big business, were under fire. There was a tremendous amount of criticism being focused on America and the American Way of Life. Much of it was justified. But in addition to this, there seemed to be so much guilt and negativism surrounding the American Way that we wanted to reaffirm our position in the minds of American consumers by building our image around the good aspects of this country and the good aspects of our cars.

We discussed this approach with the [ad] agency, and it developed a campaign around a theme that said, "We live in a great and beautiful country and our car with its instant availability gives you the opportunity to get out and see this beautiful country.". . . We put our cars in . . . beautiful settings alongside clean-cut, middle American families with whom just about everybody could identify. There were no curvaceous blondes lying prone on our car hoods, or adjusting five-speed gear shifts while clad in mini-skirts. We were not pushing the hard sell. The dealers could do that. We were trying to build a warm, friendly feeling. . . .

. . . we dipped into Chevrolet's past to resurrect the popular Chevy tune, "See the USA in your Chevrolet.". . .

The campaign was a resounding success. Not only did the division's image and sales pick up, but we got widespread approval for the theme of the campaign. We got letters from the President of the United States, senators, congressmen, and the general public lauding Chevrolet for promoting the positive and good aspects of this country. Chevrolet was obviously enhancing and cementing its favored positions with Americans. . . .

[Editorial note: This was 1973.]

—J. Patrick Wright, *On a Clear Day You Can See General Motors* (New York: Avon Books, 1980), pp. 180–181.

seen advertising that shows how a particular corporation is producing new jobs through some new program or product innovation or how a company is fighting for the environmental cause with its careful nature-nurturing activities. Corporate officialdom and its allies cannot fail to believe in a good measure of their own propaganda. Even the

BOX 16–8
The Business Press
Reacts to
Watergate

The Watergate scandals of 1973 and 1974 were unique in American history, leading to the resignation and disgrace of President Richard M. Nixon. These scandals, as is so often the case with political scandals, involved financial misdeeds. But what made them significant and unique was the exposure of a White House attack on Bill of Rights freedoms on a scale and intensity that had never been known before. In an interesting and important study, Professor Janet M. Clark of the University of Wyoming reviewed the reactions of the business press to Watergate. The publications she focused upon—*Forbes, Business Week, Wall Street Journal, Nation's Business,* and *Fortune*—had, of course, been sympathetic to Richard Nixon as president and as a candidate for the White House. It is not possible to review all her findings here, but here are some of them:

"Although it was expected that after the eruption of the Watergate scandal the level of support for President Nixon would radically decline in all of the journals from their average levels during his first term of office, it did not clearly do so." The business press, by and large, stuck with Nixon.

However, the Watergate events did cause the business press to turn to other subjects and to ignore Watergate as the embarrassments started to pile up. Clark finds that "silence may have been substituted for direct criticism as the journals waited to see how Nixon's political and economic trials would end." This leads to her conclusion that "From the substantial decrease in the number of comments about the Administration in most of the journals by early 1974, it appears that Watergate caused them to withdraw from Nixon as a controversial topic too hot to handle." It was an embarrassing period for the business press.

The business press's view of Watergate is perhaps a comment on corporate ideology. "Much of the business criticism of Watergate," according to Clark, "focused more on its economic effects than on questions of political morality." In the case of *Nation's Business,* she points out, the view was that this was just another political scandal among many in American history despite the important civil liberties implications. The *Wall Street Journal* even found a way to praise Nixon in his handling of the scandal-racked resignation of Vice Presi-

**BOX 16–8
The Business Press
Reacts to
Watergate
(Continued)**

dent Spiro Agnew, because Nixon had said—in an uncharacteristic concern for civil liberties—that he did not want to prejudge the Agnew case.

—Based on Janet M. Clark, "Moral Prerequisites of Political Support: Business Reactions to the Watergate Scandal," paper delivered at the 1974 Meeting of the American Political Science Association, Chicago, August 29 to September 2.

most cynical must feel that they are promoting some general good. One of the most important keepers and protectors of the corporate myth is the business press—*Business Week, Forbes, Fortune,* and the *Wall Street Journal* are good examples. And when the world goes awry, as it is wont to do now and then, corporate executives and their sympathizers need an explanation as much as anyone else. This, too, the business press seeks to supply from its perspective (see Box 16–8).

Political Activities of Corporations

In the autumn of 1981, a dinner was held in Washington in honor of Representative Daniel Rostenkowski, Democrat of Illinois. The purpose of the dinner was to raise campaign funds for Rostenkowski's re-election race in 1982. More than $400,000 was collected during this single evening. A few of the contributions were from personal friends, labor unions, and assorted interest groups, but the bulk of these contributions came from corporate America. Such dinners have become commonplace in Washington in recent years. This one was unusual in terms of the pledges collected, but this representative is the chairman of the House Ways and Means Committee, which writes the tax laws. Rostenkowski is therefore a key figure in the writing of tax bills. Almost incidental to this set of facts is the political situation in Rostenkowski's district: he is considered unbeatable and has never had serious opposition. He plans to use a great many of these contributions to help the campaigns of other House members with whom he is friendly.

The funding of political campaigns has become an increasingly important activity of corporations. One might logically expect the opposite, for some of the worst scandals associated with the Watergate corruption involved corporate contributions to CREP, the Nixon "committee to re-elect the president." But there was no great public outcry against these abuses, perhaps in part because some of the other Watergate scandals involved more dangerous matters. Corporations have continued to strengthen their hand in the political process, leading their critics to charge that they are pricing democracy out of the marketplace. Whether or not this is true, these activities represent the operational, ideological side of their work in politics.

The presidential election of 1980 cost approximately a quarter of a billion dollars. The same figure equals the costs of the congressional elections of that year. A huge proportion of these costs was borne by corporations through corporate political action committees and occasionally individual contributions of corporate officials. There are almost 3,000 political action committees in existence, and they spent at least $130 million in 1979–1980. The largest 100 of them spent a staggering $73 million.[6] Corporate PACs exist because corporations are not permitted by law to give money directly from their assets to political candidates or organizations. The PACs are groups of corporate officials and employees (and occasionally stockholders) who give money to a single fund that is in turn donated to candidates deemed worthy of company support. The individual contributions to the PAC fund are supposedly voluntary; we say "supposedly" because there are cases of corporate coercion applied to potential donors and, in any event, a young executive on the rise is hardly in a position to refuse to make a contribution. These contributions are ladled out according to the corporation's perception of its particular or general interests. A defense contractor, for example, may feel it is necessary to back a defense-oriented candidate. Some of the most active and effective corporate PACs are those of General Electric Company, Mobil Oil Corporation, and the Dart/Kraft Corporation. The president of Dart/Kraft, Justin Dart, is a zealous promoter of corporate political activity and is a close personal friend of President Reagan.

Corporate PACs use a variety of strategies. In some close congressional or other races, the PAC of a given company may actually contribute money to both major candidates. Or it may give a large amount to one candidate and a small "insurance" amount to the other in hopes that the corporation wins no matter how the election comes out. Until 1978, the PACs supported more Democrats than Republicans for Congress because of a strategy then known as "Shoot the Sick"—that is, support the safe incumbents of both parties. Because more Democrats than Republicans sat in Congress and the Democrats controlled the important committee chairmanships as a result of their majorities, they benefited from this PAC policy. Even at this time, however, the PACs demonstrated a willingness to shift to Republican insurgent candidates if they saw an incumbent Democrat in trouble. In 1980, this tendency became much more pronounced, and corporate PACs gave Republicans almost twice the contributions given to Democrats.[7]

[6] David Adamany, "Political Finance in Transition," *Polity*, **14**: 314–331 (Winter 1981).
[7] Ibid., pp. 322–324.

Two other observations should be made about corporate campaign spending. First, it is not only on the increase, but it is greatly disproportionate to the spending of other groups. Labor unions, for example, spent only about one seventh the amount spent by corporate PACs in the 1980 elections. The implications of this for public policymaking and legislative influence seem obvious enough. Second, a great deal of money is spent in campaigns by individuals that is derived from corporate wealth. The new record in this connection was set in 1980 when Governor Jay Rockefeller of West Virginia spent $11.75 million, or $30 per voter, in his own behalf.[8]

Corporate PAC contributions probably distort the political system in untold ways. But neither Congress nor the courts have seen fit to limit the amounts of expenditures that the PACs may make, and putting the PACs out of business altogether would undoubtedly be unconstitutional

[8] Ibid., pp. 322–324.

"ACTUALLY, I THINK IT CAME BEFORE THE VIDEO GAME"

(Copyright 1982 by Herblock in the Washington Post.)

**BOX 16–9
Ronald McDonald
Gets Congress to
Listen to Him**

In an era of grass-roots lobbying, it is easy to imagine the . . . potential of 68,000 small businessmen located in virtually every American neighborhood. . . .

Fourteen fast-food companies have chains with more than 1,000 units each, according to the National Restaurant Association. Most have ready-made communications networks initially designed for product uniformity and quality control.

Chain eateries, moreover, have built their success on marketing, a skill important in politics. . . .

The awakening of the fast-food chains . . . is not the only evidence of the clout . . . in franchised business. [There is] . . . the 1980 lobbying victory of soft-drink bottlers, another franchised industry, in a battle over antitrust legislation. Hotel and motel chains are organized for lobbying, and there is a growing franchise component in the politically active real estate industry. . . .

Here are some of the more active restaurant chains:

McDonald's has the oldest legislative department, formed six years ago. Three full-time executives . . . handle both state and federal affairs. The company has a network of 1,400 owner-operators, most of whom own more than one unit. . . . about half of them can be counted on to respond with calls, telegrams or visits when Congress needs a push on legislation that affects them. . . . the company mobilizes its entire franchisee system "a few times a year."

. . . McDonald's conducts workshops to train its franchisees in how government works and even offers courses in government affairs at its "Hamburger University" in Oak Brook, Ill.

Burger King has a three-year-old government relations office based in Miami. The office includes two full-time staffers who keep track of state legislation. . . . Burger King has elevated government affairs to a top corporate priority. The owners and managers of the company's 2,800 outlets are organized into 10 regional councils and encouraged to cultivate friendships with their lawmakers. . . .

Kentucky Fried Chicken . . . has a grass-roots network called the Franchisee Legislative Action Group (FLAG). FLAG began in 1977, during congressional debate of the minimum wage law. . . .

Pizza Hut and sister company Taco Bell, both owned by Pepsico, have a total of 5,300 outlets. Pizza Hut made a quick impression within the industry and Congress when it cooked up a lobbying effort that helped beat the dairy industry on milk-price supports.

Jerrico, the Lexington, Kentucky-based company that runs Long John Silver fish restaurants, started a government affairs office in 1976. The company's lobbying network calls on 100 franchise-holders in 40 states who in turn own 1,100 restaurants. Thirty to 40 per cent of the franchisees and shop managers will write to Congress on request, vice president Bruce Cotton said, and the letters are persuasively chock-full of personal experience.

"There's probably grease stains on the letter," he said. . . .

—*Congressional Quarterly Weekly Report*, June 20, 1981, pp. 1095–1098.

in light of the First Amendment rights of free speech, expression, and association.

The lobbying efforts of corporations have received a great deal of attention over the years. Some lobbying efforts are geared to the perceived needs of particular companies or industries—autos, trucking, fast-food restaurants (see Box 16–9). Three lobbying organizations also present a general corporate view on issues such as labor unions, consumer matters, government regulation, taxation, and the environment: the Business Roundtable, the U.S. Chamber of Commerce, and the National Association of Manufacturers. The Business Roundtable's membership consists of major officers of the 200 largest corporations in America. The Roundtable has shown a particular interest in anti-trust and consumer legislation, areas that are naturally of concern to corporate giants. The U.S. Chamber of Commerce represents nearly 100,000 large and small businesses, and its local counterparts are usually well known in their communities. The Chamber of Commerce seems generally to be interested in issues important to big business, such as anti-trust and consumer matters, but some of its positions—on taxation and labor matters, for examples—may reflect a broader business membership. The chamber has a legal arm that files lawsuits and "friend of the court" briefs, an affiliated citizens' lobby group that also promotes the chamber's objectives, and a network that promotes close contact between members and Congress. Many observers regard the chamber as an effective lobby. The National Association of Manufacturers, which has a long history of conservative policy objectives and which launched its infamous "American Plan"—a plan that simply means "no labor unions"—in the 1920s, is also regarded as a powerful business lobby that, in the main, represents big business. A number of small business lobbies also operate in Washington, some of them very effectively, and these groups often work for the same objectives as the three big business groups.

Business lobbies often work in combination on issues and occasionally draw in other allies to work with them—the Teamsters Union often works with the trucking industry, for example, and the National Auto Dealers Association often sees eye-to-eye with the auto industry.

It is necessary to reiterate a point stressed in earlier chapters: the influence of corporate interests on the bureaucracy. These interests often combine with sympathetic bureaucrats and allies in Congress who specialize in their problems to form "iron triangles" in Washington that can become formidable in fashioning and implementing legislation. (See Chapters 6 and 9 for further discussion on this vital area of corporate political activity.)

It is often assumed that because corporate interests are tied to a broad power "establishment" in this country that they are unlikely to ally themselves with political extremists or extremist movements. This impression is clearly subject to many exceptions. The John Birch Society, which adopts far Right political stances and is dominated by one man, has received important support from corporate officials, including vital financial backing. The Heritage Foundation of Washington, D.C., which has an attachment to ultraconservative economics, is a creature of corporate benefactors. Senator Jesse Helms' Congressional Club, estimated to have a war chest of $5 million or more, has many small contributors but also receives corporate funds. The Moral Majority, *Human Events* magazine, and a host of other far Right institutions and publications also receive their share. One of the wealthiest backers of extremism for many years was the late H. L. Hunt, the Texas oil magnate, who adopted "crackpot" theories on economics, race, and ethnic groups. And it has been reported that Richard Mellon Scaife has spent more than $100 million on far Right and other conservative causes (see Box 16–10).

Public Policy and Corporate Ideology

"I love to work with Congress; I think we think alike. It's fun to work with the guys." So said a lobbyist for the General Electric Corporation and more than fifty other corporations.[9]

Corporate ideology yields policy results. If this were not the case it is

[9] *UE News*, November 10, 1980.

**BOX 16–10
Richard Mellon
Scaife: $100 Million
to Ultra-Rightist
and Conservative
Causes**

Richard Mellon Scaife is probably the largest single donor to ultra-rightist and conservative causes in this country.

When one thinks of far Right political groups, there is a tendency to believe that such "fringe" viewpoints could not attract significant financial support. But Scaife proves conclusively that this is not the case. A *Columbia Journalism Review* article estimates that Mr. Scaife has delivered over $100 million to ultra-rightist and conservative causes over the years. Scaife's donations from tax-exempt charitable foundations financed by Gulf Oil, Alcoa, First Boston Corporation, and other companies currently run at the level of $10 million a year.

Some of the groups financed by Scaife include the Committee on the Present Danger, Accuracy in Media, the *American Spectator* magazine, WQLN–TV in Erie, Pennsylvania, the American Legislative Exchange Council, Americans for Effective Law Enforcement, and the antienvironmentalist Mountain States Legal Foundation. In 1979 Scaife alone supplied $900,000 through the Sarah Scaife Foundation, the Carthage and Allegheny Foundations, and the Trust for Sarah Mellon Scaife's Grandchildren, to the Heritage Foundation, a conservative think tank that is heavily relied upon by the Reagan administration for many of its ideas. As one newspaper puts it, "When Richard Mellon Scaife talks today, people don't just listen. Things happen."

—Based on various reports including *UE News*, August 24, 1980 and to the *Columbia Journalism Review* article it cited.

unlikely that corporations would involve themselves so deeply in political activities and financial commitments. Corporations do not invariably win on the issues and they do not prevail to the extent that they would like. But it is clear that corporations have managed over the years to win their way in some important policy areas including taxation and antitrust policy, while they have avoided many of the obligations of social accounting and responsibility.

Taxation and Subsidies

Taxation and subsidies are of central significance to corporations, because these matters directly affect the "bottom line" of the corporation's balance sheet. A new awareness of the privileged tax position of corporations appears to have developed over the past decade. Moreover, many citizens question the rationality of certain kinds of tax breaks for companies. The oil industry has been one of the more obvious targets of tax reformers, who point to such loopholes as "intangible drilling expenses" or the "foreign tax credit" (see Box 16–11).

It is not necessary to dwell on the perquisites of one industry to demonstrate how the inequalities of the tax system work to the advantage of corporations. Some question the fairness of the fact that the system taxes wages at a higher rate than income on investments. Capital gains taxes, that is, taxes on the profits made from the sale of capital assets, typically have been set at half the rate of wage income over the years, and the Reagan administration has increased this disparity with the passage of its 1981 tax package. Tax allowances are also generous toward depreciation of capital assets, certain "sheltered" investments, and income derived from government bonds.

The substantial tax favors for corporations written into the 1981 tax cut package will have deleterious effects on government revenue potential over the next few years. Among these favors are speed-ups in depreciation allowances that will total as much as $55 billion a year, a capital gains rate cut amounting to as much as $600 million a year, the exemption of "tax straddles" for commodity brokers that will cost $400 million a year, a "targeted jobs" tax credit of up to $500 million a year in lost revenues, and foreign tax credits of up to $1.5 billion a year. The oil industry can look forward to its special breaks: a credit against the windfall profits tax, which will cost up to $2.9 billion a year, a $400 million reduction in the windfall profits tax, a continuance rather than a phase-down of depletion allowances paid to the industry because their oil sources will run out someday (this costs the Treasury $2 billion yearly), and a tax exemption on "stripper oil production" of independent producers that will save the industry $700 million.[10] Perhaps the most controversial benefit to corporations, added to the tax code by Congress and the Reagan administration in 1981, is a provision that allows one company to sell its tax loss to another company. Companies that are already profitless do not need these in their tax statements to keep from paying taxes, but they are permitted to pass on these tax "losses" to profitable companies, usually in exchange for money. Under this arrangement General Electric Company avoided a tax bill of more than $100 million in 1981.[11] The logic of this provision is to promote corporate investment by lessening the tax load, but the unpopularity of this measure with the public could lead to its repeal. All these tax breaks can be viewed as government subsidies, but outright government grants and loans fit just as neatly into the traditional definition of a subsidy. Some of these are well known, such as the $250 million Lock-

[10] *UAW Washington Report*, September 4, 1981.
[11] *Washington Post*, March 15, 1982.

BOX 16–11
Tax Breaks for Oil
Companies

Through a transparent tax dodge enacted by a compliant Congress, the oil companies evade enough taxes each year to handle a healthy chunk of the federal budget.

The device is called "foreign tax credit." On the surface, it seems fair enough: For every dollar in foreign taxes an oil company pays, it is given a dollar of credit against its U.S. income taxes. Ostensibly, this prevents double taxation—or so the slick propagandists of Big Oil would have us believe.

The hitch is this: The foreign "taxes" are in fact part of the purchase price—the same kind of royalties an oil company might pay to private landowners in this country for the right to pump oil from their property. Overseas, the landowners are the various foreign governments, so most royalties paid to them are construed as taxes.

It makes no difference to the foreign governments. . . . But to the oil companies—and the rest of the American taxpayers—it makes a colossal difference.

Literally billions of dollars are at stake. . . . a revealing Internal Revenue Service study . . . cover[s] the tax returns of all American oil companies for the 12-month period from July 1975 through July 1976. . . . the figures show:

The 39 biggest oil companies grossed a staggering $291 billion.

The deductions worked out by their accounting wizards totaled $254 billion.

After a few further allowances, the total profit admitted to by the 39 oil companies came to an impressive $36.5 billion. For most corporations, this would mean an income tax owed of $17.5 billion.

Instead, the oil companies wound up paying about $2.5 billion in U.S. income taxes.

How could this happen? Simple enough: The oil moguls claimed foreign tax credits totaling $15 billion. So on an aggregate income of nearly $300 billion, the companies paid a total of about less than 1 per cent in income taxes—while individual American taxpayers were giving the federal government 20, 30, 40 per cent or more of their annual earnings. . . .

—Jack Anderson column, Fort Wayne, Indiana, *Journal-Gazette*, February 2, 1981.

heed loan guarantee or the $2.5 billion Chrysler bailout of recent years. There are also a wide variety of subsidies for airlines, defense contractors, and a host of other industries. Defense contractors often benefit from the further subsidies built into their contracts by the government. On many occasions, such contractors have worked out a subsidy for themselves through such practices as cost overruns or too low initial bids on projects they are awarded to complete.

Taxes and subsidies are an excellent commentary on corporate ideology. They clearly show that the mythical rhetoric of "rugged individualism" and free enterprise are eschewed in actual practice.

Antitrust Policy

The great economic power and the massive legal resources of giant corporations have thwarted many antitrust initiatives so often that most economists and legal experts in the field have concluded that antitrust laws and litigation are unnecessary.[12] Even economists associated with the liberal side of the political spectrum such as Lester Thurow of MIT have come to this conclusion.[13] Why should this be so? Is there not a need to preserve competition in the economy and to avoid the threat of monopoly?

One answer is the sheer volume of work involved in antitrust litigation. The government dropped a fourteen-year effort against IBM in January 1982 after 5,500 pages of testimony, 2,500 depositions, the work of more than 300 lawyers, and 66 million pages of documents.[14] An almost equally complicated case against American Telephone and Telegraph Corporation was settled at the same time on terms that almost all observers agree were very favorable to the communications giant. This litigation had also taken several years. Faced with such obstacles, the Federal Trade Commission and the Anti-Trust Division of the Justice Department, the two arms of the government concerned with such matters, are unlikely to take on any but the most flagrant cases.

Difficulty of prosecution should not necessarily be the central concern in antitrust matters, and so there may be another answer to the questions above: a direct concern about monopoly. And this concern should transcend a focus on single-industry monopolies because conglomerate corporations—those with interests in several different industries that ostensibly do not compete with one another—may still have the power to influence pricing and marketing decisions over a wide area. One reason for this is the possible overlap of executive personnel on the boards of these corporations. Such memberships create the opportunity for agreements, perhaps verbal rather than written, on such matters as dividing markets and setting prices. Congress has exhibited

[12] George A. Hay, "Is Antitrust Obsolete? A Forecast on the Role of Antitrust Policy in the Eighties," *Cornell Law Forum*, **8**: 2–7 (January 1982).

[13] *Newsweek*, January 18, 1982.

[14] "The Business Month," *Dun's Business Month*, February 1982, pp. 13–14.

an occasional concern with these membership overlaps and has published the numbers of overlaps to reveal the potential for monopoly practices (see Boxes 16–12 and 16–13).

Another response to the concern about the threat of monopoly is old but has added new embellishments. This response tells us that monopoly is no great threat because there is always competition from abroad, and that bigness is not necessarily bad. Some who hold this view say that big government or big labor is a threat but not big companies. The more consistent proponents of this view believe not only that antitrust laws and prosecutions should be terminated, but also claim that government must encourage corporate growth and expansion with finan-

**BOX 16–12
Interlocking
Directorates of the
Thirteen Major U.S.
Corporations**

According to a 1978 Senate Report, "Interlocking Directorates Among Major U.S. Corporations," the thirteen largest companies in America have these numbers of personnel overlaps:

	American Tel and Tel	Bank-America	Citicorp	Chase Manhattan	Prudential	Metropolitan Life	Exxon	Manufacturers Hanover	J.P. Morgan	General Motors	Mobil	Texaco	Ford
American Tel and Tel		4	21	22	11	17	10	19	18	15	13	2	9
Bank-America	4		3	2	2	4		2	2				3
Citicorp	21	3		18	14	23	7	26	30	12	9	2	3
Chase Manhattan	22	2	18		10	18	3	27	17	8	7	1	5
Prudential	11	2	14	10		6	1	8	5	8	6	1	3
Metropolitan Life	17	4	23	18	6		9	12	20	24	6	1	6
Exxon	10		7	3	1	9		3	6	15	6	2	4
Mfrs. Hanover	19	2	26	27	8	12	3		25	16	7	3	1
J. P. Morgan	18	2	30	17	5	20	6	25		11	2	1	6
General Motors	15		12	8	8	24	15	16	11		5	3	6
Mobil	13		9	7	6	6	6	7	2	5		4	6
Texaco	2		2	1	1	1	2	3	1	3	4		1
Ford	9	3	3	5	3	6	4	1	6	6	6	1	

—U.S. Senate Document 95–107, 95th Congress, 2nd session, 1978, p. 29.

BOX 16–13
Interlocking Directorates of the Seven Major Energy Industry Competitors

	Atlantic Richfield	Exxon	Mobil	Shell	Standard of California	Standard of Indiana	Texaco
Atlantic Richfield		4	3	1	2	5	2
Exxon	4		6	1	6	2	2
Mobil	3	6		3	3	3	4
Shell	1	1	3		1		
Standard of California	2	6	3	1			
Standard of Indiana	5	2	3				
Texaco	2	2	4				

—U.S. Senate Document 95–107, 95th Congress, 2nd session, 1978, p. 92.

cial, research, and other kinds of assistance. Some of these monopoly supporters have suggested that the American economy should be reorganized along Japanese lines, where the relationship between government and business is close and positive. A great many matters are overlooked in this set of assumptions, however. In the first place, there are already a host of tax breaks, subsidies, and other concessions given to corporate America by the government. Second, the old saw that we will have competition from foreign sources overlooks the fact that a great many would-be foreign competitors are subsidiaries of American corporations. The threat to economic and civil liberties by the corporate state, discussed below, also oppose this view. There are trends in corporate operations that demonstrate the continuing validity of antitrust laws and prosecutions. One of these is the acceleration of corporate mergers. Both 1981 and 1982 were record years for mergers and acquisitions, and the portents call for more. The biggest merger in the history of corporate America, DuPont–Conoco, took place in 1981, and there were others of note: U.S. Steel taking over Marathon Oil, Union Pacific–Missouri Pacific, Fluor Corporation–St. Joe Minerals Corporation, Bucyrus-Erie with Western Gear, and Celanese with Virginia Chemicals. Centralization of economic decision making is growing apace be-

Gas is flamed off an off shore oil rig. Oil exploration has increasingly turned to undersea sources in recent years.

cause of corporate ideology. The arguments for tax incentives or other forms of government assistance melt in the heat of the merger and acquisition activity because acquiring an already existing entity is not a venture capital investment: it creates no new jobs, no new products, and no new economic opportunities under most circumstances. The deleterious effects of mergers and acquisitions on employees' careers and lives and on various communities throughout the country have never been adequately studied, but these are serious and often socially undesirable. Antitrust laws and policy could be made more effective with

**BOX 16–14
The Socially
Responsible
Corporation**

THE CORPORATION AS CITIZEN

1. To be concerned with obeying the laws (even if it can get away with law-breaking profitably).
2. To aid in the making of laws, as by volunteering information within its control regarding additional measures that may need to be imposed on industry.
3. To heed the fundamental moral rules of the society.
4. Not to engage in deception, corruption, and the like.
5. As a citizen abroad, to act decently to host country citizens, and not inimically to U.S. foreign policy.

THE CORPORATION AS PRODUCER

1. To aim for safe and reliable products at a fair price.

THE CORPORATION AS EMPLOYER

1. To be concerned with the safety of the work environment.
2. To be concerned with the emotional well-being of its workers.
3. Not to discriminate.

THE CORPORATION AS RESOURCE MANAGER

1. Not to contribute unduly to the depletion of resources.
2. To manifest some concern for the esthetics of land management.

THE CORPORATION AS AN INVESTMENT

1. To safeguard the interests of investors.
2. To make full and fair disclosures of its economic condition.

BOX 16–14
The Socially
Responsible
Corporation
(Continued)

THE CORPORATION AS NEIGHBOR

1. To be concerned with pollution.
2. To conduct safe and quiet operations.

THE CORPORATION AS COMPETITOR

1. Not to engage in unfair competition, on the one hand, or cozy restrictions of competition, on the other.

THE CORPORATION AS SOCIAL DESIGNER

1. To be innovative and responsive in the introduction of new products and methods.
2. Not to close its eyes to the fact that the movies it turns out, the shows it produces, the styles it sets, have an impact on the quality of our lives, and to concern itself with that impact responsibly.

—Christopher Stone, *Where the Law Ends: The Social Control of Corporate Behavior* (New York: Harper & Row, 1975), pp. 231–232.

new legislation and a strong, determined implementation in Washington; but for the moment corporate ideology has emerged victorious.

"We prefer economic growth to clean air," was the complaint of Charles Barden, executive director, Texas Air Control Board.[15] His view has been reinforced, perhaps inadvertently, by Jerry McAfee, chairman of the Gulf Oil Corporation, who said with reference to the Three Mile Island nuclear accident, "Any complicated piece of machinery is going to have ups and downs."[16]

Since the mid-1960s corporations have been pressured to assume a stance of social responsibility on a great variety of issues. The general public and many well-known commentators have urged corporations to be concerned about the environment, to guard their employees from unsafe working conditions, to put only wholesome ingredients into their products, to provide appropriate warnings on labels, and to show con-

Policies of Social Responsibility

[15] *Rolling Stone*, November 4, 1976.
[16] *Wall Street Journal*, April 2, 1979.

cern for consumer interests generally. Fair and equal treatment of workers, customers, and contractors regardless of race, sex, religion, or national origin are also to be given a high priority. And in the eyes of the conscientious activist, corporate responsibility extends to foreign policies as well. They should not dump their pollution in Third World countries that are less able to regulate the corporations' activities. They should not invest in South Africa because of its racial policies. Nor should they support the anti-Israeli boycotts instigated by Arab states. Over the past few years, a campaign to boycott Nestle products has been carried out on the grounds that this company promotes its baby-food products to Third World mothers who are prone to mix these with the undrinkable local water.

A well-established business viewpoint on these questions says that social responsibility is something for the corporation itself to make judgments about; in some cases, those who hold this point of view state that it is irresponsible for a corporation to do anything but maximize its profits. Conservative economist Milton Friedman believes that in principle it is wrong for a corporation to give money to charities or foundations. Corporations have no money to give, he says; it belongs to their stockholders and should be allocated to dividends, capital investment, or research and development.[17] Whether Friedman's view is adopted or not, many corporation executives argue that the best way to achieve the goals of corporate social responsibility is to leave corporations alone to work their will and to maximize their profits. This, it is said, will promote the prosperity of all.[18]

A variety of responses have been given to the challenge of social responsibility. Some companies make public relations gestures to show that they are responsible; others, like Mobil, make large donations on the one hand to public broadcasting and other causes while attacking their critics with newspaper advertisements, letters to stockholders, and other publications.

Corporate Ideology in the International Arena

The Multinational Corporation

Thomas Jefferson noted the international character of capital when he said, "Merchants have no country of their own. Wherever they may be they have no ties with the soil. All they are interested in is the source of their profits." President Dwight Eisenhower made essentially the same point in 1960: "Capital is a curious thing with perhaps no nationality. It flows where it is served best."[19] Today there is a great deal of literature

[17] Gerald L. Houseman, *City of the Right*, Chapter 4.
[18] Leonard Silk and Mark Silk, *The American Establishment* (New York: Basic Books, 1980), pp. 229–230.
[19] Both quotes appear in Richard J. Barnet and Ronald E. Muller, *Global Reach: The Power of the Multinational Corporations* (New York: Simon and Schuster, 1974), p. 77.

on the multinational corporation. The term is applied to most of the Fortune 500 companies and to many lesser ones as well. It reflects not only the well-known fact of corporate operations around the globe— drilling for oil in Venezuela, manufacturing cars in Australia, or selling computers in Europe—but also the nature of the structure and organization of the corporate giants based in America and other countries. These giants are often governments unto themselves, and they have the power of governments—shifting personnel from country to country, investing with budgets much larger than those of many countries, making decisions about development, environmental measures, food production, and product quality, and shoring up their decisions with political influence exercised in a wide variety of ways.

Probably the most important characteristic of the multinationals is the one implied by the term: they have no particular loyalty to any

---

Other big German combines, like Krupp, Siemens, or Mercedes, while they regained their own dominance, went through an ordeal of public recrimination and questioning which (I believe) fundamentally affected their corporate character; and a new generation forced them to undergo some kind of corporate self-analysis. But ITT [the International Telephone and Telegraph Corporation] buried its history in a mountain of public relations, so that scarcely anyone on its staff now knows that it was ever associated with Focke-Wulf bombers or with Hitler's SS.

Most remarkable of all, ITT now presents itself as the innocent victim of the Second World War, and has been handsomely recompensed for its injuries. In 1967, nearly thirty years after the events, ITT actually managed to obtain $27 million in compensation from the American government, for war damage to its factories in Germany, including $5 million for damage to Focke-Wulf plants—on the basis that they were American property bombed by Allied bombers. It was a notable reward for a company that had so deliberately invested in the German war effort, and so carefully arranged to become German. If the Nazis had won, ITT in Germany would have appeared impeccably Nazi; as it lost, it reemerged as impeccably American.

—Anthony Sampson, *The Sovereign State of ITT* (New York: Stein and Day, 1973), pp. 45–46.

**BOX 16–15
The Multinational Corporation—With Its Dubious National Loyalties—is Not a New Phenomenon**

nation. Because the nation-state is still the dominant unit of government operating in the Western and Third worlds, there is no transnational authority to control multinationals' political activities. Governments and multinationals may cooperate at times, and there is the occasional successful government sanction against some corporate activity. In the 1930s, for example, the Roosevelt administration stopped the Curtiss-Wright Corporation when it was seeking to sell arms to some Latin American governments. This kind of event, however, is highly unusual. More often than not, governments including that of the United States aid arms producers in selling their products. Arms remain a very successful U.S. export.

The multinational corporation's lack of national loyalty sometimes has implications for American national security. The close cooperation between oil and chemical companies in America with Nazi Germany until nearly the outbreak of World War II received a great deal of publicity. Less well-known cases are the charges made by a congressional study against an oil company for payoffs to the Vietcong in Vietnam in the 1960s to keep the company's property safe from attack.[20] There is a continuing concern about the export of American technology, both from the standpoint of national security and from the worries over trade secrets and advantages (see Box 16–15).

Multinational Policies and Activities

The activities of multinationals create problems for the image of the United States and its people. In Latin America, there is a long-standing legacy of opposition by American-based corporations to any meaningful land reform programs. There is also a tradition of corporate support for some of the most repressive regimes—the Somozas in Nicaragua, the Duvaliers in Haiti, Perez Jimenez in Venezuela. In South Africa, corporations have usually acquiesced in the government's racist policies carried out in the areas of employment, housing, and education. In the Middle East, oil companies played a prominent role in the 1954 installation of the Shah of Iran, a policy that has had disastrous results. They have also sought to shift American policy toward a more pro-Arab position on the issue of Israel, and they have been somewhat successful in this attempt since the energy crisis of 1973. Elsewhere in the world, multinationals have created much suspicion as they propped up unpopular repressive regimes. Perhaps the best-documented of such activities in recent years was the overthrow of a democratically elected regime in Chile carried out with the cooperation of the Central Intelligence Agency and the International Telephone and Telegraph Corporation.[21]

Corporate ideology generally tends to support dictatorial and totalitarian regimes of the anti-Communist variety. But multinationals cast a

[20] Drew Pearson column, San Francisco *Chronicle*, March 15, 1966.
[21] Richard J. Barnet and Ronald E. Muller, *Global Reach*, pp. 23, 110.

wide net, so that it is both simplistic and incorrect to claim that this is all they do politically. Eastern European nations allied with the Soviet Union and the Soviet Union itself are business partners of American based multinationals. The tremendous Western debts of countries like Poland and Romania could only have been possible with the approval of banking interests such as Bank of America, Chase Manhattan, and Citibank. Tom Theobald, senior executive vice-president of Citibank, has asked, "Who knows which political system works? The only test we care about is: Can they pay their bills?"[22] So there is a curious "nonpartisanship" that is operated by international corporate ideology. This extends to an important say—some would say control—in the loan activities of the International Monetary Fund. The IMF ties strings to its loans that include the adoption by a borrower nation of what it considers sound economic policies that often benefit multinationals, and it gives or withholds its approval of financial aid accordingly. If IMF-approved policies are adopted, it matters little what kind of government carries them out. The same considerations also seem to govern another international institution, the World Bank, although its functions of providing development funds are quite different from those of the IMF, which seeks to stabilize national economies, banking, and currencies.

The Corporate State

The Crisis of Reindustrialization

The American economy is presently undergoing a basic restructuring. More than 10 million jobs were added to the economy in the years between 1973 and 1980 in just three areas—services, retail trade, and state and local government. These jobs account for three-fourths of all new jobs created in this period. At the same time, we have seen our domestic auto industry decline, along with its thousands of suppliers. In the last decade sales of American cars have dropped from more than 10 million a year to fewer than 4 million.[23] There is a basic problem of maintaining our industrial base and at the same time assuring that job opportunities are opened up in those industries and areas of the economy in which productivity is high and profitable.

The American corporation is caught up in the middle of these basic changes, and to some degree it has not proved to be competitive. Transistors, television sets, and some electronic products and equipment are produced in Japan, which has become the world leader in this area. Semiconductors, products that are basic to the data processing industry, are also increasingly produced in Japan. The auto industry has been hurt by Japanese and European competition. And it has been some time

[22] *Wall Street Journal,* December 31, 1981.
[23] *The New York Times,* November 22, 1981.

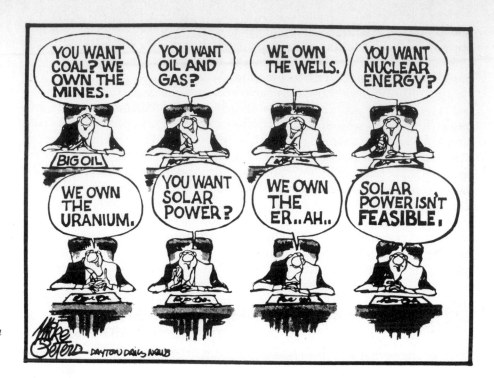

since many of the domestic shoe and textile industries were competitive.

These and other competitive shortcomings have led to some alarm in the corporate world, in the unions that see their membership declining, in the cities affected by shutdowns and layoffs, and in the financial community. There is a feeling that domestic industries are not competitive for a variety of reasons—high labor costs, outmoded plant and equipment, lapses in technological development, poor management, and too much concentration of research and development personnel and resources in the weapons industry. In the case of the multinational corporation, however, it is a simple matter of moving operations out of the country. Their factories are springing up in Hong Kong, Mexico, and Malaysia. In 1982, General Electric closed its small-appliance unit in Ontario, California, displacing more than 1,700 workers as it moved this plant to Singapore.

This practice of opening subsidiaries abroad at the expense of domestic industry has led to a call for government-industry cooperation in developing and retaining industry in this country. Senator Bill Bradley, Democrat of New Jersey, and many other politicians are calling for government aid to industry in various forms—grants, loans, tariff preferences, and a variety of tax incentives to keep industry competitive and operating in this country.

These demands could lead to the formalization in this country of the government-industry relationship into a form of the corporate state. The close and often cozy relationship that now exists between multinationals and the federal government could be made even more explicit—some libertarians would say, more dangerous—with a corporate state arrangement.

In a corporate state the organization of both the government and the economy is tied closely and formally together. The purest model of such a system in recent times is Fascist Italy under Mussolini. Individual freedom and opportunity under such a system are usually snuffed out by this great agglomeration of power. Under this system there is a syndicate for each major industry, and this syndicate is jointly run by the business interests and the state.

American politicians do not advocate the corporate state, but they see a need for government assistance to industry, and they may have models like Japan, Great Britain, or Belgium in mind. In these countries the governments lend important assistance to industry with loans, grants, tariff protection, and tax advantages. But in America the corporate state or some form of it is a possibility if an even stronger relationship than now exists between government and big business comes to pass.

In any event such an arrangement could be futile because all the corporate giants in America are multinationals and, as such, capable of divesting themselves of their American investments and commitments any time they choose. Under these circumstances it is not likely they can be induced to demonstrate national loyalty or concern.

In addition, economic forces at work limit the choices of U.S. policymakers. One of the most important of these is the natural tendency for corporations to locate their operations in countries with large surplus pools of labor, once the work force is skilled enough to perform the tasks of manufacturing. We have already seen an international trend of multinationals' moving their operations from Western countries to such Asian nations as Korea and Formosa, then again to Malaysia and Singapore. When the surplus labor market starts to dry up and wages rise in a given country, the tendency is for multinationals to move on to cheaper markets.[24]

In the face of such economic trends, the hope for the U.S. economy may well be some form of the corporate state and tariff protections. But such a development would be ominous.

[24] W. Arthur Lewis, "Economic Development with Unlimited Supplies of Labor," *Manchester School of Economic and Social Studies*, **22**: 139–191 (May 1954).

FOR FURTHER READING

BARNET, RICHARD J., and RONALD E. MULLER. *Global Reach: The Power of the Multinational Corporations*. New York: Simon and Schuster, 1974. A definitive work on multinational corporations and their implications.

BERLE, ADOLPH A., and GARDNER MEANS. *The Modern Corporation and Private Property*. New York: Harcourt, 1968. Sets out the case for regarding managerial and ownership classes as separate entities.

COLE, ROBERT E. *Work, Mobility and Participation: A Comparative Study of American and Japanese Industry*. Berkeley: University of California Press, 1979. A view from inside the Japanese factory that helps to dispel the many facile comparisons of the two societies and shows how adoption of a "Japanese model" would probably not work in the United States.

DOMHOFF, G. WILLIAM. *The Powers That Be*. New York: Random House, 1979. A description of elite rule in America that makes close connections with the corporate world and its concerns.

GALBRAITH, JOHN KENNETH. *The New Industrial State*. Boston: Houghton Mifflin, 1977. Persuasive description of the many previously unrecognized functions and emphases of corporations and the elites who run them.

GIRVAN, NORMAN, and RICHARD BERNAL. "The IMF and the Foreclosure of Development Options: The Case of Jamaica." *Monthly Review*, **33** (February 1982), 34–48. Case study revealing how the International Monetary Fund, at the behest of the multinationals, can control the economic policy of a developing nation.

GROSS, BERTRAM. *Friendly Fascism: The New Face of Power in America*. New York: M. Evans, 1980. Describes the imminent peril of the corporate state.

JENKINS, DAVID. *Job Power: Blue and White Collar Democracy*. Baltimore: Penguin, 1974. Introduction to the few but varied worker control and job enrichment schemes presently being tried in the United States.

LEWIS, W. ARTHUR. "Economic Development with Unlimited Supplies of Labor," *Manchester School of Economic and Social Studies*, **22** (May 1954), 139–191. Landmark labor power study that helps to explain the current migration of industry to underdeveloped countries.

MINTZ, BETH, and MICHAEL SCHWARTZ, "The Structure of Intercorporate Unity in American Business." *Social Problems*, **29** (December 1981), 87–103. Describes banking institutions as central to the organization of corporate interlocks in America.

SAMPSON, ANTHONY. *The Sovereign State of ITT*. New York: Stein and Day, 1973. Dated but interesting and informative look at one multinational giant and its activities.

SCOTT, JOHN. *Corporations, Classes and Capitalism*. London: Hutchinson, 1979. Dispassionate description of various theories and explanations of the modern corporation that employs a crossnational focus.

STONE, CHRISTOPHER. *Where the Law Ends: The Social Control of Corporate Behavior*. New York: Harper & Row, 1975. One of the better of many recent books on social responsibility of corporations, with fairly comprehensive treatment of the subject.

WRIGHT, J. PATRICK. *On a Clear Day You Can See General Motors*. New York: Avon, 1980. Best-selling memoirs of GM executive DeLorean that help to explain the decline of the American auto industry.

Conclusion: The Approaching Crisis

This book began on a note of paradox; it will end the same way. We have seen that the American political system, in its own terms, is working reasonably well. However, success on that score may be grounds more for concern than congratulations.

In its own terms, the system was designed for stability, to endure—and it has. It has survived triumphs and disasters that have undone many other nations. It has endured through wars and territorial expansions that led it across the continent and on to become the greatest military power on earth. In our day, only the Soviet Union comes close to matching that record, and in history only Rome equalled it. The American political system has also absorbed defeats of many kinds, especially at home—a catastrophic civil war, economic depression, an unenviable number of assassinations of public figures, gross mismanagement of natural resources, and the bungling of numerous social problems. And through all this the system survived remarkably unchanged in terms of its fundamental principles and practices.

A major reason for this record of successful survival has been the nation's isolation, both geographical and intellectual. Geographically the two oceans on either side preserved the nation from invading armies. Intellectually, the nation's persistent provincialism shielded it from the challenge of alternatives. Come triumph or disaster, the nation knew only one myth and one ideology, and it went forward to grapple with new conditions always from its narrow base of traditional political concepts.

For purposes of survival at least, these traditional concepts have proved effective. Tattered, even tainted, though it may be, our traditional national myth tells us convincingly who we are and legitimizes both us and our politics. If we fret that we are not what we mean to be, it is still the case that myth defines our hopes and we thereby still hold to it. Meanwhile, the national ideology with evenhanded effectiveness isolates the weak, fragments the strong, and divides up enough of what the government has to give among those anxious enough to snatch for it to keep any general breakdowns far from possibility. In the language of this book, the People are well "mythed," and the "barons" are getting what they must have. In this perspective, not only does the American political system work; it gives every appearance of being able to continue as it is indefinitely.

But survival is not the only criterion by which a political system may be judged. The capacity to meet major problems meaningfully is another. Deep in any nation's consciousness, not least the American, is a desire to be led with a sense that problems are being comprehended and that progress in dealing with them is being made. Over the past three decades or more, for an increasing number of Americans, that precious sense of national progression has been steadily weakening.

The Korean War, the Vietnam War, and Watergate, but also the failure to make good on the claims for racial equality, the difficulties in preserving the environment and rebuilding decaying cities, the escalating arms race and the threat of nuclear war, the steady disintegration of the social fabric in the face of increasing crime, drug abuse, and vandalism, weakening standards of private morality, and spreading evidence of a significant, long-term deterioration in the nation's industrial base under the pressures of recessionary spasms and foreign competition all have contributed to a deepening malaise. But ominous as these problems may be, there is an overriding concern among many thoughtful citizens that before them the political system stands in a virtually permanent state of immobility. The system may survive, but will the nation?

The inability of the political system to respond meaningfully and creatively to major problems afflicting the nation can be traced to three sources, in terms of the analytic framework of this book:

1. the inadequacy of the national myth in comprehending these problems;
2. the inadequacy of the national ideology in dealing with them;
3. the lack of fit between the myth and the ideology.

American political myth is filled with concern for distant goals, but because of its inherent individualism, it is ill-equipped to comprehend broad, national problems in the terms in which they arise, that is, social terms. This is a weakness of both ends and means. American myth tends to understand national problems in the vocabulary of individual needs, in terms mostly of securing individuals their rights, hardly ever in terms of anything more specific than enrolling unfortunates in job training programs or doling out welfare payments to them. Moreover, the campaigns to secure individuals these benefits are mounted mostly in terms of sudden, highly emotional crusades: "An unconditional war on poverty," "Make a new beginning," "Bring us together," "Ban the bomb," "We shall overcome," or "Split wood, not atoms." Some of these crusades may result in a burst of legislation but the programs they initiate over a few years languish from inattention.

Americans, said sociologist C. Wright Mills, lack "sociological imagination," a faculty he defined as the capacity to comprehend private troubles as public problems. It is precisely that capacity to translate the private into the public that the American political myth most lacks. It can sense our hurts and lament them mightily; but it lacks the intellectual fiber to organize our understanding of them in the broad, social terms that would permit their being attacked comprehensively. The American mythic mind simply does not see a whole range of social reality having to do with classes, structures, and forces.

Even if myth could identify and comprehend our most serious national problems, it is doubtful that our ideological resources could deal with them effectively. Those resources of institutions and practices have a good record of harmonizing the diverse claims of the competing interests. That is government of a kind. It forestalls a certain range of troubles. It also gets some things done. Interstate highways are built. Schools and other public services are provided after a fashion. Soldiers get armed and sent overseas, which was enough to win wars for much of our history. Men voyage to the moon in government programs of huge complexity. But whether these and all the other myriad operations of our 80,000 governments, federal, state, and local, add up to a coherent and comprehensive confrontation with the major issues now facing our nation is precisely the question most in doubt. Volumes of evidence suggest that our social ills are getting worse rather than better. More significantly, there is ample evidence that the ideological process of "incremental" policymaking is hit or miss on social goals and more interested in rewarding the entrenched than in solving problems.

Finally, there is the lack of fit between myth and ideology. As we have seen at many points in this book, the contradictions and tensions between myth and ideology in America can have devastating consequences, not least of which is an all too frequent cycle of challenge, anguish, immobilism, crisis, despair, and challenge again. But it is important to re-emphasize one central feature of this process. When myth sounds its brave calls for social justice, the reason ideology fails to respond is not that performance always falls short of promise. It is that ideology is uninterested in myth's goals. Ideology has its own goals, its own moral imperatives, most notably the values of personal freedom for those able and anxious to use it for their own pursuits. This disparity between the values and goals of myth and ideology is the final source of our national frustration.

An interesting but little noticed fact is that the American Revolution was fought in the name of liberty but it did not free anyone who was not already free when it began. It can be argued that because of this fact, the Civil War was inevitable. But then it must be pointed out that the Civil War did not do the job either. The problem of bringing social justice to all persons without regard to race is with us still.

Philip Roth's novel *Portnoy's Complaint* is cast in the form of a monologue delivered by a patient from his psychoanalyst's couch. The story it tells is ambiguous, tormented, and long. On the last line of the book's last page, the psychoanalyst speaks for the first time: "So [*said the doctor*]. Now vee may perhaps to begin. Yes?"[1]

Our book has been a critical interpretation of the American political system. Its emphasis has been on fact, analysis, explanation, and judgment about capabilities and limitations. It has not at any point outlined a program for political change or called for political action. It would be inappropriate for this or any similar book to attempt anything of that sort.

But as authors concerned about students, we will say this much. For readers who have been moved to think about action and change by what they have read in this book, the first concern cannot be to go out and do something straight off. The first concern must be to go back and rethink everything so far learned. To understand, it is not enough to be told how to understand. You must understand for yourself. That takes time, effort, and rethinking. Our conclusions must be your beginnings. So begin.

[1] Philip Roth, *Portnoy's Complaint* (New York: Random House, 1967).

Glossary

This glossary lists mostly concepts. More concrete terms can be located in the index.

Administrative law rules and orders issued by administrative agencies that have the force of law because they are derived from statutes passed by Congress and the president.

Adversary proceedings an arrangement in a court by which each side argues its case as vigorously as it can with the judge and/or jury to decide between them.

Appellate jurisdiction the right of a court to review the work of a lower court.

Authoritarianism the belief that final authority should be vested indefinitely in a single person or group.

Authority institutionalized power.

Bail money deposited by an accused as security to obtain release from jail while awaiting trial.

"Baron" a term employed in this book to indicate an individually situated political figure of influence and some power.

Boondoggle an informal expression for a make-work project.

Bourgeois ethos the underlying ethic of American business, preaching success for individual effort in unrestrained material pursuits.

Bureaucracy an organization of offices in hierarchical patterns according to rational and professional criteria.

California Plan a system for selecting judges that combines nomination by the governor, approval by a commission on judicial appointments, and popular election.

Capitalism   an economic system in which the means of production are owned and operated privately and investment decisions that determine future development are made primarily for private advantage.

Caucus   a meeting of like-minded individuals from a political party, legislature, or other body to formulate policy positions and plot tactics.

Chain of command   in a bureaucracy the linking of higher offices to lower ones without break so that orders can be transmitted downward and reports upward.

Charisma   the near superhuman attributes, frequently manifested in feats of physical strength and valor in battle, by which a person is enabled to unite (congregate) a community for action.

Checks and balances   a system of power allocations derived from mixed government theory that allows the various branches of a government to intervene ("check and balance") in the work of other branches.

Civil law   law regulating relationships between private individuals.

Civil liberty   a freedom for individuals, usually from state interference, guaranteed by the state itself as opposed to an ideal theory or supposed body of natural law.

Civil right   an opportunity to participate in the political process guaranteed by the state and its laws.

Civil service   the permanent, professional civilian work force of a government.

Class action   a case brought by an affected individual on behalf of himself and other members of a similarly affected and identifiable group.

Clientele   a group of people whose interests are especially served by a particular department, agency, legislative unit, or politician.

Closed primary   a party election to determine its nominee in which only party members may vote.

Cloture   a procedural motion to curtail debate and bring a substantive motion to a vote.

Collective goods   publicly secured goods that many individuals may enjoy such as parks, highways, and clean air.

Commerce clause   the clause in Article I, Section 8 of the U.S. Constitution empowering Congress to "regulate Commerce with foreign Nations, and among the several States."

Common good   the good of the whole community secured through the integrated experience and contributions of all its members.

Common law   a body of law based on custom, traditional usage, and judicial precedent rather than on statute or legal code.

Concurrent Majority   John C. Calhoun's doctrine holding that every interest in a system should be so represented that it would be enabled to block (veto) proposals by a numerical majority that might in its view adversely affect its vital interests.

Concurrent powers   powers shared by two or more authorities (e.g., the federal and state governments in the United States).

Confederalism   a system in which two or more states (nations) agree by permanent compact to set up a central authority to perform certain functions for them jointly.

Conference committee   a joint committee of the two houses of Congress created to devise a mutually acceptable version of a bill that the houses have passed in different forms.

Congressional oversight   review by Congress of administrative activity.

Constituency   a body of citizens, usually defined by residence in a particular territory, entitled to representation in a legislative body.

Constitution   the basic law of a community defining its essential political institutions, their powers, functions, and relationships, and the fundamental rights and obligations of its citizens.

Constitutionalism   a belief that the law, specifically the law of the constitution, should be sovereign and that the courts should ensure that all other political actors work within the confines of that law.

Continuing resolutions   temporary laws continuing in effect appropriation measures whose force would otherwise expire.

Criminal law   law defining certain acts as offenses against the public order and therefore subject to prosecution by the state.

Direct primary   an election in which voters choose directly a party's nominee in a subsequent election.

Division of powers   the allocation of powers between the federal and state governments and the people.

Double jeopardy   being tried a second time for the same crime although previously acquitted.

Due process   a requirement that a legal proceeding be carried out with exact regard for all specifications established for correct procedure.

Elite   a select group that dominates major political, economic, or social institutions.

Eminent domain   the power of the government to acquire by fiat private property for public use.

Equity   a body of mostly judge-made law employed to prevent injustice that might follow from the strict application of other law. It provides for remedies other than money damages.

Executive agreement   a binding agreement between the chief executives of two or more nation-states that, unlike a treaty, does not require ratification by their legislatures.

Executive order   a presidential order that does not require congressional approval.

Executive privilege   the president's right to withhold documents and other matters from review by Congress and the courts.

Federalism   a system for establishing governments within a single nation by which a fundamental law divides powers between a central government and two or more regional (state) governments.

Field of meaning   the fund of language, concepts, and understandings shared across a community that make possible political dialogue.

Filibuster   the process by which a small group of senators "talk a bill to death," that is, by dragging out the debate they prevent the bill's coming to a vote and force its withdrawal.

Fiscal policy   the policy by which taxation and other sources of public revenue are related to public spending by both amount and kind.

Full faith and credit   the requirement of Article IV, Section 1 of the U.S. Constitution that each state must accept the legal validity of the acts of all the other states.

Gerrymandering   the drawing of constituency boundaries with primary regard to party advantage.

Governance   the formal exercise of political power.

Grand jury   a panel of citizens convened to determine whether evidence is sufficient to bring a case to trial.

Grants in aid   financial help, usually from the federal government to state and local governments, to enable the undertaking of certain projects and programs.

Home rule   a form of local government guaranteeing a local authority considerable and secure autonomy from interference by the state.

Ideology   in this book, the conventionalized, routinized tradition of values and practices by which a nation operates its governmental processes.

Impeachment   the formal charging of a public official with misconduct.

Impoundment   the placement of funds or material in the custody of a court, or, similarly, the refusal of the president to allow an agency to spend funds allocated to it by Congress.

Incrementalism   the advancement of public policy in a sustained series of small steps each one of which must be individually justified and enacted.

Independent regulatory commission   a board charged with regulating in the public interest a specified sector of economic activity that operates with considerable independence from the president, Congress, and other agencies.

Indirect primary   a party election in which voters select delegates who choose the party nominee for a subsequent general election.

Individualism   a philosophy demanding that public recognition of individual life and pursuits be a primary value in the organization of society and government.

Initiative   a law proposed by popular petition and adopted by a vote of the general electorate.

Injunction   a court order requiring a person or group to do or refrain from doing a specified act.

Inquisitorial proceedings   the European alternative to adversary proceedings in which judges actively pursue truth and justice from dossiers prepared by the parties.

Institution   a formal pattern of offices or processes.

Interest group   an organization of persons having common views and needs that seeks to influence government policymaking and implementation.

"Iron triangles"   long-enduring coalitions between persons in Congress, the bureaucracy, and interest groups that are highly effective in securing their shared interests and are little subject to outside control or penetration.

Item veto   a power that allows an executive to delete particular provisions in a bill passed by the legislature.

Judicial activism   a belief that the courts should energetically exercise the power of judicial review and otherwise intervene in the political process.

Judicial restraint   a belief opposite to judicial activism.

Judicial ("constitutional") review   the right of the courts to review the work of other branches of the government, both federal and state, to determine whether it conforms with their interpretation of the fundamental (constitutional) law.

Justiciability   the qualification of a case for a court hearing.

Laissez-faire   a government policy of nonintervention in the economy.

Lateral penetration   the entry into a bureaucratic chain of command by an external agency that bypasses the nominal authorities.

Law   a uniform rule for behavior backed by governmental sanction.

Legislative veto   a right included in a law by which Congress can stay, in one of a variety of ways, its implementation by a particular agency.

Legitimation   the acknowledgment by word or action of power.

Liberal Democracy   a framework of law within which individuals are permitted to pursue their private interests with maximum possible freedom.

Lobbyist a professional representative of an interest group who attempts to influence public policymaking and implementation.

Log rolling the trading of votes in a legislature by which members promise to support each other's legislative projects.

Missouri Plan a system of selecting judges that combines nomination by a judicial commission, selection by the governor, and popular election.

Mixed government a system for organizing the powers of a government in which, within a rigid constitutional framework, the major divisions of society find independent representation in a bicameral legislative body monitored and policed by an independent executive authority.

Monetary policy policy that seeks to regulate general levels of economic activity and inflation by control over interest rates, the money supply, and the availability of credit.

Myth in this book, the conventionalized, routinized tradition of values and practices by which a nation defines and declares its historic identity and the legitimacy of its government.

Nation-state a community that shares a history and an enthusiasm as a people and also a sovereign juridical order.

Natural law a rule of conduct supposed to inhere in the rational order of nature and of humankind.

Natural rights liberties supposed to be possessed by all persons through their membership and participation in the rational order of nature.

Original jurisdiction the right of a court to hear a case in the first instance and to review both the facts and the relevant law.

Parliamentary system a way of organizing a government in which all power from the electorate is concentrated in the legislature, which in turn delegates it to an executive committee (cabinet) of, and responsible to, itself.

Participatory Democracy a vision of society in which all citizens, of every sort and capacity, are positively enabled to contribute to and participate in the fullness of the common life.

Party an organization of like-minded persons that seeks to control public policymaking and implementation by nominating and getting elected to public office some of its outstanding members.

Patronage government jobs that can be distributed by an elected official to supporters.

Petit Jury a panel of citizens selected to hear and decide on the facts at issue in a particular case.

Plea bargaining   a deal struck between an accused and the prosecution in which a guilty plea is made to reduced charges or sentencing.

Pluralism   the theory that American politics is dominated by the competition for governmental attention by a large number of diverse interest groups.

Pocket veto   a variation on the executive veto in which the president or governor fails to sign legislation after the legislature has adjourned, thereby killing it.

Police power   the right of a government to restrict individual behavior to further the common welfare, public health, and/or public morals.

Political culture   the historically shared field of meaning within which the dialogue that creates and exercises power goes on.

Political questions   issues involving the activities of the other branches of government into which the courts usually choose not to intervene.

Political socialization   the process by which the values and aspirations of a society are inculcated in and absorbed by its citizens.

Political system   the total complex of mythic and ideological institutions by which a nation-state proclaims its identity as a sovereign people and legitimizes and operates its government.

Politics   the dialogic process by which power is created and exercised in a shared field of meaning.

Power   a transactional relationship in which an acknowledged superior exercises control through language over the actions of a willing inferior.

Protestantism   the dominant, underlying religiosity in America that preaches salvation through personal repentance, faith, and a life of love, sacrifice, and devotion to the concerns of others.

Pressure group   an organization of like-minded persons who seek to influence government policymaking and implementation through lobbying efforts and arousing public opinion.

Privacy   an area ("sphere of anarchy") within which individuals can do much as they like without interference from the public or governmental authorities.

Public opinion   the passing preferences of the general public for particular politicians, policies, and parties.

Public policy   a course, plan, or program of actions designed to achieve broad social objectives consistently and efficiently.

Quorum   the number of members of a legislative body that must be present for it to conduct business legally.

Rational professional   in this book, a mentality that guides its work by a rational appreciation of how particular professional competencies can contribute to the public good.

Reapportionment   the redrawing of the constituency boundaries of a legislative body.

Recall   a system in which voters can petition for a special election to determine whether an elected official should be removed from office prior to expiration of the normal term.

Referendum   a vote by the general electorate on a proposed law or resolution.

Representative government   a system ensuring that legislators will serve ("represent") the clientele groups and interests that did the most to secure their election.

Responsible government   the core principle of the parliamentary system that requires ministers of the government, both individually and collectively, to be clearly accountable for the discharge of their duties.

Safe seat   a legislative seat for which there is little electoral competition because the victory of one of the candidates is seen as virtually assured in advance.

Select committee   a temporary legislative committee created to carry out a special investigation or other matters.

Senatorial courtesy   an unwritten rule in the Senate that it will uphold the objection of a member who wishes to block a judicial (usually) appointment being made in his state by the president.

Seniority rule   a rule in Congress that the longest-serving member of the majority party on each committee becomes its chairman.

Separation of powers   a system for organizing government in which the power to govern is distributed among three functionally differentiated branches—legislative, executive, and judicial—each of which is answerable in one way or another to the electorate but not to each other.

Social Democracy   a vision of society as united, under the congregating leadership of a charismatic hero, in pursuit of social justice and egalitarianism.

Sovereignty   final authority in a legal order that receives habitual obedience from the bulk of the population and does not render it to any external power.

Span of control   in a bureaucracy, the number of inferiors reporting to a single superior.

Speaker   the presiding officer in an assembly.

Standing committee   a permanent committee of a legislative body.

Stare decisis   literally, "let the decision stand," or judges should be guided by precedent.

Subpoena   the power granted most courts and many legislative committees to order witnesses to produce records and testify at a hearing under penalty of the law.

Substantive due process a requirement that a legal proceeding observe not only all specified procedures but also all substantive (usually constitutional) guarantees (e.g., life, liberty, and property).

Tyranny arbitrary, uncontrolled government in its own interest.

Unitary government a system in which a nation's fundamental law assigns all legitimate power to one central government, which may elect to delegate some of it to local governments inferior to itself.

Welfare state a comprehensive program by which the government seeks to meet the minimum needs of a nation's unfortunate—the aged, the abandoned, the unemployed, the poverty-stricken, the despairing, the chronically ill, and the like.

Whip the party leader in a legislative chamber charged with getting party members to vote the party position on legislation.

Writ of certiorari an order from a higher (appeal) court to a lower court to send up the record of a case for review; in the case of the Supreme Court, a discretionary device used to select cases the court wishes to hear.

Writ of habeas corpus a court order usually to police officials to bring a prisoner to a hearing to determine whether there are sufficient grounds to warrant continued detention.

Writ of mandamus a court order requiring a government official to perform a specified action.

Appendix I
The Declaration of Independence

When, in the course of human events, it becomes necessary for one people to dissolve the political bands which have connected them with another, and to assume, among the powers of the earth, the separate and equal station to which the laws of nature and of nature's God entitle them, a decent respect to the opinions of mankind requires that they should declare the causes which impel them to the separation.

We hold these truths to be self-evident; that all men are created equal, that they are endowed by their Creator with certain unalienable rights, that among these are life, liberty, and the pursuit of happiness.

That, to secure these rights, governments are instituted among men, deriving their just powers from the consent of the governed;

That whenever any form of government becomes destructive of these ends, it is the right of the people to alter or to abolish it, and to institute new government, laying its foundation on such principles, and organizing its power in such form, as to them shall seem most likely to effect their safety and happiness. Prudence, indeed, will dictate that governments long established should not be changed for light and transient causes; and accordingly all experience hath shown that mankind are more disposed to suffer while evils are sufferable, than to right themselves by abolishing the forms to which they are accustomed. But when a long train of abuses and usurpations, pursuing invariably the same object, evinces a design to reduce them under absolute despotism, it is their right, it is their duty, to throw off such government, and to provide new guards for their future security.

Such has been the patient sufferance of these colonies; and such is now the necessity which constrains them to alter their former systems of government. The history of the present king of Great Britain is a history of repeated injuries and usurpations, all having in direct object the establishment of an absolute tyranny over these states. To prove this, let facts be submitted to a candid world.

He has refused his assent to laws the most wholesome and necessary for the public good.

He has forbidden his governors to pass laws of immediate and pressing importance unless suspended in their operation till his assent should be obtained; and when so suspended, he has utterly neglected to attend to them.

He has refused to pass other laws for the accommodation of large districts of people, unless those people would relinquish the right of representation in the legislature, a right inestimable to them, and formidable to tyrants only.

He has called together legislative bodies at places unusual, uncomfortable, and distant from the depository of their public records, for the sole purpose of fatiguing them into compliance with his measures.

He has dissolved representative houses repeatedly, for opposing, with manly firmness, his invasions on the rights of the people.

He has refused, for a long time after such dissolutions, to cause others to be elected; whereby the legislative powers, incapable of annihilation, have returned to the people at large for their exercise; the state remaining, in the mean time, exposed to all the dangers of invasion from without and convulsions within.

He has endeavored to prevent the population of these states; for that purpose obstructing the laws of naturalization of foreigners, refusing to pass others to encourage their migration hither, and raising the conditions of new appropriations of lands.

He has obstructed the administration of justice, by refusing his assent to laws for establishing judiciary powers.

He has made judges dependent on his will alone for the tenure of their offices, and the amount and payment of their salaries.

He has erected a multitude of new offices, and sent hither swarms of officers to harass our people and eat out their substance.

He has kept among us, in times of peace, standing armies, without the consent of our legislature.

He has affected to render the military independent of, and superior to, the civil power.

He has combined with others to subject us to a jurisdiction foreign to our constitution and unacknowledged by our laws, giving his assent to their acts of pretended legislation:

For quartering large bodies of armed troops among us;

For protecting them, by a mock trial, from punishment for any murders which they should commit on the inhabitants of these states;

For cutting off our trade with all parts of the world;

For imposing taxes on us without our consent;

For depriving us, in many cases, of the benefits of trial by jury;

For transporting us beyond seas, to be tried for pretended offenses;

For abolishing the free system of English laws in a neighboring province, establishing therein an arbitrary government, and enlarging its boundaries, so as to render it at once an example and fit instrument for introducing the same absolute rule into these colonies;

For taking away our charters, abolishing our most valuable laws, and altering, fundamentally, the forms of our governments.

For suspending our own legislatures, and declaring themselves invested with power to legislate for us in all cases whatsoever.

He has abdicated government here, by declaring us out of his protection and waging war against us.

He has plundered our seas, ravaged our coasts, burned our towns, and destroyed the lives of our people.

He is at this time transporting large armies of foreign mercenaries to complete the works of death, desolation, and tyranny already begun with circumstances of cruelty and perfidy scarcely paralleled in the most barbarous ages and totally unworthy the head of a civilized nation.

He has constrained our fellow-citizens, taken captive on the high seas, to bear arms against their country, to become the executioners of their friends and brethren, or to fall themselves by their hands.

He has excited domestic insurrections among us, and has endeavored to bring on the inhabitants of our frontiers the merciless Indian savages, whose known rule of warfare is an undistinguished destruction of all ages, sexes, and conditions.

In every stage of these oppressions we have petitioned for redress in the most humble terms; our repeated petitions have been answered only by repeated injury. A prince whose character is thus marked by every act which may define a tyrant is unfit to be the ruler of a free people.

Nor have we been wanting in attention to our British brethren. We have warned them, from time to time, of attempts by their legislature to extend an unwarrantable jurisdiction over us. We have reminded them of the circumstances of our emigration and settlement here. We have appealed to their native justice and magnanimity; and we have conjured them, by the ties of our common kindred, to disavow these usurpations, which would inevitably interrupt our connections and correspondence. They, too, have been deaf to the voice of justice and of consanguinity. We must, therefore, acquiesce in the necessity which denounces our separation, and hold them, as we hold the rest of mankind, enemies in war, in peace, friends.

We, therefore, the representatives of the United States of America, in General Congress assembled, appealing to the Supreme Judge of the world for the rectitude of our intentions, do, in the name and by authority of the good people of these colonies, solemnly publish and declare, that these united colonies are, and of right ought to be, free and independent states; that they are absolved from all allegiance to the British crown, and that all political connection between them and the state of Great Britain is, and ought to be, totally dissolved; and that, as free and independent states, they have full power to levy war, conclude peace, contract alliances, establish commerce, and do all other acts and things which independent states may of right do. And, for the support of this declaration, with a firm reliance on the protection of Divine Providence, we mutually pledge to each other our lives, our fortunes, and our sacred honor.

Appendix II
The Constitution of the United States

We the People of the United States, in Order to form a more perfect Union, establish Justice, insure domestic Tranquility, provide for the common defence, promote the general Welfare, and secure the Blessings of Liberty to ourselves and our Posterity, do ordain and establish this Constitution for the United States of America.

Article I—The Legislative Article

Section I. All Legislative Powers herein granted shall be vested in a Congress of the United States, which shall consist of a Senate and House of Representatives.

Section 2. The House of Representatives shall be composed of Members chosen every second Year by the People of the several States, and the Electors in each State shall have the Qualifications requisite for Electors of the most numerous Branch of the State Legislature.

No Person shall be a Representative who shall not have attained to the Age of twenty-five Years, and been seven Years a Citizen of the United States, and who shall not, when elected, be an Inhabitant of that State in which he shall be chosen.

Representatives and direct [Taxes][1] shall be apportioned among the several States which may be included within this Union, according to their respective Numbers, [which shall be determined by adding to the whole Number of free Persons, including those bound to Service for a Term of Years, and excluding Indians not taxed, three fifths of all other Persons].[2] The actual Enumeration shall be made within three Years

[1]Modified by the 16th Amendment
[2]"Other Persons" refers to black slaves. Replaced by Section 2, 14th Amendment

after the first Meeting of the Congress of the United States, and within every subsequent Term of ten Years, in such Manner as they shall by Law direct. The Number of Representatives shall not exceed one for every thirty Thousand, but each State shall have at Least one Representative; and until such enumeration shall be made, the State of New Hampshire shall be entitled to chuse three, Massachusetts eight, Rhode-Island and Providence Plantations one, Connecticut five, New-York six, New Jersey four, Pennsylvania eight, Delaware one, Maryland six, Virginia ten, North Carolina five, South Carolina five, and Georgia three.

When vacancies happen in the Representation from any State, the Executive Authority thereof shall issue Writs of Election to fill such Vacancies.

The House of Representatives shall chuse their speaker and other Officers; and shall have the sole Power of Impeachment.

Section 3.   The Senate of the United States shall be composed of two Senators from each State, [chosen by the Legislature thereof,][3] for six Years; and each Senator shall have one Vote.

Immediately after they shall be assembled in Consequence of the first Election, they shall be divided as equally as may be into three Classes. The Seats of the Senators of the first Class shall be vacated at the Expiration of the second Year, of the second Class at the Expiration of the fourth Year, and of the third Class at the Expiration of the sixth Year, so that one third may be chosen every second Year; [and if Vacancies happen by Resignation, or otherwise, during the Recess of the Legislature of any State, the Executive thereof may make temporary Appointments until the next Meeting of the Legislature, which, shall then fill such Vacancies.][4]

No Person shall be a Senator who shall not have attained to the Age of thirty Years, and been nine Years a Citizen of the United States, and who shall not, when elected, be an Inhabitant of that State for which he shall be chosen.

The Vice President of the United States shall be President of the Senate, but shall have no Vote, unless they be equally divided.

The Senate shall chuse their other Officers, and also a President pro tempore, in the Absence of the Vice President, or when he shall exercise the Office of the President of the United States.

The Senate shall have the sole Power to try all Impeachments. When sitting for that Purpose, they shall be on Oath or Affirmation. When the President of the United States is tried, the Chief Justice shall preside: And no Person shall be convicted without the Concurrence of two thirds of the Members present.

[3]Repealed by the 17th Amendment
[4]Modified by the 17th Amendment

Judgment in Cases of Impeachment shall not extend further than to removal from Office, and disqualification to hold and enjoy any Office of honor, Trust or Profit under the United States: but the Party convicted shall nevertheless be liable and subject to Indictment, Trial, Judgment and Punishment, according to law.

Section 4.   The Times, Places and Manner of holding Elections for Senators and Representatives, shall be prescribed in each State by the legislature thereof; but the Congress may at any time by Law make or alter such Regulations, except as to the Place of chusing Senators.

[The Congress shall assemble at least once in every Year, and such Meeting shall be on the first Monday in December, unless they shall by Law appoint a different Day.]⁵

Section 5.   Each House shall be the Judge of the Elections, Returns and Qualifications of its own Members, and a Majority of each shall constitute a Quorum to do Business; but a smaller Number may adjourn from day to day, and may be authorized to compel the Attendance of absent Members, in such Manner, and under such Penalties as each House may provide.

Each House may determine the Rules of its Proceedings, punish its Members for disorderly Behaviour, and, with the Concurrence of two thirds, expel a Member.

Each House shall keep a Journal of its Proceedings, and from time to time publish the same, excepting such Parts as may in their Judgment require Secrecy; and the Yeas and Nays of the Members of either House on any question shall, at the Desire of one fifth of those Present, be entered on the Journal.

Neither House, during the Session of Congress, shall, without the Consent of the other, adjourn for more than three days, nor to any other Place than that in which the two Houses shall be sitting.

Section 6.   The Senators and Representatives shall receive a Compensation for their Services, to be ascertained by Law, and paid out of the Treasury of the United States. They shall in all Cases, except Treason, Felony and Breach of the Peace, be privileged from Arrest during their Attendance at the Session of their respective Houses, and in going to and returning from the same; and for any Speech or Debate in either House, they shall not be questioned in any other Place.

No Senator or Representative shall, during the Time for which he was elected, be appointed to any civil Office under the Authority of the United States, which shall have been created, or the Emoluments whereof shall have been encreased during such time; and no Person

⁵Changed by the 20th Amendment

holding any Office under the United States, shall be a Member of either House during his Continuance in Office.

Section 7. All Bills for raising Revenue shall originate in the House of Representatives; but the Senate may propose or concur with Amendments as on other Bills.

Every Bill which shall have passed the House of Representatives and the Senate, shall, before it become a Law, be presented to the President of the United States; If he approve he shall sign it, but if not he shall return it, with his Objections to that House in which it shall have originated, who shall enter the Objections at large on their Journal, and proceed to reconsider it. If after such Reconsideration two thirds of that House shall agree to pass the Bill, it shall be sent, together with the Objections, to the other House, by which it shall likewise be reconsidered, and if approved by two thirds of that House, it shall become a Law. But in all such Cases the Votes of both the Houses shall be determined by Yeas and Nays, and the Names of the Persons voting for and against the Bill shall be entered on the Journal of each House respectively. If any Bill shall not be returned by the President within the ten Days (Sunday excepted) after it shall have been presented to him, the Same shall be a Law, in like Manner as if he had signed it, unless the Congress by their Adjournment prevent its Return, in which Case it shall not be a Law.

Every Order, Resolution, or Vote to which the Concurrence of the Senate and House of Representatives may be necessary (except on a question of Adjournment) shall be presented to the President of the United States; and before the Same shall take Effect, shall be approved by him, or being disapproved by him, shall be repassed by two thirds of the Senate and House of Representatives, according to the Rules and Limitations prescribed in the Case of a Bill.

Section 8. The Congress shall have Power To lay and collect Taxes, Duties, Imposts and Excises, to pay the Debts and provide for the common Defence and general Welfare of the United States; but all Duties, Imposts and Excises shall be uniform throughout the United States;

To borrow Money on the credit of the United States;

To regulate Commerce with foreign Nations, and among the several States, and with the Indian Tribes;

To establish an uniform Rule of Naturalization, and uniform Laws on the subject of Bankruptcies throughout the United States;

To coin Money, regulate the Value thereof, and of foreign Coin, and fix the Standard of Weights and Measures;

To provide for the Punishment of counterfeiting the Securities and current Coin of the United States;

To establish Post Offices and post Roads;

To promote the Progress of Science and useful Arts, by securing for limited Times to Authors and Inventors the exclusive Right to their respective Writings and Discoveries;

To constitute Tribunals inferior to the supreme Court;

To define and punish Piracies and Felonies committed on the high Seas, and Offences against the Law of Nations;

To declare War, grant Letters of Marque and Reprisal, and make Rules concerning Captures on Land and Water;

To raise and support Armies, but no Appropriation of Money to that Use shall be for a longer Term than two Years;

To provide and maintain a Navy;

To make Rules for the Government and Regulation of the land and naval Forces;

To provide for calling forth the Militia to execute the Laws of the Union, suppress Insurrections and repel Invasions;

To provide for organizing, arming, and disciplining the Militia, and for governing such Part of them as may be employed in the Service of the United States, reserving to the States respectively, the Appointment of the Officers, and the Authority of training the Militia according to the discipline prescribed by Congress;

To exercise exclusive Legislation in all Cases whatsoever, over such District (not exceeding ten Miles square) as may, by Cession of particular States, and the Acceptance of Congress, become the Seat of the Government of the United States, and to exercise like Authority over all Places purchased by the Consent of the Legislature of the State in which the Same shall be, for the Erection of Forts, Magazines, Arsenals, dock-Yards, and other needful Buildings;-And

To make all Laws which shall be necessary and proper for carrying into Execution the foregoing Powers, and all other Powers vested by this Constitution in the Government of the United States, or in any Department or Officer thereof.

Section 9.   The Migration or Importation of such Persons as any of the States now existing shall think proper to admit, shall not be prohibited by the Congress prior to the Year one thousand eight hundred and eight, but a Tax or duty may be imposed on such Importation, not exceeding ten dollars for each Person.

Congress could prohibit it after 1808 —

The Privilege of the Writ of Habeas Corpus shall not be suspended, unless when in Cases of Rebellion or Invasion the public Safety may require it.

No Bill of Attainder or ex post facto Law shall be passed.

[No Capitation, or other direct, Tax shall be laid, unless in Proportion to the Census or Enumeration herein before directed to be taken.][6]

[6]Modified by the 16th Amendment

No Tax or Duty shall be laid on Articles exported from any State.

No Preference shall be given by any Regulation of Commerce or Revenue to the Ports of one State over those of another: nor shall Vessels bound to, or from, one State be obliged to enter, clear, or pay Duties in another.

No Money shall be drawn from the Treasury, but in Consequence of Appropriations made by Law; and a regular Statement and Account of the Receipts and Expenditures of all public Money shall be published from time to time.

No Title of Nobility shall be granted by the United States: And no Person holding any Office of Profit or Trust under them, shall, without the Consent of the Congress, accept of any present, Emolument, Office, or Title, of any kind whatever, from any King, Prince, or foreign State.

Section 10. No State shall enter into any Treaty, Alliance, or Confederation; grant Letters of Marque and Reprisal; coin Money; emit Bills of Credit; make any Thing but gold and silver Coin a Tender in Payment of Debts; pass any Bill of Attainder, ex post facto Law, or Law impairing the Obligation of Contracts, or grant any Title of Nobility.

No State shall, without the Consent of the Congress, lay any Imposts or Duties on Imports or Exports, except what may be absolutely necessary for executing its inspection Laws: and the net Produce of all Duties and Imposts, laid by any State on Imports or Exports, shall be for the Use of the Treasury of the United States; and all such Laws shall be subject to the Revision and Controul of the Congress.

No State shall, without the Consent of Congress, lay any Duty of Tonnage, keep Troops, or Ships of War in time of Peace, enter into any Agreement or Compact with another State, or with a foreign Power, or engage in War, unless actually invaded, or in such imminent Danger as will not admit of delay.

Article II—The Executive Article

Section 1. The executive Power shall be vested in a President of the United States of America. He shall hold his Office during the Term of four Years, and, together with the Vice President, chosen for the same term, be elected, as follows.

Each State shall appoint, in such Manner as the Legislature thereof may direct, a Number of Electors, equal to the whole Number of Senators and Representatives to which the State may be entitled in the Congress: but no Senator or Representative, or Person holding an Office of Trust or Profit under the United States, shall be appointed an Elector.

[The Electors shall meet in their respective States, and vote by Ballot for two Persons, of whom one at least shall not be an Inhabitant of the same State with themselves. And they shall make a List of all the Persons voted for, and of the Number of Votes for each; which List they shall sign and certify, and transmit sealed to the Seat of the Government of the United States, directed to the President of the Senate. The President of the Senate shall, in the Presence of the Senate and House of Representatives, open all the Certificates, and the Votes shall then be counted. The Person having the greatest Number of Votes shall be the President, if such Number be a Majority of the whole Number of Electors appointed; and if there be more than one who have such Majority, and have an equal Number of Votes, then the House of Representatives shall immediately chuse by Ballot one of them for President: and if no Person have a Majority, then from the five highest on the List the said House shall in like Manner chuse the President. But in chusing the President, the Votes shall be taken by States, the Representation from each State having one Vote; a quorum for this purpose shall consist of a Member or Members from two thirds of the States, and a Majority of all the States shall be necessary to a Choice. In every Case, after the Choice of the President, the Person having the greatest Number of Votes of the Electors shall be the Vice President. But if there should remain two or more who have equal Votes, the Senate shall chuse from them by Ballot the Vice President.][7]

The Congress may determine the Time of chusing the Electors, and the Day on which they shall give their Votes; which Day shall be the same throughout the United States.

No Person except a natural born Citizen, or a Citizen of the United States, at the time of the Adoption of this Constitution, shall be eligible to the Office of President; neither shall any Person be eligible to that Office who shall not have attained the Age of thirty-five Years, and been fourteen Years a Resident within the United States.

[In Case of the Removal of the President from Office, or of his Death, Resignation, or Inability to discharge the Powers and Duties of the said Office, the same shall devolve on the Vice President, and the Congress may by Law provide for the Case of Removal, Death, Resignation, or Inability, both of the President and Vice President, declaring what Officer shall then act as President, and such Officer shall act accordingly, until the Disability be removed, or a President shall be elected.][8]

The President shall, at stated Times, receive for his Services a Compensation, which shall neither be encreased nor diminished during the Period for which he shall have been elected, and he shall not receive within that Period any other Emolument from the United States, or any of them.

Before he enter on the Execution of his Office, he shall take the fol-

[7]Changed by the 12th and 20th Amendments
[8]Modified by the 25th Amendment

lowing Oath or Affirmation:-"I do solemnly swear (or affirm) that I will faithfully execute the Office of President of the United States, and will to the best of my Ability, preserve, protect and defend the Constitution of the United States."

Section 2. The President shall be Commander in Chief of the Army and Navy of the United States, and of the Militia of the several States, when called into the actual Service of the United States; he may require the Opinion, in writing, of the principal Officer in each of the executive Departments, upon any Subject relating to the Duties of their respective Offices, and he shall have power to grant Reprieves and Pardons for Offences against the United States, except in Cases of Impeachment.

He shall have Power, by and with the Advice and Consent of the Senate, to make Treaties, provided two thirds of the Senators present concur; and he shall nominate, and by and with the Advice and Consent of the Senate, shall appoint Ambassadors, other public Ministers and Consuls, Judges of the supreme Court, and all other Officers of the United States, whose Appointments are not herein otherwise provided for, and which shall be established by Law; but the Congress may by Law vest the Appointment of such inferior Officers, as they think proper, in the President alone, in the Courts of Law, or in the Heads of Departments.

The President shall have Power to fill up all Vacancies that may happen during the Recess of the Senate, by granting Commissions which shall expire at the End of their next Session.

Section 3. He shall from time to time give to the Congress Information of the State of the Union, and recommend to their Consideration such Measures as he shall judge necessary and expedient; he may, on extraordinary Occasions, convene both Houses, or either of them, and in Case of Disagreement between them, with Respect to the Time of Adjournment, he may adjourn them to such Time as he shall think proper; he shall take Care that the Laws be faithfully executed, and shall Commission all the Officers of the United States.

Section 4. The President, Vice President and all civil Officers of the United States, shall be removed from Office on Impeachment for, and Conviction of, Treason, Bribery, or other High Crimes and Misdemeanors.

Article III—The Judicial Article

Section 1. The judicial Power of the United States, shall be vested in one supreme Court, and in such inferior Courts as the Congress may from time to time ordain and establish. The Judges, both of the supreme and inferior Courts, shall hold their Offices during good Behaviour, and shall, at stated Times, receive for their Services, a Compensation, which shall not be diminished during their Continuance in Office.

Section 2. The judicial Power shall extend to all Cases, in Law and Equity, arising under this Constitution, the Laws of the United States, and Treaties made, or which shall be made, under their Authority;-to all Cases affecting Ambassadors, other public Ministers and Consuls;-to all Cases of admiralty and maritime Jurisdiction;-to Controversies to which the United States shall be a Party;-to Controversies between two or more States; [between a State and Citizens of another State][9] between Citizens of different States;-between Citizens of the same State claiming Lands under Grants of different States, [and between a State or the Citizens thereof, and foreign States, Citizens or Subjects.][9]

In all Cases affecting Ambassadors, other public Ministers and Consuls, and those in which a State shall be Party, the supreme Court shall have original Jurisdiction. In all the other Cases before mentioned, the supreme Court shall have appellate Jurisdiction, both as to Law and Fact, with such Exceptions, and under such Regulations as the Congress shall make.

The Trial of all Crimes, except in Cases of Impeachment, shall be by Jury; and such Trial shall be held in the State where the said Crimes shall have been committed; but when not committed within any State, the Trial shall be at such Place or Places as the Congress may by Law have directed.

Section 3. Treason against the United States, shall consist only in levying War against them, or in adhering to their Enemies, giving them Aid and Comfort. No Person shall be convicted of Treason unless on the Testimony of two Witnesses to the same overt Act, or on Confession in open Court.

The Congress shall have Power to declare the Punishment of Treason, but no Attainder of Treason shall work Corruption of Blood, or Forfeiture except during the Life of the Person attainted.

Article IV—Interstate Relations

Section 1. Full Faith and Credit shall be given in each State to the public Acts, Records, and judicial Proceedings of every other State. And the Congress may by general Laws prescribe the Manner in which such Acts, Records and Proceedings shall be proved, and the Effect thereof.

[9]Modified by the 11th Amendment

Section 2. The citizens of each State shall be entitled to all Privileges and Immunities of Citizens in the several States.

A Person charged in any State with Treason, Felony, or other Crime, who shall flee from Justice, and be found in another State, shall on Demand of the executive Authority of the State from which he fled, be delivered up, to be removed to the State having Jurisdiction of the Crime.

[No Person held to Service or Labour in one State, under the Laws thereof, escaping into another, shall, in Consequence of any Law or Regulation therein, be discharged from such Service or Labour, but shall be delivered up on Claim of the Party to whom such Service or labour may be due].[10]

Section 3. New States may be admitted by the Congress into this Union; but no new State shall be formed or erected within the Jurisdiction of any other State; nor any State be formed by the Junction of two or more States, or Parts of States, without the Consent of the Legislatures of the States concerned as well as of the Congress.

The Congress shall have Power or dispose of and make all needful Rules and Regulations respecting the Territory or other Property belonging to the United States; and nothing in this Constitution shall be so construed as to Prejudice any Claims of the United States, or of any particular State.

Section 4. The United States shall guarantee to every State in this Union a Republican Form of Government, and shall protect each of them against Invasion; and on Application of the Legislature, or of the Executive (when the Legislature cannot be convened) against domestic Violence.

Article V—The Amending Power

The Congress, whenever two thirds of both Houses shall deem it necessary, shall propose Amendments to this Constitution, or, on the Application of the Legislatures of two thirds of the several States, shall call a Convention for proposing Amendments, which, in either Case, shall be valid to all Intents and Purposes, as Part of this Constitution, when ratified by the Legislatures of three fourths of the several States, or by Conventions in three fourths thereof, as the one or the other Mode of Ratification may be proposed by the Congress; Provided that no Amendment which may be made prior to the Year One thousand eight hundred and eight shall in any Manner affect the first and fourth

[10]Repealed by the 13th Amendment

Clauses in the Ninth Section of the first Article; and that no State, without its Consent, shall be deprived of its equal Suffrage in the Senate.

Article VI—The Supremacy Article

All Debts contracted and Engagements entered into, before the Adoption of this Constitution, shall be as valid against the United States under this Constitution, as under the Confederation.

This Constitution, and the Laws of the United States which shall be made in Pursuance thereof; and all Treaties made, or which shall be made, under the Authority of the United States, shall be the supreme Law of the Land; and the Judges in every State shall be bound thereby, any Thing in the Constitution or Laws of any State to the Contrary notwithstanding.

The Senators and Representatives before mentioned, and the Members of the several State Legislatures, and all executive and judicial Officers, both of the United States and of the several States, shall be bound by Oath or Affirmation, to support this Constitution; but no religious Test shall ever be required as a Qualification to any Office or public Trust under the United States.

Article VII—Ratification

The Ratification of the Conventions of nine States, shall be sufficient for the Establishment of this Constitution between the States so ratifying the Same.

Done in Convention by the Unanimous Consent of the States present the Seventeenth Day in September in the Year of our Lord one thousand seven hundred and Eighty seven and of the Independence of the United States of America the Twelfth. In witness whereof We have hereunto subscribed our Names.

Amendment 1—Religion, Speech, Assembly, and Politics

Congress shall make no law respecting an establishment of religion, or prohibiting the free exercise thereof; or abridging the freedom of speech, or of the press; or the right of the people peaceably to assemble, and to petition the Government for a redress or grievances.

Amendment 2—Militia and the Right to Bear Arms

A well regulated Militia, being necessary to the security of a free State, the right of people to keep and bear Arms, shall not be infringed.

Amendment 3—Quartering of Soldiers

No Soldier shall, in time of peace be quartered in any house, without the consent of the Owner, nor in time of war, but in a manner to be prescribed by law.

Amendment 4—Searches and Seizures

The right of the people to be secure in their persons, houses, papers, and effects, against unreasonable searches and seizures, shall not be violated, and no Warrants shall issue, but upon probable cause, supported by Oath or affirmation, and particularly describing the place to be searched and the persons or things to be seized.

Amendment 5—Grand Juries, Self-incrimination, Double Jeopardy, Due Process, and Eminent Domain

No person shall be held to answer for a capital, or otherwise infamous crime, unless on a presentment or indictment of a Grand Jury, except in cases arising in the land or naval forces, or in the Militia, when in actual service in time of War or public danger; nor shall any person be subject for the same offence to be twice put in jeopardy of life or limb; nor shall be compelled in any criminal case to be a witness against himself, nor be deprived of life, liberty, or property, without due process of law; not shall private property be taken for public use, without just compensation.

Amendment 6—Criminal Court Procedures

In all criminal prosecutions, the accused shall enjoy the right to a speedy and public trial, by an impartial jury of the State and district wherein the crime shall have been committed, which district shall have been previously ascertained by law, and to be informed of the nature and cause of the accusation; to be confronted with the witnesses against him; to have compulsory process for obtaining witnesses in his favor, and to have the Assistance of Counsel for his defence.

Amendment 7—Trial by Jury in Common Law Cases

In Suits at common law, where the value in controversy shall exceed twenty dollars, the right of trial by jury shall be preserved, and no fact

tried by a jury, shall be otherwise reexamined in any Court of the
United States, than according to the rules of the common law.

Amendment 8—Bail, Cruel, and Unusual Punishment

Excessive bail shall not be required, nor excessive fines imposed, nor
cruel and unusual punishments inflicted.

Amendment 9—Rights Retained by the People

The enumeration in the Constitution, of certain rights, shall not be construed to deny or disparage others retained by the people.

Amendment 10—Reserved Powers of the States

The powers not delegated to the United States by the Constitution, nor
prohibited by it to the States, are reserved to the States respectively, or
to the people.

Amendment 11—Suits against the States

The Judicial power of the United States shall not be construed to extend
to any suit in law or equity, commenced or prosecuted against one of
the United States by Citizens of another State, or by Citizens or Subjects of any Foreign State.

Amendment 12—Election of the President

The Electors shall meet in their respective states and vote by ballot for
President and Vice-President, one of whom, at least, shall not be an
inhabitant of the same state with themselves; they shall name in their
ballots the person voted for as President, and in distinct ballots the
person voted for as Vice-President, and they shall make distinct lists of
all persons voted for as President, and of all persons voted for as Vice-
President, and of the number of votes for each, which lists they shall
sign and certify, and transmit sealed to the seat of the government of the
United States, directed to the President of the Senate;-The President of
the Senate shall, in presence of the Senate and House of Representatives, open all the certificates and the votes shall then be counted;-The
person having the greatest number of votes for President, shall be the

President, if such number be a majority of the whole number of Electors appointed; and if no person have such majority, then from the persons having the highest numbers not exceeding three on the list of those voted for as President, the House of Representatives shall choose immediately, by ballot, the President. But in choosing the President, the votes shall be taken by states, the representation from each state having one vote; a quorum for this purpose shall consist of a member or members from two-thirds of the states, and a majority of all the states shall be necessary to a choice. [And if the House of Representatives shall not choose a President whenever the right of the choice shall devolve upon them, before the fourth day of March next following, then the Vice-President shall act as President, as in the case of the death or other constitutional disability of the President].[11] The person having the greatest number of votes as Vice-President, shall be the Vice-President, if such number be a majority of the whole number of Electors appointed, and if no person have a majority, then from the two highest numbers on the list, the Senate shall choose the Vice-President; a quorum for the purpose shall consist of two-thirds of the whole number of Senators, and a majority of the whole number shall be necessary to a choice. But no person constitutionally ineligible to the office of President shall be eligible to that of Vice-President of the United States.

Amendment 13—Prohibition of Slavery

Section 1.   Neither slavery nor involuntary servitude, except as a punishment for crime whereof the party shall have been duly convicted, shall exist within the United States, or any place subject to their jurisdiction.

Section 2.   Congress shall have power to enforce this article by appropriate legislation.

Amendment 14—Citizenship, Due Process, and Equal Protection of the Laws

Section 1.   All persons born or naturalized in the United States, and subject to the jurisdiction thereof, are citizens of the United States and of the State wherein they reside. No State shall make or enforce any law which shall abridge the privileges or immunities of citizens of the United States; nor shall any State deprive any person of life, liberty, or property, without due process of law; nor deny to any person within its jurisdiction the equal protection of the laws.

[11]Changed by the 20th Amendment

Section 2.   Representatives shall be apportioned among the several States according to their respective numbers, counting the whole number of persons in each State, excluding Indians not taxed. But when the right to vote at any election for the choice of electors for President and Vice President of the United States, Representatives in Congress, the Executive and Judicial Officers of a State, or the members of the Legislature thereof, is denied to any of the male inhabitants of such State, being [twenty-one][12] years of age, and citizens of the United States, or in any way abridged, except for participation in rebellion, or other crime, the basis of representation therein shall be reduced in the proportion which the number of such male citizens shall bear to the whole number of male citizens twenty-one years of age in such State.

Section 3.   No person shall be a Senator or Representative in Congress, or elector of President and Vice President, or hold any office, civil or military, under the United States, or under any State, who having previously taken an oath, as a member of Congress, or as an officer of the United States, or as a member of any State legislature, or as an executive or judicial officer of any State, to support the Constitution of the United States, shall have engaged in insurrection or rebellion against the same, or given aid or comfort to the enemies thereof. But Congress may by a vote of two-thirds of each House, remove such disability.

Section 4.   The validity of the public debt of the United States, authorized by law, including debts incurred for payment of pensions and bounties for services in suppressing insurrection or rebellion, shall not be questioned. But neither the United States nor any State shall assume or pay any debt or obligation incurred in aid of insurrection or rebellion against the United States, or any claim for the loss or emancipation of any slave; but all such debts, obligations and claims shall be held illegal and void.

Section 5.   The Congress shall have power to enforce, by appropriate legislation, the provisions of this article.

Amendment 15—The Right to Vote

Section 1.   The right of citizens of the United States to vote shall not be denied or abridged by the United States or by any State on account of race, color, or previous condition of servitude.

Section 2.   The Congress shall have power to enforce this article by appropriate legislation.

[12]Changed by the 26th Amendment

Amendment 16—Income Taxes

The Congress shall have power to lay and collect taxes on incomes, from whatever source derived, without apportionment among the several States, and without regard to any census or enumeration.

Amendment 17—Direct Election of Senators

The Senate of the United States shall be composed of two Senators from each State, elected by the people thereof for six years; and each Senator shall have one vote. The electors in each State shall have the qualifications requisite for electors of the most numerous branch of the State legislatures.

When vacancies happen in the representation of any State in the Senate, the executive authority of such State shall issue writs of election to fill such vacancies: *Provided,* That the legislature of any State may empower the executive thereof to make temporary appointments until the people fill the vacancies by election as the legislature may direct.

This amendment shall not be so construed as to affect the election or term of any Senator chosen before it becomes valid as part of the Constitution.

Amendment 18—Prohibition

Section 1.   After one year from the ratification of this article the manufacture, sale, or transportation of intoxicating liquors within, the importation thereof into, or the exportation thereof from the United States and all territory subject to the jurisdiction thereof for beverage purposes is hereby prohibited.

Section 2.   The Congress and the several States shall have concurrent power to enforce this article by appropriate legislation.

Section 3.   This article shall be inoperative unless it shall have been ratified as an amendment to the Constitution by the legislatures of the several States, as provided in the Constitution, within seven years from the date of the submission hereof to the States by the Congress.][13]

[13]Repealed by the 21st Amendment

Amendment 19—For Women's Suffrage

The right of citizens of the United States to vote shall not be denied or abridged by the United States or by any State on account of sex. Congress shall have power to enforce this article by appropriate legislation.

Amendment 20—The Lame Duck Amendment

Section 1.   The terms of the President and Vice President shall end at noon on the 20th day of January, and the terms of Senators and Representatives at noon on the 3d of January, of the years in which such terms would have ended if this article had not been ratified; and the terms of their successors shall then begin.

Section 2.   The Congress shall assemble at least once in every year, and such meeting shall begin at noon on the 3d day of January, unless they by law appoint a different day.

Section 3.   If, at the time fixed for the beginning of the term of the President, the President elect shall have died, the Vice President elect shall become President. If a President shall not have been chosen before the time fixed for the beginning of his term, or if the President elect shall have failed to qualify, then the Vice President elect shall act as President until a President shall have qualified; and the Congress may by law provide for the case wherein neither a President elect nor a Vice President elect shall have qualified, declaring who shall then act as President, or the manner in which one who is to act shall be selected, and such person shall act accordingly until a President or Vice President shall have qualified.

Section 4.   The Congress may by law provide for the case of death of any of the persons from whom the House of Representatives may choose a President whenever the right of choice shall have devolved upon them, and for the case of the death of any of the persons from whom the Senate may choose a Vice President whenever the right of choice shall have devolved upon them.

Section 5.   Sections 1 and 2 shall take effect on the 15th day of October following the ratification of this article.

Section 6.   This article shall be inoperative unless it shall have been ratified as an amendment to the Constitution by the legislatures of three-fourths of the several States within seven years from the date of its submission.

Amendment 21—Repeal of Prohibition

Section 1. The eighteenth article of amendment to the Constitution of the United States is hereby repealed.

Section 2. The transportation or importation into any State, Territory, or possession of the United States for delivery or use therein of intoxicating liquors, in violation of the laws thereof, is hereby prohibited.

Section 3. This article shall be inoperative unless it shall have been ratified as an amendment to the Constitution by conventions in the several States, as provided in the Constitution, within seven years from the date of the submission hereof to the States by the Congress.

Amendment 22—Number of Presidential Terms

Section 1. No person shall be elected to the office of the President more than twice, and no person who has held the office of President, or acted as President for more than two years of a term to which some other person was elected President shall be elected to the office of the President more than once. But this Article shall not apply to any person holding the office of President when this Article was proposed by the Congress and shall not prevent any person who may be holding the office of President, or acting as President, during the term within which this Article becomes operative from holding the office of President, or acting as President, during the remainder of such term.

Section 2. This article shall be inoperative unless it shall have been ratified as an amendment to the Constitution by the legislatures of three-fourths of the several States within seven years from the date of its submission to the States by the Congress.

Amendment 23—Presidential Electors for the District of Columbia

Section 1. The District constituting the seat of Government of the United States shall appoint in such manner as the Congress may direct:
    A number of electors of President and Vice President equal to the whole number of Senators and Representatives in Congress to which the District would be entitled if it were a State, but in no event more than the least populous State; they shall be in addition to those appointed by the States, but they shall be considered, for the purposes of

the election of President and Vice President, to be electors appointed by a State; and they shall meet in the District and perform such duties as provided by the twelfth article of amendment.

Section 2. The Congress shall have power to enforce this article by appropriate legislation.

Amendment 24—The Anti-Poll Tax Amendment

Section l. The right of citizens of the United States to vote in any primary or other election for President or Vice President, for electors for President or Vice President, or for Senator or Representative in Congress, shall not be denied or abridged by the United States or any State by reason of failure to pay any poll tax or other tax.

Section 2. The Congress shall have power to enforce this article by appropriate legislation.

Amendment 25—Presidential Disability, Vice Presidential Vacancies

Section l. In case of the removal of the President from office or of his death or resignation, the Vice President shall become President.

Section 2. Whenever there is a vacancy in the office of the Vice President, the President shall nominate a Vice President who shall take office upon confirmation by a majority vote of both Houses of Congress.

Section 3. Whenever the President transmits to the President pro tempore of the Senate and the Speaker of the House of Representatives his written declaration that he is unable to discharge the powers and duties of his office, and until he transmits to them a written declaration to the contrary, such powers and duties shall be discharged by the Vice President as Acting President.

Section 4. Whenever the Vice President and a majority of either the principal officers of the executive departments or of such other body as Congress may be law provide, transmit to the President pro tempore of the Senate and the Speaker of the House of Representatives their written declaration that the President is unable to discharge the powers and duties of his office, the Vice President shall immediately assume the powers and duties of the office as Acting President.

Thereafter, when the President transmits to the President pro tempore of the Senate and the Speaker of the House of Representatives his written declaration that no inability exists, he shall resume the powers and duties of his office unless the Vice President and a majority of either the principal officers of the executive department or of such other body as Congress may by law provide, transmit within four days to the President pro tempore of the Senate and the Speaker of the House of Representatives their written declaration that the President is unable to discharge the powers and duties of his office. Thereupon Congress shall decide the issue, assembling within forty-eight hours for that purpose if not in session. If the Congress, within twenty-one days after receipt of the latter written declaration, or, if Congress is not in session, within twenty-one days after Congress is required to assemble, determines by two-thirds vote of both Houses that the President is unable to discharge the powers and duties of his office, the Vice President shall continue to discharge the same as Acting President; otherwise, the President shall resume the powers and duties of his office.

Amendment 26—Eighteen-year-old Vote

Section 1. The right of citizens of the United States, who are eighteen years of age or older, to vote shall not be denied or abridged by the United States or by any State on account of age.

Section 2. The Congress shall have the power to enforce this article by appropriate legislation.

Proposed Amendment—District of Columbia Full Voting Representation in the U.S. Congress

Section 1. For purposes of representation in Congress, election of the President and Vice President and Article V of this Constitution, the District constituting the seat of government of the United States shall be treated as though it were a state.

Section 2. The exercise of the rights and powers conferred under this article shall be by the people of the District constituting the seat of government, and as shall be provided by the Congress.

Section 3. The twenty-third article of amendment to the Constitution is hereby repealed.

Section 4. This article shall be inoperative unless it shall have been ratified as an amendment to the Constitution by legislatures of three-fourths of the several states within seven years from the date of its submission.

INDEX

Abington School District v. *Schempp*, 493
ABSCAM trials, 197
Acquisitions, corporate, 536–537
Adams, John (Pres.), 91, 92, 147, 206
Adamson v. *California*, 478
Administrative Procedures Act of 1946, 294
Administrative state. *See* Bureaucracy
Adversary system of trial, 128–129
Advertising, corporations and, 520–525
Affirmative action, Supreme Court and, 158
  employment and, 498–500
Agencies, of federal government, 284, 287
  attitudes toward, 106–107
  coordinating, 293, 294
  failure in, 304–306
  government corporation, 293
  independent, 288–289, 290–291
Agency for International Development (AID), 338, 341
Agriculture Department, 338
Aid to Families with Dependent Children (AFDC), 381, 388, 393, 396
Alien and Sedition Acts, 483
American Bar Association, judicial selection process and, 141
Anderson, John, 440–441, 454, 455, 456–457
Anglo-American Liberalism, 63
Antitrust
  corporations and, 534–537, 539
  laws, 356
Antiwar demonstrations, 110
Anzus Treaty, 342
Appellate jurisdiction, 144, 148

Appointments
  Congress and, 167
  president and, 139–141, 143, 167
Arms race, 334–336, 346
Artists, opinions of on political system, 115
Assassination threats, presidency and, 236–237
Assembly, freedom of, 494
Assimilation, individualism versus, 22–23
Association, freedom of, 494
Attica Prison, 274–275
Authority, partitioning. *See* Federalism;
    Mixed government theory;
    Separation of powers
Automatic stabilizers, 367–368

B-1 bomber, 336
Baker v. *Carr*, 255
Bakke decision, 158, 498
"Barons," 97, 98, 110, 273
  Liberal Democracy and, 102–104, 109
  members of Congress as, 175
  see also Elitism
Batten, William C., 118
Bay of Pigs invasion, 229
Bernstein, Leonard, 115
Bicameralism, 89–91
Bill becomes a law, 192–196
Bill of Rights, 26, 28; *see also* Civil liberties
Black, Hugo (Justice), 141, 478, 493, 505
Blackman, Harry Andrew (Justice), 141
Blacks
  civil liberties and, 474–475

Blacks (*cont.*)
    Civil Rights Act of 1964, 165, 497
    civil rights movement and, 439, 441
    education, 120, 146, 157–158, 439
        Brown v. *Board of Education*, 120,
          146, 157–158, 439, 475, 497
        busing, 497
    employment, 158, 392, 498–500
    housing, 497–498
    National Association for the
        Advancement of Colored People
        and, 439, 441, 494
    political participation, 434
    slavery and, 119, 120, 578
    unemployment, 392
    voting and, 455
    welfare services for, 392–393
Blanket primary, 462
Bourgeois individualism, 28, 29, 34, 35,
    37
    cynicism and, 422
Bradshaw, Thomas F., 118
Brandeis, Louis J. (Justice), 141, 504
Brennan, William Joseph, Jr. (Justice),
    141
Bribery, lobbying and, 197–199
Brown v. *Board of Education*, 120, 146,
    157–158, 439, 475, 497
Budget making
    bureaucracy and, 303, 306, 310–311,
        313–314
    defense, 346
    incrementalism and, 310–311, 313–314
    president and, 229, 231
    state governments and, 247
    zero-based budgeting, 313
Bureau of the Budget, 208; *see also* Office
    of Management and Budget
Bureaucracy, 6–7, 229, 279–280, 281–284
    budgetary reform in, 310–311, 313–314
    bureaucratese in, 298–299
    Congressional oversight over, 187–
        189–190
    coordinating agencies, 293–294
    federal government size and shape and,
        284–287
    Freedom of Information Act and, 312–
        313, 314–315
    government corporations, 293
    ideology and, 283
    independent agencies, 288–289, 290–
        291
    independent regulatory commissions,
        289, 291–293

    laws and, 294–295
    myth and, 283
    practices of, 302–303, 306–307
    rational professionalism in, 284, 296–
        297, 299, 302
      chain of command in, 299–300
      policy-administration dichotomy in,
        301–302
      span of control in, 301
    regulations of, 289, 291–296
    reorganizing, 307, 309–310
    sunset laws, 313–314
    see also Cabinet; Economic
        management; Foreign policy;
        Welfare state
Bureaucratese, 298–299
Burger, Warren (Justice), 141, 151, 262
Business
    ethics of, 19–20
    opinions of on political system, 48
Busing, desegregation in schools and, 497
Byrne, Jane (Mayor), 268, 270

Cabinet, 84–85, 209, 211
    departments, 286–287, 287–288
      Commerce, 338, 365
      Defense, 232–233, 326, 332, 333–337
      Energy, 309–310
      Health and Human Services, 377
      Labor, 338
      State, 232, 285, 326, 330–333
    Reagan's appointments to, 286–287
Calhoun, John C., 28, 59–60, 107–109,
    192
Califano, Joseph A., Jr. 377, 501, 503
Campaigns. *See* Elections
Canada, United States and, 324–325
Candidates. *See* Elections
Capitol, 169
Carnegie, Andrew, 31
Carswell, Harold G., 140
Carter, Jimmy (Pres.), 201
    court appointments and, 143
    economic management and, 348, 373
    election, 67, 440–441, 456–457, 459,
        463
    energy program and, 310
    foreign policy and, 325
    staff, 207
    state and local governments and, 242
    style, 215
Censorship, First Amendment and, 489–
    490

Central Intelligence Agency (CIA), 106,
  209, 325, 326, 328–330, 332
Chain of command, in bureaucracy, 299–
  300
Checks and balances, 85–87, 89
  presidential veto, 92
  see also Mixed government theory
Chief executives, 110–111, 113; *see also*
  Governor; Mayor; Presidency
Chile, 320
China, policy towards, 330, 332–333
Christmas tree legislation, 47, 108–109,
  192
Church and state, separation of, 479,
  492–493
Circuit courts of appeals, 144
City government, 257–258, 268–269
  urbanization and political
    participation, 434, 440–441
  see also State and local government
Civic education
  college level, 413, 414
  political participation and, 435
  secondary education, 412–413
Civil law, 129–130
  privacy and, 504–505
Civil liberties
  Bill of Rights, 473, 477 (*see also* First
    Amendment *below*)
    Second Amendment, 480, 481, 575
    Third Amendment, 480, 505, 576
    Fourth Amendment, 155, 480, 502–
      503, 504, 505, 576
    Fifth Amendment, 130, 155, 478, 480,
      482, 505, 576
    Sixth Amendment, 480–482, 576
    Seventh Amendment, 480, 482, 576–
      577
    Eighth Amendment, 480, 483, 577
    Ninth Amendment, 483, 505, 577
    Tenth Amendment, 240, 245, 483, 577
  First Amendment and, 28, 472–473,
    474, 477–480, 484–495, 505
    assembly and association freedom, 494
    church and state separation, 492
    "clear and present danger" test in,
      486–488
    fighting words rule, 488–489
    free speech guaranteed by, 472–473,
      474, 477, 479–480, 484–491
    libel and defamation, 490–491
    obscenity and censorship, 489–490
    religious freedom guaranteed by,
      491–492

text, 575
Fourteenth Amendment, 26, 155, 165,
  262, 477
  adequacy, 499–503
    due process clause, 478, 495–496
  equal employment, 498–499
  handicapped and, 500–501, 503
  text, 578–579
  total incorporation of Bill of Rights
    into, 478
  women and, 500
freedoms
  double jeopardy protection, 480, 482
  due process clause, 478, 480, 495–496
  equal employment opportunity, 498–
    499
  equal protection, 473–474, 495–498
  privacy, 480, 483, 503–507
  religion, 479, 491–492
  self-incrimination protection, 480,
    482
  separation of church and state, 479,
    492–493
  speech. *See* First Amendment
  states' rights, 483
  threats to, 483–484, 485
  in trials, 482–483
Civil Rights Act of 1964, 165, 497
Civil rights movement, 439, 441; *see also*
  Blacks; Civil liberties; Women's
  rights movement
Civil service, state, 267
Civil War, 117–120, 407, 474
Civilian Conservation Corps (CCC), 356
Clark, Mark (General) 109
Class action suits, 151, 153
Clear and present danger, First
  Amendment and, 486–488
Cloture vote, 195
Code of Federal Regulations, 296
College, political socialization in, 413,
  414
Commerce
  Congress and, 165, 167
  Constitution and, 354
  Supreme Court and, 150, 154, 354
  see also Economic management
Commerce Department, 338, 365
Commission system, of City Government,
  258
Commissions, independent regulatory
  289, 291–293
Committee system. *See* Congress
Common law, 480, 482

Communists, campaigns against, 29
Communitarianism, Social Democracy
   and, 111
Comprehensive Employment and
   Training Act (CETA), 388
Concurrent majority, doctrine of, 59–60,
   107–108, 192
Concurrent original jurisdiction, 144
Confederation, 70, 71, 72
Congress, 5, 86, 123, 162–164
   bicameralism and, 89–91
   bills and
      becoming a law, 192–196
      bureaucracy controlled by, 190
      committees and, 182
      ideology and, 190, 192
      myth and, 169–171
      supplementary spending, 225
   committees
      bills and, 183
      investigations of, 186–187, 188–189
      lobbying and, 196
      norms and, 182–183, 185
      oversight function of, 187, 189–190
      political organizations, 172–173, 181
      subcommittees, 182
   courts and, 164, 174
   federal bureaucracy and, 294
   foreign policy and, 167–168, 326, 341
   ideology and, 163, 164, 172
   lame duck, 581
   legislative veto of, 190
   as a legislature
      Constitution and, 164–169, 565–570
      legislative process, 169–171
      party organization and, 171–173,
         181, 183, 185–186
   Liberal Democracy and, 112–113
   lobbying, 163, 175, 178, 186, 187, 196–
      199, 327, 438
   members of, 97–98
      choosing, 166–167
      constituencies of, 175, 179
      incumbency, 179
      norms and folkways and, 182–183,
         185
      position and privileges of, 174–178
      reasons for becoming, 191
      reciprocity among, 182–183
      re-election, 179–181, 451, 452–453
      seniority system and, 181–182, 183
      terms of, 168
   myth and, 162, 164, 172
   nuclear defense and, 336

   old versus new views of, 184–185
   powers of, 164–165, 167–169
      investigatory, 186–187, 188–189
      oversight, 187, 189–190
   president and, 164, 173–174, 189, 220–
      221
      budget process and, 221, 224–227
   separation of powers and, 94
   Social Democracy and, 112–113
   see also House of Representatives;
      Senate
Consensus, 17, 18
   in business ethic, 19–20
   pluralist thesis and, 40–41
   religion and, 17–19
Consolidated Edison v. Public Service
   Commission, 487
Constitution, 150
   amending, 574–575
   Amendments, 169
      First through Tenth as Bill of Rights.
         See Civil liberties
      Eleventh, 577
      Twelfth, 459, 577–578
      Thirteenth, 578
      Fourteenth. See Civil liberties
      Fifteenth, 455, 579
      Sixteenth, 580
      Seventeenth, 580
      Eighteenth, 580
      Nineteenth, 455, 481
      Twentieth, 581
      Twenty-Second, 582
      Twenty-Third, 582–583
      Twenty-Fourth, 455, 583
      Twenty-Fifth, 583–584
      Twenty-Sixth, 455, 584
   Bill of Rights, 26, 28; see also Civil
      liberties
   checks and balances and, 86
   commerce and, 354
   Congress and, 164–169
      bicameralism and, 89–91
   courts and, 139, 143, 145, 148
   elitist bias of, 93
   federalism and, 71
   foreign policy and, 326
   freedoms guaranteed by. See Civil
      liberties
   full faith and credit clause of, 245
   legitimation of, 37
   mixed government theory and, 89, 93
   poor and, 93
   preamble of, 25

Presidency and, 92, 204, 206
    Electoral College and, 455–461
separation of powers and, 86, 87, 89
text, 565–583
Constitutional Convention of 1787, 89
    property rights and, 515–516
Constitutional review, 91, 113
Constitutionalism, 91
Consumer ethos, corporation and, 500–525
Continuing resolutions of Congress, 225
Contributory welfare programs (Social Security), 77, 357, 379, 381
Conventions, presidential nominating, 77–78, 444
Coolidge, Calvin (Pres.) 361
Coordinating agencies, 293–294
Corporate political action committees (PACs), 526–527, 528
Corporate state, 543–545
Corporations
    compensation of chief executive officers, 512
    corporate state, 543–545
    definition, 509–511
    free speech rights of, 487
    governance of, 517–520
    government versus private ownership of, 512–513, 543–545
    ideology, 519
        antitrust policy and, 534–537, 539
        multinational corporations and, 512, 540–543
        public policy and, 530–540
        social responsibility of, 536–540
        taxation and subsidies and, 531–534
    military-industrial complex and, 44, 341–346
    myth and, 519–520, 524–525
    political activities of, 525–530
    purpose of, 513–515
    roots and history of, 515–517
    socialization of public by, 520–525
Corruption
    bribery in lobbying, 197–199
    in Liberal Democracy, 104–105
Council of Economic Advisers, 209, 221, 294
Council of Environmental Quality, 211
Council-manager system of city government, 257–258
Counties, 258–259
Courts, 5, 26–27, 30, 93, 123, 125
    civil liberties and, 474

First Amendment freedoms and, 477
Sixth Amendment and, 482
Seventh Amendment and, 482–483
Congress and, 164, 174
Constitution and,
    Amendments of, dealing with courts, 576–577
    text of, dealing with courts, 572–573
constitutional review, 91, 113
English legacy of, 128–129
example of proceedings in, 136–137
as independent judiciary, 130–131, 135, 137–138
jurisdiction of, 143, 145
jury trial, 480, 482
organization of, 143
plea bargaining in, 125–128
role of, 128
Social Democracy and, 112–113
see also Judges; Law; Supreme Court
Cox, Archibald, 297, 299
Criminal law, 129–130
    privacy and, 505–507
Crisis stage of political process, 98–99, 117–118
    aftermath of, 119–120
    Civil War and, 117–120
    in political system, 117–120
Cuba, Bay of Pigs invasion of, 229
Cultural rituals, political socialization and, 420
Culture, 49

Daley, Richard J. (Mayor), 268
De facto segregation, 158, 497
De jure segregation, 497
Decision-making classification, power and, 47
Declaration of Independence, 21, 24–25, 119
    text, 561–564
Defamation, First Amendment and, 490–491
Defense budgets, military-industrial complex and, 346
Defense Department, 232–233, 326, 332, 333–337
Defense policy. See Foreign policy
Defense spending, 333–334, 338
Democracy
    participatory, 102
    popular, 63–65

Democracy (*cont.*)
  see also Liberal democracy; Social
    democracy
Democratic Party, 21, 444, 446
  conventions of, 444, 447, 449
  membership in, 450–451
  primary election and, 462
  stereotypes of, 442, 445
Demonstrations, political participation
    by, 437, 438
Desegregation. *See* Blacks; Segregation
Deterrence, 334
Dillon's rule, 244, 257
Discontent, rise of, 110–111
Discrimination
  physically handicapped and, 500–501,
    503
  religious, 492
  women, 500
  see also Blacks
Disaffection, with political system, 420–
    424
District of Columbia
  full voting representation in the U.S.
    Congress of, 584
  presidential electors for the, 582–583
District courts, Federal, 141, 143, 144,
    154
Diversity, 14–17
  business arena and, 19
  political parties and, 21
  religion and, 16
Domestic Council, 211
Douglas, William O. (Justice), 343, 478,
    505
Draft, exemption from, 492
Dred Scott case, 146, 474
Dualism, 31–32
Due process, 155
  substantive, 155
  Supreme Court and, 155, 496
  text, 578–579
Dulles, John Foster, 330

Economic indicators, 365
Economic management, 348–350, 363
  free enterprise, 350, 351
  mixed economy, 352, 353
    Great Depression, 356–358
    ideology and, 354–356
    myth and, 361–365
    post-World War II and, 358, 360
    regulation, 356

  supply-side economics, 360–361, 364,
    374
  socialism, 352–353
  tools of, 365
    fiscal policy, 365–368, 369
    jawboning, 373–375
    monetary policy, 368, 370–372; *see
      also* Supply-side economics
    wage and price controls, 375
    wage and price guidelines, 373–375
Edwards, Jonathan, 29–31
Eighteenth Amendment, 580
Eighth Amendment, 480, 483, 577
Eisenhower, Dwight D. (Pres.), 110, 415
  business and, 540
  election, 228
  evaluation, 218–219
  foreign policy, 330
  military-industrial complex and, 44,
    343
  Supreme Court appointments, 141
Elderly
  political participation and, 434
  welfare services for, 392–393
Elections, 67, 69
  campaigns, 432–433, 462–465, 466–467
    corporations funding, 525–527, 529
    costs, 454
    debates during, 431, 433
    professionals involved in, 464–465
  candidates
    creating perfect, 465, 466–467
    initiative of, 451
    nominating convention for. *See*
      Political parties
    political parties and, 444, 446, 451
    responsibility for conduct in office,
      446, 453–454
  congressional, 69, 179–181
  eighteen-year-olds and, 584
  function of, 6, 64–65
  gubernatorial, 69, 247
  judges and, 139
  meaning of, 465, 467–470
  nonparticipation in, 117
  poll tax amendment and, 583
  presidential, 67, 169, 205, 206–207
    Congress and, 169
    District of Columbia and, 582–583,
      584
    Electoral College and, 455–461
    incumbency and, 451
    nominating conventions, 77–78, 444
    primaries, 461, 462, 463

social groups and, 440–441
  terms, 582
  Twelfth Amendment and, 577–578
  Twenty-Second Amendment, 582
  Twenty-Third Amendment and, 582–583
  primaries, 461–462, 463
  senatorial, 69, 580
  separation of powers and, 88
  Social Democracy and, 113–116
  state government and, 246
Electoral College, 455–461
Eleventh Amendment, 577
Elite rule theorists, public opinion studies and, 429
Elitism, 111
  elections and, 467–469
  Liberal Democracy and, 102–104
  mixed government theory and, 89, 92–93
  power elite and, 44–45, 60–62, 104
  in state and local government, 273, 275
  see also Interest groups
Emerson, Ralph Waldo, 28
Employment, blacks and, 392
  affirmative action and, 158, 498–500
Employment Act of 1946, 192, 209
Energy Department, 309–310
Engel v. *Vitale*, 156, 493
English law, 128–129
English Liberalism, 58; *see also* Bourgeois individualism
Enterprise zone program, 390
Environmental Protection Agency (EPA), 290–291
Equal employment opportunity, affirmative action and, 498–499
Equal protection of the laws, 473–474, 578–579
Equal Rights Amendment (ERA), 500
Equality, equal protection and, 496–497
Establishment, 63
  corporate interests and, 530
Ethnic identification, political socialization and, 410
Everson v. *Board of Education*, 493
Executive agreement, president and, 168, 232
Executive Office of the President. *See* Presidency

Family, political socialization and, 409–410

Family Assistance Plan (FAP), 396
Federal aid programs, to state and local governments, 78–82
Federal Circuit Courts of Appeals, 141, 143
Federal District Courts, 141, 143, 154
Federal grants-in-aid, 263, 264
Federal Register, 294, 296
Federal Reserve banks, 371
Federal Reserve Board, 358, 370
Federal Reserve System, 354, 356, 360, 369, 370–372
Federalism, 5, 59, 67, 69, 94, 241
  definition, 70, 71
  division of power and, 71–73
  dysfunctional, 80–81
  ideology and, 78–82
  local government and, 75
  myth and, 77–78
  states' rights amendment and, 483, 515, 577
  Supreme Court and, 149–150
  see also State and local government
Federalist, 10, 50, 51, 78, 90, 137–138, 146–147, 516
Fellini, Federico, 115
Fifteenth Amendment, 455, 579–580
Fifth Amendment, 130, 155, 478, 480, 482, 505, 576
Fighting words rule, First Amendment and, 488–489
Filibuster, 195
Finance Committee, Senate, 187
First Amendment. *See* Civil Liberties
Fiscal policy, 358, 365–368; *see also* Economic management
Flag, as symbol of primary myth, 53, 56
Food and Drug Administration, 74
Food stamps, 389
Ford, Gerald (Pres.)
  campaign, 431
  economic management, 374
  election, 440–441, 463
  state and local governments and, 242
  Supreme Court appointments, 141
Foreign policy, 316–319
  Congress and, 167–168, 326, 341
  coordination, 339–341
  establishment, 325–327, 328
    Agency for International Development, 338, 341
    Central Intelligence Agency, 106, 209, 325, 326, 328–330, 332
    Constitution and, 326

Foreign Policy (*cont.*)
  Defense Department, 232–233, 326, 332, 333–337
  International Communications Agency, 338–341
  National Security Council, 209, 227, 233, 294, 326, 328, 330, 339
  State Department, 232, 285, 326, 330–333
  great power approach of, 321
  historical roots of, 320–321, 323–325
  ideology in, 319–320, 323–325
  military-industrial complex, 341–346
  myth in, 319–320, 323
  president and, 227–228, 231, 234, 326, 339, 340–341
  Third World imperialism and, 322
Foreign Service Institute, 330
Fortas, Abe (Justice), 473–479
Fourteenth Amendment. *See* Civil liberties
Fourth Amendment, 155, 480, 502–503, 504, 505, 576
Frank, Reuven, 118
Franklin, Benjamin, 29–31
Free enterprise, 350, 351; *see also* Corporation
Freedom of Information Act, 312–313, 314–315, 506–507
Freedoms. *See* Civil liberties
Friedman, Milton, 396–398
Full Employment Act of 1946, 361, 362–363

General Accounting Office (GAO), 190, 336
General Services Administration, 293–294
Gerrymandering, 254, 255
Gettysburg Address, 54–56, 111
Gibbons v. *Ogden*, 150, 154, 354
Goldberg, Arthur (Justice), 505
Government agencies. *See* Agencies, of federal government
Government corporation, 293
Government Operations Committee, House, 190
Governmental Affairs Committee, Senate, 190
Governors, 246–248, 267, 272
  election of, 69, 247
Grant, Ulysses S. (Pres.), 119

Grants-in-aid, federal, 263, 264
Grass roots democracy, Social Democracy and, 111
Great Depression, 356–358, 378–379
  New Deal and, 120, 146, 356–357, 361, 379
Great Society, 260, 379, 391
Griswold v. *Connecticut*, 504–505
Group conformity, socialization and, 410
Guatemala, 320
Guild socialism, 353
Gun control, Second Amendment and, 480, 481

Hamilton, Alexander, 147, 364, 515, 516
Hayes, Janet Gray (Mayor), 270
Haynsworth, Clement, 140
Health and Human Services Department, 377
Heinz, John (Senator), 198
Hellman, Lillian, 115
Heroes, 97, 98, 99, 101; *see also* Chief executives; Presidency
Hills v. *Gatreaux*, 498
Hiring Act of 1964, 498–499
Hispanic-Americans, welfare services for, 392–393
Hobbes, Thomas, 21, 23–24, 28, 59, 478
Holmes, Oliver Wendell, Jr. (Justice), 473, 486
Hoover, Herbert (Pres.), 223
House of Commons, 84
House of Representatives, 82, 93
  bicameralism and, 89–90, 91
  bill introduced to, 193–194
  checks and balances and, 91
  committees, 160–161, 181–182
    Government Operations, 190
    Rules, 193, 194
    Un-American Activities, 188–189
    Ways and Means, 160–161, 187
  party organization of, 170–172
  powers, 92, 164–165, 167–169
  representatives as members of Congress, 183; *see also* Congress, norms of
  Speaker of the, 170–172
Housing, desegregation efforts aimed at, 497–498
Housing Opportunity Plan, 498
Humphrey-Hawkins Act of 1978, 192, 361–362, 363

Ideology, 57–58, 65–66
  bureaucracy and, 283
  campaigns and, 464
  concurrent majority doctrine and, 59–60
  Congress and, 163, 164, 172
  corporate, 519, 530–543
  definition, 3, 50
  effectiveness of, 547–548
  elections and, 467–468
  federalism and, 78–82
  foreign policy and, 319–320, 323–325
  of Founding Fathers, 58–59
  inadequacy of, 548, 549
  legislative process and, 190, 192
  myth versus, 3–6, 548, 549–550
  New Deal and, 357
  political parties and, 447–455
  political system disillusionment and, 420
  power and, 48–51
  power elite and, 60–62
  presidency and, 202–203, 228–236, 237
  state and local government and, 242, 271–276
  welfare state and, 394–395
  welfare system and, 380
Illegal aliens, Social Security and, 385
Impeachment, Congress and, 169
Imperialism, Third World and, 322
Impoundment, 189
Income tax, state, 261
Incrementalism
  budgetary process and, 310–311, 313
  in Liberal Democracy, 107–109
Incumbency, 179–181
  re-election and, 451, 452–453
Independent agencies, 288–289, 290–291
Independent regulatory commissions, 289, 291–293
Index of Leading Economic Indicators, 365
Individualism, 5, 69
  alienation from legitimation and, 117
  assimilation versus, 22–23
  Bourgeois, 28, 29, 34, 35, 37, 58
  liberalism and, 28–31
  philosophy of, 21
  power and, 34, 35, 37
  Protestant, 28, 29, 34, 35, 37, 56, 58, 60, 88, 111, see also Legitimation; Myth; Social Democracy
  roots of, 21, 23–28

see also Federalism; Separation of powers
Industry, military-industrial complex and, 214, 341–346; see also Corporation
Inflation, 359, 360, 361, 365–366, 375
Initiative
  petition required by, 436
  in state government, 246
Inner Circle, 198
Inquisitorial system of trial, 129
Institutionalization, of the president, 206–207
Interest groups
  chief executives and, 110–111
  Congress and, 186, 187
  organization of for political participation, 438–441
  public relations programs of, 419–420
  strength of, 99
  see also Lobbying
International Commerce Commission (ICC), 355
International Communication Agency (ICA), 338, 341
International Telephone and Telegraph Corporation (ITT), 320
Interstate Commerce Clause, Supreme Court and, 150; see also Commerce
Interstate compact, government formed by, 76–77; see also Federalism
Investigations, as power of Congress, 186–187, 188–189
Iran, 320

Jackson, Andrew (Pres.), 146, 206
Jackson, Robert H. (Justice), 491
Jefferson, Thomas (Pres.), 21, 88, 148, 206, 364, 493, 515, 516, 540
Johnson, Lyndon B. (Pres.)
  Congress and, 181
  economic management and, 360, 363–364, 373
  evaluation of, 202, 204
  grants-in-aid and, 263
  Great Society and, 260, 379, 391
  national morale and, 223–224
  style, 215
  Supreme Court and, 141
  Vietnam War and, 223–224, 227, 472
  welfare and, 381

Judges
  to Federal Circuit Court of Appeals, 141
  to Federal District Court, 141
  independence of, 130–131
  qualities required of, 131, 135, 137–138
  selection of, 139–141
  Social Democracy and, 113
  to Supreme Court, 139–141
  see also Courts; Supreme Court; *specific judges*
Judicial review, 145, 146–149
Judicial system. *See* Courts; Judges; Supreme Court
Judiciary Act of 1789, 144, 148
Jury, trial by, 480, 482
Justiciability of cases, 150

Katz v. *U.S.*, 505
Kennedy, John F. (Pres.), 236
  Defense Department and, 332
  economic management and, 360, 373
  election, 431, 459
  foreign policy and, 228, 229
  national morale and, 223
  style, 215, 216
  Supreme Court and, 141
Keynes, John Maynard, 357–358, 360
King, Martin Luther, Jr., 110
Kirkpatrick, Jeane J., 325, 339
Kissinger, Henry (Secty. of State), 330, 332
Know Nothing movement, 29, 483
Korean War, 234–236
Korematsu v. *U.S.*, 146
Ku Klux Klan, 29, 106, 483

Labor, opinion of on political system, 112
Labor Department, 338
Laffer curve, 361
Laissez-faire economics, 351, 353, 355
Lame duck amendment, 581
Lance, Bert, 118
Law
  English, 128–129
  libel, 491
  civil, 129–130
    privacy and, 504–505
  common, 480, 482
  criminal, 129–130
    privacy and, 505–507
  law school curriculum, 130, 132–135
  mixed government theory and, 91

see also Courts
Lee, Robert E., 119
Legalism, 26–27, 30
Legislation, bureaucracy and, 294–296
Legislators, 97
Legislature
  bicameralism and, 89–91
  of state governments, 248–257, 267, 270
Legitimation, 57–58
  elections and, 467
  failure to give, 117
  federalism and, 70
  political parties, 442
  of power, 38–39, 41, 42–43, 45–46, 48–51, 57–58
  separation of powers and, 70
Letter writing, political participation by, 436–437
Libel, First Amendment and, 490–491
Liberal Democracy, 5, 111
  baronial elite and, 102–104
  Calhounian incrementalism in, 107–109
  civil liberties and, 474
  Congress and, 163, 174
  corruption in, 104–105
  Courts and, 128, 139, 148–149
  in political system, 420–424
  public interest in, 105, 107
  Supreme Court and, 150, 154–157, 158
Liberalism, 28–31
  Anglo-American, 63
  English, 58; *see also* Bourgeois individualism
Liberties. *See* Civil liberties
Lieutenant-governor, 247, 251
Lincoln, Abraham (Pres.), 54–56, 71, 119, 206, 236, 237
Line agency, 284, 287
Lobbying, 438
  Congress and, 163, 175, 178, 186, 187, 196–199
  corporations and, 528–530
  foreign policy and, 327
  state legislature and, 251, 253
Local governments, 240–241, 257
  city governments, 257–258, 268–269
  consolidation of, 265–266
  counties, 258–259
  federalism and, 75
  neighborhood-level, 266
  reform in, 267
  regional government, 260, 266
  special districts, 259

see also State governments; State and local governments

Locke, John, 21, 24, 28, 87, 516

Log rolling legislation. *See* Christmas tree legislation

McCarran Act of 1950, 508

McCarthy, Joe (Senator), 332, 333

McCarthyism, 483, 506

McCulloch v. *Maryland*, 149–150, 240

McKay Commission, 274

Madison, James, 28, 50, 89, 90, 137–138, 139, 148, 240, 516

Magazines, political socialization and, 419

Majority floor leaders, 172

Mansfield, Mike (Senator), 185

Marbury, William, 148

Marbury v. *Madison*, 147–148, 150

Marshall, John (Justice), 91, 141, 148, 149, 150, 154, 240, 354

Marshall, Thurgood (Justice), 140

Mass media, 413, 415–420, 465

Mayor, 258, 268

Mayor-council system, of city government, 258

Meany, George, 112

Medicaid, 381, 385, 397

Medicare, 77, 384, 385, 397

Mellon, Andrew, 31

Memoranda, bureaucracy and, 307, 308–309

Mergers, corporate, 536–537

Merit systems, for public employment, 267

Mexican Wars, 407

Middle East, 337

Military, opinions of on political system, 109; *see also* Defense Department; Military-industrial complex

Military-industrial complex, 41, 341–346

Military treaty obligations, 342

Mill, John Stuart, 28

Miller v. *California*, 489

Mills, C. Wright, 44

Mills, Wilbur (Rep.), 160–162

Minority rights
concurrent majority doctrine and, 59–60
political participation and, 434
Supreme Court and, 158
see also Blacks; Civil liberties

Mixed economy. *See* Economic management

Mixed government theory, 89, 94
bicameralism and, 89–91
checks and balances in, 91
elitist bias of, 92–93
law and, 91
state governments and, 245

Monetarists, 360, 374

Monetary policy, 358, 368, 370–372; *see also* Supply side economics

Money supply, as indicator for monetary policy, 371

Monopoly, antitrust policy and, 534–537, 539

Monroe Doctrine, 319, 321

Montesquieu, Baron de, 87

Moorer, Thomas H. (Admiral), 109

Moral Majority, 116

Moses, Robert, 268, 269

Multinational corporations, 512, 540–543

Municipalities. *See* Local governments; State governments; State and local governments

Murphy, Frank (Justice), 478

MX missile, 336

Myth, 58, 60, 65–66
bureaucracy and, 283
campaigns and, 463–464
civil liberties and, 474
components of, 406–408
Congress and, 162, 164, 172
corporate, 519–520, 524–525
definition, 2–3, 50
effectiveness of, 547
elections and, 468–469
federalism and, 77–78
foreign policy and, 319–320, 323
Gettysburg Address and, 54–56
historical development in, 407
ideology versus, 3–6, 548, 549–550
inadequacy of, 548–549
independent regulatory commissions and, 291
mass, 406–408; *see also* Public opinion
mixed economy and, 361–365
patriotism and, 51–54
political parties and, 442–447, 451, 453, 454
popular democracy in, 63–65
power and, 48–51
presidency and, 202, 203, 215–228, 234, 237
primary, 53, 56–57

Myth (*cont.*)
  state and local government and, 242,
    264–271
  Supreme Court and, 144–146, 147
  wars and, 407
  welfare system and, 380, 394, 399–400
  see also Legitimation; Political parties

National Association for the
    Advancement of Colored People
    (NAACP), 439, 441, 494
National conventions. *See* Political
    parties
National culture, 46, 48, 49
National health insurance, 385
National Municipal League, 75
National Recovery Act, 357
National security, 326, 339
  congressional role in, 167–168
  see also Foreign policy
National Security Agency (NSA), 209, 328
National Security Council (NSC), 209,
    227, 233, 294, 326, 328, 330, 339
Nationalism, Social Democracy and,
    111–112
Negative Income Tax (NIT), 396–398
Neighborhood-level governments, 266
Neoconservatives, welfare system and,
    391
New Deal, 120, 146, 356–357, 361, 379
  Great Depression and, 356–358, 378–
    379
New Left, 353
Newspapers, political socialization and,
    417–419
Nineteenth Amendment, 455, 581
Ninth Amendment, 483, 505, 577
Nixon, Richard Milhous (Pres.)
  Defense Department and, 332
  economic management and, 358, 373,
    375
  election, 459
  evaluation of, 230–231
  foreign policy and, 227–228, 333
  national morale and, 224
  Office of Management and Budget and,
    208
  as paradox, 11–13
  revenue sharing and, 263
  style, 215, 219
  Supreme Court and, 140, 141
  television and, 415, 431
  Watergate and, 11, 101, 120, 297, 299

welfare state and, 396
Nominating conventions, presidential,
    77–78, 444
Noncontributory welfare program, 385–
    390
Nonestablishment of religion clause, of
    the First Amendment, 479, 492–493
North Atlantic Treaty Organization
    (NATO), 342
Nuclear defense system, 334–336, 346
Nuclear Regulatory Commission, (NRC),
    304–306

Obscenity, First Amendment and, 489–
    490
Office of Emergency Preparedness, 211
Office of Management and Budget (OMB),
    208, 214, 221, 224, 229, 287, 294
Office of Personnel Management, 294
Office of Technology Assessment, 190
Oil companies, taxation and, 533
Olmstead v. *U.S.*, 501
Olney, Richard (Secty. of State), 321
O'Neill, Thomas P. (Speaker of the
    House), 244
Opinion sampling, for polls, 425
Original jurisdiction, 143, 145
Oversight function, of Congress, 187,
    189–190

Parkinson's Law, 307
Parliamentary system, 84–85
Participatory Democracy, 102
Parties. *See* Political parties
Pateman, Carole, 64
Patriotism, myth and, 51–54
Patronage, 269
Peace Corps, 319, 323, 338
Peer groups, political socialization and,
    411
Pentagon, 232–233, 333, 338; *see also*
    Defense Department
Petitions, political participation and,
    435–436
Physically handicapped, Fourteenth
    Amendment and, 500
Plea bargaining, 125–128
Plessy v. *Ferguson*, 120, 474
Pluralist thesis of power, 40–41
  elite and, 62

Police state, advent of, 501
Policy–administration dichotomy,
    bureaucracy and, 301–302
Political action committees (PACs), 526–
    527, 528
Political actors, classifying, 97–98
Political character, American, 13–14; *see
    also* Consensus; Diversity;
    Individualism
Political culture, 46, 48, 49
Political institutions, consensus and, 17,
    18
Political parties, 6, 442
    Congress and, 171–173, 181, 183, 185–
        186
    conventions of, 447, 449, 451
        presidential, 77–78, 444
    ideologic role of, 447–455
    individualism and, 21
    mythic role of, 442–447, 451, 453, 454
    reform in, 267
    Social Democracy and, 114–116
    state legislatures and, 254
    two-party system in, 114
Political power. *See* Power
Political process
    polls distorting, 429
    stages of the, 98–99, 117–118
Political system
    disillusionment with, 420
    diversity of claims and opinions found
        in, 118
        arts, 115
        business, 118
        labor, 112
        military, 109
    evaluation
        myth clashing with ideology in,
            548–550
        problems handled by, 548–549
    Liberal Democracy in, 420–424
Politics, 6, 37
    corporations and, 525–530
    definition, 42
    individualism in, 21
    power and, 37–42
    see also Elections; Political parties
Polls. *See* Public opinion
Poor
    mixed government theorists and, 93
    political participation and, 434
    War on Poverty, 263, 264
    see also Welfare state
Popular Democracy, America as, 63–65

Popular government, state and local
    government and, 246
Pork barrel legislation. *See* Christmas
    tree legislation
Poverty. *See* Poor
Powell, Lewis Franklin, Jr. (Justice), 141
Power, 34–37
    decision-making classifications and, 47
    definition, 38, 42
    dividing, *see* Federalism; Separation of
        powers
    establishing, 38–39
    governance and, 39, 41, 42, 48–51, 58;
        see also Ideology
    legitimation and, 38–39, 41, 42–43,
        45–46, 48–51, 57–58
    in Liberal Democracy, 103
    myth and, 48–51
    national and political culture and, 46,
        48, 49
    pluralist thesis of, 40–41
    political socialization of children and,
        409–410
    politics and, 37–42
    power elite thesis and, 44–45
Power elite, 44–45, 60–62, 104; *see also*
    Elitism
Presidency, 5, 86, 93, 97, 98, 123, 201–
    203
    assassination threats and, 236–237
    budget process and, 221, 224–227, 229,
        231
    Congress and, 161, 173–174, 189, 220–
        221
        bills and, 164, 173–174, 196
        budget and, 221, 224–227
        elections and, 169
    corruption and, 105
    day in life of, 210–211
    disability of, 583–584
    electing. *See* Elections
    Executive office of, 207, 211, 213–215,
        229, 294, *see also* Cabinet
        Council of Economic Advisers, 209,
            221, 294
        foreign policy and, 327–328
        National Security Council, 209, 227,
            233, 294, 326, 328, 330, 339
        Office of Management and Budget,
            208, 214, 221, 224, 229, 287, 294
        White House office, 207, 294
    ideology and, 202–203, 228–236
    independent regulatory commission
        and, 291

Presidency (*cont.*)
  institutionalization of, 206–207
  interest groups and, 110–111
  Liberal Democracy and, 103
  mixed government theory and, 94
  myth and, 202, 203, 215–228, 234, 237
  philosophical limitations on, 234–236
  powers, 167, 168
    appointments, 139–141, 143, 167
    as commander-in-chief, 217
    Constitution and, 204, 206, 570–572
    executive agreement of, 168, 232
    legislative veto, 173–174
    foreign policy, 227–228, 231–234,
      326, 339, 340–341
  separation of powers and, 92
  Social Democracy and, 112–113
  symbols of the, 217, 219–221
President *pro tem* of Senate, 170
Presidential primaries, 461, 462, 463
Presidential veto, 92
Presidents. *See specific presidents*
Pressure groups, 439; *see also* Interest
  groups
Primary education, political socialization
  and, 411
Primary elections, 461–462, 463
Privacy, right to, 503–507
Privacy Act of 1974, 506
Progressive Party, reform movement and,
  266–271
Prohibition, Constitutional amendments
  on, 580, 582
Propaganda, corporate, 520–525
Property rights, Constitutional
  Convention and, 515–516
Property tax, 261
Proposition, 13, 261
Protestant individualism, 28, 29, 34, 35,
  37, 56, 58, 60, 88, 111; *see also*
  Legitimation; Myth; Social
  Democracy
Proxmire, William (Senator), 190
Public assistance programs, as
  contributory welfare programs,
  381–385
Public interest, Liberal Democracy and,
  105, 107
Public opinion
  definiton, 424–425
  individual and collective conduct
    measuring, 429–430
  polls measuring, 405, 425–427
    evaluation of accuracy of, 427–429

political parties, 445
political process distorted by, 429
public policy and, 429
Public relations programs of interest
  groups, political socialization and,
  419–420
Public safety, First Amendment and,
  488–489
Pump-priming, 358

Radio, political socialization and, 413
Rallies, political participation by, 437
Randolph Resolution, 90
Random sample, for polls, 425
Rapid Deployment Force (RDF), 337
Rational-professional mode, 97, 98, 284
  Supreme Court and, 154–157
  see also Bureaucracy
Rayburn, Sam (House Speaker), 103
Reagan, Ronald (Pres.)
  budget and, 225–227, 348
  cabinet, 286–287
  defense spending and, 333–334, 336
  Department of Energy and, 310
  economic management and, 348–350,
    360, 361, 364, 366, 369, 374, 532
  election, 67, 431, 440–441, 456–457,
    459–461
  federalism and, 81, 82, 263
  foreign policy and, 323
  privacy and, 507
  regional governments and, 260
  religious discrimination and, 492
  secret fund of, 220
  style, 212–213, 215
  Supreme Court and, 141
  welfare state and, 380, 381, 382, 388–
    390, 398, 399
Reapportionment, state legislatures and,
  254, 255–257, 455
Recall election, 246, 436
Recession, 361, 366
Reciprocity, in Congress, 182–183
Red Scare, in 1920's, 120, 483
Redistributive issues, 47
Referendum, 246, 436
Regents of the University of California v.
  Bakke, 158, 498
Regional government, 76, 260, 266
Regional planning councils, 260
Regulation
  bureaucracy and, 294–295
  commissions and, 167, 289, 291–293

of economy, 356
  failure of, 304–306
  of poor by welfare system, 394–395
Rehabilitation Act of 1973, 501, 503
Rehnquist, William (Justice), 141, 152
Relief systems, 378; *see also* Welfare state
Religion
  consensus and, 17–19
  discrimination and, 492
  diversity of, 16
  freedom of, 479, 491–492
  liberalism and, 28, 29
  political participation and, 434
  political socialization and, 410
Representative government, in state and
      local governments, 272–275; *see
      also* Congress
Representatives, as members of Congress.
      See Congress; House of
      Representatives
Republican Party, 21, 444, 446
  membership in, 450–451
  stereotype of, 442, 445
Reuther, Walter P., 112
Revenue sharing, 263–264
Reynolds v. *Sims*, 255
Rickover, Hyman G. (Admiral), 109
Riegle, Donald (Senator), 191
Rights. *See* Civil liberties; Civil rights;
      Minority rights
Rio Treaty, 342
Rituals, political socialization and, 420
Rockefeller, David, 518–519, 520
Rockefeller, John D., 31
Roe v. *Wade*, 505
Romney, George (Governor), 431
Roosevelt, Franklin D. (Pres.), 227, 364,
      542
  campaigning and, 431, 433
  detention plan and, 506
  New Deal and, 146, 207, 356, 357–358,
      378–379
  style of, 215
  Supreme Court and, 496
  welfare state and, 378
Roosevelt, Theodore (Pres.), 219
Rossetti, Frank G., 448–449
Rules Committee, House, 193, 194
Rutledge, Wiley B. (Justice), 478

Sales tax, state, 261
San Antonio Independent School District
      v. *Rodriguez*, 262

Schenck v. *United States*, 486
School districts, 259
Schools
  districts, 259
  financing, 261–262
  political socialization and, 411–413,
      414
Search and seizure, law of, 480, 502–503,
      576
Second Amendment, 480, 481, 575
Secondary schools, political socialization
      in, 412–413
Segregation
  de facto, 158, 497
  de jure, 497
  see also Blacks
Senate, 93, 187
  bicameralism and, 89–90, 91
  bill introduced to, 194–195
  checks and balances and, 91
  committees
    Finance, 187
    Government Operations, 190
  elections to, 69, 580
  party organization of, 172
  powers, 92, 164–165, 167–169
    foreign policy, 227
    Supreme Court nominations and,
      139–140, 141–142
  presiding officer of the, 170
  senatorial courtesy, 141–142
  senators as members of Congress
    reasons for becoming, 191
    re-election, 179
    norms of, 183
  see also Congress
Senatorial courtesy, 141–142
Seniority system, of Congress, 181, 183
Separation of powers, 5, 59, 67, 69, 70,
      82–84, 89
  checks and balances in, 85–87
  courts and congress and, 174
  presidency and, 92
  pure theory of, 87–89, 94
  Social Democracy and, 111–112
  state governments and, 245
Seventeenth Amendment, 580
Seventh Amendment, 480, 482, 576–577
Shah of Iran, 320
Shay's rebellion, 92
Sinclair, James, 118
Single issue politics, 439; *see also* Interest
      groups
Sixteenth Amendment, 580

Sixth Amendment, 480–482, 576
Slavery, 119, 120
　prohibition of, 578
Smith, Adam, 28, 351, 364
Smith Act, 486
Social class
　diversity in, 15
　political participation and, 434, 440–441
Social Democracy, 5, 102
　civil liberties and, 474
　Congress and, 162
　courts and,
　　judges and, 131, 139
　　Supreme Court, 150, 158
　discontent and, 110–114
　elections and, 113–116
　Liberal Democracy and, 131, 135
　party organization and, 172
　presidency and, 207
　stress stage of, 113–114
　vision of, 111–113
　see also Myth
Social responsibility of a corporation, 538–540
Social security system, 77, 357, 379, 381–385
Socialism, 352–353
Socialist Party, in the United States, 353
Socialization of the public, by corporations, 520–525
Socioeconomic status. See Social class
Soldiers, quartering of and Third Amendment, 480
Southeast Asia Treaty Organization (SEATO), 342
Southeastern Community College v. Davis, 503
Soviet Union
　socialism and, 352
　United States and, 334, 335, 344, 346
Span of control, in bureaucracy, 301
Spanish-American War, 319, 321, 407
Speaker of the House, 170–172
Special districts, 259
Special interest groups. See Interest groups
Speech, freedom of and First Amendment. See Civil liberties
Spending policies, 366–367, 368; see also Economic management
Staff agency, 284, 287
Stare decisis, 137, 157
State Appellate Court, 143

State civil service, 267
State Department, 232, 285, 326, 330–333
State governments, 240–241, 266
　education spending of, 243
　public opinion toward, 271–272
　reform and, 266–271
　relationships among, 245
　structure of, 245–246
　　governor, 246–248, 267, 272
　　legislative reapportionment, 255–257
　　legislature, 248–257, 267, 270
　　popular government in, 246
　see also Local government; State and local government
State and local governments, 5, 123, 240–241
　bureaucracies of, 311
　Constitution and, 573–574
　federal aid to, 78–82
　financing, 78–82, 259, 260–264
　ideology in, 242, 271–276
　intergovernmental relations in, 242–245
　myth in, 242, 264–271
　primary elections for officers of, 462
　reform in, 266–271
　representative government in, 272–275
　social program inadequacy in, 275–276
　spending policies of, 368
　see also Local governments; State governments
State of the Union address, 174, 220
States' rights amendment, 483, 515, 577
Stevens, John Paul (Justice), 141
Stockholders, 517, 519
Stockman, David, 243–244, 369
Stone, Harlan (Justice), 486
Subsidies, corporations and, 531–534
Substantive due process, 155
Sunset laws, 313–314
Supplementary Security Income, 381
Supplementary spending bills, 225
Supply-side economics, 360–361, 364, 374
Supreme Court, 27, 73, 86, 128, 143
　cases, 127
　　Abington School District v. Schempp, 493
　　Adamson v. California, 478
　　Baker v. Carr, 255
　　Brown v. Board of Education, 120, 146, 157–158, 439, 497
　　Consolidated Edison v. Public Service Commission, 487
　　Dred Scott, 146, 474

Engel v. *Vitale*, 156, 493
Everson v. *Board of Education*, 493
Gibbons v. *Ogden*, 150, 154, 354
Griswold v. *Connecticut*, 504–505
Hills v. *Gatreaux*, 498
Katz v. *U.S.*, 505–506
Korematsu v. *U.S.*, 146
McCulloch v. *Maryland*, 149–150, 240
Marbury v. *Madison*, 147–148, 150
Miller v. *California*, 489
Olmstead v. *U.S.*, 501
Plessy v. *Ferguson*, 120, 474
Regents of the University of California
   v. *Bakke*, 158, 498–499
Reynolds v. *Sims*, 255
Roe v. *Wade*, 505
San Antonio Independent School
   District v. *Rodriguez*, 262
Schenck v. *United States*, 486
Southeastern Community College v.
   Davis, 503
Tinker v. *Des Moines School District*,
   472–473
United Steelworkers of America v.
   Weber, 499
voting to hear, 154
Warth v. *Seldin*, 151
Watkins v. *U.S.*, 188
Weber, 158
Welsh v. *United States*, 492
civil liberties and, 472–473
  affirmative action and employment
    and, 498–499
  association freedom and, 494
  blacks and, 474–475
  church and state separation and, 492,
    493
  due process and, 155, 496
  equal protection, 497–498
  Fourteenth Amendment and, 478
  freedom of speech and, 472–473, 474,
    486–490
  gun control and, 480
  physically handicapped, 503
  privacy and, 504–506
  religious freedom and, 491, 492
  search and seizure, 502–503
  Sixth Amendment, 482
commerce and, 150, 354, 356
Congress and, 165
enforcement and, 146, 156–157
federal supremacy and, 149–150
judicial review, 145, 146–149
jurisdiction of, 143, 145, 148

justices, 140, 141; *see also names of*
   specific justices
justiciability of, 150–151
legislative reapportionment and, 255
limitations on power of, 150–151, 153–
   154
  ideological, 154–155, 157–158
myth and, 144–146, 147
school financing, 262
separation of powers and, 94
Surveys, as polls. *See* Public opinion
Symbol manipulation, 53

Taxation
  Congress and, 165
    corporations and, 531–534
  policies, 366
  property, 261
  sales, 261
  Social Security, 381, 382
  state income, 261
  state and local government and, 259,
    260–263
Taylor, John, 88
Television, political socialization and,
   415–417
Tenth Amendment, 240, 245, 483, 577
Third Amendment, 480, 505, 576
Third World, American foreign policy
   toward the, 322
Thirteenth Amendment, 578
Thoreau, Henry David, 27, 28
Three Mile Island, 304–306
Thurow, Lester C., 350
Tinker v. *Des Moines School District*, 472
Treasury (T) bills, 372
Treasury Department, 372
Treaty alliances, military defense and,
   342
Triad nuclear defense system, 334–336
Trial courts, 143, 154
Trident submarine, 336
Truman, Harry (Pres.), 215, 459
Twelfth Amendment, 459, 577–578
Twentieth Amendment, 581
Twenty-Fifth Amendment, 583–584
Twenty-First Amendment, 582
Twenty-Fourth Amendment, 455, 583
Twenty-Second Amendment, 582
Twenty-Sixth Amendment, 455, 584
Twenty-Third Amendment, 582
Two-party government, 114

Un-American Activities Committee, House, 188–189
Unitary government, 70, 71, 72
United Nations, 339
United Steelworkers of America v. *Weber*, 499
Universities, military research and, 326
Urbanization, political participation and, 434, 440–441; *see also* City Governments

Vandenberg, Arthur (Senator), 185
Veto
  legislative, 190
  presidential, 92
Vice-president
  electing, 169
  as presiding officer of Senate, 170
  vacancy in office of, 583–584
Vidal, Gore, 115
Vietnam War, 120, 223–224, 227, 320, 325, 342, 364, 375, 408
  civil liberties and, 472, 474
Voice of America, 338, 341
Voting, 433, 469–470
  Constitutional amendments on, 455, 459
    Fifteenth, 579–580
    Nineteenth, 581
  reapportionment and, 254, 255–257, 455
  reason for, 468, 469–470
  registration, 455
  Voting Rights Act of 1965, 455
  women and, 581
  see also Elections; Political parties
Voting Rights Act of 1965, 455

Wage and price controls, 375
Wage-price guidelines, 373–375
Wallace, George (Governor), 459
War(s)
  Civil, 117–120, 407, 474
  demonstrations against, 110
  Korean, 234–236
  Mexican, 407
  myth and, 407
  Spanish-American, 319, 321, 407
  Vietnam, 120, 223–224, 227, 320, 325, 342, 364, 375, 408, 472, 474
  War Powers Act, 190
  World War I, 407
  World War II, 407

War on Poverty, 263, 264
War Powers Act of 1973, 190
Warren, Charles (Justice), 504
Warth v. *Seldin*, 151
Washington, George (Pres.), 206, 207
Watergate, 11, 101, 120, 297, 299, 525
Watkins v. *U.S.*, 188
Ways and Means Committee, House, 160–161, 187
Weber decision, 158
Welfare state
  attitude towards, 377–381, 387–388, 389, 405
  contributory programs (Social Security), 77, 357, 379, 381–385
  development of, 377–381
  effectiveness of, 390–392
  future of, 398–400
  ideology and, 380, 400
  liberalism and, 40
  myth and, 380, 394, 399–400
  noncontributory programs, 385–390
  Reagan and, 381, 382, 388–390
  reforming
    federalizing, 398
    Negative Income Tax, 396–398
    workfare, 398
  social needs and purposes of, 392, 395, 399–400
  substantive due process and, 155
Welsh v. *United States*, 492
Whips, 172
White House, 207
White House office, 207, 294
Wilson, Woodrow (Pres.), 181, 206, 364, 469
Winpisinger, William W., 112
Women
  peace voted for by, 345
  political participation and, 434
  voting rights of, 581
Womens' rights movement, 110
  Equal Rights Amendments and, 500
  Fourteenth Amendment and, 500
"Workfare," 398
Workplace governance, 64
Works Progress Administration (WPA), 356
World War I, 407
World War II, 407
Writ of mandamus, 148

Zero-based budgeting, 313